STANFORD
THE CAMBRIDGE JUBILEE
AND TCHAIKOVSKY

STANFORD
THE CAMBRIDGE JUBILEE
AND
TCHAIKOVSKY

GERALD NORRIS

DAVID & CHARLES
Newton Abbot   London   North Pomfret(Vt)

British Library Cataloguing in Publication Data

Norris, Gerald
    Stanford, The Cambridge jubilee and Tchaikovsky
    1. Cambridge University Musical Society – History
    I. Title
    780′.6′242659   ML28.C/

    ISBN 0–7153–7856–2

Photoset and printed in Great Britain
by Redwood Burn Limited, Trowbridge & Esher
for David & Charles (Publishers) Limited
Brunel House Newton Abbot Devon

Published in the United States of America
by David & Charles Inc
North Pomfret Vermont 05053 USA

CONTENTS

ACKNOWLEDGEMENTS

Thanks are given, for invaluable help, to Mrs Ursula Vaughan Williams, Dr Herbert Howells, Miss Irene Seccombe, Dr Edward Garden, Dr David Brown, Mr A. Vlasto, Mr C. H. S. Fifoot, Mr Charles Osborne, Mr George Hutchinson, Mme Xenia Davidova and Mr G. A. Shamkin of the Tchaikovsky Museum in Klin, Mrs Myrrha Bantock, the Verdi Institute in Parma and, not least, to the vivacious Maude Hatzfeld; for translations, to Felicity Cave, Magda-Marie Petržilková, Karen Pepper, Mary Milnes, Peter Lamb and the gifted composer John Carmichael; for other material assistance, to the author's friends Maureen Bonnell, Gillian Stormer, Richard Stormer, Penny Crisfield and Pippa Mann. It must be added that, were it not for the work of John and Laurie May and other book suppliers like William Reeves and Kenneth Mummery, much priceless information would never come to the notice of those engaged in writing about music and musicians.

CHAPTER 1

STANFORD

In the spring of 1892, Cambridge University Musical Society, which had been founded forty-nine years earlier, began to make preparations for celebrating its jubilee. The festivities were planned to take place during June of the following year. It was decided that the first step should be to invite Brahms and Verdi to come and receive honorary doctorates and participate in a commemorative concert.

That the Society should contemplate the joint attendance of the two most highly esteemed of living composers would have astonished its founders, amateur enthusiasts with few aspirations beyond that of holding pleasant musical evenings. Their original concerts, modest and informal, had been held in Peterhouse College; they initially called themselves the Peterhouse Musical Society, for nearly all their members were undergraduates from that college. They were high-spirited young men. Their very first concert came close to being their last; the junketings at supper later the same evening somehow contrived, after certain hilarious proceedings, to finish on the college roof, and their next concert had to be given in the Red Lion Hotel in Petty Cury, because the Master of Peterhouse would no longer allow them use of a suitable room within the college. At this second concert, on 8 December 1843, there was quite a large audience, consisting almost entirely of students. The orchestra, made up of eleven players, performed Haydn's Symphony No 97, the *Elisabethen* waltz of Johann Strauss senior, the overture to Auber's *La Muette de Portici*, the overture to Rossini's *Semiramide* and Jullien's *Royal Irish Quadrilles*. The programme also included a glee, some songs and a flute solo.

The first concert to be given under the new name of Cambridge University Musical Society (CUMS) was presented at the beginning of May 1844. Among the orchestral pieces played on this occasion were Haydn's *Surprise Symphony*, the overture to Auber's *Les Diamants de la couronne*, which at that very moment was opening in London, and the overture to *Le nozze di Figaro*. There were also a waltz, a quadrille, two glees, a violin solo and a comic song performed by J. B. Dykes, of

St Catherine's, from whom was demanded an encore.

John Bacchus Dykes, then twenty-one and a founder member of the Society, was to become one of the most celebrated of all hymn composers. His startling second name was inherited from his mother's side of the family. Extremely popular at Cambridge, he was a talented singer and had a delightful sense of humour. His enthusiasm for music was immense. Writing, while an undergraduate, about a concert he had attended in London, he told his sister Fanny, 'We had the Sinfonia Eroica, and upon my word, it nearly drove me mad. What a grand, wild, extraordinary, and sublime production it is.' After seeing Jenny Lind, he was even more excited.

> To say that her *Sonnambula* is *'perfection'*, *'divine'*, and anything of that sort sounds but tame, but I really cannot say anything else. She nearly drove us all crazy. The accounts you see in the papers of her are really not the least exaggerated, but (I think) far below the reality. The Queen was there last night, and Prince Albert, the Duke and Duchess of Cambridge, the Grand Duke Constantine of Russia, and the *grander* Duke of Wellington, Prince Louis Napoleon, etc., etc. Oh that angelic Jenny Lind!

Dykes became in turn secretary, president and conductor of the CUMS before leaving to take up his first curacy, at Malton in Yorkshire. In 1848 he was appointed precentor and minor canon of Durham Cathedral. His finest hymn tunes date from 1856 onwards. Among these are *Melita* ('Eternal Father, Strong to Save'), *Rivaulx* ('Father of Heaven, Whose Love Profound'), *St Aëlred* ('Fierce Raged the Tempest o'er the Deep'), *St Bees* ('Hark, My Soul! It is the Lord'), *Hollingside* ('Jesu, Lover of My Soul'), *Nicaea* ('Holy, Holy, Holy! Lord God Almighty!') and *St Oswald* ('Through the Night of Doubt and Sorrow'). He also composed *Gerontius*, to Cardinal Newman's 'Praise to the Holiest in the Height'. This hymn was the solace both of General Gordon and of Gladstone in their final hours. When Newman was once asked how it felt to have written one of the most popular of all hymns, he said, 'It is not the hymn itself, but Dykes's tune that has gained it the popularity.' The best known of Dykes's hymns is probably *Horbury* ('Nearer, My God, to Thee'), which is believed to have been played by the dance-band of the SS *Titanic* while the liner was sinking, on 14 April 1912.

Dykes led a busy life, making use of every moment. It is said that he was invariably late in leaving his home for the services at Durham Cathedral and consequently had to run part of the way. Though he always arrived on time, he was usually so winded that his colleagues had to take the responses until he could get his breath back. He died in 1876, at the age of fifty-two, exhausted not only by his many church duties, but by a protracted theological dispute with the Bishop of Durham. Despite the popularity of his tunes, which in *The Church Hymnary* amounted to thirteen more than those by any other composer, his earnings were slight. Throughout his life he sought neither profit nor fame. 'God forbid', he once said, 'that I should make these attempts from any unworthy desire to thrust myself forward. I earnestly pray that this motive may never, *never* actuate me.' His family, however, was left practically penniless. A memorial fund was opened for his widow and children and was headed by the Bishop of Durham himself. The response was remarkable, for Dykes's name proved to be well known in every corner of the globe. In next to no time £10,000 was contributed, and, having produced a fortune, the fund was closed.

Dykes was president of the CUMS in 1846–7. The first president, both of the Peterhouse Musical Society and of the CUMS, was G. E. Smith, who, more than anybody, was responsible for their foundation. An excellent cornet player, he died in 1844, while still an undergraduate. He was succeeded as president by William Blow, a descendant of John Blow. Ordained in 1847, he was a superb violinist who came in time to be regarded as one of the leading musical amateurs in Europe. He built up the most important single collection of violins in England, among which were instruments by Stradivarius, Amati, Guarnerius and many other notable makers. Blow died in 1887.

Other founder members of the CUMS included Alfred Pollock, an oboist, who became a solicitor; Charles Coombe, who played the viola and, like Dykes and Blow, took holy orders; Edward Cridge, a cellist and eventually the Bishop of British Columbia; and John Sutton, who installed in his rooms an organ that had formerly been used by Handel. Of all those who took part in the founding of the CUMS, the most illustrious was William Thomson, who was president in 1845–6, immediately after Blow and before Dykes. When Thomson was elected president, Dykes commented in a letter to his family, 'It will be no end of a feather in our caps to have such a man as our representative in the University.' Thomson's scientific genius was already recognised while he was at Cambridge. Later, as Lord Kelvin, he became one of the most admired scientists of his time.

He was appointed Professor of Natural Philosophy at the University of Glasgow in 1846, when he was only twenty-two, and occupied that post for the next fifty-three years. As early as 1848 he proposed his absolute scale of temperature. In 1851, reconciling the work of Carnot, Rumford, Davy, Mayer and Joule, he stated the principle of the dissipation of energy. From 1854 onwards he made a special study of telegraphy. This led to a marked improvement in the manufacture of cables and to his invention of the mirror galvanometer and the siphon recorder. He also interested himself in electromagnetism and in 1851 calculated the absolute electromotive force of a Daniell cell, determining, as well, the absolute measure of resistance of a wire from the heat produced in it by a known current. In 1873 he wrote the first in a series of commissioned articles on the mariner's compass. The article raised so many questions in his mind that another five years passed before he produced the second. By then, he had totally reconstructed the compass, making it impervious even to the oscillations of gunfire, invented a sounding apparatus, a tide gauge, a tidal harmonic analyser and a tide predicter, and devised simplified methods for calculating the position of a ship at sea. When working on the sounding device, he used a coil of piano wire. 'What's that for?' enquired another scientist. 'Sounding,' said Thomson. 'What note?' asked his colleague. 'Deep C,' said Thomson. In 1884, in Baltimore, he proposed the wave theory of light. In the same year he turned his attention, with far-reaching results, to the electronic theory of matter.

Thomson was knighted in 1866 and raised to the peerage in 1892. He remained unfailingly modest. 'I am not really an inventor', he said. 'I am just a dreamer sleeping in the arms of the past.' In 1899, having resigned his professorship because of old age, he enrolled at Glasgow University as 'Lord Kelvin, Research Student'.

Music was one of the great loves of his life. At Cambridge he devoted to music much of the time left over from his scientific and mathematical studies. He played the french horn in the concert at the Red Lion on 8 December 1843. Later, when the orchestra grew in size, he was happy to retreat to the comparative safety of second horn. On a visit, during the Easter holidays in 1844, to Dykes's home in Wakefield, he not only played the horn in the family concerts, but constructed a flying-machine out of umbrella whalebones, persuaded an egg to stand on its end and performed other amazing experiments. John Airey, later Rector of St Helen's, Bishopsgate, for whom Thomson made way as first horn, recalled an incident in which his friend's interests in science and music were fused. Fellow students in mathematics, they had been studying the theory of sound. In their instrumental practice, they noticed, wrote Airey, that 'the fundamental note, as ordinarily accounted and played, was an octave higher than the theoretical fundamental note of an open tube. How was this?' For Thomson, the apparent anomaly had to be reconciled – and duly was.

As I was enjoying my after-dinner pipe, he rushed in wildly, crying 'Airey, Airey, I have found it; I have found it! Where is your horn?' Whereupon, after sundry efforts, he succeeded in producing the *real* fundamental note of the open tube, and was satisfied. In fact, this note is so low, and practically impossible of production, that it is not quoted at all as *the* fundamental note, but the octave above takes its name and place in ordinary parlance. This was an early indication of the strong powers of investigation and research in the student who afterwards became the distinguished scientist.

Thomson's favourite composers were Haydn, Mozart, Beethoven, Weber, Schubert, Mendelssohn, Chopin and Schumann. He had little interest in more modern composers. A piano work by Richard Strauss was once played to him.

'The piece is by Richard Strauss, a contemporary German composer?' he asked.

'Yes', the pianist confirmed.

'Any friend of the Strauss family who wrote such excellent dance music?'

'None whatsoever.'

'No, I should not have thought so,' Thomson concluded.

The pianist then gave a short account of Strauss's abandonment of classical models and his subsequent development of the symphonic poem, a musical form created by Liszt. 'Very interesting', said Thomson.

His niece Agnes Gardner King, in her biography of Thomson, says that he had a particular dislike for Grieg, and that once, when she was at the piano, she slipped in a piece of his between Beethoven and Mozart in the hope of changing her uncle's low opinion of him. But the moment she finished playing, he declared, 'You very cleverly showed the remarkable contrast by placing that Grieg between Beethoven and Mozart.' Music-making was a common occurrence in Thomson's home, and he often listened to it balanced uncomfortably on the arm of his favourite chair, rather than disturb his dog, whose favourite chair it also was. He showed a similar concern for his parrot, to whom he devoted much time in giving him singing lessons. The parrot had a good ear and quickly picked up the beginning of a tune, says Miss King, 'but he had not Lord Kelvin's patience, and "The Quaker's Wife", which the bird always treated as a part-song with his master, was the only thing he ever perfected.' An attempt was made to learn extracts, from the *Pastoral Symphony*, that were considered to have a possible interest for the parrot. This did not prove successful, and work on the symphony was eventually abandoned; the parrot 'enjoyed the lessons immensely, but Lord Kelvin was obliged to acknowledge defeat, and in a letter he said: "I am afraid I cannot prevent his mixing it up with other things."'

Thomson had little enthusiasm for Wagner. When questioned about that composer, he invariably replied that he preferred Weber. To the suggestion that the libretto of *Der Freischütz* was extremely silly, he answered, 'Not so silly as Wagner's operas'. As for Wagner's mysticism, he asked, 'What could be more mystical than the casting of the seventh bullet in *Der Freischütz?*'

Joseph Joachim, the great violinist and friend of Brahms, knew Thomson well and spent many hours trying to interest him in Brahms, but with hardly any success. On some of Brahms's piano pieces Thomson commented, 'Very fine, very fine, but a little involved. Rather like Browning's poetry.' His single favourite composer appears to have been Beethoven, whose piano sonatas gave him particular enjoyment. He described him in a lecture at Birmingham in 1883 as 'the greatest master of sound, in the poetic and artistic sense of the word at all events, that ever lived'.

He kept to the end of his life the french horn he had used at Cambridge. In his seventies he could still play it surprisingly well and, for the Glasgow musician Archibald Henderson, he once satisfactorily performed the important solo from the overture to *Der Freischütz* and a passage from Beethoven's Horn Sonata. He seems to have regarded his lectures on the principles of sound as valid pretexts for displays of musical prowess and on such occasions he would frequently give a brief recital to demonstrate a point he was making; his students often responded with a standing ovation. He did not restrict himself to the french horn. Lectures on the principles of velocity were accompanied by rifle-shots; the nature of dewfall ended with a rubber device representing an overburdened dewdrop bursting above the heads of his pupils. All manner of gadgets and apparatus filled his lecture-room. Triple-spiral spring vibrators hung menacingly from the ceiling alongside a 12lb cannon ball suspended from a 30ft pendulum. Thomson's lectures were exhilarating. One of his students later wrote. 'He sprang like a tiger into the classroom, tearing off his professor's gown as he bounded down the aisle to the platform. "Today," he would announce, as if just arriving with the good news from Ghent, "I will lecture on the propagation of luminar motion through a turbulently moving inviscid liquid."'

With the death of G. E. Smith and the departure from Cambridge of men like Dykes, Blow and Thomson, the CUMS lost some of its initial exuberance and impetus. Nevertheless, membership, which had risen to 426 by the beginning of 1846, continued to grow. Orchestral music, principally overtures, dominated the Society's concerts, though songs and glees also featured on the programmes. The conductor was usually the president, but during 1852 professional conductors were engaged for the first time. Foremost among these was William Amps, organist of St Peter's College and the composer of piano sonatas and songs. Under his baton the Society performed, in March 1853, a short selection from Mendelssohn's *Elijah*, their first attempt at a choral work. Not long afterwards they tackled the incidental music to Sophocles' *Antigone* and *Oedipus at Colonus*, also by Mendelssohn.

The year 1856 was marked by the arrival at Cambridge, as Professor of Music, of William Sterndale Bennett, the friend of Mendelssohn and Schumann. In November of that year, he conducted a CUMS concert in which he also took the piano part in one of his chamber works. 'To engage in performances when the amateur element so strongly preponderated was a new experience for him', wrote his son John in his *Life of William Sterndale Bennett*.

The band and chorus of the University Musical Society presented, at the time, rather a motley crew. College choirs were at hand to assist; good solo-singers were generally attainable; among the members were men of intellectual ability, to whom the study and practice of music seemed to present little difficulty; the north of England, from which Cambridge draws so many of her students, contributed its due share of musical fervour. General culture and enthusiasm were, however, far in advance of actual performance, which was, and remained for many years, rough and imperfect. Music was a disturbance to the established routine of College life. Tutors and reading-men could ill afford time taken from the evening hours of teaching and of study. Rehearsals were irregularly attended. The constantly changing 'personnel' of a University prevented any steady improvement from year to year. Periods of prosperity and depression came in turn, according to the zeal and musical ability of the men of each period.

It often seemed strange that a man so sensitive, so noted for perfection of detail in his own performances, could find it tolerable to assist in such haphazard music-makings. 'Poor Sterndale Bennett,' the Rev. H. R. Haweis called him, when he wrote his reminiscences of these early concerts; and, as time went on, there were others who felt incongruity in so refined a musician taking part with them in their badly-balanced and imperfectly-prepared exhibitions . . . But whatever he felt or thought, when he was taking part in these concerts he certainly threw his whole energy into what he was doing, and he proved himself a most capable leader of irregular forces. After the first concert which he conducted, 'an old guest of the Musical Society' wrote to the newspaper: 'It was truly delightful to see the talented Professor of Music presiding over the band; his forces seemed animated with something of his own vigour, for rarely, if ever, have they more distinguished themselves than on the present occasion.'

There was a seriousness of manner, bordering upon severity, inseparable from Bennett when practising his art in public. Upon amateurs who found themselves for the first time under the influence of his musical personality, the impression was very forcible. The presence of a master was felt . . . A particular example of the wonderful control he had over himself was given by these concerts. When other musicians were occasionally invited to Cambridge to conduct their own works, their looks of anguish when they heard the orchestra strike up were involuntary and natural, but very alarming to the poor performers. Bennett's face, stern as it was, never betrayed the least sign of displeasure, or of his having taken any particular notice of failures and imperfections past remedy. No individual performer was ever disconcerted by any special recognition of what he was doing.

When the music was over he appeared in another aspect. He had the faculty, strengthened no doubt by long experience with pupils, of finding a few expressive words of temperate approval or encouragement. These never approached to flattery, seldom to unqualified praise. They were often humorous, or seasoned with a sprinkling of raillery. They were never twice alike, but adroitly adapted to the individual case, while they had a ring of truth about them that drove them home, fixing them as little treasures in the memory of those to whom they were addressed.

It is worth remembering that at this time Sterndale Bennett was a considerable figure in the world of music. Three years earlier, in 1853, when he was thirty-seven, he was offered the conductorship of the celebrated Leipzig Gewandhaus Orchestra, but had to decline the honour because of numerous engagements to which he was already committed. As a conductor alone, he played an important role in the history of music in England. In 1856 he succeeded Wagner as conductor of the Philharmonic Society of London, a post that he held for the next eleven years. During his first season he conducted the English première of Schumann's *Paradise and the Peri,* just five weeks before the composer's death. There is no doubt that he had a beneficial effect on the CUMS, who, despite their limitations, became increasingly ambitious, and, in December 1857, Mozart's *Requiem* was given under his baton. In the following year they performed Mendelssohn's *Lauda Sion* and Beethoven's incidental music to *The Ruins of Athens.* In 1859 came Beethoven's *Mass in C* and *Choral Fantasia.* In February 1860 they gave their first chamber concert. Handel's *Ode for St Cecilia's Day* was also performed during that year. One of the highlights of 1861 was a further presentation of Mendelssohn's *Antigone* music, with the verses recited by Charles Kingsley. At the beginning of April 1862 the Schumann Piano Concerto was played by the Rev John Lunn, who had been president of the Society in 1858. This was among the earliest performances of the concerto in England and appears to have been the first by an Englishman. At fifteen, Lunn had been present at the first performance of *Elijah,* conducted by Mendelssohn in Birmingham in August 1846. A Fellow of St John's, he regularly began his day by putting an egg into a saucepan of boiling water and timing it by playing on the piano the overture to *Le nozze di Figaro.*

Other notable CUMS performances of the 1860s included the finale to Act One of *Tannhäuser* (1863); the English première of Schumann's Festival Overture on the *Rheinweinlied* (1863); a selection from Handel's *Samson* (1865); Part One of Mendelssohn's *St Paul* (1867); Spohr's *God, Thou Art Great* (1869). As the Society entered the 1870s, it was approaching twenty years of existence. It was flourishing, its concerts were well attended, its performances were of a reasonable standard. Yet it was still no more than an amateur provincial music society.

In October 1870 there arrived at Cambridge an eighteen-year-old undergraduate who was to change the Society's status out of all recognition. He made his first CUMS appearance at a concert on 30 November of that year, playing piano pieces by Schumann and Heller. His name was Charles Villiers Stanford.

Stanford was born in Dublin on 30 September 1852, the son of a distinguished lawyer. Dublin was also the birthplace of John Field, in 1782, and of Michael Balfe, in 1808. In his *Pages from an Unwritten Diary*, published in 1914, Stanford described his native town.

Dublin, as I woke to it, was a city of glaring contrasts. Grandeur and squalor lived next door to each other, squalor sometimes under the roof of grandeur. Society, 'The Quality' as the Irishman calls it, had deserted its centre and made its home in the outskirts: houses of perfect architectural proportions had become tenements; Adam's ceilings and Angelica Kauff-mann's designs looked down upon squalling families in rags and tatters. The hall where Handel conducted the first performance of the 'Messiah' had become a low theatre. The two old cathedrals stood in a region compared to which the Seven Dials was a Paradise. But the well-to-do classes, who had turned their faces outwards, had built up a town which, if it had its quota of dull featureless streets, was not wanting in a good sprinkling of private houses of artistic merit, and in open spaces and squares of a beauty quite unique in this country. Best of all, they entrusted the designing of their public buildings to an architect of genius, James Gandon, who had those rare gifts, a style of his own without extravagance and an unerring sense of dignity. Two great monuments of his skill, the Law Courts and the Custom-House, with the impressive group in College Green, gave Dublin the *cachet* which distinguishes it from all its sister cities. Beauty was everywhere, dirt was everywhere too, trying its best to conceal it. A perspective of quays and bridges, which rivals that of its prototype, Pisa, looked down on a salmon river so polluted that to drive along it at low tide recalled to the passing traveller Coleridge's description of Cologne. It was an amazing tribute to the endurance of the monarch of fish that, though unable to hold his nose, he could plough through this ditch to the upper waters of the Liffey (and I have seen him jumping at the falls of Leixlip, the Lach's Leap, many miles above). To the North stretched a street of a breadth comparable to the famous Unter den Linden in Berlin, with a massive central column to Nelson's memory, which accentuated its noble proportions. To the South stood the semi-circle of the old Parliament House, the statues of Burke, of Goldsmith, and of William of glorious, pious, and immortal memory, guarding the hill up to the gloomy castle; and so one passed into Merrion Square where Medicine on the North side gazed at Law on the South, along streets upon which the distant Dublin mountains smiled and a canal lined by tall old trees where the smell of the turf was wafted from the smoke of barges from Athlone. Thus semi-consciously did famous names in the country's history become familiar to a young mind. Fitzwilliam, Carlisle, Sackville, Harcourt, Dorset, Grafton, Usher, Heytesbury, Grattan, Herbert, all these were household words. It was in Herbert Street (No. 2) I was born, and all round were names of Herbert history; Wilton, Mount Merrion, Sidney and many more.

The boy was born into a musical family. His mother, Mary, was an accomplished pianist, who had once played Mendelssohn's First Piano Concerto at a Dublin Musical Union concert; she gave young Charlie his first lessons. His father, John Stanford, was an excellent cellist. He was also a superb singer 'whose bass', wrote his son, 'with a compass from high F to low C, was one of the finest in quality and style that I have ever heard anywhere.' When Queen Victoria once visited Ireland, John Stanford was chosen to sing before her, together with Jenny Lind, at a special musical evening. He had studied abroad and spoke Italian fluently. He was a born actor, and it was only with difficulty that his Low Church family had prevented him from becoming an opera singer, thus averting 'a scandal which in their opinion would have shaken their character and traditions to the core.'

At that time Dublin was rather weak in professional music-making. Nevertheless, the younger Stanford recalled, 'I found myself in a centre of real music, where amateurs were cultivated performers who had taken their art as seriously as if it were their means of livelihood.' John Stanford was keenly interested in contemporary music and in August 1846 went to Birmingham with his friend Joseph Robinson to hear the first performance of *Elijah*. Robinson knew Mendelssohn and introduced Stanford to him. The three of them, together with Sterndale Bennett, who was one of Mendelssohn's dearest friends, had supper at the Woolpack Inn. According to John Stanford, Mendelssohn was 'as full of fun as any Hibernian'. Earlier in the day they were with him when he slid down the bannisters of a long staircase, with his feet high in the air. During supper, Stanford, who was 6ft 4in tall, performed a Punch and Judy show over the top of a door. With considerable ingenuity he fashioned a napkin into a ghost and accompanied its spectral entry by humming the Commendatore motif from *Don Giovanni*, much to Mendelssohn's delight. The elder Stanford saw Mendelssohn conduct on more than one occasion. 'His impressions of Mendelssohn's *tempi* exactly tallied', wrote his son, 'with all the other opinions which I have heard from men of his time who had experience of them. His Allegros were very quick, and his Adagios very slow. There was an entire absence of sentimentality. My father told me that the composer's conducting of *A Midsummer Night's Dream* overture was so rapid that he seemed to be whipping cream!'

Stanford senior studied the part of Elijah with Mendelssohn's reading fresh in his mind and sang it the following year in Dublin, having been chosen ahead of all the city's professional basses. Some years later his son accompanied him in Elijah's aria 'Is Not His Word Like a Fire?' and found he could hardly keep up; the pace was 'like a hurricane, but so rhythmical and clear that not a note or passage was blurred.'

The boy's musical development was equally swift. At four, he composed a Venetian dirge. When he was eight, he had a march performed in a Dublin production of *Puss in Boots*. He studied the piano, organ and violin and gave a piano recital when he was nine, playing Bach, Handel, Mozart, Beethoven, Moscheles and Mendelssohn. Another recital two years later, in which he played a Beethoven sonata and a Bach prelude and fugue, drew excellent reviews. By the age of twelve he could sight-read with complete facility. He acquired this ability through having to play a fresh Chopin mazurka at the end of every lesson. In time he worked his way through all of them. His teacher, Elizabeth Meeke, had been a pupil of Moscheles. Stanford attributed the effectiveness of her teaching method, which involved pushing forward, regardless of mistakes, to 'the principle of non-stop runs and entire unfamiliarity with the style of music tackled. At the time she placed Chopin on the desk I knew no more of his compositions than a Red Indian.' His piano technique was established by his early teens. His friend and biographer Harry Plunket Greene has left a description of it.

> Stanford's touch was the most delicious thing imaginable, impossible to define. It had a sweetness which gave one a lump in one's throat; a beauty which pervaded every note of the whole and a sparkle which made one chuckle. It never varied in this respect and seemed inviolate in crabbed passages, fifth-rate pianofortes, or moods of irritation. He never practised in later life, and yet it was just as beautiful till the day of his death. His playing was as unselfconscious as himself, his hands just following the colours of his joyous humorous imagination.

He developed his remarkable aural memory at an early age. At the first concert he ever attended, when he was seven, he heard Jenny Lind in *Messiah*. During a private musical evening in an English country house fourteen years later, he identified her voice, even though he was sitting where he could not see her, was hitherto unaware of her presence in the house and had not heard her since the *Messiah* performance. Once, when his organ teacher Robert Stewart was called away from the organ-loft before the end of a Sunday morning service in St Patrick's, he took over and played Bach's

St Anne fugue from memory. His ear was exceptionally sensitive. Attending a rehearsal in Dublin for an orchestral concert, he was so overwhelmed by the sound of the brass that he burst into tears. Charles Hallé, who was visiting Dublin and happened to be standing nearby, comforted the boy with jokes. 'I reminded him of this episode in later years', says Stanford in *Pages from an Unwritten Diary*, 'and he said it was no wonder that the Dublin brass had moved me to tears, for it nearly had the same effect on himself.'

At ten, Charlie became engaged. Twice. And to both girls at the same time. One of them was ten; the other was eight and as irresistible as the first. But, as the initial pangs of romantic ardour subsided, he became increasingly conscious of the equivocal position in which he had placed himself.

> This weighed so heavily on my tender conscience that I consulted my father as to the best means of disentangling the difficulty. He immediately said that the only way was to write fully to Judge Keatinge. The Judge replied in a formidable blue envelope inscribed 'On Her Majesty's Service', and threatened me with committal for contempt if I did not carry out his instructions. These he sent me in another long legal document, pointing out the penal consequences of bigamy and prescribing a course of action which would obviate my committing the crime.

The guilt-racked Charlie duly extricated himself from his unhappy plight, though with what pain to his fiancées and himself he never disclosed; all he would admit was that thenceforward he forever harboured 'a wholesome dread of the assizes'.

In 1862 he visited England for the first time and saw the famous International Exhibition. He became acquainted with the paintings of Millais, Leighton and Watts and the modern French school. He visited Westminster Abbey, where the first tomb for which he searched was that of Macaulay, who had died three years earlier. He deemed the singing both in the Abbey and at St Paul's 'sloppy'. He took some piano lessons from Ernst Pauer, who had been a pupil of Mozart's second son, Wolfgang. He had a single lesson from the celebrated Thalberg, whom Liszt for some while regarded as his chief rival, and was warned against raising his wrist above the flat level of his hand as he struck the keys. 'You will thump', said Thalberg. The one vexation of the trip to London was not being allowed to go and see the ravishing Marie Wilton, 'The Queen of Burlesque', who as a teenager, appearing in *King John*, had moved Charles Kemble to shout from his box, 'That girl will be a great actress.' She later became Lady Bancroft.

Back in Dublin he fell under the spell of the theatre, going to any opera or play that was presented, queueing for hours and jostling through the crowds. He also talked his way into rehearsals. From the wings, he learned much of the stagecraft that he later put to such fine effect in his operas.

In the summer of 1864 the Stanfords went to stay in Norwood so that they could be close to the Crystal Palace, where the most advanced music was performed at the concerts conducted by the great August Manns. Here, in South London, at a dinner party in the home of John Scott Russell, the builder of the Great Eastern, eleven-year-old Charlie first met Arthur Sullivan, then aged twenty-two, and George Grove, who at that time was secretary of the Crystal Palace.

> Grove was the heart and soul of Crystal Palace music, and pioneered me into the gallery of the concert-room now sacred to his and many other memories, showed me where to sit and study the orchestral instruments at rehearsal, plied me with full scores, and infected me, as he did anyone who came into contact with him, with his own enthusiasm. It was a queer mixture of experiences. Tietjens, Giuglini, Trebelli, Santley at operatic concerts in the transept; Beethoven, Schubert, Schumann, Strauss and Lanner in the concert-room, with Blondin on the tight-rope and Léotard on the flying trapeze thrown in. Blondin made me tremble, but Léotard never. Such a graceful figure of a man was never seen, his most daring feats were accomplished with an ease and a certainty which made fear impossible, and yet it was before the days of County Councils, and he had no net. He was, I believe, a French barrister, and a caricature of the time depicted Disraeli in the garb of Léotard flying into court over the wigs and gowns of judges and Q.C.'s. Our great hero, however, was a still surer acrobat than he, the chimpanzee, whose cage was in the tropical court. It was he who one Sunday morning [in December 1866] discovered the fire which destroyed the end of the Palace, attracting the attendant by his cries and pointing with quivering finger at a wreath of smoke which was issuing through the boards. He died afterwards of the fright, but he saved the rest of the building. I have his photograph still.

Meanwhile, in Dublin, 'we had flashes of good music. A chamber concert now and then, an occasional visit from Joachim, Piatti, Hallé, and one from Rubinstein whose extraordinary playing of Schumann's "Études Symphoniques" at last awoke the town to the beauties of that great master, whose works had been a sealed book to the inhabitants, and caused a furore which has seldom been equalled there.'

Stanford developed fast in his middle teens and was fortunate to have at that time, as the last of his Dublin teachers, Robert Stewart, an exceptional organist and musician. Stewart was almost wholly self-taught in both organ-playing and composition. He was familiar with the very latest works and with musical developments throughout Europe. 'How he did it', Stanford later wrote, 'is a mystery to me.' He brought a new standard of organ-playing to Ireland and greatly widened the organ repertoire. He adored Blow, Gibbons and Purcell at a time when they had yet to be rediscovered; he went against the fashion, also, by preferring Bach to Handel. 'His treatment of Bach,' said Stanford, 'which I have often heard mercilessly attacked, was only an intelligent anticipation of the principles of phrasing, upon which Schweitzer lays such stress. Stewart applied the same method of "bowing" to his organ music, that Joachim and others have laid down in practice and by precept for the violin works. He used to be sharply criticized for the rapid pace with which he played many of the Preludes and Fugues. Recent authorities have held that Bach himself played his music so quickly that his pupils despaired of imitating him.' Like Stanford, Stewart was endowed with a phenomenal memory and often dispensed with a score. He could prop up a full orchestral score and play at sight a transcription for organ. In a somewhat perverse way, he came eventually to prefer this sort of challenge to that of playing pieces written expressly for the organ. 'He did not draw the line at works which would seem the most unsuitable for the organ; but his nimble fingers and command of phrasing made one forgive him, even when he astonished his hearers by a perform-ance of the overture to *A Midsummer Night's Dream!*' Stewart was one of those who, some years later, went to Bayreuth for the first perform-ance of *The Ring*; he took Wagner, like everything else, completely in his stride and wrote a review, in the Dublin *Daily Express*, that was among the most perceptive to appear in the British press. He vastly widened young Charlie's interests and enthusiasms, helping him to lay the foundations of what was later to develop into an all-round professionalism of daunting proportions.

The boy continued to compose, writing a hymn that was taken into the Church of Ireland hymnal, and appearing at Dublin concerts, often with his father. At school he did excellently, becoming a classics scholar. His character, which changed little throughout his life, was by now fully formed. 'Master Stanford, with all his ability, is a natural, lively and unaffected boy', a critic wrote of him, following a concert directed by Robert Stewart in which his fourteen-year-old protégé's choral work *Heroes and Chieftans* was successfully introduced. It was said of him, too, that he had 'never the slightest desire to show off'. His boyhood friend Raoul de Versan has left a full description of Stanford at seventeen.

> My estimate of his character formed at that time has varied but little since. He was warm-hearted and affectionate – entirely devoid of vanity, sentimentality, or jealousy. He openly acknowledged any musical talents in others, never assuming superior airs. Being of a frank, unsuspicious nature, he was inclined to make new friends too readily and often suffered in consequence. His gravest defect was that he resented opposition to anything he proposed and which he invariably wanted to have carried out forthwith, regardless of due consideration for the wishes or difficulties of others or their points of view. When thwarted, he would show resentment and sulk for a while, but he would soon recover and be the same as ever. His disposition generally was gay; he was fond of fun and amusement, blessed with a strong sense of humour, thoroughly enjoying the good things of this life yet ever clean and straight in his mode of living. Unless they had offended him deeply, he never forgot his old friends and was most happy when he had them around him.

In the spring of 1870 Charlie and his father were in London, walking up Regent Street, when John Stanford suddenly stopped opposite Peter Robinson's and asked his son what he wanted to be. 'A musician', said Charlie. His father was silent for a moment, then gave his consent. First, though he must go to Cambridge; after that, he would pursue his musical training abroad.

He went up to Cambridge in October 1870 with an organ scholarship to Queen's College. He subsequently also won a classical scholarship. He came across many old Dublin friends, among whom were some of the most brilliant undergraduates in the entire university. It was not long before he learned about the CUMS and within a month, as we have already noted, he made his début in two piano solos. He was disappointed in the musical environment in which he found himself. 'Music in Cambridge was then in a disorganized state. There was plenty of talent, but no means of concentrating it for useful purposes. The University Musical Society, which was one of the most ancient in England, was at a low ebb.' The continuing presence in the university of CUMS luminaries from earlier, more exciting days served only to emphasise the difference between what it once was and what it had become. Of these past heroes, Stanford was delighted to make the acquaintance of the egg-timing John Lunn, who still occasionally played at CUMS concerts, but, says Stanford, 'was wont to treat his audiences as if they were troublesome undergraduates at a lecture.'

He once ascended the platform a few minutes before the concert began, sat himself down at the piano and, without striking any notes, proceeded to go through an acrobatic exhibition of wrist and finger exercises, which caused a *crescendo* of merriment amongst the assembling public. This was too much for him, and he shook an angry fist at the audience, making a face of concentrated fury the while, as he retired from the fray.

By 1870 the CUMS had developed essentially into a choral society, in which respect it was heavily handicapped by being composed exclusively of males. 'There were no sopranos save boys; the altos were a handful of choirmen; the society was neither fish, flesh nor fowl. It did not try to be a first-class Männer-Gesangverein, for which there were ample materials if they were properly worked. The bad balance of voices damped the enthusiasm of the men. There was but one hope of salvation, the admission of women into the ranks.' Having reached this conclusion, Stanford managed to convert two senior members of the Society to the same point of view. He then persuaded them to propose and second the resolution 'That ladies be admitted as performing members of the Society'. He wisely kept in the background, feeling that his lack of years might be a provocation to the older members. The resolution was placed before the Society on 5 June 1871 and was rejected by thirty votes to three. Unperturbed by this defeat, Stanford simply decided that 'other methods had to be adopted to dish the conservatives'. Moreover, help was at hand: 'the hour had come, and with it the woman.' This was Mrs Dunn, who suggested that Stanford form a new choir independent of the CUMS. She would take the responsibility of providing the women singers, and he was to be the conductor. The choir was formed with surprising ease. It was trained both by Stanford and by Sedley Taylor, a distinguished physicist, president of the Society in 1857, author of the important book *Sound and Music* and a fighter for women's rights, who had helped to found Girton College. Calling themselves the Cambridge Amateur Vocal Guild, the choir soon gave their first concert and scored an instant success. Mrs Dunn proved to be a fine contralto, whose singing of Bach later won the praise of Joachim. A second concert was held, in which, for good measure, the Guild gave the first performance in England of Bach's Cantata No 106, *Gottes Zeit ist die allerbeste Zeit*. This, too, was a triumph, and the new choir had now captured the interest of the university, to the dismay of the CUMS. At that time, Sterndale Bennett, who had been knighted in March 1871 at the instigation of his warm admirer Gladstone, was still Professor of Music. Although he always conducted one CUMS concert every year, he had no official connection with the Society and, by reason of his eminence, stood above the battle that was now being joined. He was delighted by both the enterprise and the level of performanc3 of the Guild and accordingly urged the CUMS to suggest that they combine forces. This the Society did, and their offer was readily accepted. In token of his achievement, Stanford was asked to put forward his previously defeated motion, at a special meeting held on 23 October 1872. This time it was carried by twenty-eight votes to two.

To celebrate the union, Sterndale Bennett agreed to direct the CUMS in a performance of his choral work *The May Queen*. Stanford had recently met him for the first time and in his book *Interludes*, published in 1921, described how this took place one afternoon when he was visiting a friend in Trinity.

> While we were talking, there walked into the room a small figure of a man whose dignity of bearing made him look half as tall again as his stature warranted, with a well-proportioned and squarely built head, lovely and sympathetic eyes, and an expression of unmistakable kindliness and charm, which captivated me before he opened his mouth. The dress was a little in the old style, recalling with its high collar and dark ample stock, the early drawings of Berlioz and Mendelssohn . . . It was easy to see at a glance the qualities which endeared him to Schumann and to Mendelssohn, and also the modesty which prevented his powers from being acclaimed by the mass of the public, and even stood in the way of his own exercise of them. In the few short years which intervened before his premature death in 1875, I had several opportunities of seeing him, and getting to know him both as a man and as an artist. On one occasion when I dined with him *tête-à-tête* we played pianoforte duets all the evening, and I was able to appreciate the great beauty of his touch and tone of which so many great musicians have spoken. We played the whole of his G Minor Symphony, and others of the four-handed arrangements of his orchestral works. On another, he came to Cambridge, when a much-needed revolution had succeeded (largely through his support) in substituting ladies for boys in the soprano department of the University Musical Society. We showed our gratitude to him by performing his 'May Queen', and engaged

a first-rate orchestra for the concert. He was invited to conduct, and, though in indifferent health, went out of his way to do so. Nothing, however, which I could say would induce him to believe in the efficiency of the band for accompanying the solos with enough delicacy, although the players were of the best: his memories of scratch local orchestras at the University town in old days were too painfully vivid: and he insisted upon my playing them on the pianoforte, characteristically veiling his mistrust of his forces under the euphemism, that the pianoforte would be a pleasant contrast to the orchestral accompaniments of the Chorus.

The performance, which took place on 27 May 1873, was rapturously received.

A month before the concert, there was sad news from the Isle of Wight, where John Hopkins, the noted organist of Trinity College, had retreated during the previous year, in the hope of shaking off ill health. He died in Ventnor on 25 April. Stanford and Gerard Cobb, Junior Bursar of Trinity, had shared his duties while Hopkins was away. On the recommendation of Cobb, Stanford was appointed in Hopkins' place. But there was another important music post that Hopkins had held: he had been the permanent conductor of the CUMS. To this position Stanford was also now elected; he was still only twenty years old.

As organist of Trinity, he began in earnest to build a reputation as an executant. The years with Robert Stewart, who, completely out of the blue, had just received a knighthood, served him well, and from what J. A. Fuller-Maitland remembered of him in *A Door-Keeper of Music*, it seems that Stanford modelled himself closely on his teacher.

> He was by no means a stickler for confining the music he chose, whether for services or recitals, to works originally written for the organ; he loved arrangements, and to translate the scores of symphonies and overtures into the language of the organ without preparation. It is only the purist who could object to such preferences in days when we had so few opportunities of hearing the larger kinds of music. He was almost single-handed in the work of opening the eyes of all of us to the world of music, and he gave us a sense of artistic proportion which, while shattering some old illusions, made us at least conscious of the extent of the classics . . . I doubt if at that time, before the Royal College of Music had been even thought of, there was any training in England to compare with what we got through Stanford's influence and example.

W. H. Thompson, the awesome Master of Trinity, who had little feeling for music, nevertheless declared that Stanford 'plays like

St Cecilia'. However, he rebuked him after a Sunday evening service for performing what he considered to be a popular melody. Gerard Cobb had to explain to the Master that it was, in fact, an aria from Bach's *St Matthew Passion*. Thompson once said of his young organist, 'Mr Stanford's playing always charms and occasionally astonishes, and I may add that the less it astonishes, the more it charms.'

When he took up his organist's post, Stanford transferred from Queen's to Trinity. He found himself sharing a floor with the man who was at that time a tutor and head lecturer of the college, as well as being Public Orator of the University, a position to which he had been elected five years earlier, when he was twenty-eight. This was Richard Jebb, who was already in the process of becoming one of the greatest classical scholars of the nineteenth century. He was also the current president of the CUMS. Stanford's and Jebb's rooms had once been occupied by Isaac Newton, and the rooms directly below, on the ground floor, by Macaulay and Thackeray. Jebb – who eventually became MP for Cambridge, was knighted and received the Order of Merit – vacated his rooms in 1874, when he married. Stanford and he became firm friends. When the younger man applied to Jebb, as head lecturer, to be excused from the 1873 college exams, he was given leave in the following couplet. *Quid tibi Musa neget? trutinam lacrimosa parabit, Si fugis examen, tollere Musa suam.* Some years later Jebb borrowed Stanford's key to the Fellows' Garden and forgot to return it. When Stanford reminded him that he still had it, Jebb sent it back with the message, *Clave quid ablata silvis excluditur Orpheus? Ne domitum vates auferat ipse nemus.* Both of these are quoted in Caroline Jebb's life of her husband.

Mrs Jebb, born Caroline Lane, had first married General Adam J. Slemmer, who fought on the Union side in the American Civil War. She was extraordinarily beautiful and was supposed to have accelerated her husband's promotion by going to see Lincoln personally about it, laying her hand on his shoulder as she spoke. When Slemmer, who rose from lieutenant to general in a comparatively short space of time, died in 1868, she came to Cambridge, intending merely to visit for a while with relations. She made an immediate impression; in *Period Piece*, Gwen Raverat writes that 'every marriageable man proposed to her.' It was said that she once received three proposals in one evening in the parlour of the house in which she was staying, 15 Fitzwilliam Street. She later denied this: 'that is absurd', she laughed; 'One was in the garden.' Finally she settled on Jebb, who was among the wittiest and most attractive men at Cambridge, but also one of the most retiring and unobtrusive. Thompson, for some curious reason, saw him in a completely different light. 'The time Mr Jebb can spare from the adornment of his person', he declared, 'he devotes to the neglect of his duties.' He went even further when Arthur Sullivan came up to the university in 1876 to receive his honorary degree. Seeing the composer gorgeously attired in his doctor's robes, he inquired of the junior bursar as to who that 'painted jay' might be. Thompson was pretty much prepared to insult anybody in sight. He had little regard for Charles Kingsley and was not unhappy when Kingsley resigned from the Chair of Modern History. The author of *Westward Ho!* was succeeded by Professor John Seeley, whose famous essay, *The Expansion of England*, later won him the KCMG. After attending Seeley's inaugural lecture, Thompson commented, 'I did not think we should miss poor Kingsley so soon.' On another occasion, referring to Gerald Balfour, who was then a Junior Fellow of Trinity, he remarked, 'We are none of us infallible – not even the youngest of us.' Thompson once wrote Stanford a letter in which he began, 'The College may reckon itself fortunate in the possession of so fine a musician and so skilled an organist as . . .' and here the first side of the page ended. Overleaf, it continued '. . . Gerard Cobb . . .'. Stanford was convinced that this was a calculated effect, but, recalls Plunket Greene, 'his sense of humour was tickled. He showed me the letter in the Avenue just as the old Master was driving out in his landau. As he passed, Stanford shook his fist with the letter in it at his back and said in his broadest brogue, "Y' ould scoundrel!"'

In the summer of 1873, Stanford travelled abroad for the first time, to the Schumann festival in Bonn, which took place during the third week in August. During the festival he made friends with the composer Ferdinand Hiller, then sixty-one, who, as a boy of fifteen, had been taken by his teacher Hummel to call on Beethoven and Schubert. Hummel and Hiller visited Beethoven four times during March 1827, the final month of his life, seeing him for the last time three days before he died. Beethoven had been cheered on his death-bed by a gift of £100 from the Philharmonic Society. He spoke to young Hiller of this kind action and praised the generosity of the English. He said that as soon as he was better he would go to London, which he had never visited. 'I shall compose a great overture and a great symphony for them', he resolved. Hiller confirmed that

Beethoven died during a thunderstorm; he remembered 'a dense fall of snow accompanied by violent thunder and lightning'. Hummel and Hiller had never heard of Schubert before they arrived in Vienna, and they only happened to meet him through a mutual friend. They were treated to a private performance of a number of his songs, sung by Michael Vogl, with Schubert accompanying. Schubert's technique, according to Hiller, 'was very far from being that of a master.' Vogl's voice, too, was past its best. Nevertheless, the two visitors were amazed by what they heard, and Hummel, 'who already had nearly half a century of music behind him, was so deeply moved that tears glistened on his cheeks.' Schubert told Hiller, 'I compose every morning – when one piece is finished, I start another.' Hiller was friendly, at one time or another, with Cherubini, Rossini, Chopin, Liszt, Berlioz, Meyerbeer, Spohr and, in particular, Mendelssohn and Schumann. He wrote a book about Mendelssohn, which he dedicated to Queen Victoria. Schumann dedicated his piano concert to Hiller, who conducted the first performance, with Clara Schumann at the piano. Among Hiller's pupils was Max Bruch, who was also present at the Schumann festival.

Two days after the festival finished, Stanford went to a dinner-party at Hiller's home in Cologne and met there, for the first time, Johannes Brahms, then aged forty. He was 'tawny-haired and clean-shaven'; the famous beard was not to appear until five years later. He was 'rather silent'. A few days earlier, Clara Schumann had noted in her diary that Brahms was 'not in the best of tempers, which distressed me since he meant so much to my Robert.' Stanford's first conversation with Brahms was 'short and uninteresting'; the composer was 'somewhat bored and unapproachable, and not (to tell the truth) in the best of tempers'.

> I had, however, the opportunity of studying his face, which I never again saw without the now familiar beard. The clean-cut refined beauty of his boyish features had vanished, the jowl was thick and powerful, and the mouth rather large and coarse. But his eyes, which were of an astonishingly deep and luminous violet, were fascinating, and the brow and head most noble in proportion.

On his way back to England, Stanford visited Switzerland and France. In Paris he saw Offenbach conduct *Orphée aux enfers*, 'sung with a verve, a dash and a finesse such as only France can attain. Impudent music, perhaps, but fascinating too. Offenbach always seemed to reflect in his work the spirit of his "cheeky" reply to a questioner who asked him if he was not born at Bonn. "No, Beethoven was born at Bonn; I was born at Cologne."' Sometimes he signed himself 'O. de Cologne'.

Once more in Cambridge, Stanford resumed his studies, which resulted in his gaining a BA in classics in the summer of the following year, 1874. He achieved quite modest marks in the exams, particularly compared to some of his brilliant contemporaries. However, one of these, Walter Leaf, reasoned in his autobiography that 'Charlie Stanford, with the creative musical gift, was right in treating examinations as mere obstacles to be cleared with the absolute minimum of exertion – an aim which he very successfully attained.'

Plunket Greene writes of the way in which Stanford had matured during his undergraduate years.

> Complete absence of parental control had worked wonders with his character. He had had a taste of the outer world and found it good. The moment he set foot in Cambridge he started to shed repressions, and each succeeding year set him firmer on his feet. It was the making of him that he was called upon to face responsibility at an age when the Victorian youth was still in leading-strings; and his faculty for pulling things out of the fire which we all knew so well in later times was no doubt largely due to these early days with the C.U.M.S when responsibility was like wine to him.

Stanford aimed high from the very start of his tenure as conductor of the CUMS. In June 1874 he directed a performance of Schumann's *Paradise and the Peri*. In May 1875 he conducted the English première of Part Three of Schumann's *Scenes from Goethe's 'Faust'*. The Society had now come dramatically to life and was even beginning to draw some of its audience from London. At this time the custom was initiated of engaging professional orchestral musicians, most of whom also came from the capital. This enabled the Society to perform practically anything it wanted. In the summer of 1876 the third English presentation of Brahms's *German Requiem* was given at Cambridge. This excited such enthusiasm that cricket matches were rescheduled so that those cricketers who were members of the CUMS choir could attend all the rehearsals. The number of concerts given annually was reduced, and increased attention was paid to major compositions, on which there was now time to lavish more care. The standard of performances rose higher and higher, and by 1877 the CUMS and its

young conductor were building a national reputation. Stanford was
beginning to come to the attention of musicians outside Dublin and
Cambridge as early as 1875, when Hubert Parry, then twenty-seven,
noted in his diary how his friend Robin Benson had been telling him
about 'rising men in the musical world, especially the new organist at
Trinity College, Cambridge, called Stanford, who according to him
must be a tip-top man.' Typically, George Grove had arrived at an
estimate of Stanford's worth even earlier and had enlisted his help in
1874 during the early stages of the planning of his epoch-making
Dictionary of Music and Musicians.

In 1874 Stanford, by no means satisfied with the extent of his
musical education, had determined, as his father had suggested, to
complete his studies abroad. Over the three years following his gra-
duation, he spent six months annually away from the university. This
was possible only because of the generosity both of Trinity and
Thompson, who, despite regarding music as merely 'a grade better
than dancing', was not unaware of what Stanford's growing reputation meant to the college, and himself admired the young man's
'organ-blowing'. Accordingly, in the summer of 1874, Stanford set
out for Leipzig. His departure is alluded to in Fuller-Maitland's
A Door-Keeper of Music.

> At the beginning of my second year, during Stanford's absence at Leipzig,
> I was allowed to occupy his rooms next the Chapel, the famous rooms
> once inhabited by Sir Isaac Newton, the door of which was furnished with
> two small apertures which we believed were arranged by the philosopher
> for the convenience of his cat and her kitten.
>   On Stanford's return from his studies in Germany, I was given rooms
> on the ground floor of the Great Court in what was sometimes called
> 'Mutton-Hole Corner', where, it was said, Byron kept a tame bear.

Stanford makes no mention of these apertures in his memoirs;
perhaps he was uneasy about the idea of Newton constructing two
when one would do.

In Leipzig, he became a pupil of Karl Reinecke, to whom he had
been given an introduction by Sterndale Bennett. The two older men
had both been friends of Schumann. The master dedicated his *Études
symphoniques* to Sterndale Bennett; Reinecke used to assimilate Schumann's new works with such speed that Schumann once exclaimed,
'He has my stuff by heart before I've even written it.' In 1860
Reinecke became conductor of the Leipzig Gewandhaus Orchestra

and Professor of Composition at the Leipzig Conservatoire. He had many well-known pupils, including Sullivan, Grieg, Bruch and Svendsen. Delius was a pupil of his in the eighties, and Elgar made a special trip to Leipzig in 1882, when he was thirty-five, to hear Reinecke conduct. This Danish-born musician achieved such eminence that people in the streets of Leipzig took off their hats to him as he passed. Stanford said of Reinecke, who in 1874 was fifty, 'Of all the dry musicians I have ever known, he was the most desiccated.' Others came in time to agree. Reinecke evolved inexorably from a modernist to an ultra-conservative. He turned down Grieg's Piano Concerto for performance at a Gewandhaus concert without even bothering to explain why. Grieg constantly vilified him, and Svendsen, writing to Grieg in December 1878, avowed, 'I completely share your opinions about Reinecke; yes, I go still further and maintain that not only is he envious and bloodless, as you say, but he is also in the highest degree *villainous*.' Stanford had other teachers in Leipzig, as well as Reinecke, and he was not too taken with them either. In his third year, he left Leipzig for Berlin where he became a pupil of Friedrich Kiel. He found in this delightful man 'a master at once sympathetic and able . . . I never heard him say a hard word of anyone, and he always tried to emphasize the best points even in the works of men with whom he had the least affinity . . . He was a rare man and a rare master. I learnt more from him in three months than from all the others in three years.' In May 1878 Stanford performed Kiel's fine *Requiem*, Op 20, with the CUMS – a tender tribute to his master.

While on the continent, he succeeded in visiting Vienna, 'tasting for the first time the joys of Strauss waltzes under Strauss leadership'. He also went to Salzburg, where he played on Mozart's harpsichord. On more than one occasion he found himself sitting next to Robert Franz in a restaurant in Leipzig that they both frequented, 'but conversation with him was impossible for he was stone-deaf.' He saw Wagner at the opera in Leipzig in 1874; in December of the following year he encountered him at much closer quarters and 'actually rubbed my coat sleeves against his.' Among the most exciting of his experiences was hearing Liszt at a semi-private gathering held in Leipzig.

> The moment his fingers touched the keys, I realised the immense gap between him and all other pianists. He was the very reverse of all my

anticipations, which inclined me, perhaps from the caricatures familiar to me in my boyhood, to expect to see an inspired acrobat, with high-action arms, and wild locks falling on the keys. I saw instead a dignified composed figure, who sat like a rock, never indulging in a theatrical gesture, or helping out his amazingly full tone with the splashes and crashes of a charlatan, producing all his effects with the simplest means, and giving the impression of such ease that the most difficult passages sounded like child's play . . . He had a magnetism and a charm which were all-compelling. We understood how he could meet Kings and Empeeors on an equality, and fascinate with all the wiles of the serpent. He had two smiles: the one angelical, for artists, the other diabolical, for the satellite Countesses. How innately kind he could be was proved by a little incident which occurred in Berlin shortly after his visit to Leipzig. A young lady pianist had announced a recital, advertising herself (in the hope of attracting a larger audience) as a 'pupil of Liszt'. As she had never laid eyes upon him in her life, she was horrified to read in the papers on the morning of her concert that the Abbé had arrived in the city. The only thing to be done was to make a clean breast of it; she went to his hotel and asked for an interview. When she was shown in, she confessed with many tears, and asked for absolution. Liszt asked her the name of the pieces she was going to play, chose one and made her sit down at the piano and play it. Then he gave her some hints about her performance, and dismissed her with a pat on the cheek, and the remark, 'Now, my dear, you can call yourself a pupil of Liszt.'

In the summer of 1876 Stanford travelled to Bayreuth, where the festival theatre had just been opened. He heard the second cycle of *The Ring*, which went better than the première a week earlier.

To visit the head-centre of modernity was in those days a perilous business. Partisanship ran to such fever-heat that even friendships were broken, and the friction was almost intolerable. Macfarren, the successor to Sterndale Bennett [who had died in February 1875] in the Cambridge Professorship, roundly and loudly rated me in a music-shop in Bond Street when I informed him of my approaching journey, ending with an expression of contemptuous pity for my having to sit through an opera consisting wholly of the chord of E flat on a pedal: a criticism which suggested that he did not know much of it beyond the opening pages of the 'Rheingold'. He and many others of his kidney looked upon a pilgrim to the Wagnerian shrine as a brazen-faced traitor to musical art.

When Macfarren learnt that Hubert Parry, who had been his pupil, would also be among the pilgrims, he felt obliged to caution him in writing.

I am sorry you are going to Bayreuth, for every presence there gives countenance to the monstrous self-inflation. The principle of the thing is bad, the means for its realisation preposterous. An earthquake would be good that would swallow up the spot and everybody on it, so I wish you were away.

Yours, with kindest regards,

G. A. Macfarren.

In Stanford's view, the atmosphere at Bayreuth 'was not sympathetic, and gave a feeling of polemic prejudice which militated against whole-hearted appreciation or valuable discrimination. "He that is not with me is against me" was the motto of the whole festival.' Wagner drove to each performance 'in semi-royal state' and at the conclusion of the cycle appeared on the stage, 'but happily did not make one of his unfortunate speeches.'

He contented himself with a bow, but we were able to note the influence of the 'forties upon his dress . . . and the attitude of conscious superiority, which contrasted so unfavourably with the kingly modesty of Verdi in a like position . . . I regretted seeing him in the flesh. The music was the music of Jekyll, but the face was the face of Hyde. Whatever magnetism there was in the man, his physiognomy did its best to counteract. The brow and head were most impressive, the mouth and chin equally repulsive. Together they made a most curious combination of genius and meanness which exactly corresponded to the Wagner of the Liszt letters [letters to Liszt] and the autobiography.

The most alarming incident in Stanford's three years apprenticeship on the continent happened when he offended one of the many duel-happy young Germans studying in Leipzig.

I was standing one day talking to a friend on the bridge over the ornamental water in the Johannes Park. There had been heavy snow and frost, and the ice was crowded with skaters. As I talked, my hand knocked off the parapet about as much snow as would cover a five-shilling piece, which fell unnoticed by me on the cap of one of these fire-eaters. I saw this man make for the bank and tear off his skates, and was still more surprised when he made a straight line for me and demanded my card. I happily had not got one, whereat he fixed a whole volley of abuse at me, of which I feigned as much ignorance as if it were Hebrew. As he got no change out of a foreigner on whom apparently his oratory was quite thrown away, he eventually took himself off, muttering curses upon British ignorance of foreign languages, and I felt that the tip of my nose was saved.

By far the most important episode in Stanford's German sojourn, however, was his meeting with Jennie Wetton.

He had been playing the piano one evening at a party in Leipzig, when he was asked if he would accompany an English girl in some songs. Hardly had he begun Schumann's 'Du bist wie eine Blume', when she requested him to start again and take it more slowly. Later that evening he described her to his room-mate as 'an impertinent minx'. She was nineteen years old, extremely good-looking, lively, adventurous . . . and by October 1876 they were engaged. There are many things that could have attracted her to Charlie. He was tall – 6ft 1in – dark and striking. He had a wonderful soft Leinster brogue and an ever-present sense of humour. He had, too, the gift of laughing till he cried. From his mother he inherited courtly old-world manners and genuine charm. He was inclined, when first one met him, to look forbidding, partly because he was short-sighted, in consequence of which he wore pince-nez similar to those of his countryman Yeats. It was not unknown for a woman to go in to dinner on his arm in some trepidation and to emerge two hours later starry-eyed, rhapsodising over the most delightful man she had ever met.

Charlie and Jennie may have been engaged as far as they themselves were concerned, but in his parents' eyes they were not, and there seems little doubt that the Stanfords had somebody else in mind for their only son. The outcome of this difference of opinion, after a disturbing exchange of letters to and from Dublin, was that the two young people could marry if, after a year apart – without corresponding – they were still of the same mind.

For one year, they neither met nor wrote to one another. Their friends helped out, not by carrying messages, but by reporting on the welfare of each and by bending the rules just enough to give the lovers sufficient emotional sustenance on which to survive their ordeal.

They were married on 6 April 1878 at Jennie's family church at Ockley in Surrey. In June they went over to Dublin. As Jennie stepped off the gangway, she found a huge dark man looming above her, silently scrutinising her. He looked hard at her for several seconds, then suddenly smiled and said in a deep voice, 'Come along, you little thing', slipping his arm through hers and carrying her off. 'Nothing was too good for her from that moment', says Plunket Greene. John Stanford threw dinner-parties in her honour 'and asked all the most brilliant people in Dublin to meet her – and Dublin in those days was probably the most brilliant town in the Empire.'

He gave evening parties at which she had to sing and Charles to play, while he stood by, bursting with pride. The triumphs of Gotha were nothing to it. It was hard to believe that this was the man who had condemned them to the year of starvation and held aloof from their wedding. It seemed as though he would never tire of proving to them thus the repentance which he could not bring himself to put into words – the end was well and all was well.

On 8 March 1877, the CUMS gave the first performance in England of Brahms's First Symphony. This was only the seventh performance of the symphony and it was conducted from manuscript by the composer's great friend Joseph Joachim, who was granted an honorary doctorate while he was in Cambridge. Stanford was responsible for this coup, which at once made him and the CUMS famous. Shortly afterwards, Joachim wrote to Brahms, 'Since Cambridge, the future of your work in England is assured.'

By now Stanford was also attracting attention as a composer. His first numbered works appeared in 1875, consisting of songs and piano pieces. His Op 5, *The Resurrection*, a choral composition based on Klopstock's poem, also dates from 1875 and was first performed by the CUMS. In the same year he was startled to receive a totally unexpected invitation to write incidental music for Tennyson's tragedy *Queen Mary*, the poet's first play. The commission was initiated by the poet laureate himself, then sixty-five, who had learned of Stanford from his sons Hallam and Lionel; coming from one of the titans of the day, it conferred a signal honour on the young composer. Unfortunately, there was intrigue at the Lyceum Theatre, which had just come under the management of Mrs Sidney Frances Bateman, following the death of her husband a few months earlier, and, as a result, Stanford's music was not used. It appears that the theatre's musical director, Robert Stoepel, wanted the commission for himself. Stanford may not have been aware of this. 'Many difficulties were put in the way of the performance of the music, into the causes for which I had neither the wish nor the means to penetrate', he wrote in an article, for the *Cambridge Review* October 1892, that is included in his *Studies and Memories*, published in 1908.

Finally, however, the management gave as an explanation that the music could not be performed, as the number of orchestral players required for its propee presentment would necessitate the sacrifice of two rows of stalls.

To my young and disappointed soul came the news of a generous action which would have been a source of pride to many a composer of assured position and fame. The poet had offered, unknown to me, to bear the expense of the sacrificed seats for many nights, in order to allow my small share of the work to be heard. The offer was refused, but the generous action remains, one amongst the thousands of such quiet and stealthy kindnesses which came as second nature to him, and were probably as speedily forgotten by himself as they were lastingly remembered by their recipients.

The year 1876 saw a further advance in Stanford's reputation. The Alexandra Palace, whose concerts usually consisted of pot-pourris from Italian opera, 'British Army Quadrilles with all the original effects' and similar items, was rapidly losing ground to the more progressive programmes of the Crystal Palace. In an attempt to display more resolute artistic purpose, the proprietors of the Alexandra Palace held a competition for 'the two best Orchestral Symphonies to be written by British composers'. The judges were George Macfarren and Joseph Joachim. The first prize, worth £20, was won by Francis Davenport, twenty-nine, who later became a professor at the Royal Academy of Music and the Guildhall School of Music. He was a pupil of Macfarren and married his daughter. Stanford's Symphony No 1, in B flat, took the second prize, of £5; this was performed at the Alexandra Palace, along with Davenport's Symphony in D minor, and created a good impression.

In the following year his setting of Psalm 46 was given by the CUMS under his direction. In September 1877 the *Festival Overture*, in B flat, conducted by the composer, had its première at the Three Choirs Festival in Gloucester. This was shortly afterwards performed at the Crystal Palace, where, according to one report, it was 'exceedingly well received'.

In 1878, the year of his marriage, he completed the score of his first opera, *The Veiled Prophet of Khorassan*, based on Thomas Moore's *Lalla Rookh*, and took it to Ernest Frank, director of the Frankfurt Opera, who was one of the most gifted producers of that period. Frank gave him valuable help in reconstructing some of the scenes and would have produced the opera in Frankfurt had he not soon afterwards resigned because of a quarrel with the management.

During the summer of 1878 Stanford and the CUMS gave two English premières of works by Brahms: the *Alto Rhapsody* and the *Neue Liebeslieder* Waltzes.

The first composition of Stanford's to achieve permanent popularity, the Service in B flat, appeared in 1879. During the Christmas vacation that year, he met Tennyson for the first time. It is possible to appreciate the thrill of such an encounter from a passage in Bram Stoker's *Personal Reminiscences of Henry Irving*.

In my own young days Tennyson was a name of something more than reverence. Not only was his work on our tongue-tips, but the extraordinary isolation of his personal life threw a halo of mystery over him. It is a strange thing how few of the people of his own time – and all through his long life of such amazing worth and popularity – had ever seen him. Naturally a man who knew him was envied if only from this source alone.

Stanford had been saddled 'with the appalling burthen of examining some thousand papers on music for the local examinations of the University'. One of the questions was about the oratorios of Handel and Mendelssohn. Cited among the answers was an oratorio listed as *Jacabenus*, 'a portmanteau word for *Judas Maccabaeus* and *Jack and the Beanstalk*, which was worthy of Lewis Carroll himself'. Another examinee alluded to *Judius Macabeth*. Best of all was 'a modest general-servant title of a score, which would only need to be written to command instant success, and even acceptance at the Albert Hall': *Eliza*. 'To get some Atlantic air in the intervals of this penal servitude', Stanford took himself and his exam papers to a hotel in Freshwater, on the Isle of Wight, close to Farringford, where Tennyson lived. 'From my window I saw on the first morning a figure in a large cloak, with a broad-brimmed wide-awake, pounding up the avenue in the rain and wind, in company with a young man and a grey Irish deerhound. It was Tennyson.' Stanford soon took the opportunity of introducing himself, and they were quickly on friendly terms; shortly afterwards he was invited to Farringford.

Tennyson's life was one of the most wholesome regularity. The daily walk from eleven to one and the shorter stroll in the afternoon were timed to the moment. Sometimes, on returning from his morning walk, he would find that he had taken five minutes less than his fixed two hours, and would insist upon finishing the allotted period by pacing up and down in front of the door. These two hours were the delight of those privileged to be his companions; an unceasing flow of reminiscences, of humorous stories and of wise sayings made the time pass with much begrudged rapidity . . . He had an inexhaustible fund of anecdote, at times serious, at times humorous. He would often light up a point with a turn of expression which

showed the inward fire of poetry which permeated him; such as when
describing his visit to Valentia in 1848: 'I looked out over the ocean with
all the revolutions in Europe behind me' . . . In discussing the sound of
perfect lines, he told me that he considered the best line he ever wrote to be
'The mellow ouzel fluted in the elm.' . . . He was seventy when I first saw
him on that stormy morning at Freshwater, but the mind was that of a
man in his prime, and he had the rare faculty of adapting his age to his
surroundings, a boy with boys and a man with men. He knew little about
music, but was a past-master in an art which has a vast deal to do with
music, declamation. He instinctively felt how words should be set, and his
fine ear could detect the slightest slip in an accent, or a stress which was
faulty or ill-balanced. I often accompanied him on his clockwork consititu-
tional . . . He once told me of a conversation he had with Queen Victoria,
which is so touching that it should be put on record. He was walking up
and down the terrace at Osborne with her, and was so silent that the
Queen asked him what he was thinking about. He said, 'I was thinking
how lonely Your Majesty was up there.' 'And', he said, 'she cried, and I
was sorry I had said it, but it was uppermost in my thoughts and out it
came.'

Stanford was a lifelong friend of Tennyson's and visited him on a
number of occasions, both at Farringford and at his other home,
Aldworth. Through Tennyson, he met other leading literary figures.
Francis Turner Palgrave's journal entry for the second week of
January 1885 records, 'To Aldworth, where I found Jowett. One
evening A. T. read us several recent poems in his ballad style of
extraordinary power and beauty. On the 12th Mr V. Stanford, the
agreeable musician, came.'

Tennyson had a soft spot for Jennie Stanford. She was not the least
in awe of him and once made him waltz with her round the drawing-
room at Farringford while her husband played the piano. She said
that he danced 'to perfection'. She was among the very few who
persuaded him to part with his autograph, and for her he produced
something special. In one corner of a piece of paper, he wrote his
name in short; in the next, in full; in the third, upside-down; in the
last, he put, 'To the little vivid thing'.

By the 1880s Stanford was established with a national reputation
as organist, conductor and composer. In Plunket Greene's words, 'He
was drawing crowds to Trinity Chapel; the CUMS under his stick
was setting the pace to the rest of the country; and he had composed,
and was composing, music which was ahead of his time. To the *B flat
Service* he had added the *Evening Service in A*; he had written the *Cavalier
Songs* for baritone solo and male voice chorus . . .'

The *Cavalier Songs*, settings of poems by Robert Browning, were a further feather in his cap. The poet much admired Stanford's treatment of his work. 'The whole of my poetry', he wrote, 'should be at your service – "to serve thyself, my cousin!" . . . were you able to illustrate it so happily.' Stanford met Browning for the first time when the poet travelled to Cambridge for the English première of Brahms's First Symphony. After that he saw him quite often.

> He was to all superficial observers the very reverse of what his admirers pictured him in their mind's eye. No one who met him without knowing him would have guessed him to be a poet. His matter-of-fact society manner, and his almost dapper appearance, belied the inner fire. His shell was very thick, and his oddly rasping voice gave the impression of its being very hard as well . . . Those who had once broken the shell were never again conscious of its existence.

In the spring of 1880 there was good news from Ernst Frank, who had recently been appointed director of the Court Theatre in Hanover. He wanted to go ahead and produce *The Veiled Prophet*. Rehearsals began towards the end of the year. The entire cast soon became most enthusiastic about the opera and, according to Plunket Greene, 'seemed to take a pride in doing their very best for the Engländer, from the *prima donna* to the drummer . . .' The drummer was indeed wonderfully conscientious. 'On one morning', Stanford recalled, 'I heard a curious sound in the dark theatre, and, peering round from the stage, I saw the drummer all alone practising the entire opera by himself.' *The Veiled Prophet*, presented on 6 February 1881, was an instant success, and Stanford had to take numerous curtain-calls. It was subsequently performed throughout Germany, laying the foundations of the composer's continental reputation.

'Meanwhile', Stanford notes in *Pages from an Unwritten Diary*, 'music in Cambridge was progressing steadily, and was leading the way in the encouragement of native music.'

> Hubert Parry's remarkable setting of scenes from *Prometheus Unbound*, a work far in advance of any choral work of the kind which had hitherto been created by any Englishman since the days of Henry Purcell, had been brought out at Gloucester, and was attacked by the greater part of the Press, headed by Joseph Bennett, mainly on the score of its pronounced sympathy with modern developments. The University Society cared nothing for their fulminations, and produced it, with the success anticipated by less prejudiced musicians . . .

The performance took place in March 1881 and was a triumph for Parry, who was delighted with the way the work was produced: 'the *tempi* were good, the band perfect. Stanford all along was marvellously kind and genial,' he wrote. 'He has the Irishman's characteristic sweetness in companionship and is evidently worshipped almost universally in Cambridge; as it seems with good reason.'

Despite his busy life in England, Stanford still found time for travel. In the autumn of 1881 he and Jennie went to Vienna, where he did some research on Schubert, on behalf of George Grove, who was near to completing his important life of Schubert for the *Dictionary*. Grove was a Schubert expert and, with Arthur Sullivan, had tracked down the lost *Rosamunde* music in Vienna in 1867. In 1881 he was on the trail of the 'lost' *Gastein Symphony*. He bombarded Stanford with requests for information, enclosing minute instructions concerning the various MSS that he was to examine. 'I am so sorry to bully you with all these questions', he wrote, 'but you are at the fountain head and I am thirsting in the desert.' Stanford could find no evidence to support Grove's belief in the existence of the missing work. Grove was deeply disappointed: 'I nearly wept at having to give up the 10th symphony.' Stanford had an immense regard for Grove.

> Never was Britisher less British . . . Poetry had almost as much attraction for him as music. The little green books, with which from time to time Tennyson enriched the world, were to be seen in his hand within five minutes of publication. He seized me one morning . . . hurried me into his room, and read to me, with the tears running down his cheeks, the last lines (about Edward Fitzgerald) in *Tiresias* . . . In a word he was unique: like nobody else in the world, and, both from contrast and by personal force, one of the most vivid and vivifying influences in English life . . .

The next year the Stanfords were in northern Italy, where they chanced on a sight in Venice 'which alone repaid the journey: Charles Hallé in a frock-coat and a white top hat reading the *Daily Telegraph* while seated in a gondola and floating under the Bridge of Sighs.'

Earlier in 1882, in mid-January, Stanford visited Hamburg and discovered on arrival that Brahms, too, was there, having come to perform his recently completed Second Piano Concerto.

> The reception given to the composer by his native town was as enthusiastic as we anticipated. His pianoforte playing was not so much that of a finished pianist, as of a composer who despised virtuosity. The skips,

which are many and perilous in the solo part, were accomplished regardless of accuracy, and it is not an exaggeration to say that there were handfuls of wrong notes. The touch was somewhat hard, and lacking in force-control; it was at its best in the slow movement, where he produced the true velvety quality, probably because he was not so hampered by his own difficulties. But never since have I heard a rendering of the concerto, so complete in its outlook or so big in its interpretation. The wrong notes did not really matter, they did not disturb his hearers any more than himself. He took it for granted that the public knew that he had written the right notes, and did not worry himself over such little trifles as hitting the wrong ones. His attitude at the piano was precisely that in Professor von Beckerath's sketch. The short legs straight down to the pedals, which they seemed only just to reach, the head thrown back and slightly tilted as if listening to the band rather than to himself, the shoulders hunched up and the arms almost as straight as the legs and well above the keyboard. His figure was curiously ill-proportioned. He had the chest development and height from the waist of a muscular man of five foot ten, but his legs were so short as to reduce him well below middle height. His eyes were, I think, the most beautiful I ever saw; blue, and of a depth so liquid that (as I once heard a friend of his say) 'You could take a header into them.'

The year 1882 witnessed the premières of two more orchestral works by Stanford: the Second Symphony, the *Elegiac*, inspired by Tennyson's *In Memoriam* and played at a CUMS concert, and the Serenade in G, commissioned for the Birmingham Musical Festival, which was held that August. Both pieces received a warm welcome.

In 1883 he was granted an honorary doctorate by Oxford University. In June of the same year, at a CUMS concert, he conducted the first performance of Parry's Second Symphony, the *Cambridge*. Parry, then thirty-five, was also given an honorary doctorate by the university. This was the result of an application made to the Senate by Macfarren, in his capacity as Professor of Music, but the idea was Stanford's.

On 7 May 1883, the Royal College of Music was opened. George Grove was appointed its director and simultaneously knighted. Among the professors were Jenny Lind (now Madame Lind-Goldschmidt, aged sixty-two), for singing; Walter Parratt, for organ; Frederick Bridge, for harmony and counterpoint; and Parry and Stanford, for composition. Stanford also became co-conductor, with the violinist Henry Holmes, of the Royal College orchestra; from 1885 he was the sole conductor. The decision to found the RCM, which took over the premises of the seven-year-old National Training School for Music, followed many months of discussion, but was reached in a matter of seconds. According to Albert Visetti, who was made a Professor of Singing, he and his colleagues, a number of whom had also been employed by the National Training School, were summoned by the Prince of Wales (whose favourite composer was Meyerbeer) to St James's Palace, where they all stood round a table, while the Prince, seated at the end, read out the resolution proposing the founding of the college. He then asked, 'Will those gentlemen in favour of the resolution please remain standing and those against it sit down.' Those against looked about them, but found no chairs in the room other than that occupied by the Prince. While they were considering what to do, he declared the resolution carried. There were initially forty-two paying students and fifty scholars, who included a mill girl, the son of a blacksmith, the son of a farm labourer and the daughter of a brick-maker. The election of the first scholars, Stanford recalled, was a dramatic and moving occasion.

> The examiners sat round a large horseshoe table in the Council Room of the Albert Hall, and had first to hear the performance of some of the candidates whose merits were too equal to be decided upon by the preliminary judges. When the soprano singers were brought in, Madame Goldschmidt (Jenny Lind) did not test them at the pianoforte, but sang from her seat a series of amazing roulades and cadenzas which the trembling young women had to imitate as best they could, divided between anxiety for themselves and astonishment at the Chopin-like passages which came so easily out of the throat of an elderly lady at the table. Some of them made surprisingly good attempts at the ordeal. When the names of the successful fifty were decided upon, they were ushered into the room in a body. By some misunderstanding outside, as I afterwards ascertained, they were one and all under the impression that they were those who had failed.

When Grove told them that, on the contrary, they were the ones who had passed, there was a remarkably emotional scene. Jenny Lind 'sobbed like a child . . . and most of us had a curious lump in our throats.' Grove made a memorable speech at the opening of the college, says Stanford. 'In the short ten minutes which it took to deliver, it placed the whole of English musical education on the highest plane, and gave a lofty tone to the Institution which it could not fail to live up to.'

Grove was a phenomenal man. He became director of the RCM without it ever occurring to anybody that there could be any alternative candidate for the post. 'No one seems to know how he got there', wrote Geoffrey Parratt in his life of his father, Walter Parratt, 'and no record of his formal appointment exists; it was taken as the obviously fitting thing.' Grove was originally a civil engineer and between 1841 and 1846 supervised the erection of lighthouses in the West Indies. He served under Robert Stephenson during the construction of the Britannia tubular bridge over the Menai Straits and, at the suggestion of Stephenson and Brunel, was later appointed secretary to the Society of Arts. He next became secretary of the Crystal Palace, moving permanently to nearby Sydenham in 1852. Shortly afterwards he acquired an interest in biblical research, contributing more than 800 pages to the 3,154 page *Dictionary of the Bible*, which he also helped to edit. He visited the Holy Land in 1858 and 1861 and was largely responsible for establishing the 1865 Palestine Exploration Fund. He contributed to *The Times* the first detailed report on the Oberammergau Passion Play Festival. Concurrent with this work ran his musical activities. From 1856, for nearly forty years, he prepared the programme notes for the Crystal Palace concerts. In 1873 he began editing the celebrated *Dictionary of Music and Musicians*; 'one dictionary led to another', as he put it. Almost as a side-line, he edited *Macmillan's Magazine* from 1868 until his appointment as director of the RCM. In 1876 he wrote a book on geography. At a gathering in his honour in 1880 – at which he was presented with a golden chronometer and a cheque for a thousand guineas – bible scholars, musicians, engineers, poets and novelists rubbed shoulders, many of them discovering for the first time the incredible range of his achievements. Tennyson, Longfellow, Emerson, Millais, Brahms, Balfour were among his many distinguished friends; Browning, himself a near-polymath, called him 'Grove the Orientalist, the Schubertian, the Literate in ordinary and extraordinary'. Stanford's admiration for him was practically boundless.

> Grove's fascination was extraordinary. I felt it from the first evening I saw him in the Scott Russells' drawing-room in 1864. Nature had made him from the painter's and the sculptor's point of view the reverse of beautiful. His intellect made him more attractive than many an Adonis. His walk was once graphically described to me as one of a man with two left legs and somebody else's arms; but it had more character in it than that of the best-drilled officer of the Guards . . . From his opening speech at the College to the day he resigned, he kept the highest ideals steadily before the eyes of every man and woman within its walls, and by his insistence, by his example as well as precept, upon general culture, raised the *niveau* of

musical education in England to a height to which it had never before attained. This fact alone is a monument to his memory, and to an influence which succeeding generations may find it difficult to emulate but impossible to destroy.

Stanford, too, contributed greatly towards making the RCM an immediate success. He put the stress on practical music-making, being opposed to foreign conservatoires' concentration on paper work. 'We went on the principle that a hearing of a composition is the best lesson the writer can get, and that the perspiration and agony from which a composer suffers when he hears the sounds of his own inexperience is the most valuable part of his training. School orchestras abroad were seldom complete, and were restricted in their repertoire to the most classical music, all modern developments being stringently placed upon the Index Expurgatorius. We adopted the principle that for effective training the players should know everything, old and new . . .' According to Plunket Greene, the result was that the RCM students could read anything at sight, could cope with emergencies and gained an enviable practical knowledge of masterworks from the past and present.

> One student after another passed almost automatically into the great orchestras of the country and never failed to make good. Sixty years ago [1875] British orchestras were mainly foreign; to-day they are British to a man – and the training grounds have been the R.A.M. and the R.C.M. and Stanford their greatest trainer. No one would accuse him of being a 'star' conductor. He was far too unself-conscious to associate himself with virtuosity of any kind . . . I doubt if any student orchestra in any country got such a grounding in essentials as that of the R.C.M. in his time.

The grounding even extended to 'dangerous' works, like Berlioz's *Harold in Italy,* and to light-classical favourites. Such catholicity had its pitfalls: when he conducted a waltz and polka by Johann Strauss at a Christmas concert in December 1888, one of his fellow professors, noted Parry in his diary, 'made a fool of himself by hissing them.' His ideals were shared by other prominent musicians, including Sullivan, who, when he was conductor of the Leeds Musical Festival, made the orchestra entirely English, with results, wrote Stanford, 'which somewhat amazed foreign composers when they visited that Festival. I heard Humperdinck say to him, after a very smooth reading of a new work, that he supposed that there were many foreigners in the band, and Sullivan was able to answer, "Not one," with an amused and not untriumphant smile.'

On 18 April 1884 Stanford's opera *Savonarola* was staged for the first time, in Hamburg, and scored a decided success. The critic Riccius commented, 'As regards intrinsic musical importance, fertility of imagination, clever and at the same time solid elaboration, and dramatic instinct, as well as honesty and seriousness of artistic purpose, this work far surpasses all other operatic novelties produced here during the past few years; and yet we have witnessed a good many during that period, and amongst them some of undoubted merit.' Riccius who had been a friend of Schumann, further expressed his admiration by inviting Stanford to his home, where, comments Stanford, 'if I had been a born Hamburger, I could not have met with greater kindliness.'

Savonarola was produced in London in July 1884 and was a complete fiasco. In *A Door-Keeper of Music*, Fuller-Maitland gives some of the reasons for this rebuff.

I went with Barclay Squire to Hamburg for the production of our friend Stanford's *Savonarola*, which was finely given under Sucher and very warmly received. Frau Sucher, 'doubling' the parts of a mother and daughter, was at her best, and I formed the opinion that the Prologue marked the highest point the composer had attained in dramatic music. I have since seen no reason to alter that opinion, although the single and quite inadequate performance of the work at Drury Lane under Richter a few months later, was undeniably a failure. There were many reasons for this, for in the first place Frau Sucher was not in the cast, and for some reason, connected with a lawsuit as to performing rights, the publisher of the score thought fit to put every obstacle in the way of the production. *Prima donna* after *prima donna* was struck down by one of those strange indispositions which have so often upset operatic plans. Each of Stanford's friends was provided with a candidate for the engagement, whose name had to be carefully concealed for fear of the same epidemic attacking them. Mine was a German soprano living in North London who got through a trial rehearsal with a good deal of success, but in the event a lady sang who had not been very satisfactory in the part of Magdalena in the *Meistersinger* on the night before. The representative of the title-part refused to part with his flowing yellow beard, so that Savonarola's appearance was not very convincing. The copies of the vocal score, although printed, were never issued to the public, but a few were available for the press, and appeared with the words 'Als Manuscript gedrückt' on the title-page. I fortunately possess one of these, and it is amusing to recall the innocent air with which Hueffer [critic for *The Times*] – a German by birth and education – asked me what the words meant.

One most unfortunate thing about the whole incident was that the failure killed another opera by Stanford, which had been successfully launched at the same theatre shortly before the German season. *The Canterbury Pilgrims* was given some four times under Carl Rosa, and was on its way to a real success, for the price of the seats was run up to nearly double, and every performance was quite full.

Standford wrote of the London presentation of *Savonarola*, 'I scarcely recognized the opera I had seen at Hamburg a few weeks before.' One member of the audience who did enjoy the work's single performance was Robert Stewart, on a visit from Dublin. He mentioned it in a letter to his daughter Helen.

I went to Savonarola, by C. V. Stanford, and liked it very much. *The British Philistines* rather sat on Charlie: unjustly in the extreme. I was very much pleased with it, and I wrote to his mother in high praise of it. I was quite in accord with the previous Hamburghers' criticism. She (Mrs S.) sent my letter to Charlie, who wrote me a sweet letter back, asking me: 'Did I not recognise the result of my own teaching in his orchestral scoring?' This does not look as if success has spoiled him!

During the same year, in the purer air of Norfolk, the *Elegiac Ode*, based on Walt Whitman's lamentation on the death of Lincoln, was given at the Norwich Music Festival. This made an excellent impression, winning warm reviews. In setting this poem, which dates from 1867, Stanford was much in advance of his time, for Whitman had yet to be generally appreciated. The critic of *The Musical Times*, though asserting that the music 'possesses real charm', was blind to the beauties of the poetry.

There are some who look upon Whitman as a poet of genius, while others regard him as little better than a lunatic. It is not our duty now to discuss this question, but we must say that it is long since we met with anything more eccentric than the words which Dr. Stanford has selected for treatment in his Ode . . . This may be poetry, but to ourselves we confess it is more like incoherent maundering.

It is difficult to believe that this was prompted by the lines that open, 'When lilacs last in the dooryard bloom'd'; the 'fine spirit' that Tennyson so admired in Whitman had yet to make a universal appeal.

Stanford's next major work, *The Three Holy Children*, was introduced the following year at the Birmingham Musical Festival; this oratorio was more in the tradition of English choral pieces and is less striking than the *Elegiac Ode*. It, too, was well received. The first part, a setting of Psalm 137, 'By the Rivers of Babylon', was particularly attractive and could be performed perfectly well on its own.

During 1885, Stanford was appointed conductor of the London Bach Choir in succession to its principal founder Otto Goldschmidt, the husband of Jenny Lind. He at once established with these performers the same rapport he had at Cambridge and the RCM. Plunket Greene relates,

He was once conducting a rehearsal of the Bach Choir and was insisting on the proper pronunciation of the words. His cousin, Miss Elsie Holmes, whispered to him:

'Charlie, you're finding fault with the English choir in an Irish brogue.'

'Not at all,' he said indignantly. Then turning to the choir, 'Me cousin says that I c'rect ye in 'n Irish brogue.'

During the autumn of 1885 Stanford made another trip to Vienna, where, with Richter, he called on Brahms. This visit is described in *Studies and Memories*.

He opened he door of his little flat himself, clad in a jersey and trousers, and led us through a bare outer room, and his bedroom, scarcely less bare save for a drawing of 'Anselmo's Tomb' over his very short and stumpy bed, into his study, a double room crammed with books, music, and literature of all sorts. He greeted Richter warmly, and when I was introduced gave me a most distant and suspicious bow . . . I was quite sure he was aware of who I was, but was going to measure my capacity for lion-hunting. His chance came; he offered Richter a cigar, and was then handing the box to me, when he snatched it back with a curt, 'You are English, you don't smoke!' To which I replied, with an impertinence which it required some courage to assume, 'I beg pardon, the English not only smoke, but they even compose music sometimes,' making a simultaneous dash after the retreating cigar-box. For one moment he looked at me like a dangerous mastiff, and then burst out laughing. The ice was broken and never froze again. I caught sight of some fine engravings, and he spent the best part of the morning showing me his complete collection of Piranesi engravings, and other treasures which he had picked up in Italy during the previous summer. He only mentioned music once . . .

When I next visited Vienna I went to see him without an appointment, thinking that I should surely find him at home at eleven o'clock. But his housekeeper told me that he had just gone to dinner. I was so astonished that I said to her, 'In Heaven's name, what time does Brahms eat his breakfast?' 'At five,' said the dame; 'he does all his work before eleven, and is out the rest of the day.' However, I fell in with him later, and sat with him through a rehearsal of Gluck's *Alceste* at the Opera House, over which he waxed enthusiastic. His two favourite haunts in Vienna were Strauss's band and the Opera. While there I heard of a tremendous verbal castigation which he had given at a restaurant to a young man who thought he would gain his favour by sneering at Wagner . . .

A most remarkable and extraordinary personality was Brahms. Humorous, fearless, far-seeing, sometimes over-rough to his contemporaries, but a worshipper of and worshipped by young children; with a very noble, generous, and ideal side to his character, and a curiously warped and sensual side as well. He could look like Jupiter Olympus at one moment, and like Falstaff the next . . .

In 1886, one of the most popular of all Stanford's works, *The Revenge*, for chorus and orchestra, obtained its first hearing, at the Leeds Musical Festival. This 'Ballad of the Fleet', based on Tennyson's poem of 1880, became an immediate favourite with choral societies throughout the land and firmly established Stanford in the minds of the general public as one of the foremost of contemporary British composers. *The Revenge* was performed eighteen times during the 1886–7 season. The only other works to exceed that figure were Handel's *Messiah* (64), Mendelssohn's *Elijah* (22), *St Paul* (20) and *Hymn of Praise* (19), and Haydn's *The Creation* (19), all of which are of a religious nature.

'The spirit of the poem gave him one of his natural elements, the atmosphere of the sea, in which some of his finest works were to be cast', writes John F. Porte in his book on the composer.

In *The Revenge* Stanford breaks away into his own individual genius and makes music of the most inspired and stirring type. Of all his works up to this number, *The Revenge* stands out as one of the finest. The composer appears free from conventional influence and writes music that is entirely worthy of his natural genius. The stirring lines of Tennyson's poem found a ready sympathiser in Stanford, whose power to create, not depict, the sea atmosphere in his music is inimitable. Page after page in *The Revenge* contains music full of fire and salt-sea vigour and strength. The work is very conveniently scored only for chorus and orchestra, and has never yet failed to make an impression on, and stir the enthusiasm of, the listener, for it is really made of the ingredients that create great music.

Plunket Greene agrees: 'it stirs the blood like no other sea-ballad to this day; and the man who wrote it and the *Songs of the Sea* and the *Songs of the Fleet* hated, or professed to hate, the sea! His inspiration was not drawn from pleasure cruises in the Mediterranean or buffetings off the coast of Wicklow. Words were his magic carpet.'

His love of words constantly drew him to the works of Tennyson, who was frequently able to offer valuable advice on the settings.

> Without being a musician, he had a great appreciation of the fitness of music to its subjects, and was an unfailing judge of musical declamation. As he expressed it himself, he disliked music which went up when it ought to go down, and went down when it ought to go up. I never knew him wrong in his suggestions on this point. The most vivid instance I can recall was about a line in *The Revenge* –
> 'Was he devil or man? He was devil for aught they knew.'
> When I played him my setting, the word 'devil' was set to a higher note in the question than it was in the answer; and the penultimate word, 'they', was unaccented. He at once corrected me, saying that the second 'devil' must be higher and stronger than the first, and the 'they' must be marked. He was perfectly right, and I altered it accordingly.

The year 1887 was the fiftieth year of Queen Victoria's reign, and Stanford played a prominent part in the celebrations. Tennyson wrote a *Jubilee Ode*, which, at his request, Stanford set to music. The poet asked the Queen whether the work might be performed at Buckingham Palace during one of her visits to London. To this she assented, and it was played on 11 May, when, says Stanford, 'the orchestra and singers so outnumbered the listeners as to suggest the solitary operas given before King Ludwig of Bavaria.' Tennyson, now seventy-seven, was not well enough to travel up to London for the occasion, but the Queen wrote to him three days later.

> I am anxious to tell you that your beautiful Ode was performed at Buckingham Palace on the 11th., with a full Orchestra, Solo, Gala, and choruses, and conducted by Mr. Stanford himself.
> We greatly admired the music, which was very descriptive and well adapted to the words – and it was extremely well executed. I wish you could have heard it.

Also in connection with the jubilee was a performance in Westminster Abbey of Berlioz's *Te Deum*, with the London Bach Choir conducted by Stanford. This was a daring choice on his part, for Berlioz was still regarded with suspicion, and the work had received its English première only two years earlier. Even the *Symphonie fantastique* had to wait until 1879, when Hallé conducted the first English performance, in Manchester, forty-eight years after it was introduced in Paris. In the summer of 1887 the orchestra of the Royal College of Music was commanded to give a special concert at Windsor Castle, following one of the jubilee banquets, on 25 June. Among the second violins was fourteen-year-old Landon Ronald, who recalled the occasion in his memoirs *Variations on a Personal Theme*.

> I remember quite distinctly my great indignation at my dear mother, because she would insist on my wearing a velvet knicker bocker suit which, for some ungodly reason, I possessed at the time. We were all to leave from Paddington Station in a couple of third-class coaches attached to a special train. This special train turned out to be the one which was to take the various Royalties.to Windsor Castle. I can still feel the thrills I experienced when I arrived on the platform carrying my violin, and was told by some fellow-student, 'You see that couple there? Well, that's the King and Queen of Norway and Sweden! Just standing by them is the King and Queen of Denmark. And you see these three men grouped together? Well, the old man is the Kaiser, and the man with the beard is the German Crown Prince (afterwards Kaiser Frederick), and the youngster is Prince Wilhelm.' I remember I was quite enthralled, and felt very much the same as when I was first taken to Madame Tussaud's. Only two outstanding memories remain of what occurred at the Castle that night. The first is that some kind official hoisted me on his shoulder and let me have a peep of the great banqueting hall through a tiny little window, and told me to be sure and have a look at the gold plate, which duly impressed me. The second is my intense nervousness and anxiety lest I should play a wrong note, as I was obsessed with the idea that Queen Victoria would at once detect it, and that I should be promptly sent to prison.

Stanford says that one of the RCM professors who accompanied the orchestra held republican opinions and 'sorely disgusted Grove by insisting on wearing a black tie, and would not even admit that the same courtesy should be shown to the Queen as was due to any lady at an evening party in her own house. But I observed with some amusement that he did not turn his back on the late King of Denmark when he came up and talked to him, but rather enjoyed the distinction, so much that his republican tenets went by the board.' The orchestra numbered about seventy-five, and the entire RCM contingent came to around eighty. After making the short journey from the station, they arrived in the dark at the Castle, where, writes Stanford, 'we were directed to an entrance which led into a perfect labyrinth of passages.' Grove headed the procession, striding purposefully forward on his two left legs and swinging somebody else's arms, and made for a likely-looking door 'which landed us in the kitchen. He was equal to the occasion, smiled round upon the army of white-capped officials', and set off in a different direction. He eventually marched his troops into the Tapestry Room, which seemed to be the right place, except, by the time the whole orchestra had filed in, there was hardly any space left for the royal audience. In Stanford's view, the room 'would have been roofless after the first chord.' All of a sudden the Queen herself appeared. 'She gave one look at us, turned round, made a sweeping gesture with her arm, summoned an equerry (who looked very uncomfortable at what she confided to him) and departed. We were promptly ordered out again, and with a swiftness which would have done credit to Aladdin's Djinn we found ourselves in an adequate space in the Waterloo Chamber.'

The concert turned out to be a real success, despite a veto against any preliminary tuning-up and a subsequent royal and largely foreign 'Babel of conversation' in which, conspicuously, the Queen did not take part. A few days later, Grove wrote about the concert to his friend Mrs Wodehouse; his letter appears in Charles L. Graves's *The Life and Letters of Sir George Grove, C.B.*

My young heroes rose to the occasion and I really do not think that the overture to *Ruy Blas* has been often played better. Russell sang Wood's two songs very well indeed. The mass of the room talked loud, but the Queen was very attentive and very intelligent. I and Charles Morley were taken to her afterwards by the Prince of Wales, and I understood her to say that she was very much pleased, and that she was astonished to find them playing so well. She also asked questions about the performers, but her voice was so low that I missed much of her words. It was a splendid night. Two kings at least, and lots of beautiful women of the highest rank. The most interesting thing to me was to see an Infanta of Spain for the first time in the flesh! Another very interesting thing was the transformation that occurred when the Queen said that we were not to play in the Tapestry Room but to go into the Waterloo Gallery. Just as in an Arabian Night, when you stamp your foot everything is carried away, etc., so here, on the instant (as it seemed to me), thirty or forty men appeared, carried off all the desks, seats, music, etc. at once and the change was made within five minutes.

Also during 1887, Stanford's setting of Psalm 150, 'Praise Ye the Lord', was sung at the Manchester Exhibition, for which it had been commissioned. In Cambridge, the Piano Quintet, perhaps the most beautiful of his chamber works, received its first performance. Another piece to have its première at a CUMS concert was Frederic Cowen's Symphony No 5, conducted by Stanford; his reputation, like Parry's and Stanford's, was rising quickly too.

In London, on 17 ·May, six days after appearing before Her Majesty at Buckingham Palace, Stanford directed the London Bach Choir in the first performance of Parry's magnificent *Blest Pair of Sirens*. This was instantly acclaimed. Parry admitted it 'went pretty well'; as for Grove, he jumped up and 'wrung my hand with tears in his eyes', the composer noted in his diary.

Ten days later, on 27 May 1887 came the première, in London under Richter, of Stanford's Third Symphony, the *Irish*, which many might suggest is his masterpiece. 'It is the most popular and lovable of Stanford's symphonies', observes John F. Porte, 'and when we consider the period in which it was written, its freshness and originality are remarkable.' The slow movement is one of the most moving in all British music, while the finale, riding to a brilliant conclusion with 'Let Erin Remember the Days of Old' blazing out on the four horns, is totally irresistible. The *Irish Symphony* brought Stanford world-wide fame. Within a year it had been heard three times in London, as well as in Birmingham, Bradford and Norwich. The German première in Hamburg was shortly followed by two performances in Berlin. It was also played in Brussels, Rome, Bologna and other European cities; by May 1888 it had been given twice in New York and once in Boston. When the Concertgebouw was opened in Amsterdam, the *Irish Symphony* was chosen to conclude the first concert, which took place on 3 November 1888.

The international success of the *Irish Symphony* was a source of immense pride to all British musicians of the time and particularly, of course, to the cities of Dublin and Cambridge and to everybody at the RCM. It should be mentioned that in 1866 Sullivan had also brought forward an 'Irish' symphony, though he did not actually give the work that title. 'I always meant to call it the "Irish Symphony"', he later wrote, 'but I modestly refrained, as it was courting comparison with the "Scotch Symphony".' In March 1893 he subtitled it 'In Ireland' – 'Stanford called his symphony the "Irish", so I didn't see why I should be done out of my title abroad.' Sullivan's symphony made no headway outside Britain; it was privately rehearsed in Leipzig in October 1867, but not performed publicly.

In January 1888, Stanford travelled to Hamburg to attend the

German première of the *Irish Symphony* and met there for the first time the remarkable Hans von Bülow. Bülow was one of the most famous of all living musicians; pupil of Liszt, friend of Brahms, champion of the young Richard Strauss, he was renowned both as pianist and conductor. Among many other premières, he conducted those of *Die Meistersinger* and *Tristan und Isolde*. His first wife Cosima, the daughter of Liszt, left him for Wagner in 1869; in 1882 he married the actress Marie Schanzer. He spoke a number of different languages with great ease, making puns in English and even in Cockney and producing countless *bon mots* and witticisms. He possessed an almost unbelievable memory and generally gave the impression of being superhuman. Stanford became aware of this within minutes of setting eyes on him. After arriving in Hamburg, he and a friend slipped into the morning's rehearsal unannounced and sat down in the dark at the back of the hall. He had not told Bülow that he would be in Hamburg. 'Hans was hard at work on the symphony. Whether it was second sight or brain-wave I know not, but we had not been there for a few minutes before he turned round, peered into the dark recesses at the back of the room, and called out my name. He had not heard a syllable about my coming.'

The Hamburg performance was most successful. Before going on to Berlin, where he was again to conduct the symphony, Bülow took Stanford to see a production of *Le nozze di Figaro*. Among the other members of the audience, he spotted Richard Strauss, then twenty-three, whom he introduced to his Irish colleague. 'This', he said, 'is Strauss *not* the waltz king!' Bülow and Stanford journeyed to Berlin together. With the Berlin Philharmonic, Bülow conducted both the rehearsals and the performance entirely from memory. When Stanford expressed his amazement, Bülow merely replied, 'Good for the newspapers'. The Berlin audience gave the work a rapturous reception. *The Musical Times* reported that 'Dr. Stanford was called six times, and the usually cold Berliners got up and cheered like undergraduates.' The symphony had to be repeated on the following evening.

During the summer of 1888, Bülow came to Cambridge at Stanford's invitation and gave a piano recital in King's College Hall. By now he was addressing Stanford as 'Meister', a wonderful compliment from so eminent a musician. This was not his first trip to England; he had already come several times. On one previous visit he was asked by a female admirer whether he knew Wagner. 'Why, yes,

Madame', he answered. 'He is the husband of my wife.' In *Pages from an Unwritten Diary* Stanford pays tribute to Bülow's generosity of character, alluding in particular to the numerous piano recitals he gave to raise money for the building of the Festspielhaus at Bayreuth.

His extraordinary loyalty to Wagner's efforts on behalf of German opera, in the teeth of the greatest wrong which one man can do to another, was one of the most convincing proofs of the greatness of mind which was in him. He laid many of the bricks of the Baireuth Theatre with his piano-forte recitals. He did not cease to do so, when the composer made his home desolate; for he knew and said that his work was being done for the music and not for the man; the advice of friends and the sneers of foes had no power to dissuade him from his purpose. But he never saw the Baireuth Theatre until after Wagner's death, if then. Quixotic perhaps he was, in the eyes of the man of the world, but instinct with real unadulterated nobility. He was to his finger-tips a great gentleman.

The only work of note to be introduced in 1888, after the previous *annus mirabilis*, was the concert overture *Queen of the Seas*, composed for the tercentenary of the defeat of the Spanish Armada. That summer Stanford was again in Bayreuth, where he chanced on Robert Stewart, who was on his honeymoon; his first wife had died the year before, and he had remarried. 'We met . . . Charlie Stanford. The latter poked me up in the dark of the auditorium of the Wagner Theatre, with a long umbrella, and he said he had attended seventeen performances of the *Meistersinger*, and that this was the best of all.'

Meanwhile, Macfarren had died. The matter of who was to be his successor at Cambridge was not even debated, and, at thirty-five, Stanford became the new Professor of Music. In November 1888 the university bestowed on him an honorary doctorate. At the same ceremony this distinction was conferred, also, on the Scottish composer Alexander Mackenzie.

Mackenzie was at that time regarded as highly as Stanford. He was born in Edinburgh in 1847; his early life was arduous in the extreme, and for a while he earned his living as a piano teacher and orchestral violinist. He first came to notice with his Piano Quartet of 1875, dedicated to Charles Hallé, which was much admired by Bülow and popularised by him in Germany. In 1880 the delightful *Scottish Rhapsody No 1* was introduced by Manns at a concert in Glasgow and shortly afterwards given its continental première under Nikisch in Germany. In the mid-seventies, Mackenzie and his wife moved to Florence, where they stayed for about ten years. During this period he produced many of his finest compositions, including the opera *Colomba*, presented at Drury Lane in 1883; the oratorio *The Rose of Sharon*, performed at the Norwich Music Festival in 1884; the Violin Concerto, introduced by Sarasate at the Birmingham Musical Festival in 1885; and the opera *The Troubadour*, also staged at Drury Lane, in 1886. Liszt held Mackenzie's abilities in high esteem, and the two men were on friendly terms. The last music that Liszt wrote was the opening of a fantasia on themes from *The Troubadour*. In 1886, Mackenzie received an honorary doctorate from the University of St Andrews. In February 1888 he was appointed principal of the Royal Academy of Music, succeeding Macfarren.

In his memoirs, *A Musician's Narrative*, published in 1927, Mackenzie recalls the occasion when he and Stanford received their doctorates.

The honours of that day at Cambridge were enhanced by the fact that they were shared by Charles V. Stanford, then seated in the Cambridge Chair of Music in succession to Macfarren. We met for the first time on Drury Lane stage on he *première* of *Colomba*, when the young Irishman, five years my junior, offered his congratulations. Prolonged absences prevented further acquaintance either with himself or his works until personal convictions caused the *'Irish' Symphony* to make instant appeal to my sympathy. Nor was I slow to seize an opportunity for conducting it at one of the Novello Concerts.

By that time C.V.S. had several important works to his credit (*Elegiac Ode, Holy Children, The Revenge*, and a couple of operas), and had already risen to eminence. For exceptionally dexterous workmanship, unceasing industry, and a positively staggering rapidity in composition, I have never met his equal. That he could cast off his Irish brogues at will and adapt himself to any particular subject in hand added to my appreciation of an outstanding ability. In the long and varied catalogue of his works there are many really great things which justify the high place he now occupies in our musical history.

In January 1889, Stanford returned to Berlin, to conduct the world première of his Fourth Symphony, which was warmly welcomed by audience and critics alike. Some musicians value this work more highly than the *Irish Symphony*, but it has not proved as popular. Also introduced at the same concert was the Suite for Violin and Orchestra, the exuberant finale of which is an Irish jig, similar in feeling to the hop-jig second movement of the *Irish Symphony*. The solo part was played by Joseph Joachim, to whom the piece is dedicated.

Joachim was not short of dedications. Among the violin works inscribed to him are Brahms's Violin Concerto, Hiller's Violin Concerto, Bruch's First and Third Concertos, and Sarasate's first book of *Spanish Dances*. Other works of which he is the dedicatee include Liszt's *Hungarian Rhapsody No 12* and Schumann's Fourth Symphony, which bears the inscription. 'Symphony (in D minor) for orchestra (sketched in 1841, newly orchestrated in 1853). When the first notes of this symphony came into being, Joseph Joachim was still a little boy. Since then, the symphony has grown, and the boy, even more, and thus I dedicate it to him, though only in private.' It was to Joachim that Clara Schumann entrusted the task of informing her friends of her husband's death in July 1856.

Born in Hungary in 1831, Joachim was a child prodigy who developed into a great musician. On his first visit to London in the spring of 1844, he played the Beethoven Violin Concerto, with Mendelssohn conducting. The organist Elizabeth Mounsey vividly recalled the two of them at rehearsals.

I well remember Mendelssohn's bright look of pleasure and appreciative interest in his little friend. As conductor, he turned to the young soloist, attired in a short jacket and turned-down collar, so as to follow him dutifully, Mendelssohn's own subordinate position appearing to give him a degree of amusement. But it was very beautiful to see the pleasure it gave him to regard the boy at his side, not only with admiration, but with honour.

Of the performance, the critic J. W. Davison wrote, 'Not only was it astonishing as coming from a comparative child, but astonishing as a violin performance, no matter from whom proceeding . . . No master could have read it better, no finished artist could have better rendered it.'

Through the years, Joachim acquired an enormous circle of friends; apart from Mendelssohn, Schumann, Liszt and Brahms, these included Berlioz, Spohr, Franz, Cornelius, Raff, Bruch, Hiller, Bülow, Marschner, Rossini, Spontini, Gounod, Sterndale Bennett, Grove, Dickens, Tennyson, the brothers Grimm, and Bismarck. He met Stanford for the first time in 1862 in Dublin, when he was thirty and Stanford nine. The boy listened to him perform the 'Kreutzer' Sonata and Bach's G minor fugue and felt at once 'the inevitable rightness of every note and phrase he played'. When he was presented to the great violinist, Joachim 'was in an instant as much as a boy as I, and a friendship began which lasted unbroken till his death.'

Joachim came to England for Stanford's wedding. In his letters he often called himself 'the big fiddler Jo Jo'; later, he became 'the old fiddler'. He made many appearances at CUMS concerts, and in 1889 the Society honoured him with a gala dinner to celebrate his fifty years before the public. The menu reflected the happy relationship between himself and the CUMS.

THURSDAY; MARCH 14TH, 1889

Consommé Fausse Tortue à la Corelli
Potage aux Huitres à la Paganini
*

Turbot sauce Homard à la Viotti
Cotelettes de Saumon à la Bach
*

Vol au Vent à la Bartholdy
Quenelles de Lièvre à l'Hongrois
*

Hanche de Mouton à la Stradivarius
Jambon d'York
Dinde braisé à la Spohr
*

Baba à la Beethoven
Chantilly d'Orange à la Tourte
*

Diablotins à la Tartini

In 1889 Stanford dedicated a work to his friend Bülow: the Piano Trio No 1. 'Good gracious! What wonderful progress your country is making, owing to your genius', wrote Bülow when accepting the dedication. He added that, together with Brahms's Third Violin Sonata, the Trio was one of the finest two pieces ever dedicated to him. This was indeed a compliment, for only two years earlier Dvořák had named him as the dedicatee of the Fifth Symphony.

Bülow described the Czech composer as 'a genius who looks like a tinker'; his pet name for him was 'Caliban'. Another important work of Stanford's to be introduced in 1889 was *The Voyage of the Maeldune*, for soloists, chorus and orchestra. Based on Tennyson's poem of 1880, it was first performed at the Leeds Musical Festival. The poet was pleased with Stanford's setting and told him how much he enjoyed the section 'The Undersea Isle', where it 'rippled away at the end'.

Stanford's responsibilities at the close of the eighties and the beginning of the nineties were daunting. At Cambridge, he was Professor of Music, organist of Trinity College and conductor of the CUMS. In London, at the RCM, he was Professor of Composition and conductor of the student orchestra; he was also conductor of the London Bach Choir. In addition he was now a father, with two young children, Guy and Geraldine. He nevertheless managed to produce an impressive number of works each year. In 1890 he created two major compositions. The slighter of these, *The Battle of the Baltic*, for chorus and orchestra, is generally accounted the more successful. Receiving its first performance on 20 July 1891 under Richter in London, the piece is a setting of Thomas Campbell's poem. 'The whole work is fresh, individual, and exhilaratingly swept by the keen breath of the composer's genius', writes John F. Porte. 'There is something in it that sets the blood tingling in our veins, and it has that peculiarly keen suggestiveness of the sea atmosphere that Stanford obtained so inimitably, both in preceding and later works.' The second of the 1890 compositions, *Eden*, is based on Milton's draft, dating from around 1640, of a drama called 'Paradise Lost' that antedates his epic poem by more than twenty-five years. The draft is in a workbook housed in the library of Trinity College, and it was there that Stanford read it and realised its possibilities. Since it is largely in outline, he asked Robert Bridges to produce a text that would fit Milton's scenario. The choice of authors and subject, the size of the work and the care that Stanford put into *Eden*, all these are convincing evidence that the composer intended it to be something out of the ordinary, possibly his choral *chef-d'oeuvre*. Certainly there are fine moments in it, including a beautiful *Madrigale spirituale* in five parts, *a cappella*, some lovely choruses, and attractive and varied parts for all six soloists; and, when it was presented at the Birmingham Musical Festival in October 1891, it undoubtedly created a favourable impression. Parry, to whom *Eden* is dedicated, thought it 'brilliantly effective and admirable in poetry and balance'. Nevertheless, it would not seem to represent Stanford at his most inspired. Indeed, Parry's 'effective and admirable' says much through omission. Again, Grove's comment to Mrs Wodehouse, 'Stanford's "Eden" has a great deal in it, and I desire to hear it again', is, for him, somewhat luke-warm. Out of friendship for the composer, Parry, Grove, Mackenzie and others all round something pleasant to say about *Eden* – and there is much that can be said – but George Bernard Shaw, who was then music critic for the *Star*, made use of it for one of the most memorable of his many attacks on British composers.

Who am I that I should be believed, to the disparagement of eminent musicians? If you doubt that *Eden* is a masterpiece, ask Dr. Parry and Dr. Mackenzie, and they will applaud it to the skies. Surely Dr. Mackenzie's opinion is conclusive; for is he not the composer of *Veni Creator*, guaranteed as excellent music by Professor Stanford and Dr. Parry? You want to know who Dr. Parry is? Why?, the composer of *Blest Pair of Sirens*, as to the merits of which you have only to consult Dr. Mackenzie and Professor Stanford.

Apart from regularly inveighing against Stanford, Parry and Mac-kenzie, Shaw was always ready to dispatch the other two leading British composers of the day, Sullivan and Cowen. The admiration and respect in which Sullivan was held throughout the music profess-ion and by audiences in every part of Britain – particularly at Windsor – were as chaff before the blast of Shaw's invective.

As to Sir Arthur's scores, they form an easy introduction to dramatic music and picturesque or topical orchestration for perfect novices; but as I had learned it all from Meyerbeer (not to profane the great name of Mozart in such a connection), and was pretty well tired of Offenbach before *Trial by Jury* was born, there was no musical novelty in the affair for me. Besides, Sir Arthur's school is an exploded one. Neatly or cleverly as he exploits it, he cannot get a progression or a melody out of it that is not the worse for wear.

Cowen received much the same sort of drubbing. His opera *Thorgrim*, however eagerly other critics might extol it, would not provide as much wear 'as I shall get out of my second best pair of boots before they descend into the blind cave of eternal night.' Perfect Wagnerite that he was, Shaw dutifully lampooned Brahms, whenever possible. The Hamburg master's music was 'at bottom only a prodigiously elaborated compound of incoherent reminiscences'. 'Mind', he conceded, 'I do not deny that the Requiem is a solid piece of musical manufacture. You feel at once that it could only have come from the establishment of a first-class undertaker'; the flattest of funerals, he added, 'would seem like a ballet afterwards'. When, in June 1891, Stanford conducted the London Bach Choir in the first English performance of Brahms's Three Motets, Shaw wrote that 'for the most part it was a horrible tissue of puffing and blowing and wheezing and groaning and buzzing and hissing and gargling and shrieking and spluttering and grunting . . . It was really worse than the influenza.'

In the summer of 1891, the CUMS netted their biggest fish so far, when Dvořák travelled from Prague to receive an honorary doctorate and conduct one of the Society's concerts in a programme of his own works. His first visit to England had been in March 1884, following a joint invitation from the Philharmonic Society and the Albert Hall Choral Society. The *Daily Telegraph* noted on his arrival then that he was mentioned in only a single biographical dictionary. He was listed as DWORZAK, his christian name was unknown; he had had an opera performed in 1876; beyond that, there was little to tell. On 13 March 1884 he conducted the *Stabat Mater* at the Albert Hall. A week later he directed a concert at St James's Hall, consisting of the *Hussite* Overture, Sixth Symphony, *Second Slavonic Rhapsody* and some of the *Gipsy Songs*. Two days later, at the Crystal Palace, he led performances of the *Scherzo capriccioso* and the Nocturne for Strings. The success of these concerts was colossal; within a space of ten days Dvořák had taken London by storm. A dinner-party was held in his honour by the music publisher Henry Littleton of Novello's, and 150 guests attended, including many of the country's most prominent musicians. On 21 March the Philharmonic Society gave a banquet for him at the Café Royal, when in a brief speech in English he described the previous fortnight as the happiest he had ever spent. In a letter to his father, he said, 'Everywhere they write and talk about me and say that I am the *lion* of this year's musical season in London!'

> In September I'll be coming here again, and going outside London, too. This will be to the big industrial town of *Worchester*, where I'll again be conducting the Stabat Mater. I've already got offers to come to England next year and in '86 and I'll have to write some new works.

From all this you can see how they like and value me here. There was also mention of you in some of the papers, how I came of poor parents and how my father was a butcher and innkeeper in Nelahozeves and did all he could to give his son a proper education. *Honour to you for this!*

In a letter to the music publisher Urbánek, Dvořák told him that 'the English are a good, warm-hearted, music-loving nation, and it is well known that, if they take a liking to somebody, they remain loyal to him. God grant that this may be so with me, too.' He left England with commissions to compose two large choral works, one for the Birmingham Musical Festival and the other for the Leeds Musical Festival. Three months later he was elected an honorary member of the Philharmonic Society and commissioned by them to write a symphony. With the money from these commissions – one of the choral works alone carried a fee of £2,000 – he was at last able to realise his dream and buy a house in the country, not far from the Bohemian Forest, where he could be amid nature, at peace, and free to compose without disturbance or distraction. The visit to Worcester, to take part in the Three Choirs Festival, was another triumph. The *Stabat Mater* was given at midday on 11 September in Worcester Cathedral, and in the evening he conducted the Sixth Symphony in the town hall. Among the violins in the performance of the work was Edward Elgar, aged 27. 'I wish you could hear Dvořák's music', he wrote to his friend Charles Buck. 'It is simply ravishing, so tuneful & clever & the orchestration is wonderful: no matter how few instruments he uses it never sounds thin.' Dvořák liked Worcester and enjoyed being presented 'to all the élite of beautiful ladies'. Everywhere that he went in the city 'either in the street or at home or even when I go into a shop to buy something, people crowd round me, asking for my autograph. There are pictures of me in all the bookshops . . .'

The composer's third trip to England was to conduct the world première of the Symphony No 7, the piece commissioned by the Philharmonic Society. The performance, which took place in St James's Hall on 22 April 1885, caused a sensation; the *Athenaeum* called the symphony 'one of the greatest works of this kind that have been performed in the present generation'. Dvořák's reputation now stood so high that the new composition was described as 'fully worthy of the composer's name'. In no other country outside Bohemia had his genius been so fully recognised. Also played during this visit were the Piano Concerto and the cantata *The Heirs of the White Mountain*, published by Novello's and dedicated 'with feelings of deep gratitude to the English people'. Three months later he made his fourth visit, going to Birmingham, where he conducted the first English performance of *The Spectre's Bride*, which was enthusiastically received. He wrote home that the audience's acclamation and cries of 'Dvořák' went on and on. 'Orchestra, choir and public were all cheering. I wasn't aware of what was happening to me. I was moved as I have never been before.' One critic proclaimed that 1885 'will be accounted glorious because it has brought forward such a masterpiece'. The composer was impressed with Birmingham, 'an immense industrial town where they make excellent, knives, scissors, springs, files and I don't know what else', but was wholly enchanted by a brief holiday in Brighton, 'where the wealthiest London class go in the summer'.

> The lovely view of the sea from my room, the sight of thousands of people swarming everywhere, the beautiful English women bathing (*and in public*), the *men* and *children*, the huge number of boats large and small, and here a band playing Scottish folksongs and goodness knows what else besides: all this is so charming and fascinating that nobody who has seen it could ever forget it.

His fifth journey to England took him first to Leeds, where on 15 October 1886 he conducted the world première of *Saint Ludmilla*, again winning many ovations. Also performed for the first time at this memorable festival were Stanford's *The Revenge* and Sullivan's *The Golden Legend*. During rehearsals, Sullivan made himself most helpful to his Czech colleague, whose English was still a little shaky, by frequently interpreting his wishes to the orchestra. From Leeds, Dvořák travelled down to Birmingham to conduct the Sixth Symphony. Elgar was again in the orchestra. On this visit, Dvořák also managed to squeeze in a trip to Stratford-upon-Avon. Before leaving the country, he directed two performances in London of *Saint Ludmilla* and one of *The Spectre's Bride*.

The English première of the Symphony No 8, published by Novello's, brought him to British shores for the sixth time. This work was given under his baton at St James's Hall on 24 April 1890, further enchancing his reputation. By now, indeed, he was regarded in English musical circles as one of the supreme living masters, almost to be ranked with Brahms and Verdi. In an article in the *Cambridge Review* of 11 June 1891, published on the eve of Dvořák's arrival to receive his degree, Sedley Taylor stated that he occupied 'a leading position among living composers of the first rank'; he had attained 'a high pinnacle of distinction as a composer'. Taylor even suggested that parts of the *Stabat Mater* rose to the level of Mozart's *Requiem*. The first event to take place during his visit to the university was the CUMS concert, at which he conducted the *Stabat Mater* and Eighth Symphony. There was an enthusiastic report in the *Cambridge Review* of 18 June.

The C.U.M.S. concert on the 15th., which has been looked forward to with such keen interest all the term, was a quite unparalleled success. Afte hearing that gorgeous music, there can be little doubt that Herr Dvořák occupies a foremost place among great composers; one feels that his music will always live, and ever be fresh. What strikes us is the absolute newness and originality of it, combined with a perfect mastery over every shade of feeling – it is extraordinarily sympathetic; whilst in the *Stabat Mater* it is striking, solemn, and impressive to the last degree, in the symphony in G, it is all lightness, vivacity, and sometimes intense humour . . . It is extremely gratifying also to hear that Herr Dvořák was himself very pleased with the concert, and thought it the best performance of the *Stabat Mater* that has been given; the chorus have every reason to be proud of themselves, and great credit is due to them for their untiring energy all this term in making their part of the work a complete success; not only were they thoroughly firm and sure, and their singing excellent, but they never lost pitch; this was especially creditable in the very difficult chorus *Virgo virginium*, which is largely unaccompanied and which it is said no chorus has till this occasion succeeded in singing in tune.

One of the several London newspapers that reviewed the concert extended 'very hearty congratulations' to Stanford for 'having brought the musical resources of Cambridge up to the high level at which such performances as that of Monday last became possible.' Grove, too, came up for the concert. It appears that he had met the Czech composer for the first time in 1884, when Dvořák went to the Crystal Palace to conduct the *Scherzo capriccioso* and Nocturne for Strings: they may also have met at the Worcester concerts. They saw each other once more in 1886 at Leeds, when Grove informed Mrs Wodehouse that Dvořák 'came up and spoke to me. I never thought that he would have remembered me again.' He very much enjoyed the Eighth Symphony at Cambridge. 'It was full of feeling and beautiful tune, reminiscent of Schubert here and there – (Trio strongly so), but distinctly a master work and delightful.'

After the concert, Dvořák went to tea in the rooms of Arthur Tilley, where he treated the assembled company to a riveting display of another of his accomplishments by consuming a truly vast quantity of sandwiches. One of music's most powerful and dramatic trencher-men, he concluded this feat with the remark 'Now my stowmack is betterer.' It is little wonder that he endeared himself to the English. On an earlier visit, when it once began to rain heavily, his face lit up with pleasure; it would be good, he said, for the potatoes in his garden back home. On the evening of the concert, effortlessly recapturing his tea-time exuberance, Dvořák did more than justice to the gala banquet held in his honour. He and his wife stayed the night with the Stanfords at 10 Harvey Road, and, says Stanford, somewhat sur-prised their hosts the following morning.

> I heard a noise in the garden in the small hours and saw the pair sitting under a tree at 6 a.m. He and Brahms must have had in common the gift of being satisfied with from four to five hours of sleep. Dvořák's interest in contemporary music was, as far as I could gather, very limited. The only composer of his time who seemed to rouse his enthusiasm was Verdi. Of Brahms . . . he scarcely spoke, and that little was not what I expected him to say.

The degree ceremony began at noon on the day after the concert. Dvořák had been looking forward to it since the arrival of Stanford's letter the previous November. 'It is, so I am told, a rare distinction', he confided to a friend, after receiving the good news, 'and the only other foreign artist to have received it is Joachim. It goes without saying that I shall accept.' Also receiving honorary degrees at the ceremony were the Russian biologist Ilya Mechnikov, who discov-ered the white corpuscles in the blood and propounded the theory of phagocytes, winning the Nobel Prize for Medicine in 1908; the Marquess of Dufferin and Ava, under whose viceroyalty India annexed Burma; Sir William Flower, Director of the Natural History Museum; Sir Archibald Geikie, President of the Geological Society and Director of the Practical Geology Museum; Sir Alfred Lyall, authority on Indian government and ideology; and the Irish historian William Lecky, author of the eight-volume *History of England in the Eighteenth Century*. The only one of the honorary doctors to be greeted by the undergraduates with more than polite applause was Dvořák, who, however, was so nervous and overcome with emotion that he hardly knew what was going on. He was 'on pins and needles' he later told his students at Prague Conservatoire.

All the faces around me were so serious, and nobody seemed capable of speaking anything but Latin. I looked to my right and I looked to my left, but I couldn't find out who I was meant to be listening to. When I finally realized it was me they were talking about, I felt as if I was drowning in hot water and I was so ashamed at not being able to understand what was being said.

It was a pity that Dvořák could not understand, because John Sandys, who succeeded Richard Jebb as Public Orator, made a flattering and eloquent speech, mentioning in particular the *Slavonic Dances*, the symphonies, the *Gipsy Songs*, *The Spectre's Bride* and the *Stabat Mater*.

As a souvenir of the occasion, Dvořák took home to Bohemia his 'lovely' doctor's cap and gown. Shortly afterwards he received from Cambridge a photograph of himself in his robes, taken at the time of the ceremony. For the Czechs, this has always been a favourite picture of their most famous composer. In return, he made the university a richer gift, dedicating to it his wonderful overture *Amid Nature*, which he completed three weeks after bidding goodbye to his new-found friends in Cambridge.

CHAPTER 2
BRAHMS

By 1892 the CUMS had gained an enviable reputation; the success of Dvořák's visit to Cambridge had further increased their standing. Their conductor was now a famous composer, held in esteem throughout Europe. Their president, too, was a man of distinction, the Reverend Augustus Austen Leigh. Born in 1840, he was educated at Eton and Cambridge, becoming Provost of King's College in 1889. He held notably liberal views and was an educational reformer who left his mark on the university. Stanford entertained the deepest respect for Austen Leigh, who was elected president of the CUMS in 1883. The following tribute by Stanford is taken from the book *Augustus Austen Leigh*, written by Augustus's brother William and published in 1906.

The position of President of the Musical Society is never a sinecure and was more than usually difficult at the time of his acceptance of it. The Society had reached a high level of excellence, and had come to be regarded, in the words of Sir George Grove, 'as one of the powers of the country.' The organization had for some time been centred in the hands of Mr. Gerard Cobb, a man of very exceptional administrative ability. When he retired from the Presidency it became a very difficult and delicate matter to re-apportion the different duties among a number of men who were unfamiliar with them, and so to lighten the task of the incoming President . . . Without his tact and unfailing courtesy the Society might have had a very difficult and dangerous crisis; but his immediate grasp of the old conditions, and the methods necessary to retain their good results while altering the constitution, made the transition from an autocracy to a limited monarchy almost imperceptible. It is characteristic of the subtle influence which he exercised upon bodies over which he presided, that on no single occasion can I remember a warm (still less a heated) controversy in Committee during his *régime*. His touches of genial humour often enlivened a dull and dry discussion. In the drafting of some circular when (after the manner of Committees) almost every sentence had been twisted out of all recognition, he would wind up by saying, 'And now let us give it all to Jenkinson (later University Librarian) to translate into English.' It was not only in administrative matters that he was so invaluable to the

66

Society; he also took a deep interest in its influence upon music generally, and warmly encouraged its efforts to preserve the highest standard of performance, and to keep in touch with the greater world of art outside.

Austen Leigh was also president of the University Cricket Club and of the University Golf Club. Here, again, he appears to have exerted a conspicuously beneficial influence, for, commented *Granta* in April 1893, he 'has been known at Fenner's to turn the tide of victory simply by appearing.' He was, in addition, an excellent tennis player, and when new tennis courts were opened at Cambridge in 1890, he and a Mr Ewbank of Clare College were selected to play the inaugural match on them. His other accomplishments included cycling and ice-skating.

As president of the CUMS, he seems to have been a good deal more than a mere figure-head. Stanford mentions his desire 'to keep in touch with the greater world of art outside', so we may conclude that Austen Leigh was keen to have foreign composers come to Cambridge. However, the idea of persuading Brahms and Verdi to take part in the CUMS fiftieth anniversary celebrations appears to have originated with Stanford, for William Austen Leigh, a talented pianist and himself president of the Society in 1865–6, states that 'To invite composers of European fame to Cambridge, and to rely on the University to present them with degrees seemed to Stanford and the other authorities of the Society the most suitable way of marking the importance of the epoch.' With his customary reticence regarding his own contribution to the CUMS's activities, Stanford, in *Pages from an Unwritten Diary*, simply remarks, 'In the Spring of 1892 we set on foot the organization of the movement to celebrate the Jubilee of the University Musical Society in 1893. The first step taken was the invitation of Verdi and of Brahms to become *honoris causa* Doctors of the University, and the programme outlined was Verdi's *Requiem* and Brahms's C minor Symphony.'

So impressive had been the Society's achievement in recent years that nobody in Cambridge, or even in London musical circles, looked on this plan as unduly ambitious; neither did they find anything fanciful about an attempt to bring together, for the first time in their lives, the world's two most respected contemporary composers.

England first learned of Brahms through Schumann's famous article in the October 1853 edition of *Neue Zeitschrift für Musik*. Schumann, then forty-three with less than three years left to him, entitled the article 'New Paths'. Ten years, he said, had passed since he had last contributed to the magazine – which he had founded in 1834 and for several years edited. During the last decade, he had noted the emergence of many talented young composers.

> It seemed to me, who followed the progress of these chosen musicians with the greatest interest, that under such circumstances there must suddenly and inevitably appear one whose destiny would be to give the highest and most ideal expression to the spirit of the times, one who would reveal his mastery not in gradual evolution, but would spring, like Pallas Athena, fully armed from the head of Zeus. And now he has come, a young man over whose cradle the Graces and Heroes have kept watch. His name is *Johannes Brahms*; he is from Hamburg, where he has worked in quiet obscurity, though trained in the most difficult laws of his art by an excellent and enthusiastically devoted teacher [Schumann's footnote: 'Eduard Marxsen of Hamburg']. He was recently introduced to me by a revered and well-known artist [Joachim, then twenty-two]. It was made clear to us by every sign, even by his outward appearance, that he is one of the elect.

With an introduction from Joachim, the twenty-year-old Brahms had called on the Schumanns, Robert and Clara, in Düsseldorf towards the end of September 1853. Robert at once invited him to perform one of his compositions, but hardly had the young man seated himself at the piano and played a few bars than his host begged him to stop. 'Clara must hear this', he said and left the room to fetch her. Together they then listened, completely enraptured. Over the next few days, Brahms played them a number of his compositions, none of which had yet been published, including piano pieces and chamber works. Through these, Schumann was able to see into the future with astonishing accuracy, as his article on Brahms reveals.

> Should he only point his magic wand to where those massed forces, both of chorus and of orchestra, may lend him their power, yet more wondrous glimpses into the spirit world await us. May the highest genius strengthen him to this end. His fellow musicians hail him on his first step through a world where wounds perhaps will be his lot, but also palms and laurels. We welcome him as a strong champion.

Writing to Joachim, Schumann said, 'This is he who was to come.' He immediately sent letters, as well, to Brahms's father, expressing his belief in his son's genius, and to music publishers, recommending Brahms's compositions to them.

The 'New Paths' article at once provoked immense curiosity throughout the musical world. By 6 November 1853, Liszt was enquiring in a letter to Joachim, 'Did you see Brams [sic] in Düsseldorf?'; by 9 December, Berlioz was writing from Leipzig, where he made a point of meeting the young musician, 'Brams has had a great success here. He made a deep impression on me the other day at Brindel's [at the home of Brendel, the editor of the *Neue Zeitschrift*] with his scherzo and his adagio. I am grateful to have made the acquaintance of this shy young man who is audaciously bent on writing modern music. He will have much to endure.' Berlioz was so moved by what he heard that he embraced Brahms and pressed him to his heart. Brahms wrote to Joachim, 'Berlioz praised me with such great warmth and affection that the rest of them humbly followed suit. Yesterday evening at Moscheles' he was just as friendly. I have much to thank him for.' Liszt had by now met Brahms. 'Je m'intéresse sincèrement', he wrote to Bülow.

By the beginning of 1854, Brahms was in print, with his Piano Sonata No 1, dedicated to Joachim, and his Piano Sonata No 2, dedicated to Clara Schumann; these two friends would be his most devoted interpreters for more than forty years. Other early publications included songs, the scherzo that Berlioz had so admired and the Piano Sonata No 3, the adagio of which Berlioz had also liked. In March 1854 Bülow embarked on his first concert tour as a piano recitalist and in Hamburg performed the opening movement of Brahms's Piano Sonata No 1.

In November 1854, Brahms's song 'Liebestreu', from Six Songs, Opus 3, was published in London a little over half a year after its original printing in Germany. The English critics were ready and waiting. The anti-Schumannite, H. F. Chorley, was among the first to pounce: 'Gratuitous ugliness, uncouthness, difficulty and affectation have hardly ever been more firmly combined and in larger quantity', he asserted. There was resistance on all sides, extending also to the typesetters of London's musical journals, who regularly converted Brahms into Braham, a name much better known to them, for

John Braham, the original Huon in Weber's *Oberon* and the composer of the popular song 'The Death of Nelson', had for many years
been a familiar figure in London's musical life. In years to come, it
would be Braham's name that would suffer at their hands. 'Braham'
was not the least of the distortions that lay in store: when Clara
Schumann played a sarabande and gavotte by Brahms at a recital in
London in July 1856, *The Musical Times* identified the composer as
Brackens, which comes remarkably close to being a direct translation
from the German. Reporting this concert for *The Times*, the fire-
breathing, Schumann-hating critic J. W. Davison declared, 'The
Sarabande of the "new man" Johannes Brahms, is extremely difficult,
extremely uncouth.'

Such was the tenor of the opening salvoes, but throughout the
fifties and early sixties Brahms's piano pieces and songs were unob-
trusively and systematically introduced to London audiences by a
small group of admiring English and German artists. By the mid-
sixties, more substantial works were played, including the First
Sextet, in May 1863, and the Piano Quartet No 2, in July 1865. More
notably, on 25 April 1863, Manns conducted three movements from
the First Serenade at the Crystal Palace. By 1870 the sextet had been
performed twice more. During the seventies, the tide began to turn
strongly in Brahms's favour, and this decade witnessed his establishment, in British eyes, as one of the leading contemporary composers.
In 1871 the *German Requiem* was introduced; in 1872, the First Piano
Concerto, conducted by Manns, the Second Sextet and the First
Serenade in its entirety. In 1873, Florence May, who later became
Brahms's first important British biographer, played the *Handel Variations* at the Crystal Palace, and in this year, too, the Piano Quartet No
1 received its English première. The Second Serenade was featured
on a Philharmonic Society programme in 1874. In March of the same
year, the *Song of Destiny* was given at the Crystal Palace. The review in
The Musical Times is indicative of the degree to which opinion had
changed in twenty years.

> It was recognised by its hearers as a work of genius of the highest order,
> and in this opinion we cordially agree. The verdict which had been given
> by nearly the whole of musical Germany upon the composition was on this
> occasion unanimously endorsed by perhaps the most critical audience ever
> assembled at Sydenham; and Herr Brahms may reckon at least upon a
> cordial reception being accorded to any future work from his pen.

The year 1874 saw the introduction, as well, of the *Hungarian Dances*, the *Schumann Variations* and the First String Quartet. His pieces were now being played with increasing frequency, and in an article in *The Musical Times* Joseph Bennett, the critic for the *Daily Telegraph*, described him as 'the typical composer of the present'.

We do not intend here to insist on his genius, or to enter upon comparisons between him and others, preferring rather to indicate the character and influence of his works.

In character, Brahms's music . . . is not mathematical in the sense that form and rule are made primary considerations, but it is emotional, reflective, aesthetic – an attempt to excite feeling, convey impressions, and even stimulate definite thought. Here, then, we have the ideal of the latest development of 'pure' music. The works of Brahms, and those of his fellows who stand nearest to him, embody modern principles in their most artistic shape. They stand apart from surrounding exaggerations, and they are also clearly separable from the creations of the past.

This being so, it is a matter for rejoicing that Brahms is not absolutely a 'bogey', even to musicians of conservative taste. He puzzles them, at the outset, but in the result, his works grow upon them, and only within the last two or three years we have seen this 'modern German composer' rapidly passing into the ranks of accepted masters, cheered on by a well-nigh unanimous public voice. This is a matter for congratulation apart from any question as to the exact degree of Brahms's genius, and the precise status which will ultimately be his. It shows that modern musical development, in the hands of a thoughtful and conscientious composer, does not necessarily lead to incoherence, and to flagrant offence against the true principles of art.

By 1875, London had almost completely caught up with Brahms's principal compositions, and from now on the first English presentations of his major works followed rarely more than a year behind the original premières, and often a good deal less. The *Variations on a Theme of Haydn* arrived by 1875; the First Symphony, by 1877; the Second Symphony, conducted by Manns, by 1878; the Violin Concerto, played by Joachim and Manns, by 1879; the *Academic Festival Overture* and *Tragic Overture*, conducted by Manns, by 1881; the Second Piano Concerto, again under Manns, by 1882; the Third Symphony, by 1884 (with a performance, the following year, conducted by Sullivan); the Fourth Symphony, by 1886; the Double Concerto, by 1888. Such was Brahms's standing towards the end of the eighties that British premières were sometimes only a few months behind the German. In February 1889, Brahms and Joachim gave the first performance of the Violin Sonata No 3; by May, it had been played in London. In January 1892, the Clarinet Quintet was first presented; this reached London by the end of March and was repeated five days later.

In 1887, Grove wrote to Brahms, 'I only speak the sentiments of a great many Englishmen when I thus thank you most warmly for the invaluable benefits that we derive from you, and for which we are so deeply indebted to you.' During the previous year, Liszt had died, and three years earlier, in 1883, Wagner. It was generally considered in England that Brahms was now the world's leading contemporary composer and worthy of his place as one of 'the three Bs', the triumvirate to which Bülow had assigned him, together with Bach and Beethoven. The *Cyclopedia of Music and Musicians*, published in 1888, traces Brahms's rise to world supremacy from the appearance of his First Symphony.

> His first symphony, upon which he had been at work for ten years, off and on, came almost like a thunderclap out of a clear sky when it was brought out at Carlsruhe, Nov. 4 1876. No composition ever made more, or more immediate, noise in the world; Brahms found himself suddenly world famous. His fame was still increased by his Deutsches Requiem and his second symphony. He stands to-day almost undisputed as the foremost composer in the world. He represents the climax of modern musical thought; he is the legitimate successor to Schumann. His style is marked by great elaboration, and there is in his music a stoutness of construction, a warmth of sentiment, and a real profundity of thought (which has often been misconstrued into abstruseness) such as no other living composer can lay claim to.

Two books in preparation during 1892, at the time of the CUMS's decision to invite Brahms to Cambridge, further illustrate how highly he was regarded. In the first of these, *Masters of German Music*, J. A. Fuller-Maitland declares:

> It is difficult to see what quality of greatness is absent from this composer's work; the grandeur, wealth, and originality of his ideas, and the ease and power with which he uses forms already invented, or develops them into new organisms full of suggestion and opportunity for those who may come after, are, perhaps, the most striking of his peculiar attributes; but there is also a deep expression as well as an exquisite beauty in the greatest of his works. He is sometimes accused of neglecting the merely pleasing side of music, and, as far as some of his earlier compositions are concerned, it is certainly possible to find passages where sensuous beauty

of melody is not easily to be discovered. Taking the whole of his work into consideration, however, it is quite impossible to agree with the charge, for no composer, past or present, has invented lovelier melodies, or has set them in more delightful surroundings; and they are to be found in nearly all his works, scattered through them with no niggard hand. Of course, if the only function of music is to appeal to the lower emotions of the less cultivated classes, then Brahms cannot rank with the great masters at all; but in that case the whole of musical history must be re-arranged, and Beethoven must be recognised as the artistic inferior of Offenbach or the compiler of the last street song. Where the usual tests of musical merit are fairly applied, there must Brahms rank with the masters of the first order. There is one test which it is a little dangerous to apply, since it takes from certain popular idols their long-held position of supremacy: it can only be of real value when all allowances are made for circumstances and the influence of the outer world upon the artist's life. It is the test that is applied to a chain, the strength of which is judged by that of its weakest link; in matters of art it resolves itself into the question, 'Does a man's work contain examples altogether unworthy of himself at his best?' This does not, of course, imply a dead level throughout his work, for such a level must be one of mediocrity; but it requires the absence of any composition obviously written to order or against the grain, or of anything a composer would be ashamed of in his better moments. We need not take into account the posthumous compositions of any master, for these may be merely the contents of his waste-paper basket, thrust into publicity by injudicious survivors; but the Devil's Advocate will have to expel many a famous name from the list of the supreme masters, and in fact, putting aside the old composers, whose weaker works may very likely have disappeared, there will remain few beside Bach, Beethoven, Schumann, and, curiously enough, Chopin. In the case of Mozart and Haydn, it must be remembered that the conditions of the musical world in their day made it imperative upon them to write in and out of season. This high test, it is not too much to say, is fulfilled by one living composer alone, and his name is JOHANNES BRAHMS. Through the long list of his works we may search in vain for music that he need blush to own; naturally some are far better than others, but in the least attractive we shall find signs of the master's genius, whether in the manipulation of an unpromising theme or the exact portrayal of some subtlety of expression. The felicitous combination of intense earnestness of aim and nobility of ideal with the passionate ardour that is characteristic of Southern countries, may well have its origin in the circumstances of his life: the first possibly comes from his North German birth, the second from the artistic atmosphere of Vienna, the city of his adoption.

The other book being prepared during 1892 was the four-volume *Famous Composers and their Works*. The section on Brahms is by Louis Kelterborn, who takes a view similar to that of Fuller-Maitland.

Greatness indeed remains Brahms's characteristic feature, wherever we look at him or at his works; greatness in ideas, purposes and powers; greatness in self-criticism and faithfulness to the dignity of his art; greatness in the devotion to past masters and independence of contemporary influences; greatness in the sincerity and simplicity of his manners and relation to the outer world. Never appearing as a revolutionary spirit, yet he has himself introduced many strong innovations in various fields . . . patiently has he waited, till the world has come to him to respect in him the noblest musical genius of our time.

Stanford was fifteen when he first heard a piece of Brahms, in 1867.

I shall never forget the amazing effect which was produced upon me by hearing the variations on a theme of Handel, or how much of my small pocket-money I spent in buying as many of his works as I could get. I knew nothing of the Schumann article, nor anything about him save his music, and the grip it took of me at fifteen has never relaxed since. My first sight of the composer himself was at the remarkable Schumann Festival given at Bonn under the direction of Joachim in 1873, where he sat, tawny-haired and clean-shaven, beside his 'second mother', Clara Schumann.

While the *Handel Variations* were, for Stanford, the beginning of his love of Brahms, they were, by coincidence, the last of Brahms's works to excite any enthusiasm in Wagner. The two German composers met in February 1863 at Wagner's home in the Vienna suburb of Penzing, and Brahms played the *Handel Variations* at Wagner's request. Another guest wrote, 'I can remember with what unhypocritical warmth Wagner (who could never praise a work unless it appealed to him) showered appreciation on the young composer and with what conviction he discussed every detail of it. "One can see," he concluded, "what can yet be done with the old forms when somebody comes along who knows how to use them."' In *On Conducting*, published in 1869, Wagner recalled, 'Herr Johannes Brahms once had the kindness to play me one of his compositions, which I found first-rate, and from which I could tell that he was hardly a joker.' Of Brahms's piano playing, Wagner's other guest said it assumed 'that genial, splendidly plastic quality that used to come most to the fore when Brahms was among musicians or friends who were sympathetic towards him.' Wagner described it as 'painfully dry, inflexible and wooden'.

In his writings, Stanford became a stout defender of Brahms, showing nothing but admiration and loyalty for the contemporary whom he ranked above all others. To Wagner's assertion that Brahms's importance 'lies in his not wishing to create any striking effects', he replied that Brahms 'did not lay himself out to capture taste with eccentricity or theatricalism'. Wagner's charge that Brahms was humourless Stanford dismissed as an opinion that would have been about equally true of Sydney Smith. As for Wagner's suggestion that Brahms was Jewish, Stanford not only showed it to be entirely unfounded, but proved, through analysis of Wagner's music, that it was in fact he who was Jewish. He even provided Brahms with a dazzling musical pedigree that is outlined in his essay *Brahms and His Music.*

His master, Edouard Marxsen of Altona, was first a pupil of Clasing, the pupil of Schwenke (the successor of Philip Emmanuel Bach of Hamburg), and afterwards of Seyfried, the pupil of Mozart. Moreover, as Seyfried studied also under Albrechtsberger, he could claim kinship with that famous theorist's greatest pupil, Beethoven. The educational family tree may be set out thus:

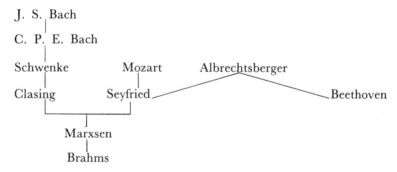

It could not have been long after returning from the 1873 Schumann Festival at Bonn that Stanford set his heart on bringing Brahms to England for the first time and, more particularly, to Cambridge. He realised that to achieve this end, it would be necessary to convert Sterndale Bennett, then Professor of Music, into a Brahms supporter. In theory, this should have been an easy task. Sterndale Bennett had received his training in Germany, he had a great affection for Schumann and he was moderately open-minded. Stanford was probably entitled to feel that he would succeed in recruiting Sterndale Bennett to his cause.

In 1873 the appreciation of Brahms was beginning to make itself widely felt in England, and I made many attempts to interest him in the famous *Requiem*, in the chamber-works and pianoforte compositions of that master, thinking that their common friendship for Schumann and Schumann's warm championship of the younger man would arouse interest and sympathy in Bennett. But he remained practically impervious to any appeal. This is the more curious as in one respect at least, their methods, though varying fundamentally in style, were alike in principle. Passage writing for the pianoforte had before their time become mainly a medium for display, irrespective of any intrinsic merit or relevancy. To this snare even Mendelssohn, the then leader of musical fashion, had fallen a victim. With Bennett it became part and parcel of the musical idea and a natural development from it, a system Brahms carried out with unvarying force throughout his life. Bennett's harmonic scheme was diatonic, but he was exceptionally chromatic in passage writing: another point of similarity. Finally he was very prone to *arpeggio* writing, as in *The Fountain*, a form of ornament to which the German master was equally partial.

Sterndale Bennett died in February 1875, unconverted to Brahms. He was succeeded in the Cambridge professorship by George Macfarren, a man who hated Liszt and Wagner. In a concert programme note of 1872, Macfarren suggested to the listener that the Prelude to *Lohengrin* should be regarded 'rather as a study of orchestral effect than as a composition'. In 1874, he advised the organiser of a series of historical concerts not to include Liszt or Wagner. 'These writers are working a great evil on music . . . To bring them into notice is to applaud their pretensions . . . Were you to preach temperance at a gin-shop door, and let your congregation taste the poison therein, that they might know its vileness, they would come out drunkards. You must represent the art of now by music of Brahms, perhaps of Bruch, or even of Gounod.' So numerous were Macfarren's musical prejudices that even Sterndale Bennett, the most accommodating of men, found it difficult to converse with him. However, towards the end of his life he discovered a subject 'which does not lead to argument – we talk about our grandchildren.' Wagner met 'Mr. Mac-Farrinc, a pompous, melancholy Scotsman', when he came over to conduct the Philharmonic Society concerts in 1855. On 11 June, he conducted Macfarren's overture *Chevy Chase*, which he quite enjoyed, though its composer, says Wagner in his autobiography, was 'too proud' to discuss matters of interpretation.

Stanford much preferred Sterndale Bennett as a man, but Macfarren was more likely to support the idea of inviting Brahms to

Cambridge. Indeed, he turned out to be all that Stanford could have wished for, becoming a total convert – with the result that in April 1876 the following letter to Brahms was dispatched from Cambridge.

My dear Sir,
The Council of the University of Cambridge yesterday agreed to sanction a grace, offering the honorary Degree of Doctor of Music to you, and I must request the favour of your informing me within three weeks from this date if it will be agreeable to you to accept the same. This is the only country in which the Faculty of Music is represented in its Universities, and acknowledged by scholastic Degrees, and England has thus the opportunity of making recognition of your high services to art, in which all earnest musicians will concur. For myself, I am happy on this occasion to address you, which enables me to thank you for the great pleasure that I have experienced from your works.

I am, my dear Sir,
Yours with the highest esteem,

G. W. Macfarren

P.S. The ceremony of conferring the Degree can take place on the 8th of May or on the 1st. of June, the former being preferable. There will be a performance of your *Requiem* by the University Musical Society on the 23rd. of May, to which your presence would give extra interest, and the members of the Society would be especially proud and pleased if you could be induced to conduct your work. It will be particularly fortunate if the ceremony and performance could combine to bring you to Cambridge.

Stanford also persuaded Macfarren to offer Joachim an honorary degree. The violinist, who was then Brahms's closest friend, was expected to be a staunch ally in prevailing upon him to come to Cambridge. Joachim's friendship with Stanford since the Dublin days, when young Charlie remembered his being announced in stentorian tones by a butler as 'Mr. Jehoiakim', was another asset. It may have been at Stanford's suggestion that Joachim, who was in England at the time of Macfarren's letter to Brahms, also wrote to the composer.

Professor Macfarren (Bennett's successor as Professor of Music at Cambridge and Director of the Royal Academy of Music in London) will have written to you on behalf of the Vice-Chancellor of the University to ask whether you will accept the distinction of Honorary Doctor of Music, which they would like to confer on you. The University wants to honour me in the same way, and I have said 'Yes'. It's the first time that the title of Doctor has been offered to a foreigner. Grove tells me that Haydn had

to compose the prescribed exercise for Oxford before he was made a
Doctor, and I think Grove is knowledgeable about such matters . . .
However, I feel it would have been better if they had offered the distinction to you alone. Nevertheless, I think you should accept it. It's proof,
after all, of how highly they prize you there, and, indeed, throughout the
entire English musical world. All you need do is write a letter, in German
– using Roman characters – to Macfarren, saying you accept the honour
with pleasure (or that you are delighted to accept), adding, if you like, that
you value it as an indication of the esteem in which they hold you. The
next point is whether you actually come to England so you can be made a
Doctor (a solemn ceremony at which the whole University is present).
Without this, you cannot become a Doctor. I shan't be able to manage it
myself this year and have postponed my visit to Cambridge until next
year . . . I am curious to know what you will decide . . . There's something
fine in the thought of being accepted by a body of men that has included
Bacon, Milton, Newton, Byron, etc. Remember this and don't look at it
from too modern a point of view.

Brahms's initial reaction was favourable; he told Joachim that he
was 'highly delighted with this great adventure'. He seems, though,
to have used the postponement of Joachim's ceremony as an excuse
for delaying his own. He wondered, too, whether it was really necessary for him to appear in Cambridge, but Macfarren confirmed that
the degree could not be bestowed unless he was 'personally admitted
to it'. The intention, it seems, was that he should be made a Fellow of
Trinity (Stanford's College); and to Gerard Cobb, then Junior Bursar
of the College and Chairman of the University Board of Musical
Studies, Brahms now put further questions. Cobb at once assured
him of his sympathy for his fears regarding the journey to England,
recognising that it must inevitably involve 'the necessity of submit-
ting to the excitement of London'. He assured him that he would do
his utmost 'to induce the Vice-Chancellor to dispense with personal
attendance on the occasion of the conferring of the Degree'. But
nothing could be done, and on 12 December 1876 Cobb had to tell
the composer that the University 'had no such powers' to depart from
the statutes relating to the degree ceremony.

It must have been exasperating for the twenty-four-year-old
Stanford to have to stand by and watch Brahms slowly slipping
through his elders' fingers. He therefore now took matters into his
own hands and promptly pulled off a coup. Through Joachim, he
secured Brahms's consent to allow the first English performance of
the Symphony No 1, which had just received its première in Carls-

ruhe, to be given by the CUMS. Moreover, by gaining the additional support of Clara Schumann, he was able to induce Brahms into reconsidering the trip to England and even into contemplating the idea of himself conducting the Cambridge performance. At that stage, as Stanford later wrote, Brahms 'intended to visit Cambridge only, and to leave London severely alone.' Had he gone to London, he professed that his chief interest would have been 'to explore the East End and the docks', an understandable desire for a man who had been brought up in the great German port of Hamburg.

Harry Plunket Greene tells of the excitement created by this new turn in events: 'the whole musical world of England sat up. Brahms was coming to receive his honorary degree and to conduct the first performance in this country of his (MS.) *C Minor Symphony* – not in London or Manchester or any other great city but at a C.U.M.S. concert at Cambridge!' But it was not to be, as Stanford relates.

The rumour of Brahms's approaching visit got about with disastrous speed, and the Crystal Palace authorities publicly announced that they hoped for a special concert of his works conducted by himself. This ill-timed advertisement reached his ears and effectually stopped his coming . . . As soon as he saw what the Crystal Palace meant to do, he retired into his shell, and the opportunity was lost for good.

Jeffrey Pulver, in his book on Brahms, published in 1926, is doubtful whether the composer's change of heart can be explained as simply as Stanford suggests.

. . . it is scarcely to be supposed that this advertisement alone was sufficient to keep him away. It was more likely to have been the 'commercialism' and the musical taste in England at the time, as exhibited to him in Joachim's letters, and his own lack of sympathy with England and English politics, that rendered him a little indifferent to the honour offered him.

To this can be added further possibilities advanced by Karl Geiringer in *Brahms: His Life and Work*, published in 1934.

Brahms may have had a very prosaic reason for his refusal: he seems to have been afraid of seasickness. It is well known that he left a ship in Genoa, on which he and his companion had already taken passage, at the last moment, making the hot railway journey through the whole of Italy to Naples in order to avoid the sea. He may have heard gruesome accounts of

storms in the Channel from Clara Schumann, so that he, who laid so little
stress on outward honours and material gain, could not understand why
he should expose himself to such inconvenience. Apart from this fear, his
inability to learn foreign languages discouraged him from visiting
countries in which a strange tongue was spoken.

The score and parts of the First Symphony were sent by Brahms to
Joachim, whom he asked to conduct the Cambridge performance,
and preliminary rehearsals began in London at the Royal Academy
of Music in Tenterden Street, Hanover Square, at the end of
February 1877. The symphony was still in manuscript; the autograph, according to Stanford, who took the very first rehearsals,
'showed its age on the face of it; the first movement dated in its
original form from 1862.' Brahms was still loth to hand the symphony
over to Simrock, his publisher, for printing, even four months after
the first performance, feeling that he might yet decide to make some
last-minute adjustments or alterations. By the time he did pass it for
publication, shortly afterwards, there could be no doubt of the work's
importance, and Simrock paid him 15,000 marks, the largest amount
that had ever been given for an orchestral piece.

The symphony gave the CUMS orchestra a good deal of trouble for
a while. This, says Stanford, was 'partly owing to the short and
somewhat jerky beat of Joachim, which his own men [in Berlin]
followed with ease but which was enigmatical to English players';
another cause was 'the inferior technique of the horn-players, who
were then the weak spot of British orchestras.' A number of familiar
artistic figures, including Robert Browning, Frederick Leighton,
Manns and Grove, attended the London rehearsals.

The concert took place in Cambridge on 8 March 1877. The first
half of the programme consisted of Sterndale Bennett's overture *The
Wood Nymphs*, Beethoven's Violin Concerto, Brahms's *Song of Destiny*,
some violin pieces by Bach, and Joachim's *Elegiac Overture*. Joachim
conducted his overture and was soloist in the violin works. Stanford
took the baton for all the items not conducted by Joachim. In the *Song
of Destiny*, the CUMS choir amounted to 150. 'The Guildhall was
somehow induced to hold 51 players and 150 singers', recalled Harry
Plunket Greene, 'and, as experience invariably shows us, overcrowd-
ing keyed up both performers and audience to a high pitch of excitement. The concert marched from one success to another, and ended
in a demonstration of affection for the two conductors (*aetat* 24 and 45
respectively).' The ovation followed Joachim's excellent interpreta-

tion of the First Symphony, which was the sole item in the second half
of the programme. 'This performance', wrote Stanford, 'put the
crown on Joachim's unceasing and loyal efforts to win for Brahms an
abiding place in this country. Never had a composer a more trusty
friend.'

> The Cambridge performance of the C Minor Symphony attracted almost
> every musician of importance in England [Hallé had a concert in
> Manchester], and much interest was excited among Cambridge men by
> the curious coincidence that the horn theme in the introduction to the last
> movement was, nearly note for note, a quotation of the famous hour-
> chimes of St. Mary's (the University Church) bells. Brahms' music had
> long been more deeply appreciated in England than in Germany owing
> probably in a measure to the fact that we had no serious battle-ground of
> Wagnerian and anti-Wagnerian parties; the performance of this
> symphony set an imperishable keystone on his fame among Britons. I had
> myself the curious good fortune to compare the attitude of an English and
> a German audience towards one of his orchestral works. In 1875 I heard
> within a few weeks two performances of his Serenade in A (without
> violins), first at the Philharmonic Society of London, and afterwards at the
> Gewandhaus in Leipzig. In London the enthusiasm was so great that two
> movements (the scherzo and the minuet) had to be repeated. In Leipzig
> the entire work went literally without one hand being raised to applaud.

Fuller-Maitland was another who was immediately struck by the
horn-call, and he states that 'the actual phrase came down from St.
Mary's tower while the symphony was going on.'

The programme note, which betrays the heavy hand of Macfarren,
defines the symphony as 'a work of whose beauties many and the
greatest are imperceptible on a single hearing'.

> Its depth of purpose is manifest to the most superficial observation, and it
> abounds in incidents which may serve as landmarks for the hearer's atten-
> tion, points of interest to be remembered before the work as a whole can
> stamp itself on the mind . . . The auditor can alone do justice to the new
> Symphony and to himself by faith in the unrevealed on the warrant of
> what is manifest, and by employing all coming opportunity of hearing and
> reading the music till he thoroughly masters its intricacies.

This portentous admonition seems to have left its mark on the critic
of *The Musical Times*.

> With regard to Brahms's Symphony, I shall say little beyond an express-
> ion of opinion that it is worthy to rank among classic things. So great a
> work ought not to be judged with authority and definiteness, after a single

hearing under exciting circumstances; and as it is announced for production in London on more than one occasion, there is everything to gain by
the exercise of patience. Enough now that the Cambridge Symphony of
the German master made an extraordinary sensation, and sent the
audience away with a consciousness that they had just heard for the first
time music which the world will not soon let die.

Such serious, respectful and open-minded judgement, which was then
quite out of the ordinary in concert reporting, must be partly ascrib-
able to the influence both of Macfarren's weighty prose and of Stanford's fervent propaganda; its tone was adopted, in relation to
Brahms, for many years to come by much of the British Press, and
traces of it survive even today. After hearing the second English
performance of the symphony, conducted by Manns at the Crystal
Palace, the same critic of *The Musical Times* explained that 'as the
score is not at present published, no opportunity for a thorough study
and analysis of the work has yet presented itself. Our remarks must
therefore be considered simply a record of impressions and in no
degree as a final verdict upon the composition.' Nonetheless, the
piece was 'unmistakably one of the greatest symphonic works of
modern times'.

The ceremony at which Joachim was awarded his honorary doctorate took place at 2.00 pm on the afternoon preceding the evening's
concert. As was traditional, the undergraduates whistled, made loud
comments and, in the words of one reporter, 'generally behaved
themselves as though the whole affair had been got up for the amusement of an idle hour.' 'But', wrote *The Musical Times* correspondent,
in more unbuttoned mood, 'the young fellows meant no harm.'

It is their way when they can have their way; and if anybody unused to
such irreverence felt annoyed, all was surely forgiven as the appearance of
Herr Joachim in the scarlet robe and white hood of his new degree evoked
enthusiastic applause. The business of introduction to the Vice Chancellor
might have been better managed than by permitting Herr Joachim to
advance to the daïs before taking his place with the Public Orator at the
lower end of the Hall. As it was, the new graduate retraced his steps, and
standing in front of the Vice Chancellor, though separated from him by
the whole length of the benches on either hand, waited while Mr. Sandys
held forth upon his work in approved University Latin. Mr. Sandys is new
to his post as Orator, and, though there was nothing to find fault with in
his formal speech, he appeared ill at ease. Noting this, the sympathetic
men above flung down a few coppers by way of encouragement. Then
everybody laughed, and Mr. Sandys, brightening up, got safely to the end

of his task. Though brief, the oration was comprehensive, and touched upon everything that fairly came within its scope . . . it ended, amid loud applause, by presenting Joseph Joachim to the robed dignitary who, enthroned on the centre of the daïs, gravely listened, while everybody else laughed at the humour of the gallery. The Public Orator then conducted Herr Joachim to the Vice Chancellor, who, rising from his seat, shook him warmly by the hand, amid renewed and general cheering. With this the special ceremony ended, and after some gentlemen, about whom nobody seemed to care, had received degrees, the Congregation broke up, the undergraduates taking the opportunity as it did so of groaning with much vigour at some obnoxious person – no doubt a proctor.

The concert and the ceremony combined to make this not only an important event in Cambridge's musical history, but also a social occasion of some prominence, attracting a good deal of society to the university, many of them friends of Joachim, who was a frequent guest in London's leading salons. Typical of these visitors was Mary Gladstone, the twenty-nine-year-old daughter of the statesman. Her great passion was music, the love of which she inherited from both sides of her family. Her mother had taken piano lessons from Liszt when she was at finishing school in Paris; her father possessed an attractive baritone voice. He was a founder member of the London Bach Choir. Joachim, Jenny Lind and other notable musicians often came to the Gladstones' home in London. Mary Gladstone was brought up in an atmosphere of music and was on the friendliest terms with Parry, Joachim, Clara Schumann and many others. She was well acquainted, too, with a number of politicians and literary figures, whom she met continuously at parties and similar gatherings. It was not uncommon for her to find herself seated at dinner between Tennyson and Browning, with somebody like Lord Acton, Joachim or Carlyle opposite. She was physically very attractive. She was also one of those characteristically English girls who, finding herself burdened with more than her fair share of sex appeal, conscientiously attempted to keep it down to manageable proportions – which, of course, to certain men, merely made her increasingly irresistible. The normally reserved Ruskin was stimulated into overt flirtation with her, while Tennyson went even further. When she was at Farringford for a visit in June 1879, she noted in her diary, 'He came down after breakfast and stood staring at my face. "Those wonderful eyes of yours. I do believe they are grey." I put all this down because I am unused to personal remarks, having an ordinary face, and it is so *very* odd.' On another occasion, 'He suddenly began to stroke my nose,

having discovered it was a "petit nez retroussé", and declared it
meant all sorts of naughty things.' On the following day, 'Went to his
sanctum and had some alarm. *He kissed me* . . . Told us that when the
Queen took him all over the Mausoleum the only thing he was conscious of was the creaking of his boots.' Browning, too, was somewhat
taken with her, though he does not appear to have been to her taste.
An entry for March 1874, 'Browning brushed my face with his
beard', elicits no comment.

Mary's visit to Cambridge, 'to see Joe made a Doctor', may be
likened to Zuleika Dobson's arrival at Oxford, with broken hearts the
order of the day. The man who fell hardest seems to have been the
Rev Augustus Austen Leigh, then thirty-six, who made every attempt
to monopolise her. She wrote to her sister Lavinia that a number of
others were also often in her company, with 'Nose (Mr. Grove) very
much to the fore'. As for Browning, 'He talks everybody down with
his dreadful voice, and always places his person in such disagreeable
proximity with yours and puffs and blows and spits in yr. face. I tried
to think of *Abt Vogler* but it was no use – he couldn't ever have written
it.' Stanford and she got on moderately well; she seems to have liked
Jennie better, finding her 'a dear little soul'. She was disappointed
not to see George Eliot, who could not come because of illness.

Browning, another good friend of Joachim's, found the day enjoyable, but hectic, partly owing to the fact that he had accepted invitations to six separate meals. Two years later, he, also, was made an
honorary doctor at the university; he received a similar distinction at
Oxford in 1882, and it was during this ceremony, that an undergraduate dropped a red cotton nightcap on his head. After the evening's
concert, he and a number of other celebrities, including Joachim and
Grove, gathered in the rooms of the Rev Coutts Trotter, a chemist
and tutor of Trinity, for still further refreshment. Stanford was there
as well, and in *Pages from an Unwritten Diary* he speaks of a warm
controversy that took place over Beethoven's last quartets.

The member of the party who talked most and knew least about the
subject was, curiously enough, Browning . . . his arguments explained to
me that the true reason of the obscurity of many references to music in his
poems was the superficiality and exiguity of his technical knowledge.
When Jebb was writing his masterly Greek translation of 'Abt Vogler', he
too became well aware of this weakness and was able with infinite skill to
gloss over the solecisms of the original. 'Sliding by semitones, till I sink to
the minor' is indeed the refuge of the destitute amateur improviser. But

Browning was too consummate a master of his own craft to commit such blatant blunders as others of his day, when they ventured upon the perilous paths of an art they did not know ... even George Eliot, most careful of writers, spoke of 'a long-drawn organ-stop', comparing a piece of wooden mechanism with a sound. *The Times* too once described the organ on the Handel Festival platform as possessing 'wonderful ramifications of fugues and diapasons.'

It is questionable whether Stanford is not being a little hard on Browning here, and certainly, had he wished, he could have cited as another oddity, from Tennyson's *The Brook*,

> I chatter over stony ways
> In little sharps and trebles.

'Abt Vogler' is also generally recognised as one of the finest poems ever written on the nature of music. This is not especially surprising, since Browning not only had an intense interest in music, but received a thorough musical training. 'His love of music, which was marked even from earliest childhood, came to him from his mother, a sympathetic and accomplished musician who loved to sit at the piano in the gloaming', writes W. Hall Griffin in *The Life of Robert Browning*. His teacher was John Relfe, who was much admired in his time, and the boy was taken through 'the whole arcana of the science, so as completely to analyze any regular composition'. He gained a sound knowledge of musical theory and was able to compose songs, including a setting of Donne's 'Go and Catch a Falling Star', fugues and other pieces; before he was twenty-one, he even contemplated writing an opera. 'I was studying the grammar of music', he told his friend Mrs Ireland towards the end of his life, 'when most children are learning the multiplication table, and I know what I am talking about when I speak of music.' He developed into a good pianist and frequently played Beethoven and Handel for his wife's enjoyment. Griffin says that he played other keyboard instruments as well.

From the days when as a mere child he stole downstairs from bed to listen to his mother at the piano, and, as she ceased, flung himself into her arms, whispering, amid sobs, 'Play, play', until the days when he drew music from the organ at Vallombrosa, or charmed his intimate friends with his improvisations on the piano, or wrote *Abt Vogler, Master Hugues of Saxe-Gotha* and *A Toccata of Galuppi's*, and became the friend of Joachim and Clara Schumann, Browning remained a music-lover. At Asolo, during the last months of his life, he would sit in the little *loggia* of his friend Mrs. Bronson, and in the gathering twilight would discourse old-time melodies upon the little tinkling spinet which his hostess had provided for his pleasure.

Browning had a keen interest in modern music; his trip to Cambridge was not just a social outing. Various lines in his poems tell us of his taste, which from our vantage-point would seem exemplary. 'Schumann's our music-maker now', in *Dis aliter visum*, dates from 1864, at a time when H. F. Chorley and other English critics were still laying into the poor, dead master; while

> And to-day's music-manufacture, – Brahms,
> Wagner, Dvorak, Liszt, – to where – trumpets, shawms
> Show yourselves joyful!

from 'Charles Avison', published in 1887, shows, despite its grotesquerie, a sure grasp of contemporary musical worth, all the more remarkable in a man of seventy-five. Perhaps we should give the final word on Browning to Hallé, who writes of him in his autobiography.

During my annual sojourns in London I made the acquaintance of Robert Browning and his gifted wife, who were both passionate lovers of music, and especially of Beethoven's sonatas, which I had often the privilege of playing to them at my own house in Mansfield Street. Browning formed an exception to the rule that poets and literary men care less for music than painters, in whom the love of our art seems almost invariably to be inborn [Browning and Hallé both had sons who were talented painters]. Thackeray and Dickens had a certain liking for music, but Tennyson listened to it with great indifference, and his loud talk whilst I was playing some superlatively fine work has now and then 'agacé' my nerves. Browning knew the whole literature of music, had an unfailing judgement, and sometimes drew my attention to pieces by old masters which had escaped my notice and which I have always found worth knowing. He must have been a good pianist himself, but I could never prevail upon him to give me a proof of his power as such. I enjoyed his friendship to the end of his days, and he endeared himself to me especially through the kindness with which he forgave my incapacity to understand his poetry – an incapacity which I frankly confessed to him more than once.

It was another twelve years before Stanford approached Brahms on the matter of coming to England, and this was to invite him to the Leeds Musical Festival of 1889 to conduct the *German Requiem*.

Stanford seems to have been acting in an unofficial capacity, but probably with the Festival Committee's blessing. He told Brahms that the best plan was to come to Cambridge via Harwich; then the two of them would travel incognito to Leeds and back – 'but he was not to be stirred.'

This was hardly surprising; it was the tail-end of an unfortunate exchange, between Brahms and the Leeds Festival Committee, that had started two years earlier. At the beginning of February 1887, the Committee had sent him an invitation to write a new work for the 1889 Festival. But as Stanford points out, Leeds had hitherto wholly neglected Brahms's compositions. At the previous Festival, in 1886, Sullivan had refused to conduct Brahms's Second Symphony and replaced it with Mendelssohn's *Scottish*. When Fuller-Maitland was appointed music critic of *The Times* early in 1889, Sullivan called him 'a dangerous man, who admires Brahms and Wagner'.

Brahms's reply to the Committee's request for a new work was, in Stanford's words, a 'very pretty *riposte* and a thoroughly dignified specimen of epistolary satire'. It ran as follows.

I cannot really decide to promise you a new work for your Festival.

Should you deem one of my existing pieces worthy of the honour of a performance, it would give me great pleasure. But if this, as it appears, is not the case, how could I hope to satisfy you with a new one?

However, should the charm of novelty be an absolute necessity, then forgive me if I confess that I fail either properly to appreciate or fully to sympathize with such a distinction.

Respectfully,
J. Brahms

Upon receipt of this letter, the Yorkshire committeemen, after giving due consideration to its contents, reached a unanimous decision that it was 'not altogether positive in its refusal'. The secretary accordingly wrote a second letter to Brahms, informing him, 'We are sure that universal interest would be felt in the production at our great Festival of a new work from you – whether vocal or instrumental is left to your choice; so also would be the length of the work – though the committee favour, for a vocal composition, one lasting not more than an hour and a half. Should you comply, we need hardly say that your visit here personally to conduct the work would be made (as far as we could make it) both pleasant and memorable.'

Since no reply was forthcoming, the committee applied to Gustavus Nathan, the British Consul-General in Vienna, to contact the composer and obtain his answer. Nathan had once lived in Leeds, and it was suggested that he acquaint Brahms with the attractions of that city. However, on 11 November 1887, he had to report to the committee, 'I regret to be compelled to inform you that Johannes Brahms' present nervous condition will not allow him to compose a new work for your Festival, which he himself regrets very much indeed, feeling highly honoured by your request.' In the circumstances, one cannot wonder at the fact that Stanford later failed to make Brahms change his mind about Leeds.

The 1889 Festival was attended by Otto Lessmann, correspondent for the *Allgemeine Musikzeitung*, who heard the *German Requiem* conducted by Sullivan. He wrote that the choral performances were more beautiful than any he had known on the continent. He cautioned German readers 'not to underrate, as formerly, the pains bestowed upon the cultivation of music in England.'

Stanford, as he sat poised in February 1892 to invite Brahms once more to Cambridge to receive an honorary degree, must have taken up his pen with a heavy heart. All attempts to lure the master to England had so far failed, not only his own, but those of several others as well. Yet he was probably not without some small measure of optimism, for he had two prizes to offer Brahms. The first was a meeting with Verdi, whom Brahms so much admired, but had never met. The second was the award of an important honour from a country that since 1876, when last the same distinction was offered, had proved beyond any doubt to be genuinely sympathetic to his music, perhaps even more so than his native Germany. And this honour was not given away lightly. He could not doubt the warmth and sincerity of the offer. It came from a society that had done much to popularise his works and from a fellow musician whom he knew and liked, a man who, himself, had won a European reputation.

Moreover, the Brahms of 1892 was a mellower, less defensive person than he had been sixteen years earlier. He was by now well used to accepting honours and would not fail to recall that Cambridge had been the first institution that wished to show him honour. Since then, he had been made a Doctor of Philosophy, in 1879, at the University of Breslau, for whom he composed the *Academic Festival Overture*. In 1886, the Emperor of Germany had dubbed him Knight of the Order, *pour le mérite*, for Arts and Sciences – at the same time as

Verdi received his knighthood *in absentia*. In 1886, too, he was elected a member of the Berlin Academy of Arts. In 1889, he was granted the freedom of the city of Hamburg, a distinction that affected him profoundly. Other honours included the Order of St Leopold, from the Emperor of Austria, and the Maximilian Order of Arts and Sciences, from the King of Bavaria. When Wagner heard of this latter award, he resolved to return his own Order, but his wife persuaded him to keep it.

Brahms quite liked people occasionally to mention his honours. His friend Joseph Widmann has left an account of how, when they were staying with the Duke of Meiningen at his palace, Brahms was not averse to drawing attention to them.

> Though it was usually no slight effort for Brahms to put on gala dress, still here he enjoyed appearing at table in the splendour of his many orders: and this did not seem to me to be a contradiction of his plebeian principles, but, rather, a confirmation of the same, since such decorations and the accompanying honours were in his eyes merely the tribute paid to genius -- that nobility of the mind which is as much a gift of God as any high birth -- honours that in former days had been denied to a Mozart and a Schubert, sons of the people. This is no vague supposition of mine, for I know, from several observations that he made, that such was Brahms's feeling on this point. For instance, he once remarked, alluding to the almost princely honours showered upon Wagner, that every musician's lot had thereby been raised to a higher plane, 'and although he had the lion's share, yet all have indirectly reaped the benefit.'

———————————

So Stanford wrote to Brahms and waited for an answer. It was no more than an exploratory letter; the vice-chancellor would send official invitations to Brahms and Verdi later in the year. Stanford suspected that Brahms might need softening up, but he seems to have been unaware of the extent of Brahms's refusals to come to England. Had he known, he might well have thrown in the towel straight away.

Among the first to invite Brahms was, predictably enough, the intrepid Manns, who, as we have seen, was responsible for the premières of a number of Brahms's works in this country. He had a quite exceptional pioneering record, comparable to that of Stokowski in our own century; his only peer in England at the time was Hallé. Born in Germany in 1825, he worked his way up through military bands and dance orchestras, and in 1854 came to the Crystal Palace as sub-conductor of the wind band. By the following year he was conductor. In time, the band became a full orchestra, and Manns, with Grove's inestimable support as secretary to the Crystal Palace, thereupon proceeded to introduce one new work after another to English audiences. He did much to establish, against fierce opposition, Schumann's reputation in London and also played Wagner and Liszt when they were looked on as 'dangerous'. In 1897, when he was past seventy, he unleashed Richard Strauss's *Also Sprach Zarathustra* on disbelieving British ears. In a letter of thanks, the composer told him, 'I heard . . . that you brought about its first performance with personal sacrifice and, by means of your transcendent skill, secured for the piece a wonderful performance.'

It is uncertain when precisely Manns invited Brahms to the Crystal Palace, though it seems to have been about 1873, when the German composer was conductor of the Vienna Philharmonic Society. His letter of reply is dated 7 September, but the year is not stated.

Dear Sir,
    Herr Joachim has just forwarded to me your letter, which I hasten to answer. Unfortunately, it is not possible for me to accept your kind invitation, and I hope you will believe me when I say how much I regret not being able to do so. My conductor's duties here last from 13 October to the end of April, and I cannot be away for more than a fortnight because of rehearsals and preparations for the concerts.
    I want to take this opportunity to tell you what great pleasure it gives me to know of the warm interest that you show in my music and to learn from my friends of your splendid performances of them. I therefore regret all the more strongly, as I have mentioned, that the situation here does not leave me free to make this journey.

With the greatest esteem,
Yours very truly,

J. Brahms

Brahms turned down the offer of another engagement at the Crystal Palace in 1876; this was the occasion of the unfortunate advertisement in *The Times* that backfired on the Crystal Palace proprietors. It is unlikely that Manns or Grove were involved.

In 1876, Brahms was also contacted by Novello's, who offered him 15,000 marks for an oratorio of the same size as Mendelssohn's *Elijah*. Nothing came of this. During the following year, the composer was awarded the Gold Medal of the Philharmonic Society. He declined the opportunity of coming to London to receive it in person. In 1878, the society invited him to conduct at one of its concerts. His friend the Handel scholar Friedrich Chrysander, who was then living in London, assured him on 30 December 1878, 'You need not be afraid of being pestered. You'd be surprised how quiet and undisturbed a life you can lead right in the middle of London.' Brahms replied that circumstances did not permit him to come at present. Chrysander pointed out to the society that this was not a cut-and-dried refusal: 'He has given me his promise to visit England.' He added, 'Since he has not hitherto given this promise to anyone else, you may depend upon him, with his disposition, that he will keep his word. In the meantime he gives Joachim, who is coming to London now, his new violin concerto, and wishes that his English friends will consider this as a sign of his gratitude for the kindness and the lively interest that they take in him and his works.' Joachim played the concerto at Philharmonic concerts on 6 March and 20 March 1879, but he gave the first English performance with Manns at the Crystal Palace on 22 February. It received a more enthusiastic reception in London than it had yet been accorded anywhere else. Chrysander informed Brahms that it had been listened to 'with the greatest intelligence – while, the other day, the good people of Hamburg still had no idea how they should take it.' In 1880, the society offered Brahms an engagement to conduct three concerts during the 1881 season. He replied, after a telegram had also been sent to him, on 9 December 1880.

Unfortunately I cannot make up my mind to accept your kind invitation. My partiality for concerts is very small. I already have more than I would like of them both here [Vienna] and in Germany. This prevents me from resolving to undertake a long journey for further concerts, though it is my ardent desire to see and hear for myself what I have so often heard praised by my friends. Please accept my warmest thanks for sending me so cordial an invitation.

At the end of 1883, the society asked the composer to come to London to conduct his latest symphony, the Third. Replying on a postcard, he regretted that this would be impossible.

Another who attempted to bring Brahms to England was his good friend the singer, conductor and composer George Henschel, who settled in London and in 1890 became a naturalised Englishman. Born in Breslau in 1850, he was a pupil of Reinecke. He first met Brahms in 1874 when, as a baritone, he took part in the Cologne Festival. In 1881, he was appointed conductor of the newly founded

Boston Symphony Orchestra. In 1886, he succeeded Jenny Lind as Professor of Singing at the Royal College of Music and, in the same year, established the London Symphony Concerts.

In July 1876, Henschel joined Brahms for twelve days at the holiday resort of Sassnitz on the Isle of Rügen in the Baltic. He kept a diary during his stay, and much of it makes delightful reading.

Sunday, July 9.

Early yesterday morning Brahms came up to go bathing with me. There was a fine surf on, and the temperature of the water being rather high, we stayed in it for nearly half an hour, enjoying ourselves hugely. I greatly admired Brahms's burly, well-knit, muscular body, which is only rather too much inclined to stoutness, I fear.

In the water he drew my attention to the possibility of keeping one's eyes open wide when diving. It is not only possible, he said, but also very agreeable and strengthening for the eyes. I at once followed his advice to try, succeeding immediately, and we greatly amused ourselves by throwing littler copper coins into the water and diving for them . . .

Brahms is looking splendid. His solid frame, the healthy, dark-brown colour of his face, the full hair, just a little sprinkled with grey, all make him appear the very image of strength and vigour. He walks about here just as he pleases, generally with his waistcoat unbuttoned and his hat in his hand, always with clean linen, but without collar or tie. These he dons at table d'hôte only. His whole appearance vividly recalls some of the portraits of Beethoven. His appetite is excellent. He eats with great gusto and, in the evening, drinks his three glasses of beer, never omitting, however, to finish off with his beloved Kaffee.

July 11.

We stretched ourselves out in the low grass – it was a very warm evening – lit cigarettes and lay listening [beside a frog pond] in deepest silence, not a breath of wind stirring, for fully half an hour. Then we leaned over the pond, caught tiny little baby frogs and let them jump into the water again from a stone, which greatly amused Brahms, especially when the sweet little creatures, happy to be in their element once more, hurriedly swam away, using their nimble little legs most gracefully and according to all the rules of the natatory art. When they thought themselves quite safe, Brahms would tenderly catch one up again in his hand, and heartily laugh with pleasure on giving it back its freedom . . .

July 15.

Today I read out, from a Berlin paper, the news of the death, at Bayreuth, where *The Ring* was being performed for the first time, of a member of the Wagner orchestra. '*The first corpse*', said Brahms, dryly . . .

July 17.
'I sometimes regret,' he said to me after some moments of silence, 'that I did not marry. I ought to have a boy of ten now; that *would* be nice. But when I was of the right age for marrying, I lacked the position to do so, and now it is too late . . .'

July 18.
Yesterday, when, after our usual swim, we leisurely strolled to the Fahrnberg for dinner, a button on Brahms's shirt suddenly came off. As it was the one which served to hold the collar in its place, Brahms was greatly embarrassed. I proposed to help him out, and we went to my room, where I took out of my valise a little box containing sewing materials which my mother had given me to carry with me when travelling. The amusing situation of my sewing the button on to Brahms's shirt while he had it on, again recalled memories of his youth. 'When *I* went on my first journey,' he said, laughingly, 'my mother also put such a little box into my bag, and showed me how to use its contents. But I remember quite well, when I tore a hole in my trousers, I repaired it with sealing wax! It didn't last long, though . . .'

In the train to Berlin July 19.
This morning, at five o'clock, I left Sassnitz. Strangely enough, it again poured in torrents, as on the night of my arrival. A horrid, chilly morning. Brahms was up at the Fahrnberg a little before five, and, to my delight, accompanied me in the diligence as far as Lancken, some three miles from Sassnitz. There he got out, we shook hands, and parted. For a long time I looked after him out of the carriage window in spite of the wind and the still pouring rain. It was a picture never to be forgotten. As far as the eye could reach, nothing but moor, and clouds, and – Brahms.

In later life, Henschel retired to a manse in Aviemore, by the Spey, in Inverness-shire. There, one afternoon in the summer of 1933, John Barbirolli called on him, so that Henschel could 'show me how to do the Brahms symphonies', and spent a wonderful few hours with the old man. In 1956, Henschel's daughter Helen presented Barbirolli with her father's marked scores of the symphonies. He was deeply touched. 'Of course I shall use them for conducting and draw inspiration from the knowledge that I have before me the possession of a very great and noble man and artist.'

Henschel had not been in London long before he discovered that the English really meant what they said about Brahms: for them, he was indisputably one of the great composers, and they listened to his music with obvious enjoyment and understanding. Henschel recounted this to Brahms and told him he should look more favourably on invitations from England. The composer replied, 'I shall not easily be persuaded to come. I have too great an aversion to concerts and similar disquietudes. It has nothing to do with the question of whether I like English politics or English globe-trotters or not.'

It was a commonly held belief during the 1870s and 1880s that Brahms had little respect for music-making in London. What other reason, the English argued, could explain his continued refusal to visit the capital? Henschel himself reached the same opinion, and he asked Brahms if this was true, adding, 'London doesn't take second place to any other city in its admiration for you.' This inquiry, dispatched in 1879, seems to have irritated the composer, who replied:

The chief point of interest as regards myself is that at least *you* should give up believing the rumour that I have a special dislike for English concert rooms.

No more so than for others. Into none of them do I ever go with pleasure, and people ought to be able to see how much easier it is for me to be caught now and then in the snare of a German invitation than to undertake a long journey to England, followed by a restless stay there. Surely, once in a while, you could explain to people things as they really are?

I have quite enough to do with concerts, anyhow, and fight against it here just as much as over there . . . If only I could come over and stroll around with you incognito! But that would be treating in rather an ungracious way the many kind invitations I have had.

For several years afterwards, Henschel appears to have dropped the subject of a visit to London, but in 1887 he wrote to Brahms, offering him the remarkable fee of £500 to conduct a number of the London Symphony Concerts. Somewhat undiplomatically, he again referred to the idea that the composer found London musical life little to his taste. Brahms was once more annoyed by this suggestion.

I thank you for your kind invitation, but am rather vexed at having to hear from you, too, the common rumour of my dislike for the English, etc.

You really ought to know – I've told you often enough – that *solely* love of comfort – laziness, if you prefer – and aversion to concerts prevent my going to England, but equally so to St. Petersburg or Paris.

I am perfectly aware that my persistent refusal is open to misinterpretation. However, it would be hopeless to try to explain this and to tell people how it has nothing to do with music if we, on the one hand, have a Bohemian Cabinet or you, over there, have a magnificent Opium War, etc., etc.

It's all vanity, anyhow!

London and Leeds were by no means the only cities to occasion a negative response from Brahms. Bradford and Cardiff also received refusals. The Birmingham Musical Festival, too, tried and failed, despite the following sympathetic and imaginative appeal to an intermediary from one of the Festival's directors, George Johnstone.

> I fear that the rumours which have reached Dr. Brahms of our strict adherence in this country to certain social conventionalities have hitherto been the main obstacle to his visiting England. Please therefore assure the great man that if he will do me the distinguished honour of being my guest during the festival, he will find my house to be Liberty Hall itself, that smoking goes on all over it and that I myself have been seen in the drawing-room not only in my dressing-gown, but even without a shirt collar.

Notwithstanding Mr Johnstone's spirited endeavour, Brahms replied, 'Neither a German nor an English Musical Festival could tempt me to undertake such a journey; a country like Sicily, totally bereft of this species of culture, would attract me more.'

Hallé failed to get Brahms to Manchester. They met at one of the Rhenish Musical Festivals, and Hallé urged the composer to come to England and conduct a concert of his works. On his return to Manchester, he wrote, fixing a date, but, says Brahms, he 'offered me a fee lower than what I was receiving in some of the smallest towns in Germany. Had I been asked to go merely for the honour, I might have accepted, but it was the meanness of the offer, after all his big talk, that made me refuse it with indignation.' Hallé, born in Westphalia in 1819, and the friend of Berlioz, Chopin and Liszt, was one of the most generous of men. Since founding his orchestra in 1857, he had impressed artists from all over Europe, including Bülow, Joachim and Henschel, with both his open-handedness and his integrity. His son writes of this in his biography of the great conductor.

> To bring his band, by training and careful recruitment, as near perfection as possible was the hobby of his life, and to this end he spared neither trouble nor expense. He never for a moment allowed any question of money to stand in his way, and his agents were often driven to despair by his engagements at ruinous terms of artists who did not make the difference of a sixpence in the receipts; indeed, to my certain knowledge, he several times gave cheques to members of the band, or to singers whom he engaged for the concerts, on his private banking account, so that he might escape the 'talking to' he knew he so well deserved, if Messrs. Forsyth [the Hallé Orchestra managers] had got wind of his goings on.

When Hallé and Brahms met again in Vienna in October 1880 they got on excellently. 'Brahms is the most delightful and good-natured creature imaginable', Hallé wrote to his daughter, 'and what a musician! . . . We have dined together every day at the coffee house ('Der Igel') where Beethoven used to dine, spent a few hours afterwards in talk, met again in the evening and remained together till midnight.' When he left Vienna a few days later, Hallé was able to say, 'Brahms has taken to me like a duck to water (of which I feel not a little proud); he hardly ever left me, and on Monday afternoon even went to the station – a very long way indeed – to see me off.'

Hallé's interest in modern music and the high quality of his orchestra are touched on in a letter, dated March 1877, from Joachim to the composer Ernst Rudorff.

> I have spoken to Manns and Hallé . . . about your Serenade. The latter knows it already and means to do it without fail this autumn . . . Next to Manns', his orchestra is the best in England. I have had no definite promise yet from Manns, but I feel sure that he, too, will do it. I shall also draw Stanford's attention to it.

Hallé introduced vast quantities of Brahms to his Manchester audiences during the 1880s and acquainted them, too, with the latest works of Dvořák, Grieg, Saint-Saëns, Sullivan, Stanford, Bruch and many other contemporary composers. In the sixties and seventies, he had done the same for Liszt and Wagner. In 1874, with Bülow, he gave the first performance in England of the two-piano version of the *Haydn Variations*. In 1882, at the age of sixty-three, he took the solo part, at a concert in Manchester, in Brahms's Second Piano Concerto, almost exactly a year after the première in Budapest.

Brahms, whether he liked it or not, was often asked, by English people who met him, when he would be coming to London. Among the first to put this question was Florence May, who saw a good deal of him when she was a pupil of Clara Schumann in Baden-Baden in 1871. Did he intend visiting England? she inquired.

> 'I think not,' he immediately replied, as though his mind were definitely made up on this point. I ventured to pursue the subject, telling him he ought to come, in order to make his compositions known. 'It is for that they are printed,' he said rather decidedly, and with these words he certainly gave me some real insight into his character . . . His want of familiarity with our language may have had something to do with it; he could

read English a little, but I never heard him attempt to speak it. He had a horror of being lionized and of involving himself in an entanglement of engagements; perhaps, also, he was possessed with an exaggerated notion of the inflexibility of English social laws, especially as to the wearing of dress-clothes and the restrictions with regard to smoking. Before and behind all such superficial considerations, however, I suspect that early in his career the idea had taken root in him, right or wrong as it may have been, that to visit England would not further his artistic development.

Although Brahms told Miss May that his compositions could become known without any need of his coming to England – 'It is for that they are printed' – Robert Haven Schauffler mentions in his biography of Brahms that 'he never wearied of urging his publisher to bring out the songs *without* English words. "I am indifferent," he would exclaim, "to everything connected with England!"'

Another pupil of Clara Schumann, the pianist Mathilde Verne, recalls in *Chords of Remembrance* an inquiry similar to Florence May's.

I remember another evening when Brahms was present and Caroline Geisler-Schubert asked him: 'Why don't you go to England where everyone loves music?' He shrugged . . . 'Ah, in England it always rains, rains, rains, and in England one always has to wear evening dress.'

In her book *Another Way of Music*, Eva Ducat relates how the singer William Shakespeare, his wife and daughter Mimie visited Brahms in Vienna. Mimie told Miss Ducat, 'He ate too much, and I couldn't get over it.' Mrs Shakespeare spoke of how she taxed Brahms with the old familiar question.

Then as I was going, I asked Brahms if he would not come to England. 'No, that can I not,' he cried emphatically. 'I hear that in England everybody wears patent leather shoes in the evening. Now I have never worn such things in my life. I can never come.'
'Ah, but Herr Doktor, come,' said I; 'we shall all love you whether you wear patent leather shoes or not!'
'Well,' said he, smiling, 'if I come, it will be to your house.'

Brahms once told Joseph Widmann that 'the chief reason why he declined the most pressing invitations to England was that "one has to live in a dress suit and white tie."' The composer Ethel Smyth maintained that he was strongly prejudiced against England because of his fear of being lionised. 'I know how you went on with Mendelssohn', he said.

.

Of course, the charming, graceful and aristocratic Mendelssohn, with his perfect command of English, acquitted himself with almost effortless brilliance in English society. In many ways, the salon was his natural milieu. This was not so with Brahms, and it could be suggested that it was not the evening dress and patent-leather shoes that worried him, but the conduct and behaviour which were expected to go with them. Lionised he would certainly have been in England, but the stars of London society during the seventies, eighties and nineties were writers and painters, not composers, as in Vienna. In the Austrian capital, he was an undisputed god; in London, he could well have found, at a party or dinner, that people like Tennyson, Browning, Carlyle, George Eliot, Leighton or Millais attracted equal, if not greater, attention. Brahms may well have feared that he might not necessarily have been granted the centre of the stage in London, as of right. In *Music and Manners*, published in 1887, W. Beatty-Kingston, formerly Austrian correspondent for the *Daily Telegraph*, writes about the artistic circle in Vienna.

Johannes Brahms, whenever he joined it, became at once the central point and chief personage – partly in virtue of the prestige earned for him by his indisputable genius, and partly by reason of his own innate masterfulness of disposition, which enabled him, in eleven cases out of twelve, to take and keep the lead in society, no matter of what class. An imperious man, restrained from self-assertion by no reluctance to wound his neighbours' sensibilities, if he be endowed with real talent, and have done things universally acknowledged to be great, finds little difficulty in establishing himself as a social despot amongst people of average brains and courage. Having a rough side to his tongue, and being quite unscrupulous with respect to his use of it, his domineering is frequently submitted to by those who are his equals in intelligence and his superiors in breeding, but either too timid or too indolent to resist his assumption of superiority. Such an one, when I first met him some eighteen years ago, was Johannes Brahms – loud, dictatorial, a little too obviously penetrated with a sense of his surpassing greatness, violently intolerant of opinions differing from his own, curiously blunt of speech and 'burschikos' – a German adjective comprehensively descriptive of the roughness characterising University manners throughout the Fatherland – but none the less a jovial spirit, strongly addicted to the pleasures of the table, and taking keen delight in highly-salted 'after-dinner' stories, of which he was an ever-ready narrator, at once boisterous and unctuous. As long as he was allowed to have his own way, without let or hindrance, whether in an oracular or anecdotal mood, he was an exceedingly amusing companion, being extremely well read, clear-headed, and humorous. But he could not stand competition; a shared social throne had no charms for him, and other people's brilliancy 'put him out'. When by any extraordinary accident he found himself relegated to the position of 'the other lion' who 'thought the first a bore', his irritation too often betrayed him into actual rudeness towards people for whom he had the highest regard. At one of the W—s' select musical parties I remember an instance of how badly he could behave, even to such a man as Joseph Joachim – a prince of executant art and his intimate personal friend. Joachim had very amiably volunteered to play, and there happened to be no violin music handy except one set of the Beethoven P.F. and Violin Sonatas (that dedicated to Salieri), which was brought by our hostess to the great *virtuoso* with the request that he would ask Brahms – she had not the courage to do so – to take the pianoforte part. Turning towards Brahms, Joachim smilingly asked, 'Dear master, will you vouchsafe to play this with me for the amusement of our friends here?' 'I am not an accompanist,' growled Brahms, and abruptly turning his back upon Joachim, strode angrily off into another room. The Hungarian violinist merely shrugged his shoulders, and looked around for a volunteer pianist. I may perhaps be pardoned for mentioning *en passant* that I had the good fortune to be accepted as Brahms' substitute, much to my gratification. Nobody except myself seemed the least surprised at the latter's pettish outburst and *sortie*.

To a look of inquiry I was unable to supress, Joachim replied, 'It is his way when he is vexed; he means nothing by it'; and this view of the incident was evidently the one adopted by all present.

That Brahms was 'strongly addicted to the pleasures of the table' is corroborated by Liza Lehmann, who mentions in her autobiography how she met him while studying with Clara Schumann in Frankfurt.

While I was there Johannes Brahms came on a visit for a few days; but he took no interest whatever in the 'English Miss', which was his way of referring to me, and my charming hostess was quite offended with him because he never asked to hear me sing. *I* was very thankful; for, truth to tell, his rather bluff and coarse manners made me shrink into my shell; and when, one morning at breakfast, he gobbled up a whole tin of sardines and made assurance doubly sure by drinking the oil from the tin at a draught, he, so to say, finished *me* off as well as the sardines!

Returning to the subject of Brahms and England, we find in his excuses to the concert promoter Edward Speyer, recounted in Speyer's *My Life and Friends*, another intriguing reference to Sicily.

I asked Brahms how it was he could never make up his mind to visit England, where he was sure to be received with warm sympathy, and where, moreover, he could not fail to find much that would interest him apart from music. 'Ah, no,' he replied jokingly. 'If I must travel, I prefer Taormina [in Northern Sicily]!' . . .

Part of Brahms' antipathy to the English was due to the bad impression made upon him by the parties of tourists ['English globe-trotters'] he saw so frequently. This was the only personal contact he had by which to judge the English.

Brahms's love of Sicily was genuine. He visited the island on three occasions, and Taormina was his favourite spot. During the first trip, in 1878, his companion Billroth wrote a letter to the critic Hanslick, describing the beauties of the place.

Five hundred feet above the murmuring waves! Full moon! Intoxicating scent of orange blossoms, red cactus blooming as luxuriantly on the huge picturesque rocks as moss does back home! Forests of palms and lemons, Moorish castles, a well-preserved Greek theatre! The broad line of snow-capped Etna, the pillar of fire! Add to this a wine called Monte Venere! Above all, *Johannes in ecstasy*!

Sicily was about as far as Brahms ventured from mainland Europe, and for him it had the same attraction as the many books he used to read on travel, voyages of exploration and polar expeditions. These included factual narratives like Stanley's *In Darkest Africa* and novels like Defoe's *Robinson Crusoe*, of which he never tired. He liked Sicily, too, because of the almost complete absence of the autograph-hunters who normally plagued him in Germany, Austria, Switzerland and Italy, where he also took holidays. The lengths to which people would go to inveigle him into signing his name are described by Widmann.

Needless to say, even in Thun [in Switzerland], Brahms received many visits from German and Austrian acquaintances, as well as from conductors, young composers and lady pianists. The last mentioned hoped for a word of praise, which they would have used as further recommendation, but, through long experience, Brahms had perfected the art of politely preventing them from sitting down at the piano. Of course, there was also at Thun no lack of inquisitive admirers and autograph-hunters, some of whom set to work with considerable cunning. One day he showed me a missive received from Solingen [the Sheffield of Germany] that ran as follows: 'YOUR ORDER FOR TEN DOZEN RAPIERS GENUINE SOLINGEN-MAKE TO BE DISPATCHED WITHIN NEXT 48 HOURS: PLEASE MAKE PAYMENT THROUGH POST OFFICE.' But the calculation that Brahms would immediately refuse to receive the supposed order, and thereby furnish the sought-after autograph, was made without knowledge of his perspicacity. He simply put the communication in his pocket and sent no reply. When neither rapiers nor demand for payment arrived, it became clear how correctly he had recognised this as no more than another attempt to extort an autograph from him.

CHAPTER 3

VERDI

Brahms's reply to Stanford, dated 23 February 1892, was not long in coming.

My dear and very honoured Sir,
  I find it hard to take up my pen, for how can I speak of my deep gratitude and at the same time say 'No'? And yet I am earnestly and sincerely grateful to you for your kindness and to your university for the signal honour that it offers me, but it would still have to be 'No' in July [by which time Stanford asked for a final decision], whether I keep the fact from you and from myself today or whether I later try to talk myself out of it.
  But please think kindly of me; I cannot come to Cambridge without also going to London, and how much there would be for us to see and do together in London — but all at the height of beautiful summer, when you, too, would surely prefer to go walking with me beside some lovely Italian lake.
  How tempted I am to accept your invitation. I know it will be an especially charming musical festival. Yet would I not run the risk of being put to shame by old man Verdi, who would probably surpass and abash me in both youthfulness and gratitude?
  But were I now to yield to my inclination and promise you I would come, I know only too well that, when the time at last arrived, I should find it impossible to face the journey and all that it must inevitably entail.
  Please forgive me in as kind and friendly a spirit as you can. Scold me a little, laugh at this ponderous stick-in-the-mud, but never think of me as either indifferent or ungrateful.

Your sincerely devoted,

J. Brahms

So there it was: the most cordial and conciliatory of replies, yet one offering small hope. The allusions to the youthfulness of 'old man Verdi' and to his own unwieldiness were, in fact, justified. Brahms, who was by now fifty-eight, looked and moved like a man many years older. On the other hand, Verdi, at seventy-eight, was still remarkably spry, showing few signs of age. The contemporaneous *Famous Composers and their Works* describes him as 'agile, vigorous, endowed

with an iron constitution and an energy of character that promise
lifelong virility . . . he is still young, still vivacious.' As to walking
beside an Italian lake, Brahms was to be a guest that summer of the
Duke of Meiningen at the Villa Carlotta in Cadenabbia on the
western shore of Lake Como in Lombardy. At the end of the summer,
he would decline an invitation to conduct at the Chicago Exhibition
of 1893, informing Theodore Thomas, 'I cannot make up my mind to
accept . . . for at the last moment I know resolution would fail me and
I should ask to be released from my promise. Kindly excuse, then,
this stick-in-the-mud who cannot undertake the long voyage . . .'

Stanford had, of course, half-expected that Brahms would reply as
he did, which was why he wrote to him so far ahead of time and why
he asked for an answer by July, though none was really necessary
until the end of 1892. He now took the obvious next step and enlisted
the aid of Joachim, who was in England during March and April of
that year. The great violinist discreetly pleaded Stanford's cause. On
30 March, he wrote to Brahms from London, 'It would delight you to
see how all the good musicians here – Stanford, Hubert Parry, Grove,
etc. etc. – love and admire you.' On 5 April, he mentioned that
Stanford was captivated by the Clarinet Quintet, which had just
reached London and had already been performed twice, and, for
good measure, he added that the Irish composer 'was as much taken
with it as are, too, Hubert Parry, Hallé and his wife, Grove, Chappell, etc.'

All was not yet lost. In November, there would be the official
invitation from the vice-chancellor, and by then Brahms might have
been persuaded to change his mind. Nevertheless, at this stage, Verdi
was clearly a better prospect.

In 1892, Verdi's name had been known to English music lovers for
almost fifty years. He established his reputation on the Continent in
1842 with *Nabucco*, and, in an article published that year in the *Athenaeum*, H. F. Chorley, who, as we have seen, was later to be the
scourge of Schumann, Brahms, Liszt and Wagner, alerted his readers
to the emergence of the young Italian.

> Recent occurrences and appearances having called the attention of our
> English public to the modern style, or rather no-style, of Italian singing, it
> may be as well for the critic to see what is doing in the world of Italian
> vocal composition; and, since the name of Giuseppe Verdi has begun to

circulate widely as the *maestro* most likely to become popular, we will avail ourselves of such opportunities as persual of his compositions here published affords us, to offer a word or two concerning his operas.

But, first, we must remind the reader that the distinctive basis of Italian opera, from its outset, has been melody – melody in recitative, in air, in concerted piece, and in chorus – the dramatic expression being largely left to the singer. Even in the German musical drama, though the voice has been often assigned tasks too ungracious to be ever well performed, under the notion of rendering it a mere instrument in the composer's hands, and the adaptation of sound to sense has been more closely studied, still melody has been indispensable to success – in the orchestra if not on the stage . . . Now it appears to be the fancy of the modern European school to throw overboard what is essential because of the accidental; and, since invention just now seems to be at the lowest ebb of exhaustion, musicians denounce the old manner of satisfying the ear as mere excitement *ad captandum*. In France, for instance, M. Berlioz . . . Then there is Herr Wagner, the young Dresden composer, whose operas we have heard rapturously bepraised, because they contain no tunes which any one can carry away . . . Signor Verdi's concerted music strikes us as a shade worthier and more individual than his songs . . . For new melody we have searched in vain, nor have we found any variety of form, indicating an original fancy at work as characteristically as in one of Pacini's, or Mercadante's, or Donizetti's better cavatinas. All seems worn and hackneyed and unmeaning . . .

However, despite this warning, *Ernani*, the first of Verdi's operas to arrive in England, was given a warm welcome by London opera-goers when it opened at Her Majesty's Theatre on 8 March 1845, a year after its successful première in Venice. It had also scored a triumph in Vienna, where Donizetti, as director of the Italian Opera, supervised its production. The teenage Hans von Bülow was bowled over by Verdi's 'richness of melodic invention and genius for theatrical effect'.

On the strength of the enthusiastic reception of *Ernani*, *Nabucco*, first given in Milan in March 1842, was brought to London in March 1846. To meet the demands of censorship relating to the representation of Biblical subjects on the stage, the opera was retitled *Nino, King of Assyria*, and the names of the characters were altered. The opera was so successful that a second London theatre took it up, staging it as *Anato*. Such popularity must have amused Verdi, for English critical opinion, led by Chorley, was still against him. *Ernani* had received only one favourable review, in the *Observer*. This, interestingly enough, was written not by the regular music critic, who was unable to attend the première, but by a cub reporter who knew nothing of opera but went along and enjoyed it. His name was William Howard Russell, who later became an outstanding war correspondent.

For Chorley, *Nino* was merely confirmation of his earlier assessment of Verdi. 'With every sympathy in favour of a new style and a new master, our first hearing of *Nino* has done nothing to change our judgement of the limited natures of Signor Verdi's resources. He has hitherto shown no powers as a melodist.'

Two months after *Nino*, came *I Lombardi*, in May 1846; this had been originally presented in Milan in February 1843. So high was his popularity by now that Verdi was commissioned by Her Majesty's Theatre specially to write an opera for London; the work was *I masnadieri*, produced in July 1847, and the composer himself made the trip to conduct it. Three months earlier, *I due Foscari*, introduced in Rome in November 1844, also received its English première. In addition, *Ernani* was revived – with a famous contralto taking the baritone role of Don Carlo. Such disregard for dramatic truth typifies the state of opera in London in the 1840s. Singers reigned supreme and were expected to improvise cadenzas and embroider arias as a display of virtuosity. Stage and auditorium were both illuminated by gas, with the auditorium only a little the darker of the two. The public, despite their comparative lack of interest in the dramatic elements of opera, were nevertheless keen and informed judges of singing. There were a good many real enthusiasts among them who were quite content to let the critics tear Verdi to shreds as long as the flow of his operas to London was not impeded. Theatrical managers became their allies, for Verdi had become excellent box-office, with money also to be made on revivals, like that of *Anato*, which was re-introduced at Covent Garden in 1850, directed by the star conductor of the day, Michael Costa.

The next arrival after *I due Foscari* was *Attila*, reaching London in March 1848, exactly two years after its première in Venice. Chorley bestowed his customary greeting.

It would be difficult to fancy a worse opera than *Attila*, even from Verdi. The force of noise can hardly go further, unless we are to resort to the device of Sarti's cannon fixed to time his Russian *Te Deum* on the taking of Ochakov, or imitate the anvil chorus which Spontini introduced in one of his operas . . . May we never hear its likes again.

Rigoletto was introduced in May 1853, with Costa conducting; it was by then a little over two years old. Critical opinion was now beginning to move in Verdi's favour: even those who gave *Rigoletto* a drubbing cited *Ernani* and other early operas to prove that he could actually write melodies if the mood took him. When the two-year-old *Il trovatore*, replete with anvil chorus, arrived in May 1855, conducted by Costa, *Rigoletto* was in turn used as a stick with which to beat it. Though the *Observer* spoke of its 'gay and voluble melodies', there were still those who found this latest Verdi opera quite unacceptable. *Musical World* led the way.

> Il Trovatore is written in contempt of all rules . . . no temporary success can atone for the want of refinement, the coarseness of style, the habitual contempt for pure forms, which are as apparent as in any of the previous attempts of the composer . . . they render it impossible to hope for any newly awakened desire on the part of Signor Verdi to become essentially an artist. Verdi should communicate with Richard Wagner – the other red republican of music, who wants to revolutionize the art after a fashion of his own . . . The firm of Wagner and Verdi would then be able to export their musical wares to all parts of the earth.

Musical World was a magazine driven almost senseless by the inexorable advance of modern music and, 'red in tooth and claw', it struck out in all directions against composers 'like Liszt-madmen, enemies of music to the knife, who, not born for music, and conscious of their impotence, revenge themselves by endeavouring to annihilate it.' Wagner 'was born to feed spiders with flies'; *Lohengrin* was 'poison – rank poison'.

> All we can make out is an incoherent mass of rubbish, with no more real pretension to be called music than the jangling and clashing of gongs and other uneuphonious instruments with which the Chinamen, on the brow of a hill, fondly thought to scare away our English 'blue-jackets'.

Even Chorley rarely matched this sort of vituperation, but he comes near to doing so in his evaluation of Schumann, written in June 1856, a month before the composer died in an asylum near Bonn.

> Dr Schumann is not possessed of that musical organization without which all the talent and ingenuity in the world avail nothing . . . For years Schumann reigned a high authority on musical matters; but in an evil hour he fancied he could compose . . . The asylum at Düsseldorf can tell the sequel.'

Despite having Schumann, Berlioz, Liszt, Wagner and, since 1854, the 'new man' Brahms on his hands, Chorley did not neglect his duty regarding *Il trovatore*.

> Time increases our conviction that in England and France the operas of Signor Verdi only pass because there is nothing else, and that the first more elegant and gracious Italian composer who arrives can sweep them away to the limbo of forgotten frenzies.

In effect, such a composer did arrive in May of the following year, 1856, when *La traviata*, dating from March 1853, was produced in London. With its delicacy and wistfulness, it revealed, in greater measure than before, facets of Verdi's genius that had hitherto gone largely unnoticed. The *Observer* declared the opera to be 'unquestionably among the principal works of its composer' and 'full of melody'. However, on this occasion, it was not so much the musical content – which Chorley, predictably, found 'trashy' – but the subject matter that prompted adverse criticism. *The Times* called it 'foul and hideous'. The public thought otherwise, as the *Spectator* reported ten weeks later.

> The favourite opera of the season has been *La Traviata*. The highest society in England has thronged the opera house night after night to see a very young and innocent-looking lady [the beautiful Marietta Piccolomimi] impersonate the heroine of an infamous French novel, who varies her prostitution by a frantic passion . . . We should have thought the production of *La Traviata* an outrage on the ladies of the aristocracy who support the theatre, if they had not, by crowding their boxes every night, shown that they did not notice the underlying vice of the opera.

By the summer of 1856, London had seen *Rigoletto, Il trovatore,* and *La traviata,* and Verdi's popularity was established once and for all. There now followed *Luisa Miller,* in June 1858; *I vespri siciliani,* in July 1859; *Un ballo in maschero,* in June 1861; and *Don Carlo,* conducted by Costa, and *La forza del destino,* both in June 1867. To Dublin fell the honour of giving the first performance in Britain of *Macbeth,* which was produced in March 1859, with Pauline Viardot as Lady Macbeth. Before the sixties were out, London had staged no less than fourteen of Verdi's operas, several of which had permanently entered the repertory of more than one company. What is astonishing is that, as yet, not a single opera by Wagner had been presented. All that was known of him was what could be heard in the concert hall, consisting of various orchestral excerpts, preludes, overtures and a handful of arias. The first of his operas to be staged was *Der fliegende Holländer*, in July 1870, which was sung in Italian and entitled *L'olandese dannato*. *Lohengrin*, also sung in Italian, was introduced in May 1875, and *Tannhäuser*, again in Italian, in May 1876. Thus, at the time of the first Bayreuth Festival, in August 1876, not one of Wagner's operas had been heard in German. In January 1879, *Rienzi* arrived, sung in English. *Der fliegende Holländer* had taken 27 years to reach England; *Lohengrin*, 25 years; *Tannhäuser*, 30 years; and *Rienzi*, 36 years.

A month after the English première of *Tannhäuser*, *Aida* was presented at Covent Garden, in June 1876. *The Times* welcomed it in flattering terms, acknowledging Verdi as 'a dramatic composer, who for some thirty years has been one of the chief entertainers of our opera-going public.' Moreover, he did not appear to be tainted with Wagnerism: 'He is, happily, still the Verdi of our long rememberance, our own Verdi in short, and may he continue to remain so.' During the previous year, London had heard the *Requiem* for the first time and greeted it warmly. The *Pall Mall Gazette* considered this to be the finest sacred work since Mozart's *Requiem*. By now, it was beginning to dawn on people that, apart from being immensely popular, Verdi might possibly also be a great composer. By February 1887, when, after a silence of more than twelve years, *Otello* was produced in Milan, such a conclusion became practically universal. Musicians came from all over the world to be at the première. They were amazed at what they heard: an advanced, modern work revealing still further development in the genius of the seventy-three-year-old composer. The nineteen-year-old Arturo Toscanni, who played one of the second cellos at the first performance, told his mother when he got home, '*Otello* is a masterpiece. Go on your knees, Mother, and say "Viva Verdi!"', and this he compelled her to do.

Otello was given in London, amid great excitement, in July 1889. By now, Verdi dominated the world of opera. When Wagner died in February 1883, Verdi wrote to his publisher Ricordi, 'Sad Sad Sad!' The words were penned in a trembling hand, and, in the shock of the moment, he spelled Wagner's name as Vagner, just as he would have pronounced it. Though they had never met, he was deeply moved. So, too, was Brahms. He was taking a choral rehearsal in Vienna when a note announcing Wagner's death was handed to him. He laid down his baton and said, simply, 'Today we sing no more. A master is dead.' Wagner finally conquered London in the year of his death.

Das Rheingold was presented on 5 May 1882; *Die Walküre*, on 6 May; *Siegfried*, on 7 May; *Götterdamerung*, on 9 May; *Die Meistersinger*, on 30 May; and *Tristan und Isolde*, on 20 June. *Parsifal* was given in a concert performance in 1884 so as not to infringe the Bayreuth copyright in regard to stage productions.

Notwithstanding the excitement provoked in London by this deluge of masterpieces, *Otello* gained a formidable success and was critically acclaimed. Verdi was particularly anxious about the English première and was relieved and delighted to learn by telegram of its triumph. 'Praise given in Shakespeare's own country is valuable indeed', he remarked.

With Wagner's death and Liszt's in 1886, Verdi found himself the sole surviving representative of that group of great composers, including, also, Berlioz, Mendelssohn, Chopin and Schumann, who were born in the period 1803 to 1813. In 1892, he was no less famous than Brahms. Indeed, interest in him was perhaps even greater, for it had recently been discovered that he was busy on yet another work, *Falstaff*, his first comic opera in nearly fifty years. This was scheduled for performance in Milan early in 1893.

The idea that Verdi might like to follow the première of *Falstaff* with a trip to England to receive a high academic honour must have seemed a reasonable one to Stanford and the other leading members of the CUMS. Verdi's name was now indissolubly linked with Shakespeare's; such a visit would perfectly round off a long and distinguished career. England, too, had been among the first countries outside Italy to welcome his talent, and *I masnadieri*, performed in London in 1847, was the first of his operas to have its première outside of Italy. This 'most popular musician of the nineteenth century', as the contemporary English critic Crowest called him, was no stranger to accepting honours. In 1859 he became a member of the French Académie des Beaux Arts; in 1862 he was decorated with the Grand Cross of the Russian Order of St Stanislaus; in 1872 he received the Order of Osmanie from the Khedive of Egypt; in 1875 he was awarded the Cross of Commander, and Star, of the Austrian Order of Franz Joseph, and was nominated, in Paris, a Commander of the Legion of Honour. During the eighties, the list of titles grew even larger and more resplendent. The journey to Cambridge could surely hold no terrors for him, as it did with Brahms, for he had visited England on several occasions.

He made his first trip for the production of *I masnadieri*, which was presented at Her Majesty's in July 1847. He intended to come quite early in the year, but was delayed by ill-health, brought on by overwork. In his characteristic, businesslike way, he forwarded doctors' certificates to Benjamin Lumley, manager of Her Majesty's, as proof of his indisposition. He sent on ahead his loyal pupil and assistant, the high-spirited and impressionable young Emanuele Muzio, to arrange accommodation and make contact with Lumley. He himself at last arrived on 5 June 1847, exactly twenty-one years to the day after the poor, frightened Carl Maria von Weber expired amid the fog and fumes of London, having seen *Oberon* safely through its première. Soon after his arrival, Verdi wrote to the wife of Andrea Maffei, the librettist of *I masnadieri*.

> I have been in London barely two days . . . I can say nothing about London, because yesterday was Sunday and I haven't yet seen a soul. The smoke, though, and the smell of coal annoy me awfully: it's like being on a steamboat all the time. . . .

Muzio also wrote home to Italy.

> What chaos is London! What confusion! Paris is nothing by comparison. People shouting, poor people weeping, steam engines, steamboats racing along, men on horseback, in carriages, on foot, and everybody howling like the damned . . .
>   On Sunday there is not a soul in the streets, they are all at church, where they have the sermons. Many, however, stay in bed practically all the day, so I hear, while others go into the country or just outside London for amusement and debauchery. The English say that on Sundays only dogs and Frenchmen are to be seen in the streets of London, and certainly all one sees are travellers and foreigners . . .
>   It's cold in London, it does nothing but rain, and it's always windy. The Maestro doubts whether there's any sun at all, for he's never seen it shining because of the mist, which is continuous . . .
>   Byron says: 'In England there are nine months of winter and three months without sun' [*The English winter – ending in July, / To recommence in August*]; and it's Byron, England's greatest poet, who has written this! . . . We get up at five in the morning and we work till six in the evening, which is supper-time. Then we go to the theatre for a while . . . they look at nobody but Verdi. He's already as much a celebrity in London as he is in all Italy . . . and then we come back at eleven to go to bed, so we can be up early next morning . . .
>   We in Italy imagine that the English don't love music; this is a mistake. It is said that the English only know how to pay for the pleasure of listening to great artists, but that they do not understand anything. This is a story invented by the French.

Muzio was worried about Verdi's health. 'The heavy, damp climate affects his nervous system and makes him more eccentric and melancholy than usual. He's always afraid of coming down with some illness or other.' Also, there was 'this perpetual smoke that poisons the air, blackens your face and makes your eyes smart.' Muzio was anxious, too, about the Maestro's diet: 'he can't eat those meals full of drugs and pepper, and all the cold dishes and the wine that's so strong it's like rum.'

Verdi had postponed orchestrating *I masnadieri* until he came to London, and it was this that was keeping him so busy. At the end of June, he was still hard at work, but by now he had seen something of the capital.

> Long live our sunshine, which I have always loved so much, but which I now positively worship since I've been plunged into this fog and smoke that suffocates and depresses me. However, apart from this, what a wonderful city! There are things here at which you stop and stare, as if turned to stone – but this climate takes everything out of such beauty. Oh, if only the sky of Naples lay overhead, you wouldn't have to dream of Paradise. I haven't started rehearsals for my new opera, because I haven't yet had time . . .
>
> The theatres are packed, and the English pay so well!! Oh, if only I could stay here for a couple of years, I'd be able to carry away sackfuls of those most holy pounds. Still there's no point in having such lovely thoughts, because I would never be able to stand the climate . . .
>
> In London my health is really not too bad, only I'm always afraid of being about to fall ill.

Verdi found himself working more slowly than usual; the climate drained even his enormous vitality. Its effect on men of frailer constitution, like Weber and Chopin, could be fatal. Shortly before his death, Weber wrote to his wife that 'this is a day on which to shoot oneself, with such a thick, dark, dank yellow fog that it is almost impossible to exist without candles. The sun has no rays; it is simply a red point amid the fog. It is terrifying.' A year after Verdi's visit, Chopin wote, in October 1848; 'The winter is already approaching, and what will happen to me I can't yet tell . . . I have been ill for the past 18 days, ever since returning to London. I have not once left the house.' Verdi speaks in one of his letters of 'this infernal climate that robs me of all desire to work.' This was echoed by Wagner, who says in his autobiography that his recollections of his visit to London in 1855 were 'merged in the all-absorbing memory of practically uninterrupted ill-health'.

I had a perpetual cold and therefore followed the advice of my friends by taking a heavy English diet in an attempt to resist the effects of the climate, but this totally failed. For one thing, I could never get my rooms sufficiently warmed, and the work I had brought with me was the first to suffer. The orchestration of *Die Walküre*, which I had hoped to finish, advanced a mere hundred pages . . . In absolute despair, I plunged into Dante, making my first serious attempt to read him. In that London climate, the *Inferno* became, indeed, a never-to-be-forgotten reality.

I masnadieri eventually had a glittering and triumphal première, on 22 July 1847. Early that day, there was such excitement that people rushed the doors and broke into the theatre. Verdi had not wished to conduct the opera, but was persuaded to do so by the Russian ambassador and a number of English noblemen. The first performance, according to Muzio, 'created a furore'.

From the prelude to the finale there was nothing but applause, *hurrahs*, recalls and encores. The Maestro himself conducted, sitting on a chair higher than all the others, baton in hand. As soon as he appeared in the orchestra pit, applause broke out, lasting for a quarter of an hour. Before it had ceased, the Queen arrived, together with her consort Prince Albert, the Queen Mother, the Duke of Cambridge, uncle of the Queen, the Prince of Wales, son of the Queen, and all the royal family and countless lords and dukes. It goes almost without saying that the boxes were packed with the most elegantly dressed ladies, and the pit was so crowded that nobody could remember seeing so many people. At half past four the doors were opened, and the crowd burst into the theatre with an enthusiasm never before witnessed . . . The takings amounted to £6,000 and were even more than on the evening when the Queen attended a gala performance. The Maestro was cheered, called on to the stage, both on his own and with the singers, and pelted with flowers. Nothing was to be heard but 'Evviva Verdi! Bietifol!'

Muzio observed, however, that the English 'never gave way to enthusiasm like the Italians'. They were 'a formal and thoughtful people'. A few days earlier, when he went to see a play, he noticed some of the audience 'with the printed tragedy in their hands, not watching the actress, but looking to see if she said all the words.'

The star of *I masnadieri* was Jenny Lind. Her singing and acting were much praised. The *Illustrated London News* reported that 'bouquets innumerable were thrown to the Swedish songstress . . . Her acting; her exquisite perception of the character; her delicious execution of the music, written, we suspect, rather with a view to its performance by *prime donne* of a less extended compass of voice, and therefore not embracing her higher notes, but to which she gives an inexpressible charm; all this would afford matter for a long dissertation . . .' To Muzio, she confided that 'she hates the theatre and the stage; she says she is unhappy, and will experience contentment and a little pleasure only when she no longer has anything to do with theatre people or with the theatre itself. On this point, she is much in agreement with the Maestro, who also hates the theatre and can't wait for the moment when he can retire from it.' In Muzio's opinion, 'her voice is a little harsh in the high notes, weak in the low ones.' Chopin, who saw her a year later in *La sonnambula*, came to a different conclusion. 'She sings with amazing purity and certainty, and her *piano* is so steady – as smooth and even as a thread of hair.' Queen Victoria noted in her diary, 'Lind sang and acted most exquisitely', adding that she 'looked very well and attractive in her several dresses'. She found the music 'inferior and commonplace', which may have been not so much her own opinion as Prince Albert's. After all, the Verdi of *I masnadieri* hardly sounded like Mendelssohn. In fact, Mendelssohn took an interest in Verdi's music and, much to Chorley's disgust, admitted to a partiality for Italian opera. He much admired Rossini and once startled Chorley by humming a tune from *Il barbiere di Siviglia*. Of Donizetti's *La Fille du régiment*, he said, 'It's so merry, with so much of the real soldier's life in it. They call it bad, but, to be sure, it's surprising how easily one can become used to bad music!' Chorley was naturally on hand for the première of *I masnadieri* and struck his best vein. 'We take this to be the worst opera which has been given in our time at Her Majesty's Theatre. Verdi is finally rejected. The field is left open for an Italian composer.'

Verdi conducted one further performance of the opera, and then the Irish composer, conductor and singer, Michael Balfe, whom Rossini chose to play Figaro in *Il barbiere* in Paris in 1827, took over the baton. He had also conducted the first performance of *Nino*. Verdi appears to have admired Balfe's skill as a conductor, according to Balfe's biographer William Barrett.

In Verdi's estimation, 'without having caused a furore, *I masnadieri* was well received.' As a result, he was invited to compose for Her Majesty's one opera a year for the next ten years. This he was not anxious to do, and he therefore proposed terms that Lumley found too excessive to accept. A week later, Verdi and Muzio took their leave of the English capital. Writing from Paris to a friend in Italy, the composer looked back on his not unpleasant stay.

Though I found the London climate horrid, I took, despite this, an extraordinary liking to the city. No, it isn't a city; it's a world. Nowhere else can compare with it in size, richness, the beauty of its streets and the cleanness of its houses. One is struck dumb with astonishment and made to feel insignificant when, in the midst of all this splendour, one surveys the Bank and the docks. Who could resist such a nation? The surroundings and the countryside outside London are marvellous. I'm not so keen, though, on some of the English customs, or, rather, they don't suit us Italians. How silly it looks when· people in Italy try to imitate the English!

Verdi again came to England in the mid-fifties, making flying visits in 1854, 1855 and 1856. These were essentially business trips, necessitated by the need to protect certain copyright interests and to protest against a projected unauthorised production of *Il trovatore*. The laws at that time were extremely complicated. A legal action relating to an unauthorised presentation in London of *La sonnambula*, which had dragged on for twelve years, was eventually resolved in August 1855 by the House of Lords, who ruled, among other things, that, unless a composer personally supervised the production of his opera in England, he could not receive copyright protection. 'This means', Verdi informed his lawyer in October 1855, 'that publishers understandably now find it easier to appropriate our operas, without it being necessary to negotiate with the composer.'

> During my two trips to London, they suggested that I should apply for citizenship of either England or France, or even Piedmont (since France and Piedmont have international agreements with England), but I prefer to be what I am, in other words, a peasant from Roncole, and I prefer to ask my government to make an agreement with England. The Parma government has nothing to lose through such an agreement, this being purely artistic and literary: it will merely have to go to the trouble of asking for it through its representative in England, who is, I believe, either the Austrian or Spanish ambassador. When you next go to Parma, I would be grateful if you would be kind enough to look into this.

Verdi's plight was the same as that of many other opera composers. As George Martin writes in his book on Verdi, 'At the start of Rossini's career, 1810–20, the composer had no royalties for a copyright in his work. The opera belonged for a period of two years to the impresario who commissioned it; after that it became public property. The composer hoped for another commission to start the cycle again, and neither he nor the impresario cared, for any financial reason, what happened to the previous opera after the first two years.' In this instance, the Parma government did not act on Verdi's suggestion, and, for the time being, his problems continued.

On his 1855 trip to London, the composer was accompanied by the singer Giuseppina Strepponi, who had been living with him in Busseto since 1851. They married in 1859, but she was generally known as Signora Verdi for some while before then. With them on this occasion was Verdi's Italian publisher, Ricordi, and his French agent, Escudier. They went to the first English production of *Il trovatore* and were much impressed by the performance of Pauline Viardot as Azucena. Another outing was to the Crystal Palace: this was reported in the 1 August 1855 edition of *The Musical Times*.

> The celebrated composer has visited all the sights of London during the week, and on Thursday paid a visit to the Crystal Palace. He appeared greatly delighted with the magnificent building and grounds, and expressed his astonishment and pleasure in the most rapturous terms to those who accompanied him. Herr Schallehn having learned that the Italian *maestro* was present, paid him a graceful compliment, in performing a selection from his latest operas, *Il Trovatore* and *Luisa Miller*. This little attention was duly appreciated by Signor Verdi, who complimented Herr Schallehn on the efficiency of his band.

Three months later, Schallehn was dismissed from his post and replaced by young August Manns. This came about in an interesting way. A year earlier, Manns had been sub-conductor and, at Schallehn's request, had written a quadrille on national airs to celebrate the Anglo-Franco-Turkish Alliance. This work, *The Alliance Quadrille*, over which Manns took such pains that it made him ill, was performed at the Crystal Palace in the presence of the Queen and a large audience, and scored a huge success. Schallehn then asked Manns to make a piano arrangement, and shortly afterwards the piece was published. But, to Manns' surprise, the composer was advertised as Schallehn, who received £50 for the quadrille, a sum almost equal to Manns' yearly salary. When Manns demanded an explanation, Schallehn dismissed him for insubordination. Although secretary to the Crystal Palace, Grove was at the time unable to improve the situation, because of a special clause in Schallehn's contract. Meanwhile, Manns, who was forced to find employment as a violinist in Leamington and then Edinburgh, wrote to the *Musical World*, who printed an editorial article that fully acquainted its readers with this injustice. As a result of public opinion and the discredit that Schallehn had brought on the Crystal Palace, the directors requested his resignation, and Grove had the pleasure of inviting Manns to take his place. He also asked him what works he intended to play, and Manns accordingly outlined some projected programmes. Grove's answer to his proposals reveals that, even at this early stage in their careers, they were both joyously hell-bent on bringing new music to people's attention.

> I am much obliged to you for sending the programmes; when you write again, send me a few more. I like them very much, and would give a great deal to have such music done in the Crystal Palace. The overture Op 124 [Beethoven's *The Consecration of the House*] has only been done once in London in my recollection. Weber's 'Clarinet Concerto', *never*. Berlioz's 'Invitation à la Valse', *never*. Nor do I ever remember hearing of Mozart having written a finale to Gluck's *Iphigenia*.

Such programmes, he concluded, did Manns 'the highest honour'.

Verdi's second extended trip to England was in 1862, for the International Exhibition, which was held in London. Her Majesty's Commissioners for the Exhibition decided that, for the opening on 1 May, they would have a concert with four new works, each by a different composer, to represent France, Germany, Italy and England. For Italy, they selected Verdi. To conduct the concert, they chose the baleful and ubiquitous Michael Costa, who, at the mid-century, dominated the English musical scene.

Costa was born in Naples in 1808. He came to England in 1829 and quickly built a reputation both as composer and conductor. He wrote operas, ballets and other works that were often highly successful, and his oratorio *Eli* was still being performed up until the end of the century. It was as a conductor, though, that he was best known. In 1846, he took over the conductorship of the Philharmonic Society concerts and of the Italian Opera at Covent Garden. In 1848, he became conductor of the Sacred Harmonic Society concerts and, in 1849, of the Birmingham Musical Festival. To these responsibilities he added the Bradford Musical Festival in 1853 and later the Leeds Musical Festival. One almost gains the impression that, at this time, any musical performance in London was more likely to be conducted by Costa than not. Yet, despite his wide range of activities, he introduced few works of note to England. He directed the première of *Rigoletto*, in 1853, and, during the same year, Schumann's *Overture, Scherzo and Finale*, and, in the following year, Schumann's First Symphony. Both these orchestral works, however, were programmed by the Philharmonic Society, and, as its conductor, he was required to perform them. He seems to have had few ardent admirers; the most prominent was Chorley, who left him £50 in his will. He was a martinet who would brook neither opposition nor interference and commanded respect without really earning it.

In an article on Costa, Grove maintained that his lifelong objective was '"make yourself safe". Surround yourself with the best possible agents, the best assistants that you can obtain, quite regardless of expense, and success is certain.' Grove adds, though, that this method was extremely costly, and, in fact, crippled the Sacred Harmonic Society. It was his further opinion that Costa completely lacked the ability to train and develop orchestral players or to educate them, as Manns and Hallé did. Moreover, he set a bad example by tampering with scores, making vulgar and unnecessary emendations, even in supreme masterpieces. Nevertheless, says Grove, 'He was a splendid drill sergeant; he brought the London orchestras into an order unknown before. He acted up to his lights, and was thoroughly efficient as far as he went, and was eminently safe.' Grove had several personal memories of Costa. He asked him on one occasion how his friend Captain Lyon was coming along, after breaking his leg. 'He will walk on crotchets', Costa assured him.

Once he told me an anecdote which was probably questionable so far as Mendelssohn was concerned. He went into a room in the old Queen's Theatre and found Mendelssohn, Moscheles and Meyerbeer together. 'What are these old Jews about?' was his manner of addressing them, which I do not think would have pleased Mendelssohn particularly. One day he said to me, 'Is there any overture or other piece which you would like to hear at the opera concerts? because if so, I should have great pleasure in putting it into the programme.' Now I had heard a few months before Beethoven's *Coriolan* overture and was thirsting to hear it again, and accordingly suggested it. 'Oh, I do not know it,' said Costa, 'but I will put it in for you,' and he inquired the name a second time. In those days Costa did not *rehearse* the opera concerts himself – that was done by Sainton, his leader [he also left the ballets in operas to the leader]. *Coriolan* closed the concert and I went into Costa's room with a bursting heart to thank him for it. 'I will never play that piece again,' he said in his harshest voice. 'It ends *pianissimo*, and it is impossible to make any effect with it.'

Costa was a most strict disciplinarian. He had ordered his librarian at Covent Garden never to lend any parts or pieces from the Library. On one occasion, however, Manns had borrowed from the librarian in question the parts of *Fidelio*, but to his surprise he found the *obbligato* horn parts pasted over. Of course he tore them off. Costa required them within a day, and his wrath may be imagined when he found that the cancels had been destroyed. He discharged the librarian on the spot and never employed him again.

Stanford also recounts this story, concluding in high drama.

COSTA.   'Send for the librarian.'
            (Enter that official trembling.)
            'What have you done with my parts?'
LIBRARIAN. 'They were lent to the Crystal Palace and Mr. Manns must
            have restored them.'
COSTA.   'You are dismissed!' (And he was.)

Costa's misdemeanours were legion. When Meyerbeer came to London in 1849 for the first English production of *Le Prophète*, at Covent Garden, and made some suggestions during rehearsals, Costa not only ordered him off the stage, but out of the theatre. Hallé, in his memoirs, recalls another incident involving Costa and Meyerbeer, when he was with them at a dinner-party.

The conversation fell on Mozart's 'Zauberflöte', which had been given at Covent Garden a few days before. Lady Hastings had not enjoyed the performance and abused the work in unmeasured terms. Especially was she angry with the recitatives; 'those interminable, monotonous, unmeaning recitatives', she called them. Meyerbeer looked puzzled, Mozart's opera containing no recitatives, and asked quietly: 'Quels sont donc les récitatifs dont Lady Hastings parle?' 'Ils sont de moi, monsieur,' said Costa, and Lady Hastings began to talk of something else.

Costa, as one could guess, had no regard for Wagner, referring to the swan in *Lohengrin* as 'dat goose!' The score from which he conducted the second English production of the opera – given in Italian, like the first – was later found by Richter to contain more than 400 mistakes. Richter attributed these not to carelessness, but malice. 'He had a Corsican vendetta in him', says Stanford; 'he carried his quarrel with Sterndale Bennett even beyond the grave.' Stanford also suggests that Costa once fired Sullivan from his post as organist at Covent Garden in the early 1860s, because of his lateness at rehearsals, though it seems that Sullivan was soon afterwards reinstated. He adds, 'Costa was, however, for all his tyranny, a true friend of the orchestral player. He raised his status and fought battles to do.' Vaughan Williams, writing in Grove's *Dictionary* at the turn of the century, supports this view. 'Perhaps the exaggerated respect paid to Costa during his lifetime has caused too violent a reaction since his death. There can be no doubt that he was a very fine band-master, whatever may have been his shortcomings as an interpreter.' Nevertheless, Jenny Lind never allowed him to accompany her, and one newspaper of the day commented that Costa did not so much beat time, he threshed it. Indeed, Sterndale Bennett, alluding to Costa's pell-mell tempi, wrote that 'we might hear the whole of Beethoven's symphonies in one night and still have time for supper.'

Naturally, there were a number of people who genuinely admired Costa, even though they recognised his failings. In his reminiscences, *Student and Singer*, the baritone Charles Santley writes sympathetically of the famous conductor.

Somewhat cold and distant in manner – an attitude he always maintained in business – he was quick even to curtness in his remarks and directions, by which he acquired the unmerited name of 'tyrant'; he had an impassive countenance, in which it was impossible to read his thoughts; the only visible sign of approbation or the contrary which he ever vouchsafed was a peculiar twist of the back of his neck. Clear-headed, systematic, and punctual, he never wasted a moment of time at rehearsals; the work once arranged was carried on by clockwork. Out of business he was affable, or merry, according to the society in which he found himself. He liked a good dinner and good wine, and knew how to enjoy them; and in a quiet *tête-à-tête*, of which I have had many with him, he delighted in a bit of gossip or mild scandal. He made me no promises, but told me he was sure I should make a good career, and if at any time it was in his power to do me a service, he would do all he could for me. This he carried out; I found him always a staunch friend, adviser, and monitor.

He had two hobbies – watches and horses. Of the latter I do not think he was rich enough to own many, but of the former he possessed several, some of them valuable as curiosities. He also possessed a chronometer, a very appropriate and necessary article for one who prided himself on his punctuality . . .

He had a method of reading a score for the first time in the orchestra, which, as far as my observation goes, was peculiar to himself. It is the usual practice to read a bar or more ahead of, but he read a bar or more behind, the orchestra. I remarked it at a rehearsal for Birmingham festival . . . I had to sing a hymn by Rossini never performed before, and as I had not been provided with a copy, I was reading from the full score from which Costa was conducting. I, of course, had to read a bar ahead, and as he did not turn over in time, and I could not very well guess what was coming, I was forced to leave out a bar or two each time we arrived at the bottom of a page. I then noticed it was a systematic plan, which I think is well worth the consideration of young conductors. It is much easier to correct mistakes after hearing them than before.

That the Commissioners of the 1862 International Exhibition should appoint Costa as the musical director of their inaugural concert was perhaps inevitable. But, because he was quite out of sympathy with three of the composers – Verdi, Meyerbeer and Sterndale Bennett – from whom they ordered works, it was also a recipe for disaster.

With the fourth composer, invited to represent France, Costa appears to have had no particular grudge. This was Auber, who responded to the commission with a typically spirited *Marche triomphale*. Now aged eighty, he was a practised hand at this sort of thing, having produced dozens of such pieces, including funeral marches for Napoleon and other worthies, and numerous cantatas celebrating royal marriages, royal baptisms and victories like Sebastopol and Magenta. He was by no means finished with the stage, either; he wrote another three comic operas before he died in 1871 and, of these, *Le Premier Jour de bonheur*, presented in February 1868, had run for over 150 performances by the time of his death.

Meyerbeer, chosen for Germany, was seventy. Perhaps we should note that Wagner, then forty-eight, was still not as well recognised as Meyerbeer; nor was Berlioz, at fifty-eight, yet considered the equal of Auber. The work that Meyerbeer composed for the International Exhibition was an overture in the form of a march. Like Auber, he was familiar with writing such pieces, the most recent of which had been a Grand March for the Schiller Centenary Festival.

The Commissioners had hoped to prevail upon Rossini, who was also seventy, to compose something for Italy, but he declined, apologising, 'If I were still of this musical world, I would consider it a duty and a pleasure to show on this occasion that I am not unmindful of England's noble hospitality.' In this reply, he was remembering his visit to England, from December 1823 to July 1824, when he was entertained in London and Brighton by George IV, with whom he sang *buffo* duets. He was also fêted by the Duke of Wellington and many other notables. During his six and a half months in England, he made around £7,000 through personal appearances, giving lessons and conducting operas and concerts. One of these concerts featured a work, *Il pianto delle muse in morte di Lord Byron*, commemorating the poet's recent death in Missolonghi. In July, the same month as the concert, he travelled to Cambridge for the annual musical festival. He played the organ of St Mary's in a concert of sacred music and in a secular concert in the Senate House sang a duet, with Angelica Catalani, from Cimarosa's *Il matrimonio segreto* and accompanied himself on the piano in 'Largo al factotum' from *Il barbiere di Siviglia*. Whether, like Haydn in 1791, he had a chance to look around the colleges is not known. 'During my stay in England', Rossini later told Ferdinand Hiller, 'I received attentions that it would be difficult to find paralleled anywhere else.' Though Rossini pleaded to the Commissioners in June 1861 that his composing days were over – it was now thirty years since his last opera, *Guillaume Tell* – he composed, towards the end of 1861, a choral work, *Le Chant des titans*, for a Paris concert designed to raise funds for a monument to Cherubini. In 1862, he also wrote a hunting chorus with which the Baroness Rothschild welcomed Napoleon III to her country estate. In 1867, he produced a choral work, for the Paris Exhibition, which Costa conducted in Birmingham six years later.

Verdi was the obvious choice after Rossini to represent Italy. He normally refused to write these '*pezzi di circonstanza*', as he called them, but on this occasion his fervent patriotism led him to accept, because he felt that Italy might otherwise go musically unrepresented at the Exhibition's inaugural concert. When he learned that Auber and Meyerbeer would be writing purely orchestral items, he determined, for the sake of variety, to compose a work for chorus and orchestra, and commissioned a text from a young compatriot, Arrigo Boito, whom he had met in Paris, where he and Giuseppina were living at the time.

The English contribution was requested from Sterndale Bennett. He seems to have been surprised to have received the commission. 'I thought Balfe would be asked', he said. He was required to compose a piece to verses especially written by Tennyson for the concert. The poet could not always be relied upon to supply texts for such ceremonies. Seven years earlier, when the Crystal Palace was moved down to Sydenham, Grove was dispatched to the Isle of Wight by his directors, who hoped he could persuade the laureate to produce an appropriate ode for the reopening. It was Grove's intention to approach Berlioz with a request to set the ode. But Tennyson was not forthcoming.

He received me with the greatest cordiality, but he could not see his way to writing the poem; and the net result of my visit was the beginning of a truly delightful and valuable friendship, and his explanation of the difference between a 'cowslip' and an 'oxslip', which I asked him *apropos* of his lines

'As cowslip unto oxslip is,
So seems she to the boy.'

This he answered by picking one of each in the copse behind the house, and showing me how the one stood erect and the other drooped its head.

Tennyson's ode for the 1862 Exhibition was ready by November 1861. The poet sent a message to Sterndale Bennett as soon as he had completed it, but admitted, says Sterndale Bennett's son, that he was not entirely happy with it.

Thereupon Bennett went to the chambers in the Temple where Tennyson was stopping with a friend. He was fascinated by the quaint occupation in which he discovered the poet completely absorbed, viz. that of drying tobacco on the hobs of the grate; he thought, as a listener, that the reading of the poem was curiously monotonous; but when, before leaving, he ventured to confide his own anxiety and spoke of public criticism as sitting at his elbow when he tried to compose, then the words of sympathy which followed, and Tennyson's assurance that he himself knew that feeling only too well, went to his heart.

In December, at which time Sterndale Bennett secured the Commissioners' permission to employ an orchestra for his setting, the Prince Consort died. Feeling that he should recognise Albert's death in the ode, Tennyson added the lines that begin.

O silent Father of our Kings to be,
Mourn'd in this golden hour of jubilee . . .

He invited Sterndale Bennett to Farringford to discuss the additions and another slight alteration, informing him that, at first, the Queen did not want any references to be made to Albert's death, but 'now I hear (none of my instigating) that Lord Granville showed them to H.M. and she wished them to be included.' The composer accordingly made a short visit to the Isle of Wight. Tennyson seemed anxious to confer with him, says J. R. Sterndale Bennett, 'but for what purpose, beyond that of conveying to him his own emphasis of the words by reciting them in his presence, is not clear.'

Tennyson made a habit of inviting composers and other musicians to the Isle of Wight and then turning them into captive audiences. He was still doing it thirty years later, as his guest Hubert Parry discovered in 1892.

He soon set to work reading, and began with *The Lotos-Eaters*. It struck me at once that it was not a prepared or careful performance, as he frequently ignored stops, and ran phrases into one another, with little apparent regard for the sense, but he evidently greatly enjoyed himself. This manner of reading is most strange – I should think something after the manner of the ancient professional reciters of epics and songs amongst barbarous peoples. He pitched his voice rather high for average intoning and raised and dropped it for special words. Moreover he was much given to a rather commonplace lilt – a sing-song method of enforcing the accents which rather jarred with my sense of the rhythmic variety of the written verse. If I had heard him read before I read his works I never should have thought him capable of such exquisite effects of subtle variety in the treatment of his metres. But it was a most interesting experience. After *The Lotos-Eaters* he began talking about *Maud* and then read a great deal of that too. Then he got discussing critics again, and the variations of the sense of measure and rhythm in poets generally. Of Browning he said: 'It's strange: Browning was a musical man, and understood music, but there's no music in his verse. Now I am unmusical and I don't understand music, but I know there's music in my verse.'

During Sterndale Bennett's visit to Farringford, Tennyson invited him to point to any words in the *Exhibition Ode* that might cause difficulties, but, when it actually came to the question of making changes, he proved to be 'very inflexible'. He was, however, prepared to alter the opening, substituting 'thousand' for 'hundred' in the first line, which thus became

Uplift a thousand voices full and sweet
In this wide hall with earth's invention stored . . .

The completed ode was in the composer's hands by the third week of January 1862, with the inaugural concert scheduled for 1 May. He made an immediate start. The work was not needed for another fifteen weeks, but after only five weeks he was being pestered for the finished composition. 'Costa called here to-day', wrote the secretary to the Commissioners on 20 February, 'and was anxious to know whether I had received your contribution to the musical part of the opening Ceremony.' On 3 March, the secretary wrote again. 'I have just had Costa here, very uneasy as to the Music for the opening. When may I hope to have your part of the work?' A month later, Sterndale Bennett was stunned to learn that he would have to conduct his work himself, for it now transpired that Costa, 'when engaged as conductor eight months before, had made it a condition of his services being available, that he should not be expected to conduct any work by Bennett in the event of the latter being asked to furnish one.'

The reason for Costa's vendetta against Sterndale Bennett goes back to an incident that took place fourteen years earlier, in May 1848. The composer's overture *Parisina* was to be performed at a Philharmonic Society concert on 29 May. On 27 May, Costa rehearsed the piece and, according to J. W. Davison, music critic of *The Times*, took great pains with it, but, somewhat uncharacteristically, played it too slowly. When Sterndale Bennett was told of Costa's leisurely tempi, he wrote a note, on the afternoon prior to the concert, to Charles Lucas, a director of the Philharmonic Society and a friend of Costa's.

> You would very much oblige me if you would ask Costa to take my Overture a little faster. I have not been able to explain my idea of the time to him, but you have often done it, and I am sure he would not take it amiss – the middle parts especially, with the syncopations, want keeping up to time – Be so good as to do this for me – it is of some consequence to me.

To this, Sterndale Bennett added some relevant bars from the overture, over which he wrote, 'all fast'. Lucas, deeming the note totally inoffensive, passed it to Costa shortly before the concert was to begin. Costa became immediately incensed. He was already annoyed that the overture, which he would have liked to have had more time to study, had not reached him until just before rehearsals. Indeed, it was said that he first set eyes on the score when it was handed through the window of his carriage as he set off for the concert hall. Now, at the last moment, he was given a note, which was not even addressed to him, stating how the piece should go. The final blow – in a sense, self-inflicted – was that he misconstrued the words 'all fast', reading Sterndale Bennett's 's' as an 'r'. The letter looks not unlike an 'r', but is clearly an 's', and corresponds with the composer's usual method of producing the letter. How Costa could imagine that the mild, correct and fastidious Sterndale Bennett would set down such a word is puzzling. 'Tales have been told', writes the composer's son, 'of the effect produced upon Costa at the sight of it, how he burst into a frenzy of rage, how he raved and stamped.' Taking his cue, perhaps, from what appeared to be Sterndale Bennett's manner of expression, he then proceeded to indulge in 'strong language' and, noting the words 'but you have often done it', shouted at Lucas, 'If you have often done it, you shall do it now!' He refused to conduct the overture, and Lucas was forced to take his place.

Sterndale Bennett was much distressed by this misunderstanding and on more than one occasion suggested a meeting between Costa and himself to patch things up, but he received no response. The sad outcome was that he felt obliged to resign from the Philharmonic Society and over the next eight years he appeared at none of their concerts. He was then at the height of his powers as a pianist; his interpretations of the Mozart concertos were already legendary. His touch had been compared to Chopin's, and Ferdinand Hiller described his playing as 'full of soul and fire'.

The situation was aggravated in 1853, five years later, when the pianist Arabella Goddard was invited to make her début with the Philharmonic Society and chose to play Sterndale Bennett's Concerto in C minor. Costa refused to conduct it, and Miss Goddard, a pupil of Thalberg, was asked to select another work. This she would not do, and her engagement was cancelled. She was at once offered the opportunity to perform the concerto at a concert of the recently formed New Philharmonic Society, and Sterndale Bennett was invited to play his Concerto in F minor at a concert of the Orchestral Union. In reviewing this second concert, the *Musical World* spoke of Sterndale Bennett's 'magnificent performance'; the Hanover Square Rooms were packed out: 'a significant expression of public opinion about a recent event which has made much noise in the musical world.' The affair also reached the notice of *Punch*, which supplied its own comment.

Sterndale Bennett was Indignant with Costa
For not playing Bennett's Composition faster;
Costa flew into Excitement at Lucas
For shewing him Bennett's Order, or Ukase,
Haughtily Resigned the Seat which he set on,
And Contemptuously told Lucas himself to Take the *bâton*,
Moreover Stipulated this Year with the Directors
That Nobody was to read him any more Lectures:

Also, he made it a Condition Strict,
He was Only to conduct what Pieces of Music he lik'd,
Whereby this Year Costa doth Prevent
Any performance of Music by Sterndale Benn't:
Likewise excluding the young and gifted Miss Goddard,
Whom with Admiration all the Critical Squad heard:-
All to be Deplored, and without more Amalgamation,
The Philharmonic will Tarnish its Hitherto Deservedly
High Reputation.

Costa's relationship with the Philharmonic Society continued to worsen and in 1854, the year after this latest incident, he resigned. Berlioz was asked to take over, but he was unable to release himself from future commitments: the job eventually went to Wagner, who was a disappointment and was not re-engaged. In 1856, Sterndale Bennett, who three years earlier had been forced to turn down the conductorship of the Leipzig Gewandhaus Orchestra because of previously scheduled engagements, was appointed as conductor, holding the post until 1866. Costa never forgave Sterndale Bennett. In 1867, Lucas begged Costa to shake hands with the composer when all three were present at a performance of Sterndale Bennett's *The Woman of Samaria* in Birmingham. Costa replied, 'Lucas, remember 1848.' On Sterndale Bennett's death in 1875, Macfarren asked Costa to add his name to a petition for the composer to be interred in Westminster Abbey, but, as Stanford has said, 'he carried his quarrel with Sterndale Bennett even beyond the grave' and refused. The petition was successful, and Sterndale Bennett lies in Westminster Abbey, close to Purcell. When the Dead March from *Saul* was featured as a tribute to Sterndale Bennett in a concert given shortly after his death, Costa, who had been engaged as conductor some months earlier, handed over the baton to Sainton, the leader of the orchestra.

At the time of the 1862 International Exhibition, Sterndale Bennett was somehow under the impression that Costa had ended his rancorous feud, but now he found him to be as implacable as ever. There could be no question of his conducting the *Exhibition Ode*. The Commissioners asked the composer himself to conduct it or to name somebody in his place. Sterndale Bennett declined the offer to conduct, adding, 'I cannot help feeling disappointed that it should be proposed to present my work in a different manner to the works of other composers invited to write for the occasion.' He named nobody in his place. The secretary now requested him again to do so. He replied, 'I cannot on any consideration undertake to name a conductor of my music in the place of Mr Costa.' At this stage, there was every prospect of his piece being withdrawn, but the press got wind of what was happening and came to the composer's aid, severely attacking both Costa and the Commissioners. The *Daily Telegraph* made Costa the subject of a leading article.

> Suddenly he turns round upon us and won't play Professor Bennett's music, or wave the bâton to a note of his cantata. Fêted and feasted for years and years on English soil, he has interposed his contemptible private bickerings on this solemn occasion. The spoiled child of the easy English public, he slaps its sensibilities in the face upon this exigency. The man whom we made something from nothing, famous from obscure, selects the moment when we show him our greatest favour, to show us his greatest arrogance.

Punch again also joined the fray. 'We don't think that STERNDALE BENNETT has a right to complain that Mr. COSTA will not conduct him at the Inauguration. Costa sometimes does not even know how to conduct himself.'

The secretary to the Commissioners was, nevertheless, 'still at a loss to understand why you will neither conduct your own work or name any person except Mr. Costa to act for you.' But Sterndale Bennett had no more to say, and, a week before the ceremony, Sainton was chosen. Costa, meanwhile wrote to *The Times*, pointing out that, as far back as the previous July, 'I made it a distinct condition of my services being available that I should not be expected to conduct any work of Dr. Bennett, if he should be invited to furnish one for performance on the occasion of the opening.' The Commissioners, as a result of this letter, made a public apology to Costa, but another month passed before they apologised, though not in public, to Sterndale Bennett. Even then, the secretary felt it necessary to inform the composer that he could quite easily have learnt of Costa's intentions – though the Commissioners themselves apparently failed to – by reading the newspapers: 'a statement appeared in some of the public journals in the month of July, 1861.'

Meyerbeer, whom Hallé admired for 'his high-bred manners, his cultured *esprit*, invariable tact, and great *savoir-faire*' and whom Costa had ordered out of the theatre at Covent Garden, managed on this occasion not to incur the conductor's wrath, principally because Costa did not bother to rehearse the German composer's overture, leaving it to his assistant Alfred Mellon. Meyerbeer did, however, ask Costa for ten rehearsals – to be informed 'You shall have *two.*' Mellon, who later became conductor of the Liverpool Philharmonic, felt that the overture would be enhanced by the addition of a battery of percussion instruments. Meyerbeer disagreed. However, he, too, was eventually coerced into acceding to the Commissioners' wishes and retired to the York Hotel in Albermarle Street, where he added the necessary parts to the score. He attended the rehearsals not only of his own work but also of Sterndale Bennett's *Exhibition Ode.* The first rehearsal turned out to be a triumph for the English composer, as Davison reported in *The Times.*

> After the Ode had been gone through once, a general cry for 'Bennett' was raised, and the Professor, at length making his appearance, was led into the orchestra by M. Sainton. The greeting he received was such as he will possibly never forget. We remember nothing more hearty, nothing more spontaneous. There was one universal burst of cheering, accompanied by waving of hats and handkerchiefs, the thousand ladies of the chorus being conspicuous in their manifestations of enthusiasm. About the extraordinary popularity of Professor Bennett, if there had ever been a doubt, this would have dispelled it.

So animated was the demonstration that Meyerbeer, who was not unused to wild applause, was 'quite astonished', according to Davison.

Auber did not come over for the playing of his march, but stayed at home in Paris. He was an exceptionally shy man, so shy that he never attended any public performances of his operas. 'If I were to be present at a performance of one of my works', he once confessed, 'I wouldn't be able to write another note of music.' He was also entirely without conceit; 'if I had any, I'd have more talent', he said. The success of his operas allowed him to live in great luxury, but he rarely left his own home, except to go riding in the Bois de Boulogne on his favourite English horses. As a young man, the son of a publisher, he had come to London to learn English, staying for sixteen months, until the rupture of the Treaty of Amiens in May 1803 forced him to return to France. He was introduced to Queen Victoria and Prince Albert in August 1855 during their state visit to Paris, this being the first occasion on which a British soverign had set foot in the French capital since the coronation of Henry VI in 1431. Charles Dickens met the composer a few months later, at the home of Auber's librettist Eugène Scribe, with whom he collaborated on thirty-eight stage pieces. Dickens's biographer John Forster has left an account of their meeting.

> One of the guests was Auber, 'a stolid little elderly man, rather petulant in manner', who told Dickens he had once lived in 'Stock Noonton' (Stoke Newington) to study English, but had forgotten it all. 'Louis Philippe had invited him to meet the Queen of England, and when L. P. presented him, the Queen said "We are such old acquaintances through M. Auber's works, that an introduction is quite unnecessary."'

Dickens, Auber and Scribe met again on 23 February 1856 at a supper given by the French translator of *David Copperfield*, Amédée Pichot. Lamartine, who was also present, complimented Dickens on his excellent French, 'whereat your correspondent blushed modestly.' When he visited Paris with Dickens seven years later, Arthur Sullivan, an accomplished linguist, came to a different conclusion. 'His French was not particularly good. It was quite an Englishman's French.' However, 'he managed to make himself understood, and interviewed everybody.' The night of Pichot's supper-party was also the first night of Auber's *Manon Lescaut*. Scribe, who wrote the libretto, left early to be at the premiére, but Auber stayed where he was. A week later, Dickens also went to *Manon Lescaut*, which he found 'charming throughout'. Of Auber's other operas, he particularly enjoyed *La Muette de Portici* and *Fra Diavolo*. Among his very best loved operas were *Il barbiere di Siviglia* and *Il trovatore*. In Paris, he also heard *Orphée aux enfers* and Gounod's *Faust*, which prompted him to write that Gounod 'must be a very remarkable man indeed'. Apart from opera, he was fond of the orchestral and instrumental works of Mozart, Mendelssohn and Chopin. His own instrument seems to have been the accordion, with which he entertained his fellow passengers on board the *Britannia* during his trip to America in 1842. 'The steward lent me one on the passage out, and I regaled the ladies' cabin with my performances. You can't think with what feelings I play "Home, Sweet Home" every night, or how pleasantly sad it makes us.'

Dickens also met two other composers, Halévy and Meyerbeer. Halévy came to dinner with Dickens at 1 Devonshire Terrace, along with Scribe, when the two were over for the première of their *La tempesta* in May 1850. Dickens and Meyerbeer were fellow guests at a dinner-party given by the Secretary of the Colonies, Lord John Russell, on 7 July 1855, when the novelist inveighed against the Lord's Day Observance Act: 'I gave them a little bit of truth about Sunday that was like bringing a Sebastopol battery among the polite company.' When dinner was over, Meyerbeer complimented him by saying, 'Ah, my illustrious friend! How fine it is to hear you speak with such a high moral tone at the table of a Minister!' A week earlier, Meyerbeer had a sudden encounter with Wagner, who was then conductor of the Philharmonic Society and had just published his notorious *Judaism in Music*. On another occasion, finding himself called on to conduct Mendelssohn's *Italian Symphony*, Wagner had ostentatiously donned kid gloves for the performance, removing them for the other items on the programme. Not a word passed between Meyerbeer and Wagner when they met, which was in the presence of a mutual acquaintance; there was nothing left to be said.

The musician that seems most to have appealed to Dickens was Joachim. They met just before the International Exhibition, in March 1862, and the novelist was so taken with him that he invited him down to his home at Gad's Hill, near Rochester. Dickens spoke of Joachim as 'a noble fellow'; the violinist, for his part, was delighted with Dickens's 'vigorous, unaffected manner'. Joachim spent two days at Gad's Hill, where, he wrote back to Germany, 'Falstaff's knavery, of jovial memory, took place.' He played a number of works for Dickens, but Tartini's *Devil's Trill* Sonata made the deepest impression. Dickens's daughter later wrote of how profoundly it affected her father.

> I never remember seeing him so wrapt and absorbed as he was then, on hearing him play; and the wonderful simplicity and *un*-self-consciousness of the genius went straight to my father's heart, and made a fast bond of sympathy between these two great men.

Joachim, says Stanford, made 'a host of friends' in England, including Dickens, Tennyson, Browning, Thackeray, George Eliot, Gladstone, Darwin, Leighton, Grove and many more. With Carlyle, he was unable to achieve much rapport, as he later recalled.

> Early in the seventies Brookfield, a friend of mine and Thackeray's, took me to Carlyle's house in Chelsea and introduced me to him as 'the well known musician' and then left me there, pleading an engagement elsewhere. Carlyle, who was about to start on his morning constitutional,

begged me to accompany him, which I did. During our long walk in Hyde Park, the Sage of Chelsea poured forth a stream of conversation about Germany, the King of Prussia, Bismarck, Moltke, the war, etc. At last I thought I ought to say something, so I innocently asked the irascible gentleman if he knew Sterndale Bennett. 'No,' he answered abruptly, and added after a pause: 'I can't bear musicians as a rule, they're such an empty-headed, wind-baggy set of people!'

According to Tennyson 'Mr. and Mrs. Carlyle on the whole enjoyed life together, else they would not have chafed one another so heartily.' He and Joachim got on excellently, as Hallam Tennyson has attested.

My father was fond of asking Joachim to play to him. . . One particular evening I remember, at 86, Eaton Square. My father had been expressing his wonder at Joachim's mastery of the violin, – for Joachim had been playing to us and our friends numberless Hungarian dances, – and by way of thanks for the splendid music I asked him to read one of his poems to Joachim. Accordingly after the guests had gone he took the great musician to smoke with him in his 'den' at the top of the house. There they talked of Goethe, especially praising a poem of Goethe's old age, 'Der Westöstliche Divan', and then my father read 'The Revenge'. On reaching the line

> And the night went down, and the sun
> smiled out far over the summer sea,

he asked Joachim, 'Could you do that on your violin?' – the peace of nature after the thunder of the battle. There was no more reading however that night, for he suddenly turned round to me, saying, 'I must not read any more, else I shall wake up the cook who is sleeping next door.'

Arthur M. Abell, in his *Talks with Great Composers*, relates how he was once present when Joachim told Brahms about some of his conversations with Tennyson. The composer of *The Song of Destiny* was apparently fascinated with Tennyson's concept of creation, also finding much in the poet's views on the immortal soul that coincided with his own thinking. Joachim told him that Tennyson said, 'The soul, on the next plane, remains a separate independent individuality. This is what I had in mind, when I wrote my *Crossing the Bar*.'

At this juncture, Brahms went to the piano again and played the first theme of the Eroica Symphony, declaring,
'This is my homage to Tennyson. Did he give you any hints, Joseph, in regard to his conception of the nature of the future abode of the soul?'
'Yes, I asked him that question, and his reply was so original as to fill me with wonder again.'. . . .

Tennyson attended the opening of the International Exhibition on
1 May. One newspaper reported that he was 'clothed in his green
baize'. Verdi, who had arived a fortnight earlier, was also among the
vast concourse. The London musical season was now in full swing,
having started on 8 April with Italian opera at Covent Garden.
Berlioz has left a memorable description of this annual phenomenon.

> But after the French Season, 'the London Season! the London Season!' is
> the cry of all the Italian, French, Belgian, German, Bohemian,
> Hungarian, Swedish and English singers; virtuosi from all nations fervent-
> ly repeat it while boarding their steamboats – just as the soldiers of
> Aeneas, when they too, clambered into their boats, shouted, 'Italiam!
> Italiam!' Nowhere else is so much music consumed in a season as in
> London. Thanks to this, all artists of real talent, after a few months of
> getting themselves known, are certain to find work there. Once the public
> has got to know them, they are expected to return every year; it is taken for
> granted that they will reappear, just like the pigeons in North America.
> And never, even to the end of their lives, have they been known to disap-
> point the expectations of the English public, that model of fidelity, always
> ready to welcome, applaud and admire, 'without noting the irreparable
> ravages of the years.' One must actually witness the rush and turmoil in
> the lives of these favourite artists when they are in London to be able to
> appreciate it.

Giuseppina Verdi reached London a little ahead of her husband
and at once started practising her English by writing to their friend
the poet Maggioni, who worked as a translator at Covent Garden. 'If
you can and it does not derange you too much be so kind as to lend
me during my abode in England a French and Italian Dictionary.
Laugh at me at your pleasure, but I will read, write and speak in
English at random till I shall be able to understand this infernal
language.' In inviting Maggioni to dinner soon afterwards, she held
out the promise of 'a Leg of Lamb, a Fish, Soup, Salade, *at your
service*'. The day following Verdi's arrival, she informed Maggioni,
'He desire to grasp your hand. Then come, I beg you, as soon as you
can. Without doubt, you must dine with us. Good morning.' Apart
from improving her English, she also spent time shopping. 'Did you
see', she wrote to a friend in Paris, 'that a most charming, brand new
dress in a first-class establishment in Regent Street can be had for
£5 10s 0d.?'
No sooner had Verdi arrived in London than he was told that his
cantata would not be performed at the Exhibition. He was given this

amazing news by the Commissioners, but behind them, of course, loomed Costa. It may well be that Costa felt he himself should have been chosen for Italy. In 1862, he had a considerable reputation as a composer. He had written a number of operas and ballets that had pleased the public. Of his *Don Carlos*, brought out in 1844, Chorley wrote, 'it is full of good music: the orchestra is handled with a thorough knowledge of effect and colour.' In 1855, he scored his biggest success, with the oratorio *Eli*, commissioned by the Birmingham Musical Festival. *Eli* became a popular work, performed by choral societies throughout the country until the end of the century. On Costa's death in 1884, *The Musical Times* wrote: 'Certain it is that we look in vain among the successors of Mendelssohn for an Oratorio which more nearly approaches the standard of "Elijah" than "Eli". In this fact is an honour by no means small.' *Eli* supplied, in its 'March of the Israelites', one of the only two marches that the Victorians did not deem it undevout to play on the Sabbath, and so, along with Mendelssohn's 'War March of the Priests' from *Athalie*, it received a vast number of performances. Costa the composer was assuredly not lacking in admirers, and among these, strangely enough, was Rossini, who corresponded with him for many years. There are more than forty letters in existence that Rossini wrote to Costa, many of them whimsical and affectionate. He often addressed Costa as 'My adored son'. In return, the conductor used to mail him English cheeses that sent the gourmet Rossini into ecstasies, even inspiring quasi-philosophical musings. 'Now, more than ever, I am confirmed in my opinion, which is that frequently eating Stilton (as I imagine you do), one must compose classical oratorios and trot down to posterity with one's brow garlanded with laurel. Continue then, my beloved son, in the speciality that renders you unique, and thus become the Glory of the Fatherland and the Consolation of your Genitor.' One particular 'chedor chiese' was accounted 'worthy of a Bach, a Handel, a Cimarosa . . . for three successive days I have enjoyed it moistened with libations of the best wines from my cellar . . . I swear that I have never eaten anything better.' In truth, he seems to have enjoyed Costa's supply of cheeses rather more than his compositions. When Costa sent him *Eli* accompanied by a cheese, Rossini, commenting on the double gift, said, 'The cheese was delightful.' After Verdi's death in 1868, Costa directed a memorial concert at the Crystal Palace, attended by 18,500 people, at which the *Sabat Mater* was performed by 3,000 singers and instrumentalists.

It seems certain that Costa was partly or wholly responsible for the rejection of Verdi's cantata. Various reasons have been put forward as to why the piece was refused performance at the Exhibition. The official explanation, wounding to Verdi's justified pride in his consistent professionalism, was that the score had been delivered late. It was also held that Verdi had originally been asked to submit a march, not a cantata. A letter written some months earlier to Verdi by the secretary to the Commissioners bears directly upon these contentions.

> The object in naming so early a date as the 1st. of February 1862 for the transmission of the scores was to prevent the possibility of any failure in the execution of the music in a manner that should be worthy of the eminent composers who had been requested to represent their respective countries on such an occasion as the opening of a great International Exhibition. Her Majesty's Commissioners, however, would regret to think that the naming of a particular date was in any way likely to interfere with the prospect of their being favoured with a work from your distinguished pen. They are quite willing to leave it in your own hands to fix the time at which you will be able to send the music of the march.

The cantata reached the Commissioners on 5 April 1862. It lasts approximately fifteen minutes and is for tenor solo, chorus and orchestra. Verdi did not regard three and a half weeks as too short a time in which adequately to prepare it for performance. His reason for not composing a march has already been mentioned: knowing that Auber would be producing a march, and Meyerbeer an overture in march style, he understandably felt that yet another march could hardly give the concert variety. What is interesting in this respect is that the secretary's first letter to Sterndale Bennett, dating from as far back as July 1861, states that the four works to be performed would be an anthem 'of about the same length as Handel's Coronation Anthem [*Zadok the Priest*], a chorale, a triumphal march and march for wind instruments. In broad outline, this is exactly what the Commissioners eventually received: the two Sterndale Bennett-Tennyson and Verdi-Boito choral pieces and the two Auber and Meyerbeer orchestral works in march-time.

Incensed to discover that both his labour on the cantata, *Inno delle nazioni*, and his and Giuseppina's trips to London had been undertaken to no purpose, Verdi wrote to *The Times*. The letter was translated into English by Maggioni. The composer said that the Commissioners had told him that twenty-five days were insufficient rehearsal time. In his opinion, a whole new opera could be learned in that period. He had delivered the score in what he considered to be good time. 'I wish this fact to be known, not in order to give importance to a matter of such little account, but only in order to correct the error that I did not deliver my composition.' The press and the public took Verdi's side. In a leading article, the *Morning Post* apologised to him for the way in which he had been treated by the Commissioners, assuring him of the great indignation felt by the London public. He had probably believed, said the paper, 'that the Exhibition Committee was gifted by Providence with common sense, and with some ability to appreciate art and the intentions of the artist. We are sorry for Signor Verdi, the most widely esteemed composer in Europe, and for ourselves as Englishmen and compatriots of that anything but gentlemanly Committee, to find that in these two perfectly legitimate hopes he has been entirely deceived.'

The public, of course, knew that Costa must be involved in the suppression of Verdi's *Inno delle nazioni*; they had also recently witnessed his treatment of Sterndale Bennett. Though often required to conduct Verdi's operas, Costa was known to hold little regard for them. Conceivably, he saw himself as Verdi's equal as a composer, or even superior, and better suited to tackle a choral work. And indeed, at this stage, Verdi had no large-scale choral piece to his credit with which to challenge the popularity of *Eli*. Costa would have perhaps expected to represent Italy at the Exhibition. The idea of substituting for Rossini would certainly have appealed to him. What could be more natural than for the 'adored son' to take the place of the father who could no longer carry out the task? However, he may really have found twenty-five days insufficient time for rehearsal, though, bearing in mind his continual and efficient deployment of assistants like Sainton and Mellon, this seems unlikely. Nevertheless, it was 'The London Season', and, between 8 April and 16 August, he directed no fewer than seventeen separate operas, including four performances of *Un ballo in maschera*, four of *Il trovatore*, two of *Rigoletto* and one of *La traviata*. There were also other commitments, principally to the Sacred Harmonic Society and the Handel Festival. That even he could not cope with this work-load can at least be mooted.

However, there was no doubt in the public's mind about what had been going on, and Verdi was inundated with letters. He now came to rue the publication of his letter to *The Times*, as he confided to his friend Count Arrivabene.

I wish I hadn't done it! It's been a millstone round my neck and, on the following day, it brought me a deluge of letters, raining the wrath of God on the Commission and Costa; and, what's more, requests for autographs from all quarters, in a very odd and totally English manner. In other countries, people who want autographs either get themselves introduced or else have their album presented by a friend. Over here, nothing of the sort: I get letters through the post, and inside is a stamped envelope addressed to the person for whom I'm meant to be signing the autograph. Who the hell they are, I've not the slightest idea. On top of this, the letters are in English (because of that damned letter in *The Times*) and that's another millstone, for Peppina, since she's got to translate them for me.

The inaugural concert opened with Meyerbeer's Overture and was followed by Sterndale Bennett's *Exhibition Ode*, which Verdi described as 'strictly English in inspiration and style, a conscientious, talented work showing the influence of Mendelssohn'. In conclusion, came Auber's 'lively, sparkling, fiery march, which carried the day'. Writing to Escudier in Paris, Verdi told him that he had no regrets about not providing yet another march, which 'would have bored the balls off me and everybody else'. He found the Exhibition itself completely chaotic: 'So far, the most interesting items are broken crates, rollers, mounds of straw, porters you have to avoid unless you want to get your ribs cracked, and drops of water that drip from the glass roof to refresh the noses of the curious. The place is utterly dismal in all its vastness.'

Sterndale Bennett's *Exhibition Ode* was immediately published and was soon being performed throughout the country; the final section was frequently encored. The two march pieces were hardly ever played again, though Auber's would make a pleasant addition to the repertoire. Meyerbeer left London early in the morning after the concert, catching the Paris Mail. Before leaving, he astonished Mellon by knocking on his door at 7.00 am and demanding his extra percussion parts, for fear that they might be used again. Mellon was forced to hand them over.

As for Verdi's *Inno delle nazioni*, the astute and resourceful impresario Henry Mapleson decided to perform it at Her Majesty's. He describes, a trifle disingenuously perhaps, how this transpired.

One day. . . . in coming from my house at St. John's Wood, I met Verdi, who explained to me that he was very much disappointed at the treatment he had received at the hands of the Royal Commissioners, who had rejected the cantata he had written for the opening of the exhibition. I at once cheered him up by telling him I would perform it at Her Majesty's Theatre . . . At the same time the work was purchased by a London publisher, who paid a handsome price for it. Verdi appeared very grateful and promised me many advantages for the future.

Verdi kept his word and selected Mapleson to stage the English première of his recently completed *La forza del destino*.

The performance of *Inno delle nazioni* was scheduled for 24 May, the Queen's forty-third birthday, to follow the evening's production of *Il barbiere di Siviglia*. The tenor part had been specially written for Enrico Tamberlik, a handsome Italian who had sung Manrico in the English première of *Il trovatore* and had also played the title-role in London in Berlioz's *Benvenuto Cellini*, which, according to Berlioz, Costa had successfully sabotaged. Tamberlik, however, was under contract to Covent Garden, where the musical director was Costa; there could be no question of his being released to perform at Her Majesty's. The biggest star who was then under contract to Mapleson was Thérèse Tietjens, a tall and striking soprano, and so, at the impresario's request, Verdi rewrote the tenor part for her; she later played Leonora in the first English version of *La forza del destino*. Mapleson's musical director was Luigi Arditi, and in *My Reminiscences*, compiled with the help of his friend Baroness von Zedlitz, he speaks of how thrilled he was to work with Verdi. The Baroness states that there was only one general rehearsal.

> The Maestro himself was present, and was amazed and delighted to find that the English musicians were such capable men. They read their parts so admirably, and indeed, faultlessly, that the whole Cantata, from the beginning to well-nigh the end, proceeded without a hitch. In the final part, however, a grave mistake occurred, and Signor Arditi, for the first time, stopped the orchestra.
>
> The Maestro, who had listened in perfect silence to the rehearsing of the Cantata, could not help exclaiming, 'Che peccato!' ('What a pity!') and afterwards warmly congratulated Signor Arditi on the efficiency of his conducting, and the superiority of his orchestra.

The first performance, on 24 May, went well. Arditi describes the occasion with great charm.

> The feelings which were entertained with regard to the Maestro's composition rose to a tremendous pitch of enthusiasm during the performance. Tietjens' solos were magnificent; indeed, they were so perfectly rendered that it was hard to realize that they had been composed for any other voice than hers. . .

In recognition of the manner in which the Cantata was produced the Maestro was good enough to speak in highly flattering terms; he sent me a fine portrait of himself, to which he added a few affectionate words. I spent many pleasant hours in his quiet retreat in St. John's Wood in those early days of our acquaintance, days to which I look back in happy retrospect.

The production was a memorable one in many respects, and it will live long in the hearts of all who, having been present on the occasion, watched the Maestro's subsequent triumphs.

The entire work was at once encored, and five further performances were given during the next three weeks. Verdi was given six curtain-calls at the première. The newspapers took pains to describe him, as well as his music, and this is how he appeared to one of the reporters.

A soft, thoughtful face, mellow and olive-tinted; cavernous eyes, dreamy yet full of subdued power, which hint at the true artistic embers glowing steadily behind; an air of that romantic dignity, dashed with a tone of melancholy which somehow fills every Italian face; a short, dark beard, trained heart-shape, out of Titian or Pordenone; a spare figure; a stature over middle size. This is the famous Guiseppe Verdi, the most popular composer in Europe.

Inno delle nazioni makes use of two revolutionary songs, the 'Marseillaise' by Rouget de Lisle and the 'Inno di Mameli' by Michele Novaro. These, today, are the national anthems of France and Italy, but neither was in 1862, and their incorporation in the cantata may have shocked a number of people. At the conclusion of the work, they are, in addition, combined with 'God Save the Queen'. Furthermore, though being a 'Hymn of Nations', the cantata contains no German melody. The Commissioners may possibly have rejected the composition because they thought it too republican in nature. The verses by young Boito urge peace, brotherly love, the rights of man and the fellowship of nations, but they also represent a clear call for a free and united Italy – reason enough why no German tune should be included. Verdi liked the text and showed his appreciation by giving Bioto an elegant watch, with the message, 'In thanking you for the fine work that you have written for me, permit me to offer you, as a token of esteem, this modest watch. Please accept it in the friendly spirit in which it is given. May it recall to you my name and the value of time!' Boito did not come over to London for *Inno delle nazioni*, but travelled to Poland to visit relations. He was thus presumably unaware of *The Times* review that spoke of his verses as 'the somewhat bombastic stanzas of the poetaster whom it has been the fortune of the popular Italian composer to immortalize.' The work was on the whole highly praised. Combining the three national melodies in the finale was described by one critic as a feat 'rarely heard' in Verdi's operas. The correspondent for the French newspaper *Le Nord* was less impressed.

> The sonorousness has been designed for a large area, such as that of the Crystal Palace. In a theatre, the brass nearly makes one's ears bleed. In addition, the patriotic *maestro* has conceived the idea of crossing and intertwining different national melodies one with the other . . . there is not the least *entent cordiale* between the *Marseillaise* and *God Save the Queen*. Have you ever found yourself at a review, between two or three military bands playing different tunes? That is the effect of the *Inno delle nazioni*, or something very like it.

Toscanini was an admirer of the cantata, conducting it in Milan during the First World War and in New York, at Madison Square Garden, during the Second. He also directed a performance on film.

It was June before the Verdis took leave of the little house and garden in St John's Wood, to which Giuseppina, in particular, had become attached. Despite the composer's initial problems, they enjoyed their stay in London. They also found time to make a trip to the Lake District. In London, Verdi purchased two excellent guns, a small double-barrelled shotgun and a carbine, for duck-shooting in the marshes along the Po.

Around the time the Verdis were travelling home, Sterndale Bennett journeyed to Cambridge, where his ode for the installation of the new chancellor was to be performed. The words were by Charles Kingsley, who asked him, 'Are you still alive? or has Costa pistolled you in despair of harming you by any less direct means?' The undergraduates hailed Sterndale Bennett's return with an almighty cheer, but he was too shy to be able to express his thanks. 'Groans for Costa' were then called for, and these were undertaken by the students 'with keen relish'.

Verdi made a further, brief trip to London in June 1874, to finalise arrangements for the English première of his new *Requiem* during the following year. While he was there, he took the opportunity of going to the Handel Festival, at the Crystal Palace, which he had never previously attended. Hardly anybody was aware of his presence in the country, but he was spotted at the Crystal Palace by his friend Albert Randegger, who in 1880 conducted the first performance in English of *Aida*. Their meeting is related in *Thirty Years of Musical Life in London* by Herman Klein, music critic of the *Sunday Times* during the eighties and nineties.

> Mr. Randegger has told me that his surprise was indescribable when he came across Verdi at the Crystal Palace with a score of *Israel in Egypt* tucked under his arm. He insisted, however, that his presence should be concealed; and he seems to have returned to Paris as mysteriously as he came.

The triennial Handel Festival was one of the foremost events in Victorian musical life and was famous throughout the world. It owed its inception indirectly to Prince Albert, who insisted, when the Crystal Palace was rebuilt at Sydenham and reopened in the summer of 1854, that the inaugural concert should be fully worthy of the occasion, unlike the musical arrangements at the Great Exhibition of 1851, which he found 'beneath criticism'. Costa, who had played no part in the ceremonies at the Great Exhibition, was commanded to take charge of the concert. He was faced with a difficult problem, for the building, constructed entirely of steel and glass, was also exceptionally large and therefore had poor acoustics. He reached the conclusion, as we also might, that these obstacles could be best overcome by sheer numbers, using huge orchestral and choral forces. He still had the worry, though, of whether a soloist would be able to make any impression across the immeasurable wastes of the building. Accordingly, he asked the famous soprano Clara Novello to help him by putting this to the test, and, one Sunday morning, she, her husband and two other members of her family travelled down to Sydenham to meet Costa. They found the place dauntingly cavernous and empty, as she relates in her memoirs.

> On arriving, we found Costa waiting, who gave me no time to be overcome by the vastness of the space, but made me a sign to begin 'God Save the Queen', from the entrance where I was standing, he remaining in the centre. The result surpassed his hopes, but to make doubly sure I told him and my party to go to the extreme opposite end, and when they had reached it I sang again, purposely altering one line of words, which alteration was distinctly heard by them, though I was hardly visible to the eye.

The opening concert took place on 10 June 1854, Clara Novello's thirty-sixth birthday, and was a stunning success, attended by an audience of 30,000. 'Immediately behind us', the Queen wrote in her diary, 'rose the enormous orchestra . . . led most beautifully by Costa. I cannot describe the splendid effect of the music, it was beyond all description . . . Clara Novello's fine voice sounded so well in that large space.' The performers numbered 2,000 and, in the national anthem, they were joined by the audience. 'Never, perhaps,' said *The Times*, 'was this noble anthem heard with more overpowering effect. Many shed tears, many more found it difficult to restrain them.'

The enthusiastic reception given to the concert was borne in mind when plans were being made to commemorate the centenary of the death of Handel. It was decided to hold a three-day festival in his honour in June 1859. The committee engaged on this matter met as early as 1856 and was of the opinion that the festival 'would fail in one of its most important features, if it did not exhibit Handel's genius to assembled thousands on such a scale as would be referred to in after years as a proper standard by which his giant powers had been measured.' And so the Crystal Palace became the obvious venue. The next step was to hold a preliminary festival in 1857 that 'would excite great public interest, and, as it were, preparing for the commemoration of Handel in 1859, would decide satisfactorily some important points, which otherwise would be open to future discussion.' Costa was appointed conductor. For this occasion, he settled on a choir of 2,400. The orchestra consisted of 300 strings, with woodwind and brass in proportion, among which were three ophicleides and nine serpents and bass-horns. The percussion included Distin's Monster Drum, which stood upright, seven feet high, and emitted a sort of subterranean roar that must have had a most disturbing effect on the organist, behind whose seat it was placed.

The 1857 preliminary festival opened on 15 June with a performance of the *Messiah*. The *Musical Times* reported that the Crystal Palace was packed to overflowing.

> An immense crowd of people was collected outside the building, and remained there during the whole performance. They were certainly not unrewarded, for during the choruses the peal of voices seemed to swell from the building, and fill the air, as though the Palace itself were a vast musical instrument.
>
> The 'Hallelujah Chorus' could be distinctly heard nearly half a mile

from Norwood, and its effect, as the sound floated on the wind, was impressive beyond description, and sounded as if a nation were at prayers . . . The unison of the voices on the words, 'For the Lord God Omnipotent reigneth', brought out the full force and power of the orchestra – while the reposeful passage which immediately follows displayed to great advantage the precision of the performers. A burst of applause, which could no longer be restrained, attested, at its conclusion, the overpowering effect of this colossal interpretation of the 'Hallelujah Chorus'.

At the second concert of the preliminary festival, *Judas Maccabaeus* was given, during which, by nodding her head, the Queen authorised Costa to repeat the chorus 'See the Conquering Hero Comes', which had been clamorously received by the audience. The third and final concert, on 19 June, was devoted to *Israel in Egypt*. In the concluding national anthem, Clara Novello's superb ringing high note 'in the last cadence' (according to *The Musical Times*), became the talk of the town.

The second festival, the official Handel Commemoration Festival of 1859, was an even greater success, with 27,000 attending *Israel in Egypt* on the final day, and it was decided soon afterwards that this should become a triennial event. This proved extremely profitable to the Crystal Palace, who encouraged people to regard each concert as part of a whole-day outing and to spend the rest of their time in looking at the many other attractions that the vast building had to offer. On the last day of the 1859 festival, the audience, in between listening to the plight of the captive Israelites, sustained themselves with 19,000 sandwiches, 14,000 pies, 65,000 buns, 32,000 ice creams, several thousand lobster salads and more than 800 gallons of coffee, tea and chocolate.

Costa conducted the Handel Festival again in 1862, 1865, 1868, 1871, 1874, 1877, and 1880. By the seventies, it was firmly established as a part of the English way of life, and its fame had spread to all parts of the globe. The size of the forces employed grew each year under Costa's leadership. By 1874, when Verdi visited the festival, the choir was over 3,500. In 1883, because Costa was then in his final illness, Manns took over, and conducted the festival until the turn of the century. Apart from correcting the numerous discrepancies in the scores he inherited from Costa, he raised the standard of performance to the highest levels.

After going to the Handel Festival, Verdi wrote to Léon Escudier in Paris, on 28 June 1874, telling him of the arrangements that he had

made for the peformance of the *Requiem* in London during the following year. To the Handel Festival, he devoted but a single sentence, as
part of the postscript to the letter. 'These three or four thousand
performers', he said, 'amount to nothing more than a gigantic confidence trick.'

Verdi came to conduct the English première of his *Requiem* in 1875.
The chorus had been trained by Joseph Barnby, composer of the song
'Sweet and Low'; John Stainer, whose *The Crucifixion* was published
in 1887, played the organ in the first performance, which took place
in the Albert Hall on 15 May. The work was praised on all sides, and
the *Pall Mall Gazette* called it 'the most beautiful music for the church
that has been produced since the Requiem of Mozart', echoing
Brahms, who described it as 'a work of genius'.

Herman Klein attended the final rehearsal with a family friend,
Signor Deliguoro, who had been a fellow student of Verdi's in Milan
in the early 1830s. The two men had not met for more than thirty
years. Deliguoro told Klein, 'Giuseppe and I were like brothers. We
ate, drank and worked together the whole of the time. His harmony
exercises always had more mistakes than mine, and he could never
master the art of writing a really good fugue. I wonder whether he has
dared to put one into his "Requiem"! We shall see . . .' Klein, then
eighteen, mentions in *Thirty Years of Musical Life in London* that this
was his first sight of the composer.

> I sat with Deliguoro not far from the orchestra. He was so excited that I
> had the utmost difficulty in restraining him from climbing over the barrier
> and taking Verdi in his arms there and then. Nor were my own feelings
> altogether calm as I gazed for the first time upon the man who had
> composed 'La Traviata', 'Rigoletto', and 'Aida'. He was then sixty-three
> [sixty-one] years of age, and his closely cut beard was fast turning grey;
> but he was as active and robust as a youth, his eyes were keen and bright,
> and his clear, penetrating voice when he addressed the choir (in French or
> Italian, I forget which) could be heard all over the hall.
>
> At the end of the fugal chorus, 'Sanctus Dominus', which my neighbour
> declared to be more scholarly than anything he had anticipated, Verdi
> came around to speak to his friends among the select audience, and ere
> long I could see that he was staring in an uncertain way at Deliguoro.
> Then all of a sudden he appeared to make up his mind, and took a
> 'bee-line' over the stall chairs to the spot where we were standing. 'Tu sei
> Deliguoro, non è ver?' exclaimed the maestro. 'Si, si, son Deliguoro,'

replied his old friend, his eyes brimming over with tears. And then
followed a close embrace that I thought would never end. It would be hard
to say which of the two former classmates evinced the fuller measure of
joy.

Before leaving London, where he conducted two further performances of the *Requiem*, Verdi 'sent a substantial money gift to the less
fortunate friend of his youth, who was destined to survive only a year
or two longer.'

The première of the *Requiem* remained for Klein one of the supreme
memories of his musical life.

Surely none who heard that magnificent performance of the 'Requiem' can
have ever forgotten the combined effect of the beautiful music, the superb
singing of the Albert Hall choir, the wonderful voices of the soloists, and,
pervading all, the subtle magnetic influence induced by the presence and
personal guidance of the composer . . .

Since May 1875, Verdi had not again journeyed to England. The
Requiem was followed in 1887 with the triumph of *Otello*. During the
winter of 1892, the musical world looked forward with eager anticipation to the première of *Falstaff* in Milan in February of the following year.

By now, Verdi was a man heaped with honours too numerous to
mention. Recently, when he went to Paris for the French première of
Otello, the President decorated him, in a box at the Opéra, with the
Grand Cordon of the Legion of Honour. Only England, among the
leading countries of Europe, had so far failed to pay him honour. But
the University of Cambridge intended making good that deficiency
with an honorary doctorate, a distinction that Verdi, with his
modesty and patriotism, would no doubt regard as being conferred as
much upon Italy and Italian music as upon himself.

It was the beginning of November 1892, and the time had come for
John Peile, Vice-Chancellor of Cambridge and Master of Christ's
College, to send official letters of invitation, on behalf of the Senate of
the University, to Brahms and Verdi.

CHAPTER 4

GOUNOD

It can readily be imagined with what anxious expectation Stanford, Austin Leigh, Sedley Taylor, Gerard Cobb and the other members of the CUMS awaited the replies from Vienna and Genoa.

Verdi's was the first to arrive. He had answered with customary promptitude; his letter was dated 9 November. It made disappointing reading.

> I am quite unable to put into words my gratitude and surprise on receiving the offer of the honorary doctorate that the Senate of the University of Cambridge wants to bestow on me.
>
> I wish that I were able to accept this very rare distinction, yet I must, despite myself, refuse, not daring, at my advanced age of almost 80, to undertake so long a journey.
>
> I would be deeply obliged if the Senate and the Vice-Chancellor would accept as valid this excuse, together with the expression of my profound thanks.

So Verdi would not be coming. But hope was not lost, for Brahms might still decide, at long last, to make his first trip to England. It was agreed that, if he accepted, nobody else would be invited to take Verdi's place. The festivities would be built entirely around Brahms.

It was 25 November before his reply to John Peile finally came. The Vienna postmark was dated 23 November.

> Though I have already had the pleasure of writing to Mr. Stanford at greater length, it still remains for me to express to you my most humble and cordial thanks for the exceedingly high distinction with which you wish to honour me. Mr. Stanford will no doubt inform you of my letter, and you will not be pleased by its vagueness. It does not perhaps say 'No', yet neither can this be interpreted as 'Yes'. In as much as your kindness permits, please accept the apologies of a man who has always been accustomed to keeping himself to himself and who finds that this habit has tended to become more pronounced with the years.
>
> Since it would be impossible to doubt my gratitude towards you, I do not need to make any request in that respect. In conclusion, I earnestly ask for your indulgence.

No Brahms; no Verdi: this was the sad outcome of so many months' hopes and fears. Yet the jubilee celebrations were still to take place, and it was now even more urgent that a famous composer, or composers, be found who would come to Cambridge and add glamour and excitement to the occasion. But who?

The almost automatic choice would have been Dvořák, but, of course, he had already received his honorary doctorate. Possibly the Society might have contemplated building the celebrations around him, despite no longer having any degree to offer. But there would have been little likelihood of his accepting their invitation, for by November 1892 he had taken up his post as director of the National Conservatory of Music in New York and was settled in an apartment at 327 East 17th Street where, over the coming months, he was to write the 'New World' Symphony. A visit to Cambridge, involving a round trip of more than 7,000 miles, would obviously have been out of the question.

The next most popular composer after Brahms, Verdi and Dvořák was Gounod, whose fame rested almost entirely on his opera *Faust*. He was the favourite living composer of Queen Victoria and, indeed, of a large proportion of the general public, but many professional musicians were antipathetic towards much of his music. These conflicting reactions and the widespread reservations about the ultimate value of his achievement are reiterated in writings of the time. In the 1879 edition of Grove's *Dictionary*, Gustave Chouquet acknowledges that the introduction of *Faust* in Paris on 19 March 1859 'placed Gounod at once in the first rank of living composers.' However, in his very next sentence, he makes reference to the opera's apparent shortcomings.

> The fantastic part of 'Faust' may not be quite satisfactory, and the stronger dramatic situations are perhaps handled with less skill than those which are more elegiac, picturesque, or purely lyric, but in spite of such objections the work must be classed among those which reflect high honour on the French school. The Kermesse and the garden-scene would alone be sufficient to immortalise their author.

Chouquet's article, which, interestingly enough, is longer than that on Brahms in the same edition of the *Dictionary*, concludes in the following way.

To sum up, Gounod is a great musician and a thorough master of the orchestra. Of too refined a nature to write really comic music, his dramatic compositions seem the work of one hovering between mysticism and voluptuousness. This contrast between two opposing principles may be traced in all his works, sacred or dramatic; and gives them an immense interest both from a musical and psychological point of view. In the chords of his orchestra, majestic as those of a cathedral organ, we recognise the mystic – in his soft and original melodies, the man of pleasure. In a word, the lyric element predominates in his work, too often at the expense of variety and dramatic truth.

Around the same time that Chouquet was preparing his article, Verdi expressed similar views to his friend Arrivabene in a letter dated 14 October 1878.

I know little about Gounod's success. But let's not delude ourselves. We must take men as they are. Gounod is a great musician, a great talent, who composes excellent chamber and instrumental music in a manner entirely his own. But he isn't an artist of dramatic fibre. *Faust* itself, though successful, has become small in his hands ... his treatment of dramatic situations is weak, and his characterization is poor.

It is worth recalling, in relation to Verdi and Gounod, that, when the Khedive of Egypt invited Verdi, in 1870, to compose *Aida*, he had Gounod in mind as his second choice, should Verdi refuse the commission. His third choice was to have been Wagner, which gives us some idea of Gounod's world-wide popularity. Across the Atlantic, *Faust* was so frequently performed at the Metropolitan in New York that the critic W. J. Henderson eventually dubbed that theatre 'Das Faustspielhaus'. Wagner had scant regard for Gounod and spoke of his 'unflagging and nauseous garrulity', a particularly damning indictment.

    In assessing Gounod's standing at precisely the moment when the CUMS received Brahms's and Verdi's letters, we are fortunate in being able to draw on two valuable essays that were then in preparation. They offer appraisals of the composer that remind us very much of the opinions of Chouquet and Verdi, dating from more than a dozen years earlier. The first comes from the book *Masters of French Music*, in which the distinguished critic Arthur Hervey places Gounod at the head of living French composers.

To be the composer of 'Faust' is in itself sufficient to establish a claim upon the sympathy and gratitude of many thousands, as well as to enjoy the indisputable right of occupying a niche by the side of the greatest and most original composers of the century.

There are but few creative musicians whose individuality is so striking that it leaves its impress, not only upon their own productions, but upon those of their contemporaries. Their genius is reflected, their mode of thought copied, and even their mannerisms are reproduced by numberless admirers and conscious or unconscious imitators.

As it was with Mendelssohn, Schumann and Wagner, so it has been with Gounod. A higher tribute of praise it is indeed impossible to offer.

After more than sixty pages of analysis of Gounod's compositions, Hervey arrives at the following conclusion.

In summing up the qualifications of a great composer – and as such there can be no doubt that Gounod must be reckoned – it is evidently better to dwell on that which he has actually achieved than upon what he may have left undone.

The composer of 'Faust' has imprinted his mark in an unmistakable manner upon his epoch. He has struck a note that had not previously been heard, and if he has perhaps reiterated this note somewhat too frequently, thereby attenuating its effect, the credit of having been the first to employ it must not be refused him.

In *Famous Composers and their Works*, also in preparation during 1892 and 1893, the leading French critic Arthur Pougin has no hesitation in calling Gounod 'the greatest living musician of France'.

However little enthusiasm his detractors – for he has them – may feel for his genius, they are none the less obliged to acknowledge that genius, and the power and the influence exerted by him upon the public – a public which everywhere, in all the countries of the world, has applauded his works. The artists who are sharply discussed are usually the ones who possess true worth. More noble than majestic, more tender than pathetic, more pensive than enthusiastic, more deliberate than spontaneous, the immense talent of the author of 'Faust' glitters with a multitude of rare qualities . . .

In 1892, Gounod was seventy-four and at the very height of his fame. In youth, he had considered entering the Church, and for a while he used to preface his letters with the sign of the cross and call himself 'Abbé Gounod', though he had not actually taken holy orders. Now, in later years, he adopted semi-clerical garb and led a life of great piety in his magnificent mansion outside Paris. His huge study, rising the height of two floors, was panelled in oak and vaulted like a church. At one end, on a platform, was a large organ, the bellows of which were worked by a hydraulic machine in the basement. In the centre of the organ was placed a medallion representing the head of Christ. His work-desk, which stood beneath a big stained-glass window, had a movable keyboard that could be slid backwards and forwards underneath. The study's Renaissance mantelpiece was richly carved in high relief, representing scenes of the Passion, and decorated with massive iron ornaments and a bronze medallion of Joan of Arc. He had a deep reverence for *La Pucelle*, and once intended to compose a mass in her honour, kneeling, throughout the writing of the work, on the stones of Rheims Cathedral where she herself had stood. He later decided that this was impracticable, but, nevertheless, in 1887, completed the mass, which draws on incidental music he had written fourteen years earlier for Barbier's *Jeanne d'Arc*. His study also held a large grand piano. One entire wall of the room was lined with bookcases, full of books on theology and philosophy.

Gounod, who referred to himself as 'the musician of love', was worshipped by many of his countrymen as the world's greatest living composer and was adored by thousands of female opera-goers whose passion for *Faust* was as intense as Wagner's loathing for this 'sugary, vulgar, sickening, bungling piece of work'. Such was the fervour of their admiration that one woman, who discovered a button from his trousers on the floor, took it to her jeweller and had it encased in an exquisite locket that she wore constantly around her neck. Another votaress purloined a discarded cherry-stone from his dessert-plate, hid it in her glove and later had it set as the centrepiece of a diamond brooch.

Parisian salons were well-nigh insatiable in their desire to learn of Gounod's latest opinions and pronouncements on practically any topic under the sun. 'Holiness', he might asseverate one morning, 'is a pre-celestial translucence, an intimation of the immateriality of the life to come', and, by evening, the news would be across the town. In his engaging biography of Gounod, James Harding suggests that the composer's remarks sometimes 'took on the surrealist quality of those apocalyptic announcements credited to Victor Hugo in his rambling old age.' Harding recounts the time that Gounod sat to the painter Duran and meditated aloud, as he often did when a number of people were within earshot.

Art, he mused, was life and love – to be in love was all that mattered. Art was also the heart intellectualized. Besides Goodness and Truth, he went on, there was Beauty, which proceeded from the other two as the Holy Spirit from the Father and the Son. A crowd of reporters diligently noted his statements.

His judgements on new works of music, were also avidly canvassed. These lucubrations, unlike his philosophical meanderings, often took on an almost gnomic density. When asked what he thought of Massenet's *Hérodiade*, after attending the Paris première in February 1884, he declared, 'It's rhomboidal.' At the first performance of César Franck's Symphony in February 1889, he is said to have described the work as an 'assertion of impotence raised to the level of dogma.'

It seems unlikely that Stanford and the CUMS would have considered inviting Gounod to receive an honorary degree, but this must remain a matter of conjecture. More important is the fact that there would have been little chance of his reaching Cambridge, even if he accepted the invitation. In all probability, he would have been arrested either at his port of entry or in London. The reason for this will shortly become apparent.

H. F. Chorley was among the first Englishmen to take an interest in Gounod. He met him in Paris in March 1850, when the composer was thirty-one and still to make a reputation. An entry in Chorley's diary states, 'It was a great pleasure to me in Paris to add to my list of sensations Gounod, of whom the world will one day hear as *the* composer, or else H. F. C. is much mistaken.'

Gounod made his first trip to England for a concert given on 15 January 1851, at St Martin's Hall in Long Acre, when John Hullah conducted four sections from what was later to become the *Messe solennelle Sainte-Cécile*. Taking time off from the vilification of Schumann, Verdi and Wagner, Chorley penned a fulsome review.

Within our critical experience we do not recollect any first appearance under parallel circumstances. The first performance of music, new in style, by an untried composer, totally unknown to fame, in the presence of an audience entirely strange, and largely made up of musicians and artists, very few of whom by any possibility could have any partiality for a total stranger, made up a case of ordeal at once more sudden and severe than most recorded in the history of art. The success was decided, and this, said a veteran musician near us, more accustomed to blame than to praise, marks the commencement of a new career in music.

Chorley was especially moved by the religious fervour of the music, but the critic of the *Musical World* was rather less affected.

> It is never an agreeable task to record a disappointment, following on the heels of unbounded expectation, but it is our duty at present, and we must not shrink from it . . . Mr. Gounod has notions of harmony and instrumentation which dissatisfy without exciting surprise; his treatment of the orchestra is singularly monotonous and tame, in the midst of a tendency to extreme noise . . . there is nothing to impress the hearer with deep emotion; occasionally, indeed, as in the *Sanctus*, it is common and theatrical, not to say vapid. At other times, in the *Hosanna in Excelsis*, its distinguishing trait is a sort of pedantic triviality – pedantic because making a pretence to a quality it does not possess, and trivial because destitute of all evidence of elaboration and depth.

Gounod's second visit took place a few months later when he came over with Pauline Viardot and her husband for the English première of *Sapho* on 9 August 1851. The famous singer had just taken leave of her beloved house-guest Turgenev, who had temporarily returned to Russia. She was the star of *Sapho*, and it was her decision to appear in the opera that was responsible for its being staged. Also in the London cast was Enrico Tamberlik; the conductor was Costa. The opera ran for two performances. It had been a failure in Paris, too, though Gounod maintained that he had seen Berlioz weeping with emotion on the first night. In *The Times*, J. W. Davison saluted the arrival of *Sapho* in a veritable saturnalia of extirpation.

> The characteristics of his music are want of melody, indecision of style, ineffective treatment of voices, inexperience in the use of instruments, accompanied by an affectation of originality disclosed in strange and unsuccessful experiments, excess of modulation, monotonous in itself and proceeding from inability to develop phrases, contempt of established forms, and general absence of continuity, vexing the ear with beginnings that rarely arrive at consummation.

Pauline Viardot's own performance was well received. As April FitzLyon has written in *The Price of Genius*, the thirty-year-old diva 'had only one really hostile critic – Gounod himself, who wrote to a friend that Pauline was, as a singer, "already nearing her end, and singing out of tune all the time."'

'London is not my sort of town', Gounod had written to his mother in 1851, but he changed his mind when, as the famous composer of

Faust, he made his third trip to the capital to attend the first English presentation of the opera. He arrived on 11 June 1863, the day of the performance, and during his visit stayed at 62 Avenue Road, St John's Wood. Arditi, who conducted the première, expected him to come earlier. 'I had ardently hoped, and indeed Gounod had given me his promise, that he would himself come to London in order to superintend the rehearsals of "Faust", and it was with no small amount of trepidation that, day after day, I looked for his coming and was continually disappointed.' Arditi had given him up, when, just as he was about to raise his baton, 'I looked round, and, to my intense surprise and pleasure, caught sight of Gounod, who was seated in the stage-box.' During the first act, Gounod turned to his publisher Choudens, who had accompanied him from Paris, and said, 'Praise be to God! *This* is my *Faust!*' The audience and critics seemed equally delighted.

On reaching Her Majesty's Theatre, the composer had made no apology for not coming earlier to supervise the production. Mapleson later recalled that 'all I heard from him was that he wanted a good pit box in the centre of the house. With this, for reasons which I will at once explain, I had no difficulty whatever in providing him.' The fact was that only a very few seats had been sold; the English public were at first curiously indifferent to *Faust* and its growing reputation. Mapleson discovered this in the nick of time.

One afternoon, a few days before the day fixed for the production of the opera, I looked in upon Mr. Nugent at the box-office and asked how the sale of places was going on. 'Very badly indeed,' he replied.

Only thirty pounds' worth of seats had been taken.

This presaged a dismal failure, and I had set my mind upon a brilliant success. I told Mr. Nugent in the first place that I had decided to announce *Faust* for four nights in succession. He thought I must be mad, and assured me that one night's performance would be more than enough, and that to persist in offering to the public a work in which it took no interest was surely a deplorable mistake.

I told him that not only should the opera be played for four nights in succession, but that for the first three out of these four not one place was to be sold beyond those already disposed of. That there might be no mistake about the matter, I had all the remaining tickets for the three nights in question collected and put away in several carpet bags, which I took home with me that I might distribute them far and wide throughout the Metropolis and the Metropolitan suburbs. At last, after a prodigious outlay in envelopes, and above all postage stamps, nearly the whole mass of tickets for the three nights had been carefully given away.

I at the same time advertised in *The Times* that in consequence of a death in the family, two stalls secured for the first representation of *Faust* – the opera which was exciting so much interest that all places for the first three representations had been bought up – could be had at twenty-five shillings each, being but a small advance on the box-office prices. The stalls thus liberally offered were on sale at the shop of Mr. Phillips, the jeweller, in Cockspur Street, and I told Mr. Phillips that if he succeeded in selling them I would present him with three for the use of his own family. Mr. Phillips sold them three times over, and a like success was achieved by Mr. Baxter, the stationer, also in Cockspur Street.

Meanwhile demands had been made at the box-office for places, and when the would-be purchasers were told that 'everything had gone', they went away and repeated it to their friends, who, in their turn, came to see whether it was quite impossible to obtain seats for the first performance of an opera which was now beginning to be seriously talked about. As the day of the production approached the inquiries became more and more numerous.

'If not for the first night, there must surely be places somewhere for the second,' was the cry.

Mr. Nugent and his assistants had, however, but one answer, 'Everything had been sold, not only for the first night, but also for the two following ones . . .'

The second night, *Faust* was received more warmly than on the first, and at each succeeding representation it gained additional favour, until after the third performance the paying public, burning with desire to see a work from which they had hitherto been debarred, filled the theatre night after night. No further device was necessary for stimulating its curiosity; and the work was now to please and delight successive audiences by its own incontestable merit. It was given for ten nights in succession, and was constantly repeated until the termination of the season.

Three weeks after the opening at Her Majesty's, a rival version of the opera was staged at Covent Garden. Gounod consented to supervise the production for a fee of £100. The conductor was Costa, and the organist was twenty-one-year-old Arthur Sullivan. One night a tricky situation developed; this is recounted by Charles Willeby in his essay on Sullivan in *Masters of English Music*, published in 1893.

All went well until the church scene, in the midst of which the wire, connecting the pedal under Costa's foot with the metronome stick at the organ, broke. In the concerted music this meant disaster, for the organist could hear nothing but his own instrument. Quick as thought, whilst he was playing the introductory solo, Sullivan called a stage hand. 'Go,' he said quickly, 'and tell Mr Costa the wire is broken and that he is to *keep his ears open and follow me*.' No sooner had the man flown to deliver his message than the full meaning of the words flashed upon Sullivan. True, there had been no time for choice of expression, but what would Costa say to a message thus delivered by a stage hand, which, moreover, would certainly gain nothing of elegance in the telling? The scene, however, went well, but at the end of the act Sullivan realised more fully than ever the arrogance (as it seemed to him) of his message, and approached his chief with no little nervousness. He commenced to apologise profusely. Costa, to his great surprise, stopped him at once, and shaking him by the hand said: 'No, no. Good boy, you kept your head and did quite right.'

Faust soon became the opera of the day, and the composer's presence in London was fully exploited for publicity purposes, so that he complained of having been turned into 'a walking advertisement poster'. It became even more popular during the seventies and eighties, better known than any single opera by Verdi or Wagner. Queen Victoria was one of its greatest admirers. Herman Klein was at Windsor in the summer of 1900, when she attended a royal command performance of the work. 'From the beginning to the end the Queen remained deeply interested, and never stirred from her chair upon the dais.' Her face lit up 'and her lips parted with a transient smile of recognition whenever some well-known phrase occurred.'

In January 1864, *Faust* was heard in the English language, in a translation by Chorley. The singers, reported *The Musical Times*, 'whether with or without the author's permission we have no means of knowing, continually substituted other words, as good for the sense as, and infinitely better for the sound than, those in the printed copy.'

Gounod's longest visit to England began in the middle of September 1870, when he, his family and his mother-in-law arrived in Liverpool, having sailed from Dieppe twelve days after the capture of Louis Napoleon at Sedan. The Franco-Prussian War was responsible for the flight to London of a number of musicians, including, also, Pauline Viardot. Turgenev came over with her and went into rooms in Bentinck Street. The Gounods stayed initially with friends in Blackheath, shortly afterwards transferring to a rented house nearby, at what is now 15 Morden Road. Their next move was to Paddington, where they lived at 9 Park Place.

Gounod was by then widely regarded as France's greatest living composer – Berlioz had died the previous year, in March 1869. His comings and goings were noted in the newspapers. His plans for new works were constantly reported. He was, said reliable sources, about to write an opera with Victor Hugo; now he was composing a

'Francesca da Rimini', though it would depart a little from Dante.

Meanwhile, he was invited to produce a composition, on behalf of France, for the inaugural concert of the 1871 International Exhibition. Drawing the text from the Bible, he wrote the oratorio *Gallia*, and this he conducted at the concert on 1 May 1871 in the Albert Hall, which had been opened a month earlier. At that moment, the French capital was in the hands of the Commune. *Gallia* was well received.

Representing Germany at the Exhibition was Ferdinand Hiller, who contributed a Festival March. Meyerbeer had died in 1864, and Wagner and Brahms were not yet established in England, although Wagner, now sixty, was only a year younger than Hiller. Hiller was a wise and safe choice, whose reputation was not inconsiderable, and is worth remembering that he was held in high esteem by Berlioz, Mendelssohn, Liszt, Verdi, Stanford, Hallé and many other musicians. He was enthusiastically regarded, too, by musical amateurs. When, in the autumn of 1860, William Rossetti and Vernon Lushington called on the Brownings in Siena, the conversation touched on Hiller. Lushington, whom Browning had not previously met, expressed an admiration for Hiller's works. 'Ah, now I understand who you are', said the poet. 'When I find a man who shares with me a liking for Hiller's music, I can see into him at once; he ceases to be a stranger.'

Chosen to represent Italy was Ciro Pinsuti, Professor of Singing at the Royal Academy of Music. Rossini had died in 1868, and, apart from Verdi, Italy had few composers of note. The great advantage of selecting Pinsuti, a pupil of Rossini, was that he was on hand; and, to avoid any repetition of the controversy caused by *Inno delle nazioni*, he was furnished with the text that he was to set. This was the poem 'O, People of This Favoured Land', which was commissioned from Lord Houghton, who, in P. J. Keating's words, 'was justly renowned for his wit, kindness to struggling writers and vast collection of erotica.'

England was represented by Arthur Sullivan, the Queen's favourite British composer, who was in the process of overtaking Sterndale Bennett in general estimation. He had already made his mark nine years earlier at the age of nineteen, when Manns conducted his incidental music to *The Tempest* at the Crystal Palace. This provoked such a storm of enthusiasm that it was repeated a week later, creating a record attendance. Charles Dickens was in the audience and afterwards came round to the artists' room, shook Sullivan vigorously by the hand and told him, 'I don't profess to be a musical critic, but I do know that I have listened to a very remarkable work.' In 1869, the Queen wrote to Sullivan and asked him to send her a complete set of his compositions; this was an honour that she had not even conferred on Mendelssohn.

Sullivan's Exhibition piece was a choral work, *On Shore and Sea*, which he dedicated to Grove. The verses were supplied by Tom Taylor, the prolific dramatist, art critic for *The Times* and contributor to *Punch*, of which he became editor in 1874. His popular comedy *Our American Cousin* was the play being performed when Lincoln was assassinated at Ford's Theatre in Washington in 1865. *On Shore and Sea* takes as its subject a marine adventure set in the Mediterranean, for which the composer was severely upbraided after the concert, the *Graphic* being among his sternest critics.

> Surprise has been expressed that Mr. Arthur Sullivan, upon whom devolved the championship of England, should have gone out of England for the subject of his cantata, *On Shore and Sea*. We share that surprise to the fullest extent. It was expected that, on such an occasion, Mr. Sullivan would have been intensely national, as are Sterndale Bennett in *The May Queen*, and Mr. Macfarren in *May Day*. Instead thereof, he accepted a libretto . . . which laid the action in an Italian port, on the Mediterranean Sea, and among the barbarians of Northern Africa. Having made his choice it was fitting that he should pay due heed to the veracities involved, and write music as much Italian or Moorish in style as knowledge or aptitude allowed. This Mr. Sullivan has done, the result being wholly unsuggestive of England or English art.

In the packed audience at the inaugural concert was the delectable Mrs Georgina Weldon. She had once caught the eye of Thackeray and provoked the painter Watts into admitting to being 'in a fidget about the wild little girl'. Her husband, Harry Weldon, developed into rather a dull person, and Georgina had often to seek her own amusement. In this, she was aided by having a lovely singing voice, which brought her into contact with a number of well-known musicians. Among those who succumbed to her charms was the usually circumspect Arthur Sullivan. All her admirers, however, paled into insignificance beside Gounod, whose music sent her into ecstasies. Sullivan's *On Shore and Sea* was, for her, totally eclipsed by *Gallia*.

I and Harry went to the Albert Hall. It is the most magnificent hall I ever saw – splendid for sound. First was sung Pinsuti's *Chorale*, then Gounod's *Gallia* which is too heavenly. I cried bitterly at the 'Vide, Dominum, afflictionem meam'. It is all so divine, the finest thing he has written, though *all* he has done is *so* wonderfully beautiful.

Georgina and Gounod first met two months before the concert, at the home of Julius Benedict, the favourite pupil of Weber, through whom he was introduced to Beethoven. Georgina had loved Gounod's music from as far back as she could remember; it summoned up visions 'of cathedrals, of incense, of anthems, of plain chant, of processions. It spoke of simple farm-yards, of courtly castle yards, of hell, of heaven.' Gounod was immediately captivated by her good looks. He sat at the piano and sang one of his love songs, his eyes steadfastly gazing into hers. 'I did not know which way to look', she confessed in her diary. 'My tears, which had begun to flow at the first line, had become a rivulet, the rivulet had become a stream, the stream a torrent, the torrent sobs the sobs almost a fit.' Fortunately, Gounod, an experienced philanderer, was adept at handling this sort of situation. When a dewy-eyed young admirer asked him how he was able to compose such wonderful tunes, he replied, 'God, Madame, sends me down some of His angels, and they whisper sweet melodies in my ear.' Three days after their encounter at Benedict's, Georgina and Gounod met again. This time their roles were reversed: she sang; he wept. His wife wept, and her mother wept too. All around, people wept. Gounod pressed Georgina's hands, his eyes brimming with tears. Then he sat down at the piano and began *Faust*. 'Gounod and I sang it right through from beginning to end! Thereupon followed bravos and sighs without end. Madame Gounod became enthusiastic; she told me herself that I was "born for Gounod" . . . Gounod was jubilant . . . I was in ecstasies!' Thereafter, Georgina and Gounod began to see much more of each other; he told her she was the inspiration behind *Gallia*. She was enraptured by his genius and, so she discerned, his beatific soul, but she does not appear to have been drawn very much to him physically. He, however, left her in no doubt of what sort of relationship he wanted. She gently deflected him, though, with the protestation 'You are not a *man*! You are a *god*!'

Nevertheless, as one might guess, Madame Gounod became bitterly jealous, and, since hostilities had ceased in France, she took the rest of the family back to Paris. The Weldons thereupon offered the composer a room in their house, and, on 19 June 1871, he gratefully joined them, having determined, he said, to part from his wife. The Weldon's residence, Tavistock House, in Tavistock Square, was the home of Dickens between 1851 and 1860, before he moved out to Gad's Hill. It was a capacious building. One room had been large enough to accommodate an audience of a hundred when, in January 1857, Dickens and Wilkie Collins took part in a production of the latter's play *The Frozen Deep*. Hans Christian Andersen stayed with Dickens at Tavistock House in June of the same year, often puzzling and irritating his host by his unworldliness and inability ever to find a language in which satisfactorily to communicate. 'His unintelligible vocabulary was marvellous', Dickens declared. Andersen could not speak English, French or German, maintained the novelist, and, in the opinion of his interpreter, could not even speak Danish. During his stay, said his host, the great weaver of fairy-tales 'got into a wild entanglement of cabs'. One day, he amazed everybody by returning to Tavistock House completely lame in both legs, says Dickens.

> It turned out that a cab driver had brought him back from the City, by way of the unfinished new thoroughfare through Clerkenwell. Satisfied that the cabman was bent on robbery and murder, he had put his watch and money into his boots – together with a Bradshaw, a pocket-book, a pair of scissors, a penknife, a book or two, a few letters of introduction, and some other miscellaneous property.

At the start of his visit to England, Andersen had journeyed up by train from Dover; 'we went through tunnel after tunnel and soon we saw the great Crystal Palace, glittering in full sunshine, and London, swathed in smoke, looming on the horizon.' Dickens took him to the Crystal Palace, which enchanted Andersen, who noted down everything he saw: the wide paths, the blaze of flowers, the trees and statues, the rooms from Pompeii, the French galleries, the sun on the glass roof. It was at the time of the preliminary Handel Festival, and the two men heard Costa conduct the *Messiah*. 'The wind whispered outside', Andersen wrote, 'and, when the singing and the music rolled, it vibrated in my heart; I was close to tears.' He also attended a performance of *The Frozen Deep*, staged at the Gallery of Illustration in Regent Street to help raise money for the family of the dramatist Douglas Jerrold, who had recently died. Andersen was thrilled to see in the audience the Queen, Prince Albert, the Prince of Wales, Prince Alfred, the Princess Royal, Princess Alice, the King of the Belgians,

Princess Charlotte of Belgium, Prince Frederick William of Prussia, the Prince of Hohenzollern-Sigmaringen and the Count of Flanders. He thought that Dickens 'performed his part in the drama with striking truthfulness and great dramatic genius.' In the death scene, Dickens was so affecting that Andersen, along with many others, burst into tears. Afterwards, he recalled, 'the whole company gathered for a lively, cheerful supper – we drank champagne.' When the time came for Andersen to return to Denmark, Dickens drove him to the station and drew a route of his journey, so that he should not get into any further 'entanglement', and they embraced and parted.

Tavistock House was to be Gounod's home for three years. He moved in, bearing gifts for Georgina: a rosary and a copy of *The Imitation of Christ*. During the summer of 1871, he returned briefly to Paris on business and rejected an offer of the directorship of the Conservatoire. The same autumn, he again travelled to Paris, to conduct the French première of *Gallia*. Georgina accompanied him; she sang the principal part in the oratorio and also appeared in two stage presentations of the work.

Over the next two and a half years, the composer became completely absorbed into the Weldon household. He was not an easy man to look after, because he was often unwell. When they came back from Paris at the end of November 1871, he was ill for several days; Georgina wrote that 'he crouched down in his bed like a poor hunted animal.' Congestion of the lungs and bronchial tubes was diagnosed, together with eczema and the possibility of a cerebral attack. It was recommended that he should be made to perspire, and he was therefore enveloped in wet sheets, blankets, furs and waterproofs, and placed in a specially heated room. There were also frequent hot baths. The side-effects of this treatment, which lasted for two months, were rheumatism, colic, glandular swelling and dysentery. The eczema was aggravated, and the patient systematically scratched his scaly skin until it snapped. Yet, he was eventually returned to full health, thanks to the constant nursing and attention that he received from the Weldons. In future, there would be more illnesses, though none quite so bad. Concomitant chronic disorders included hallucinations, amnesia and incipient deafness.

Gounod's relationship with the Weldons often partook of the elements of Dadaist comedy. Georgina's diary and her later reminiscences vividly capture many of these moments, which are reproduced in Edward Grierson's marvellous book, *Storm Bird: The Strange Life of Georgina Weldon*. The first of these extraordinary scenes took place one morning in the early spring of 1872, when Gounod was composing his opera *Polyeucte*. He and Georgina somehow managed to work up an argument over nothing, and Gounod said he could not stay cooped up in the house with her; he had to get out. 'You can't go out', she told him. 'You are ill, you have a bad cold, the weather is awful. I do beg and implore you not to stir out, my dear old man.'

> Gounod went to dress. He put on his winter coat, my sealskin cap, his strongest boots; he rummaged the things on my table for a bit, hoping it would give me the chance of saying something which would enable him to recommence his 'row'. But I held my head down, my eyes fixed on my books. I was nearly crying. He went off without another word. I heard him go downstairs; I heard the front door shut. I went and gazed at the great black plane trees swaying to and fro their branches, and the horrid dark cold weather.

He returned shortly after 2.00 pm. Harry Weldon was now also in the house, having come home for lunch. Gounod was bathed in perspiration. Georgina made him sit down, took off his hat and started mopping his brow. She had him keep on his coat for a while, in case he caught cold. She rang for the maid to bring in his broth. But, in an instant, he was up and off again, with Harry in pursuit. Harry managed to collar him just as he was reaching the street and dragged him back into the house, where he settled him in another armchair. Gounod now seemed to have quietened down, so Harry felt free to return to work. However, no sooner had he left the house than 'the black fury of Gounod burst out in all its violence.'

> In vain I tried to calm him. I tried to take him in my arms and coax him; he pushed me brutally away, almost with blows. 'Don't touch me,' he shrieked, 'it is *you* who have invited your husband to insult me, to outrage me, to defy me. I will die,' he shrieked, 'and all shall perish with me!' I was terrified. The thought struck me that he meant to set the place on fire but I followed him with my eyes, hoping that my looks might subdue him. He rushed like a madman to the cupboard where the orchestral score of 'Polyeucte' was carefully stored away. He seized hold of it, crying out, 'Polyeucte first; Polyeucte shall burn!' It was his custom, at the least contrariety, to burn the manuscript he was composing. It was his best way of getting anything he wanted out of me. It made me wretched to see him destroy his work.

With strength lent me by the horror of despair, I threw myself on Gounod with all my weight; I knocked him down; I rolled on him; we tussled violently for possession of the treasure. I tore it from him; I flung it on the sofa; I suddenly picked myself off the floor; I sat upon it and screamed: 'You shall kill me first, but you shall not burn Polyeucte!' My strength then gave way, I burst into sobs, I stretched out my arms to him — 'My old man! My old treasure! why are you so wicked to me?' . . .

Gounod, to whom the fight had done good, had calmed down, thank God: the score of 'Polyeucte' was saved.

This altercation was the first of several, and, after a while, Gounod took to keeping a small travelling bag, packed ready for immediate departure, in which he stowed away, among other items, a loaded pistol. One day, Harry accused him of humbug, because Gounod always showed such exaggerated affection for everybody, even kissing on both cheeks people whom he had known only for a few minutes. The composer observed that he disliked being insulted by 'this dragoon who never says one word louder than the other'. It was time to go for his bag and be off again.

Twenty minutes after this Gounod returned. He had completely dressed himself anew. He had put on his best trousers, his new waistcoat, his black frock coat, his neatest shoes, his red socks, a clean white shirt, a black neckerchief (the bows most carefully tied), and he had on his head his Algerian fez. Under his arm he carried some music paper. He entered ceremoniously. He approached the table; he stood opposite my husband . . . took off his fez and made a profound salaam.

'Sir,' he said deliberately, 'I have reflected that it must be as disagreeable for you to have a humbug in your house as it is for me to remain in it. I have the honour of wishing you a very good morning.'

He replaced his fez on his head; he walked slowly with inexpressible dignity towards the door. My tears began to flow; I joined my hands together and I looked at my husband in the most imploring manner. My husband understood; he flew towards the door; he turned towards Gounod, with his back to the door, and, fixing his bright eyes on him, he said, 'You shall not go out.'

| GOUNOD: | To-day I am a prisoner; the other day I was brought back by you by the arm before all London; another time I was a *glutton*; another day I am a *liar*; now, to-day I am a *humbug*. Open the door, if you please. |
| MY HUSBAND: | Come, my dear-old man, what has come over you this morning? |

So saying, Harry drew near to Gounod, who at once took him in his arms, burst into tears, hugged him with all his might, and fainted. After being revived, he begged forgiveness, tears coursing his cheeks. Georgina and Harry told him they were intrigued to know what he had been intending to do with the music paper. 'Well,' he confessed, 'I meant to spend the day in the underground railway and note down on the way musical ideas, which I think would have occurred to me.' Georgina kissed him through her laughter. 'You funny old man, that you are!'

During the summer holidays, Gounod's seventeen-year-old son Jean sometimes came over to stay. He was present at the card-table, partnered by his father, when another memorable scene took place. Jean unintentionally precipitated it by swearing after losing a hand of whist. Georgina promptly accused him of being coarse. Gounod inferred that her remarks were also addressed to him, and things got under way. The game broke up. Georgina went to her room and prepared for bed. Soon there was a knock at her door. 'You can't come in.' Nothing happened for five minutes, then there was another knock, and in trooped Gounod and Jean. 'I only came to tell you that Jean heard exactly as I did', said Gounod. Georgina ordered them to leave her room and added that tomorrow Jean would have to find somewhere else to stay. 'So, then,' Gounod exclaimed, 'you turn me out of doors!' and away he went to pack. A few moments later Georgina followed him to his room.

He had pulled my sealskin cap over his ears; he had on his thick winter overcoat (the weather was very fine and hot – 16th August 1873), he had his little travelling bag, which contained his loaded pistol, in his hands, his warm trousers, his thick shoes; he was sitting on his bed with his legs hanging down. He took no notice of Jean, who was sitting crying on the portmanteau. Never were seen two beings so profoundly miserable.

At this point, however, Gounod suddenly threw in the towel. Georgina went over to him, and he put his arms around her. 'You – have – turned – me – out – of – doors!' he sobbed, having decided to stay.

Though within the walls of Tavistock House Gounod and Georgina engaged in these extraordinary skirmishes, they presented a united front to the outside world, waging war on concert promoters and music publishers. Georgina acted as his business manager, at which she was exceptionally competent, and even, in court, as his defending counsel. She booked a large number of concerts for him and founded a choir to take part in programmes devoted almost exclusively to his pieces. She wrote a number of extravagant propaganda articles and pamphlets about him and his music. The result of this fanatical advocacy was that the composer and his works soon became anathema to much of the musical establishment. The management of the Albert Hall eventually barred him from appearing there, and Novello's sued him for libel. Acting for Gounod, Georgina pleaded his case so skilfully that the jury, though finding against the composer, set the damages at a mere £2. Costs, however, amounted to £100. Georgina advised him not to pay them, and Gounod was prepared to go to prison as a martyr. He cursed the fact that he did not possess Verdi's well-known business acumen, which, he felt, would have enabled him to take advantage of publishers, rather than see things happen the other way round. 'At the present day,' he declared, 'vampires are said to inhabit only certain villages in Illyria. Nevertheless, it is by no means necessary to undertake so long a journey to engage in conflict with monsters of this kind. They come across us in all parts of civilized Europe, in the form of Music Publishers and Theatrical Managers.' Proceedings designed to place Gounod behind bars advanced a good way before the Lord Chief Justice, mindful of this squalid treatment of France's greatest living composer, deferred the committal order. This did not stop Gounod and Georgina producing a pamphlet on the subject of 'the various ways publishers have of thieving from composers'. Gounod was disappointed not to go to prison. He had particularly looked forward to working on *Polyeucte* during his incarceration and to orchestrating the scene in which the hero is imprisoned prior to his martyrdom.

Despite the distractions of London, squabbles with publishers and theatrical managers, holidays in Margate, Hastings and St Leonards, and the unusual course of life at Tavistock House, which latterly included nocturnal walks in his nightshirt, accompanied by the emission of 'unearthly cries', Gounod succeeded in composing a voluminous amount of music while he was in England. This consisted of *Polyeucte*, music for Barbier's *Jeanne d'Arc*, ten psalms and anthems, *Gallia*, a mass, twelve choruses and more than sixty songs and short pieces, among which were settings of poems by Byron, Shelley, Kingsley and Longfellow, and of Lord Houghton's 'Stanzas in Memory of Livingstone'. He also wrote a *Te Deum* commemorating the recovery of the Prince of Wales from a serious attack of typhoid.

He informed John Goss, organist of St Paul's and composer to the Chapel Royal, that he would be happy to have this work performed in St Paul's. While thanking him, Goss wrote, 'In all candour I must confess to you that I do not wish it to be accepted . . . for the very natural reason that there are yet Englishmen in existence who are capable of, and would be expected to produce, the music required for the ceremony. I am quite sure that their hearts would be in the music . . .' The official *Te Deum*, commissioned from Sullivan, was conducted by Manns at the Crystal Palace on 1 May 1872 in the presence of royalty and an audience of 30,000.

Of Gounod's London pieces, the song 'Oh, That We Two Were Maying', to verses by Kingsley, proved very popular, but the most famous work was *Funeral March of a Marionette*, which was incorporated in the ballet scene from *Jeanne d'Arc*. The incidental music for this play was dedicated to 'my two dear and courageous friends' – Georgina and Harry – 'in memory of the stake at which public malice has condemned them to burn with me.' The composer originally meant the march to be a musical caricature of H. F. Chorley, who for more than twenty years had been such a loyal champion of Gounod's works. It is ironic that this piece, which was given its title by Georgina, should have been written by one of the few composers whom the critic had not savaged. It is not clear why Gounod was inspired to parody Chorley, but both he and Georgina hated him, and Georgina once described Chorley's movements as those of 'a stuffed red-haired monkey'. When Gounod first played the march to Georgina, it made her 'nearly die of laughter'. Within two years, it earned Gounod more than £350.

Chorley's appearance was indeed simian. 'Bah! Don't talk to me of Chorley!' once cried his fellow critic John Ella. 'He looks like a sick monkey.' In *Memories of Half a Century*, published in 1908, Rudolph Lehmann recalls Chorley, whom he used to see at his parents' house. 'He was tall and thin. His eyes blinked and twinkled as he spoke; and his quaint pecking gestures and high staccato voice made an impression which caused one of his friends to describe him as the missing link between the chimpanzee and the cockatoo.' Alice Mangold, in her *Musical Memories*, describes him as 'tall, spare, pale, with colourless eyelashes shading light gray eyes . . . with the nervous habit of blinking his eyes and slightly twitching his lips.' She also mentions his red hair and high-pitched voice, which Georgina called 'thin, sour, high-pitched, sopranoish'.

Chorley had a wide circle of friends who, despite his vitriolic writings and unfortunate physical appearance and mannerisms, were genuinely attached to him. We can perhaps begin to understand why this should be, by noting a passage from the Rev J. E. Cox's *Musical Recollections of the Last Half-Century*.

> Mr. Chorley, though not a regularly trained musician, had, generally speaking, a singularly clear appreciation of the art itself, and of the requirements for its legitimate progress, although he not infrequently permitted his prejudices – as some may have been inclined to designate many of his expressed opinions – to overrule his judgement. In spite, however, of this peculiarity – the result more of temperament, perhaps than of affectation or ill-feeling – it is impossible to say of him that he ever pandered to the whims and caprices of *artistes*, however intimate he might have been personally with them, or made himself subservient to their desire for unworthy or undue commendation. Although an eccentric, he was essentially an honest and an upright man. This is a testimony I am only too happy to be able to pay to Mr. Henry F. Chorley's memory, although, whilst having had merely a passing acquaintance with him, I never was numbered amongst those whom he especially looked upon and esteemed as his friends.

We may infer that, like so many Victorians, Chorley had a passionate concern for the 'legitimate progress' of music, and this was at the root of all his criticism. It was his misfortune to lack real musicality and Darwinian perspective, and to be possessed of an acerbic prose style with which he over-zealously belaboured any composer who seemed to him, with his limited vision, to menace that 'legitimate progress'. It would be reasonable to suppose that a large number of his readers held views precisely the same as his. Those who were on the side of the angels – Grove, Manns, Hallé – appear to have regarded him with indulgence, and even pity, recognising that he was no more than the banner-waver for the legions of the benighted. Indeed, Hallé, who devoted his whole life to championing the very composers whom Chorley damned, says simply of him, 'He was a man of strong views, fearless in his criticism, perfectly honest, although often and unconsciously swayed by personal antipathies and sympathies.'

One of the best full-length portraits of Chorley comes in the reminiscences of Frederick Lehmann, which are reproduced in the *Memoirs* of his son Rudolph.

Chorley, the musical critic of the *Athenaeum*, was in appearance and manner one of the strangest of mortals. His face was all out of drawing, and his high voice and curious angular movements made him a very conspicuous figure wherever he went. . . . No single critic could now [1884] make or mar a musical reputation, but in the antediluvian days of which I speak Chorley, as the mouthpiece of the *Athenaeum*, was master of the situation and ruled supreme. I am bound to add that he was thoroughly honest, and, though he had his favourites, he wrote without fear. But he had neither the natural gifts nor the education necessary for so responsible a position . . . There can be no doubt that by his ignorant but constantly expressed detestation of Schumann's music he for many years prevented that great composer from becoming properly known and appreciated in this country. On the other hand, Chorley adored Mendelssohn, and went so far as to consider any admiration of Schumann a slight upon his idol . . .

At his little house, 13, Eaton Place, West, he saw very good company and gave many pleasant dinners, to which he invited artists and literary men of eminence. At the same time he had a curious way of alluding to those whose rank and means made it unnecessary for them to live by their brains as 'real people' . . .

Chorley was really a most hospitable man, but his hospitality sometimes took strange forms. Once, I remember, he asked me whether I was engaged upon a certain date, and upon replying 'No', he somewhat astonished me by saying that he would come and dine with me on that day. 'I shall have a blue-coat boy staying with me,' he continued, 'and I will bring him with me; it will do the lad good.' Chorley was as good as his word. On the appointed day he and his *protégé* dined with me at my house in Westbourne Terrace . . . Chorley, however, was, I am bound to say, profuse in his invitations to dinner at his own house, but occasionally his stream of dinners would cease, though he never consented to abdicate altogether the position of Amphitryon. For instance, he would meet you in June and say to you, 'I have quite made up my mind to have a little dinner on Guy Fawkes day; will you come?' And through all these intervening months Chorley would never meet you without reminding you that you were engaged to him for the 5th of November. This became a standing joke amongst his intimates . . .

In his later days poor Chorley became very feeble, and used often to forget where he was, and to imagine when dining out that he was dining at his own house.

On one occasion, when Charles Reade, Wilkie Collins, and others were dining at our house near Highgate, a curious incident happened. When Chorley arrived before dinner he showed that he was not quite at his ease by saying to my wife, 'Dear friend, where am I?' To which she replied reassuringly, 'Oh, Mr. Chorley, you must consider yourself at home.' I take the following amusing account from a letter written at the time by my wife:

'At last Chorley didn't in the very least know where he was, and again asked me confidentially if I could tell him. I said he was at Woodlands. He said, "Where's that?" During dinner he appeared to have settled it in his own mind that he was at home; consequently he kept on ringing the bell, giving Martin all sorts of orders, and calling him Drury (his own man's name). He was quite vexed with me for ringing once and giving an order myself. At the end of dinner he tottered up, held on for a moment as if the chair was a mast and he was crossing the Channel, asked me to be good enough to take care of his guests for him, and particularly to see that Mr. Collins got what wine he liked, feebly said "Drury", whereat Martin took his arm – and so vanished to bed. Afterwards when I went up, I took a peep at him through the door, and saw him asleep in a large highly coloured turban. He was all right the next day, and is right now and most delightful, like his fine, bright old conceited self again. To-night we have a dinner-party in his honour, Charles Reade, Tuckie, Wilkie Collins, Mrs. Procter, Mr. Bockett, and one or two others.'

Next day. 'I told you in my last letter about the dinner we had arranged for Chorley. When we sat down, his delusion of being at his own table came on again. We were all known to him except Mr. Bockett. I saw him now and then puzzling over Mr. Bockett, unable to account for Bockett, but in his old-fashioned, chivalrous way with the greatest stranger, sending all the dishes round to Bockett, pressing things upon him. "Take the champagne to Mr. Bockett, please," &c., &c. After dinner, when Wilkie was proceeding to light his cigar, Chorley at once interfered, declaring that he never allowed smoking in his dining-room. There was, I believe, a little scene, but matters were amicably arranged afterwards. Afterwards, in the music-room, Chorley asked me how his dinner had gone off, was it good? Then he said, "I shall certainly ask Mr. Bockett again, he's ver-r-y nice." "But," said Kitty, "have you ever seen him before?" "Well," said Chorley, meditating, "no – but then" (with an important little snigger) "this little dinner of mine has been a complete –" perhaps he meant a complete surprise to himself, but he waved off the end of the sentence. Every now and then he quite recovered himself, and told us how confused he had been. During one of these intervals he went up to Wilkie and most touchingly apologised to him, but in a short time again he would ring the bell and think himself at home.'

Chorley led a lonely bachelor life, waited on by Drury and by a tippling housekeeper, Mrs Drake. Charles Dickens, whose penchant for grotesques may have attracted him to Chorley, was one of his best friends and describes in a letter to Nina Lehmann, Frederick's wife, how he called on Chorley one day at his tiny house, 'the tiniest in London, perhaps', according to Hallé. It was 1869, and by now Chorley had become an exceedingly heavy drinker.

I saw Chorley yesterday in his own home. A sad and solitary sight. The widowed Drake, with a certain incoherence of manner, presented a blooming countenance and buxom form in the passage; so buxom indeed that she was obliged to retire before me like a modest stopper before I could get into the dining room where poor Chorley reposed like the dregs of last season's wine.

Chorley's bibulousness was partially responsible for his bouts of oblivion. At times he became totally *hors de combat* and, on a holiday in Biarritz and Spain with Frederick Lehmann, he was frequently forced to retire to his room. One evening, Lehmann was so taken with a small-town Spanish band, playing music of the region, that he hauled the semi-stupefied critic out of bed to listen to it. However, on Chorley's arrival, the band went into a selection from *Il trovatore*, and so he turned round and staggered back to the hotel again. On another occasion, during the autumn of 1864, he arrived, totally drunk, for dinner with Dickens and his family, before going on to a play. The novelist's daughter Mamie told Nina Lehmann about the incident, and she passed on the news to Frederick in a letter that is reprinted in John Lehmann's *Ancestors and Friends*.

When he entered the room, they saw in an instant he was gone. He was long past speech, and it is Dickens's idea that he has been in this state all the time he has been alone in Biarritz . . . At dinner he couldn't speak, so the three Dickens's talked to each other without minding him . . . He got to the theatre alone somehow, went into Mr. Oxenford's box and fell on the floor. The box-keeper picked him up, and was going to take him away, when Mr. O. said, 'Oh, never mind, he's an old friend of mine, leave him.' During the evening he made his way half asleep to Dr. de Mussy's box, and gradually recovered *slightly*.

Chorley often showed his non-critical writings – novels, hymns and other pieces – to Dickens for his approval, and the novelist took great pains to help him. In March 1862, Dickens even attended a lecture on the national music of different countries that Chorley delivered, and then wrote to him, giving him his reactions.

. . . I hope I may venture to tell you that I was extremely pleased and interested. Both the matter of the materials and the manner of their arrangement were quite admirable, and a modesty and complete absence of any kind of affectation pervaded the whole discourse, which was quite an example to the many whom it concerns. If you could be a very little louder, and would never let a sentence go for the thousandth part of an instant until the last word is out, you would find the audience more responsive.

A spoken sentence will never run alone in all its life, and is never to be trusted to itself in its most insignificant member. See it *well out* – with the voice – and the part of the audience is made surprisingly easier . . . I take the liberty of making the remark, as one who has fought with wild beasts (oratorically) in divers arenas. For the rest nothing could be better. Knowledge, ingenuity, neatness, condensation, good sense, and good taste in delightful combination.

Chorley died in February 1872, at the age of sixty-three. Mamie Dickens, in her contribution to H. G. Hewlett's biography of Chorley, pays tribute to his friendship with her father.

He was very grateful for any love and attention shown to him, and never forgot a kindness done to him. I believe he loved my father better than any man in the world; was grateful to him for his friendship, and truly proud of possessing it, which he certainly did to a very large amount. My father was very fond of him, and had the greatest respect for his honest, straight-forward, upright, and generous character. I think, and am glad to think, that the happiest days of Mr. Chorley's life – his later life, that is to say – were passed at Gad's Hill.

After my father's death, and before we left the dear old home, Mr. Chorley wrote and asked me if I would send him a branch off each of our large cedar-trees, as a remembrance of the place. My friend, and *his* dear friend, Mrs. Lehmann, saw him lying calm and peaceful in his coffin, with a large green branch on each side of him. She did not understand what this meant, but I did, and was much touched, as, of course, he had given orders that these branches should be laid with him in his coffin. So a piece of the place he loved so much, for its dear master's sake, went down to the grave with him.

Without knowing it, Chorley had the last laugh on Gounod. *Funeral March of a Marionette* was composed while he was still alive, but, at the time of his death, it had not yet been offered to a publisher. Thus, there could be no question of any reference being made to him, either in the title or dedication, as Gounod had originally intended.

At length, Gounod decided he should return to his wife and family and on 8 June 1874 he sorrowfully took his leave of Georgina and Harry Weldon. They saw him off at Charing Cross. He was wearing one of Harry's panama hats, 'so he had something of ours.'

The old man cried as if his heart would break, but as for me, I kept up my courage to the last, I did not shed one tear, nor even had tears in my eyes . . . The railway clock marked 1.20. Gounod was in the carriage; my husband and I both stood near the door.

He sobbed, he yet held our hands tight in his, without being able to utter a word. 'Come, my dear old man,' said my husband to him tenderly: 'don't cry so much.'

The train moved off, and Gounod was gone. Georgina and Harry lunched at the station and then went back to Tavistock House. She wrote in her diary, 'I hope he won't cry long. I took care not to cry. I came home and went to bed for four hours. Jean Gounod 18 years old to-day.'

Before parting, Gounod had pledged that he would die in Georgina's arms and he gave her to understand that one way or another he would eventually return to her and Harry. But the vision quickly faded. A month after his departure, a solicitor acting on his behalf informed Georgina that the composer intended to open legal proceedings to recover possessions, including the score of *Polyeucte*, that he had left behind at Tavistock House. This resulted in the usual misunderstandings, aggravated by an increasingly rapid and bitter exchange of letters. The correspondence ultimately reached the stage where Georgina asserted that he owed them more money than the value of his belongings that remained in their possession. In reply, Gounod invited her to send him a bill covering his entire stay at Tavistock House.

So I was to make out my bill.
I had been his sick nurse.
I had been his secretary.
I had been the round of the publishers for him.
I had written all sorts of puffs and adverts for him.
I had been his poet.
I had spent my money.
I had been general agent for all M. Gounod's affairs.
I had sung at all his concerts.
I had always sung his compositions.
I had played the devil so that he might appear an angel.

A bill he most certainly received, and a formidable document it turned out to be. The principal figure was £5,000, 'as compensation to some extent for the injury done by infamous calumnies, lies and libels.' The sum of £3,000 was listed as compensation for her being prevented from continuing her career as a singer, at which she could with ease have earned £1,000 a year during the three years of Gounod's stay. To this basic £8,000 was added a number of other items, including £45 for medical expenses, £8 for subscription and entrance fee to the Royal Yacht Club, £25 for 'a kind of advertising cart', £5 for harness, £6 18s 6d for 'a square wooden affair on wheels'. The final total was £9,791 2s 9d.

Gounod did not attempt to pay this bill, but, for the moment, Georgina hardly cared and made no move to enforce payment. She saw herself as a woman deserted and wronged. She dreamt, says Edward Grierson, 'of seeing her husband horsewhip Gounod on the steps of the Grand Opéra, a scene of which Paris was unfairly deprived through the failings of Harry's phlegmatic character.' Harry failed her in other ways, as well, and shortly afterwards they separated; she received £1,000 a year and the use of Tavistock House. By now, she saw Gounod for what he was, but her affection for him did not lessen. When a friend described him as the greatest hypocrite alive, she merely commented, 'So he is, poor darling old man.'

Reunited with his family in Paris, Gounod set about regaining the leading position he had previously held in French musical life. Offenbach saluted his return by staging *Jeanne d'Arc*, and a performance was given of *Gallia*. *Faust* was still immensely popular, being presented, on average, seventy times a year in Paris. By 1893, it was on the brink of its thousandth performance at the Opéra.

Established once more as France's principal musician, Gounod honoured his young friend Bizet by attending the première of *Carmen* in March 1875. During the second interval, he ardently embraced '*cher* Georges'. 'It's monumental', he proclaimed, showering him with compliments; 'What a work this is!' After Micaela's third-act aria 'Je dis que rien ne m'épouvante', he leaned forward and ostentatiously applauded over the edge of his box. Then, sitting back, he remarked that the melody was in fact his own. 'Georges has robbed me; take the Spanish airs and mine out of the score, and there remains nothing to Bizet's credit but the sauce that masks the fish.' This was overheard by the young Jacques-Emile Blanche. The embraces he had just seen Gounod give Bizet were, he later wrote, 'my first lesson in duplicity'. Three months later, Gounod delivered the eulogy over Bizet's grave. His voice shook with emotion; eventually he broke down and was unable to finish. He had now been back in Paris exactly a year.

Another seven years passed before Gounod returned to England, in August 1882, to conduct the first performance of his oratorio *Rédemption* in Birmingham. The Festival Committee offered him the amazing sum of £4,000 for the work, on which he had been engaged for several years. The magnitude of this payment gives us a good idea of Gounod's continuing popularity. With the contract finalised, he deleted the original dedication to his mother and his children (it did not include his wife) and put Queen Victoria's name in their place.

Rédemption and the price that had been paid for it attracted widespread interest. *The Musical Times* reported that the initial rehearsals, in London, of the oratorio were listened to by 'a considerable audience of privileged persons, among whom was his eminence Cardinal Newman'. Also present was Mary Cowden Clarke, who in *My Long Life*, says that after the first rehearsal, 'Gounod mustered sufficient English to address the orchestra with these kindly, courteous words: – "Gentlemen, I could rather have believed to have been a second performance than a first rehearsal, so correctly have you played."' Herman Klein was also at the first rehearsal.

Gounod said to me later, 'They are wonderful readers, these English players. There is scarcely a mistake that is due to inaccurate deciphering of the notes. And what makes it even more remarkable is that my work is so full of awkward chromatic progressions.' I ventured to observe that since he was last in London our orchestras had been turning their attention somewhat extensively to Wagner.

Gounod retorted quickly, 'Yes, I know that. But you will not tell me that Wagner's four semitones in "Tristan" or his slurred notes (*notes coulées*) in "Tannhäuser" required more delicate care than my "framework of the augmented fifth"' – an allusion to the peculiar harmonic structure which the composer had avowedly employed as the predominant feature of the accompanying chords in the 'Redemption'. I thought I detected a slight touch of scorn in his voice, and made no attempt to argue the point . . .

Gounod was one of the most fascinating men I have ever spoken with. His manner had a charm that was irresistible, and his kindly eyes, soft and melting as a woman's, would light up with a smile, now tender, now humorous, that fixed itself ineffaceably upon the memory. He could speak English fairly well, but preferred his own language, in which he was a brilliant conversationalist; and he could use to advantage a fund of keen, ready wit. He was influenced at that time by a recrudescence of that religious mysticism which had so strongly characterized his youthful career; but his tone, though earnest and thoughtful when he was dwelling upon his art, could brighten up with the lightness and gaiety of a true Parisian.

Also to have its première at the Birmingham Musical Festival was Stanford's specially commissioned Serenade in G, one of the key works in his early rise to fame. The conductor-in-chief of the Festival was Costa, who was now in the grip of his final illness. Like Gounod, Stanford would be conducting his own work at the Festival. Costa went out of his way to help him.

I got a message from the great man to call upon him at Eccleston Square, and found him in his study clad in a rather antique dressing-gown and surrounded by what looked like architectural maps and plans. He quite belied my anticipations of a haughty and stand-off reception, and was most genial and hospitable. He apologized for not conducting my work, on the score that he never made himself responsible for living writer's compositions, though he had none the less read through my MS. He then produced the plans, in order to instruct me where each instrument was placed, and who the players were. He had the seating (to an inch) both of St. George's Hall, where the London rehearsals were held, and of the Birmingham Town Hall, and described to me with great accuracy the height of the players above the conductor at the latter room. When I went up to rehearse in St. George's Hall, he planted himself at my elbow following every note of the score, and giving me a secret prod when he wanted a passage repeated which I had passed over. The first movement (in ¾ time) ended with a long *accelerando*, which I could not get to move on to my satisfaction. It was my own fault, for I continued beating three to a bar. Costa prodded, and whispered to me under his breath 'One beat will do it.' So it did, and his next prod was one of satisfaction accompanied by a most un-Costa-like wink. His care not to let the band know that he was coaching me was excessive, and both in London and in Birmingham I had good reason to be grateful for his tactful kindness.

He was not at all so kindly to Gounod, who conducted the first performance of the 'Redemption' on the same occasion. He disliked the Frenchman's pose and resented the suggestion of 'The Assumption of Gounod' which his attitude pictured. I fully expected to see a miracle: the opening of the Town Hall ceiling and the ascent of the composer into a layer of Black Country fog. There was nearly an open breach about the number of harps. Gounod wanted six, Costa would only consent (with many grumbles) to four. The secretary came to Costa in despair saying that 'M. Gounod insists on six harps.'

COSTA: The old fool! he thinks that he will go to Heaven with six harps! He shall have four' (*banging the table*).

During the Festival, Costa surprised Stanford by performing Mozart's Symphony No 40, not with a vast orchestra, but with no more than forty-five players. 'Costa loved a big noise,' Stanford wrote, 'but he had a sense of proportion.'

Gounod sat in front of me at this concert, and his ravings over Mozart were too exaggerated and theatrical to ring true. I could not help recalling the description given to me by Charles Hallé of his powers of *blague*. Hallé had visited Paris to give a recital, which took place at the Salle Érard in the afternoon; and he had gone to a party in the evening where he met Gounod. Gounod seized him by both hands and thanked him profusely for the pleasure his recital had given him, instancing one passage in a Beethoven Sonata which he hummed, which proved to him that 'no one – no one, my dear friend, except you could have interpreted that passage in so masterly a way. Even with my eyes shut, I should have known that Hallé was playing.' Immediately after, up came Madame Gounod, who began by apologizing for her and her husband's absence from the concert owing to a previous engagement. Hallé used to act to perfection the slow and silent vanishing away of Ch.G. after this *exposé*.

Costa, says Stanford, 'was a martinet, but could be a very kindly one.'

He was in his place to the second both at rehearsal and at concert, and woe to any player who was late. His first bassoon was once an hour behind time, and when Costa asked the reason, excused himself by reporting the arrival of an additional future bassoon in his family.

COSTA: 'Very well, Mr.———, I will excuse you this time, but do not let it occur again.'

The Birmingham Musical Festival of 1882 was Costa's last major engagement. He died in Hove in April 1884 at the age of seventy-six. In taking leave of him, we should remember that he made an important contribution to English musical life. He introduced badly needed discipline into orchestral playing, which in London in the 1830s and 1840s was often disastrously slack and haphazard, with star players vying with each other in their solos and not bothering to attend rehearsals. He subordinated every player to his will, thereby achieving integrated, accurate performances, the like of which, in his early days, had never before been heard in London. He was not an imaginative interpreter, but he had an impeccable stick technique and crystal-clear directions, as one would expect of a man who could successfully lead 4,000 musicians at the Handel Festivals. He undoubtedly prepared the way for more gifted interpreters by instilling a tradition of discipline in English orchestras that his successors might have been unable to provide. It is doubtful whether the Philharmonic Society orchestra that Wagner conducted for the 1855 season would have been able to satisfy his wayward demands, had it not been for their many years of training under Costa. They did not achieve much under Wagner, partly because they had been spoilt by the lucidity of Costa's directions and found it difficult to adapt to Wagner's eccentric gesticulations. Under Berlioz, however, they rose to almost undreamt-of heights. Meyerbeer, despite the way that Costa treated him, told the Rev J. E. Cox that he considered Costa to be 'the greatest *chef-d'orchestre* of the world'. He said this at the time of the preliminary Handel Festival in 1857, at which he heard finer massed singing than he had ever heard before, and he repeated it on the occasion of the 1862 International Exhibition, when Costa's orchestra, under Mellon, played his overture at sight without making a single mistake.

In the opera-house, too, Costa did valuable work, curbing the vagaries and extravagances of the great stars and redirecting them to the printed score. There was virtually no other conductor of his day who had the force of personality to be able to do this. Whatever his aversions to certain composers, he frequently produced excellent performances. When he conducted the English première of *Don Carlos* at Covent Garden in June 1867 (Costa had composed his own *Don Carlos* in 1844), it eclipsed the world première presentation in Paris three months earlier. Learning of this from Léon Escudier, Verdi wrote, 'So the London production is a success? If it is, what will they say at the Opéra, seeing that in London a work is staged in 40 days, whereas they take four months!! However, you are telling me nothing new when you say that Costa is a great conductor . . .'

Apart from subjugating singers, orchestral players, composers and virtually anybody else who crossed his path, Costa must be credited with having disciplined opera audiences, as Mapleson testifies.

> His love of order, punctuality, regularity in everything stood him in good stead. At many operatic theatres the performance begins some five or ten minutes after the time announced; at no theatre where Sir Michael conducted did it ever begin a minute late. The model orchestral chief arrived with a chronometer in each of his waistcoat pockets; and when, after consulting his timepieces, he saw that the moment for beginning had arrived, he raised his baton and the performance began. He did not even take the trouble to see that the musicians were in their places. He knew that, with the discipline he maintained, they must be there.

One of Costa's most devoted admirers was William Spark, who knew the conductor for thirty years and worked with him at the Bradford and Leeds Musical Festivals. He recalls him in this extract from his *Musical Memories*, published in 1888.

Undoubtedly he was the most popular *chef d'orchestre* that ever resided in England. I must confess that as a young man I felt somewhat frightened at the austere manner and sharp conversation of this famous *maestro*. For instance, I remember asking him after dinner whether he considered two conductors desirable for a musical society which was then about to be established in Leeds, whose duties should be exercised at alternate practices and performances. 'Consent to nothing of the sort,' he said, very rapidly. 'You must not do so, that is not business. If you are a conductor and wish to be somebody, stick to your own power and divide with nobody. You must assert your independence, and your men must be entirely under your own control if you wish to succeed.' No doubt it was acting upon this principle of cool and determined action in all he did that helped to secure for him the very high position which he occupied. At the same time, it must not be denied that very frequently his exhibitions of sharp temper, quick speech, and over-ruling manner led him to be regarded both with fear and jealousy by many who did not understand his real character . . .

No one, excepting perhaps his own devoted brother Raphael, ever knew to what an extent Sir Michael Costa extended his charity and generosity. Scores of impecunious, unfortunate members of his band owed him their very existence from his timely aid in sending them away to Hastings, St. Leonards-on-Sea, Eastbourne, or some other health-restoring, beautiful coast residence, entirely at his own expense . . .

Sir Michael Costa was never married. He was once engaged, I believe, to the mother of Mdme. Parepa Rosa [Euphrosyne Parepa Rosa, the wife of Carl Rosa; her mother was the singer Elizabeth Seguin], but the wooing was not successful, the engagement was broken off, and he declared he would 'never again be troubled with a woman.' . . .

No more truly loyal subject existed than Sir Michael Costa. From the time he gave pianoforte lessons to the Princess Royal, the future Empress of Germany, he was always imbued with a spirit of loyalty to her most gracious Majesty the Queen, and to all the members of the royal family. For many years he annually visited the Princess in Berlin, and used to tell me on his return of the happy moments he spent with her in playing over some of the old duets, especially his favourite Rossinian overtures, *William Tell, La Gazza Ladra, Il Barbiere*, etc.

He was never a great pianist, but an admirable accompanist and a sweet singer. He spoke and wrote English in a remarkably neat style and finish; his music copying was as clear and beautiful as Mozart's, and those who have seen the latter (as I have at Carl Reinecke's in Leipsic) will know what praise is here. The plate and presents he possessed were really extraordinary, chiefly from royalty; and he was decorated with orders from the Sovereigns of Germany, Turkey, the Netherlands, Würtemburg, Italy, etc.

At his beautiful house in Eccleston Square, I have had the honour and the enjoyment of many a good dinner with this truly great man. He was always animated and cheerful, full of racy anecdotes, and a willing listener to others; surely the friendship of such a man was worth having and gratefully remembering.

Sir Michael Costa died in May 1884, and was buried in Kensal Green Cemetery, in the presence of an immense concourse of musicians, nobility, friends, and the general public. I felt it to be my duty to go to town on purpose to attend his funeral. At the close of the beautiful Church of England service for the dead, wreaths and other floral tributes were cast upon the coffin by affectionate hands, and then the mourners followed the body to its last resting-place [not far from where Sir John Barbirolli now rests]. Those who witnessed the sad ceremony of his funeral must have come away with the conviction, as I did, that Sir Michael Costa was held in high and general esteem; for not only were tears shed by women over the coffin, but the eyes of many men were moistened with grief.

The 1882 Birmingham Musical Festival was one of the most successful festivals in which Costa ever took part; his long connection with Birmingham was later commemorated by naming after him Costa Green, near the town centre. Hailé was at the Festival and wrote to his daughter, 'Gounod was very nice and kissed me, *à la française*, which I thought unnecessary . . . Poor Costa looks awful, but gets through his work in spite of his illness; there is indomitable pluck in the old fellow.' Thanks to Costa's coaching, Stanford's Serenade in G was very well received; this carried his name across the Atlantic, and the work was conducted in New York in January 1884 by Theodore Thomas. It was *Rédemption*, however, that dominated the Festival and was such a colossal success that the Festival Committee were able to sell the piece to Novello's and make a handsome profit on their £4,000 outlay. Novello's, in turn, made a small fortune from it, much to Gounod's disgust and fury, for he had sold it outright. Over the coming year, performances took place in cities all over the world. Nevertheless, it proved to be little to the taste of a large number of musicians and critics, and their judgement has so far been adopted by posterity. Hallé found it 'a dull work and monotonous in the extreme'. *Musical Opinion*, after calling it 'a stagy imitation of Bach's sublime "Passions Musik"', said, 'The impression after listening to Gounod's "ouvrage de ma vie" [as he termed it] must be faithfully chronicled – it is one of dull monotony.' George Bernard Shaw wrote, 'I have no more to say generally than that, if you will only take the precaution to go in long enough after it commences and to come out long enough before it is over, you will not find it wearisome.'

Gounod spent nearly a week in Birmingham, conducting *Redempt-ion* twice, on 30 August and 1 September, and being fêted on all sides. At one dinner party to which he had been invited, Mary Cowden Clarke, who, like so many women, idolised him and his works, was thrilled to find herself sitting next to him. She at once spoke of her admiration for *Rédemption*, 'and when I began to ecsta-sise on the sublimity of the work, he owned that he nearly shed tears as he wrote its concluding bars, so intensely had he felt the delight of composing it.'

When I told him how keenly I sympathised with this feeling, and how I thought that, upon the completion of a work into which one has put one's heart, one feels inspired to commence another, he said, '*Commencer une oeuvre d'art qu'on aime, est comme un mariage d'amour.*' And as he uttered the words, what sparkling expression there was in his eloquent eyes!

After dinner he accompanied his daughter Jeanne in the song, 'Loin du Pays', by himself, and afterwards in the song, 'Souviens toi que je t'aime' from his opera 'Mireille'. She sang with charming sentiment and feeling. Just before he began accompanying her she made us laugh by saying '*Non, papa, tu te trompes*', because he had made some slight variation in the opening passage. The idea of telling my adored Gounod that he tripped in music seemed to me beyond measure strange and droll . . .

He was altogether fascinating to me personally as well as compos-erly . . .

One morning I had the pleasure of hearing Mr. Barnby try over the 'Sanctus' in Gounod's just-composed MS. Mass, and I heard that Gounod had said, in his finely imaginative way, 'When I composed that "Sanctus" I seemed to see the assembled multitude kneeling in devout contemplation of the holy mystery.'

Before returning to Paris, the triumphant composer made a short stay in London, where he visited the Lyceum to see Henry Irving and Ellen Terry in *Romeo and Juliet*. The incidental music was by his old friend Julius Benedict, at whose house he had first met Georgina. At the end of the third act, he went round to Irving's dressing-room and chatted with both the celebrated actor and his secretary, Bram Stoker. Stoker, the future author of *Dracula*, engaged the cherubic, loquacious Frenchman in conversation while Irving was on stage.

I asked him what in his estimation were the best words to which he had composed music. He answered almost at once, without hesitation: '"Oh that we two were maying!" I can never think of those words without emotion! How can one help it?' He spoke the last verse of the poem from *The Saint's Tragedy*:

'Oh! that we two lay sleeping
In our nest in the churchyard sod,
With our limbs at rest on the quiet earth's breast,
And our souls at home with God.'

As he spoke, the emotion seemed to master him more and more; at the last line the tears were running down his cheeks.

Stoker also asked him who he thought was the world's greatest composer.

'Mendelssohn! Mendelssohn is the best!' Gounod replied. 'But there is only one Mozart!'

In the eight years between Gounod's departure from Tavistock House and his return to England to conduct *Rédemption*, Georgina rose to national prominence as the result of a series of bizarre legal actions and other escapades in which she had been involved. At first, the public, who were forever avid to read of her latest adventures, saw her as a figure of fun, but in time they came to regard her with admiration. She was aided by her good looks, which hardly diminshed over the years. In 1882, she was forty-five and still remarkably pretty. Five years later, she appeared in an advertisement that was posted far and wide and on every London bus. This bore a picture of her and the words I AM 50 BUT MY COMPLEXION IS 17 – THANKS TO PEARS' SOAP.

During the late 1870s, she engaged in an extraordinary legal battle with her husband, who, roused out of his usual torpor, endeavoured to terminate their wranglings by having her committed to a private madhouse. He even initiated a kidnap attempt that she managed to evade by barricading herself in Tavistock House. Horrified at how easily she could have been captured and put away, with any number of mock-doctors ready to accept bribes to declare her insane, she became a fierce and popular campaigner for lunacy reform. She entered into litigation with several other people besides Harry and in 1880 went to prison for five weeks for libel. She was severely handicapped by being unable to proceed in civil action unless joined as plaintiff with her husband, to which he, of course, never consented, but so adroitly did she acquit herself in her legal affairs, and so persuasively campaign for the causes she espoused, that reform groups often sought her support, and she became a prominent member of the Land Reform Union. She had an excellent grasp of public relations and was imaginative in her use of the tools of advertising, once raining leaflets from the balcony of a concert hall on the stall-holders below.

As yet, she had done nothing about Gounod, apart from returning to him the score of *Polyeucte*. In August 1882, she journeyed up to Birmingham to hear *Rédemption* and to set eyes again on her 'poor darling old man'. But her reputation went before her, and the Festival Committee had prepared for her arrival. As she was approaching the Town Hall, a steward handed her a note informing her that she would not be allowed to enter. The committee plainly feared that she might stage some sort of demonstration or cause a disturbance. She ignored the note and pressed forward, to find her way barred by another steward and a plain-clothes policeman. She at once went to a local magistrate, but without success. She was also denied access to the second performance and so returned to London without having heard a note of *Rédemption*.

A fortnight later she purchased a copy of the official publication relating to the Married Woman's Property Act, which had just been passed through Parliament. This document now became her bible, the answer to all her troubles, for the Act ruled that a married woman could proceed in her own right in a civil action without requiring her husband to be co-plaintiff. Georgina's forensic career now blossomed overnight; she put forth a proliferation of writs in a widespread onslaught against those who, she deemed, had at some time or other caused her wrong. She set up in an office at 9 Red Lion Court with a staff of three. Before long, she was engaged in seventeen simultaneous actions, most of them in the High Court. Practically all of these she pleaded herself, astonishing everybody with her command of court procedure and her cogent advocacy. She was immediately successful, winning damages for £1,000 and £500. These were followed by a further £500 for a libel in respect of her eviction from Birmingham Town Hall. The barrister and dramatist Frank Philips first met her a few months after she had moved into Red Lion Court, and, in *My Varied Life*, has left an interesting account of his visit to her office.

The inner room was her sanctum and here she made tea and received her visitors. She was not at all the kind of person you would have expected to meet. She welcomed you pleasantly, put a few shrewd questions to you as to your business, and when she was satisfied would enter into conversation very freely. Her dress was plain, and with a certain picturesque primness about it, but was in perfect taste. As she talked she threw one knee over the other and rested both her palms upon it as a man might have done. The attitude was masculine, but perfectly natural. Her hair was cut short. Her features, which were public property, were extremely vivacious, and her eyes strangely brilliant and piercing. It was no flattery to say that if a woman is never older than she looks, Mrs. Weldon must then have been still young. Her conversation was no incoherent recital of grievances. You were surprised to find that she was singularly exact and precise. Dates, figures, facts were ready with her for anything. She could tell you with the lucidity of a practised counsel what her case was, what she considered her due, and what she believed to be her chance of getting it. You saw at once that any attempt to draw her out or to make her commit herself to an extravagance or exaggeration would be promptly detected and promptly resented. You might put to her the case against her as strongly as you pleased. You might tell her exactly the kind of things that were said of her. She would take it all with perfect good nature and absolute self-possession . . . She was confident of success. The Press, she used to tell you, began by attacking her, or else ignoring her. It was now beginning to think that there might be something in what she had to say. At this time she was winning all her cases, and she used to tell one that she intended to win them – every one. Her law was so much at her fingers' ends that she could spare some of it to those whom she considered oppressed . . .

That she was strangely unlike most other women was evident at once. Her manner, no doubt, was feminine and tender. One could understand in a moment the power she claimed to exercise over children and animals. But with all this there was a strange masculine thread in her character. She behaved like a woman, but she thought and expressed herself as a man would, and could beyond all question make herself extremely disagreeable if she chose to do so. In speaking of those against whom she has had to pit herself, her tone was as trenchant as the pen of George Eliot, and she used it mercilessly . . .

Without saying anything definite, and while she was occupied in pouring out tea and dispensing wafer-like slices of bread and butter, Mrs. Weldon managed to impress you with the idea that her work was planned out, and that she saw her way to carry it through. If you complimented her upon her success as an advocate, she would laugh and tell you that barristers as a rule were very poor creatures, and that they took very little interest in the cases entrusted to them . . . Mrs. Weldon did not believe in paid advocates. She regarded them as shams, and, indeed, she had a very wholesome detestation for every form of imposition or pretence. She saw the world moving round and round like some vast piece of machinery, and she saw that in the course of its motion are worked numberless acts of infinite oppression and wrong. It was useless to tell her that the machinery as a whole worked admirably. You could not divert her from the particular case of injustice in which she was at the moment engaged. Her attitude was that of the old knight-errant who did not trouble himself very much about the abstract principles of law or justice, but rode out to discover individual cases of oppression and to decide them on his own authority and to redress them according to his own judgement. Mrs. Weldon practically became the recognized legal adviser of women who had been wronged and ill-treated. Her two rooms in Red Lion Court came to be known as a sort of legal dispensary, where more or less reliable advice was always to be obtained.

All this with her was a pure labour of love. It was a part of her mission and she gloried in it. Difficulties as to her status did not daunt her in the least. She was ready at any moment to appear in Court and to argue any question. I may add that throughout all her fighting she was perfectly fair and bore no malice whatever.

One of the first people towards whom she turned her litigious attention was the comparatively inoffensive conductor Jules Rivière. They had given some concerts together, but had fallen out after a petty misunderstanding that Georgina somehow contrived to magnify into awesome proportions, leading her eventually to regard him as a fiendish monster steeped in every conceivable shade of depravity and moral turpitude. She libelled and slandered him on and off during the late seventies, at length calling him, somewhat inventively, 'an escaped felon and a trigamist'. This was too much for poor Rivière, and he took her to court. It was this case that resulted in her being sent to Newgate Prison for five weeks for libel. Thanks to the Married Woman's Property Act of 1882, she was now much better placed to start harrying him all over again, principally by dragging him frequently through the law courts, where she was able to make rings round him.

Rivière, who was born in France in 1819, had led an eventful life. As a young army bandsman in Verdun, he was compelled to witness the execution of a trombonist who had struck a bandmaster with his trombone. He recalled this tragic occurrence in *My Musical Life and Recollections*, published in 1893.

A deal of sympathy was expressed for the young fellow, who had been punished by the bandmaster, a German, for an imperfect rendering of a certain passage on his trombone, the punishment inflicted having been two days' confinement. This unjust and tyrannical treatment led the trombone player to commit the offence, for which he suffered death in presence of all the troops of the garrison; the different regiments being drawn up in a large square on the Place d'Armes, in front of the citadel, twelve soldiers firing at the word of command, and sending their comrade into eternity. The preliminary was first gone through of the sentence being read over to him, and the buttons torn off his coat. I shall not forget the scene.

Rivière took all kinds of different jobs connected with music, managing to work his way up to conductor. In his capacity as director of the afternoon concerts in the Jardin d'Hiver in Paris, he met Offenbach, with whom he had a fight. There seems to have been some confusion over whether or not a singer from Offenbach's theatre had his permission to appear at one of Rivière's concerts. Rivière understood that Offenbach had given his permission, but at the last moment this was apparently denied.

Not in the best of tempers I called in the evening to see Offenbach at the stage door of the theatre, and asked him for an explanation, but, as this was not forthcoming, and as my rage, I suppose, was increasing, from words we soon came to blows. It was an undignified scrimmage, of course, as all such scrimmages are, but in moments of passion men sometimes lose self-control. Except that we each had to look for our hats that had rolled upon the floor, to set our collars in order, and pick up the spectacles that each had lost, no serious results ensued from the undignified scuffle that had taken place.

Rivière came to England in 1857 and during the next two decades built a reputation as a conductor of light-classical music. He did well in London, but his greatest successes were in Blackpool and Llandudno in the eighties and nineties. His showmanship was much to the taste of provincial audiences. His arrival on the platform was always marked by the deferential salutations of a uniformed commissionaire, who, stepping forward, tendered an ornate baton and white gloves on a silver salver. Having graciously availed himself of these, Rivière would lower himself into a luxurious armchair, facing the audience, from which he would conduct the music. His lapel sprouted flowers. In *Memories and Music*, Dan Godfrey stated that the conductor 'received so many floral offerings from his fair admirers that he had a special collar made to his coat for the purpose of holding at least twenty buttonholes.' The young Henry Wood went to a Rivière concert on the Esplanade at Llandudno, later recording the event in *My Life of Music*.

As I took my seat I saw an elderly gentleman seated in a gilded arm-chair, *facing* the audience. He was elegantly dressed in a velvet jacket on the lapel of which reposed a huge spray of orchids more fitted for a woman's corsage. He held a bejewelled ivory baton in his hand from which dangled a massive blue tassel. This he wound round his wrist. He bowed ceremoniously to the audience and tapped loudly on his golden music-stand. Still seated, he began the overture to *Mignon*.

It was a sad day for the conductor when he first provoked Georgina's displeasure, and he drew scant consolation from winning his cases against her: 'I still have reason to remember Mrs. Weldon all my life, for the litigation she drew me into cost me no less a sum than £4,000.'

Having cut her teeth on Rivière and several other minnows, Georgina decided it was time to go for the biggest fish of all, Gounod. She sued him for libel, basing her case on a number of calumnious statements he had made about her since his return to the safety, so he imagined, of Paris. And she had not forgotten the bill covering his stay at Tavistock House, in regard to which she also sought compensation.

Weldon versus Gounod, an exceptionally involved case, was a long time unfolding. Gounod's lawyers put up a tenacious defence, causing delay after delay, so that little progress was achieved. Months of inactivity would often be followed by the briefest of hearings, with Georgina in and out of court in a matter of moments. At length, however, in the spring of 1885, the final round was reached, and the case was tried in full at the Middlesex Sheriff's Court in Red Lion Square. Unfortunately, at this vital moment, Georgina could not be on hand to plead the case. A few months earlier, Rivière had once again decided he had taken more than he could stomach. He sued for a fresh libel, and this time Georgina was put away for six months, being detained in Holloway from March to September 1885. Despite her low opinion of barristers, she had occasionally employed them in the past, for the simple reason that, with such a welter of litigation on her hands, she could not be in two places, or courts, at the same time. Now, she instructed two barristers to act for her: Frank Philips, whom she much admired, and the distinguished advocate William Bowen Rowlands. Gounod's defence was led by Alfred Lyttleton, who was later Colonial Secretary under Balfour. Through a special dispensation, Georgina was able to attend the hearing, accompanied by a 'lady-in-waiting'.

Bowen Rowlands made a brilliant concluding address, which left nobody in doubt that Georgina would win the case. After the jury retired, Bowen Rowlands speculated with Philips on how much they might expect to be awarded. 'Just write down what damages you think they will give', he told Philips, 'and I will do the same, and we will see who is nearest.'

> I wrote down £2,000 and he wrote down £1,000. 'Oh,' he said, '£2,000 is absurd. They will never give that. The Sheriff's jury, if they give £100, think that they have set up the plaintiff for life.' 'Well,' I answered, 'I think they will give at least £2,000, and they certainly ought to after your speech. If ever I saw a man get hold of a jury, it was you on that occasion.' They shortly returned to Court and gave a verdict of £10,000, as far as I know the largest that had ever been given for libel up to that time.

To this were added two further sums, amounting to £1,640, as compensation for expenses incurred during the time of Gounod's residence at Tavistock House.

Outside the court, Georgina was cheered as she began her journey back to Holloway. She happily contemplated 'the excitement in Paris and the rage of the old man!' Now she would be able to 'bother him for the remainder of his life'. It later proved impossible to gain a similar judgement in Paris. As long as the composer kept outside England, he would be able to avoid paying the £11,640, but, if he once set foot on English soil, he would be liable for the entire amount.

This caused him an immediate problem, for he was already committed to travelling to Birmingham in August 1885 to conduct the first performance of his new oratorio *Mors et Vita*, for which Novello's were paying another £4,000. Dvořák, who was just beginning to make his way in England, was so alarmed to learn of this colossal figure that he wrote to the publishers, beseeching them, 'Pray do not pay Mr. Gounod, who truly does not need it, so immense sums, for what would be left for me?'

Gounod had no alternative other than to withdraw from his Birmingham engagement. This made headline news in England and France, and even as far afield as the United States. Had it been a matter of £1,000, Gounod might well have come, but £11,640 was clearly too high a price to pay. The première was therefore conducted by Richter, Costa's successor at the Festival, scoring a handsome success, with receipts of £25,000, and prompting the Queen to send a message of congratulations to the absent composer. Like *Rédemption*, the work was not well received by many musicians. Hallé said of the 'Tubae ad ultimum judicium', 'If they play that music at the Resurrection, I shall refuse to rise.' Parry found the oratorio 'sentimental, dawdling, pointless'. Richter himself commented 'Horrendum est!', echoing the first words of the text. Nevertheless, *Mors et Vita* proved almost as popular as *Rédemption,* and the Queen ordered a performance to be given at the Albert Hall. Discreet inquiries were made, to ascertain whether Georgina might be prepared to waive her legal rights for the occasion and thus permit Gounod to come and conduct the work, but she refused. Londoners took to the new oratorio, and *Mors et Vita* nights at the Albert Hall soon vied with *Rédemption* nights in the size of audience they could attract. In his *Portraits et Souvenirs,* Saint-Saëns wrote, 'I have seen, on one of those dreadful black and rainy nights in which London specializes, the enormous auditorium of the Albert Hall packed to its upper galleries with an audience of 8,000 silent and attentive people listening devoutly, while their eyes followed the text, to a monster performance of *Mors et Vita* given by a thousand performers, a gigantic organ and the finest soloists in England.'

Far from allowing Gounod to come to England, Georgina added a few more touches to her case; one step on English soil, and he would now be arrested and imprisoned. But his popularity continued to rise, as F. F. Buffen's *Musical Celebrities,* published in 1889, makes plain.

Had Gounod produced nothing save his *Faust,* that most beautiful of modern operas, he would, by all lovers of music, have been regarded as the first of living composers, and earned the applause of the musical world. The poetic and mystic character of Goethe's legend has so much in harmony with the temperament of the French composer, and the exquisite love-music, with which he has let 'all heaven into our eyes', is so enchanting as not only to cast into shade the numerous settings of this subject by others, but has served to raise Gounod to a pinnacle of fame unattainable by any of his contemporaries.

In altered circumstances, might Gounod have been invited to Cambridge? Progressive opinion viewed his music with lukewarm enthusiasm, and even undoctrinaire composers like Sullivan and Cowen, with whom he had much in common, were less than ardent admirers. Sullivan applied the adjective 'morbid' to Gounod, and Cowen wrote of his 'monotony and triviality'. Perhaps we can best make up our minds by turning to Stanford's *A History of Music,* published in 1916.

Charles Gounod, a Parisian *pur sang*, was a curious compound of music and theology, picturesque and superficial in both, endowed with a gift of melodic invention and a certain poetry which showed itself at its best in his first book of songs, the well known, *Vingt Mélodies*. He played with the fringe of great things, but was clever enough to avoid swimming in deep water. He was attracted to the lurid, but was often 'frightened with false fire.' He produced one opera which is an abiding success, *Faust*, and many others which are quite forgotten, though not devoid of a charm which was very far-reaching in its day, and was especially noticeable in *Mireille*. Later in life he betook himself to oratorio writing, and produced (with much trumpeting) two works, the *Redemption* and *Mors et Vita*, both of them (to quote Carlyle) 'poor husks of things', but sufficiently sentimental temporarily to capture the unthinking part of the English public, appealing alike to Catholics, Anglicans, and the Salvation Army. In his own country these excursions into realms so foreign to himself and his countrymen had no success. But his early songs and *Faust* remain, and prove his right to a high position in the French school.

CHAPTER 5

RUBINSTEIN

November 1892 drew to a close. The jubilee was now no more than six months away. Brahms and Verdi were not coming; Dvořák was in America; Gounod could not be considered.

Whom next to invite? The *Cambridge Review* of 1 December 1892 gave thought to the matter.

> That Signor Verdi should have declined is not to be wondered at, considering that he will be eighty next year, and that the acceptance would have meant the fatigues of a journey to England. It is now sixteen years since a similar honour was declined by Herr Brahms.
>
> If the Senate wish to confer an honour upon a composer outside the British Isles, it is difficult to see to which quarter to turn. It is hazardous to make conjectures, but the names which most readily occur to mind are possibly those of Rubinstein and Edvard Grieg: but, except for the reasons which should make next year a memorable one in the history of Cambridge music, there is no reason why such an honour should be held out with too lavish a hand; and the reasons already alleged may have quite their full weight with the eminent composers whom we have mentioned.

It is worth noting the words, 'If the Senate wish to confer an honour upon a composer outside the British Isles . . .' There seems to be an implication here that any honorary doctorates could, or should, go first to native musicians. This echoes the strong feeling of the time that Britain's composers were a match for those of any other country. Alexander Mackenzie expressed such a view as early as December 1886 in an address delivered in Manchester to the National Society of Professional Musicians. 'We may certainly say', he told his audience, 'that England can now hold her own against the Continental nations.' Citing Sullivan, Parry, Stanford, Cowen and other British composers, he suggested that 'excepting Verdi, Gounod and Brahms, of whom only the last may be said to be in full activity, the Englishmen named by me are the peers, if not more than the peers, of their musical contemporaries in other countries . . . I use the word (English) in the comprehensive sense in which it is current on the Continent.'

187

The same opinion is forcefully advanced in H. C. Banister's essay
The Music of the Victorian Era, based on lectures that he gave during the
nineties.

And the English composers of this generation, no longer marked or
fettered by the insularity and self-containedness of the time anterior to
that which we have been considering, but keenly alive to all external
influences, quick to assimilate, eclectically, whatever finds affinity in their
own minds, but withal having English characteristics of their own, are
writing – not, as was said by some critic a few years ago, German music,
nay, nor English music, but *music*. They are expressing 'the spirit of the
age', very hard to define or characterize, in artistic matters. They are,
somewhat defiantly, almost petulantly, throwing off what they esteem
pedantic fetters, ridding themselves of what they think antiquated formu-
laries or formalities, even forms, and are, so to speak, exploring, launching
out, experimentalizing – shall I say annexing and colonizing? – and thus
exhibiting English characteristics. While we have among us writers with
the enthusiasm and ability of Arthur Seymour Sullivan, Alexander
Campbell Mackenzie, Frederic Hymen Cowen, Charles Villiers Stanford,
Charles Hubert Hastings Parry, and others who show their English
nationality, not by insular narrowness, but by their all-embracingness, we
may well believe and hope that upon English music, as upon the British
empire, the sun will never set, until the cataclysm occurs that shall bring
the New Zealander to the ruins of London Bridge.

Sullivan, Mackenzie, Cowen, Stanford, Parry: again and again
during the 1890s we find these five linked together as the leading
English composers of the time. In Charles Willeby's *Masters of English
Music*, published in June 1893, there are five chapters, one each on
Sullivan, Mackenzie, Cowen, Stanford and Parry; nothing in the
introduction suggests that the choice could have been otherwise.

Many people would no doubt have supported the *Cambridge
Review*'s desire for a British composer to be honoured during the
CUMS celebrations. However, an unfortunate situation had arisen.
Sullivan had received his doctorate in 1876, Parry was given his in
1883, and Mackenzie and Stanford had theirs in 1888. This left only
Cowen. But to honour him on this occasion – and certainly there was
no other British candidate of his stature – would have been to give the
impression that he stood first in the ranks of contemporary native
composers. Moreover, there could have been few who would have
relished the idea of making Cowen the star of the jubilee, for, much as
his music was admired, he excited little enthusiasm as a person.
There have been handed down to us an abundance of amusing anec-

dotes and affectionate reminiscences of Sullivan, Stanford, Mackenzie and Parry, but of Cowen we have next to none. The few tales that we do have of him come almost exclusively from his own pen, in his memoirs *My Art and My Friends*. This is actually a very pleasant autobiography, but the fact remains that Cowen was, on the whole, an outsider, possessed of acquaintances rather than friends.

Frederic Cowen was born in Kingston, Jamaica, in January 1852, of English and Jewish blood. He came to London at the age of four, when his father was appointed treasurer to Her Majesty's Theatre. He exhibited highly developed musical abilities from an early age, playing the piano before Thalberg when still a child and giving his first recital at eleven. At thirteen he won a place at the Leipzig Conservatoire, where he studied under Moscheles, Reinecke and Ferdinand David. In *My Art and My Friends*, he recalls one of Moscheles' oddities – 'namely, a fastidiousness with regard to the height of the piano-stool or chair on which he sat that bordered almost on eccentricity, and he would increase or lessen this height with the help of a book, or a single piece, or even a single *sheet* of music, until he literally found his level to the fraction of an inch.' Cowen went to a number of Reinecke's Gewandhaus concerts. He found him capable, but uninspiring, 'and he had a peculiar way when he was conducting of beating time with his head in inverse ratio to his baton, so that when the latter was up his head was down, and *vice versa*, which reminded one for all the world of those little Chinese figures that, once set wagging, take a long time to stop. Domestically, he was blessed with a very numerous progeny – I think he had thirteen or fourteen of them. At all events, I know that whenever one went to his house they were all over the place . . .'

During his early teens, Cowen made great strides as a composer and, at fifteen, had an overture performed at one of Alfred Mellon's promenade concerts at Covent Garden. His next period of study was in Berlin, where he became a pupil of Tausig, whom Liszt so admired. It was there, at the home of Eugen Franck, that he made the acquaintance of George Henschel, then eighteen, who recalled their first encounter in *Musings and Memories of a Musician*.

The meeting between the young Englishman and me, at a supper-party arranged for the occasion by our mutual friend, developed in the course of the evening into something like an Olympic contest. Evidently bent on doing credit to his master, the young Englishman, a striking-looking, handsome boy of sixteen, with finely-cut features and very pleasant manners, played wonderfully well, thus spurring me on to do my best when *my* turn came. So we went on, actually for hours, he playing and I singing, to the great delight of our host, who, equally interested in us both, confessed to being baffled as to which of us in his opinion had the greater talent, until, at the end of a most enjoyable evening, he had to be satisfied with declaring that both Frederic Cowen – for that was the boy's name – and I had the chance of a brilliant future before us . . .

At the end of 1868, Cowen returned to London and completed his training, under Hallé. In December 1869, his First Symphony and First Piano Concerto were performed at St James's Hall. Though not yet eighteen, he was already becoming well known in the London musical world, both as composer and pianist. He was also doing well enough to be able to take rooms almost next door to Robert Browning, who 'was a conspicuous figure in our neighbourhood by reason of the curious habit he had of always walking with his umbrella or stick over his shoulder as if he were carrying a gun.'

For a time, like Sullivan before him, he became one of Costa's assistants at Covent Garden.

Sir Michael ruled everyone with a rod, or rather, baton of iron. He was scarcely what one would call a genial man, but he was very just, and of a not unkindly nature at heart, though he usually hid it under an abrupt and far from prepossessing manner, which made us all very frightened of him. One day at rehearsal, after I had been waiting about on the stage for some time to know if I had any duties to perform, I went up to him and asked him if there was anything he wished me to do, to which he replied in a loud angry voice, his eyelids twitching nervously, as they always did: 'Yes; go home and work, and don't stop idling your time here!' But he could unbend at times, and I remember quite a pleasant chat I had with him at his own house, in the course of which he told me some of his early experiences, and took out of a drawer a card with some tiny toy razors on it that had been sent to him satirically when, as a beardless youth, he first stepped into the conductor's seat at the opera. That he had treasured these for nearly fifty years showed that he was not entirely without sentiment o humour. It was also to him that I owed my first important festival com mission – *i.e.*, my cantata, 'The Corsair', produced at Birmingham in 1876.

It is worth recalling that Costa was also among the first to commiss ion anything from Sullivan, inviting him to write music for the balle *L'Île enchantée*, presented at Covent Garden in May 1864, when the composer was twenty-two.

The Corsair was well received at the Birmingham Musical Festival, and four months later, in December 1876, Cowen's opera *Pauline* created like enthusiasm when it was introduced at the Lyceum. His reputation was then undoubtedly higher than that of Stanford, his junior by eight months; he was not far short of emulating the speed with which Sullivan had established himself a decade earlier.

During the late seventies, he continued to gain attention through his compositions and piano-playing. He also developed into an excellent conductor, and in 1880 was appointed to direct both the Saturday evening concerts at St James's Hall and the promenade concerts at Covent Garden. More notably, during the same year, he brought out his delightful Third Symphony, the *Scandinavian*, which scored an instantaneous success and took his name across Europe. The *Scandinavian Symphony* was the most widely played symphony by a British composer until the advent, in 1887, of Stanford's *Irish Symphony*, which it closely rivalled in popularity throughout the nineties. Its successor, Symphony No 4, the *Welsh*, dating from 1884, also became well known. In *Half a Century of Music in England*, published in 1889, Francis Hueffer, the music critic of *The Times* and a champion of Berlioz, Liszt and Wagner, wrote that 'Mr. Cowen's symphonies – particularly the 'Scandinavian' and the 'Welsh', which have made their way to most European and American concert-rooms – I am prepared to class amongst the best specimens of symphonic writing that could be produced by any living master at home or abroad.' Many practising musicians also had the highest respect for Cowen, and the following passage from *My Musical Recollections* by the conductor Wilhelm Kuhe, published in 1896, reflects the esteem in which he was held.

> To enumerate even a tithe of the oratorios and other sacred works, operas, symphonies and drawing-room pieces with which Frederic Cowen has enriched the world would be a formidable task indeed. No reference to the distinguished composer, no matter how brief, should, however, omit mention of that beautiful, descriptive, richly-coloured, and pre-eminently scholarly work, the Scandinavian Symphony, a composition which, not only in this country, but in every part of the Continent, is rightly regarded as a *chef d'oeuvre*.

As Hueffer mentions, the *Scandinavian Symphony* entered the repertoire, too, of a number of American orchestras. In Boston, for instance, it was performed four times before the turn of the century, the première, in that city, having been conducted by Henschel in 1883; the first performance in the United States was given in New York in November 1882 under Theodore Thomas.

Apart from his symphonies and other orchestral works, like the charming suite *The Language of Flowers* (1880), Cowen also achieved success during the eighties with three choral compositions, the oratorios *St Ursula* (1881) and *Ruth* (1887), and the cantata *The Sleeping Beauty* (1885). A number of his salon pieces proved extremely popular as well. By 1882, his growing reputation both as composer and conductor afforded him the opportunity of travelling abroad, and in that year he went to Vienna to hear Richter conduct the Austrian première of the *Scandinavian Symphony*; he then journeyed on to Budapest, where he himself directed the work. Through visits like these, he was able to get to know Brahms and Liszt. In Milan, he became acquainted with Rubinstein, and in Copenhagen, Gade. His participation in the Birmingham Musical Festival enabled him to meet Dvořák.

Cowen's abilities as a conductor developed so propitiously that, when Costa died in 1884, Sullivan regarded him as the first choice (with Stanford, the second) to take over the conductorship of the Birmingham Musical Festival. Richter's eventual appointment to the post was 'an affront to all of us English', Sullivan wrote to his friend Joseph Bennett, music critic of the *Daily Telegraph*. To Herman Klein, he again expressed his regret that a foreigner had been selected. 'If we had no men who could do the work, I would say nothing – but we have . . .'

However, in 1888, Cowen's talent with the baton was fully recognised when he was made permanent conductor of the Philharmonic Society, in succession to Sullivan, who was influential in securing his appointment. Nevertheless, this still only came about after offers to Bülow, Rubinstein and Joachim had been declined. Also in 1888, Cowen went to Australia for six months, where, for the remarkable fee of £5,000, he took up the position of musical director of the Melbourne Centennial Exhibition. The trip proved to be a huge success; he was fêted on all sides, constantly besieged by deputations and other well-wishers, and made the recipient of banquets and all manner of hospitalities.

He excited similar enthusiasm in his initial concerts with the Philharmonic, and at the conclusion of his first season the general meeting of the society put it on record that the orchestra's performances had been 'of unsurpassed excellence'. He continued to delight

Philharmonic audiences with his conducting for a further four years, but at the end of the 1892 season he was dismissed after an incident at a concert that took place on 15 June of that year. The final item on the programme was Beethoven's *Pastoral Symphony*, for which only a single rehearsal had been allowed – 'time insufficient', Cowen later wrote, 'for what I considered an adequate preparation of the music.'

> This thought was still in my mind when the hour of the concert arrived, and wishing to justify myself with the audience, I turned round to them before beginning the symphony (it was the Pastoral) and asked them to excuse any shortcomings there might be in the rendering of the work, as the rehearsal had not been as thorough as I could have desired. It was a thoughtless and unwise thing to do, as events proved, but one's impetuosity often gets the better of one's judgement, and this was so in my case. The directors took umbrage at my action, and, perhaps, not quite without reason, although from what I afterwards heard, their grievance was not so much against what I had said as against the fact of my having made a speech at all, an act which they contended was their own prerogative and no one else's. They said nothing to me at the moment about the matter, but a few weeks later I received an official letter from them, giving me my *congé*, and it was some years before my name again appeared in any of their programmes.

Cowen's dismissal, a much publicised event, was still fresh in people's memories six months later. In such circumstances, for Cambridge to offer him an honorary degree, to be received in June of the following year, would inevitably involve the CUMS and the university in musical politics. Furthermore, a number of progressive musicians of the day, including Stanford, were not particularly impressed by Cowen's overall achievement. They were neither jealous of the popularity of his music, nor impervious to its undoubted charms, but they detected in Cowen a lack of the earnestness and artistic aspiration that were then so highly prized in composers.

Stanford certainly seems to have admired Cowen's music and valued it to a greater degree than did many of his contemporaries; otherwise he would hardly have commissioned Cowen's Fifth Symphony for the CUMS. It was in connection with the première of this work that Cowen somehow came under the impression that, on the occasion of his visit to Cambridge to attend the performance, he was to be given an honorary doctorate, along with Alexander Mackenzie and Arthur Goring Thomas, each of whom also had pieces being played. At that time, June 1887, Macfarren was still Professor of Music, but had only five months to live.

The concert was held during Commemoration Week (1887) and it was hoped (as I was privately informed) that the University would avail itself of our presence in Cambridge to confer on us the Honorary Degree of Musical Doctor. This did not come to pass. Our names were indeed submitted to Macfarren, who as Professor of Music had to be consulted in the matter; but he raised an unexpected difficulty by adding two or three more names to the list – a wholesale order that the Senate did not feel disposed to carry out.

As we have seen, Mackenzie received his degree a year later, at the same time as Stanford. For Cowen, there had since been no further intimation of impending honour, and there was none, either, for Goring Thomas, who in March 1892 committed suicide by throwing himself under a train at West Hampstead Station. He had been deranged by a terrible accident in which he fell on his head, he had lost his fiancée and had fears of going blind. Stanford orchestrated his unfinished cantata *The Swan and the Skylark*.

Beyond Sullivan, Mackenzie, Stanford, Parry and Cowen, there were, in December 1892, no British composers who bulked very large in the musical world, though Edward German, at thirty, already had a promising reputation. So, if Cowen was not to be honoured, there was really no question of any other native musician being considered in his stead.

————————

'It is hazardous to make conjectures,' suggested the *Cambridge Review*, 'but the names which most readily occur to mind are possibly those of Rubinstein and Edvard Grieg.'

That Anton Rubinstein should have been mentioned ahead of Grieg reflects the high opinion then held of him in many quarters. The renowned Russian composer and pianist, now sixty-two, had made his London début at the age of 12, giving his first recital in Hanover Square in May 1842. Moscheles noted in his diary that the boy 'has fingers light as feathers, and with them the strength of a man.' Throughout his initial stay in the capital, young Anton made a favourable impression on all who heard him, including William Ayrton of the *Examiner*, who, as former music director of the King's Theatre, had staged the English premières of *Don Giovanni*, *Così fan tutte* and *Die Zauberflöte*.

In private parties he has displayed his powers as a performer on the pianoforte, and excited the astonishment not only of those who are easily and willingly surprised by youthful genius, but of professors who judge of a performance by its own ability. This lad – who is small for his age and very slenderly made, though his head is of large dimensions – executes with his hands the very same music in which Thalberg excels, and to perform which, it has been jocosely said, this celebrated artist has been furnished with five fingers and two thumbs to each hand, put in motion by steam power. We have heard Rubinstein play some of these pieces, and can answer for the unimpeachable correctness of his performance; and, what is still more remarkable, for the force by which, through some unparalleled gift of nature, he is enabled to exert a degree of muscular strength which his general conformation, and especially that of his arms and hands, would have induced us to suppose he could not possibly possess. To gratify those whose taste leads them to prefer fashionable music, he plays the fantasias of Liszt, Thalberg, Herz, etc.; but when exhibiting before real connoisseurs he chooses for his purpose the elaborate compositions of the old German school – the learned and difficult fugues of Sebastian Bach and Handel – all of which he executes with an ease as well as a precision which very few masters are able to attain; and, to add to the wonder, he plays everything from memory, this faculty being apparently as fully developed in him as it is now and then, though rarely, in adults who have perfected it by long practice.

Rubinstein performed in the highest circles, even before the Queen, whom he described as 'young and pretty'.

Shortly after his visit to London, he had his first composition published. This was reviewed by Schumann with the characteristic generosity that he showed towards all young musicians. He found nothing extraordinary about Rubinstein's *étude*, but 'since the little piece is predominantly melodious, without actually presenting us with a fine or novel melody, we are led to hope that he has already begun to understand the true essence of music and may continue to develop his talents happily in this sense.' Schumann maintained his interest in the young Russian to the end of his life; even during his final, pathetic confinement in Endenich, he asked Joachim for news of Rubinstein.

The boy prodigy was soon moving in rarefied musical society, mixing with Mendelssohn, Meyerbeer and Liszt and later with Wagner and Brahms. He got on well with all of them, though, as he wrote to Liszt, he could not make up his mind about Brahms as a person. 'I find it difficult to describe precisely the impression he has made on me; for the drawing-room, he is not polished enough; for the concert-hall, he is not fiery enough; for the country, he is not simple enough; for the city, not cultured enough . . .'

By the time Rubinstein returned to England in May 1857, he was a European celebrity. On this occasion, he played his Third Piano Concerto at a Philharmonic Society concert conducted by Sterndale Bennett. His performance was well received, but the concerto was not. Among the audience was Arthur Sullivan, then fifteen, and he, too, was unimpressed by Rubinstein the composer.

> I enjoyed the Philharmonic very much last Monday, all except Rubinstein. He has wonderful strength in the wrists, and particularly so in octave passages, but there is a good deal of clap-trap about him. As for his composition, it was a disgrace to the Philharmonic. I never heard such wretched, nonsensical rubbish; not two bars of melody or harmony together throughout . . .

At this stage in his career, Rubinstein was usually accorded a warmer reception if he avoided his own compositions. When he returned to the Philharmonic the following year and performed Weber's *Concertstück* and solos by Mozart, Beethoven, Field and Mendelssohn, he was greeted with wholehearted enthusiasm. 'Dashing, fiery, and forcible throughout', wrote Chorley of the Weber interpretation; 'the last movement was taken with whirlwind speed.'

His next visit to London was not until 1867, when he appeared at a Philharmonic concert conducted by William Cusins and played his Piano Concerto No 4. This was destined to become his most popular orchestral work, though it had to wait until memorable performances by Paderewski, in 1891, and by Sapellnikov, in 1892, finally established it as a part of London musical life. He visited London again in 1869, playing Schumann's Piano Concerto and a piece by Handel at another Philharmonic engagement.

During the 1870s, his popularity as a composer grew appreciably, and he became a familiar name on English concert programmes. By now, works like the *Melody in F*, the so-called 'Rêve angélique' from *Kammenoi-Ostrov*, the Romance in E flat major and other small-scale piano pieces, as well as a number of songs, were being regularly bought for home consumption, while the Piano Trio No 3 was frequently featured in chamber recitals. His best known orchestral work was the *Ocean Symphony*, No 2, dedicated to Liszt. First heard in Leipzig in November 1854, it received its English première at a Musical Art Union concert in May 1861, when it was conducted by

Karl Klindworth. Manns played it for the first time at the Crystal Palace in 1871, and Hallé, in Manchester, in 1877. Rubinstein himself directed the symphony at the Crystal Palace in 1877; in 1879, it was performed at a Philharmonic Society concert, with Cusins conducting. By then the work had been heard frequently in Russia and also in Vienna, Paris and other European cities. It was played in New York in 1871 and in Boston in 1873; the Boston Symphony Orchestra performed it six times between 1883 and 1896, which compares favourably with eight hearings for each of Brahms's first two symphonies during the same period. Nevertheless, despite all these performances, the *Ocean* did not sufficiently capture the imagination of the concert-going public to gain a permanent place in the orchestral repertoire.

Rubinstein's trip to London in May 1876 proved to be his most successful so far. He and Cusins performed his Fifth Piano Concerto with the Philharmonic on 1 May; he also played two solos, by Haydn and Beethoven, during the same concert and acted as accompanist for two of his songs. He gave piano recitals on 3, 10, 16 and 25 May and took part in a chamber concert with Wieniawski on 20 May, which included a memorable interpretation of the 'Kreutzer' Sonata.

His 1877 visit made him a fortune. 'In a tour throughout England, Scotland and Ireland, and in a series of pianoforte recitals in London, Rubinstein realized in three months £12,000!' wrote his friend John Ella in *Musical Sketches*, published in 1878; 'No such amount was ever obtained by vocalist or actor in England in the same space of time.' In Edinburgh, he enthralled young Alexander Mackenzie, who immediately attached himself to the great pianist.

The astounding impression made upon me on hearing Anton Rubinstein for the first time is difficult of description. When he rose after completing the first part of the programme, I fully expected him to leave the platform with the Erard grand tucked under his arm, like any violinist with his instrument. His own (unwritten) arrangement of the Overture to *Egmont* and the Sonata *Appassionata* were performances the like of which I have never heard since . . . In conversation the composer-pianist showed himself to be an extremely well-read, cultured man of abundant humour; and, while direct, sometimes even to brusqueness, his manners were unaffectedly simple . . . I can see his fork raised on high with a large pickled cucumber (dear to all Russians) on its prongs, and hear the mock solemn pronouncement:- '*Das ist die hohe Poesie von Goethe!*' (That is Goethe's sublime poetry).

One night I initiated him (with the assistance of the 'cellist, Carl Drechsler-Hamilton) into the mysteries of reels and strathspeys, with the result that on the following evening he rose before the end of the dinner and insisted upon my taking him to the Waverley Market, where the regimental pipers were playing these exciting dances to a Saturday-night audience. In spite of the fact that it rained heavily, he, obstinately disdaining a cab, preferred to take my arm for the whole length of Princes Street and back in the dark. I then realized how dim his eyesight was becoming, when he heedlessly and deliberately stepped into every puddle that lay in his way.

After these exhausting recitals Anton liked nothing better than a quiet meal with cards to follow, and could show a righteous temper if these pleasures were disturbed by the officious or curious.

Mackenzie again saw Rubinstein when the Russian was in London. 'I spent a delightful evening in his company at Dieudonné's Hotel. My recollections of the great pianist are of the most agreeable nature.'

In Dublin, young Charlie Stanford was also enraptured. Rubinstein's 'extraordinary playing of Schumann's "Études Symphoniques" at last awoke the town to the beauties of that great master, whose works had been a sealed book to the inhabitants, and caused a *furore* which has seldom been equalled there.'

Cowen, too, was another young man who fell under Rubinstein's spell. 'He at once captivated me by his wonderful Beethovenish appearance, his simple nature and unspoilt manner, almost as much as he did afterwards by his playing.' There was nobody, 'before or since, who has combined all the qualities of a really great pianist as he did'.

He could, at will, move you to tears, thrill you with emotion, or make you shiver with excitement. It was no longer a piano he played on, but an entire orchestra, in which power, sweetness, and great execution vied with each other to produce effects totally unlike the efforts of any other single instrumentalist I have ever heard. . . . The magnetism he exercised over his audiences was quite extraordinary, and I have seen them roused to such a pitch of excitement and enthusiasm that they could not sit still, but had perforce to rise from their seats to watch as well as listen to him. No one could help being absorbed in his performances; indeed, he was so himself . . . any extraneous sound or movement would easily upset him and break the thread of his inspiration.

I can recall one memorable afternoon at one of his recitals at the old St James's Hall, when just as he had begun to play Chopin's Funeral March – no one ever played it like him – a post horn from a coach in Piccadilly suddenly sounded. This so disturbed him (and no wonder) that he took his hands off the piano and dashed them down again pell-mell on to the keys in a fit of rage and disgust. After a while he commenced the piece again, but the spirit of the music had left him, and for that at least we were deprived of the beauty of his rendering.

By now, Rubinstein was well enough regarded as a composer to give a concert devoted entirely to his own works – 'a compliment which we cannot recall to have been paid at the Crystal Palace to any other living composer', said the *Monthly Musical Record*. This took place on 21 April 1877 and included the *Ocean Symphony*, Second Piano Concerto, the overture to the opera *Dmitri Donskoi*, piano solos and vocal items. Rubinstein conducted the symphony and overture; Manns directed the orchestral accompaniment for the concerto. The reviews of the concert were mixed, but most of those present seem to have succumbed to Rubinstein's personal magnetism. In her *Musical Memories*, Alice Mangold writes of the powerful effect created by his conducting of the *Ocean Symphony*.

The band followed his beat like one man . . . each . . . striving to do his best, as if his very life depended upon his performance. The first movement over, the whole of those assembled rose and cheered. They were deeply stirred. At such moments analysis is impossible. They could not have told whether they cheered Rubinstein the composer, or Rubinstein the conductor, or Rubinstein the pianist . . . or, as was probably the case, all in one. But he had gripped their sympathies, he had held their hearts as he had held his *bâton*, and they cried out – that spontaneous admission of being under the power of another which means so much.

Whether that iron man was affected by this outburst of involuntary homage, perhaps even those nearest him – the players in the orchestra – could not have told. There might have been a contraction of the pupils, a grimmer tightening of the thin, firm lips – that was all. Meanwhile the mental intoxication grew. Recalled and shouted at time after time at the close of the symphony, the concerto – his second – heard in the hush which follows such an ebullition of feeling, seemed to rouse an even greater rage of enthusiasm . . . At the close of this extraordinary scene, never certainly surpassed in England, if repeated, Rubinstein played his transcription of the march in 'The Ruins of Athens', where – commencing in so faint a *pianissimo* that ears must strain to hear the theme – he gave a gradual *crescendo*, a prolonged increase of sound as of an advancing army, until the march was thundered out with all that vast volume of tone at his command, dying away afterwards with a *diminuendo* as astonishing as the *crescendo*.

An ovation followed, people standing on the seats and shouting themselves hoarse. Long before it subsided, Rubinstein left the building.

Mary Gladstone, who, a month earlier, had attended the English première of Brahms's First Symphony at Cambridge, was also at the concert, but she was by no means as impressed as Alice Mangold and the other Rubinstein devotees. 'Such a real rotten concert, bad, flashy, vulgar, worthless music played to perfection, such a sarcasm, it was fun watching him and his marvellous performance on the P.F. but *really* as a composer!' Of another concert, she wrote that 'he and his pupil, Mlle. Menter, just thumped till we were deafened.' On a further occasion she found his playing 'simply diabolical. I have never heard such relentless thumps before, and yet he can play, perhaps in Heaven where the instrument would have endless capacities.' Parry, too, had reservations.

> Sometimes he plays like a wild beast, and sometimes like an angel. The Turkish March, from Beethoven's *Ruins of Athens*, which is one of his great feats, is almost incredibly beautiful: some of his Chopin playing is quite astounding, and when he does not run wild his power and richness of tone are quite beyond anything I have heard before . . . He does glorious things out of the fulness of his heart. When it comes to playing things which need self-control or intelligent conscious interpretation, he is disappointing, and even at times when nothing but enthusiasm and feeling are required he often goes beyond the limits of good taste.

During his extended visit of 1877, Rubinstein gave another concert at the Crystal Palace and six recitals in London. He more than held his own against Wagner, Joachim and Clara Schumann, who each appeared in the capital in this same period. Herman Klein heard him for the first time at the Crystal Palace and, completely bowled over, then went to the recitals. His initial reactions are recorded in his *Thirty Years of Musical Life in London*.

> Universally acknowledged to be the greatest pianist of his time, the public simply worshipped Rubinstein as an artist and gathered in crowds whenever he appeared. His technique bordered upon the miraculous; his interpretative gifts were worthy of a musician who was himself no mean creative genius; his style, the reflex, as it were, of his massive leonine aspect, was at once the most noble and most original of any pianist I have ever listened to. The fire and passion in his soul poured out at his fingers' ends; and yet his touch could be as gentle and caressing as a woman's.

Francesco Berger, the secretary of the Philharmonic Society, who was himself a superb pianist, was equally enthusiastic, as he makes clear in *Reminiscences, Impressions and Anecdotes*, published in 1913.

His playing was, taken all in all, the most *wonderful* I have ever heard. A delicate, even, round tone, combined with irresistible fire. His reading of the 'Waldstein' and the 'Appassionata' was masterly, while he was equally great in Field's Nocturnes, Chopin, and Schumann. He and Thalberg could literally 'sing' upon the Piano. There was a 'liquidness' about their *touch* which no other Pianist of my experience possessed [Berger knew Liszt, but never heard him play], and which I should compare to the 'liquid light' of a planet.

One of his great 'battle-horses' was his own arrangement of the March from Beethoven's 'Ruins of Athens'. In it his *crescendos* and *diminuendos* were unique.

Grove was another who unreservedly admired Rubinstein, particularly for the tenderness of his playing: 'it is *so* very tender.' In a letter to his sister-in-law, he makes specific mention of Rubinstein's interpretation of the Liszt transcription of Schubert's *Erlkönig*, which he says he actually preferred to the original. Rubinstein's performance created 'an almost *terrible* impression . . . like a storm or a great fire or any thing that is all beyond one's control, and that, if it comes near you, you must be overwhelmed.' It was this work that threatened to engulf Queen Victoria at Windsor in April 1877, as George Henschel relates in his *Musings and Memories*.

Anton Rubinstein and I had received the Queen's command to go to Windsor Castle one afternoon and play and sing to her. After receiving us most graciously, Her Majesty seated herself near the tail-end of the piano, evidently in order to be able to see Rubinstein's face as he played. In the distance the only other listeners were seated, two or three ladies-in-waiting. The great pianist began with some Chopin nocturnes and other soft sweet things, which greatly pleased the Queen. After that I sang, and then Rubinstein played again, this time some louder things. I thought I could detect faint signs of uneasiness in Her Majesty's face as she seemed to realize the alarming nearness of the huge concert grand, the open lid of which threw the sounds back in the direction of Her Majesty's chair with redoubled force. Then I sang again, and then, to my dismay I confess, for I had heard him do it before, Rubinstein settled down to the playing of Liszt's arrangement of Schubert's *Erl-King*. At the first outcry of the frightened child, 'Mein Vater, mein Vater', I was prepared for the Queen asking me to close the lid, when there happened the most touching act, or rather a succession of most touching acts on the part of her indeed Most Gracious Majesty. Every now and then she would, unnoticed by the player, gently push her chair farther and farther away from the piano, the sounds issuing from which were growing more and more terrific from bar to bar, until, during the last frantic ride of the horror-stricken father, keys, strings, hammers seemed to be flying through the air in all directions, dashed into fragments by the relentless hoofs of the maddened horse. By that time, however, the Queen was at a safe distance, and a charming smile of pleasure and relief stole over her serious, wonderfully impressive features when at last home was reached.

Rubinstein was lionised by London society, which he seems to have enjoyed, for he was a very sociable man. He met a number of literary celebrities including Browning and Oscar Wilde. The former warned him of the unlikelihood of any of his operas based on religious subjects being staged in England. Among these were *The Tower of Babel*, *The Maccabees*, *The Shulamite*, *Moses* and *Christus*. This cautionary advice proved well founded; by 1893, none of them had been presented. Only *The Demon*, after the poem by Lermontov, was performed in London during Rubinstein's lifetime. The composer himself conducted it at Covent Garden in June 1881, when it was given in an Italian translation. It was staged again in London in 1888 by a Russian touring company, becoming the first opera to be sung in Russian in the capital. Despite an initially enthusiastic reception, the work failed to find a place in the repertoire of any British opera company.

In *Memories of a Musician*, the conductor Wilhelm Ganz writes warmly of Rubinstein's generous nature and of how, 'after each concert, he used to invite his friends to a reception at the Hotel Dieudonné in Ryder Street, to which I also received an invitation.' The violinist Leopold Auer also pays tribute to Rubinstein's engaging sociability in *My Long Life in Music*.

> Very simple in his manner, without any affectation of importance, he was charming in his relations with all artists, and indeed, with all whom he regarded as devoted to the true cause of music. In the little French hotel where he resided, near St. James's Hall, then the largest concert hall in London, he usually kept open house for his friends in the good old Russian Style of bygone days, transplanting the hospitality of his native land to English soil. His unostentatious manner of life, his daily receptions, unheralded and unadvertised, nevertheless had a touch of the lordly, emphasized perhaps by the cordiality with which Rubinstein received his guests.

Rubinstein always felt very much at home at the Dieudonné, making friends with many of the other people who came to stay or eat there. Among these were the two little Douste sisters, Louise and Jeanne, who later became popular musical entertainers. He was introduced to them by their piano teacher Mortier de Fontaine, and on their first meeting, writes Edouard Garceau in his book on the sisters, Rubinstein took Jeanne, then six years old, on his knee and 'amused himself by stuffing her with asparagus, making her bite off the tops one by one.'

The children often went to the Dieudonné; not to lunch off asparagus, but to play to the great pianist. He afterwards continued to give them help and advice both in London and Paris, as chance favoured their meetings in the cities where the same art brought them together.

Through never missing an opportunity of hearing Rubinstein, whether he were at the Dieudonné practising or at his concerts, the sisters knew him in many moods, in good and bad humour. If sometimes it happened that the accuracy of his playing was not impeccable (as for instance at one of his concerts where, tired and sullen, he was recalled to play one of his own valses, his favourite, in which the treble note in the right hand is repeated in a jump, his little finger on this occasion fell without exception on the note next to the correct one!) he was, whatever the mood of the moment, superb; great in his understanding of the souls of the masters. Beethoven, Bach, Chopin, Schumann, all relived under his touch . . .

Rubinstein worked very hard . . . His method of rehearsing his programme was unique [Rakhmaninov later adopted a similar method]. Some hours before appearing in public he went to the piano, and there, playing as softly as possible so that he could hardly be heard in the adjoining room, he went through all the pieces he was to play, without stopping, without the least expression or shade of meaning . . .

At one of his concerts some of his admirers had transformed the platform into an altar of flowers. Even the piano was crowned with masses of them. The artist appeared, stopped abruptly, frowning. Suddenly he surveyed this florists' display, then went brusquely to the piano, hurled the sheaves that covered it to the floor, kicked over those too near the piano-stool, and finally, more bear-like than ever, began his programme.

On another occasion, having probably some 'grouch' against his public (who nevertheless applauded him to the echo), Rubinstein came off the platform and with upraised arms precipitated himself towards the little Doustes (who had been listening devoutly to the concert from the doorway of the artists' room), exclaiming:

'Oh, my children, what a gang! What a gang!'

The extent of Rubinstein's friendships and the scale on which he entertained are described in Edward Speyer's *My Life and Friends*.

During Rubinstein's visit to London, we had sent him an invitation to dine with us at Denmark Hill, but his numerous engagements prevented him from accepting. In a charming letter conveying his regrets he at the same time invited us to dine with him at the Hotel Dieudonné in Ryder Street, his habitual residence when in London, and where in princely fashion he used to give a great number of these entertainments. We found ourselves in the company of some twenty-four guests, and I remember Sir John Millais, Sir Laurence Alma-Tadema, Sir Charles Hallé, Madame Normann Neruda, Sir Felix Semon and his wife, formerly Augusta Redeker, the charming singer. After dinner the company moved into the large drawing-room, where soon afterwards they were joined by some thirty or forty other people. In the centre of the room a card-table had been placed, at which Rubinstein and Sir John Millais, with two other men, took their seats, and, amidst the indescribable hubbub and turmoil of the surrounding guests, continued playing whist quite unperturbed. Later on Millais, handsome, of robust build and huge stature, rose, saying in a stentorian voice, 'Rubie, it is time for me to go to my little bed,' and left the assembly, which soon afterwards broke up.

Herman Klein was present on a similar occasion.

In private life his chief amusement was a game of whist. He loved the game and played it well – as I discovered for myself one evening when I visited him at the old Hotel Dieudonné, in St. James's. Quite a number of friends dropped in after dinner, but Rubinstein simply ignored their presence until he had finished his rubber. Then he went round and warmly welcomed them. After a time he sat down to the piano, and never left it till midnight, giving us a treat that will never fade from my memory as long as I live.

It appears that Rubinstein especially enjoyed the companionship of Millais. This is mentioned by Alice Millais in John Guille Millais' biography of their father.

Rubinstein in his various visits to London always came to dine with him, and it used to be with us a subject of conjecture whether my father would tempt Rubinstein to the piano, or Rubinstein detain my father at the card-table.
Rubinstein fancied himself as great a whist-player as he was a pianist.
I recollect one evening in the studio in Palace Gate, Rubinstein had set himself down to a game, and was playing rather worse than usual. My father suffered acutely through one or two rubbers, until at last he rose in desperation, saying, 'If you don't stop I will go and play the piano.'

Whist seems to have been the bait with which the great pianist could be enticed into London's drawing-rooms, but, as H. Sutherland Edwards makes clear in his *Personal Recollections*, he was also susceptible to other allurements.

I have often heard Rubinstein in private houses, where, under pretence of being summoned to a game of whist, he would be brought into a room in which a fine piano had been left open. Calling himself a passionate whist player, he took no interest in the game unless he had a pretty woman for a partner, and two pretty women for antagonists. But after a game or two the open piano would be sure to attract him from the card table; and then, playing of his own accord and because he was in the mood, he would play divinely. It was better, however, not to ask him.

'Anton did not drink', wrote Louise Héritte-Viardot in *Memories and Adventures*. 'He had another passion, which in the course of years became a vice – the fair sex. He respected very few women . . . he, like Liszt, had been admired, spoilt and pursued by women from his youth upwards. He once told me in confidence: "If I had to educate and provide for all my children, the fortune of two Rothschilds would scarcely suffice".' That his amorous propensities could be easily aroused is affirmed in Maude Valerie White's *Friends and Memories*. At a dinner-party, 'happening to sit beside a lady with a very beautiful white neck, his feelings got the better of him, and he bent down and kissed it. She was furious.' He, however, seemed quite unaware that he had done anything unconventional. 'Just a little Russian custom', he explained.

One famous Englishwoman who seems to have been fascinated by both Rubinstein and Liszt was George Eliot. She met Rubinstein for the first time in Weimar in September 1854, when she was thirty-four. She and George Lewes were visiting Liszt at the time, and it was he who introduced Rubinstein to them. Liszt, who was then at the pinnacle of his fame, was of course the primary attraction, and George Eliot gave him most of her attention.

My great delight was to watch Liszt and observe the sweetness of his expression. Genius, benevolence and tenderness beam from his whole countenance, and his manners are in perfect harmony with it . . . Then came the thing I longed for – Liszt's playing. I sat near him so that I could see both his hands and face. For the first time in my life I beheld real inspiration – for the first time I heard the true tones of the piano. He played one of his own compositions – one of a series of religious *fantaisies*. There was nothing strange or excessive about his manner. His manipulation of the instrument was quiet and easy, and his face was simply grand –

the lips compressed and the head thrown a little backward. When the music expressed quiet rapture or devotion, a sweet smile flitted over his features: when it was triumphant, the nostrils dilated. There was nothing petty or egoistic to mar the picture.

She found Liszt's conversation 'charming. I never met with a person whose manner of telling a story was so piquant.' His replies, too, 'were always felicitous and characteristic'. During her stay in Weimar, she saw him conduct *Der Freischütz* and also heard performances that he directed of *Der fliegende Holländer* and *Tannhäuser*, which she enjoyed, and the more recent *Lohengrin*, which she found wearisome. There was further pleasure, though, in Verdi's *Ernani*. 'Liszt looked splendid as he conducted the opera. The grand outline of his face and floating hair were seen to advantage as they were thrown into dark relief by the stage lamps.' At this time, Liszt was engaged in a maelstrom of activity; while George Eliot was in Weimar, he completed a large part of his *Faust Symphony*, worked at an article on Schumann, read Raff's book *The Wagner Question* and carried on a lengthy correspondence with Berlioz, Wagner and Bülow. Apart from preparing and conducting the operas already mentioned, he took part as well in a number of concerts. At one of these he conducted Schumann's *Manfred* Overture, Fourth Symphony and Piano Concerto. The soloist in the concerto was Clara Schumann, who was in a terribly depressed state because of Robert's recent confinement in the asylum at Endenich. 'My money is at an end,' she wrote in their family diary on 30 September, 'and I cannot bring myself to sell any of Robert's investments. God knows what is going to happen.' She was consoled by the presence of Brahms and Joachim, who did much to help her, but on 19 October, during a performance in Leipzig of the First Symphony of Gade, whom Schumann so loved, she broke down and wept. Liszt was touchingly kind to her at Weimar a week later, and the concert was a great success, but nothing could assuage her misery. George Eliot was introduced to her by Liszt, but does not seem to have been fully aware of the awfulness of Clara's situation. She describes her in a journal note of 28 October as 'a melancholy, interesting creature' and adds, 'Her husband went mad a year [eight months] ago, and she has to support eight [seven – and the youngest was only four months old] children.'

The reason for Rubinstein's appearance in Weimar was that Liszt intended staging his one-act opera, *The Huntsmen of Siberia*, in mid-November. Liszt had a profound admiration for Rubinstein, regarding him, in terms of piano-playing, as his true successor. Like everybody else, he was much taken with his young colleague's striking good looks, often addressing him as Van II because of his similarity in appearance to Beethoven. (Bülow called Rubinstein 'the Michelangelo of Music'.) Since, as a boy of eleven, Liszt had played before Beethoven and been taken up in his arms and kissed by him, he was clearly well qualified to judge of any resemblance: he also possessed Beethoven's death-mask. Rubinstein must have made a powerful impression on George Eliot, for, twenty years later, she put him into *Daniel Deronda* as the commanding and somewhat menacing musician Julius Klesmer, with his imposing physique and 'grand features'. Gordon S. Haight, in his biography of George Eliot, notes that 'Rubinstein had Klesmer's massive features and thick mane of hair, which he threw backward when he played in conscious imitation of his hero, "the king of musicians, Liszt".' Mr Haight also observes, in comparing 'the irascible Klesmer' with Rubinstein, that 'Brusqueness is the trait in which they resemble each other most closely.'

In describing Klesmer's piano-playing, George Eliot writes that 'he certainly fetched as much variety and depth of passion out of the piano as that moderately responsive instrument lends itself to, having an imperious magic in his fingers that seemed to send a nerve-thrill through ivory key and wooden hammer, and compel the strings to make a quivering lingering speech for him.' She was herself a highly competent amateur musician and had been the best pianist in her school in Coventry, where she used to be called upon to play for visitors. Not content with this accomplishment, she also took up the violin, though with less success. She continued to study the piano after leaving school and in January 1864, when she was forty-four, was taking lessons in accompaniment from Leopold Jansa, who numbered among his pupils Wilma Norman-Neruda, later Lady Hallé. That this instruction proved worthwhile can be gathered from the reminiscences of Frederick Lehmann, which are reproduced in Rudolph Lehmann's *Memories of Half a Century*.

In the winter of 1866 my wife and family were at Pau, while I was alone in London. George Eliot was a very fair pianist, not gifted, but enthusiastic, and extremely painstaking. During a great part of that winter I used to go to her every Monday evening at her house in North Bank, Regent's Park, always taking my violin with me. We played together every piano and violin sonata of Mozart and Beethoven. I knew the traditions of the best players [notably Joachim] and was able to give her some hints, which she always received eagerly and thankfully. Our audience consisted of George Lewes only, and he used to groan with delight whenever we were rather successful in playing some beautiful passage.

As well as performing music, George Eliot loved to go to concerts. She saw Mendelssohn conduct *Elijah* in London in May 1847, six months before his death. As time went by, she came greatly to admire Joachim and Clara Schumann, with both of whom she eventually became very friendly. Among her favourite operas was Gounod's *Faust*; she was 'much thrilled by the great symbolical situations, and by the music'. The most famous composer she ever met was Wagner (by chance, she once found herself sitting opposite Berlioz in a hotel restaurant in Brussels, but they did not introduce themselves). The German master was in London in the spring and early summer of 1877 to give a series of concerts of his music in order to raise money to finance the Festspielhaus at Bayreuth. Cosima Wagner, Liszt's daughter, visited George Eliot in Regent's Park, bringing a letter of introduction from her father and complimentary tickets for the first concert. During her stay in London, Cosima went to many museums and galleries, and called at the studios of a number of important painters. Her visit to Watts was spoilt when the artist showed her his portrait of Joachim, who was *persona non grata* in the Wagner canon, because of his allegiance to Brahms. Wagner himself was received at Windsor and also met Browning. George Eliot saw the Wagners on several occasions, at parties and other functions. She was able to converse satisfactorily with Wagner, thanks to her excellent command of German. No doubt, in speaking to Wagner, George Eliot steered clear of any reference to her recently published *Daniel Deronda*, with its Jewish subject matter, though she did remark to Cosima, 'Your husband does not like Jews; my husband is a Jew.' Wagner, for his part, treated her and George Lewes, one evening at the home of Edward Dannreuther, to a reading of his entire *Parsifal* libretto, which he had just completed. This was delivered, according to the novelist, 'with great spirit and like a fine actor'. She went to at least three of his rehearsals, which were largely presided over by Hans Richter, who shared the conducting with Wagner. At one of these, Wagner came and sat next to her. Also with her on that occasion were

William Morris, Edward Burne-Jones and Frederick Leighton. Morris was an imperfect Wagnerite, since Wagner's 'theories on musical matters seem to me, as an artist and non-musical man, perfectly abominable.' Burne-Jones got more out of the rehearsal, for he spotted among the audience an attractive girl who afterwards agreed to pose for him.

It was in May 1876 that George Eliot met Rubinstein again. Remembering him from Weimar, twenty-two years earlier, she described him in *Daniel Deronda* as 'not yet a Liszt, understood to be adored by ladies of all European countries with the exception of Lapland'. By now, of course, he had indeed become a Liszt – and perhaps more, since Lapland lies not far north of St Petersburg. She and George Lewes were invited by the Lehmanns to a dinner-party at which Rubinstein was also a guest. Accepting the invitation, George Lewes told Nina Lehmann, 'We shall so like to renew our acquaintance with Klesmer, whom we met at Weimar in '54!' Despite being unwell, the novelist made a special effort to attend the party to see Rubinstein again. When he was in London the following year, the opportunity arose of meeting him at a party given by Felix Moscheles, the son of the pianist. Unfortunately, because of a severe attack of kidney stone, there was no question of her going, and Lewes went on his own. This proved to be her last chance of seeing him. She died at Christmas 1880, six months before his next trip to London.

Rubinstein made three visits during the eighties. The first of these, in 1881, included a concert at the Crystal Palace, before a capacity audience, in which he and Manns performed the Schumann Piano Concerto; this was followed by his own Violin Concerto, which he conducted, with Leopold Auer as soloist. The programme concluded with *The Tower of Babel*, presented as an oratorio. Ten days later, on 21 June 1881, he conducted the English première of *The Demon* at Covent Garden.

The climax of all his visits to London came in 1886, when, during May and June, he gave a series of seven 'historical concerts'. His arrival in the capital was saluted in the opening article of the June *Monthly Musical Record*.

Anton Rubinstein has commenced a series of pianoforte recitals in London, unheralded by the flourish of bombastic newspaper paragraphs, and relying simply and solely upon his own genius for due recognition. He has not visited London for making an exhibition of himself, or to excite a fictitious interest in works that have neither artistic value or are incapable of awakening human sympathy. His mission is genuine, and his own exposition of it is manly and clear, and such as will entitle him to the respect and admiration of all but the envious. There is no need for him to pose so that he may be regarded as a hero. He is one, in his way, for he can afford to trust to the impressions which his genius and talents create in and of themselves. Unstayed by charlatanism, not puffed out by the breath of romance, not surrounded by the opalescent halo of aesthetic immorality, he stands fairly in the light of day, fearlessly independent, conscious in the rectitude of an honest career, honestly pursued, using his extraordinary gifts in the best manner, and triumphantly secure of recognition and encouragement from all to whom such qualities commend themselves.

The article goes on to point out that, while Liszt 'ranks with the memories of the past', Rubinstein is 'the greatest, most versatile, and most artistic pianist of the present age'.

Rubinstein had already given the 'historical concerts' in St Petersburg, Moscow, Berlin, Hamburg, Leipzig, Dresden, Vienna, Paris and Brussels. In every city, they had been acclaimed. The first concert covered the history of music up to and including Mozart; the second was devoted to Beethoven; the third consisted of Weber, Schubert and Mendelssohn; Schumann was the subject of the fourth, while the fifth largely dealt with Liszt; the sixth featured only the works of Chopin, who was also represented in the final concert, which, in addition, included pieces by Glinka, Rubinstein himself and some of his younger Russian contemporaries. In Berlin and some other cities, he gave the series twice: once for the paying public and once for music students, who were allowed in free. In London, the seven concerts at St James's Hall yielded £6,000, which was a record for those days. These were followed by an eighth recital, the proceeds of which Rubinstein divided among various London charities. He performed the entire series from memory. 'No one save Rubinstein would have attempted the Herculean feat involved in the execution of such programmes', wrote Herman Klein. Nor were the programmes anything less than generous. The first contained 31 separate works. The Beethoven concert included no less than 8 sonatas. In the sixth concert, there were 30 items by Chopin, and the seventh began with 11 of his *études*.

The 'historical concerts' were intended as a finale to Rubinstein's career as a travelling virtuoso and, on returning to Russia, he announced his retirement and resumed his post as director of the St Petersburg Conservatoire, which he had founded in 1862. He also set up the International Piano Competition, endowing it with 25,000 roubles. During his lifetime, he gave more than 300,000 roubles to charity.

His position in the musical world in the early nineties was exceptionally high. Liszt had died in July 1886, a month after Rubinstein left London. Only Joachim now held as august a reputation as a soloist. Bülow was celebrated both as pianist and conductor, but, by 1892, his eccentricity was sadly and inexorably degenerating into madness. As a composer too, Rubinstein was well regarded. In *Famous Composers and their Works*, which was in preparation in December 1892, he is allotted 13 pages. This compares very favourably with the 16 for Verdi, 14 for Gounod and 13 for Brahms; it is also 6 better than Dvořák and 8 better than Stanford. In this four-volume work, the author of the article on Rubinstein is the gifted and perceptive Henry Finck. His assessment of the Russian composer is a valuable contemporary opinion.

Rubinstein, the pianist, is still much better known to the public than Rubinstein, the composer, although his activity as a musician is even more astounding than his skill as a virtuoso. On the occasion of his Jubilee the publisher of most of his works issued a 'Rubinstein Katalog' . . . This catalogue contains forty-eight pages, and in looking through it one never ceases wondering why so few of these pieces are known to the general public, and where the composer found time, amid his labours at the Conservatory, and his constant travels as virtuoso, to write such an enormous number of pieces . . .

In all his chamber music Rubinstein shows such remarkable skill and true musical instinct in the treatment of instruments that one would expect to find him in his orchestral works one of the greatest masters of instrumentation. But his orchestration, while often fine, and sometimes superb, is, on the whole, his weakest point; and the cause of this must be sought in his stubborn and persistent hostility to the innovations of Wagner, Liszt and Berlioz – even to those which other conservative composers have approved and appropriated. His most important orchestral works are six symphonies, an overture triomphale, three musical 'character-pictures,' *Faust, Ivan the Terrible* and *Don Quixote* (the last with fine humorous touches), and an *Eroica Fantasia*. Here may also be mentioned the exquisite ballet music which he wrote for the operas *Feramors, Demon* and *Nero*, the last named being especially fascinating and piquant. In this department Rubinstein has no rival, either among the dead or the living . . .

His critics have pointed out with tiresome iteration that the gold in his works is mixed with too much alloy. This is doubtless true, but criticism should not be synonymous with fault-finding, and where there is so much melodic gold as in Rubinstein, critics would be more just if they more frequently called attention to that, and to the distinct vein of true creative genius that runs through most of his works . . .

Rubinstein was unfortunate in appearing with his operas at a time when Wagner was teaching the world the magic power of genuine dramatic music. At an earlier period, when musical interest alone, without dramatic realism, sufficed to make operas popular (as witness the success of the Italian composers), he might have been the hero of the day. He knew instinctively what the trouble was and consequently hated Wagner cordially. Had he been more sensible and tried to *learn* from Wagner, his operas would not have been such failures. At the same time it must be said that with all their dramatic shortcomings these operas deserve to be heard more frequently, for the sake of their often ravishingly beautiful music.

We can compare this with what Grove had to say in his *Dictionary* ten years earlier. He begins by suggesting that Rubinstein's compositions 'are not yet sufficiently mellowed by time for us to judge them fairly'; nevertheless his subsequent remarks are so discerning that they were carried over, almost word for word, even as far as the third edition of the *Dictionary* in 1927.

Their style may be considered as the legitimate outcome of Mendelssohn; there is a fine broad vein of melody which is supported by true and natural harmony, and a thorough technical skill. But there is also the fatal gift of fluency, and the consequent lack of that self-criticism and self-restraint which alone make a composer great. Rubinstein has written in every department of music, but as yet his songs and chamber-music are all that can be called really popular, excepting always his 'Ocean Symphony', which is known all over the world . . . His Pianoforte Concertos are very brilliant and effective, especially that in G (Op. 45); they will perhaps in time take a permanent position . . . The numerous drawing-room pieces which he has written for the piano are far superior to most of their class, his writing for the instrument being invariably most brilliant, as is but natural in so great a pianist . . . His operas and oratorios have as yet met with but qualified success, seeming to lack dramatic force. This is in some measure due to his antagonism to the theories and practice of Wagner and the modern German school.

It would perhaps be not unreasonable to suppose that Stanford's opinion of Rubinstein the composer roughly coincided with Grove's. He would, no doubt, have liked a number of the 'drawing-room pieces', some of the songs, the piano concertos and probably the *Ocean*

Symphony, which has many moments of undeniable beauty and, in the first movement, a magnificent Schumannesque tune that alone should ensure the work's survival far beyond our own times. Nevertheless, Stanford was a progressive, while Rubinstein was very much a conservative, whose musical idiom was generally little in advance of Mendelssohn's and Schumann's. Moreover, Rubinstein had firmly set his face against Wagner and was quite out of sympathy with Brahms, none of whose works he included in the 'historical concerts'. In fact, by 1892, Rubinstein, as a composer, was considerably out of date. For this reason, it seems unlikely that the CUMS would have decided that, purely on the strength of his compositions, he was worth an invitation. However, his contribution, as a pianist, to the musical life of the second half of the nineteenth century clearly marked him out as one of the greatest musicians of the age. He was deservedly among the most famous and glamorous men of his time. Already, three books had been written about him, and, such was the aura that had built up around him, that, in one of these, published in 1889, the author, Lillian Macarthur, claimed that on Rubinstein 'the mantle of Schubert has fallen, and as a melodist he has no rival and equal to-day, for just as Brahms is the contrapuntal, Wagner the dramatic, so is Rubinstein the lyric genius of the age.'

We may therefore conclude that he would have been a popular choice and worthy of the occasion. His standing as a composer would not have lessened his claim; after all, the university had been perfectly happy to award Joachim an honorary degree fifteen years earlier, and *his* achievements as a composer were negligible.

But Rubinstein was not chosen. And the reason for this seems to lie in a passage from his autobiography, which was published in 1891. It partakes of the brusqueness that had always been one of his less endearing characteristics.

> The relative knowledge of music among the Germans, French and English, stated arithmetically, would be somewhat as follows: of the German people, at least 50% understand music; of the French, only 16%; while among the English – the least musical of people – not more than 2% can be discovered who have any knowledge of music. Even the Americans have a higher appreciation of music than the English.

To this should be added the fact that Rubinstein took no interest in English music, unlike Bülow, for instance, who once purchased three piano pieces by Sterndale Bennett that were previously unknown to

him, learned them on the train down to Brighton and played them by
heart at a concert the same evening – all because he discovered it was
Sterndale Bennett's birthday. Joachim and Richter also put themselves at the service of contemporary English music, but Rubinstein
wanted no part of it. 'You have no composers', he told Mackenzie.

The second candidate suggested by the *Cambridge Review* was Grieg,
who was regarded in an altogether different light. By 1892, in which
year he celebrated his forty-ninth birthday, he had established
himself, in the opinion of one contemporary writer, as 'the most
popular muscan in the home life of England since Mendelssohn'.
This was an interesting phenomenon. In the concert hall, Grieg's
works were infrequently performed, less so than Rubinstein's; indeed,
by May 1888, when the Norwegian composer made his first
appearance in England, his Piano Concerto was the only piece to
have entered the orchestral repertoire. Even this composition took a
while to be accepted. First performed by Dannreuther and Manns at
the Crystal Palace in April 1874, it was greeted, according to *The
Musical Times*, 'with the warmest applause'. Yet, when Dannreuther
again played it, with Cusins conducting, at a Philharmonic concert in
February 1877, it was received far less favourably. On this occasion,
reported the same journal, 'the composition left a sense of weariness
upon the audience', even though Dannreuther performed it 'with an
earnestness and artistic finish which indicated that he estimated the
work at a higher value than did the majority of his auditors.' Nevertheless, the concerto gradually became better known and liked,
without becoming especially popular.

    With the piano pieces and songs, however, it was a very different
matter, and, by the middle of the eighties, these were being bought in
large quantities for domestic consumption. Despite this drawing-
room popularity, which was far in excess of that achieved by Brahms
or Rubinstein with their piano works, Grieg was in no way looked
upon as one who pandered to public taste. The freshness and novelty
of his musical idiom, and its often striking modernity, were argument
enough against such accusation. Indeed, for an older generation,
Grieg was decidedly too advanced, though Queen Victoria was one of
his great admirers. Imogen Holst tells us that, in 1886, when Gustav
Holst was twelve, he 'had a passion for Grieg, but he always had to
wait until his father was out of the house before venturing to play the

Lyric Pieces.' Grieg's reputation was bright among his fellow musicians, particularly in England, and, as early as 1876, when on a concert tour of Norway, Cowen made a point of calling on him in Bergen.

During the late seventies and throughout the eighties, Grieg was, therefore, in a sense, an 'underground' composer, and nobody could adequately assess how high he stood in general esteem, though many suspected it might be very high. The full extent of his popularity at last became apparent when he stepped through the orchestra doorway on the occasion of his London début, at a Philharmonic concert in St James's Hall, on 3 May 1888. The packed auditorium immediately erupted in a storm of applause of such intensity that it lasted for more than three minutes. The astonished composer was completely taken aback: 'I had no idea what to do.' He was not the only one to be surprised by this tremendous demonstration. The *Daily Telegraph*, which had long felt that he had a large following, was amazed at the pitch of enthusiasm. Slightly recovering himself, but still overcome, Grieg bowed repeatedly to every part of the hall until the uproar subsided.

The concert contained four of his works, beginning with the Piano Concerto, in which he played the solo part, with Cowen conducting. As early as May 1875, a year after the Crystal Palace première, the *Monthly Musical Record* confidently predicted that the concerto would 'eventually take its place as a stock piece among the best pianoforte concertos.' By 1888, this had not yet happened, but the revelatory performance by Grieg and Cowen settled the matter. The concerto was followed by two of Grieg's songs, with the composer accompanying the soprano Carlotta Elliott. He concluded by conducting his *Two Elegiac Melodies*. All these works were welcomed with the wildest excitement. The critics were also full of praise. Commenting in *The Times* on the performance of the concerto, Francis Hueffer wrote, 'The French speak of a *voix de compositeur*; in the same sense there is a composer's touch on the piano which, when applied to his own works, gives them a peculiar charm of their own . . . Both in a technical and in an intellectual sense his rendering was perfect . . .' *The Musical Times* was equally enchanted.

Nothing could be more neat, clear, and intelligent than his rendering of the solo [in the concerto]. In it the artist predominated over the mere executant, and the audience were held closely observant by what seemed to be, in Grieg's hands, a new work. The success gained was immense, while its causes were the most legitimate conceivable. Grieg, as a conductor, gave equal satisfaction. The little pieces styled 'Elegiac Melodies' acquired a significance under his direction such as had not been suspected previously, and the performance – a triumph of delicacy and refinement – left absolutely nothing to desire. Of the applause showered upon the Norwegian musician it would be vain to speak in attempt at description. Grieg, though personally a stranger, seemed intimately known to the audience, and appeared to have all their sympathy. This was no doubt due to the charm of the songs and pianoforte pieces which long since made his name a household word. It is now to be hoped that the greatest musical representative of 'old Norway' will come amongst us every year.

Apart from being overjoyed by the success of the concert, Grieg marvelled at the capabilities of the Philharmonic orchestra. He found the string playing better than anything he had come across in Germany. Of the orchestra's performance of the *Two Elegiac Melodies*, he said, 'There were things in it to bring tears to the eyes – they sounded so fine.' He told the directors of the Philharmonic that theirs was the best orchestra he had ever heard.

In the passage devoted to Grieg in his memoirs, Cowen ultimately reveals more about himself than about Grieg, making it easier for us to understand why he never inspired the widespread affection that Sullivan or Stanford received. 'Grieg was not a great pianist', says Cowen, in referring to the Philharmonic concert, 'but he could play his own music with much effect.'

The popularity of his compositions, too, made everyone curious to see him in *propria persona*, and added not a little to the success he achieved. He and his wife (who was a very capable singer) were an interesting couple. They were both quite short, with bright intellectual faces and rough grizzly hair, and looked more like brother and sister [they were cousins] than husband and wife. They had simple, unaffected natures, and seemed as much attached to each other as they were to the art they both followed. He was perhaps the more simple-minded and ingenuous of the two. Once I published a set of doggerel verses in a musical paper, and added a postscript to the effect that having at last found my real vocation in life, I was thinking seriously of abandoning the career of the musician for that of the poet. Grieg got hold of this, and immediately wrote to me saying how sorry he was to hear of my decision, and hoped I would reconsider it. I replied that I had not yet definitely made up my mind about the matter, but was awaiting the success of the big epic poem I was writing before taking the fatal step. What he finally thought of me I cannot say, but I doubt if it ever entered his head to look on the thing as the silly little joke it certainly was.

On the day following the concert, the Griegs had dinner at the Hotel Métropole with Frederick Delius. The meeting had been arranged a week earlier, after Grieg had declined an invitation to visit Delius in Bradford. Delius, who had loved Grieg's music from childhood, had become acquainted with the Norwegian composer during the summer of the previous year. Some months later, in March 1888, when Grieg was passing through Leipzig, where Delius was studying with Reinecke, he attended a private performance of the younger man's *Florida Suite*, which was conducted by Hans Sitt, who orchestrated Grieg's *Norwegian Dances*. Grieg was impressed by the work. He also liked Delius the man, confiding in a letter to a friend, 'I must tell you that I've very rarely met anybody who's brought me so much pleasure.' Delius was then still trying to find himself as a composer, but his principal concern was whether his father was going to withdraw his allowance, as he now threatened to do. The purpose of the meeting at the Métropole was to enlist Grieg's support in an effort to persuade Delius senior not to carry out his threat. Accordingly, Grieg invited Delius's father, who was shortly coming to London on business, to dine with him, his wife and Delius, to discuss something 'of utmost urgency'. This illustrious invitation was naturally accepted, and, over another dinner at the Métropole, it was agreed that the allowance should continue.

A fortnight later, Grieg gave his second London concert, again at St James's Hall. He was assisted by his wife Nina and the violinist Wilma Norman-Neruda, who two months afterwards married Charles Hallé. Nina's excellence as a singer had not been generally known to the English before her arrival in London. In *A Door-Keeper of Music*, Fuller-Maitland recalls hearing her sing after a luncheon-party. 'Mme. Grieg had not intended to appear in public in England, but her singing of her husband's songs made so individual an impression on some friends who heard her in private that she was persuaded to sing at a "Pop". The expedients adopted by some English ladies to turn one of her gowns at a few hours' notice into something resembling the conventional evening dress of the period were amusing . . .' *The Musical Times* described her interpretation of Grieg's songs as an experience that would become a 'life-long memory'. Hueffer, in *The Times*, was once more full of praise.

We previously tried to convey some idea of Grieg's playing by comparing it to what the French call *voix de compositeur*. The poetic and indefinable charm of his manner was again felt by the audience in such pieces as 'On the Mountains' or the 'Norwegian Bridal Procession', which even those most familiar with them thought they had never heard before, so instinct with individual life was the reading here presented. Almost the same remark applies to the singing of her husband's songs by Madame Grieg – a *voix de compositeur* in a different meaning of the words . . . in such charming lyrics as 'My Song shall be Thine' and the impetuous 'Good Morning' she was – in the same sense and for the same reason as Grieg on the piano – unsurpassable. Madame Norman-Neruda . . . materially contributed to the success of one of the most interesting concerts of the year.

After this second triumph, the Griegs took a short holiday on the Isle of Wight and then returned home. Their next visit came only three months later, for Grieg had been invited to appear at the Birmingham Musical Festival, during which he was to conduct his overture *In Autumn*, which he especially revised for the occasion, and the *Holberg Suite*. Initial rehearsals were held in St George's Hall in London. Frederick Bridge, whose cantata *Callirhoë* was also to be presented, recalls in *A Westminster Pilgrim* that 'Grieg was rather a terror to the orchestra at the London rehearsals. Extremely fastidious, and demanding the most minute attention to the nuances in his music, he kept the band at it for a very long time – when he had finished, appearing a complete wreck from his exertions.' On 22 August, Grove, too, was at the rehearsals; he was so taken with Grieg that he noted down his impressions.

> Such men cannot be judged by the standard of ordinary men – of Englishmen particularly. They are free from conventions which bind us, they are all nerves, they indulge in strange words, and make everyone laugh, till we find that the gestures and looks and words are the absolute expression of their inmost feeling, and that that inmost feeling is inherent in the music and must be expressed in the performance. And they get what they want. Those who have seen Grieg conduct will know what I am attempting to describe.

In Birmingham, the Griegs stayed with one of the festival directors, George Johnstone, who, we may recall, made a creditable attempt to lure Brahms to England. Another guest was the sixteen-year-old Adelina de Lara, who was a pupil of Clara Schumann. Her recollections of Grieg and 'his sweet little wife' are preserved in her autobiography *Finale*.

I can see him now as he sat at the piano in a worn brown velvet coat which he loved. He had dreamy grey eyes and his manner was gentle and very quiet. He was a most beautiful pianist . . .

Every morning Grieg would come into the music-room, and if I were there, he would make me play with him. He could never leave the piano for long, but would sit for hours, extemporizing or playing through a song or some other work of his own. He would make me play after him, or if it were the Concerto we would take it in turns to play a movement. Grieg did not like the last movement of his Concerto played too fast; it had to be super-rhythmical, particularly in the left hand. I do not think he dreamed how often it would come to be played, and how this would have pleased him, for he loved his own music quite openly. Even I had heard the story of how sometimes, when conducting . . . he would put down his baton and listen in rapture to the orchestra while they played on without him! . . .

Sometimes his wife would join us and I sat enchanted as she sang to his accompaniment. Their devotion to each other and common passion for music was more than touching.

Grieg conducted *In Autumn* at the Festival on 29 August, and it was well received. 'How he managed to inspire the band as he did and get such nervous thrilling bursts and such charming sentiment out of them I don't know', Grove wrote to his future biographer Charles Graves. On the following evening, he directed the performance of the *Holberg Suite*. Parry, whose oratorio *Judith* was being given for the first time at the Festival, was in the audience, and his diary entry refers to the concert.

Grieg turned up to conduct his Suite – a most characteristic little object, with about the sweetest expression I ever saw on a man's face. And he is altogether of a piece with his music – on a tiny scale, so tiny that a big stool had to be brought for him to stand on. His conducting is very funny to look at, but it is very good all the same.

'It was a wonderful specimen of conducting', declared John Francis Barnett in *Musical Reminiscences and Impressions*. 'One could never have divined that such novel effects could have been produced out of these instruments [strings alone] unaided by the wind.' Barnett had been a fellow student of Grieg's at the Leipzig Conservatoire, thirty years earlier, but had apparently forgotten the fact until they met in the artists' room in St James's Hall at the time of Grieg's first London concert the previous May. It was Grieg who reminded him. Another fellow student was Sullivan, of whom Grieg had the clearest memories. He recalled them in his modest and engaging autobiographical sketch, *My First Success*.

Sullivan at once distinguished himself by his talent for composition, and for the advanced knowledge of instrumentation that he had acquired before he came to the Conservatoire. While still a student, he wrote the music to Shakespeare's *The Tempest*, a few bars of which he once inscribed in my album, and which displays the practised hand of an old master. Although I did not come across him much, I once had the pleasure of passing an hour with him that I shall never forget. It was during a performance of Mendelssohn's *St. Paul*. We sat together and followed the music from the score – and what a score! It was Mendelssohn's own manuscript, which Sullivan had succeeded in borrowing for the occasion from the director of the Conservatoire, Conrad Schleinitz, who was, as is well known, an intimate friend of Mendelssohn's. With what reverence we turned from one page to another! We were both amazed at the clear, firmly written notes, which so well expressed the ideas of the composer.

That Sullivan should have been able to inveigle Schleinitz into parting, however briefly, with such a priceless treasure is further testament to his enormous charm. We find, also, that, at seventeen, on meeting Liszt for the first time at a large dinner-party in Leipzig, he finished the evening by playing whist with him. The other members of the four were Hans von Bronsart, who gave the first performance of Liszt's Second Piano Concerto, and Ferdinand David, for whom Mendelssohn composed his Violin Concerto. Afterwards, Liszt and Sullivan walked home together. Sullivan became friendly, too, with Moscheles, who also taught Grieg. But, with the 'envious, bloodless and villainous' Reinecke, he seems to have drawn a blank.

Grieg's next visit to England, in the spring of 1889, began with a concert, at St James's Hall, in which the composer accompanied his wife in five of his songs and conducted his first *Peer Gynt Suite*, which had received its English première, under Henschel, four months earlier. The fourth movement, 'In the Hall of the Mountain King,' had to be played twice. *The Musical Times* reported that the suite caused a sensation. 'The performance was most masterly, the splendid Philharmonic orchestra seconding the composer-conductor to a marvel. No more striking and picturesque effects have been produced in our concert-rooms for a long time.' Bernard Shaw, 'the perfect Wagnerite' himself, attended the concert on behalf of the *Star*. As usual, his criticism is highly subjective.

Hitherto I have not been a great admirer of Edvard Grieg [Shaw had purposely not gone to some of Grieg's earlier concerts, telling his readers that there were other, more important musical events that should be brought to their notice]. He is a 'national' composer; and I am not to be imposed on by that sort of thing. I do not cry out 'How Norwegian!' whenever I hear an augmented triad; nor 'How Bohemian!' [a swipe at Dvořák] when I hear a tune proceeding by intervals of augmented seconds; nor 'How Irish!' when Mr. Villiers Stanford plays certain tricks on subdominant harmonies . . . All good 'folk music' is as international as the story of Jack the Giant Killer or the Ninth Symphony [Wagner: 'Hail to thee, Schiller, thou who gavest to the reborn spirit the stature of the "German Youth", who stands disdainful of the pride of Britain, the sensuous wiles of Paris! Who was this German Youth? Has anybody heard of a French, an English Youth? And *yet*, how plain and clear beyond mistake we understand this "German Youth"! This Youth, who in Mozart's virginal melodies beshamed the Italian capons; in Beethoven's symphony grew up to courage of the man, for dauntless, world-redeeming deeds! And this Youth it was who threw himself eventually upon the battlefield . . .] Grieg is very fond of the augmented triad; but his music does not remind me of Norway, perhaps because I have never been there. And his sweet but very cosmopolitan modulations, and his inability to get beyond a very pretty snatch of melody, do not go very far with me; for I despise pretty music . . .

However, let us be just. The pretty snatches are not only pretty, but both delicately and deeply felt by the composer. And they are at least long enough to make exquisite little songs, which Madame Grieg sings in such a way as to bring out everything that is in them. There is a certain quaintness about the pair. Grieg is a small, swift, busy, earnest man, with the eyes of a rhapsode, and in his hair and complexion the indescribable ashen tint that marks a certain type of modern Norseman. For Madame's appearance I cannot answer so fully, as I have had no opportunity of observing her quite closely . . .

The principal conductor at this concert was Mackenzie, whose *Burns Rhapsodie* concluded the programme. Earlier, during breaks in rehearsals, the two composers established a pleasant relationship, as Mackenzie recalls in his memoirs.

From Grieg I gathered that, at the outset of his career, it was owing to Liszt's advice that he had developed his talents in the direction of Norwegian folk-song and had adhered consistently to the national idiom to which his popularity is in great measure due. My *Burns Rhapsodie* led him, of Scottish extraction himself, to expatiate on the similarity of our countries' melodies and their characteristics. I am not, however, yet convinced of the existence of so striking a likeness as he seemed to discover.

Extremely particular regarding the smallest details when rehearsing, none could fail to appreciate the Scandinavian composer's artistic sensitiveness.

A fortnight later, on 28 March 1889, Grieg took part in another Philharmonic concert, that was, to all appearances, a gathering of Reinecke prentices. Cowen was the conductor of the evening, but Stanford was also on hand to direct his Violin Suite, with Joachim (to whom Reinecke dedicated his Violin Concerto) as soloist. In the second half, Grieg conducted his Piano Concerto; the solo part was performed by Agathe Backer-Gründahl, a Norwegian pupil of Bülow (her son, born three years earlier, also played the concerto under Grieg's baton, in Amsterdam in 1906).

Apart from these two orchestral concerts, Grieg gave three chamber music recitals. Prominent among the many works that he played was the piano version of the *Holberg Suite*. Nina sang a large number of the songs and found the courage to join her husband in piano duets, performing some of the *Norwegian Dances*. Also featured were the three Violin Sonatas. Greig took the piano part in each of these, while the violinists were Lady Hallé in the first, Joachim in the second and Johannes Wolff in the third. Wolff, a Belgian, was such a favourite with Queen Victoria that she once kept him at Balmoral for nearly five weeks.

All these orchestral and chamber concerts excited such enthusiasm that, for a month, London was in the grip of 'Grieg fever', according to one commentator. Nina became a celebrity in her own right, nearly stealing the limelight from her husband. At the final concert, people were queueing from eleven o'clock in the morning – 'quite as in the old Rubinstein days', reported a newspaper. In the midst of this frenzy, the Griegs travelled up to Manchester for a Hallé concert. Heralding their arrival, the *Manchester Guardian* devoted a leader to this signal occasion. The programme included the Piano Concerto, the *Two Elegiac Melodies*, the First Violin Sonata and six songs. Hallé had first performed the concerto, as soloist, in 1876, when the *Manchester Guardian* was so delighted by the work that it predicted, 'from this composer we have the right to expect much more in the future.' Now again, Hallé, who was but six weeks short of his seventieth birthday, took the solo part on Grieg's insistence. 'You are so much the better player', the composer told him. 'I don't play well enough for Manchester.' Grieg conducted both the concerto and the *Two Elegiac Melodies*. The concert was a huge success, the Griegs and Hallés being overwhelmed with applause.

Spurred on by their English triumphs, the Griegs made their début in Paris later in 1889 and were once more wildly acclaimed. A return visit the following year provoked the same reaction. The French capital took Edvard and Nina as much to its heart as London had done. In 1892, the writer Joseph Péladan proclaimed Grieg to be the world's greatest living composer, and, in 1893, Gabriel Fauré wrote in *Le Figaro*, 'Among the most famous living musicians, I know of none whose popularity equals, with us, that of Grieg; none whose works have entered our innermost musical life to the same degree.'

By December 1892, Grieg, who had not since returned to London, was established in the English musical consciousness as a powerful rival to Brahms, Verdi, Gounod and Dvořák. His inclusion in Lydia T. Morris's *Famous Musical Composers*, published in 1890, is indicative of the esteem in which he was held, for, of those composers alive at the end of 1892, only Brahms, Dvořák, Rubinstein and Bülow also received entries. The selection of Bülow is odd, since, as a composer, he amounted to nothing. The omission of Verdi and Gounod is equally perplexing, but perhaps Lydia T. Morris was not an opera-goer. Nevertheless, for Grieg to be ranked alongside Brahms, Dvořák and Rubinstein was achievement enough.

We may therefore conclude that Grieg was now an obvious choice for the CUMS jubilee. And, indeed, chosen he was.

But Stanford, Sedley Taylor, Austen Leigh and their colleagues did not leave it at that, and issued invitations to no less than four others. There are two possible explanations for this sudden largesse. Having originally set their sights on Brahms and Verdi, they may have felt that Grieg, or Grieg and one other, hardly amounted in terms of musical avoirdupois, to their initial grandiose concept. After all, as Mozart once reminded a fellow composer who spoke slightingly of Haydn, 'Sir, if you and I were melted down together, we would still not come to enough to make a Haydn.' The CUMS may therefore have decided that it would take five other composers to compensate for the absence of Brahms and Verdi. The alternative explanation is that time was now running short, and it was vital to get *somebody*. Brahms and Verdi had declined the offer; there was no knowing whether Grieg might not do the same. And so it could go on. However, by sending out five invitations, there was the probability that one reply, at least, would be affirmative – and, of course, the more acceptances, the better.

Of the four other composers whom the university approached, only one was accounted to come within hailing distance of Brahms, Verdi, Dvořák, Gounod and Grieg. This was Camille Saint-Saëns.

CHAPTER 6

SAINT-SAËNS

In his book *Masters of French Music*, completed in July 1893, Arthur Hervey begins the section on Saint-Saëns by observing, 'There probably does not exist a living composer who is gifted with a musical organisation so complete as that of Camille Saint-Saëns.' Oscar Comettant concludes his essay, in the exactly contemporaneous *Famous Composers and Their Works*, with similar praise.

> We cannot more fitly terminate this sketch of the great personality of Saint-Saëns than by adding that he is one of the most masterly readers of piano and organ music who has ever lived, and an improviser of the first rank.
>
> As a child pianist and composer, Camille Saint-Saëns was what is called an infant prodigy. The child has come to man's estate and is, at the present moment, one of the most learned and able artists in every branch of his art, that can be found in the ranks of modern musicians. Since the death of Beethoven, Schumann and Mendelssohn, he wields in Europe the sceptre of symphony; he is renowned as a composer for the church and the theatre, and as an organist; and the mastery he has shown in the concerto, the oratorio and chamber music, of which he has produced a large number of works, is of world-wide fame.

Saint-Saëns also possessed vast extra-musical erudition. He published poetry, a book of philosophy and an essay on the Roman theatre. He delivered an address on astronomy. He contributed occasional articles on literature and painting, and had a play performed. He carried out research in physics and natural history. He was widely travelled, a superior linguist and an accomplished amateur archaeologist. He was a passable magician, a brilliant mimic and a deft caricaturist. His conversation, punctuated by witticisms and allusions to classical literature, was delivered like gunfire. He was not only an infant prodigy, he was an adult prodigy too.

He could read music and play the piano at two. He was writing waltzes at three. At four, he gave his first public recital. By the age of five, he was studying full orchestral scores. When he was nine, he was able to offer, as an encore to his recitals, any of the thirty-two piano sonatas of Beethoven, playing from memory whichever one was chosen. Yet he was totally devoid of showmanship; his playing was always neat and unostentatious. He would come on to the platform, sit down and begin to play, almost in one continuous movement; when he had finished, he would bow briefly and depart.

He made his mark with his First Symphony, performed in 1853, when he was eighteen. This was highly praised by Berlioz, who later described his young colleague as 'one of the greatest musicians of our epoch'; on another occasion, he perceptively remarked, 'He knows everything, but lacks inexperience.' At twenty-one, he was appointed organist of the Madeleine, one of the most coveted posts in Parisian musical life. He at once gained a reputation as an executant of incomparable ability, and both Liszt and Rubinstein declared him to be the finest organist of the age. Another early admirer was Bülow, who with characteristic generosity readily conceded that his own awe-inspiring knowledge and powers of memory were eclipsed by Saint-Saëns'.

There does not exist a monument of art, of whatsoever country, school, or epoch, that Saint-Saëns has not thoroughly studied. When we came to talk about the symphonies of Schumann [this was in 1859; these works were then hardly known in France], I was most astonished to hear him reproduce them on the piano with such a degree of ease and exactitude that I was dumbfounded in comparing this prodigious memory with my own, which is often praised. In talking with him, I discovered that nothing was unknown to him, and what made him appear still greater to me was the sincerity of his enthusiasm and his complete modesty.

A year later, Bülow went so far as to pronounce Saint-Saëns the most important living musician after Liszt and Wagner.

During his visit to Paris for the production of *Tannhäuser* in 1860, Wagner made the acquaintance of Saint-Saëns, who played to him on the piano extracts from the master's operas. Wagner was delighted by the excellence of his playing and staggered by his feats of memory.

I thus learned to appreciate the skill and talent of this young musician, which was simply incredible. With an unparalleled sureness and rapidity of glance, with regard to even the most complicated orchestral score, this young man combined a no less marvellous memory. He could not only play my scores by heart, including *Tristan* [which had not yet been performed; Bülow conducted the première, from memory, five years later], but could also reproduce their several parts, whether they were leading or minor themes. And this he did with such precision that one could imagine him to have had the actual music before his eyes.

Some years later, finding himself in the company of a number of French musicians, Wagner drank to the health of Saint-Saëns, who was not present, referring to him as 'the greatest living French composer'. At this time, it should be borne in mind, though, that 'the theatrical parody' *Faust* was occupying plenty of time and space in Europe's opera-houses. The toast may have been intended as one in the eye for Gounod, but it was nevertheless good publicity for Saint-Saëns.

In 1868, came the first of the orchestral works that were to carry Saint-Saëns' name around the world: the Second Piano Concerto, commissioned by Rubinstein for one of his Paris concerts and completed in seventeen days. At the extremely successful première, Saint-Saëns took the solo part, and Rubinstein conducted. From now on, his works themselves, rather than the praise of fellow musicians, were to become his most powerful recommendation.

His first visit to London, as a fully fledged composer, took place in the spring of 1871, when he escaped from Paris during the Commune. Like Bizet, he had joined the National Guard a year earlier, at the time of the Franco-Prussian War. He was wise to leave when he did, for the Communards regarded his military service with disfavour. His escape was just in time, for, on the following day, the railways and ports were closed. This was a period of real danger. Fauré, who had enlisted with Massenet in a rifle regiment, came under fire at Champigny and later only avoided being pressed into the Commune army by using a false passport to cross the federal lines and make his way to the safety of Rambouillet. A friend of Saint-Saëns, the painter Henri Regnault, was killed at Buzenal, and to him the composer dedicated his *Marche héroïque*. Another casualty was Auber, who, having threatened to live forever, died of a broken heart at the age of eighty-nine while watching his beloved Paris being destroyed successively by the Prussians and the Communards. His death was reminiscent of that of Haydn, who expired in his seventy-eighth year during the French bombardment of Vienna in 1809, after weakly struggling to the piano each day, defiantly to play the national anthem he had written for his country. Auber's distress was perhaps the greater, for the hostilities affected him personally. 'The only things I like', he once told Wagner, 'are women, horses, the boulevards and the Bois de Boulogne.' He always owned magnificent horses, being particularly proud of his English breeds, which he loved to ride in the Bois. Shortly before his death, his two favourite horses were appropriated by the Communards; Almaviva was given a cart to draw in St. Denis, and Figaro went to the butchers. Conditions were appalling then: dogs sold at a franc a pound; rats, at a franc each. More than 20,000 lives were lost during the Commune, and many people were frightened to leave their homes. In his book on Charles-Valentin Alkan, Ronald Smith quotes from a letter, written by the composer to Hiller, describing what life was like: 'For forty-nine days and nights without respite I have been living in the midst of cannon balls and bullets. All I have is a shutter and a piano with a hole through them. I have hardly eaten at all.' César Franck, with a family to look after, was forced to venture out in search of food and once pushed a barrow right across Paris in order to collect coal. Henri Duparc's family had to exist for a while on nothing but chocolate.

Even those whose lives were not imperilled by the Franco-Prussian War, and immediately ensuing Commune, frequently suffered great anguish. The plight of Offenbach, who had been born in Cologne, aroused much sympathy. Bewildered by the turn in events, he fled to Italy. 'Alas!' he wrote, 'What despair I feel that I was born on the Rhine and am linked with these savages . . . Alas, my poor France!' A less serious outcome of these troubled times was that the scenery and props for *Aida*, which were being made in Paris, could not be moved out of the city, thus delaying the première in Cairo for a year. But this was of small consequence to Verdi; his pity was for the French people. 'This disaster for France desolates my heart', he wrote. 'And now that Bismarck says that Paris will be spared, I fear more than ever that at least in part it will be destroyed.' He contributed 2,000 francs, from his advance on *Aida*, for the benefit of wounded French soldiers.

The principal casualty among French musicians was Salvador Daniel. After Auber's death on 12 May 1871, he was appointed to replace him as director of the Conservatoire. A fortnight later, he was shot by the Communards. Daniel was in turn succeeded by Ambroise Thomas, then sixty, who had nursed Auber through his final days. Gounod would have seemed the obvious choice to be director, but he had long since departed for London, to the undisguised contempt of many of his colleagues. Bizet was of the opinion that Gounod would not have been appointed anyway, for 'his private life is really not pure enough to allow them to consider trusting him with a school for young ladies.'

Gounod was among the first people whom Saint-Saëns contacted on his arrival in London. He needed money quickly, and Gounod consented to his producing a piano transcription of *Gallia*, for which Saint-Saëns received five guineas. Apart from this, he also wrote a number of short piano pieces and songs, all of which found a ready market. Grove helped by engaging him for an organ recital at the Crystal Palace. This was followed by an appearance, as a pianist, in a chamber concert at St James's Hall.

Saint-Saëns was particularly happy to see, among the other refugees, Pauline Viardot. The famous singer, for whom Berlioz had once felt strongly, had come over with her husband and Turgenev, and was staying in Devonshire Street. It was through Pauline Viardot that Saint-Saëns had been introduced to Rossini, who adopted him as one of the leading performers at the celebrated musical evenings he used to give in his luxurious apartment on the corner of the Boulevard des Italiens and the Rue de la Chaussée d'Antin. Now Pauline Viardot took him into London society and invited him to her own musical evenings. Among the other frequent guests was the violinist Leopold Auer, who pays tribute to the singer in *My Long Life in Music*.

> . . . thanks to her personal charm, and to her standing as a great artist in the musical world, she became the leading spirit of the little circle of French refugee artists. One evening a week her friends gathered at her home; and I, who had become acquainted with the Viardot family in Baden-Baden, was received there as a Russian friend. On entering the Viardot salon, the guest was welcomed by the mistress of the house, surrounded by her family and friends: her husband, Louis Viardot, her two daughters, one of whom was a sculptor of remarkable talent, and only son Paul, an admirable violinist; the famous Russian novelist, Ivan Tourgueneff; Charles Gounod; Camille Saint-Saëns – then very young, very much alive, and practically unknown – as well as many others whose names I no longer recall. We had music, with Saint-Saëns, a real master, at the piano, while I played some of the attractive little pieces composed for the two instruments by Mme. Viardot and dedicated to her son. For me the most interesting moment of the evening would come when Mme. Viardot asked Gounod to sing some of his songs. Without much urging,

the composer of 'Faust' would seat himself at the piano, and after a few measures by way of prelude would recite – for it was narration rather than song – a group of his songs with a small, clear voice, in the most delightfully artistic manner. The enthusiasm of his auditors may be imagined.

As was traditional in the Viardot household, there were also evenings of charades and private fun-making to which only a select few were invited. At their country home, the Château de Courtavenel, near Rozay-en-Brie, they had formerly put on full-length plays. Pauline's daughter Louise took part in these and, in her *Memories and Adventures*, she refers to 'a very successful performance of Beaumarchais's *Mariage de Figaro*', in which the actors were Turgenev (Almaviva), Gounod (Figaro), Désirée Artôt (The Countess), Pauline Viardot (Suzanne) and Louise (Chérubin). C. E. Hallé, artist son of Sir Charles, was another who attended the Viardot gatherings. He was a friend of Pauline's brother, Manuel Garcia, the singing teacher and inventor of the laryngoscope, who sang duets with Rossini, when the composer visited London in 1824, and died at the age of 101 in 1906. In *Notes from a Painter's Life*, Hallé has left a delightful account of the Devonshire Street festivities.

> One evening there was a charade. The subject was Daphne flying from the advances of Apollo, who rose in the character of the sun from behind Mount Olympus. Mme. Viardot was Daphne, Manuel Garcia, with his cheeks puffed out, and the rays of the sun in gilt paper round his head, was Apollo. Tourguenieff, who was very large, was the mountain, and Gounod did the incidental music. It was a performance not to be forgotten!

Saint Saëns' speciality, probably given when Gounod was not present, was to sing Marguerite's 'Jewel Song' from *Faust* in a falsetto voice, attired in bonnet and long blonde tresses. In a double act with Turgenev, he donned pink tights and played a corpse, while the author of *A Nest of Gentlefolk*, taking the part of a doctor, studiously attempted to dissect him. Henry James was once witness to similar presentations; he found it 'strange and rather sweet' to see the great Russian writer so obviously enjoying the dressing-up and playing about, sometimes even on all fours.

Clara Schumann visited Pauline Viardot and was distressed to discover her friend in such alien and reduced circumstances. 'I pitied her so terribly that, when I was there the other day, I had to fight to keep back my tears. It's a good thing she didn't suspect anything; she would certainly have laughed in my face.' During her stay in London, to give concerts, Clara noted in her diary on 27 January 1871, 'Capitulation of Paris. If only we could have been in Germany today. We meet with no sympathy here.' She wrote to Brahms of 'the anti-German feeling of the English, who sympathize (which in itself is a nice thing to do) with the weaker side, and therefore with the French. At first I thought it must be jealousy on their part because we Germans had for once shown how great we were, but the Germans who live here assure me it's not this, but compassion.' Brahms, for his part, composed the *Song of Triumph*, for baritone solo, chorus and orchestra, with its reference to Revelation XIX, Verse 2, 'For true and righteous are his judgements: for he hath judged the great whore, which did corrupt the earth with her fornication . . .' – the whore being either Paris or France.

At the end of May 1871, the Commune having fallen, Saint-Saëns at once returned to the ravaged French capital, while, as we have already seen, the Gounodyssey continued, with its hero preferring to remain comfortably ensnared by the charms of Georgina Weldon. Two months later, Saint-Saëns was back in London. He had made such a good impression that he was invited, for a flattering fee of £50, to take part in the performances that inaugurated the organ of the newly opened Royal Albert Hall. He was now described as 'an exceptional and distinguished performer'.

Henceforward, he became a frequent and increasingly popular and respected visitor to England. His first Philharmonic concert was in 1874, when he played Beethoven's Fourth Piano Concerto, with Cusins conducting. Walter Macfarren, the brother of George Macfarren, notes in his autobiography, *Memories*, that Saint-Saëns performed 'with fluency and insight; although he did not efface from my memory the rendering of that beautiful work by Mendelssohn [in 1847, with Costa], or, in my opinion, equal the refinement of Charles Hallé in this particular composition.' Two years later, Macfarren heard Rubinstein in the same work; and to have heard Mendelssohn, Hallé, Saint-Saëns and Rubinstein is no mean achievement.

Saint-Saëns returned to London in 1876. He played his Beethoven Variations with Marie Jaell at a Musical Union concert and appeared in a programme of his works at St James's Hall. Among the pieces performed were the First Piano Trio and a two-piano arrangement of the *Marche héroïque*. He took part in a further Musical Union concert in 1877, and in 1878 played his Second Piano Concerto, with Wilhelm Ganz, at the New Philharmonic. Earlier in the same season,

Sarasate had introduced the *Introduction et rondo capriccioso* to London audiences. At a New Philharmonic concert, in 1879, Saint-Saëns conducted his Second Symphony and played the Fourth Piano Concerto. During the visit, he also performed the Second Concerto, with Cusins, at the Philharmonic and, as organist, played Bach's Prelude and Fugue in A minor. At the Crystal Palace, he was again the soloist in his Second Concerto, which was by now firmly established in the international repertoire; he also conducted the *Le Rouet d'Omphale*. A few months afterwards, he travelled to Birmingham for the première of his specially commissioned *La Lyre et la harpe*, a cantata with words by Victor Hugo, with whom he was on the friendliest terms. Costa happened to be in unusually affable mood and was most helpful; the choir sang superbly, and the work was a success. Saint-Saëns was full of praise for the Birmingham choral singing and, in a newspaper article, ridiculed the charge that the English were unmusical. The choir, he said, 'have everything: intonation, perfect rhythm, fine shading of dynamics and a lovely sound. If people like this are unmusical, they nevertheless perform as if they were the best musicians in the world.' In 1880, he played the First Piano Concerto at a New Philharmonic concert, took part in a chamber concert at which the *Marche héroïque* was performed in an arrangement for eight hands, and gave a Steinway Hall recital of his own works and those of his pupil Fauré. During the same year, the famous Cello Concerto was introduced at the Crystal Palace. On 8 July 1880, Saint-Saëns was received at Windsor by Queen Victoria, who greeted him with outstretched hands. He gave a brief organ recital in St George's Chapel, played some of his piano pieces, and accompanied Princess Beatrice in an aria from his opera *Étienne Marcel*. The Queen noted in her diary that he 'plays and composes beautifully'.

He continued coming to London over the following decade. Among the highlights of these trips were Philharmonic performances of Beethoven's Fourth Piano Concerto and Mozart's Twenty-Second Piano Concerto, both of which were conducted by Sullivan, whom Saint-Saëns much esteemed. At a concert in 1887, he was soloist in his first four piano concertos. 'He played them all by heart', wrote Wilhelm Ganz, who was the conductor, 'and, when he had finished, seemed as fresh as if he had done nothing at all.' The seal was set on his English reputation with the première, in May 1886, of the magnificent Third Symphony, commissioned by the Philharmonic Society and dedicated to Liszt, which prompted a great demonstration of enthusiasm from the St James's Hall audience. By December 1892, when he was fifty-seven, he had reached the peak of his fame, which was as securely rooted in England as in any other country in the world.

In terms of their popularity at the time, Grieg and Saint-Saëns would probably have been perfectly acceptable substitutes for Brahms and Verdi. But, as we have seen, this was an age of intense national consciousness, and, whereas Brahms and Verdi were generally thought to transcend national considerations, Saint-Saëns was not regarded in the same light. He was a French composer, and the CUMS therefore plainly deemed it politic to balance his selection with an invitation to a German composer as well. Had the choice been, say, Grieg and Dvořák, the problem would not have arisen, for honouring, in effect, Norway and Bohemia would have offended nobody. But France and Germany were major powers, which was a different matter.

The CUMS chose Max Bruch to represent Germany. That this was a logical and predictable choice is made apparent in Fuller-Maitland's *Masters of German Music*, which was in preparation at the time.

> It is not easy to estimate the exact distance which separates him [Brahms] whom the wisest critics call the greatest of living German composers from the master whom most of these would agree in placing nearest to him in order of artistic merit; nor is it likely that if the relative greatness of the two could be assessed, all or even the majority of those whose opinion is best worth having would measure it in the same way. They would, I think, agree in one thing; that a very great interval should be placed between MAX BRUCH and the rest of his German contemporaries. For my own part I should not hesitate to place Bruch midway between Brahms and the other composers of their country, and to make both intervals wide.

Famous Composers and their Works, in similar vein, speaks of Bruch's 'right to admission to the ranks of the masters'.

Bruch was born in 1838, three years after Saint-Saëns and five years before Grieg. He studied with Reinecke and Hiller. His first big success came in 1864 with the choral work *Frithjof Scenen*, for soloists, male chorus and orchestra. This is based on six episodes from the Swedish poet Tegnér's *Frithiofs Saga*, which was a modernisation and Christian reinterpretation of the old Norwegian pagan saga of

Frithiof the Bold. Within a year, Bruch had conducted this work, which is dedicated to Clara Schumann, throughout Germany; shortly afterwards, he directed performances in Brussels and in Paris, where he met Rossini and Berlioz, both of whom expressed their admiration. In 1866, he brought out his celebrated First Violin Concerto, dedicated to Joachim, who gave the first performance of the final revised version two years later in Bremen. Bruch also dedicated to Joachim his Third Violin Concerto and Second Symphony (the First Symphony is dedicated to Brahms). By the beginning of the seventies, he had acquired a high reputation in Germany and was often held to be the equal of Brahms, who had not yet completed his own First Symphony – while both of Bruch's were already in existence. Around this time, young Alexander Mackenzie, still toiling away as an orchestral musician, met Bruch in Sondershausen.

With him I conversed much and was sharply questioned about the state of music in London, particularly regarding the Philharmonic, upon which society most German musicians seemed to keep a longing eye.

His *Violin Concerto* (No. 1) had recently met with the success it richly deserves, and the manly 'Frithjof Scenes' had already secured fame for him in his own land. When he assured me of his interest in Scottish folksong, saying, 'Es hat mich eigentlich zum komponieren veranlasst' (It really incited me to compose), I hardly realized how much truth the statement contained until I heard the once popular prelude to his own *Lorelei*. A prominent subject in that piece consists of four bars of the second part of 'Lochaber no more' . . .

And the opening bars of the often sung *Ave Maria* in *Das Feuerkreuz* are clearly recognizable as our old song, 'Will ye gang to the ewebucts, Marion' . . .

Apart from his great ability as a conductor, the impression created by Bruch's personality on me was that of a highly-cultured, musically-gifted man, somewhat cynical of speech and brusque of manner.

Bruch once told Louis Elson, who wrote the section on him in *Famous Composers and their Works*, that he was familiar with over 400 Scottish folksongs. In the choral work *Schön Ellen*, composed directly after the *Frithjof Scenen*, he makes extensive use of 'The Campbells Are Coming'.

In 1872, Bruch produced his *Odysseus*, ten scenes from Homer, for soloists, chorus and orchestra. This was widely acclaimed, and Fuller-Maitland calls it 'the masterpiece of Bruch's genius'. He followed it with several other successful choral works, including

Arminius (1875) which is dedicated to Henschel, *Das Lied von der Glocke* (1878) and *Achilleus* (1885). At this time, Bruch was looked upon, first and foremost, as a choral composer. The 1879 edition of Grove's *Dictionary*, after describing him as 'one of the most eminent living German composers', concludes that 'Bruch's real field is concert music for chorus and orchestra; he is above all a master of melody, and of the effective treatment of the masses. These two sides of his artistic activity, so to speak, play into each other's hands, and have brought him deserved success.' Elson, writing fourteen years later, suggests, 'In the latter part of the nineteenth century probably no composer has done more for the development of the chorus, and especially of the *Maennerchor*, than Max Bruch.'

Edward Speyer, author of *My Life and Friends*, met Bruch in Berlin in 1878, when the composer was forty and approaching the height of his fame.

Bruch was appallingly ugly. He had an unusually large forehead with a marked backward slant and protruding fishy eyes. Although one could not help being impressed by his intelligence and sensibility, and his prominent gifts as a conversationalist, his personality was unattractive. During his three years' sojourn in Berlin I had occasion to meet him several times, and in particular remember an evening when he dined with me. Of course, we talked almost exclusively of music, and, discussing the great classical masters, we ended with Brahms. 'Brahms,' said Bruch, 'consistently continues to adopt the sonata form in his compositions; I myself consider this form to be exhausted; in fact, nothing really new can be created within its limits. No, I have returned to the art of Handel, and for myself can only see further progress in music in choral works.' He followed this up by alluding to his disagreeable experiences with Brahms owing to the latter's freakish and unmannerly behaviour, of which he gave the following example:

'The first performance of my Second Violin Concerto in G Minor [D minor] took place in a semi-private manner in Baden-Baden last summer. All the prominent musical personalities who generally assemble there at that time of the year were present, and among them Brahms. The Concerto, against the rule usually adopted, commences with a slow movement. The work had a great success, and at the end of the performance I was warmly congratulated by all present with the exception of Brahms, who only exclaimed, "My dear Bruch, how can one commence a Violin Concerto with an Adagio?" Not content with this, he followed me round during the afternoon and kept on tugging at my coat-tails and repeating the words, "How can one commence a Violin Concerto with an Adagio?" An unsupportable fellow.'

Here is another story about the two. Brahms chanced to visit Bruch in

Cologne, and Bruch put into his hands a MS. score of considerable dimensions with a request for his opinion and a solemn admonition to secrecy. It was the score of an oratorio entitled *Arminius*, founded on an episode in early German history, which eventually enjoyed a short-lived popularity. Bruch waited anxiously for the verdict, but all Brahms said after a seemingly close scrutiny was: 'I say, what splendid music-paper this is! Where did you get it?' A few days later Brahms and Bruch met again at a large dinner-party as the guests of a wealthy patron of music. When the sound of a barrel-organ in the street reached the ears of the company, Brahms called across the dinner-table in stentorian tones: 'Listen, Bruch. The fellow has got hold of *Arminius*.'

Speyer's description of Bruch was put down after the composer's death. Elson, writing during his lifetime, felt the need to temper accuracy with tact. 'In personal appearance Bruch is by no means as majestic as one would suppose from his works', he allowed. 'He is small of stature, and his dark eyes peer through his spectacles with the sharp glance of a teacher rather than of a creator of heroic cantatas. He is quick and nervous in motion and, when directing an orchestra or chorus, his gestures are spontaneous and expressive.' The work by which Bruch is now best known, the First Violin Concerto, was introduced to London audiences in 1868 by Ludwig Straus, who, seven years later, became leader of the Hallé Orchestra: Joachim gave the first performance in Manchester in 1869. Bruch made his English début, conducting the concerto, with Sarasate as soloist, and the prelude to *Die Loreley*, at a Crystal Palace concert in October 1877. Ten days afterwards, he conducted *Odysseus* in Liverpool; its English première had taken place in Manchester in 1875. On returning to London at the beginning of November, he conducted the world première of his Second Violin Concerto, again with Sarasate, at the Crystal Palace. He next visited London the following year, conducting the *Frithjof Scenen*. This was very well received and, as a result, he was invited to contribute a choral composition for the 1879 Birmingham Musical Festival. He was not able to produce a new piece in time, so, instead, directed the first English performance of *Das Lied von der Glocke*. At this same festival, Saint-Saëns, we may recall, conducted his *La Lyre et la harpe* and was so impressed by the choir.

Bruch was now making a noticeable impact on the English musical scene, and, in 1880, he was offered the conductorship of the Liverpool Philharmonic, following the retirement of Sir Julius Benedict. He accepted the offer – which, for Liverpool, was a major coup. With Hallé in Manchester and Bruch in Liverpool, Lancashire was thus entitled to consider itself a musical match for London. Bruch stayed in Liverpool for two and a half years, before leaving for Breslau in the spring of 1883. His departure was little regretted; he was respected, but not liked. He raised standards of performance to a very high level. However, his treatment of the orchestra and choir lacked warmth, and he had a rigid intolerance for anything less than perfection. Unlike Benedict, who came from Stuttgart, he made only a token attempt at mastering the English language, which further weakened the unsatisfactory liaison between himself and the performers. Yet, the Liverpool period was productive for Bruch. The proximity of Scotland rekindled his interest in that country's folksongs, and he composed at this time his *Scottish Fantasy*, for violin and orchestra, conducting the first public performance of the work in February 1881 in Liverpool, with Joachim as soloist. His next composition, the *Kol Nidrei*, for cello and orchestra, is another of his more popular pieces. He also found a wife in Liverpool, marrying Clara Tuczek, a singer from Berlin.

Before taking up his new conducting post in Breslau, Bruch accepted an invitation to conduct his works in America, where he stayed for two months. He was in Breslau for eight years before moving to Berlin, where, in 1891, he became director of composition at the Hochschule, of which Joachim was head. He was now Herr Professor Bruch, internationally famous, widely respected and well worth inviting to Cambridge. That he would not be quite such a social asset as the picturesque Grieg or the nimble-witted, myriad-minded Saint Saëns was of small consequence compared to his eminent position in the musical world. The courteous Fuller-Maitland gives perhaps the fairest idea of the man.

If a somewhat blunt manner and an amount of self-centredness that is not common even amongst musicians prevent his making friends very quickly, or being what is called popular in general society, those who know Bruch best know how whole-hearted is his devotion to his art, how pure are his aims, and how honest and upright he is in every artistic matter, as well as in those which concern everyday life.

From our vantage point, almost a century later, it is not difficult to understand why, in 1892, Gounod and Saint-Saëns should have been valued more highly in England than their living compatriots Thomas, Massenet, Fauře and Chabrier. One notes, in addition, that by then, Bizet, Delibes, Lalo and Franck were all dead and that Debussy, Satie and Ravel had yet to establish themselves. With regard to German composers of the time (Fuller-Maitland and most other critics made no distinction between German and Austrian), it may seem surprising, however, that Bruch was ranked above Bruckner, who, by December 1892, had already completed his Eighth Symphony. In the section on German Music in *Famous Composers and their Works*, there are leading articles on Brahms, Bruch, Goldmark and Rheinberger, with a mere two sentences on Bruckner. In *Masters of German Music*, Fuller-Maitland writes at length on Brahms, Bruch, Goldmark and Rheinberger, concluding with a chapter that briefly reviews the achievements of lesser known contemporary composers, including Kirchner, Bargiel, Hofmann, Draeseke, Sommer, Kistler – and Bruckner – among which minor figures, 'judging from the quality and value of his work, rather than by its pretensions, Anton Bruckner finds here his legitimate place.' In regard to the strength of contemporary German music at this time, it is interesting to observe that the only piece by any of these composers, excluding Brahms and Bruch, to find acceptance in England was Goldmark's *Rustic Wedding Symphony* (1876), which Hallé performed five times in Manchester between 1877 and 1892; and Goldmark was Hungarian.

On 18 December 1892, Bruckner's Eighth Symphony, conducted by Richter, received its première in Vienna and was warmly applauded. By then, all his symphonies, apart from No 5, had been performed, and each of these had been heard in Vienna. No 3 had also been played in The Hague, Utrecht, Amsterdam, Prague, Linz, Salzburg and New York; No 4, in Munich, Graz and New York; No 7, in Munich, Karlsruhe, Graz, Hamburg, Cologne, Berlin, Dresden, Amsterdam, Budapest, New York, Boston and Chicago. In July 1891, the University of Vienna conferred on Bruckner the honorary degree of Doctor of Philosophy, its first such award to a composer.

Yet, in England, Bruckner was almost completely unknown. The first of his symphonies to be performed was the Seventh, which Richter conducted in London on 23 May 1887, four days before he directed the première of Stanford's *Irish Symphony*. The work met with no success whatsoever, even though it had been eagerly awaited by a number of informed enthusiasts. *The Musical Times*, in admitting that the cold reception was not undeserved, nevertheless expressed sympathy for Bruckner. 'There is reason for unfeigned regret at the failure of the much-vaunted Symphony, since every man with a heart in him must desire success for a composer of sixty-three [sixty-two], who has vainly struggled after fame all his life.'

By December 1892, the Seventh Symphony was still only one of two Bruckner symphonies to have been heard in England. The Third was performed in London by Richter on 29 June 1891, occasioning an equally cool reception. It was not until November 1936, incidentally, that the original version of the Fourth Symphony was given its first London performance, when Karl Böhm conducted it at a Royal Philharmonic concert. In the circumstances, one can hardly wonder at the fact that the CUMS chose Bruch in preference to Bruckner.

Oddly enough, Bruckner's sole visit to England was an uncontrovertible triumph. He came over in the summer of 1871, to represent Austria in the recitals connected with the inauguration of the new organ at the Royal Albert Hall. Saint-Saëns, we may recall, also took part in these recitals. Bruckner arrived on 29 July. He stayed at Seyd's Hotel, 39 Finsbury Square, which catered for German-speaking guests. He was excited to see that, on posters advertising the recitals, his name was displayed 'in letters bigger than myself!' His first recital was on 2 August, at which he performed Bach's Toccata in F major and Handel's Fugue in D minor, with improvisations on both works, as well as on Bach's Fugue in E minor. This was a great success, and by the time he left London at the end of August, he had given five more recitals at the Royal Albert Hall and, at the invitation of Manns and Grove, a further four at the Crystal Palace, where, on 19 August, an audience of 70,000 gathered to hear him. He wrote to a friend in Linz about the 'enormous applause, always endless. Encores requested. Two improvisations in particular I often had to repeat. The same at both halls. Lots of compliments, congratulations . . . Kapellmeister Manns of the Crystal Palace said he was astounded and I was to come back again soon . . .'

Plans for a return visit unfortunately fell through, but Bruckner never abandoned the idea of making a second trip. It was at Seyd's Hotel, incidentally, that, on 10 August, he embarked on his Second Symphony, beginning with the composition of the final movement. As the years passed, his London triumphs became golden memories in a life increasingly blighted by scorn and lack of recognition (Bruckner's 'symphonic boa constrictors', said Brahms, were 'a swindle that will soon be forgotten'). Such was his desire for the success of the Seventh Symphony in London, that he even contemplated coming over for the première, in the belief that his presence might remind people of his recitals in August 1871 and persuade them to receive the work more kindly. He was saddened by the symphony's failure, but lived in hope of eventual English recognition, inspired by the medal, commemorating his participation in the Royal Albert Hall recitals, which he assigned a special place among the dozens of certificates, diplomas, citations, testimonials, depositions, and other tangible evidences of his musical ability, that were so touchingly necessary in helping him sustain his faith in himself.

An honorary degree from Cambridge would have been paradise itself for Bruckner. Indeed, not long after Brahms had declined his doctorate in 1877, Bruckner made inquiries to discover if he might be considered for such a distinction, though no formal application seems to have reached Cambridge. During the mid-eighties he sent petitions to the universities of Philadelphia and Cincinnati, who were among the first American universities to bestow honorary doctorates in music, but neither found itself able to grant his request.

In 1892, Richard Strauss, too, had yet to make his name in England. *Famous Composers and their Works* describes him as 'by far the most interesting and the most promising' of the younger German composers. Fuller-Maitland writes, 'On the whole, he is one of the most interesting figures among the younger musicians of Germany, and it may, of course, be that those who regard him as a genius of the first order will be some day proved to be right. Time will show.' Time did show, but not in England until 1896, when Manns, then seventy-one, gave the first English performance of *Till Eulenspiegel*, four months after its première in Cologne. In a brief speech to the wildly enthusiastic Crystal Palace audience, that remarkable conductor admitted that it was the most difficult work he had ever directed. *The Musical Times* called the piece 'sensational'. Performances of *Don Juan* and *Also sprach Zarathustra* quickly followed at the Crystal Palace, and, in 1897, at the age of thirty-three, the composer made his London début, establishing himself, in English eyes, as a modern master.

Like Strauss, Mahler's day was yet to come. By December 1892,

when he was thirty-two, he had only completed the first of his
symphonies, and this was not published until 1899. But like Bruckner, he had already made his sole journey to England, arriving on 26
May 1892, conducting eighteen opera performances at Covent
Garden and Drury Lane, and departing on 23 July. He learned
English especially for his visit and endeared himself to everybody by
his painstaking attempts to stick to this language, whatever the difficulties. In *The Golden Age of Opera*, Herman Klein recalled meeting
Mahler while the composer was in London.

> I found him extraordinarily modest for a musician of his rare gifts and
> established reputation. He would never consent to talk about himself or
> his compositions. Indeed the latter might have been non-existent for all
> that one ever heard about them; but his efforts to speak English, even with
> those who spoke German fluently, were untiring as well as amusing,
> though they tended to prolong conversation.

It was not until after his death, in 1911, that Mahler's music made
any headway in England.

Before taking leave of the German and Austrian composers of the
time, let us remember that, in December 1892, Johann Strauss, the
man whom Wagner once described as having 'the most musical mind
in Europe', and who was warmly regarded by Liszt, Brahms, Verdi,
Rubinstein, Bülow and many other leading musicians, was still alive,
residing in Vienna, where he had been born sixty-seven years earlier.
In 1890, an opinion poll found him to be the third most popular
person, after Queen Victoria and Bismarck, in Europe. His compositions commanded a wider audience and were more frequently performed than those by any of his contemporaries. When he died in
1899, he was mourned by the entire world and buried next to Beethoven, Schubert and Brahms. He, too, had already made his only
visit to London, which lasted from the middle of August to the end of
October 1867, during which time he conducted no less than sixty-
three concerts at Covent Garden, winning tumultuous applause and
being fêted by society. Yet Fuller-Maitland could find no place for
him in *Masters of German Music*. To its great credit, *Famous Composers
and their Works* allots him ten pages, only three less than for Brahms,
and chooses the estimable Henry T. Finck to write about him. 'And
why should the erudite historians honour with their attention', asks
Finck ironically, 'a mere Strauss, who was only a *man of genius* and
never constructed any symphonies, oratorios, or opera?' And, for

'historians', we can substitute 'Cambridge University'.
In addition to Grieg, Saint-Saëns and Bruch, the CUMS chose the
composer-poet-librettist Arrigo Boito. This was a good choice, for
Italy's place in the history of music and growing political strength
needed to be recognised. Moreover, as we shall see, Boito was clearly
chosen to represent not only Italy but Verdi, too.

Boito's claim to fame, as a composer, rested solely upon his opera
Mefistofele, because, to all intents, he had written nothing else. In this,
he was, and remains, a unique figure, as Arthur Pougin makes clear
in *Famous Composers and their Music*.

Arrigo Boito presents the peculiar example of a musician high in distinction in his own country, with a fair measure of fame in other lands, who,
though past the age of fifty years, has thus far produced but a single work,
his *Mephistopheles*. This work, having at first met with a sad repulse in
Italy, recovered itself in a brilliant fashion some years afterwards, and has
since run successfully on almost all the large stages of Europe [and in
Boston and New York]. He is perhaps the only known example of a
composer who owes his reputation to a single work, and the uniqueness of
the case makes it worthy of mention.

How high his reputation stood can be gauged from the four-and-a-
half-page entry in Grove's *Dictionary* (Gounod receives two pages, as
does Rubinstein), written by Giannandrea Mazzucato for the 1889
edition, which was largely edited by Fuller-Maitland.

It is rather early days to pronounce *ex cathedra* an opinion as to the place
which Arrigo Boito will take amongst the great masters; yet one thing is
beyond doubt, and that is, that Boito has a right to a conspicuous place
amongst the greatest living artists. There are certainly in Europe, and
perhaps even in Italy, poets of higher attainment than he: and confronted
as a musician with Brahms, Goldmark, Dvořák, Saint-Saëns, amongst
foreigners, and Sullivan, Stanford, and others, amongst Englishmen, it is
very probable that he will not bear off the palm; yet, amongst these few
privileged artists, who, like the Provençal troubadours, can say 'trove il
suono col il moto'? Boito, since Wagner's death, has no rivals . . .

Boito was born in 1842 in Padua, the son of an Italian painter and
a Polish countess. At fourteen, he entered the Milan Conservatoire.
By the age of eighteen, he had made such disappointing progress in
his music studies that he came close to being expelled. Meanwhile, in
his spare moments, he worked through the classics of literature from

Greek and Roman times onwards, turning himself into an exemplary prose stylist and poet, with equal facility in both Italian and French. His early published poetry was much applauded by the Italian press, and an essay in a French journal brought a flattering letter from Victor Hugo. When he was twenty, he supplied the verses for a cantata composed by his friend and fellow student Franco Faccio. This work proved so successful that the two young men were given state grants to study abroad for two years. They spent most of their time in Paris, where Boito, by reason of his formidable intellect, artistic gifts, good looks and charm, was able to mix in the highest circles, meeting Berlioz, Gounod and other celebrities. Faccio and he had introductions to Verdi and Rossini, on whom they naturally called at the earliest opportunity. Verdi was impressed with Boito and, as we have seen, commissioned him to write the verses for *Inno delle nazioni*, which Faccio went over to London to hear, while Boito travelled to Poland to see relations. Rossini was greatly taken with the young men, and they frequently visited him. When they finally took their leave, at the end of their stay in Paris, he gave them each two little packages, telling them, 'Everything is useful to the young.' Opening them in the street, they discovered that Rossini had saved all their calling cards, which, in accordance with etiquette, they had left each time; these usually proved expensive to replace when one was abroad. Each of them also received a signed photograph of the Master. The inscription on Boito's read, 'To my cherished colleague A. Boito.' Rossini later told the important Italian publisher Ricordi how much he liked Boito and Faccio. He said of Boito, 'I feel he's got the stuff in him for something out of the ordinary.'

Following his return to Italy, Boito set to work on *Mefistofele*, which he had begun to sketch in Paris. He continued to devote himself to literature and journalism, becoming increasingly looked on as the embodiment of young Italy. During this period, he published a novel and had a play produced in Turin. An essay praising Mendelssohn, at the expense of the less desirable traditions of Italian opera, resulted in a duel from which he was fortunate to escape with nothing more than an injury to his arm. In 1866, he and Faccio enlisted under Garibaldi in the war to free Italy from Austrian rule. Once the campaign was over, he again visited Paris, where he considered remaining, but he then travelled on to Poland to stay with his sister. Here, cut off from the distractions of Milan and Paris, he concentrated on *Mefistofele*, making such good progress that he was able to report to friends in Italy that there was now the possibility, previously unenvisaged, of the vast work actually being finished. So illustrious was his reputation in Italy, that the managers of La Scala, catching wind of the opera's near completion, offered to produce it in the winter season of 1867–8. This was quite astonishing, when one recalls that he had yet to prove himself as a musician. Many an established composer would have given his right arm to see one of his operas at La Scala.

Boito naturally jumped at the offer. The première was scheduled for 5 March 1868, and he had to labour hard to finish the opera in time for rehearsals. Because of *Mefistofele*'s complexity and modernity, the managers of La Scala, waiving the theatre's longstanding rule, permitted the young composer to conduct his own work. He also took complete charge of the stage rehearsals. Mazzucato writes of the favourable impression Boito made on the performers.

> The process of rehearsing at La Scala is a very long one, as it is done in the most conscientious manner: in the case of 'Mefistofele', it was extraordinarily long, owing to the enormous difficulties the chorus and orchestra had to grapple with; partial and general rehearsals amounted, if we remember right, to fifty-two, and during the many weeks spent in this way, all the interpreters had grown so accustomed to Boito's style, and his music had become so clear and familiar to them, that their heart warmed toward the young composer, they thought him the greatest composer in Italy . . .

Rumours leaking out from rehearsals bruited the advent of an Italian Wagner, and, though tickets had been raised to an unprecedented price, all seats and standing room were sold more than a week before the first night. On the day of the première, those with unnumbered tickets began to gather outside the theatre from 2.00 pm onwards, to make sure of good seats.

> Boito's appearance was the signal for an applause as spontaneous as it was unanimous, that began simultaneously in all quarters of the house, and lasted several minutes. During all the prologue, perfect silence was maintained, and an attempt to applaud the 'vocal scherzo' was instantly suppressed; the chorus and orchestra sang and played magnificently, and the effect seemed irresistible, and yet even towards the very end not the slightest guess could be given as to the result, so that the nervousness of all the admirers and friends of Boito was increasing every minute; but when the choir gave out the last chord of E major, there came such a sudden thunder of applause that the last bars were perfectly inaudible, though played *fortissimo* by the full orchestra and military band. Six times Boito had to bow his acknowledgement, and yet the sound of applause still rang

for minutes through the house; the cheering was taken up in the piazza outside the theatre, and it even reached the surrounding *caffès*, where hundreds of musicians had gathered with their friends to be in advance of any intelligence.

Despite this sensational and auspicious start, the originality and tough intellectual matter of *Mefistofele* proved too much for the majority of the audience, who had been nurtured on Rossini, Bellini and Donizetti. At 1.30 am, after a performance lasting six hours, the opera ended in a free fight. As the orchestra rose to its feet, cheering the exhausted composer, a large block of the audience surged towards the pit, surrounded Boito and hounded him out of the theatre. His supporters put up a spirited resistance, applauding even more fervently and baiting the baying traditionalists with such vehemence that challenges were exchanged, followed, on the morrow, by a number of duels. Two further performances of the opera were given later in the week, but *Mefistofele* was now a recognised *casus belli*, with La Scala its battleground, and the police accordingly issued an order for it to be withdrawn.

Boito spent the next seven years revising *Mefistofele* and working on another opera, *Nerone*, to which he had been giving thought for many years. In October 1875, a much amended and shortened *Mefistofele* was produced in Bologna, which city was known as the Italian Bayreuth because of its forward-looking attitude towards music. *Lohengrin*, the first of Wagner's operas to be staged in Italy, had been successfully presented at Bologna in 1871. A year later, the freedom of that city was conferred on him. He told Boito, in a letter written shortly after the *Lohengrin* première and intended for publication, that Italian music would benefit now it had made the acquaintance of 'sublime' German music. *Lohengrin* was the catalyst that would bring artistic union between Germany, who had produced 'the world's loftiest genuises', and Italy. Wagner later called *Mefistofele* 'the embroidery of a charming young woman', an inimitable way of thanking the man who had translated *Rienzi* and *Tristan und Isolde* into Italian.

The new version of the opera triumphed in Bologna and was soon being successfully performed throughout Italy. Thus, at thirty-three, Boito justified the faith of his many supporters, establishing himself as the chief Italian rival to Verdi. The publication, two years later, of his collection of poems, *Il libro dei versi*, secured his position as one of the leading literary artists of his time.

In 1876, Ponchielli's *La gioconda*, for which Boito supplied the libretto, was introduced in Milan and immediately acclaimed. In writing this libretto, Boito used the pen-name 'Tobia Gorrio', an anagram of Arrigo Boito. It was a sobriquet he adopted for all his journalistic and critical articles, short stories and, in fact, for most of what he wrote. He reserved 'Arrigo Boito' for those few of his creations that seem to have answered satisfactorily the demands both of his innermost being and of his dauntingly rigorous and frequently annihilative self-criticism. It is interesting to note that Boito was not christened Arrigo, but Enrico. He changed his name to Arrigo, the diminutive of Enrico, while he was at the Milan Conservatoire. Arrigo is an uncommon name in Italy and was associated with legends of romance and chivalry. Henri Beyle, alias Stendhal, who died a month after Boito was born, lived in Milan from 1814 to 1821 and wrote about that city with such poetic charm, also took the name Arrigo, at the moment of his death. The legend on his tombe in Montmartre, which he wrote himself, reads 'Arrigo Beyle, Milanese, Scrisse, Amò, Visse.' It seems likely that Boito, whom Benedetto Croce called 'the only romantic of Italy', was influenced by the author of *La Chartreuse de Parme*.

During the summer of 1880, Boito came to London to supervise the English première of *Mefistofele*, produced on 6 July at Her Majesty's Theatre. His fame had gone before him. 'The greatest pains were taken to give such a representation of this opera as would be worthy of the composer's high reputation', wrote the impresario Mapleson in his memoirs. 'The success of this opera is doubtless fresh in the minds of most lovers of music. I look upon it as one of the most memorable on record.' The work was conducted by Luigi Arditi, who had graduated from Milan Conservatoire in the year of Boito's birth. He recalled, 'Boito, poet and composer *par excellence*, was more than delighted with the way in which the opera was mounted and produced, and I remember with much pride all the pleasant things he said about the efficiency of my orchestra.'

Around this time, Boito renewed his early friendship with Verdi, who, to all appearances, had retired, his last opera being *Aida* (1871). However, Boito now wrote for him the libretto of *Otello*, which many hold to be the finest libretto in the history of opera. The beauty and drama of Boito's verses inspired Verdi once more to take up his pen. When *Otello* received its première at La Scala in 1887, the reputations of both men were lifted still higher, and Verdi's art exhibited further development and refinement. Inspired by this success, which was seen as the capstone of Verdi's long and glorious career, the two men then embarked on *Falstaff.* Much as Verdi tried to keep the opera a secret – for he was doubtful whether, in his late seventies, he had the power to complete it – practically the whole musical world was aware by 1892 that *Falstaff* was on the way, and there was added excitement in that this was to be his first comic opera in fifty years. Boito's role in revitalising the veteran master was recognised and applauded throughout Europe.

By 1892, hard though it was to believe, Boito, who typified the idealism and romance of youth, was fifty. He had imperceptibly become an august figure, continually invited to sit on important committees relating to the arts, yet still sought out by younger artists hoping to gain his approval or recommendation. He delighted in helping young composers. He championed Zandonai, who went on to write *Francesca da Rimini* and *Giulietta e Romeo*; he supplied a libretto for Catalani; he had a cantata by the sixteen-year-old Busoni performed in Bologna; he gave his support to Puccini and introduced him to Verdi. Though a national figure in Italy, he remained modest and unaffected by his fame, as Mazzucato relates.

Arrigo Boito has, since 1867, resided in Milan, where he lives with his brother Camillo. He does not occupy any official position, and leads a quiet and retired life. Though he is good-humoured, a pleasant companion, and of a kind and cheerful disposition, he carefully shuns fashionable society. The Italian Government has conferred upon him first the title of 'Cavaliere', then of 'Ufficiale', and lately of 'Commendatore'; but though he does not make a cheap show of pompous independence by refusing these titles, he does not like to be addressed otherwise than by his simple name, and even on state occasions he is never known to have worn the decoration to which he is entitled.

All the while, Boito had been working away at *Nerone*, which was now a topic of conversation throughout the musical world, with 'the newspapers announcing each year that it is about ready for representation', as Arthur Pougin writes in *Famous Composers and their Works*. In his excellent book *Masters of Italian Music*, published at this time, R. A. Streatfield concludes the chapter on Boito with an assessment of the composer that displays a clear understanding of his artistic psyche.

From time to time the world has been entertained with the rumours of a finished 'Nerone'. A few favoured mortals have been permitted to hear occasional extracts from it in the dreadful secrecy of the composer's study. But whether it is ever to see the footlights is a question between Boito and his conscience.

If the long-promised work is ever actually performed – and it must be ten years since it was announced as completed – we may expect in it to find Boito fully abreast of the latest development of opera. But musicians have almost given up hope of a successor to 'Mefistofele'. The fact is, that Boito is really too acute a critic to be a composer. He knows so well what good music is, that he mistrusts his own powers. He is so determined that we shall have nothing from him but the very best that we end by getting nothing at all, and I fear that on the whole we must part from him with the words which were written of another poet, Thomas Gray, whose fastidious self-criticism so fatally stunted his productive power – 'He never spoke out.'

It should be mentioned that, by December 1892, both *Cavalleria rusticana* and *Pagliacci* were already making their way in the world, although Mascagni and Leoncavallo could obviously not yet be considered as rivals of Boito. *Cavalleria rusticana* was presented in Rome in May 1890, reaching London in October 1891, when it was conducted by Arditi. *Pagliacci* was produced for the first time in May 1892 in Milan, with Toscanini conducting; its London première was scheduled for the spring of 1893. Puccini's *Le villi* had been given in Milan in May 1884, winning the praise of Verdi; *Edgar* received its first performance in Milan in April 1889, conducted by Faccio; *Manon Lescaut* was currently in rehearsal in Turin, where it was to be presented in February 1893. None of Puccini's operas had yet been performed in England. Indeed, in *Famous Composers and their Works*, Puccini is not even mentioned. Streatfield, however, with his customary acumen, devotes a lengthy section to him in *Masters of Italian Music*, maintaining, 'Puccini is undoubtedly the most fully equipped of the younger generation of Italian composers. He has an undeniable gift of melody, strong dramatic power, a cultivated sense of orchestral colour, and little inclination for those sensational and meretricious tricks which are so often apparent in the work of his contemporaries.' He possesses qualities, Streatfield asserts, that 'under the proper conditions ought to develop into something near akin to genius.' With Puccini's first real success, *La Bohème*, still three years away, this is perceptive critical writing.

The composer who, at the time, most nearly approached Boito in public esteem was Giovanni Sgambati, one year his junior. In *Famous Composers and their Works*, Arthur Foote declares, 'For what he has done as composer, pianist and conductor, and because of the strong and wholesome influence he has exerted upon the musical life of his countrymen, the name of Giovanni Sgambati will be an honoured one in the history of Italy for the last half of this century.' This eulogy seems to have been prompted by the fact that Sgambati took no interest in opera, and composed only orchestral and chamber music, thereby reminding his countrymen that the concert hall, as well as the opera-house, had pleasures to offer. Foote points out that, 'while for extravagance of expression we look to the new men of Germany, France and Russia', Sgambati's compositions exhibit a Brahmsian 'sobriety and reticence'. This Italian composer made his first trip to London in 1882, playing his Piano Concerto in G minor at a Philharmonic concert and conducting his First Symphony at the Crystal Palace. He returned in 1891 and directed an entire concert of his works – 'a most impolitic proceeding', says Streatfield, 'which put the affection of even his warmest admirers to an uncommonly severe test.' He also conducted his Third Symphony at a Philharmonic concert, taking up so much rehearsal time that, to Cowen's fury, various other items had to be omitted and a cello concerto had to be given merely with piano accompaniment. This was followed by a chamber concert at the Prince's Hall and a visit to Windsor to play for Her Majesty, which would have pleased the composer's mother, who was English. Sgambati did not interest himself in the younger generation. When Alfredo Casella took him the first movement of his First Symphony, Sgambati 'leafed through it with an air of supreme condescension and said that he understood nothing in any of the music of the young men. He hastily shook hands and went back to his lessons.' Streatfield places Sgambati at the end of *Masters of Italian Music*, after Mascagni, Puccini and Leoncavallo. Sgambati, he says, 'is an admirable composer of the second rank.'

The CUMS chose, as their fifth and final composer, to represent the growing might of Russia, Piotr Tchaikovsky, whom we can reasonably look upon as a substitute for the wayward Rubinstein. This composer, now fifty-two, was rather an unknown quantity. He was spoken of, in some quarters, as one of the more important of modern

SAINT-SAËNS 249

symphonists, but none of his symphonies had yet been performed in England. The first orchestral work to receive a hearing was the First Piano Concerto, which was played at the Crystal Palace on 11 March 1876, with Edward Dannreuther as soloist and Manns conducting. The piece had been given its première five months earlier in Boston, when Bülow took the solo part.

Dannreuther, a pupil of Moscheles, was an extremely progressive musician. Born in Strasbourg in 1844, he went with his parents to Cincinnati at the age of four. From 1859 to 1863, he studied in Leipzig and then took up residence in London. He was an ardent supporter of Wagner, founding the Wagner Society in 1872 and translating into English a number of Wagner's prose works. During the master's visit to London in 1877, he received him in his home in Orme Square; there, on 16 May, George Eliot attended the reading of *Parsifal* – 'a day to have lived for', as Hubert Parry, who was also present, wrote in his diary. Dannreuther not only championed Wagner, but espoused the cause of modern music in general, giving the first English performances, besides the Tchaikovsky concerto, of Liszt's Second Piano Concerto and, as we have seen, the Grieg concerto, too. He was, in addition, an influential writer on music, contributing to the first edition of Grove's *Dictionary* the articles on Berlioz, Chopin, Alkan, Glinka, Wagner, Grieg, Gade and several other modern composers. He was also responsible for the entry on Tchaikovsky, which we will come to shortly. His first piece of writing about Tchaikovsky appears to be the programme note for the première of the First Piano Concerto. This became the primary English source of information on the composer and was frequently quoted or paraphrased by other writers, until it was superseded, thirteen years later, by the article in Grove's *Dictionary*. After presenting biographical information about Tchaikovsky, including reference to his being a pupil of Anton Rubinstein at the St Petersburg Conservatoire, the note addresses itself more particularly to the piano concerto and to the nature of his compositions.

In the work of a highly educated musician like M. Tschaïkowsky, it would be vain to look for anything narrowly national, specifically Russian. Though he does not dream of serving up the songs and dances of his country in all their rude and crude beauty, his music nevertheless bears the unmistakable impress of a Slavonic temperament – fiery exaltation on the basis of languid melancholy. Like most Slavonic poets, Polish or Russian, he shows a predilection for huge and fantastic outlines, for subtleties of diction and luxuriant growth of words and images, together with an oriental delight in gorgeous colours. In the full sense of the word, a master of the *technique* of the modern orchestra, as well as of the pianoforte, M. Tschaïkowsky appears as one who has something to say and knows how to say it; there is no timid restraint or fear of an excess, no blinking through other men's glasses or reflex of other men's work.

The First Piano Concerto was well received, and *The Musical Times* reported favourably on its performance.

A Pianoforte Concerto, by the Russian composer, Tschaïkowsky, was the novelty on the 11th. This is a most interesting work, of decided originality and considerable power. The solo part, which is excessively difficult, was most admirably and artistically played by Mr. Dannreuther. We trust that the very decided success of this work may induce Mr. Manns next season to bring forward other compositions from the same pen. M. Tschaïkowsky has written three symphonies, besides other orchestral works; and, if they are at all equal to this concerto, the sooner we hear them the better.

This was an auspicious start for Tchaikovsky in England, and, four months later, on 4 July 1876, the First Quartet, presented at a Musical Union concert in St James's Hall, excited still greater enthusiasm. The piece had been brought to the attention of the Union's founder, John Ella, by Leopold Auer, who played first violin in the performance. The *Athenaeum* declared that 'rarely has any new quartet created such a sensation' and forthwith pronounced Tchaikovsky to be 'one of the most promising of the musicians of the day'. The *Monthly Musical Record* was equally commendatory.

Hitherto the name of M. Tschaikowsky has only been known to English audiences by one or two pianoforte pieces played here by Dr. von Bülow, and by the admirable concerto brought forward last winter by Mr. E. Dannreuther at the Crystal Palace, and which we had hoped ere this to have heard again. The high opinion which we had formed of this composer from his concerto was fully borne out in this quartett, which, though an early work, is strikingly original, clear in its construction, and even on a first hearing by no means difficult to appreciate. Indeed, we have seldom listened to a new quartett which on a first performance has met with so warm a reception. At the close of the andante the applause was so general that Professor Ella put it to the vote whether it should be repeated. Its second hearing was carried *nem. con.*

On 4 November 1876, Manns introduced *Romeo and Juliet*, published five years earlier. The work seemed to please the Crystal Palace audience. *The Musical Times* called it 'a most elaborate composition, which requires repeated hearing and careful study in order to be appreciated. It is full of beauties, but at the same time contains much that is hard to be understood. The performance, under Mr. Manns, was remarkably fine.' The *Monthly Musical Record* also found the overture difficult to grasp, because it was 'unusual in form' and had a 'strange sequence of its tonalities'. Nevertheless, the piece was 'in every way a remarkable one' and of 'striking originality'.

In March of the following year, the concerto was given its second hearing when it was played at St James's Hall by the Danish pianist Frits Hartvigson. A pupil of Bülow, Hartvigson had been living in England since 1864, with the exception of the years 1873—5, which he spent in St Petersburg, where he had become acquainted with Tchaikovsky. In 1873, he was appointed pianist to the Princess of Wales. Like Bülow, he gave concerts to raise money for the building of the Festspielhaus at Bayreuth. At St James's Hall, the concerto met with little success, despite the fact that Hartvigson was, if anything, a better pianist than Dannreuther. On this occasion, *The Musical Times* described it as 'a rambling piece of musical incoherence'.

The next work to be introduced was the Third Quartet, played at the Royal Normal College and Academy of Music for the Blind in Westow Street, Norwood, on 26 July 1877. Hartvigson, a professor at the college, was probably responsible for the performance. The *Monthly Musical Record* warmly welcomed the quartet, which deserved 'to be heard again and again'.

After such a bright beginning, Tchaikovsky's progress in England now came to a complete halt. His name appeared before the public again on 10 May 1879, when Pablo Sarasate and Manns introduced the *Sérénade mélancolique* at the Crystal Palace, but this did little to increase interest in his compositions. On 3 March 1881, his music was heard in Manchester for the first time when Hallé gave the English première of *Marche slave*. A year later, on 8 May 1882, the Violin Concerto was introduced at a Richter concert in London, with Adolf Brodsky as soloist. Brodsky, who had been a professor at the Moscow Conservatoire during the late 1870s and was friendly with Tchaikovsky, had given the world première of the work, again with Richter, in Vienna the previous December. It was this performance that prompted the critic Hanslick to observe that, 'Tschaïkowsky's

Violin Concerto gives us for the first time the hideous notion
that there can be music that stinks to the ear.' The programme note
for the London première mentions that the first of the composer's
works to be performed in England was the First Piano Concerto, but
it 'has not been since repeated, except upon one occasion, viz., by Mr.
Frits Hartvigson; nor has it led to so many of Tschaikowsky's compositions being brought forward as its merit seemed to demand. This
composer having therefore remained a comparative stranger to
London concert-rooms, a few particulars respecting his antecedents
will not be out of place . . .'; the note then goes on to quote, almost in
its entirety, what Dannreuther had written for the Crystal Palace
programme six years earlier.

Brodsky was warmly applauded by the audience at St James's
Hall, but the concerto itself seems to have made much less of an
impression. *The Musical Times* reacted coolly.

We cannot refer to the Concerto in terms of unqualified admiration. It is
long, pretentious, and entitled to boast of certain original features, but of
genius to correspond we do not see precisely an adequate measure. The
deficiency is not unusual in our day, when composers have an idea that it
is possible by excessive elaboration, and by use of what may be called the
mechanism of art, to make up for a deficiency of the subtle spirit which
cannot be manufactured, and evades analysis.

The year 1883 saw the publication of *A Handbook of Musical Biography*, compiled by the Scottish composer and writer David Baptie. The
entry on Tchaikovsky runs to three lines. 'TSCHAIKOWSKY, Peter
Fljitsch von. B. Ural, 25th April, 1840. Operatic composer of talent
and celebrity.' We can compare this with forty-two lines for Wagner
and twenty-six for Rubinstein.

Also, in 1883, came the publication in London, by Augener and
Co, of a number of Tchaikovsky's piano pieces. These included the
'Chant sans paroles' from *Souvenir de Hapsal*, Op 2; the Romance,
Op 5; the Mazurka from *Trois Morceaux*, Op 10; the 'Scherzo humor-
istique' and 'Feuillet d'album' from *Six Morceaux*, Op 19; the Barca-
rolle and Troika from *Les Saisons*; the 'Chanson triste' from *Douze
Morceaux*. They were followed shortly afterwards by a few more short
piano works, some vocal duets and, in 1886, by the song 'None But
the Lonely Heart', Op 6 No 6, which was published by Stanley
Lucas, Weber and Co. All these piano pieces did much more to
acquaint people with Tchaikovsky than the orchestral works had

done. They achieved nothing like the popularity of Grieg's piano pieces, nor of Rubinstein's, with which they have a good deal in common, but they effectively established Tchaikovsky in the English musical consciousness. 'Chant sans paroles' became the best known and, in 1887, was also published by R. Cocks and Co. By 1886, these assorted piano items had made sufficient headway for Augener to release the complete *Douze Morceaux*. Their publication, in July 1886, occasioned a complimentary review in the *Monthly Musical Record*.

In each of these twelve pieces we meet with something original. This originality lies especially in the tonality, manifested in melody and harmony – less in the rhythm, although this, too, is now and then striking. Of the younger generation of Russian composers, Tschaïkowsky has – outside his native country at least – found the largest audience. His productions belong to various branches of the art, but of course the pianoforte pieces are the best-known ones . . . What ought to be noticed [in the *Douze Morceaux*] is the fact that the piquancies are not studied refinements, but natural expressions attributable to the individuality and nationality of the composer, whose simplicity and ingenuousness – in this case, at any rate – cannot be denied. Lovers of unconventional pianoforte music will give these twelve pieces a hearty welcome.

The orchestral works, meanwhile, were making extremely slow progress in the concert room, with no single composition becoming noticeably popular. On 5 December 1885, Manns conducted the English première of *Capriccio italien*. *The Musical Times* reported, 'the absence of distinction in the melodies of Tschaikowsky's Capriccio Italien is not compensated for by their clever orchestration. Of the various sections of this work the opening Andante is much the most attractive.' On 1 May 1886, the hitherto rare occurrence of a Tchaikovsky work receiving a second hearing took place at St James's Hall, when Sarasate again performed the *Sérénade mélancolique*. On 28 October 1886, in Manchester, Hallé introduced the second and third movements of the Second Piano Concerto, taking the solo part himself. On 2 July 1887, the Italian conductor Enrico Bevignani gave the second English performance of the *Capriccio italien*, at the Royal Albert Hall. *The Musical Times* now took an entirely different view of the work.

This admirably written and interesting composition should serve to introduce a better knowledge of the labours of the composer, who is one of the foremost among the rising Russian musicians. His pianoforte works are known in England, but the best expressions of his artistic mind are to be found in those of his productions in which the orchestra is employed. London amateurs will thank Signor Bevignani, who conducted with consummate skill, for having been the means of calling their attention to a new pleasure.

One gains the impression that the reviewer may have regarded this as the first English performance of *Capriccio italien*. Such a mistake seems hardly surprising, since Tchaikovsky's works were so infrequently played and, as yet, so infrequently repeated. By now, however, Manns had conducted the *Capriccio* in Edinburgh and Glasgow.

On 13 December 1887, Henschel conducted the first London performance of *Marche slave*, and, in February 1888, the *Sérénade mélancolique* was once more played at the Crystal Palace, by the Bohemian violinist František Ondříček, who in the same concert introduced Dvořák's Violin Concerto. Interest in Tchaikovsky's orchestral works was now just beginning to grow, and, shortly afterwards, Manns repeated the First Piano Concerto and *Romeo and Juliet* at the Crystal Palace. On 22 March 1888, the composer himself made his first appearance before a British audience, conducting the Serenade for Strings and the final movement from the Third Suite, at a Philharmonic Society concert in St James's Hall. There was a full audience, since, suggested Joseph Bennett in the *Daily Telegraph*,

Nothing in the musical world is more interesting than the achievements and promise of the Sclavonic peoples, who only within a recent period have attracted notice to themselves in any special degree. That they are now closely watched by amateurs of thoughtful and far-seeing minds is due to the appearance among them of unusual talent, and to the steady manner in which Sclavonic compositions are making progress. It is impossible to say with any confidence what results will follow the occupation by Eastern Europe of an influential place in music, but there can be no risk in assuming for them great importance. A mighty and numerous race, endowed with a temperament having fiery vigour and languid melancholy as its extremes, and possessed of strong musical instincts, cannot enter the arena without making its presence felt. Considerations like these gave Mr. Tschaikowsky's advent in St. James's Hall a more than personal interest. The Russian composer there represented a new and increasing power within the domain of his art – a power at present hardly more defined than the destiny of his country, but impressive all the same. Mr. Tschaikowsky chose to address his English audience through two compositions not too liberally endowed with special characteristics . . . Authors are seldom the most correct judges of their own works, and we are not disposed to accept the composer's preference in the present case, even though it be strongly marked. We feel sure that Mr. Tschaikowsky has written music more able than this to account for the position he holds, and, at the same time, more distinctive in character. It may be that he determined to feel his way with works comparatively *ad captandum*. If so, he made a mistake . . . Mr. Tschaikowsky is an admirable conductor, with a clear, decided beat, and a *coup d'oeil* that allows no point to escape watchful observation. He was loudly applauded after each piece, and, on being recalled, gracefully indicated his obligation to the splendid orchestra which had so well interpreted his music.

In the *Sunday Times*, Herman Klein also expressed his disappointment that the composer had chosen to conduct works which, though previously unheard in England, added nothing to his reputation.

M. Tschaikowsky made his first bow – or, rather, the first of several very profound and rapid bows – before an English audience at the Philharmonic Concert on Thursday. A hearty reception awaited him as was fitting in the case of one of the most distinguished of Russian composers . . . M. Tschaikowsky is not quite forty-eight, but he looks older, his hair and close-cut beard being perfectly grey. By his intelligent and animated beat, I should judge him to be a good conductor. It was a pity, though, that he should not have been represented in Thursday's scheme by a work of first-class importance, instead of a Serenade for strings and a movement from a suite, neither of them worthy his genius in its highest phase. The predominant impression left behind is tinged with a certain coarseness, not to say vulgarity of treatment. M. Tschaikowsky had to respond to two recalls after the Serenade, which brought out the tone of the Philharmonic strings with wonderful sonorousness and purity of quality.

Similarly, the *Daily News* commented, 'The two pieces from Tschaikowsky's pen performed last night were obviously not altogether fair specimens of the Russian composer's talent.' *The Musical Times* also hoped 'that they are not the best works in his catalogue . . . Amateurs would have preferred music of greater pretence, and in character adapted to allow a comparison between the Russian master and his contemporaries on the ground of the highest art.'

Two months later, on 18 May, Hallé, his future wife Wilma Norman-Neruda, and her brother the cellist Franz Neruda gave the first English performance of the Piano Trio, in London. This was very warmly greeted, and *The Musical Times* stated, 'We regard this Trio as one of the most effective produced for a long time, and concert-givers have been unwise to neglect it. The impression it produced on the audience was unmistakable, the applause being more than usually enthusiastic.' During the summer of 1888, a very keen but unworldly

Russian touring opera company, conducted by Giuseppe Truffi, arrived in Liverpool, where, on 6 August at the Alexandra Theatre, they presented *Mazeppa*, which thus became the first of Tchaikovsky's operas to be heard in England. The company then took the work to Manchester, where it was performed at the Comedy Theatre on 27 August. It had a good reception in both cities, 'being considered by those who heard it extremely dramatic and picturesque', according to Klein. By September, the company had reached London, but without having arranged any bookings. In desperation, they hired the Royal Albert Hall, where, dressed in their national costumes, they gave a series of concerts that were poorly attended and financially disastrous. At length, they succeeded in renting a theatre, the Novelty, and announced that they would be performing *The Demon, A Life for the Tsar*, and *Mazeppa*. They opened, on 22 October, with *The Demon*, but soon afterwards their funds ran out and the troupe, now destitute, disbanded. However, there was great sympathy for their plight, and a public appeal raised enough money to finance their return to Russia.

On 15 January 1889, in London, Henschel conducted the first performance in England of *1812*. To Klein, 'it seemed a noisy, bombastic composition, and sadly needed an explanatory analysis', but the audience welcomed it rapturously, and Henschel repeated the work three weeks later.

On 11 April 1889, Tchaikovsky made another appearance in London, again at a Philharmonic concert in St James's Hall, conducting the English première of his First Suite and accompanying the Russian pianist Vasily Sapellnikov in the First Piano Concerto. In the *Daily Telegraph*, Joseph Bennett once more reflected on the future of Russian music.

Mr. Peter Tschaikowsky's second appearance in this country has a particular interest for those who are watching his career, and concerns, on wider grounds, many who speculate as to the prospective influence of Sclavonic Art. It is a remarkable fact, indicating, perhaps, much more than casual observers perceive, that the mission of creative music seems to be passing from central Europe to the east, north, and west. Scandinavia is actively at work in the persons of men like Gade, Grieg and Svendsen; the various branches of the Slav family are becoming more and more prolific; while even England, so long, in this respect, the scorn of her Continental neighbours, is rapidly regaining the place she held in the 'spacious days' of the later Tudors. With what the first and last of these people may ultimately achieve we are not now directly concerned. Mr. Tschaikowsky represents the second, and in that capacity is a very suggestive personage indeed. But even with regard to the development of Sclavonian music it is possible to do little more than speculate since Russia, that 'dark horse' in the race of nations, has not been long afield. At the present the art of Russia is somewhat nebulous. Full of energy and overflowing with enthusiasm, but wanting settled principles and a defined purpose, it is in just the position and mood to take up with every form of extravagance. Hence we find in many works by composers of that nationality not only a reflection but an exaggeration of much in the modern art of other countries that has not yet stood the test of time, and is regarded by serious observers as of doubtful value. Thus does young musical Russia sow her wild oats; by and by, no doubt, she will steady herself, and deposit grain of a better quality. Mr. Tschaikowsky may fairly be accepted as an illustration of the remarks just made. His art, too, is nebulous, without definite purpose; and, as his overture, '1812', testifies, extravagant, sometimes, to the point of incoherence. Nevertheless, it is music not wanting in great qualities such as interest and attract. The defects are principally those of style and method, the merits are substantial, and belong to the true foundation upon which, with long and painful labour, the art of a nation is built.

Mr. Tschaikowsky was represented in the latest Philharmonic programme by a pianoforte concerto in B flat minor and a Suite in D. Of these the first-named is, perhaps, the most typical in the sense of the remarks already made . . . We do not suppose that the Concerto will often be performed in this country, but, given a pianist competent to the task, connoisseurs cannot but receive it with interest whenever it does come . . .

Mr. Tschaikowsky's suite in D was played at the Philharmonic Concert for the first time in England. It consists of five movements, with an appendix styled 'Marche Miniature', introduced on Thursday last, in the place of a dropped Scherzo . . . The 'Marche Miniature' should be regarded as a mere *jeu d'esprit* . . . It was this pretty trifle, however, that the audience liked best, and insisted on hearing twice. The final movement (gavotte) ends the suite rather tamely, but the work will nevertheless stand as a good example of its composer. Mr. Tschaikowsky was loudly applauded several times during the evening.

We can see from this review that the First Piano Concerto had still not established itself in the repertoire: 'We do not suppose that the Concerto will often be performed in this country . . .' Nevertheless it was now on the verge of doing so, and enthusiasm for Tchaikovsky seemed to be continuing to grow, as Klein makes clear in the *Sunday Times*.

The representative of the advanced Russian school received a hearty welcome, and in course of the evening was the hero of several cordial demonstrations, which he acknowledged by a profusion of those singularly vigorous and rapid bows that might be accurately described as 'half measures', did they not dip to the whole depth that a bow with safety can dip. M. Tschaikowsky brought with him a clever young countryman, M. Sapellnikoff, to play the solo in his B flat minor pianoforte concerto, Op. 23; and right well did the *débutant* justify his selection for that purpose. His magnificent *technique* and extraordinary wrist-power were precisely the *desiderata* for this work of brilliant display and grandiose effects – introduced at the Crystal Palace by Mr. Dannreuther (most indefatigable of searchers after novelty) so long ago as March 1876. Hence an unalloyed triumph alike for composer and interpreter, made manifest by numerous recalls and acknowledged by the former with a profundity of obeisance which his youthful companion strove in vain to emulate.

Tschaikowsky was more worthily represented this time than in the scheme of the Philharmonic Concert at which he made his first appearance a year ago. Besides the concerto he conducted his suite in D, Op. 43, a novelty brimful of the characteristics that distinguish his music and, down to a certain point, the most interesting orchestral work from his pen that we have yet heard . . . The so-called Gavotte which furnishes the finale is a feeble inspiration; it brings the work to a 'lame and impotent conclusion'. The coda is positively vulgar – dragged in just like the reminiscence from 'Tannhäuser' at the climax of the Intermezzo, without the slightest regard for appropriateness or symmetry.

It is by such errors of judgment – and the instances quoted are not solitary ones – that Tschaikowsky frequently mars the beauty of his happiest conceptions; enforcing the impression that he does not mind sacrificing artistic truth for the sake of mere sonorousness and pomposity of effect. But for this failing, allied to a certain lack of breadth and nobility in the outline and structure of his works, Tschaikowsky might stand in the same relation to the creative geniuses of the world as he does to the musicians of his native land.

The Musical Times again regretted the choice of pieces. 'For some inexplicable reason, the Russian composer, when he appears among us, refuses to be heard in any of his numerous works of importance which have not yet been introduced to the notice of English musicians.' This refers, of course to the five symphonies that Tchaikovsky was known to have written; in those days, symphonies were, in the realm of orchestral music, 'works of importance' *sans pareil*. *Musical Opinion*, however, seemed unconcerned that there was no symphony: the concerto and suite

unfolded an absolutely astounding wealth of beautiful ideas. Where other men would use one subject, Tschaikowsky lavishes half a dozen, most of them remarkably original, all highly attractive, the *soupçon* of triviality attaching to a few being altogether nullified by piquant rhythm or harmony, and an orchestration which – for novelty, variety and charm of instrumental effects – defies description. The quaint freak of fancy, 'Marche Miniature,' for high strings and woodwind, triangle and bells – worthy of H. Berlioz at his best – in the suite, had to be repeated.

Shortly after this concert, the fourth and final volume, *Sumer Is Icumen In to Zwischenspiel*, of the first edition of Grove's *Dictionary* was published. The entry for Tchaikovsky runs to about half a page, and in much of it Dannreuther keeps, word for word, to what he originally wrote for the Crystal Palace programme in March 1876.

TSCHAIKOWSKY, PETER ILTITSCH, one of the most remarkable Russian composers of the day, was born April 25, 1840, at Wotkinsk in the government of Wiatka (Ural District), where his father was engineer to the Imperial mines. In 1850 the father was appointed Director of the Technological Institute at St. Petersburg and there the boy entered the School of Jurisprudence, into which only the sons of high-class government officials are admitted. Having completed the prescribed course in 1859, he was appointed to a post in the Ministry of Justice. In 1862, however, when the Conservatoire of Music was founded at St. Petersburg, he left the service of the state, and entered the new school as a student of music. He remained there till 1865, studying harmony and counterpoint under Prof. Zaremba, and composition under Anton Rubinstein. In 1865 he took his diploma as a musician, together with a prize medal for the composition of a cantata on Schiller's ode, 'An die Freude.' In 1866 Nicholas Rubinstein invited him to take the post of Professor of Harmony, Composition, and the History of Music at the new Conservatoire of Moscow; he held this post, doing good service as a teacher, for twelve years. Since 1878 he has devoted himself entirely to composition, and has been living in St. Petersburg, Italy, Switzerland, and Kiew. M. Tschaikowsky makes frequent use of the rhythm and tunes of Russian People's-songs and dances, occasionally also of certain quaint harmonic sequences peculiar to Russian church music. His compositions, more or less, bear the impress of the Slavonic temperament – fiery exaltation on a basis of languid melancholy. He is fond of huge and fantastic outlines, of bold modulations and strongly marked rhythms, of subtle melodic turns and exuberant figuration, and he delights in gorgeous effects of orchestration. His music everywhere makes the impression of genuine spontaneous originality.

Tchaikovsky is also mentioned in the section on piano music, where it states, 'PETER TSCHAIKOWSKI (1840–) is known by a grand concerto, an impromptu and scherzo russe, and 8 other original pieces.' A further reference occurs in the article on song.

Even the greatest Russian composers, the style of whose other works is cosmopolitan, adhere to national peculiarities in their songs. The florid passages on one syllable, already noticed, are often met with in the songs of Rubinstein; and Tschaïkofsky frequently reproduces the characteristic harsh harmony of the old folk-songs. These two composers' German *Leider* are of such beauty as to have found favour with every nation devoted to music.

Tchaikovsky had made no further visit to London by December 1892, but Sapellnikov came again in the spring of 1890, when, on 26 April, at the Crystal Palace, he and Manns gave the first complete English performance of the Second Piano Concerto. It failed to excite the same degree of interest as the First. George Bernard Shaw, writing in the *Star*, did not like it at all.

It is impulsive, copious, difficult, and pretentious; but it has no distinction, or originality, no feeling for the solo instrument, nothing to rouse the attention or to occupy the memory. It left me without any notion of Sapellnikoff's rank as a player: he is, of course, swift and powerful with his fingers; but six bars of a Mozart sonata would have told me more about his artistic gift than twenty whole concertos of the Tschaikowsky sort.

And let me here remark that whenever you hear of a great composer from Russia, or from Hungary, or from any other country which is far behind us in social development, the safest plan is not to believe in him.

As 1890 passed into 1891, the interest in Tchaikovsky's works, which had previously seemed to be growing and was stimulated by his two visits to London, gave every appearance of declining or, at best, of standing still. Tchaikovsky had gained no real acceptance in the British concert room; neither were there any invitations from cities like Leeds or Birmingham or Worcester to take part in their festivals – and no summons to Windsor, which even Sgambati received. In such circumstances, the following snippet from the 'Facts, Rumours and Remarks' section of the July 1891 edition of *The Musical Times* must have surprised many of that magazine's readers.

Mr. Tschaikowski, who makes little way in England as a composer, has been accepted in the United States. The *American Art Journal* observes: 'His example as a composer cannot be too highly commended. Not that it would be wise or justifiable to imitate the compositions of the great Russian any more than those of any other man, but the hearing of his works gives us new confidence; *first*, because it shows that the springs of melody have not yet run dry; *second*, because he demonstrates the fact that music can yet be written that will be fresh and original and yet be true to the fundamental principles of anti-Wagnerian [*ante*-Wagnerian?] times, without running into the dry pedantry of Brahms and his followers.'

The unthinkable and tastelessly provocative reference to Brahms naturally absolved the English reader from taking this intelligence seriously; in which regard, it is not inappropriate to present a sonnet that appeared three months earlier in *The Musical Times*.

BRAHMS

Brahms, strong, self-governed soul, be this thy praise, –
That in a fitful age thou didst refrain
From methods false, from liberties profane;
For thou hath gathered in tradition's ways
The flowers of full-blown thought that crown thy days.
Hark, in thy mellow music, strong and sane,
Beethoven's harmonies vibrate again,
And fill our listening spirits with amaze.
His mantle rests upon thee. Art not thou
High Priest of Music's mysteries in his stead,
The jealous guardian of the laws divine?
So men shall call thee Master; even though now
They follow after other gods than thine,
And trample out the footprints of the dead.

Tchaikovsky's stock continued to remain low in 1892, and, when the young Scottish pianist Frederic Lamond played the First Piano Concerto at the Crystal Palace, in April of that year, *The Musical Times* called the work 'a striking example of the inability of the Russian musical temperament to adapt itself to the classical forms. It contains some excellent tunes, but the working out is intensely patchy and tedious. Nothing could be more inartistic than the way in which the enormously long cadenza in the first movement is introduced. It is not led up to, it is simply lugged in anyhow.'

In the autumn of 1892, *Eugene Onegin* became the second of Tchaikovsky's operas to be performed in England and the first to reach London. It opened, in an English translation, at the Olympic Theatre on 17 October, but only managed a short run, which was terminated when the affairs of the impresario Lago collapsed and he took flight from his creditors, leaving the cast and the twenty-two-year-old conductor, Henry Wood, unpaid. The opera met with a chilling reception, and its failure contributed towards Lago's ruin. George Bernard Shaw managed to catch the opera before it came off. It reminded him of Boucicault's *The Colleen Bawn* (1860).

Something in the tailoring, in the scenery, in the sound of the hero's name (pronounced O'Naygin, or to put it in a still more Irish way, O'Neoghegan) probably combined with the Balfian musical form of the work to suggest this notion to me. There is something Irish, too, as well as Byronic, in the introduction of Eugene as an uncommonly fine fellow when there is not the smallest ground for any such estimate of him. The music suggests a vain regret that Tschaikowsky's remarkable artistic judgement, culture, imaginative vivacity, and self-respect as a musical workman, should have been unaccompanied by any original musical force. For, although I have described the form of the opera as Balfian, it must not therefore be inferred that Tschaikowsky's music is as common as Balfe's – ballads apart – generally was. Tschaikowsky composes with the seriousness of a man who knows how to value himself and his work too well to be capable of padding his opera with the childish claptrap that does duty for dramatic music in the Bohemian Girl. Balfe, whose ballads are better than Tschaikowsky's, never, as far as I know, wrote a whole scene well, whereas in Eugene Onegin there are some scenes, notably those of the letter and the duel, which are very well written, none of them being bungled or faked (factitious is the more elegant expression; but the other is right). The opera, as a whole, is a dignified composition by a man of distinguished talent whose love of music has led him to adopt the profession of composer, and who, with something of his countryman Rubinstein's disposition to make too much of cheap second-hand musical material, has nothing of his diffuseness, his occasional vulgarity, and his incapacity for seeing when to drop a worn-out theme.

Granville Bantock's *New Musical Quarterly*, though, found much to praise in *Eugene Onegin*.

Musically, the opera is a triumph; dramatically, we cannot but regard it as a failure. The ineffective closes to each Act, the disposition of the story, the modern colloquialisms with which the libretto abounds, these reasons and others in no wise tend to impress an audience favourably. The only reason for its success lies in the power and wealth of melody which is contained in the music. As in the memorable case of *Die Zauberflöte*, Mozart had to contend against the absurdities of a pantomimical extravaganza, so in this case Tschaikowsky has had to cope with the inefficiency of a weak libretto, and has therein proved himself a master of his art. The rhythmical element is particularly noticeable in the music of *Eugene Onegin*, as also is the composer's fondness for modulation and richness of orchestral colouring.

Originality of ideas and the methods of their developments are not the common property of every musician, but with Tschaikowsky all seems to come naturally. Complicated rhythms and contrapuntal devices are handled with the same grace and ingenuity that characterize all the best known works of this master.

Although, at this stage, Tchaikovsky's music seems to have appealed most to younger musicians, including the perennially youthful Manns and Hallé, there were nevertheless a fair number of older men who were also attracted to it. In *My Musical Life and Recollections*, which was published in 1893, Jules Rivière, then in his seventies, writes, 'Lago's unfortunate season at the Olympic, in 1892, though it ended in disaster for him, will also be pleasantly remembered by musical amateurs owing to the novelty recorded in connection with it. I refer to the production of Tscharkorosky's *Eugène Onégin*.'

Considering the many different spellings of Tchaikovsky's name that we have so far encountered, it is not surprising to find Rivière and his publishers concocting this rather flamboyant variation. At the same time, when an active and successful conductor like Rivière can arrive at 'Tscharkorosky', we gain a useful insight into how well known the composer was in 1892 and 1893. The prevailing lack of familiarity with Tchaikovsky's achievements can be inferred from an article, entitled 'Pierre-Iljitsch Tschaïkowsky', in the November 1892 edition of the *Monthly Musical Record*. Occasioned by the presentation of *Eugene Onegin*, its purpose is simply to remind its readers of who Tchaikovsky is.

The production of an opera by this composer again calls attention to one of the foremost musicians of the modern Russian school. He was born in 1840, but it was only at the age of 20 that he began seriously to devote himself to music. He studied at the Petersburg Conservatoire [etc] . . . Although he has written several symphonies (five are mentioned in 'Grove's Dictionary'), not one, so far as we are aware, has been heard in London. When the composer came here in 1888, and appeared at the Philharmonic, he only gave a Serenade for Strings, and a Theme with Variations from a Suite in G, and in 1889, when he came again, the Suite in D (Op. 43), and thus favourable opportunities of hearing one of his important orchestral works were lost . . . He is, of course, best known by his pianoforte pieces, and of these the short ones, such as *Chant sans Paroles* in F, *Feuillet d'Album*, Troïka, *Chanson triste*, *Au Village*, &c., have become household words. Then, too, there are his songs and vocal duets, many of which have become favourites. [In a review of *Eugene Onegin* in the same month's edition of *The Musical Times*, there is a reminder that 'The Russian composer enjoys considerable fame in his own country, but here he is principally known by his songs and short but graceful pianoforte pieces.']

There is general agreement as to the great merits of Tschaïkowsky's compositions — taking melodies, striking rhythms, skilful harmonies, and, in works written for orchestra, picturesque scoring. And to all this the Slavonic element, now of excitement, now of depression, adds a certain

charm, for in the works with which we are acquainted it is never introduced to excess. A certain tendency to diffuseness seems to be his chief
weakness, and it, perhaps, is somewhat characteristic of modern Russian
composers generally. But whatever his merits or demerits, Tschaïkowsky
deserves the high esteem in which he is held, both in his own country and
abroad.

One familiar piece that this article does not mention is the *Andante
cantabile*, which was popular in several different arrangements.
Eduard Strauss conducted it for Queen Victoria when he gave a
command concert at Windsor Castle in 1885. It is worth remembering, incidentally, that articles of a similarly informational nature
about Brahms had not been required since the early seventies, twenty
years earlier; Verdi, of course, had been accepted in England for forty
years. Even Grieg, who made his London début six weeks after
Tchaikovsky, in the spring of 1888, was now an acknowledged
master, as far as the English were concerned.

In December 1892, a Tchaikovsky symphony was at last scheduled
for performance when the Fifth was announced for the winter season
of Hallé concerts in Manchester. It was given on 2 February 1893
and passed practically unnoticed. *The Musical Times* devoted one line
to it, remarking that Hallé's performance of Beethoven's Fourth
Piano Concerto 'atoned to a great extent for the weariness and noise
of Tschaikowsky's Fifth Symphony in E minor.' The *Manchester
Guardian*, like the audience, was more enthusiastic, but admitted to
disappointment in 'a certain thinness of general construction which
forces itself increasingly upon us'. The second movement, however,
was 'an exquisite movement and made a deep impression upon the
audience.' Manchester thus became the first city in England to have
heard a symphony and an opera by Tchaikovsky. Hallé took the
symphony to Bradford two months later. The second movement,
reported the Yorkshire correspondent of *The Musical Times*, was
'remarkable for its impassioned melody and rich orchestration'; the
finale was noisy, but 'full of interest and vigour'.

Hallé, as we have seen, took part in the English premières of four
works by Tchaikovsky, and did as much as any musician, apart from
Manns, to bring the composer's music to the attention of concert-
goers. We would probably, therefore, not underestimate Tchaikovsky's popularity in England during the eighties and early nineties
if we were to investigate how many times his name appeared on the
programmes of Hallé's concerts in Manchester. Hallé first per-

formed a Tchaikovsky composition, *Marche slave*, on 3 March 1881. Let us take the twelve-year period from 2 March 1881 to 2 March 1893 and note how often Brahms, Dvořák, Gounod and Rubinstein were also represented. This gives us the following figures.

Gounod	52
Dvořák	44
Brahms	36
Rubinstein	26
Tchaikovsky	6

We may thus account Tchaikovsky fortunate, with regard to his popularity in England, to receive an invitation to Cambridge.

As soon as Grieg, Saint-Saëns, Bruch, Boito and Tchaikovsky had been settled on by the CUMS, Austen Leigh proposed their names for degrees to the Academic Council, of which he was a member. The motion was agreed to, and the Vice-Chancellor, John Peile, accordingly wrote to each of the composers, informing them of the Council's resolution and inviting them to Cambridge. The following is a translation of the letter received by Tchaikovsky; the original is in French.

Christ's Lodge,
Cambridge,
England.
12th December, 1892.

Sir,
It is with quite exceptional pleasure that, in my capacity as Vice-Chancellor of the University of Cambridge, I am carrying out the wishes of our Academic Council by inquiring whether you would accept from the Senate of the University the degree of Doctor of Music *honoris causa*. I must tell you that the acceptance of this degree would require your presence in Cambridge, to receive it in person from my hands at a meeting of the Senate. Would it be possible, Sir, for this award to be made to you during the first fortnight of next June?

If, as we fervently hope, you assent to our ardent desire to see you among us, then our University Musical Society, which at exactly that time will be celebrating the fiftieth anniversary of its existence, would be honoured to include one of your compositions in their concert.

In asking you for a reply as soon as you find it possible, I take this opportunity of offering you my deepest regards,

Dr. John Peile
Vice-Chancellor and Master of Christ's College

CHAPTER 7

STANFORD

The first reply came by return of post. It was mailed in Paris, dated 13 December, 1892, and written in French.

Sir,
The University of Cambridge, in offering me the degree of Doctor of Music, pays me a great honour, and I accept its offer with the most heartfelt gratitude.
I am most willing to come to Cambridge, but unfortunately next June I shall be in Chicago; would there not be a meeting of the Senate in May? In this way, it would be possible for me to be present. Please accept my deepest regards,

C. Saint-Saëns

There must have been a dreadful sense of *déjà vu* about this letter, with its apparent acceptance, but practical refusal. Saint-Saëns was, in fact, scheduled to take part in concerts at the World's Fair in Chicago in June. So the CUMS had still advanced no farther. However, on the following day, a letter for John Peile arrived from Berlin; this was in German.

Dear Sir,
To your very friendly letter of the 12th. of this month I have the honour of replying most respectfully herewith that it is a great distinction for me to receive the title of Doctor of Music hon. causa from your highly esteemed University.
Recognizing that personal attendance by the recipient of this august degree is essential, I declare myself with pleasure prepared, on the occasion of the fiftieth anniversary celebrations of the University Musical Society in the first fortnight of June 1893, personally to conduct one of my compositions and to accept at your hands, Vice-Chancellor, the honour that has been conferred upon me.
Please allow me to make a modest inquiry as to whether news of this award is to be published in England in the near future and, further, whether the Senate of the University wishes the matter to be treated confidentially, for the time being, in Germany.

In asking you, Sir, to express my deepest thanks to the Senate of the University for its most cordial resolve, I beg to remain with the most sincere respect your humble servant,

Max Bruch

Despite Bruch's question about the confidentiality of the university's offer, a week later Brahms was writing in reply to their mutual publisher Simrock, 'Should we congratulate him on his doctorate? The hat is on another head! (Between us: it was also offered to me, and to Verdi; the latter cannot make the journey because of his great age, and I, because of the tawdriness of the honour.)'

Happy though the CUMS must have been to receive at last a definite acceptance, there was now the chance that it might be the only one – a less than ideal prospect. Fortunately, Boito's reply, which arrived from Pegli, near Genoa, two days later, safely redeemed the situation. His letter was in French.

Most Honourable Sir,

It is with feelings of heartfelt gratitude that I hasten to thank the illustrious Senate of the University of Cambridge for my election as Doctor of Music. This supremely courteous act touches me deeply and commands my acceptance.

I shall therefore have the honour of presenting myself to you during the period mentioned in your letter, that is, in the first fortnight of June, and of taking part in the jubilee of your Musical Society.

Please accept, Vice-Chancellor, my best thanks for the warmth of your regard for me and the assurance of my profound respects.

Your devoted servant,
Arrigo Boito

Tchaikovsky's reply, from St Petersburg, was, like Boito's, also dated 16 December and written in French.

Vice-Chancellor,

It would be difficult to put into writing how proud and happy I was to read the letter you were kind enough to send me. The supreme honour that the Academic Council of the University intends bestowing on me is too great, too flattering for me not to be eager to come, at the time you mentioned, to receive it personally from you.

I therefore have pleasure in telling you that, if the good Lord grants me life and health, I shall be coming to Cambridge during the first fortnight in June.

Meanwhile, please accept, Chancellor, the deepest respects of your devoted servant,

P. Tschaikovsky

(We may note here the promotion of John Peile to Chancellor and the composer's use of v, rather than w, in his signature.)

Tchaikovsky's letter arrived on 19 December, just as the university was going down for the winter vacation. Stanford and the other members of the CUMS must now have looked forward to Christmas with gladdened hearts; and there need be no anxiety over Grieg's reply, for, with three acceptances, the success of the jubilee was largely assured.

The Norwegian composer's letter reached Cambridge on Christmas Eve and was readdressed to John Peile's home at South Cliff, Bournemouth. It was written in German and was posted from Leipzig on 22 December.

> Dear Sir,
>
> I naturally regard it as an exceptional honour to receive the degree of Doctor of Music from the University of Cambridge and I accept with joy your invitation to come in June 1893, in the hope that my health, which unfortunately at present is rather poor, will have improved by that time.
>
> Your kind letter has, I see, made a long journey, first to Norway and then here. Hence the belated reply.
>
> With the deepest respect,
>
> Edvard Grieg

It was now necessary to arrange the works to be performed at the jubilee concert, and Stanford entered into correspondence with all five composers; he still had hopes that Saint-Saëns might be able to come. In the meantime, he received a letter from Boito, with whom he was already on friendly terms. It was dated 17 December and was in French.

> I have heard from my friend Visetti that it is to your initiative that I owe my election at Cambridge; this all the more increases my delight in receiving the award. It is to you, therefore, Dear Colleague, that I owe my first thanks, and I offer them with all the sincerity of my gratitude.
>
> Although I shall indeed be in Cambridge during the first fortnight in June, I hope to have the chance of seeing you before then; you half-promised to come to the first performance of *Falstaff*; add the other half of the promise and come to Milan at the beginning of February, but don't forget to let me know as soon as possible, so that I can arrange to keep a seat for you.
>
> I'll be staying here on the Genoa Riviera until the New Year; I'll be in Milan for the whole of January.

Stanford accepted Boito's invitation and asked which of his works he would like to have performed at Cambridge – perhaps there was something in *Nerone?* Boito replied on 30 December.

> ... You mention the June concert in Cambridge, and I am grateful to you for wanting to play one of my compositions; I can discover in my musical baggage only one item that could possibly be presented in the concert hall, and this is the Prologue to *Mefistofele*, but it needs choirs and a bass-baritone soloist.
>
> In *Nerone*, there's nothing suitable so far; and, in what's to come, there won't be anything that could be taken out and given by itself. As regards orchestral works, I don't have any; in Italy we usually don't write for the orchestra on its own, or very rarely, because our orchestral concerts, alas, are rather few. The stage swallows up all our music.
>
> Goodbye, then, until we meet in the company of fat *Sir John*, when I look forward to the honour of meeting your wife, to whom I beg you to offer my respects.

It was agreed, therefore that the CUMS would perform the Prologue to *Mefistofele* and that Boito would conduct it.

In a much briefer correspondence, Stanford and Grieg settled on the latter's *Peer Gynt* Suite No 1. With Bruch, too, it was quickly decided that he should conduct the Banquet Scene from *Odysseus*.

The exchange of letters with Saint-Saëns was of a different nature. It now became apparent that his World's Fair engagement had not yet been confirmed. Stanford, ever optimistic, therefore suggested that, since there was still a faint possibility of his being able to come to Cambridge in June, it would do no harm to plan for such an eventuality. Saint-Saëns concurred with this and said he would be prepared to conduct his setting of Psalm 18. Stanford then informed him that, with two choral works already scheduled for inclusion in the concert, there would be no room for another one; it would have to be a purely orchestral work. He regretted this, but the situation was made difficult by the fact that Boito had composed no orchestral pieces. Saint-Saëns was not pleased by this information.

> I recognize that it is difficult to arrange a concert for five composers, but you will see, too, that it is unfortunate for me that M. Boito has written, as you tell me, nothing other than *Mefistofele*, and that I should therefore be forbidden to give a large-scale vocal work and thereby be forced to let him produce the biggest and most impressive musical effect of the concert. It would be possible, it seems to me, to remove the Septet, which is very long, from the Psalm; one could even cut it short at the end of the chorus in A flat; one would then have something sufficiently abridged to allow M.

Boito to spread himself to his heart's content.

If, however, you really must have an orchestral piece, well, then we cannot think in terms of the Symphony in C minor, which is too long, but we could have *La Jeunesse d'Hercule* or I could play my Fourth Concerto. I leave the choice to you, and I beg you not to see in any of this the slightest trace of ill temper towards anybody, particularly towards M. Boito, for whom I have held the deepest regard for many long years.

This letter, dated 18 January, was written from Algiers, where Saint-Saëns was spending the winter. His next letter, posted six days later, brought the news that he was no longer going to Chicago and would be able to come to Cambridge. In fact, his engagement had fallen through, but he seems to have seen it more in terms of his having cancelled it. 'Everything is arranged with America, I am free, and you can count on me for the great occasion in Cambridge. I trust that the efforts I have made to respond to the University's invitation will not go unrecognized and that I shall not be confined to a diminished role in the concert, as your last letter caused me to fear.'

Delighted, as he was, to learn that Saint-Saëns would now be able to take part in the jubilee, Stanford nevertheless had to confess that the Fourth Piano Concerto would be too long. He very much liked the idea of Saint-Saëns' performing one of his works for piano and orchestra. Perhaps there was something shorter – a new piece, possibly – that he could play? Saint-Saëns replied on 2 February.

Believe me when I say that I understood, from the very beginning, the difficulties you would encounter in organizing your programme; consequently, in the general interest, I am resigning myself to a piano solo, which will not only bring variety to the whole occasion, but will have the advantage of tiring me much less than would anything else.

Since you require something new, let me offer you my fantasy, 'Africa'. It is certainly less substantial than a concerto; however, at the Lamoureux concerts, where the audience is difficult (and even rather stuffy), it scored such a triumph that it had to be given a second time; at Liège and at Baden it succeeded to the same degree, and I enclose a review of this latter performance, which was sent to me recently. The work lasts, I believe, about 15 minutes, and this should be a perfect length.

All I ask, in return for my act of abnegation, is that the orchestral accompaniment should be rehearsed with as much care as if the work were a symphony, because it is of great importance and not just a mere accompaniment. There are, in particular, some extremely delicate oboe solos . . .

If you deem it appropriate, I could also play my 'Wedding Cake' Caprice, with quartet accompaniment, which lasts five minutes *at the most*. Do whatever is best.

The review of the Baden performance of *Africa* was cut out of a Mannheim newspaper; on it, Saint-Saëns had written, 'Understanding nothing of this literature, I leave it to your erudition.' Though Stanford's knowledge of German was unlikely to have exceeded his fellow composer's brilliant command of that language, he would nevertheless have had no difficulty in picking out phrases like 'unmistakably a work of genius', with which the Mannheim reviewer described the work. He told Saint-Saëns that he would be very happy for him to play *Africa*; but there would be no room on the programme for the *Wedding Cake Caprice* as well. In a concluding letter, dated 15 February, from Algiers, Saint-Saëns said he would use an Érard piano, to be chosen in London and sent to Cambridge.

Stanford wrote for the first time to Tchaikovsky on Christmas Eve, sending his letter, which was in French, to the address of the composer's publisher, Jurgenson, in Moscow.

> Do you remember me, perhaps, from Berlin, at the home of Herr Wolff?
> We are delighted you'll be honouring us with a visit in June. At the moment I'm preparing a programme for our concert. Your colleagues for this occasion will be Saint-Saëns, Boito, Bruch and Grieg. We are going to give one piece by each composer, under his direction.
> Would you choose for us the work you'd like to have played? Either for choir and orchestra, or for orchestra alone, or for soloist and orchestra. Will Sapellnikoff perhaps be over here then? If so, you could perform your Piano Concerto. However, whatever you decide upon, I promise I'll do my utmost to ensure it gets a satisfactory performance.

Stanford and Tchaikovsky had met, once, at a dinner-party, given by the German impresario and concert agent Hermann Wolff, on 3 February 1888. Three days later, Bülow conducted the first performance in Berlin of Stanford's *Irish Symphony*. Tchaikovsky attended the première and noted in his diary, 'Huge success of Stanford's symphony'. We see from Stanford's letter that Tchaikovsky is offered the opportunity of performing a choral work. At this stage, neither Boito nor Bruch had indicated what they would like to have played.

After a space of more than three weeks, Stanford had received no reply from Tchaikovsky. By now, Boito and Bruch had chosen to conduct choral works, Grieg had selected his *Peer Gynt* Suite and Stanford was persuading Saint-Saëns to accept 'a diminished role' in the proceedings. He wrote to Tchaikovsky on 16 January.

The concert at Cambridge will be on Monday, 12th. June. The first rehearsal, in London on Thursday, 7th. [8th] June or Friday, 8th. [9th] June. Probably Friday. The 'Doctorate', probably on 13th. June.

I have written you a letter regarding the work you could choose for the concert.

Since I haven't heard from you, I've ventured to announce your Piano Concerto.

Mr. Leonard Borwick, a pianist of the highest calibre, is ready to play it, if that's all right with you. You will be much taken with this artist (the finest of Madame Schumann's pupils).

Please be kind enough to drop me a postcard, and I'll go ahead and engage Mr. Borwick straight away. He has so many engagements that we'll have to book him in good time.

Borwick, then twenty-four, was, indeed, a magnificent pianist – possibly the best English pianist of his day. He later went on to become a leading interpreter of Debussy and Ravel.

Another three weeks passed without any response. Stanford now dispatched a third letter. In the meantime, Saint-Saëns had at last been pinned down to *Africa*, and Stanford had been requested to perform one of his own compositions at the concert, possibly to represent Britain on the programme. The third letter, posted from Milan on the day before the première of *Falstaff*, is dated 8 February. Time was now running short.

I have written twice to Jurgenson's address in Moscow, but I'm afraid my letters cannot have arrived. It's vitally important to decide at once which of your works you'll do us the honour of conducting at Cambridge on 12th. June. Since we're going to perform something by each of the new 'Doctors', we won't be able to devote more than 15 to 20 minutes a piece. I have, in my letters, spoken of the concert. Saint-Saëns has decided to play his concert fantasy, 'Africa', so I must ask you to choose a work for orchestra alone. I'm sure you appreciate the difficulties involved in making up a programme like this and that my letters going astray has added to those difficulties.

Here is the programme as it stands at present:

Scene from 'Odysseus' *Max Bruch*
Concert Fantasy for Piano and Orchestra, 'Africa' *Saint-Saëns*
Prologue to 'Mefistofele' *Boito*
??? *Tschaikowsky*
Suite, 'Peer Gynt' *Grieg*
Ode by Swinburne (10 minutes) *Stanford*

I've put myself at the end because everybody will be leaving by then!

Rehearsals:
in London, Royal College of Music, next to the Albert Hall, Friday, 9th. June at 4 p.m.; in Cambridge, Monday, 12th. June at 10.30 a.m.

Concert:
Monday, 12th. June at 2.30 p.m.

Doctorates:
Tuesday, 13th. June at 2 p.m.

A number of people have made a request for your work for string orchestra. I believe this was given at the Philharmonic in London. But is it not, perhaps, too long?

Almost a fortnight elapsed before a reply at last arrived from Russia, by which time Stanford had returned to Cambridge. Tchaikovsky's letter, written, like Stanford's, in French, was dated 17 February, the day after he started sketching the Sixth Symphony.

I've just got back home after a rather long trip, and by an unfortunate combination of circumstances it's only today I've received your three letters, which, instead of being forwarded, were held for me. Now let me hasten to tell you, Dear Colleague, that I leave entirely to you the choice of the piece to be performed in the concert at Cambridge. Since you have announced my Piano Concerto, I ask no more than to be allowed to conduct it myself. I shall be delighted to make the acquaintance of Mr. Borwick, but just in case this artist is unable to accept your invitation, I can recommend Sapellnikoff, who, as it happens, will be in England when I arrive for the rehearsals in London.

I look forward to the pleasure and honour of renewing our very cordial acquaintance and remain, Dear Colleague, your devoted servant

P. Tschaïkovsky

My apologies! I've just re-read your letter from Milan and I see that the concerto must be ruled out. Let's decide, then, on one of my symphonic poems. I suggest *Francesca da Rimini*, which, however, is difficult and needs a first-class orchestra. As for the *Serenade for Strings*, I think it lasts more than 20 minutes. So let me play *Francesca* – it's a work I prefer above all the others that I've written in this genre.

The trip to which Tchaikovsky refers was occasioned by engagements in Brussels and Odessa, which did not permit him the opportunity of returning home in between. In Odessa, he posed for the portrait by Kuznetsov, which Modest Tchaikovsky later described as the most 'living' painting ever made of his brother.

Stanford replied to Tchaikovsky on 22 February.

> A thousand thanks for your letter!
> So. 'Francesca'.
> It now only remains for me to ask if the scoring demands any extra instruments in addition to those listed below. I am actually engaging the orchestra at the moment. I think you will be pleased with it. At least, I hope you will!

The instruments listed are strings, piccolo, two flutes, two oboes, two clarinets, two bassoons, double-bassoon, four horns, three trumpets, four trombones, triangle, timpani and two harps. Like *Africa*, *Francesca da Rimini*, which was composed in 1876, had not yet been performed in England.

Stanford had to wait another fortnight for Tchaikovsky's reply. It arrived on 11 March, three months before the jubilee celebrations.

> Once again I have been slow to answer you, owing to the nomad life that I've been leading recently. Thank you for letting me play *Francesca*. Other than the instruments you've mentioned in your letter, I would like a *cor anglais* and a fourth trumpet. As for the percussion, I'd like a *tam-tam*. I beg you, therefore, Dear Colleague, to do me the kindness of engaging for this piece three extra artists. (The *cor anglais* cannot be played by the second oboist; it will need a further woodwind player in addition to the two oboists.)

This time, the delay was caused by rehearsals and concerts in Moscow, which gave Tchaikovsky no opportunity of returning to his home in the country. These engagements also interrupted work on the Sixth Symphony, the sketches for which were completed on 5 April. The composer then put these to one side, having decided to carry out the orchestration after his return from Cambridge. In the intervening weeks before the trip to England, he wrote eighteen piano pieces and six songs.

On the same day, 16 December 1892, that Tchaikovsky wrote to John Peile, accepting his invitation to Cambridge, he also sent a letter to Francesco Berger, secretary of the Philharmonic Society, telling him the good news and asking whether, during his visit to England, he might have the opportunity of appearing again at one of the Society's concerts. He did not mention any particular works that he would like to perform.

By reason of his position, Berger was an influential figure in English musical life. He was born in London on 10 June 1834, the son of an Austro-Italian father and a Bavarian mother. His father had emigrated from Trieste to London, which was where he met his wife. Young Francesco showed early musical promise and was fortunate in being given encouragement and support by his parents, who made sure he had the best teachers. By his mid-teens, he had developed into such a fine pianist that he attracted the attention of Costa, about whom he writes in his *Reminiscences, Impressions and Anecdotes*, published in 1913, two years after his retirement as secretary to the Philharmonic.

It was he who advised my father to send me to Leipzig, and on my return he continued to take a lively interest in me, asking to be shown the results of my work there, and remaining my friend and patron to the last. His day for receiving friends in Eccleston Square was Sunday morning, and his attire on these occasions was a dressing-gown, no trousers, and top-boots worn over his drawers!

He was a great Conductor, and a strict disciplinarian; woe to the man who appeared late at rehearsal, for the Chief had never been known to do so himself. He was extremely courteous to all, but very imperious too. When he asked you to dinner, it was *not an invitation*, but a *command* to attend.

In Leipzig, Berger became a pupil of Moritz Hauptmann, who had been appointed a professor of counterpoint and composition at the Conservatoire on Mendelssohn's recommendation. Hauptmann also taught Joachim, Bülow, Sullivan and Cowen. After several years in Leipzig, where he became good friends with Charles Dickens junior, who was there to learn German, Berger returned to England, by which time he had published a number of songs and piano pieces. He took piano pupils and found concert work; he also composed songs for Clara Novello, Sims Reeves and other leading singers of the day.

In 1854, at the age of twenty, he was invited to a dinner-party at Tavistock House by Charles Dickens junior and met the novelist. Berger was a remarkably handsome and entertaining young man – a fellow student at Leipzig, Edward Bache, described him as 'the cleverest young musician I have ever yet met with' – and it was not long before he was on friendly terms with the entire Dickens family. In the winter of 1855, he was invited to compose an overture and incidental music to the Christmas play, written by Wilkie Collins, that Dickens put on at Tavistock House. The overture proved so successful that

Manns performed it at the Crystal Palace. In 1856, Dickens asked Berger to compose the music for *The Frozen Deep* in which the novelist gave his most famous theatrical interpretation. When the Queen (and Hans Christian Andersen) attended the special performance at the Gallery of Illustration in Regent Street in July 1857, she was presented with a copy of the overture elegantly bound in satin. This work was dedicated to Dickens, who, in thanks for the incidental music, gave Berger a set of three shirt studs that had diamonds set in blue enamel; on the back of each was engraved 'C.D. to F.B.'. A short while afterwards, Berger accepted an invitation from Dickens to dine with him at the Garrick Club. As they were finishing dinner, 'a tall, square-shouldered man entered the room. Dickens immediately rose, went to greet him, and brought him to our table. It was Thackeray!'

Berger made his way rapidly, becoming a regular recitalist in London, frequently taking part in chamber music concerts and accompanying famous singers. He also toured extensively throughout the British Isles. Many of his songs became popular. In August 1864, he married the singer Annie Lascelles, who was much admired by Queen Victoria; they were sufficiently well off to be able to move into an attractive house at 6 York Street, Portman Square, which was to be Berger's home for the rest of the century. In 1859, he was elected an associate of the Philharmonic Society and, in 1871, a member. In 1880, he became a director of the society and, in 1884, the secretary. In 1886, he was appointed Professor of Piano at the Royal Academy of Music and, in the following year, he took up a similar post at the Guildhall School of Music.

In his capacity as secretary of the society, he corresponded with many well-known composers, including Brahms, Gounod and Rubinstein, and became friendly with such eminent musicians as Joachim, Bülow and Sarasate. Bülow was one of his particular favourites.

He was a very eccentric man, and I do not think he objected to having his eccentricities recorded. It was his custom, when playing in public, even in the daytime, to mount the platform with white kid gloves on, and carrying an opera-hat. Once, when he had accepted an engagement to play at a Concert of the Philharmonic Society, when date, fee, and *Concerto* had been fixed, I wrote to him inviting him to 'honour the Directors' of that Society by dining with them during his visit to London, and asking him to name his own day. He replied, 'What have I done, that, besides playing at your Concert, I should also be expected to dine with your Directors?'

Another favourite was Dvořák.

Great Musicians are mostly unconventional people, and he was no exception to this rule, his unfamiliarity with the usages of London life sometimes having amusing results. Thus, walking along Pall Mall one day, feeling very hungry, he saw a palatial building, through the open windows of which small tables could be seen set out with appetising dining apparatus. So he walked in, took his seat, and gave his orders to the astonished servant, neither of them being able to understand what the other said. It took him some time before he could realise the nature of his mistake, and that it was a *Club* he had entered, not a hotel.

Berger was delighted to receive Tchaikovsky's letter of 16 December. The Russian composer's two Philharmonic concerts had both been well attended, and he had not been to England for four years; there was every prospect that his next appearance in London would again fill the house. On top of this, the two men had already exchanged several letters and became friendly. Berger therefore offered him 1 June and asked which of his works he would like to conduct. Tchaikovsky replied on 16 January, in German.

> I thank you affectionately. I will accordingly conduct in the concert, on 1st June, my Fourth Symphony. (I would prefer to conduct the programme symphony *Manfred*, but, since it is very difficult, I'm afraid it wouldn't be possible to get it ready in just two rehearsals.) I shall see to the parts.

By the beginning of January, Berger had discovered that Boito, Bruch, Saint-Saëns and Grieg would also be in London the following June. This presented opportunities that were not to be missed, and he at once wrote to each of them, offering engagements. Boito was the first to reply, in Italian. (German and Italian were Berger's two best foreign languages.)

> I am very grateful for the kind invitation that you have extended to me in the name of the most celebrated musical society in Europe. Had I no more than my own wishes to consider, I would hasten to accept your precious offer, but my engagements prevent it.
> After my brief trip to Cambridge, I shall have to return immediately to Italy. Please be kind enough, Dear Sir, to tender my apologies and warm thanks to the management of the Philharmonic Society and to express my disappointment in being unable to accept.

A day later, came Bruch's reply, dated 14 January and written in excellent English. 'I shall feel much pleasure in accepting your Society's kind invitation', he said; but he was not yet decided on which date would be convenient, or which work he would conduct. However, 'You are authorized to announce that I have accepted your Society's invitation.' Berger replied by suggesting 15 June and the First Violin Concerto. On 2 February, Bruch wrote, now in German, to say that this was not entirely to his liking.

> I reply herewith most humbly to your respected lines of 27th. January of this year by stating that it is not my wish after ten years' absence from England to conduct, at a concert given by England's most distinguished musical society, nothing more than a violin concerto; anybody can do that equally well – for instance, your excellent Mr. Cusins. It is unnecessary for the composer to do it. Therefore I ask you to include, in addition to this old concerto, which has been in existence for 25 years, the *Three Pieces for Orchestra* from my secular cantata *Achilleus*. These last, in all, only 7 to 8 minutes, they are very effective and make no unusual demands on the receptive faculties of your, as you have described them, conservative public.

Berger was pleased to learn that Bruch would also like to conduct the pieces from *Achilleus*; for the Violin Concerto, he would book Ladislas Gorski. Bruch replied to this, again in German, on 12 February.

> I am glad that your committee has accepted the pieces from *Achilleus* and I give you herewith my definite confirmation that I shall conduct these *Three Pieces for Orchestra* as well as my First Violin Concerto in G minor, op. 26 – providing that Mr. Gorski is *very good* and already well known in England. Joachim will unfortunately not be in England in June, but might it not be possible to get my good friend Sarasate, who is always in London during the season? This would, of course, be very desirable for you, but I do not insist upon it in case Mr. Gorski (surely a Pole?) is already engaged.

Berger went ahead and engaged Gorski.

The third to reply to Berger's invitation to appear at a Philharmonic concert was Saint-Saëns. Berger had suggested the Second Piano Concerto and an orchestral work of the composer's choice. Saint-Saëns gave his answer, in French, on 18 January.

> As I wrote to you last year, I no longer wish to perform in public [his final concert took place in Dieppe on 6 August 1921], but this exceptional event, the Chicago Exhibition, having persuaded me to shed my reserve, I see no reason for refusing to appear one last time on the programme of the Philharmonic Society. I shall therefore play, since it is your wish, my Concerto in G minor, unless you would prefer something new, in which case I would propose my fantasy, *Africa*, which has had a huge success at

the Sunday Concerts at the Châtelet [Colonne Concerts] and at the Cirque des Champs-Élysées [Lamoureux Concerts]; I leave the choice to you. For the orchestral work, I shall conduct the symphonic poem in A, 'La Jeunesse d'Hercule'.

What pleasure I shall have in meeting you again and finding myself once more in London, which I have not seen in five years! It's really going to rejuvenate me.

You mention the terms of engagement. I ask merely that they be worthy of the famous society that is inviting me, and of myself; the pleasure is, above all, artistic, and I prefer to leave to the judgment of the committee the practical side of the matter.

By the time he had received Saint-Saëns' letter, Berger was in a much better position to see how he was going to fit him and Tchaikovsky and Bruch into the season's programmes. The Philharmonic concerts took place once a fortnight from the beginning of March to the middle of June. Bruch was scheduled for the final concert, to appear together with Melba and Paderewski, on 15 June. Berger therefore decided to put Saint-Saëns on the same programme as Tchaikovsky, on 1 June. To ask him to perform in the concert prior to that, on 18 May, almost a month before the Cambridge celebrations, was hardly likely to meet with a favourable response. He informed Saint-Saëns and was sent a reply at the beginning of February.

Since Mr. Tchaïkowsky is to conduct his symphony, it seems to me that, unless you have any other suggestion, it would be fair for me to play a second work for piano; this way, it will not look as if we are competing against each other – something that is always rather unpleasant – for we will then be, as far as possible, on different ground from each other.

I therefore suggest to you, as my second piece, my fantasy, *Africa*. However, it is also in G minor, or at least begins in that key before passing into many others and finishing in G major. It is an extended piece, in which the orchestra is important. If you see any problem in the similarity of keys, you can replace the 2nd. Concerto with the 4th. (in C minor); as far as I'm concerned, I don't see any problem, assuming that presumably Tchaïkowsky's symphony will come in between the two pieces; unless that, too, is in G minor!

I accept the 25 guineas.

Very truly yours, [in English – an ending used by Stanford]

C Saint-Saëns

P.S. This fantasy, *Africa*, that I am offering you, has had an absolutely remarkable success in Paris, also in Liège and in Baden, which is why I would like it to be given a hearing in London.

Berger was agreeable to the change suggested: Tchaikovsky's symphony was not in G minor; *La Jeunesse d'Hercule* would be replaced by *Africa*. But, in a letter dated 16 February, Saint-Saëns had further thoughts.

> I have received your letter in which you accept my new arrangement. It would now only remain for me to thank you, but since the last time I had the honour of writing to you, I have reflected; and the idea of *not* conducting your fine orchestra, of forgoing such a rare pleasure, is really too distressing to me. May I once again offer a change of plan? Don't you find me really rather a ninny? I'd like, after having played my Concerto in G minor, to conduct *Le Rouet d'Omphale*.
>
> If the programme arrangements demand that *Le Rouet d'Omphale* should precede the concerto, I don't mind either way.

We learn from Berger's *Reminiscences* that he had the warmest regard for Saint-Saëns: 'With the solitary exception of Mendelssohn, modern times have produced no Musician of such varied eminence as Dr Camille Saint-Saëns . . . he has done everything that a Musician can do, and done it successfully.' Of the fifth of his correspondents, Grieg, he had a somewhat lower opinion.

> My personal reminiscence of him is not particularly happy. I found his conceit amounted almost to snobbishness, his want of courtesy almost to rudeness. Whatever small services I rendered him (and felt proud to render), he received quite as 'a matter of course' and seemed unwilling to say 'thank you' for. This does not detract from my admiration of his talent, nor from the high esteem in which I hold his music.

Like Bruch's initial reply to Berger, Grieg's, too, was in English; it was dated 23 January.

> Dear Sir,
> If my health shall permit me to do so, I intend to visit London end of May and should be very glad to renew the acquaintance with the excellent Philharmonic Orchestra. I hope to be able to bring a manuscript orchestral work, not before performed, and, if you also wish to hear the melodies elegiaques or the newly edited melodies for stringed instruments, Op. 53, I shall with pleasure be at your service.
> My terms will be £50.
>
> > Yours respectfully,
> >
> > Edvard Grieg

Berger replied that, unhappily, his directors would not permit him to offer as much as £50. Costs were such that twenty-five guineas was all the Society could pay, and this was a sum reserved only for the most distinguished artists. Grieg answered on 31 January, 'I claim the amount I have stipulated, neither more nor less.' Berger wrote back, on 7 February, 'The Directors desire me to say that the offer contained in my recent letter to you was final on their part, and I regret that it does not meet with your acceptance.' Grieg replied by return of post, 'I regret very much that I shall have to forgo the honour of appearing with the Philharmonic Society.'

The news that so many famous composers would be taking part in the CUMS celebrations caused great excitement. In its announcement of this event, the *Cambridge Review* of 26 January began with the words 'They are all coming now' and then went on to describe at length how each composer would be conducting one of his own works. Later on in the article, it was stated that Stanford had retired from his post as organist of Trinity College.

> We have lost Dr. Stanford, who played his last service in Trinity on Christmas Day. But the coming production of his incidental music to 'Becket' at the Lyceum, with which we learn he is now very busy, comes fitly under the heading of Cambridge news. His Mass, mentioned in this column last term, is to be produced at the Brompton Oratory . . . His 'Revenge' was performed last month at Greenock, and his Irish Symphony is down for performance at the Philharmonic Society.

When Stanford went up to Cambridge in 1870, he was a promising young musician. By 1893, he was an internationally renowned composer. During those years, he had become organist of Trinity, conductor of the CUMS and Professor of Music; in London, he was Professor of Composition at the Royal College of Music and conductor of the student orchestra and the Bach Choir. He was now forty, still in his prime as a composer, and with a wife and two children, Geraldine, ten, and Guy, eight, with whom he found he was spending all too little time. He had also come to prefer London, the most musically active city in the world, to Cambridge. And so, at the end of 1892, he made London his home, moving into 50 Holland Street, Kensington, and resigning as organist of Trinity. He decided also to resign as conductor of the CUMS, but agreed to stay on until the jubilee concert. He was succeeded in the Trinity organ-loft by Alan Gray, who had played the organ at Stanford's wedding. He was by now moderately well off and could therefore afford to keep on his house in Cambridge, at 10 Harvey Road, until the jubilee was over. He remained Professor of Music, retaining his rooms in Trinity. There was nothing untoward in his holding that position and living in London. Sterndale Bennett, when he was professor, had also lived in London; his situation was somewhat different, though: the professorship carried no salary in his day, and it is questionable whether he could have afforded a house in Cambridge as well.

Because of the pressure of his many duties and concert engagements, Stanford's output had slackened in the early nineties. Yet he still managed to produce a number of excellent works, particularly the beautiful Mass referred to in the *Cambridge Review*. An amusing piece of minor importance is the *Installation March* of May 1892, composed for the installation of the Duke of Devonshire as Chancellor of Cambridge University. This not only quotes the 'Cambridge Chimes', 'Auld Lang Syne', 'Rule, Britannia' and 'Let Erin Remember the Days of Old', but eventually sets 'Gaudeamus igitur' in hilarious counterpoint with 'D'Ye Ken John Peel', a droll way of introducing the Duke to his Vice-Chancellor, John Peile.

Despite his many commitments, Stanford was still able to squeeze in visits to Italy, a country that had such happy memories for him. It was in Venice, we may recall, that he espied a sight 'which alone repayed the journey: Charles Hallé in a frock-coat and a white top hat reading the *Daily Telegraph* while seated in a gondola and floating under the Bridge of Sighs'. In Florence, in the spring of 1892, he saw Bülow for the last time. That luminous and lovable man was now close to his final, clouded days, which ended with his death in Cairo in February 1894.

On our return [from Rome] we spent a week in Florence. The first morning I was standing at the top of the staircase of the Uffizi, talking to a friend about Hans von Bülow, when as if by magic he came up the steps, seized me by the arm, and rushed me along the passages to the room where the portraits of painters from their own brush are hung. He took me straight up to those of Leighton and Millais, and said, 'There you have the characters of the two men as they are.' Then he pointed to that of Watts, and said, 'Your English Titian.' In the afternoon he carried me off to see Madame Hillebrand, the widow of the author who translated the first English edition of 'Grimm's Fairy Tales', beloved of my youth. While I was talking to her, Bülow crawled round the bookshelves on his hands and knees until he discovered the well-known volumes, and deposited them on my lap . . .

The last I saw of this witty, brilliant, and broad-minded man was the waving of his handkerchief from Madame Hillebrand's steps. The world will be much older before it contains his equal.

Stanford's next visit to Italy was to Milan for the world première of *Falstaff* on 9 February 1893.

The Scala Theatre was a wonderful sight, crammed to the roof with an audience gathered from the four corners of the earth. The excitement was so tense that the least little point of danger set everyone on edge. So keen were the listeners for the success of the old hero, that they resented a single lapse from perfection. The performance had not started for two minutes before Maurel [Victor Maurel, the French baritone, who played Falstaff] produced a high note in a way which displeased the stall. In an instant they all shouted out 'Basta! Basta! Basta!' in most angry tones. I thought the next thing would be a rapid descent of the curtain, but Maurel paid no attention and went ahead. A few bars farther on he sang the same note with the right effect. 'Ah! Ah! Ah!' said the stalls, equally loudly, with the unmistakable suggestion in their voices that he had better go on in the same style or it would be the worse for him. It was not ill-nature, obviously; the interruption sprang from pure and simple eagerness that everyone should do his level best; and it was the first and last hostile outburst of the evening. The number of times which Verdi had to appear were impossible to count, but on each entry he preserved the same dignified demeanour; he might have been a king receiving his subjects at a levée. There was no suspicion of arrogance, no suggestion of false modesty. He knew that his audience understood him and he acknowledged their tribute with the grace and nobility of a born leader of men . . . The morning after the performance I went to see him with Boito, and he was pacing the room, thoroughly out of temper. Boito asked him what was the matter, and he tossed him a telegram from the King. It contained the offer to make him Marchese di Busseto.

BOITO. 'Well, Master, what have you said?'

VERDI. 'I have answered him, "Musician I was born, musician I remain."'

Having delivered his soul, the Italian quicksilver asserted itself and he beamed upon us again.

The première of *Falstaff* was one of the great musical events of the latter half of the nineteenth century, attended, as Stanford mentions, by musicians from all over the globe. Mackenzie and Cowen were also there. Cowen recalled the occasion in his memoirs.

It was the most exciting scene I ever took part in. The house was crammed from floor to ceiling with all that was fashionable and artistic, music lovers having come from all parts of the world to hear the work, and the applause, encores, and enthusiasm, were continuous throughout the whole evening. But the most moving sight of all was when the grand old octogenarian of music came before the curtain after each act, and amid the cheering and waving of handkerchiefs, made his bow – smiling, and as erect as if he were his own young self of fifty years back, witnessing the triumph of his 'Nabucco' or 'Lombardi'.

Cowen tried hard to obtain an introduction to Verdi, but – ever the outsider – failed to meet the master, who 'was so overwhelmed, however, with callers on the same errand as myself, that, beyond his few intimates, he would see no one: therefore, after one or two visits to his hotel, I had not the courage to persist any further in my desire, and relinquished the attempt.' He did succeed in meeting Boito, Puccini, Mascagni and Leoncavallo. 'Of Boito I saw perhaps more than any of the others, as we not only used to meet frequently at the opera and at his favourite café, but also at the houses of mutual friends. He was a charming man, distinguished looking, quiet and refined, and with the polished manner of a thorough gentleman.' A few months later, when Cowen's opera *Signa* was presented at the Teatro dal Verme in Milan – 'the first English opera, I believe, that had been produced in Italy for over thirty years' – he managed so to infuriate the impresario and publisher Edoardo Sonzogno that the Italian 'was supposed to have said that if he ever met me again he would put a bullet through me. (It was suggested to me to wear a coat of mail under my waistcoat for protection, but I thought it a cowardly thing to do, so refrained.)' This was not such a light matter as Cowen implies, for Boito somehow got drawn into the affair, and Sonzogno challenged him to a duel. Boito accepted, and the two men travelled to Naples, where honour was to be settled. Since both of them lived in Milan, the choice of venue seems odd, but perhaps Naples had a romantic association for the knightly Boito. Fortunately, no sooner had he reached Naples, than Sonzogno, faced with the prospect of dispatching one of Italy's favourite sons, gallantly asked the Commendatore Boito to accept his apologies; they shook hands, and that was that. Cowen says he suffered 'many sleepless nights' on Boito's account. However, when it was all over, he received 'a charming letter' from his Italian colleague.

Cowen was not commissioned by any of the English newspapers to report on the première of *Falstaff*, but Stanford and Mackenzie were. Stanford acted as correspondent for both the *Daily Graphic* and the *Fortnightly Review*. It was in the latter that he wrote of 'the seven-leagued boots which carried Verdi from *Nabucco* to *Aida*', boots which now proved capable 'of taking another stride, and a longer one'.

Three days before *Falstaff* in Milan, the first performance took place in the Lyceum Theatre in London of Tennyson's *Becket*, for which Stanford had composed the incidental music. Henry Irving played Becket, and Ellen Terry acted the part of Rosamund de Clifford. We may recall the unhappy circumstances of how, seventeen years earlier, Stanford's music for Tennyson's *Queen Mary* had never finally been used; but this was more than compensated for by the enthusiasm with which his score for *Becket* was greeted.

Tennyson had written *Becket* as far back as 1879, and, by the 1890s, had come to accept that it would be extremely difficult to perform effectively and was unlikely ever to reach the stage. But Irving, after many years' thought about the tragedy, at last worked out how it could be presented. He finalised his plans during his annual holiday in Holy Week, 1892, and, on his return, immediately discussed them with his secretary, Bram Stoker. 'We sat that night until four o'clock, talking over the play and the music for it', wrote Stoker in his *Personal Reminiscence of Henry Irving*. 'Irving thought that Charles Villiers Stanford would be the best man to do it' – with which Stoker agreed.

The next step was for Stoker to go down to Freshwater to show Tennyson the acting version that Irving had prepared. He crossed over to the Isle of Wight on Easter Tuesday, 19 April 1892. His visit lasted three days, giving Tennyson the chance to study Irving's many cuts and alterations. The poet was by now in the grip of his final illness, and his son Hallam acted as host and, on the morning following Stoker's arrival, showed him round the grounds at Farringford.

> After breakfast, Hallam and I walked in the beautiful wood behind the house, where beyond the hedgerows and the little wood rose the great bare rolling Down, at the back of which is a great sheer cliff five hundred feet high. We sat in the summer-house where Tennyson had written nearly all of *Enoch Arden*. It had been lined with wood, which Tennyson himself had carved; but now the bare bricks were visible in places. The egregious relic-hunters had whittled away piecemeal the carved wood. They had also smashed the windows, which Tennyson had painted with sea-plants and dragons; and had carried off the pieces! When we returned I was brought up to Tennyson's room.

He was not feeling well. He sat in a great chair with the cut play on his knee, one finger between the pages as though to mark a place. He had been studying the alterations; and as he did not look happy, I feared that there might be something not satisfactory with regard to some of the cuts. Presently he said to me suddenly:

'Who is God, the Virgin?'

'Who is *what*?' I asked, bewildered as to his meaning; I feared I could not have heard aright.

'God, the Virgin! That is what I want to know. Here it is!' As he spoke, he opened the play where his finger marked it. He handed it to me, and there to my astonishment I read:

'I do commend my soul to God, the Virgin' . . . When Irving had been cutting the speech, he had omitted to draw his pencil through the last two words. The speech as written ran thus:

'I do commend my soul to God, the Virgin, St. Denis of France, and St. Alphege of England, And all the tutelary saints of Canterbury.'

In doing the scissors-work, he had been guided by the pencil-marks, and so had made the error.

The incident amused Tennyson very much, and put him in better spirits. He went downstairs into what in the house is called the 'ballroom', a great sunny room with the wall away from the light covered with a great painting by Lear of a tropical scene intended for *Enoch Arden*. Here we walked up and down for a long time, the old man leaning on my arm.

Towards the end of his stay, Stoker mentioned the question of incidental music for *Becket*. 'When I asked Tennyson what composer he would wish to do the music for his play, he said: "Villiers Stanford!" He and Irving had independently chosen the same man. How this belief was justified is known to all who have heard the fine *Becket* music.'

At first, Stanford offered to write the music for nothing, out of his regard for Tennyson, but Stoker told him that Irving, an exceptionally generous man, would never countenance such a proposal. Stoker asked Stanford to name a figure. When he refused, Stoker suggested £200. Stanford said it was far too high. They went to see Irving, who agreed, yes, £200 was wrong; it should be £300. Stanford said there was no question of his accepting £300. 'Then you shan't write the music', Irving told him. When Stanford eventually received his cheque, it was for 300 guineas.

Stanford referred to *Becket* in his contribution to *Tennyson and His Friends*, edited by Hallam Tennyson and published in 1911.

The best reproduction of the peculiar quality of Tennyson's reading which I have heard was Irving's rendering of the lines about the bird in the last act of 'Becket':

> *We came upon*
> *A wild-fowl sitting on her nest, so still*
> *I reach'd my hand and touch'd; she did not stir;*
> *The snow had frozen round her, and she sat*
> *Stone-dead upon a heap of ice-cold eggs.*

The mastery of sound-painting in these lines, the chilly 'o's' and 'e's' which the Poet knew so well how to place, Irving declaimed with a quiet reverence which made the sentence so pathetic that it will always live in the memory of those who heard it. It is interesting to record that all the actors I have met who witnessed the play invariably hit on those lines as the high-water mark of Irving's powers.

Irving was deeply impressed with Stanford's score for *Becket* and always went to listen behind the curtain to the last *entr'acte*, the funeral march depicting Becket's martyrdom, so that he could put himself in the right mood for the final scene.

'I can trust Irving – Irving will do me justice', Tennyson said shortly before his death. He knew that he would not live to witness the production of *Becket*. When the end was near, he asked his doctor, 'I suppose I shall never see it?' 'I fear not', the doctor answered. Stoker and his wife visited Farringford just before Tennyson died.

The lessening twilight and the moveless flame of the close-set candle showed out his noble face and splendid head in full relief. The mullioned window behind him with the darkening sky and the fading landscape made a fitting background to the dying poet. We said good-bye with full hearts.

Outside, our tears fell.

Queen Victoria was anxious to see *Becket*, which was performed by royal command in the Waterloo Gallery of Windsor Castle on 18 March 1893. Among the audience were the Prince of Wales and the Empress Frederick of Germany. 'It is a very noble play', the Queen told Irving afterwards. 'What a pity that old Tennyson did not live to see it.' Later, she commented on the performance in her diary.

The last scene, when Becket refuses to fly and defies his murderers, is very fine and his death and the way he falls down the steps, very striking. The language is very beautiful and so is the incidental music, expressly composed by Stanford.

CHAPTER 8

LONDON

On 25 May 1893, Tchaikovsky left St Petersburg, departing from Warsaw Station.

Russian trains and railways were now again being improved, after a period of relative inactivity. Rail travel had been introduced slowly in Russia, and, by 1850, the country possessed no more than 370 miles of track. Not until the following year were St Petersburg and Moscow connected, the 400 mile line having been laid under the direction of George Washington Whistler, the painter's father. For several decades, passengers setting out from either city had to arrive an hour ahead of departure. They were required to remove their hats in the station, show their passports and have their baggage weighed; a police certificate granting permission to leave the city was also necessary. The journey itself could be harrowing, and friends would wave goodbye in the belief that this was a final farewell. The carriages were connected by chains, and, whenever the train stopped, people were hurled from their seats. There was no heating. On his way to St Petersburg to supervise rehearsals for *La forza del destino* in 1861, Verdi had the unhappy experience of watching his glass of Bordeaux turn to ice. 'Now I understand the meaning of *cold*', he wrote to Enrico Tamberlik. At stations between Moscow and St Petersburg, insufficient information was given to those boarding trains, and many people unwittingly caught whichever 'giant samovar' turned up first. During the early fifties, a tale gained currency in which two friends found themselves seated next to each other. 'Where are you going?' inquired the first. 'To Moscow', replied the second. 'I'm for Petersburg', said the first and then reflected enthusiastically, 'But what an amazing invention this is! Here we are in the same carriage, yet bound for opposite ends of the line!'

By 1880, there were still only 15,000 miles of track in Russia and, by 1893, little over 20,000. Trains had much improved by the nineties; the locomotives, which had previously been imported and adapted, were now being designed and constructed in Russia. The

Stanford at the time of the Cambridge Jubilee

Stanford towards the end of his life – in Herbert Howells' opinion, 'the best likeness of the composer in his later years'

A cartoon of Stanford in his early fifties, from *The Illustrated London News*

Tchaikovsky during his last visit to London

Tchaikovsky's signature and a fragment from the Fourth Symphony, inscribed for Alexander Mackenzie

An autograph, with an extract from the *Serenade for Strings*, given by Tchaikovsky to Francesco Berger

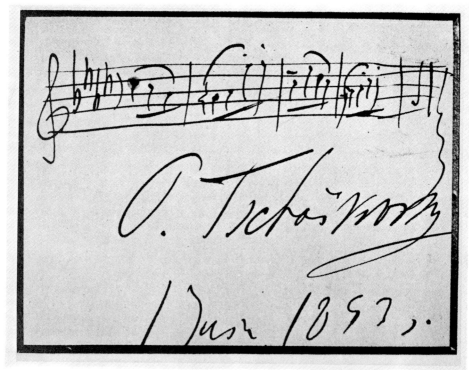

Camille Saint-Saëns

Two great champions of new music: *above*, George Grove and *right*,
August Manns, cartoons from *The Illustrated London News*

Harry Plunket Greene, biographer of Stanford and the finest interpreter of his songs

Michael Costa, one of the first and most successful dictators of the baton

The signatures of the four honorary Doctors of Music, 13 June 1893

Mus. D. Charles Camille Saint-Saëns

Mus. D. Max Christian Friedrich Bruch.

Mus. D. Pierre Ilitsch Tschaïkovsky

Mus. D. António Arrigo Boïto

train on which Tchaikovsky travelled in May 1893 is likely to have
been drawn by an N class 2-6-0 locomotive, designed principally by
Professor N. L. Shchukin and capable of moving 400 tons at 50 mph.

Tchaikovsky reached Berlin on 27 May. He arrived in London
during the early hours of 29 May, travelling via Ostend. The Channel
crossing, which was calm, took three hours. He booked into the Hotel
Dieudonné, where he had stayed on his previous two visits; it was the
height of the season, and the hotel was very full, but a room was
nevertheless found for him.

This was his fourth visit to London. His first took place in August
1861, when aged 21 he accompanied a friend of his father's on a
business trip, acting as his interpreter and speaking French and
German. Five months earlier, Tolstoy, too, had made his first – and
only – trip to London. His biographer Henri Troyat has written, 'The
foggy, smoky town, with yellow gaslamps glowing here and there,
impressed him by its orderliness, discipline and tedium. Not one
curious glance in the street, not one over-hasty movement, not a cry,
not a smile. Nothing but measured, sober citizens hiding their souls
and going about their business with no concern for that of others.'
Tolstoy went to hear Dickens – 'a genius born once in a hundred
years' – give a reading in St James's Hall. This was from a series of
six, delivered in March and April 1861, that netted over £500 – 'a
very great result', Dickens informed John Forster. Due to his limited
grasp of English, the Russian novelist understood this reading to be a
lecture on education. He later called on the revolutionary-in-exile,
Alexander Herzen, who was living at Orsett House, Westbourne
Terrace, and somewhat disappointed Herzen's daughter by arriving
in a top hat and palmerston coat and launching enthusiastically into
descriptions of a cock-fight and boxing match that he had recently
witnessed. Tolstoy 'is stubborn and talks nonsense', Herzen wrote to
Turgenev, 'but is a naive and good man.' Nine months later, Herzen
welcomed to his home the anarchist Mikhail Bakunin, who had
escaped from Siberia and now weighed twenty stone. Seven months
after that, in July 1862, he received another survivor from Siberia,
Dostoyevsky, who was, like Tolstoy, on his first and last visit to
England. Though London filled Tolstoy with 'a loathing for modern
civilization', this paled beside Dostoyevsky's disgust for a people who
'prostrate themselves before Baal'. For him, London was 'a kind of

biblical picture, something like Babylon, some prophecy out of the Apocalypse coming to pass before your very eyes ... This is the complete triumph of Baal, the ultimate organization of an anthill.' The city appeared to him to be in constant motion, day and night, with trains running above the houses ('and, soon, under them, as well'), with everything in apparent chaos, 'which is actually capitalist order in the highest degree.' The Thames was polluted, the air was impregnated with coal fumes, the slum dwellers were 'half-naked, savage and starving'. The plight of the children particularly moved him. He was so touched by the wretchedness of one little girl whom he passed in the Haymarket that he retraced his steps and gave her a sixpenny piece. 'She seized the small silver coin, threw me a crazed look of surprise and then ran off as fast as her tiny legs could carry her, perhaps terrified that I might take the money back again.'

In a letter of 10 August 1861, Tchaikovsky told his father that London was extremely interesting, but 'it makes a gloomy impression on the soul. You never see the sun, and it rains at every step.' He and his father's friend, Vasily Pisarev, took in all the principal sights. They visited the Houses of Parliament and Westminster Abbey and also ventured inside the Thames Tunnel, 'where I was nearly sick, it was so stuffy.' We now know this as the Rotherhithe Tunnel, which extends under the river to Wapping. It was constructed by Marc Isambard Brunel.

Tchaikovsky seems to have been most excited by the pleasure gardens at Cremorne, which Pisarev and he inspected on Thursday, 8 August. 'I've never seen anything like it', he wrote to his father. Occupying almost sixteen acres between the Thames and King's Road, Chelsea, the gardens could be approached from the river, and people would often arrive by steamer; the main entrance was in King's Road. 'When you go in, it's like magic', Tchaikovsky reported, and, indeed, it was. Cremorne had just reopened, after extensive improvements, and, at night-time, was a blaze of light and colour. A huge star illuminated the pay-box, while, inside, tens of thousands of lights created a veritable fairyland. Yet there was never any feeling of glare or unnatural brightness, and many lovely trees broke up the light and cast their shadows across the lawns and paths. Scattered among the grounds were ornamental walks, leafy avenues, a superb pagoda decked with hundreds of coloured lanterns, statues, fountains, temples, Swiss chalets, a maze, an American bowling-alley, a Turkish pavilion, side-shows and shooting-galleries. There was also organised entertainment on a prodigious scale. Near the main entrance was the Crystal Platform, a dance-floor with capacity for 4,000 dancers; the forty-strong orchestra was under the direction of Jules Rivière. In other parts of the gardens were two military bands, one of which was conducted by Dan Godfrey senior. Equestrians and acrobats performed in the Cirque Oriental; a troupe of dogs and monkeys, in the Octagon Theatre. Ballets and light-classical concerts took place in the main theatre, alternating with music-hall concerts and speciality acts. Popular among the latter were Cristoforo Buono Core, the 'Fire-King' or 'Italian Salamander', who could emerge unscathed from a furnace, and Natator, the 'Man-Frog', who, while immersed in a water-tank, would stand on his head, eat a sponge-cake and smoke a pipe. Other unusual acts included the Bosjesmans, who were bushmen from South Africa, and Audrian, the 'Dog-Faced Man' and his son 'from a Russian forest'. De Groof, the 'Flying Man', was a daring balloonist who once lost control, but landed safely in Brandon, Essex; he eventually plummeted to his death in Sydney Street, just outside Cremorne; his assistant managed to stay aloft, finally descending on the Great Eastern railway line in Springfield, Essex, narrowly missing a train. Another balloonist, Henri Latour, met his end in Tottenham marshes. The Cremorne career of Madame Poitevin, who, in the guise of Europa, ascended into the sky on the back of a heifer attached to a balloon, was terminated at Ilford Sessions, when she was prosecuted for cruelty to animals; her plea, that in Paris she was able to use bulls and horses as well, proved an inadequate defence. The most famous artist whom Tchaikovsky saw was Jules Léotard with his spectacular trapeze act; he was already acquainted with the legendary Frenchman's thrilling feats, which he had witnessed in St Petersburg.

Spectacular firework displays were another popular feature. Whistler was fascinated by them and often used to watch from a boat on the river. His paintings, 'Nocturne in Blue and Silver: Cremorne Lights'; 'Nocturne in Black and Gold: The Fire Wheel' and 'Nocturne in Black and Gold: The Falling Rocket' all reflect his great interest in Cremorne. 'The Falling Rocket' prompted Ruskin to accuse him of 'flinging a pot of paint in the public's face', which led to the celebrated court case resulting in Whistler being awarded damages of a farthing – which coin he later sported on his watch-chain. Cremorne was much frequented by artists, young men about town and prostitutes. It had a very racy atmosphere, yet, despite all the noise and colour and activity, somehow managed to retain a rural charm. Residents living nearby eventually forced its closure in 1877.

As well as going to Cremorne on 8 August, the two tourists earlier in the day travelled down to the Crystal Palace, which, Tchaikovsky told his father, was, from the outside, 'really magnificent, but, inside, it's a bit too showy.' Their visit coincided with the Metropolitan Charity Children's Annual Festival and Choral Performance, conducted by Henry Buckland, Vicar of St Paul's. Their programme was listed as follows:

> Old Hundredth Psalm
> Luther's Hymn
> Haydn's Hymn to the Emperor
> Hallelujah Chorus
> Chorale from Eli
> Jerusalem the Golden
> Sleepers Awake from St Paul
> God Save the Queen

The concert began at 3pm and lasted for about an hour and a half. The 5,000 children of the Metropolitan Charity Schools in their various colourful uniforms, made an attractive sight – 'the most beautiful coup d'oeil imaginable'. In an article for the 18 November 1872 edition of the Moscow paper *Russian News*, Tchaikovsky referred to this performance of the 'Hallelujah Chorus', writing, 'I cannot convey in words the overwhelming effect of strength and power that it produced on the listener.' An hour after the concert, there was a display of the fountains. 'In the present fine weather they are unusually beautiful', ran an advertisement, 'and as the terraces and gardens will be filled with thousands of children in their holyday dress, the effect will be greatly enhanced.'

On the next day, 9 August, they took a second trip to the Crystal Palace, to hear Adelina Patti in a concert, also at 3pm, conducted by Manns. The eighteen-year-old soprano had made her English début at Covent Garden three months earlier, becoming the sensation of the season. Her last opera performance in London that year was as Zerlina in *Don Giovanni* on 2 August, but Tchaikovsky and Pisarev appear to have arrived three or four days too late to see Patti in this role. This was perhaps for the best, since *Don Giovanni* was Tchaikovsky's favourite opera, and the conductor was Costa. In his memoirs, Berlioz states, 'In London, you hear *Don Giovanni, Figaro* and *The Barber of Seville* with additional parts for bass drum, trombone and ophicleide supplied by Costa.' He mentions, in an article in the *Journal des Débats*, that an ophicleide solo was introduced during the supper scene in *Don Giovanni*. Costa's version of Mozart, he says in *Les Soirées de l'orchestre*, is 'trombonized, ophicleided – in a word, copper-bottomed like a ship of the line.' To Pierre Duc he posed the question, 'Does this not lead to the utter ruin and destruction of art?'

Writing home, Tchaikovsky said that Patti 'is creating a great furore in London, though she made no particular impression on me.' During the previous eleven weeks, she had appeared twenty-five times at Covent Garden, in six different operas, and it is possible that her voice was showing signs of wear. In the December 1861 edition of *All the Year Round*, Dickens refers to those critics who increasingly felt that her voice was not 'as fresh in tone as a voice aged nineteen [sic] should be'. The programme on this occasion was hardly designed to demonstrate much of her interpretive abilities. She sang five numbers: 'Regnava nel silenzio' from Donizetti's *Lucia di Lammermoor*; Eckhart's 'Swiss Echo Song'; 'Ah, non giunge' from Bellini's *La sonnambula*; Hook's 'Within a Mile of Edinburgh Town'; Martini's 'Vada si via di qua'.

Tchaikovsky seems to have spent about a week in England during his first visit. 'On the whole, I passed the time very pleasantly', he wrote from Paris to his father on 14 August. 'I very much like their food. The dishes are simple – plain, even – but filling and tasty.'

His second trip to England, in March 1888, was prompted by the belief that only through appearing personally to conduct his works would they gain popularity outside Russia. As we have seen, Brahms and Verdi, in the middle and later parts of their careers, had no problems of this sort; their compositions were immediately performed the moment they became available. Nevertheless, as late as 1881, Brahms visited seventeen European cities as soloist in his newly completed Second Piano Concerto. Personal appearance counted for much in the second half of the nineteenth century. Verdi came to London, to conduct the English première of his *Requiem* in 1875, and Wagner came in 1877 to recoup his Bayreuth expenses. Similarly, Cowen went to Vienna and Budapest to conduct the *Scandinavian Symphony*. Most strikingly, perhaps, it was Dvořák's personal appearance in London which helped to establish his colossal reputation in England almost within a matter of weeks. Saint-Saëns' standing, too, owed much to his frequent visits to London.

Tchaikovsky was not without his champions outside Russia, but none of them, apart from Walter Damrosch in New York, really exerted much influence or pressure, particularly when compared to the powerful advocacy of Joachim for Brahms or Clara Schumann for her husband. The man who possibly did the most was Bülow. He seems first to have become acquainted with Tchaikovsky's music in March 1874, when, on a recital tour of Russia, he renewed his friendship with Karl Klindworth, who, like Bülow himself, had been a pupil of Liszt's at Weimar in the early fifties. Six years earlier, Klindworth had been appointed Professor of Piano at the Moscow Conservatoire, becoming a colleague of Tchaikovsky, who was Professor of Harmony. He greatly liked Tchaikovsky's music and expressed his enthusiasm to Bülow, playing several of his pieces to him. Bülow was immediately won over. 'Tchaikovsky is a great talent', he declared and, three weeks later, performed the Variations, Op 19 No 6, at a concert. In November 1874, he gave the English première of the work in a recital at St James's Hall. 'The Variations by Tschaikowsky struck us as remarkably clever, original, and effective', said the *Monthly Musical Record*. During the same year, he published an article in Volume 148 of the *Allgemeine Zeitung*, comparing Tchaikovsky that he regarded him, along with Brahms, Saint-Saëns, Raff stein. He refers to the First Quartet, the piano pieces, the First and Second Symphonies, 'and an uncommonly interesting overture to *Romeo and Juliet*, which commends itself by its originality and luxuriant flow of melody.' Tchaikovsky was highly flattered by Bülow's efforts on his behalf and, after Nikolay Rubinstein had poured scorn on the First Piano Concerto in December 1874, he changed the dedication in favour of Bülow, who gave the first performance, in Boston, in October 1875. Bülow sent a telegram to Tchaikovsky, telling him of its success and later wrote to say that the First Quartet had also been well received in Boston. He went on to play the concerto in a number of major European cities. In addition, he informed Tchaikovsky that he regarded him, along with Brahms, Saint-Saëns, Raff and Rheinberger, as having 'the most marked individuality of our time'. Tchaikovsky was pleased to be compared to Brahms, Saint-Saëns and Raff, but was less happy regarding the mention of Rheinberger.

In the coming years, Bülow continued to play Tchaikovsky's works and to send him letters and press cuttings reporting any successes. In December 1878 he published, in the *Signale für die musikalische Welt*, a further article, extolling 'this young master, whose significance grows with every work' and describing him as 'a real tone-poet'. Here, he speaks of the Third Quartet, the Second Symphony and *Francesca da Rimini*, which 'have delighted my fairly blasé ear with their freshness, depth, originality and strength.' Tchaikovsky was proud of Bülow's high opinion of him and told Madame von Meck, in a letter of 6 February 1879, that Bülow 'is truly interested in Russian music and in me. He is the sole German musician who admits the possibility of the Russians rivalling the Germans as composers.'

Bülow continued to give Tchaikovsky his support throughout the 1880s. He visited the composer in January 1885, writing home to his wife, 'Tchaikovsky was much moved when I played his compositions for him and said "You interpret my thoughts wonderfully."' On 24 January, Bülow conducted, in St Petersburg, the first performance of the Third Suite, which electrified the audience. 'Never before', wrote Modest Tchaikovsky, 'had any of Tchaikovsky's works been received with such unanimous enthusiasm.' Bülow was not only a magnificent interpreter of the composer's pieces, but he was also one of the first clearly to detect his influence on other composers. That same year, he wrote to Klindworth, 'Do you know Fauré's piano music, full of meaning, very original, and it has the same relationship to Tchaikovsky as Saint-Saëns' has to Anton [Rubinstein]?' On another occasion, he observed that Rimsky-Korsakov 'is somewhat indebted to Tchaikovsky, as Tchaikovsky is to Glinka.' These were remarks that showed a perception in advance of the times.

Not even Bülow, however, could single-handedly build Tchaikovsky's European reputation for him; moreover, his range of sympathies was so wide, beginning with Liszt, Wagner, Berlioz and Brahms and later embracing Richard Strauss, Stanford and other modern composers, that it would be a mistake to suppose that he devoted more than a very small proportion of his time to his Russian friend. Tchaikovsky therefore realised that he would have to go out into the world and conduct his own works. The trouble was that he had received next to no training in conducting, and, worse, it terrified him. He made his first public appearance as a conductor on 2 March 1868 at a charity concert in Moscow in aid of the Famine Fund, directing a performance of the 'Dances of the Hay Maidens' from *The Voyevoda*. He was paralysed with fear. According to Kashkin, he protested, just before the concert, that he was not at all nervous, but,

> When Tchaikovsky actually appeared on the platform, I noticed that he was quite distracted; he came on timidly, as though he would have been glad to hide, or run away, and, on mounting to the conductor's desk, looked like a man who finds himself in some desperate situation. Apparently his composition was blotted out from his mind; he did not see the score in front of him and gave all the leads at the wrong moments, or to the wrong instruments. Fortunately, the orchestra knew the music so well that they paid no attention whatever to Tchaikovsky's beat, but, laughing to themselves, got through the dances very creditably in spite of him. Afterwards Piotr Ilyich told me that, in his terror, he had a feeling that his head would fall off his shoulders unless he held it tightly in position.

Laroche confirms that Tchaikovsky's attitude, then, towards conducting was one of almost mindless dread. 'He declared that having to stand at the raised desk in front of the orchestra produced such nervous terror that all the time he felt his head was coming off his shoulders; in order to prevent this catastrophe, he held his chin firmly with his left hand and conducted only with his right.' Nevertheless, says Laroche, Tchaikovsky was not as bad as he imagined; he assumed he had no aptitude for conducting, but, significantly, he was an excellent accompanist at the piano.

Another nine years passed before he again took up the baton, directing a performance of *Marche slave* in a special concert at the Bolshoi. 'I have lately found courage to appear as a conductor', he reported to his sister Alexandra on 6 March 1877. 'I was very unskilful and nervous, but still managed to conduct my "Russo-Serbian March" in the Opera House with a certain amount of success. From now on, I shall take every opportunity to conduct, for, if my plan of a concert tour abroad comes off, I shall have to be my own conductor.'

But his fear of conducting had not really abated, and his next attempt did not occur until a further ten years had elapsed. On this occasion, he directed, with considerable success, the première of his opera *Cherevichki*, which was staged in Moscow on 31 January 1887. Prior to rehearsals, he took lessons from Ippolit Altani, who had conducted the first performances of *Mazeppa* and *1812*. He seems now to have approached the task with greater confidence, largely brought about by the encouragement of his friends, to whom he pays tribute in *An Autobiographical Account of a Journey Abroad in 1888*.

. . . I, myself, clung obstinately and steadfastly to the belief that I was completely incapable . . . my timid efforts, on two earlier occasions, to conquer my morbid nervousness and appear before the public had ended most disastrously, to my complete embarrassment. If, however, my well-wishers, including Altani, desired, in spite of this, to help me overcome my shyness and were anxious that I should make one more effort, in my declining years [he was then forty-six], to become a conductor, they were doubtless guided by the sincerest affection and by a firm conviction that my lack of talent as a conductor was a great hindrance to the spread of my works; they believed that, if I once conquered myself and succeeded in conducting – if only tolerably – some of my works, this could result in greater popularity for my music and a marked increase in my reputation as a composer . . . I still think I have no positive gift for conducting. I am aware that I do not possess that combination of moral and physical qualities that make an ordinary musician a conductor of the first rank; but this attempt – and all subsequent ones – proved that I could direct, more or less successfully, the performance of my compositions – and this was all that was necessary for my future success . . . Only one thing . . . was of importance to me: to be able to conduct my own works no worse than any other mediocre conductor would have done.

Surprised, slightly disbelieving, but delighted over the success of the première of *Cherevichki*, Tchaikovsky found the courage to conduct an entire programme of his pieces in St Petersburg seven weeks later, on 17 March. His diary entry on the day of the first rehearsal states 'Nervousness, horror'. In his biography of his brother, Modest Tchaikovsky writes, 'Henceforth, to the very end of his life, it was not the concert itself so much as the first rehearsal that terrified him.' By the third rehearsal, Tchaikovsky was able to record in his diary, 'My conducting passable'. The concert, which included the Second Suite, an aria and dance from *The Sorceress*, two movements from the Serenade for Strings, *Francesca da Rimini* and *1812*, was a complete triumph.

His new-found determination to succeed as a conductor came at an appropriate moment, for, in June 1887, he received an invitation from the Hamburg Philharmonic Society to appear at one of their concerts in the following January. He at once accepted. Preparing himself further for this ordeal, he conducted the first performance, on 1 November 1887, of *The Sorceress* in St Petersburg (with Stravinsky's father, Fyodor, in the role of Mamirov). On 26 November, he conducted his first concert in Moscow, which included *Francesca da Rimini*. The programme was repeated on the next day, when the composer's confidence suddenly collapsed just before the concert. He became flustered, was on the verge of withdrawing, but at the last moment pulled himself together – and conducted better than ever before.

By now, he was in touch with the resourceful, though somewhat unreliable Berlin concert agent Hermann Wolff, who acted on Anton Rubinstein's behalf in Europe. Wolff used the Hamburg engagement as a point from which to negotiate appearances in other major European cities, and the longed-for European tour became a reality.

Tchaikovsky set out from St Petersburg on 27 December 1887, arriving in Berlin two days later. On 5 January 1888, he conducted in Leipzig; on 20 January, in Hamburg; on 8 February, in Berlin. Meanwhile, Wolff had been in contact with Francesco Berger, expressing the hope that a place could be found for Tchaikovsky on one of the season's Philharmonic Society programmes. Berger, who was already a great admirer of Tchaikovsky's music, answered enthusiastically, but told him that his plans for the season were almost finalised and that they would have to act quickly to find a suitable date and to determine what was to be performed. Through Wolff, Berger and Tchaikovsky therefore entered into correspondence. In a letter of 6 February from Berlin, the composer suggested that he conduct the Third Suite, 'if you haven't got anything against it.' On 12 February, he moved on to Prague, and, on the same day, Berger wrote to him there, agreeing to the suite, but admitting concern over finding a date. 'It is very sad that the agent Wolff lost so much time in acquainting us with your plans.' However, either 15 or 22 March still looked possible. On 16 February, he sent a telegram, saying that he was able to fit him onto the programme for 22 March.

By this time, Tchaikovsky was in the midst of what was perhaps the happiest ten days of his life, for the Czechs displayed a love and knowledge of his music that seemed to surpass anything he had experienced even in Russia. It took him completely by surprise. He had imagined, on his way to Prague, that he was simply about to fulfil another routine engagement, in which his nerve-racked efforts would be commended with polite applause, as in Germany, and he would then take his leave, doubtful whether anything had really been achieved. The first indication of what lay in store occurred when he was officially welcomed at the Bohemian border. A second deputation greeted him at a stop just outside the capital, and, on arriving in Prague itself, he was received with speeches on the railway platform, and children presented him with flowers. A representative of the Russian Club travelled from Vienna to pay his respects. A suite of rooms at the Hotel de Saxe was provided by the Artists' Club of Prague. There were more speeches when he reached the hotel, followed by a supper reception. He was fêted throughout his stay, serenaded by students and given many presents. His portrait, surrounded by laurel leaves, was displayed. On one occasion, he was shown around the Town Hall and into the Council Chamber. It happened to be in session, and the entire body of members rose to greet him. He conducted two concerts, both of which were wildly successful. On 19 February, he wrote in his diary, 'On the whole, I believe this is one of the most memorable days of my life. I have become very fond of these good Czechs. And, indeed, with reason!!! Heavens! How much enthusiasm! Though, of course, not for me, really, but for dear Russia.'

One of his greatest joys was meeting Dvořák, whom he saw on eight of his ten days in the city. At Dvořák's home he also met Anna Dvořák, 'a simple, charming woman and an excellent hostess'. Dvořák presented him with the manuscript orchestral score of his Seventh Symphony, signed 'In memory of Prague'.

While in Bohemia, Tchaikovsky's thoughts turned to the London concert, and he came to the conclusion that all four movements of the Third Suite might be more than the audience could take. Accordingly, he sent a letter to Berger on 20 February, writing in German, the language that Berger had used.

I am so glad that you've allowed me to appear at the concert on 22 March. I will arrive in London on the 20th and will be staying at the *Hotel Dieudonné*.

I wonder if it would be possible to do my Serenade for Strings, instead of the entire Third Suite, and then just the last movement from the Suite (which is a Theme and Variations). I believe that in many ways this would be advantageous. The Serenade for Strings consists of four movements, none of which is long. For both these pieces, I have the parts ready [he conducted them, the following day, in Prague], but I do not know anything about your string sections. I have 6 parts for first violin, 5 for second violin, but Dvořák tells me that you have 15 first violins. Is this so? If it is, then extra parts will be needed. (The Serenade is obtainable from Rahter in Hamburg, and the Suite, from Bote & Bock in Berlin.) Would you like me to get them, or will you do it? Please write to me in Paris, where I arrive on 24 February (14 Rue Richepanse). See you soon,

P. Tschaikovsky

I shall be very grateful if you will let me do the Serenade and the Variations from the Suite.

The composer left for Paris on 22 February. He remained there for almost a month, being lavishly entertained, though on nothing like the scale that he had experienced in Prague. Berger's reply arrived on 28 February.

> I entirely agree to everything you have suggested. It is to be the Serenade for Strings and the finale from the Third Suite. Of course, you are thinking of performing them in separate halves of the concert.
> We have 14 first violins, 14 second violins, 10 violas, 9 cellos, 9 double-basses.
> Over here, two musicians play behind one desk. Please be kind enough to order the missing orchestral parts and bring them with you. Would you also be so kind as to send me both full scores for Mr. Bennett (who prepares the programme notes), so that he can look at them? Do you need any unusual instruments, such as, for instance, harp or tuba or English horn or anything else?

Tchaikovsky answered by return, indicating which extra instruments would be needed for the Theme and Variations, assuring him that the suite had proved popular elsewhere and thanking him again for allowing him to alter the programme. Their correspondence concluded with a brief exchange of letters relating to the fact that Berger had already booked a room at the Dieudonné and that Tchaikovsky would be coming a day earlier than he had previously suggested.

The composer left Paris on the morning of 19 March. The weather was appalling. After Amiens, it became worse. 'A snowstorm forced our train to a standstill for a long time in open country', he wrote to Madame von Meck. It reached Calais two hours late, by which time all the passengers were frozen. The Channel turned out to be so rough 'that every moment we expected some catastrophe.' 'The crossing was terrible,' he told Modest. 'Everybody was sick except me. Now I'm finally convinced that I don't suffer from seasickness. I reached London at midnight, instead of at seven. Everywhere there is masses of snow, just as we have in January.' After taking a cab from Charing Cross, he had dinner at the Dieudonné. 'It was very pleasant; chatted gladly with the servants', he noted in his diary.

The hotel, which, we may recall, was always used by Tchaikovsky's teacher Rubinstein, was staffed entirely by French. In his *Dinners and Diners*, published in the 1890s, Lieutenant-Colonel Nathaniel Newnham-Davis, who worked for the *Sporting Times* under the pseudonym 'The Dwarf of Blood', wrote, 'Before Dieudonné's became the handsome hotel and restaurant it is now, it was a boarding-house which stood in high favour with such of the French artists and sculptors and singers and actors who crossed the silver streak to perfidious Albion. The *table-d'hôte* dinner, at which Mdme. Dieudonné took the head of the long table, was a celebrated institution. No one could come without being vouched for by some of the habitués, and most of the people who might be found at the board were of European celebrity.' Situated in Ryder Street, off St James's Street, the Dieudonné was near several art galleries and within easy reach of Bond Street, Regent Street and Christie's. It was also no more than a four-or five-minute walk away from St James's Hall, in Piccadilly. J. B. Booth recalls the hotel in *Palmy Days*.

Dieudonné's, in Ryder Street, now the home of the Eccentric Club, started its career as a boarding-house, under the direction of Madame Dieudonné. Her establishment was patronised chiefly by the artists and actors who came over from France, and, as she possessed an excellent *chef*, non-residents who appreciated good cooking began to ask permission to join the *table d'hôte*, which was served at a long table at the head of which sat Madame. Permission was never given as a matter of course. The would-be guest had first to be presented and approved by the proprietress, and if approved, would in due course receive an invitation which made him free of the house. Later, if the guest was approved on further acquaintance, he was invited to join Madame in her sitting-room after dinner for coffee and talk, in a circle which included musicians, actors and painters from her land who were staying in her boarding-house. It was part of the ritual that such a guest, on his first visit to the holy of holies, should place his signature on the wall. If he were a musician or a painter he was asked to embellish it with some bars of music or a drawing. And so, in time, a section of the wall became a little museum of autographs and personal souvenirs.

In course of time Madame Dieudonné died, the boarding-house blossomed into an hotel with a restaurant attached, and under Monsieur Guffanti, an *hotelier* of character [eventually going to prison], whom I remember chiefly for the majestic sweeping curves of his moustache ends, took in several of the adjoining houses, and it became the large building of white stone and red brick, with windows gay with flower-boxes, so familiar to the London of the day.

But in the course of reconstruction Madame's little sitting-room was thrown into the entrance hall, and, in spite of Guffanti's efforts to preserve it, the portion of wall with the precious signatures was destroyed. And now Dieudonné's itself, as an hotel and restaurant, is only a memory.

In Jacques-Emile Blanche's *Portraits of a Lifetime*, there is further information about Madame Dieudonné.

It was more than an hotel for travellers that Madame Dieudonné (the buxom matron and widow of a wine-grower in the Gironde district) kept, together with her sister, Madame Beuzelin. A boarding-house such as Balzac pictured in the Latin quarter would better describe it, but it was definitely provincial, one might even say regional: Madame Dieudonné was Bordeaux transplanted . . . She was dark and had piercing brown eyes; she was talkative and did not mind either the familiarity or ribaldry of her customers. Marie Beuzelin and Juliette Dieudonné knew the hidden aspects of life in England. They lent penniless compatriots and artists a helping hand on countless occasions and in manifold ways, and well deserved their gratitude. But never did these French natures become assimilated with the English, any more than oil mixes with water . . .

In spite of having three floors, the house had not many rooms, only one bathroom, French menservants with long white aprons, who had to be rung for at least ten times, who shouted in the passages, who complained of being overworked and whose sweeping was perfunctory. There was no lift; it was an untidy inn, but it was propped up by its cookery, its carefully prepared dishes, its stews with nourishing sauces – a spread for the gastronome.

Among those who habitually stayed at the Dieudonné were Whistler, George Moore, Rops, Rodin, Legros, Sargent, Sickert, Saint-Saëns, Massenet, Sarasate and many other celebrities. It was usually full. 'The dining-room was packed with small tables surrounding a large one, at the head of which sat Juliette and Madame Beuzelin', writes Blanche; 'I still wonder how we all squeezed in.' Around this time, the Dieudonné had sixteen bedrooms. Luncheon cost 3s 6d; theatre dinner, 6s; special dinner, 8s; theatre supper, 5s. The luncheon, says an advertisement in *Dinners and Diners*, 'is pronounced to be the best in London.' The Dieudonné was essentially a family hotel, where, The Dwarf of Blood maintains, 'ladies can dine by themselves, without fear of any inconvenience.' Nevertheless, Edward VII, when Prince of Wales, frequented the hotel, which according to Charles Graves, in *Leather Armchairs*, was 'a very fashionable *maison de rendezvous*'.

The Dieudonné's single bathroom was apparently difficult to locate. 'Futile search for toilet', Tchaikovsky records in his diary on his first night; presumably one of the overworked menservants had to reveal its whereabouts.

On the following day, Tuesday, 20 March, he spent the morning trying to read the '*Dayly-Télégraphe*' (says his diary) and catching up on his correspondence. In a letter to Rimsky-Korsakov, he confesses that his concert tour has been gruelling; he has reached 'such a state of exhaustion and mental and physical anguish that, were it not for the money I am to get here [£20], and of which I am in great need, I would not have come to London.'

He lunched at the hotel and then went for a walk. 'A French Jew pestered me, but I got rid of him in the Strand', his diary records. He then took a cab and called on Berger in York Street, leading off Baker Street. On returning to the Dieudonné, he prepared the orchestral parts of the Serenade for Strings and the finale of the Third Suite, ready for the first rehearsal on Wednesday morning. He dined at the hotel and afterwards strolled over to Leicester Square and attended a performance of the ballet *Enchantment* at the Alhambra Theatre. In Moorish style with an odd sort of square-shaped, pseudo-Saracenic dome, the Alhambra began life as a museum, the Royal Pantopticon of Science and Art, which opened in 1854. Apart from many interesting exhibits, it was distinguished by a central fountain, whose single jet of coloured water rose 100 feet into the air, and by a monster organ. When the museum ran into difficulties, the premises were taken over by Howes and Cushing's American Circus, and the organ was sold to St Paul's Cathedral. In 1860, the circus was replaced with a ballet and music-hall programme. Leotard made his English début at the Alhambra in May 1861, three months before Tchaikovsky saw him at Cremorne; Blondin also appeared there, fresh from crossing the Niagara Falls on a tightrope. During the 1860s, the theatre established itself as the country's leading home of ballet, though not artistically very good ballet. It also won renown as a place where men could meet a higher class of prostitute: women were admitted unescorted to the upper promenade, and this became one of the Alhambra's main attractions.

In *The Alhambra Ballet*, Ivor Guest says of this period, 'Over the years the theatre acquired the reputation of being one of the finest music halls in Europe, both for the excellence of its programs and for the comfort it offered its patrons, and in no time, even Parisians were speaking with envy of "l'Alhambr-r-ra de Londres".' The artistic standards of the establishment began to improve after the appointment in 1872 of Georges Jacobi as musical director. This distinguished artist, like so many Frenchmen, fled to England during the Siege of Paris, settling with his wife, the dancer Marie Pilatte, in London and taking a house in Camden Road; in time, he became a professor of the Royal College of Music and president of the Association of Conductors in England. He was also an accomplished composer, and the first of his ballets given at the Alhambra was introduced in August 1873. His *Enchantment* received its première on 24 December 1887, with choreography by Eugenio Casati and Jacobi conducting. The principal dancer was the 'opulent' (to use George Bernard Shaw's adjective) Emma Bessone, who had been prima ballerina in St Petersburg five months earlier, creating the leading role in Petipa and Ivanov's *The Tulip of Haarlem*. Tchaikovsky was not much taken with *Enchantment*. He returned to the hotel and worked again on the orchestral parts before going to bed. There is nothing to indicate that he was aware of a concert that day in Princes' Hall at which Benno Schönberger (a pupil of Bruckner and Liszt) played 'Chant sans paroles' and the Variations, Op 19 No 6.

After a good night's sleep, he awoke to find himself 'very little agitated' about the forthcoming rehearsal. A little before 10.30 am, Berger called for him, and together they walked to St James's Hall, which stood on the site now occupied by the Piccadilly Hotel. He was introduced to Cowen and the orchestra. Of the two-hour rehearsal, he noted, 'They read excellently at sight. The acoustics were worse than at the Châtelet, something was lacking.' The Châtelet was the concert hall in which he had conducted both his Paris concerts a few weeks earlier. Despite the conspicuous applause of Gounod, French critics were not impressed by Tchaikovsky's music. They found it too German. (The Germans had found it too French.) William Apthorp attended the first of these concerts, on 4 March, and, in his book *By the Way*, left a valuable description both of Tchaikovsky and of his conducting of the Theme and Variations from the Third Suite.

Tchaikovsky's appearance at the head of an orchestra was striking. Tall and slim of figure, with short, thick iron-grey hair, moustache, and imperial, there was something military in his bearing, in the grave, dignified response he bowed to his reception by the audience. You felt instinctively that here was a man who knew what he was about, and was not to be trifled with . . . His beat in conducting was unostentatious, he used his left arm but little. But his down-beat was admirably clear and precise, and, whenever he gave the signal for the thunder to break loose, the whole orchestra seemed to shiver. It soon became evident that the man was positively an electric battery, launching lightning-flashes right and left from that terrible baton of his, egging his men on to the utmost fury of fiery intensity.

I shall never forget the terrific onslaught of the first violins upon one variation in rapid sixteenth notes. It was like Anton Rubinstein, at his devilmost, playing the pianoforte! Yet throughout the concert the orchestra played with as fine a finish as I ever heard them do under Colonne, their regular conductor. It took no Russophilism to help him work the audience up to the frenetic pitch of delight . . . Tchaikovsky and his Châtelet audience were like two logs in the fire, mutually keeping each other hot!

The rehearsal at St James's Hall having finished, Tchaikovsky returned to the Dieudonné for lunch and afterwards went for a long walk, followed by a nap. He then 'sat downcast, conscious of inability to do anything, even to write letters.' He had dinner at the Bergers', and it was possibly sometime during the evening that he wrote out and autographed for Berger the opening bars of the principal theme from the first movement of the Serenade for Strings, adding the date *21 Mars 1888*. According to his diary, there were four other guests: Annie Berger's sister, 'a Jewish lady', and the Czech violinist František Ondříček and his wife. Ondříček was to play Mendelssohn's Violin Concerto and Ernst's *Hungarian Airs* at the concert the following day. Already internationally famous, he had given the first performance of Dvořák's Violin Concerto in Prague in October 1883, when he was twenty-four, also introducing the work in Vienna and London. His brother Karel, who was soloist in the première of Dvořák's *Romantic Pieces*, Op 75, in March 1887, held the position of first violinist at the National Theatre in Prague, and Tchaikovsky had met him during his trip to Bohemia a month earlier. Ondříček, like Tchaikovsky, was a great admirer of Dickens. When Berger took him round Westminster Abbey, 'his first remark on entering the sacred building was: "Wo liegt Tikkenz?" On being shown the spot, he knelt down and reverently kissed the stone, remarking as he rose: "Das war ein Mann." '

'Homesickness', records Tchaikovsky's diary, was his uppermost feeling while at the Bergers'. He left at eleven and went to the Empire Theatre in Leicester Square. Opened in 1884, the Empire was intended as a rival to the Alhambra. It stood where previously there had come and gone The Astronomical Panorama, Miller's Mechanical and Beautiful Representations, and other entertainments. A contemporary account, appearing in Mander and Mitchenson's *The Lost Theatres of London*, states that, for a time, 'The establishment became so divided by different interests that few could tell whether it was a theatre, wine vaults, a billiard-room, a coffee-shop, a gunsmith's, or a Royal Academy . . . it is only by taking refuge in the lowest apartment, which partakes of a coffee-room, a cabin, and a cellar, that you

will find repose.' During one period, it became successively, but never
successfully, Grand American Hall, El Dorado Music Hall and Café
Chantant, Royal Living Marionette Theatre, Salle Valentino, Saville
House Gymnasium, Walhalla and the Alcazar.

As the Empire, it at once specialised in ballet. The *ambiance* was
altogether more appealing than that of the Alhambra, which the
Empire quite quickly overtook in popularity. W. Macqueen-Pope
affectionately recalls the Empire in *The Melody Lingers On.*

There was never any hustle or bustle, everyone moved as if eternity
stretched around; always there was that air of rich calm which accompanies good living and good dinners. The liveried attendants were as
efficient and soft-voiced as the servants in one of the best clubs; indeed, the
Empire was a Club. You paid the subscription fee every time you went
there and there was no subscription, but nevertheless, it was a club, and it
proclaimed itself one on its programmes, The Cosmopolitan Club of the
World. And that is exactly what it was. All nations and races went there.
It was the first spot to which a Briton home from abroad, from some
outpost of the Empire when there was an Empire all over the world as well
as in Leicester Square, made for on his first evening in London. It was an
almost odds on chance that he would meet a friend. They had dreamed of
the Empire when overseas and they hurried to it. It never failed them . . .

All classes, all grades of Society, the wealthy, the well-to-do, those of
moderate means, those who had saved up to pay a visit, all met at the
Empire. It was the centre of London's night life when London was the
centre of the world. Foreigners visiting this country made a beeline for it,
they all knew about the Cosmopolitan Club. A great traveller who had
reached the city of Vladivostok, very far off indeed in the 1890's, handed
his papers to the Cossack officer in charge for investigation. The officer
looked at him 'You come from London?' he queried and his eyes sparkled
at the answer, 'London, ah, yes,' he sighed, 'London — The Empire.' It
was as famous as that.

It had atmosphere, an atmosphere of its own. You walked around, there
was plenty of room at the back of that Circle and a big bar behind as well.
You sat at a table or on a lounge (some called the Promenade the Lounge)
and you were brought your drink by a footman either in black or blue and
gold livery. The air was of a celestial blue with the smoke of the best
cigars, and the scent of the cigars mingled with the aroma of champagne
and the best whisky and old brandy. The golden light from the stage beat
upwards in subdued glow and from the depths came the sound of the fine
orchestra . . .

To the ultra-respectable and to the Puritan . . . the Empire Promenade
was anathema, a cesspool of Vice. Few of them had been there to see, but
those who had, the scouts sent to make reports, certainly saw an eyeful of
the Ladies. There was no secrecy about it, there was indeed nothing to

hide. The Ladies were there for all to see and a great portion of the world went there to see. They made no secret of their profession and did not pretend to be respectable (it was their living not to be) yet they comported themselves, when in the Empire, with great dignity and decorum.

. . . Other theatres of variety, other music halls had their Promenades but not even the Alhambra could match that of the Empire, it was always a peg or two below. For the women of the Empire were the aristocrats of their 'profession'. And they looked it. Amazing creatures, amazingly dressed, of all races and speech, blondes, brunettes, redheads, they moved quietly and slowly to and fro, with a rather feline grace. A tiger pacing its cage has such a gift of movement. They were quite unmistakable, yet their manners were excellent. They never accosted a man, at the most he might feel the soft touch of a hand against his or the faint pressure of a silk-clad body if he stood by the rail watching the show.

There was never any loud chatter, shrieking laughter or bad language. These women might have had no character outside but they had one to lose in the Empire. One complaint to the management and they were barred. And that was, for them, tragedy, irrevocable loss of prestige and descent to the depths. There were all types for all tastes, from the regally majestic, to the quiet and demure; from the bold, flashing, merry eye to the modestly downcast eyelid. But there was allure everywhere. Some of those women met sad ends but, believe it or not, some of them married men they had met at the Empire in the way of business and settled down into truly excellent wives and mothers, the author knows of several such cases. And as they moved to and fro, with silken swish and gleam of jewels, the scent of frangipanni and patchouli would be apparent as a kind of aura, it lingers in many nostrils still. The Promenade was unique – and the Ladies of the Empire were unique too.

The principal ballet being performed on the evening of Tchaikovsky's visit was *The Sports of England*, with music by Hervé and choreography by Katti Lanner. It had opened on 22 December 1887 and was the theatre's first big success. Ivor Guest writes, in *The Empire Ballet*, that 'it depicted cricket at Lord's (with female representatives of the MCC and Australian elevens), yachting on the Solent (a *pas du "mal de mer"*), football at Kennington Oval, polo at Hurlingham, hunting at Melton Mowbray, boating at Hammersmith, boxing, and Derby Day at Epsom'. Tchaikovsky's diary discloses, 'Various goings-on. Boredom.'

The following day was the occasion of the composer's first concert in England. 'Slept restlessly; my tooth hurt a lot. Felt dreadful in the morning. Conquered myself and went to the rehearsal. Ondříček. There were a few people. It went well.'

Some credit for the success of this second rehearsal must go to

Cowen, who, apart from accompanying Ondříček in Mendelssohn's Violin Concerto and Ernst's *Hungarian Airs*, conducted a Haydn symphony and Svendsen's *Second Norwegian Rhapsody*. In *My Art and My Friends*, he recalls Tchaikovsky's Philharmonic début.

His name was then little known here except among musicians, although he had already given to the world many of his finest compositions. The works he selected for the occasion – his Serenade for Strings and the Variations from his Third Suite – were scarcely what would now be considered representative of his genius at its best, and though the reception they met with was favourable enough, there were few if any signs of the phenomenal success his music was destined later to obtain, not only here, but all over the world. His visits to London (he returned the following year) were so brief that I had little opportunity of being in his company except at the rehearsals and concerts. This I much regretted, for he seemed a man of a pleasant and friendly disposition and enthusiastic temperament, to whom one would be attracted more and more as one got to know him better. He did not speak English, and I had to stand at his side all the time and translate his wishes to the members of the orchestra. This I had to do with nearly all the foreign composers who came over. In fact, I was as much interpreter-in-chief to the society as I was its conductor.

Tchaikovsky lunched at the Dieudonné with the Ondříčeks and 'a Jewish journalist posing as a Czech'. Afterwards, he took a stroll, met Ondříček again briefly, had a nap, dressed for the concert and went over to St James's Hall. He and his works were warmly received, as we have already seen. 'Conducted well. The Serenade a big success; the Suite less so.' Berger was so pleased that he persuaded the directors of the Philharmonic to increase the composer's fee from £20 to £25. Grove offered him an immediate engagement at the Crystal Palace, but he declined; he had paced himself to complete the tour, which concluded with the Philharmonic concert, and he was now totally drained, lacking reserves with which to endure any further ordeal. In a letter to his publisher Jurgenson, he wrote, 'I have expended a great deal of money, and even more health and strength. In return, I have won some celebrity, but every hour I ask myself: Why? Is it worth it? And I come to the conclusion that it is far better to live a quiet life, without fame.' In a second letter, he added, 'My tour was certainly not a financial success; but I did not undertake it for the purpose of making money.'

After the concert, he had supper at the hotel with the Ondříčeks. Also present were 'Mme. Dieudonné and her sister. The latter sat and chatted with us. Johnson, the correspondent of *Le Figaro*, and his wife.' Johnson, known as either Thomas Johnson or Tony Johnson, was, despite his name, French and supposedly a baron. Edouard Garceau writes of him in *The Little Doustes*, the biography of Louise and Jeanne Douste.

Mr. Tony Johnson, the London correspondent of the *Figaro* at the time when the Little Doustes made their first steps in their musical career, was a demi-god; a sort of small sun towards whose orbit gravitated all the big stars of Art, Literature and Politics when once they had crossed the Channel.

It would have been impossible at this period to find in England another 'Salon' containing at one and the same moment so many celebrities as were to be found in the small house in the Fulham Road occupied by the Johnsons . . .

. . . Mme. Johnson was simplicity and agreeableness itself; nor had the degree of fame enjoyed individually by her guests any effect upon her smile. She received with the same charming grace, the same apparent satisfaction, a diamond brooch offered by a star of the first magnitude who had definitely 'arrived', or the little bunch of violets from the less fortunate. Among the crowd of notables who were crushed into her little dining-room there was not one who did not exert himself or herself to please her and pay her court amidst friendly rivals.

Every evening during the Opera season saw the critic and his wife take the horse-drawn omnibus to Covent Garden: while the following morning the neighbours, if they rose early enough, saw Mrs. Johnson go down her long garden to tend her fowls.

In spite of having lived for thirty years in England she never learnt English. Among the few, more ordinary words that she had mastered at last, the three that came most easily to her lips were 'No', 'Yes', and 'Dirty'. With such a vocabulary it was difficult for her to get on with her maids, who coming in on Monday or Tuesday, inevitably left abruptly the following Saturday night. Thus when Sunday, her 'At Home' day, arrived, the hosts impressed the guests into their service, and the first arrivals waited on the late-comers.

On one of these famous Sundays in June when the crush was greater than usual, the weather being magnificent, the pleasant lawn in the garden was used as a reception room. But the kitchen was empty of maids, and to crown the misfortunes there were not enough cups to go round. The hostess was already fully engaged in receiving her guests and could not attend to anything more. The more energetic therefore of her visitors undertook new rôles. Jean de Reské opened the door and announced the arrivals; Edouard de Reské and Louise Douste washed cups in the kitchen and made the tea, which was served by M. de Rochefort. Jeanne collected the dirty cups and Coquelin *aîné* carried them down to the kitchen and brought the clean ones to de Rochefort.

Among the other famous artists who regularly visited the Johnsons were Sarah Bernhardt, Sarasate, Patti, Calvé, Maurel, Nilsson, Paderewski, Wieniawski and Pachman.

Johnson enjoyed a brief period of prominence in February 1887, when, after attending the latest Gilbert and Sullivan operetta, *Ruddygore* (later *Ruddigore*), he took exception, in his column in *Le Figaro*, to some of the lyrics in Richard Dauntless's 'miserable Parley-voo' song. S. J. Adair Fitz-Gerald, in *The Story of the Savoy Opera*, recalls, 'The French correspondent of the Paris *Figaro*, who bore the very un-Gallic name of Johnson, and, although he lived in our midst for many years, never mastered the subtleties of the English language, and who was entirely deficient in humour, saw a studied insult to his beloved compatriots and said so. It did not quite become a national affair, however, but it caused a lot of friction for the moment, and it was stated in several quarters that Gilbert himself had been challenged to mortal combat!' The matter was serious enough for Gilbert and Sullivan to write a letter of apology to *Le Figaro*, pointing out that the offending lines had 'précisément autant de sens que "rosbif" et "goddam" employés pour ridiculer les anglais dans une comédie-burlesque française.'

After the evening of his meeting with the Johnsons, Tchaikovsky slept 'with difficulty, restlessly' and awoke feeling ill. At midday, he went to the bank and collected his £25 Philharmonic fee. He lunched at Gatti's, 52 The Strand. This restaurant, one of the most successful in London, specialised in a particularly delicious macaroni, which was among the composer's favourite dishes.

Carlo Gatti, who was born in Switzerland, came to London as a young man, having already tried his luck in Paris. After a brief period in the artificial flower trade, he sold waffles and roast chestnuts in Battersea Park. He did so well that he was soon able to open a shop in Villiers Street, where he cooked and sold waffles all through the day and evening. Before long, he acquired further premises and expanded into other areas of catering. He eventually handed over the business to his nephews Agostino and Stefano, who, in turn, vastly increased the range of operations, buying the Adelphi and Vaudeville Theatres, staging pantomimes at the Royal Opera House, and putting on prom-enade concerts in Covent Garden. For the concerts, they hired Rivière as their first conductor and, after him, Sullivan and Cowen. Rivière was successful enough, but Sullivan raised the levels both of the performances and the programmes, playing Beethoven's Ninth

Symphony to a packed house. The concerts continued to prosper under Cowen's leadership. Following Manns' example at the Crystal Palace, he introduced excerpts from Wagner in the early eighties, a decade ahead of the Wagner boom in London. By then, the Gatti family had become extremely wealthy.

It may have been Cowen who recommended Gatti's, the premier restaurant in the Gatti empire, to Tchaikovsky. This establishment was always personally supervised by a leading member of the Gatti family, and at the time of the composer's visit, Agostino held court there, interviewing playwrights, actors and musicians who could be used in the entertainments side of the business. In *Dinners and Diners*, The Dwarf of Blood recalled when both Agostino and Stefano presided over the restaurant, sitting at an oval table, 'to which each waiter brought every dish that was to be served, and there was a mysterious interchange of what looked like metal tokens. All the theatrical demigods of my subalternhood used to be at the tables too. There I first (off the stage) saw Nelly Power, whose photograph had adorned my room at Harrow . . .'

'Gatti's', Tchaikovsky put in his diary. 'Ate unwisely and felt sick. Decided not to travel to-day' – an indication, apparently, that he had previously intended leaving London that Friday. A surfeit of macaroni may possibly have occasioned the change of schedule. He returned to the Dieudonné, received a visit from Ondříček, and then, feeling feverish, took to his bed. He fell asleep and, on waking, found himself to be much improved. 'Throughout his life', says Laroche, 'he did not like to turn to doctors for help, preferring to cure himself, taking medicines unwillingly and as rarely as possible. Above all, he relied on good hygiene.' After having dinner at the hotel, he went to see Benoît Coquelin and his company in *Tartuffe* at the Royalty Theatre in Dean Street, the site of which is now occupied by Royalty House. French companies had been performing during the winter season at the Royalty since 1884, attracting larger audiences than the theatre could command at any other time of the year. 'Au Royalty', wrote Johnson in *Le Figaro* on 28 March 1888 (five days after Tchaikovsky saw *Tartuffe*), 'tout le monde pleurait et riait à la fois.' Perhaps it was Johnson who advised the composer to go to Coquelin's interpretation of Molière's odious imposter. Tchaikovsky seems to have enjoyed himself. 'A marvellous troupe', says his diary. The final entries for 23 March are 'Pestering . . . Read *Le Figaro* and *Le Gaulois*.'

The pestering may perhaps refer to a surprise visit by the nineteen-year-old Granville Bantock, which is recounted in Myrrha Bantock's biography of her father.

> . . . Granville attended one of the Philharmonic Society concerts conducted by Tchaikovsky, who had been invited to come to England for this purpose. My father was so enthralled by those of Tchaikovsky's works included in the programme that he made up his mind to meet the great composer. He searched the hotels of London until he found him.
>
> 'What can I do for you?' asked Tchaikovsky in French, when the young man had presented himself. Granville, pale with excitement and enthusiasm, spoke of his determination to become a composer himself.
>
> 'Then you must be prepared to work hard,' said the great man.

Myrrha Bantock is not able to give an exact date to this meeting, other than to say that it took place before September 1889, when her father became a student at the Royal Academy. It could, of course, have followed Tchaikovsky's concert in April 1889, but, on that occasion, the composer left London at 8.20 on the morning after the concert, which would have given Bantock little time in which to locate him. With his thirst for modern music, Bantock, we may assume, would not have missed the 1888 concert; probably he went to both, but his desire to meet Tchaikovsky seems more likely to have stemmed from the first. He may well have traced him to the Dieudonné by the evening of 23 March and waited there until the composer returned from *Tartuffe*.

On the morning of Saturday, 24 March, Ondříček called again 'and invited me to the Crystall-Pallast.' This invitation was declined: 'Hesitating. Wrote letters' – in one of which he told Modest, 'London is a very sad and depressing town.' He did, however, have lunch at the Dieudonné with the Ondříčeks and afterwards 'escorted them to the railway station', where they presumably caught the train to Sydenham.

> From there, went back on foot through unfamiliar streets. The weather cleared up. Bought various things. Hotel. Packing and weariness. Dinner by myself at 6 downstairs. The Ondříčeks dropped in. Said good-bye to them, to the sister of the proprietress, to the staff and then started out for the railway station. Commotion and my fears. All the way to Dover, it was rather crowded. On board ship, it was even more crowded. Excellent crossing. Made two acquaintances:

1. an English aristocrat from Nice and
2. a Russian cattle merchant, very talkative, who managed to tell me everything about himself. Calais.

Thus Tchaikovsky's diary records the conclusion of his second trip to England. During the five days of his stay in the capital, the dinner at the Bergers' represents his solitary entry into society. The Ondříčeks seem to be the only other people to have offered him companionship. Three days after leaving England he told Dvořák, in a letter written from Vienna, 'The orchestra in London is very good, especially at sight-reading. Berger and I have talked about you a lot, and we're impatiently awaiting your symphony [No 5, conducted by Manns on 7 April 1888]. Ondříček played beautifully at the concert.'

In September 1888, Berger wrote to Tchaikovsky, inviting him to make a second Philharmonic appearance, during the 1889 season. He also asked whether he would accept a commission to compose a symphony for the society. We may recall that Beethoven's Ninth Symphony, Dvořák's Seventh and Saint-Saëns' Third were all Philharmonic commissions. Replying on 1 October, Tchaikovsky assured Berger that he was 'really delighted and flattered in the highest degree' by the idea of the commission. However, 'I have just finished a symphony (my fifth) and would be very happy to introduce it in London, but it had been my intention to dedicate it to a greatly esteemed German musician, who is a friend of mine.'

The German musician was Theodor Ave-Lallemant, whom the composer had met in Hamburg the previous January. Ave-Lallemant, in his eighties, and his wife had entertained Tchaikovsky in their home one evening. The old man told him he did not think much of his compositions, but that it was not Tchaikovsky's fault, for he came from a backward country. He urged him to settle in Germany, where, under the beneficial influence of German culture, his work would improve. All this was said with such obvious friendliness and concern that Tchaikovsky was deeply touched, and he decided to dedicate his next symphony to his host. German culture unfortunately did little for Ave-Lallemant's own musicianship. 'He has a frightful habit of always philosophizing about music and musicians', Brahms once told Clara Schumann; he added in a letter of

8 December 1855, 'Wagner is his God – and evidently a benign one, for he blasphemes him with impunity through the most atrocious transcriptions.

Once having made up his mind to dedicate the Fifth Symphony to Ave-Lallemant, Tchaikovsky felt he could not now offer the work instead to the Philharmonic Society. He therefore gave Berger 'an indefinite promise to write another symphony for the Society in the near or distant future.' He had to admit, though, that his present schedule of commitments made the prospect appear more distant than near. On the other hand, he would be delighted to appear at a Philharmonic concert during the coming season.

Lightly setting aside for the moment the matter of the commission, Berger fixed Tchaikovsky's engagement for 11 April. It was next agreed that the concert would feature the British première of the Fifth Symphony. Then, on 1 March, with only six weeks to go, Tchaikovsky asked whether he could conduct something other than the symphony, which, in the meantime, on 17 November, had received its first performance, under his direction in St Petersburg.

> I am not quite happy with the orchestration of the symphony, and I would like to change it this summer. Moreover, since I am not very well known in London, I am a little anxious about appearing with a symphony that is very complicated and difficult. It would be better if you were to let me do my First Suite. This piece is much easier and has the advantage of generally pleasing the public. Unless I am mistaken, it has not yet been played in London and is thus, in addition, a novelty.

In a quick exchange of letters, it was arranged that Tchaikovsky would conduct the First Suite and accompany Vasily Sapellnikov in the First Piano Concerto. Nevertheless, wondered Berger, perhaps the composer would like to include the Fifth Symphony *as well*. No, said Tchaikovsky; the first two items would be quite enough for the Philharmonic audience. Yet,

> If it's your steadfast wish, I could also do the Fifth Symphony, but, as it's very complicated and I am not too happy with the orchestration, I'm afraid it would not get any applause; on the other hand, the First Suite, which would also be completely new to London, should certainly give people something to enjoy, more or less. My dear Mr. Berger, please don't be angry with me. Let me first of all gain a firm footing in London, and thereafter I can play everything you want. Sapellnikoff would very much like to do the First Piano Concerto, because this piece can make a big

impression, though I prefer the Second myself. If we both have a success, then let us come again next year, and we can play my Fifth or Fourth Symphony and Second Piano Concerto.

This correspondence concluded with settling on how many extra instruments would be needed for the First Suite, the scherzo of which the composer decided to omit.

After the agonies of the 1888 concert tour, the first he had ever undertaken, it is perhaps surprising to find Tchaikovsky embarking on a second a year later. But he was still motivated by a desire to increase the popularity of his works; he had also made many friends on his first tour and grown in stature as a conductor. There was more to look forward to, and less to fear. The second tour largely duplicated the first, with concerts in Cologne, Frankfurt, Dresden, Berlin, Leipzig, Geneva, Hamburg and Paris, finishing again in London., As before, he spent three weeks in Paris, his favourite European city. There, he met Massenet, Fauré, Widor, Delibes, D'Indy, Pierné, Augusta Holmes, Diémer, Paderewski, Pauline Viardot and other notable musicians, with many of whom he was already acquainted. He felt closer to the French composers of his generation than to those of any other nation save his own. Fauré he found fascinating. That composer, in turn, deeply admired his Russian colleague and presented him with signed copies of his First and Second Piano Quartets, the latter being inscribed 'To my dear master and friend P. Tchaikowsky from his affectionately devoted Gabriel Fauré'. Tchaikovsky was pleased to renew his friendship with Pauline Viardot, who, three years earlier, had shown him her autograph manuscript of *Don Giovanni*. 'It was as if I'd shaken hands with Mozart himself and chatted with him', he told Madame von Meck. She also reminisced about Turgenev, whom she had moved to tears with her singing of 'None but the Lonely Heart'. Tchaikovsky was also delighted to see again his cousin, Sanya von Vizin; on 9 April 1889, the day of his departure for England, he notes that she came to see him off: 'How lovely she is,' he comments in his diary.

This time, he embarked from Boulogne, sailing on 'the marvellous steamer "Folkestone".' Sapellnikov, who accompanied him, was violently seasick. Tchaikovsky was unaffected by the rocking, 'which wasn't actually all that marked.' They were both staying at the Dieudonné. 'Pleasant reception.' After dinner, the composer visited Berger. '"*Grieg ist unartig*,"' states the diary, reporting a comment of

Berger's. This can be translated as 'Grieg is rude', which recalls Berger's *Reminiscences*: 'I found his conceit amounted almost to snobbishness, his want of courtesy almost to rudeness.' In private, Berger seems to have dispensed with the 'almosts'. Tchaikovsky may have agreed with Berger's opinion. In his diary entry for 1 February 1888, he writes of 'Grieg's rude card' and admits in Paris, on 7 April 1889, 'Was avoiding Grieg'. Yet, despite Grieg's often excessive brusqueness, Tchaikovsky greatly liked the man and his music. Indeed, he dedicated his symphonic poem *Hamlet* to him. Interestingly enough, in his letter of thanks, dated 26 May 1888, Grieg asks, 'Is there really something in the rumour that you will perhaps visit Birmingham in August?' Richter had taken over the conductorship of the Birmingham Festival in 1885, and perhaps he recommended Tchaikovsky to the Festival Committee. If he did, they apparently took the matter no further.

'Drunkenness in private' concludes the composer's diary entries for 9 April. On the following morning, the first rehearsal for the next day's concert was held at St James's Hall. When it finished at just after midday and Tchaikovsky and Sapellnikov stepped out into Piccadilly, they were amazed to find themselves in total darkness. 'Before anything else', the composer wrote to his nephew Bob, 'let me tell you that I have now truly become acquainted with London fog.'

Last year here, I enjoyed the fog daily, but I never dreamt of the sort of thing we had today. When I went to rehearsal this morning, it was rather foggy, the way it often is in Petersburg. But when, at midday, I left St James's Hall with Sapellnikov and went into the street, it was blackest night – as dark as a moonless autumn night at home. This made an extraordinary impression on both of us. London is, anyway, very unattractive to me (for God's sake, don't tell Miss Eastwood [the English governess in Bob's family]). I get the feeling I'm sitting in a subterranean dungeon. It's now 4 o'clock. It's got a little lighter, but it's still dark. That this should happen in the middle of April is fantastic. Even the Londoners are astonished . . .

Here, I know almost nobody (and don't really want to get to know anybody, because I'm so exhausted from meeting and getting to know people) . . .

In Paris, I became nervous by having to be with people every day, but what a cheerful, enchanting, wonderful town compared to London!

Once he returned to Russia, he concluded, he would probably never want to leave it again.

After the rehearsal, he had lunch on his own and then took a walk
'in the darkness and the rain'. London's weather had changed little in
the hundred years since Haydn had written of the fog being so thick
that 'you could spread it on bread.'

Tchaikovsky spent the rest of the afternoon at the hotel, took
dinner there with Sapellnikov and afterwards, walked with him along
the Strand. Returning to the hotel, he read *Nana* before retiring. He
had mixed feelings about Zola. While reading 'the despicable *La
Terre*' a year earlier, he had remarked in his diary, 'I absolutely hate
this beast, despite all his talent.' He expressed his disgust for
L'Assommoir by ripping his copy to pieces.

On the following morning, Tchaikovsky received an invitation from
Ethel Smyth, with whom he had become friendly in February 1888 in
Leipzig. Now thirty, she was just beginning to make her way as a
composer. In April 1890, Manns conducted her Serenade in D at the
Crystal Palace; in October 1890, Henschel introduced the Overture
to *Antony and Cleopatra* at the London Symphony Concerts. She and
Tchaikovsky had met at the home of the Russian violinist Adolf
Brodsky, who, with Richter, had given the first performance of Tchaikovsky's Violin Concerto, in Vienna in 1881. The Brodskys were
among the composer's favourite friends outside Russia. In *Recollections
of a Russian Home*, Mrs Brodsky has left one of the most important
first-hand accounts we have of Tchaikovsky on tour.

In the summer of 1887 the Gewandhaus Committee invited Tschaikovsky
to conduct some of his own compositions, and as he had received similar
invitations from other towns in Germany, he decided to accept them and
so, for the first time, came abroad to conduct his own works. He arrived in
Leipzig on Christmas Eve [New Year's Eve], it was a cold frosty evening,
and the snow lay thick on the ground. My husband went to the station to
meet Tschaikovsky, and my sister Olga and her little son who were our
guests at that time helped me to prepare our Christmas tree. We wished it
to be quite ready before Tschaikovsky arrived, and to look as bright as
possible as a welcome for him. As we were lighting the candles we heard
the sound of a sledge, and soon after Tschaikovsky entered the room
followed by Siloti and my husband.

I had never seen him before. Either the sight of the Christmas tree or
our Russian welcome pleased him greatly, for his face was illuminated by
a delightful smile, and he greeted us as if he had known us for years. There

was nothing striking or artistic in his appearance, but everything about
him – the expression of his blue eyes, his voice, especially his smile, spoke
of great kindliness of nature. I never knew a man who brought with him
such a warm atmosphere as Tschaikovsky. He had not been an hour in
our house before we quite forgot that he was a great composer. We spoke
to him of very intimate matters without any reserve, and felt that he
enjoyed our confidence.

The supper passed in animated conversation, and, notwithstanding the
fatigues of his journey, Tschaikovsky remained very late before returning
to his hotel. He promised to come to us whenever he felt inclined, and kept
his word. [His diary records the visit, 'At Brodsky's. His charming wife
and sister-in-law. Christmas Tree. Hotel. Slept well.']

Among his many visits one remains especially memorable. It was on
New Year's Day [the day afterwards, in fact]. We invited Tschaikovsky to
dinner [lunch], but, knowing his shyness with strangers, did not tell him
there would be other guests. Brahms was having a rehearsal of his trio
[Piano Trio in C minor] in our house that morning with Klengel [Julius
Klengel, principal cellist of the Gewandhaus Orchestra] and A. B. – a
concert being fixed for the next day. Brahms was staying after the rehearsal for early dinner. In the midst of the rehearsal I heard a ring at the bell,
and expecting it would be Tschaikovsky, rushed to open the door. He was
quite perplexed by the sound of music, asked who was there, and what
they were playing. I took him into the room adjoining and tried to break,
gently, the news of Brahms' presence. As we spoke there was a pause in
the music; I begged him to enter, but he felt too nervous, so I opened the
door softly and called my husband. He took Tschaikovsky with him and I
followed.

Tschaikovsky and Brahms had never met before. It would be difficult to
find two men more unlike. Tschaikovsky, a nobleman by birth, had something elegant and refined in his whole bearing and the greatest courtesy of
manner. Brahms with his short, rather square figure and powerful head,
was an image of strength and energy; he was an avowed foe to all so-called
'good manners'. His expression was often slightly sarcastic. When A. B.
introduced them, Tschaikovsky said, in his soft melodious voice: 'Do I not
disturb you?'

'Not in the least,' was Brahms' reply, with his peculiar hoarseness. 'But
why are you going to hear this? It is not at all interesting.'

Tschaikovsky sat down and listened attentively. The personality of
Brahms, as he told us later, impressed him very favourably, but he was
not pleased with the music. When the trio was over I noticed that Tschaikovsky seemed uneasy. It would have been natural that he should say
something, but he was not at all the man to pay unmeaning compliments.
The situation might have become difficult, but at that moment the door
was flung open and in came our dear friends – Grieg and his wife, bringing, as they always did, a kind of sunshine with them. They knew Brahms
but had never met Tschaikovsky before. The latter loved Grieg's music
and was instantly attracted by these two charming people, full as they

were of liveliness, enthusiasm and unconventionality, and yet with a simplicity about them that made everyone feel at home. Tschaikovsky with his sensitive nervous nature understood them at once. After the introductions and greetings were over we passed to the dining-room. Nina Grieg was seated between Brahms and Tschaikovsky, but we had only been a few moments at the table when she started from her seat exclaiming: 'I cannot sit between these two. It makes me feel so nervous.'

Grieg sprang up, saying, 'But I have the courage'; and exchanged places with her. So the three composers sat together, all in good spirits. I can see Brahms now taking hold of a dish of strawberry jam, and saying he would have it all for himself and no one else should get any. It was more like a children's party than a gathering of great composers. My husband had this feeling so strongly that, when dinner was over and our guests still remained around the table smoking cigars and drinking coffee, he brought a conjurer's chest – a Christmas present to my little nephew – and began to perform tricks. All our guests were amused, and Brahms especially, who demanded from A. B. the explanation of each trick as soon as it was performed.

After dinner Brahms beckoned my little nephew to his side and putting his arm around him made all kinds of fun. I remember hearing him ask: 'Are you collecting autographs?'

'No,' the boy said, 'I collect stamps.'

The answer pleased Brahms immensely who said again and again, 'What a wise boy you are.'

Brahms was a great friend of children though he was sometimes fond of teasing them.

Once when he was walking with Brodsky in the streets of Leipzig they met a boy whom Brahms stopped with the question, 'Where did you lose your green feather?'

The boy caught anxiously at the feather and looked at Brahms in astonishment. It did not occur to him that Brahms could not have known of the green feather had it not been still there.

We were sorry when our guests had to go. Tschaikovsky remained till the last. As we accompanied him part of the way home A. B. asked how he liked Brahms' trio.

'Don't be angry with me, my dear friend,' was Tschaikovsky's reply, 'But I did not like it.'

A. B. was disappointed, for he had cherished a hope that a performance of the trio in which Brahms himself took part, might have had a very different effect and opened Tschaikovsky's eyes to the excellence of Brahms' music as a whole. Tschaikovsky had had very few opportunities of hearing it, and that was perhaps one reason why it affected him so little. [The composer's diary states, in regard to this visit, 'With Sasha (Zil [oti]) to Brodsky. Meeting with Brahms, Grieg, Fritzsch [a music publisher] etc. Suffered greatly. Grieg and his wife awfully charming. Brahms's trio. My interference in the performance. Took a nap at the hotel.']

During Tschaikovsky's frequent visits to Leipzig we saw him in every possible mood, in all his ups and downs, and always loved him more as we knew him better.

Being of an exceedingly nervous temperament, he passed from one mood to another very rapidly. One night I remember well. It was the evening before his début [public rehearsal on 3 January 1888] in Leipzig. A. B. was absent, playing in Cologne. My sister Olga and I had finished our supper some time before when Tschaikovsky suddenly called on us, apologising for being so late. We were struck by the sadness of his expression and thought he must have heard some bad news. We gave him a warm welcome without asking any questions, and did our utmost to cheer him. ['Evening at the Brodskys'. Sweet and kind women.'] We soon succeeded, and he told us it was the thought of to-morrow's concert which had depressed him so greatly, and that, if he could, he would have been glad to give up all his engagements and return to Russia immediately.

Such excitements were often more than he could bear; they brought on moods of terrible depression in which he seemed to see death in the form of an old woman standing behind his chair and waiting for him. Tschaikovsky often spoke of death and still more often thought of it.

He was greatly attached to life and loved many things passionately: people he knew, natural beauty, and works of art. He had no firm belief in a future life and could never be reconciled to the thought of parting with all that was beautiful and dear to him.

On another occasion his extreme sensitiveness revealed itself in a different way. A telephone wire had just been laid between Berlin and Leipzig. Tschaikovsky and Brodsky arranged to speak through the telephone, the former from Berlin and the latter from Leipzig. At the appointed time [on the morning of 4 February 1888] Brodsky went to the telephone office hoping to have a chat with his friend, but he had only uttered a few words when he heard Tschaikovsky say in a trembling voice, 'Dear friend! Please let me go. I feel so nervous.'

'I have not got you by the buttonhole,' said A. B., 'You can go when you please.'

Later on Tschaikovsky explained to us that as soon as he heard his friend's voice and realised the distance between them his heart began to beat so violently that he could not endure it. [A year later, in 1889, Bülow, after performing a Chopin mazurka for Edison's recording machine, was said to have fainted when he heard the playback.]

Sometimes Tschaikovsky would send us a telegram from Berlin, or any other town where he happened to be, to this effect: 'I am coming to see you. Please keep it a secret.' We knew well what this meant: that he was tired and homesick and in need of friends. Once after such a telegram Tschaikovsky just arrived in time for dinner [at 7.00 pm on 2 March 1889]; at first we·had him quite to ourselves, but after dinner, as he was sitting in the music room with his head leaning on his hand as was his custom, the members of the Brodsky Quartette [Brodsky, Klengel, Hans Becker, Otakar Nováček] quietly entered the room bringing their instruments with them as had been previously arranged. They sat down in silence and played Tschaikovsky's own String Quartette No. 3, which they had just carefully prepared for a concert. Great was Tschaikovsky's delight! I saw the tears roll down his cheek as he listened, and then, passing from one performer to the other, he expressed again and again his gratitude for the happy hour they had given him. Then turning to Brodsky he said in his naïve way: 'I did not know I had composed such a fine quartette. I never liked the finale, but now I see it is really good.'

This time he did not reproach us for having disobeyed his wish about the incognito. ['My Third Quartet phenomenally performed. Supper. Klengel (his wife has just given birth). Returned to hotel at 1 am. Homesickness has calmed down a little.']

He was very fond of meeting the Griegs at our house and, knowing this, we arranged it as often as possible. The dinners were usually followed by music. Madame Grieg would sing her husband's beautiful songs and he himself would accompany her at the piano. She always put great enthusiasm in her singing and stirred us deeply. It was a treat to hear her, and Tschaikovsky never failed to express his delight.

The composers soon became intimate friends and, as a token of his great esteem, Tschaikovsky dedicated to Grieg his Overture to Hamlet, a tribute which the latter highly esteemed.

On 29 January 1888, after again meeting Tchaikovsky that day at Brodsky's, Grieg wrote to his friend Frants Beyer, 'In Tschaikowsky I have gained a warm friend of my art. He has as great a sympathy for me as I have for him, both as artist and man.' On the occasion of his sixtieth birthday, in June 1903, Grieg, learning that a bust of himself was to be placed in the foyer of the Leipzig Gewandhaus, told his publisher, 'I hope I may have the luck to stand near my honoured friend Tschaikowsky. He is a master after my own heart.' After reading the English edition of Modest Tchaikovsky's life of his brother, Grieg noted in his diary on 31 December 1905, 'What a noble and genuine personality. And what a melancholy pleasure to renew in this way the personal friendship of those unforgettable days in Leipzig in 1888. It was just as if a friend were chatting with me.' In writing to Beyer a week later, he said of the book, 'It goes to my heart. Often it's as though I were looking into my own soul. There's so much of him that I see in myself. He is melancholic – almost to madness. He is a fine and good man but – an unhappy man, which I didn't realize when we met so long ago.'

Tchaikovsky wrote to Jurgenson, on 5 January 1888, that Grieg 'has altogether won my heart.' In *An Autobiographical Account of a Journey Abroad in 1888*, he says,

I rejoiced in the depths of my heart when we were introduced to each other and it turned out that this personality, which was so inexplicably sympathetic to mine, belonged to a musician whose warm emotional music had long since won my heart . . .

I think I am right in saying that just as Brahms is perhaps undeservedly disliked by Russian musicians and audiences, so Grieg has known how instantly to capture Russian hearts for once and for always. There exists in his music a fascinating melancholy that seems to reflect all the beauty of Norwegian scenery, now immense and sublime in its vast expanse, now grey and muted, but always full of charm for Northern souls . . .

Grieg is probably by no means as great a master as Brahms; his range is less extensive, his aims are less wide, and an inclination towards obscurity seems altogether absent; nevertheless, he stands nearer to us and is more approachable and intelligible, because of his humanity. Hearing Grieg's music, we instinctively recognize it to have been written by somebody who has been impelled to release in sound a flood of feelings and moods of a deeply poetic nature that obeys no theory or principle and bears no impress other than that of a vigorous and sincere artistic feeling. Perfection of form and strict and irreproachable logic in the development of his themes . . . are not perseveringly pursued by the celebrated Norwegian. But what charm, what inimitable and rich musical imagery! How much warmth and passion in his melodic phrases, how much teeming vitality in his harmony, how much originality and fascination in the turn of his piquant and ingenious modulations and rhythms, and, in everything else, what infinite interest, novelty and independence!

It was through Grieg that Tchaikovsky also met in Leipzig the young members of the Grieg circle, Sinding, Halvorsen and Delius. He also became acquainted with Busoni, whom he found 'very talented'. Apart from Grieg and Brahms, though, the person who seems most to have captured his interest was Ethel Smyth. He devotes a section to her in *An Autobiographical Account*.

> . . . while we were all sitting round the tea-table at Brodsky's, a beautiful dog of the setter breed burst into the room and began greeting in turn the host and his little nephew. 'This means that Miss Smyth will appear directly,' everybody exclaimed together, and in a few moments a tall Englishwoman, still young, not handsome, but with what people call an 'expressive' or 'intelligent' face, came into the room, and I was at once introduced to her as a fellow-composer. Miss Smyth is one of the comparatively few women composers who may be seriously reckoned among those active in this sphere of music. She came to Leipzig a few years ago and has studied theory and composition very thoroughly; she has composed several interesting works (the best of which, a violin sonata, I heard excellently played by the composer herself and Mr. Brodsky [Joachim found this sonata, Op 7, 'unnatural, far-fetched, affected, and poor in

sound'.]) and gives promise of a serious and talented career. Since no Englishwoman is without her originalities and eccentricities, Miss Smyth has hers, which are: firstly, the superb dog, which is quite inseparable from this lonely woman and invariably announced her arrival, not only on this occasion, but at other times when I met her [Marco's most dramatic entrance was at Brodsky's, where, arriving at speed, he bowled over Klengel's music-stand while the cellist was taking part in a performance of Brahms's Piano Quintet – much to the amusement of the composer, who was at the piano]; secondly, a passion for hunting, on account of which Miss Smyth occasionally returns to England; and, thirdly, an incredible and almost passionate worship for the enigmatic musical genius of Brahms. From her point of view, Brahms is the supreme pinnacle of all music, and everything that has gone before has served merely as preparation for the embodiment of absolute musical beauty that manifests itself in the figure of this Viennese master.

Ethel Smyth writes engagingly in *Impressions that Remained* of her time in Leipzig. She met everybody there. She admired Grieg for his absolute honesty; she was convinced that, despite appearances to the contrary, Brahms 'had a heart of gold'; she found herself not impervious to the 'demoniacal charm' of the young conductor of the Leipzig Opera, Mahler. Of English composers, she was most smitten with Sullivan: 'My one idea . . . was to see him whenever I could.'

But of all the composers I have known the most delightful as a personality was Tschaikowsky, between whom and myself a relation now sprang up that surely would have ripened into close friendship had circumstances favoured us; so large minded was he, that I think he would have put up unresentingly with all I had to give his work – a very relative admiration. Accustomed to the uncouth, almost brutal manners affected by many German musicians as part of the make up and one of the symptoms of genius, it was a relief to find in this Russian, who even the rough diamonds allowed was a master on his own lines, a polished cultivated gentleman and man of the world. Even his detestation of Brahms's music failed to check my sympathy – and that I think is strong testimony to his charm! He would argue with me about Brahms by the hour, strum passages on the piano and ask if they were not hideous, declaring I must be under hypnotic influence, since to admire this awkward pedant did not square with what he was kind enough to call the soundness of my instinct on other points. Another thing was my devotion to Marco, of whom he was secretly terrified, but this trait he considered to be a form of English spleen and it puzzled him less than the other madness. For thirty years I have meant to enquire whether dogs play no part in the Russian scheme of life or whether Tschaikowsky's views were peculiar to himself; anyhow it amused me, reading his Memoirs, to find Marco and Brahms bracketed together as eccentricities of his young English friend.

It is worth mentioning here that Marco was a very big powerful dog: today, a music-stand; tomorrow, a composer, perhaps. Tchaikovsky, in fact, adored animals, but he told Madame von Meck in a letter that he thought he was probably an unusual sort of dog-lover.

> Firstly, I prefer mongrels; secondly, I can't keep a dog in my house, and in all my life I've only had one house-dog . . . This is because I worry about them all the time; I continuously imagine that they are hungry, that they want something and can't say so, that they are sick, etc., etc. Moreover my Alexey does not like them, and when servants are not attentive and patient enough with animals, then they can't be happy.

He once pondered the idea of abducting Madame von Meck's parrot, to whom he became greatly attached while he was at Brailov, but when he found that one of the parlourmaids also liked the bird, he dropped his plan for fear of hurting her.

Unhappily, in April 1889, Tchaikovsky was unable to accept Ethel Smyth's invitation to visit her, because he was off early on the following morning. He left the writing of his reply until the afternoon and went with Sapellnikov to the second of the two rehearsals for that evening's concert. On the previous day he had rehearsed the First Suite. Today was to be the First Piano Concerto. It was his strong hope that Sapellnikov, whom he held in considerable esteem, would score a triumph at the concert and prove that Russia had more Rubinsteins to give the world. But the rehearsal was brief and disappointing. 'Cowen took up too much time. I got cross. Musicians were very cold, as they were yesterday.' However, Cowen, we recollect, said of Tchaikovsky, 'He did not speak English, and I had to stand at his side all the time and translate his wishes to the members of the orchestra.' He also alludes, in his memoirs, to 'the amount of time taken up by the foreign composers in rehearsing their works, to the detriment of the rest of the programme . . .'

> My foreign *confrères* did not always recognize the receptiveness of our players, and, glad as I was to show the former every possible courtesy, it became just a little tiring when, in response to their requests, I used to have to say continually to the orchestra, 'Please, gentlemen, Mr. ——— would like this again'; and the passage would be repeated over and over, even after it was perfect, until the patience of the performers was often wellnigh exhausted, and, what was worse, little time left us to rehearse the rest of the programme.'

Because of his general diffidence, Tchaikovsky tended to under-rehearse, and it seems unlikely that he would qualify as 'Mr. ———'; it is much more probable that Cowen had composers like Grieg and Sgambati in mind. But Cowen's principal grievance, which ultimately led to his dismissal, lay with the Philharmonic directors, who, he was never backward in declaring, were simply not prepared to allot sufficient time for rehearsals. Berger's policy of engaging so many guest composer-conductors undoubtedly made life difficult for the resident conductor. On this occasion, Cowen had to conduct Mozart's Symphony No 39, Wallace's overture to *Lurline* and accompany three arias, amounting to about fifty minutes' music. Tchaikovsky's two pieces lasted about sixty-five minutes, and the First Suite was entirely new to the orchestra. It is hardly surprising that there was not enough time. It seems likely that neither Cowen nor Tchaikovsky was to blame in this matter; nor, indeed, the orchestra. 'They read excellently at sight', Tchaikovsky had noted in his diary a year earlier, and, after the 1888 concert, he told the orchestra's manager, William Cummings, that the Philharmonic was the finest orchestra he had ever heard. On the other hand, Tchaikovsky's diary entries are usually accurate and fair. Perhaps Cowen *did* take up too much time.

After the rehearsal, the composer and Sapellnikov went out to lunch. Tchaikovsky then returned to the hotel and, in French, replied to Ethel Smyth.

Dear, Good and Much Respected Miss Smyth,

I would so much like to take advantage of your kind invitation, but, dear Mademoiselle, I leave tomorrow, Friday, at 8.20 a.m., and so it will be impossible for me to come and see you. Let's hope I get a better chance when I'm next in London. Though, to tell the truth, I strongly doubt whether I'll be coming again, for there's no possibility of doing things properly when one has only two rehearsals and when the orchestra's conductor has scarcely time to do justice to the other pieces on the programme! . . . Still, let's hope I'll be able to return, and then my dearest wish will be to come and visit you. Tomorrow, I'm travelling to Marseilles and from there I'll be taking the steamer all the way to the Caucasus; the passage will last a fortnight!

A month ago, I was with Mr. Brodsky and his dear wife, and it goes without saying that we talked a lot about you. In Hamburg, I spent an entire day with *your Idol* . . . JOHANNES BRAHMS!!! He was charming to me. He's a very likeable man, though my estimation of his talent doesn't correspond to yours . . .

Au revoir, dear Mademoiselle; I hope you've been composing some
beautiful works and I wish you every sort of prosperity.

P. Tschaikovsky.

I hope your *dear dog* is well!!

There is no criticism here of Cowen, whose problems Tchaikovsky
clearly appreciated. The final straw came at the Philharmonic
concert of 15 June 1892, when Cowen was granted just one rehearsal
in which to prepare Wagner's *Siegfried Idyll*, Bruch's Second Violin
Concerto, Rubinstein's Fourth Piano Concerto and Beethoven's
Pastoral Symphony. His speech to the audience precipitated his dis-
charge, as we have read earlier.

The sentence 'I hope you've been composing some beautiful works'
could be regarded as patronising. But we must remember that Tchaikovsky, standing, like Bruch and Saint-Saëns, against all the different schools and theories of the day, consistently advocated one
objective: the creation of beauty. Mussorgsky, for one, found this idea
obnoxious and, after meeting Tchaikovsky in St Petersburg in
December 1872, wrote to Stasov, 'I've had to pass all these days in
the company of worshippers of absolute musical beauty and have
experienced a strange *feeling of emptiness* in conversation with them.'
In Mussorgsky's opinion, Tchaikovsky probably spent his time
'dreaming of Turkish sweetmeats', always riding 'the same hobby-
horse: "Our aim in music must be beauty – nothing but beauty!"'
Tchaikovsky was less hard on Mussorgsky, whom he mentions to
Madame von Meck in a letter of January 1878.

> This Mussorgsky, for all his ugliness, speaks a new language. Beautiful it
> may not be, but it is fresh. This is why we can expect Russia some day to
> produce a whole cluster of strong talents who will open up new paths for
> art. Our ugliness, anyhow, is better than the pitiful impotence, mas-
> querading as serious creative power, of Brahms and other Germans.

In regard to this final sentence, we can usefully turn to *Life and Liszt*
by Arthur Friedheim, who met Tchaikovsky in Leipzig early in 1888.
'But for Tschaikowski, as for Saint-Saëns, Brahms did not exist, and
neither nationality nor race had anything to do with it.' Tchaikovsky
viewed Brahms as an accomplished manipulator of form, but not as a
creator of 'beautiful works'.

The day that he spent with Ethel Smyth's '*Idol*' was 12 March

1889. Tchaikovsky was in Hamburg, the city of Brahms's birth, to conduct the first performance outside Russia of the Fifth Symphony. On arriving on the night of the 11th, he discovered that he was not only staying at the same hotel as Brahms, but in the room next to him. The German composer had been visiting Hamburg and had prolonged his stay so that he could listen to the first rehearsal of the Fifth Symphony. This took place on the following morning, and often after the rehearsal the two men lunched together at the Pfordte Restaurant.

Brahms had also attended a rehearsal during Tchaikovsky's first tour a year earlier, listening to the First Suite in Leipzig on 3 January 1888. In his diary of the tour, Tchaikovsky wrote that Brahms 'made no encouraging remarks; I was told he was very pleased by the first movement, but did not praise the rest, especially the "Marche miniature".' The Germans tended to dislike the march; one critic called it 'a mere pattern of sounds'; another said it was 'tea-caddy-decoration style of art applied to music'. The first movement, Introduction and Fugue, won many admirers, though, including Clara Schumann, who had heard the work six years earlier in Frankfurt, entering in her diary on 3 February 1882, 'Suite by Tschaikowsky; a good deal of talent and ability; the national flavour which runs through it often makes it interesting, but only in places. The first movement – introduction and fugue – interested me most, it seemed to me the most finished.' Clara had previously been entertained by Tchaikovsky when, as a student at the St Petersburg Conservatoire, he played the flute in one of Kuhlau's chamber works that was featured in a musical evening welcoming her to the capital in March 1864. Another musician who particularly liked the first movement of the suite was Madame von Meck's eighteen-year-old pianist, Claude Debussy. 'Among all modern fugues, I've never come across anything so fine', he told his employer, after they had played it through together in August 1880; 'Mr. Massenet [his teacher] could never equal that.' A few months later, he published his first composition, an arrangement for piano duet of the Spanish, Neapolitan and Russian Dances from *Swan Lake*.

After their first meeting, in January 1888, Tchaikovsky described Brahms to Jurgenson as 'very pleasant and not as vain as I expected.' He later wrote more fully about him in *An Autobiographical Account*, as follows.

Brahms is rather a short man, with an impressive fullness of figure and possessing a very sympathetic appearance. His handsome head, almost that of an old man, recalls the type of a handsome, benign elderly Russian priest [a photograph of Brahms's head was reproduced, to illustrate 'the typical Caucasian', in Baenitz's *Lehrbuch der Geographie* in the Velhagen and Klasing schoolbook series] . . . A certain softness of outline, pleasantly rounded, rather long and slightly thin hair, kind grey eyes and a thick greying beard – all these at once brought to mind the sort of pure-bred Great Russian so often encountered among our clergy.

Brahms's manner is extraordinarily simple and free of arrogance, his disposition is cheerful, and the few hours spent in his company left me with a very agreeable recollection. Unfortunately I am forced to confess that, despite a rather extended stay among them in Leipzig, I did not get on very well with the most prominent representative of modern German music. The reason was as follows. Like all my Russian musical friends, without exception, I only respected in Brahms an honourable, energetic musician of strong convictions; but, in spite of all desire to the contrary, I never could, and never can, admire his music. Brahmsism is very widespread throughout Germany; there are a number of authoritative people and an entire musical institution specially consecrated to the Brahms cult, and he is considered a great composer, almost equal to Beethoven. But there are anti-Brahmsians in Germany and everywhere beyond the German frontier, with the exception perhaps of London, where, thanks to the vigorous propaganda of the violinist Joachim, who is unusually popular in England, the greatness of Brahms is also largely accepted. Everywhere else, as I say, there reigns complete ignorance and neglect of Brahms. But nowhere, perhaps, has he made less headway than in our fatherland. There is something dry, cold, vague and nebulous in the music of this master that is repellent to Russian hearts. From our Russian point of view, Brahms possesses no melodic invention whatsoever. His musical thought never reaches a conclusion; hardly have we heard an allusion to some tangible melodic phrase, when it disappears in a whirlpool of almost meaningless harmonic progressions and modulations, as though the composer's special aim was to be incomprehensible and profound. Thus he excites and irritates our musical feeling, as it were, yet does not want to satisfy its demand; he seems ashamed to put things plainly, to speak clearly and reach the heart. Hearing his music, we ask ourselves: is Brahms deep, or does he merely wish to appear deep in order to mask the ultimate poverty of his imagination? The question can never be precisely answered.

It is impossible to say of Brahms's music that it is weak or unremarkable. His style is always elevated. Unlike other contemporary musicians, he never has recourse to purely external effects; he never tries to surprise us, to strike us by some new and brilliant orchestral combination; nor do we find in his music anything trivial or directly imitative. All of it is very serious, very distinguished, apparently even original, but, nevertheless, the chief thing is lacking – beauty! This is my own view of Brahms, and, as far as I know, it is shared by all Russian composers and all the musical public in Russia. However, a few years ago, when I frankly expressed my opinion of Brahms to Hans von Bülow, he replied: 'Wait awhile, the time will come when you will enter into the depth and beauty of Brahms. Like you, it was long before I understood him, but gradually I was blessed by the revelation of his genius. It will be the same with you.' And so I wait, and still am waiting, and the revelation has not come. I revere Brahms's artistic personality. I bow to the purity of his musical aspirations and admire his firm and proud renunciation of all the tricks that solemnize the Wagnerian cult – and, to a lesser degree, the worship of Liszt – but I do not care for his music.

The reader will understand that this prevented me from seeking the closest acquaintance with the deeply sympathetic personality of Brahms. I met him constantly in the company of devoted admirers . . . and it would have been unseemly – in view of the fact that I was a stranger and did not share in the worship of their idol – to bring any discord into the complete harmony of these devout believers in this musical dogma. On the other hand, Brahms himself, as though he instinctively understood or even knew that I did not belong to his camp, made no effort to become at all close. He was perfectly straightforward and polite to me, as he was to everybody else, but nothing more. Meanwhile, all that I have heard of Brahms as a man has made me doubly regret that the 'revelation' predicted by von Bülow has not yet been granted me. He is an unusually noble and attractive man, and all who have come into close contact with him are inspired by the warmth of his personality. The celebrated Czech composer Dvořák used to speak with tears in his eyes of the strong interest Brahms showed in him at a time when his works were finding neither publishers nor performers, and what vigorous and powerful support he gave him, and what energy he showed in sounding the depths of the undiscovered genius of his Slavonic brother-in-art! Brodsky, too, related incidents that revealed the sympathetic side of Brahms's character, especially his rare and pleasing modesty. It is well known that Wagner treated his contemporaries with the greatest animosity and always showed himself particularly caustic towards Brahms's works. Once, when somebody reported to the latter a fresh sarcasm that Wagner had levelled at him, he exclaimed, 'Good heavens! Wagner, honoured and triumphant, takes up most of the highroad. How can I, ploughing my own little furrow, be any hindrance or annoyance to him? Why can't he leave me in peace, since we are never likely to clash!'

Brahms's early German biographers, who knew him personally, intimate that, at the first meeting between the two composers, Tchaikovsky made no particular impression on Brahms, who regarded him simply as a pupil of Rubinstein. The small amount of Tchaikovsky's music with which he was acquainted had not led him to value him as one of his more important contemporaries, to be compared, for instance, with Dvořák, Grieg or Goldmark. He found it difficult to take seriously somebody who seemed to waver unhappily between European culture and Asiatic barbarism.

During lunch at the Pfordte Restaurant, Brahms told Tchaikovsky, 'with frankness and simplicity', that he tended to like the Fifth Symphony, except for the last movement. Tchaikovsky appears to have attached great importance to this opinion, soon becoming convinced that the finale was no good, and confiding to Modest, 'I, too, find it odious.' He was relieved, however, that Brahms and he had at last got round to discussing each other's music, and he at once made a clean breast of things and confessed that he was out of sympathy with Brahms's music and did not really understand it. This broke the ice between them, and Tchaikovsky, in his capacity as a director of the Russian Musical Society, then went on to invite Brahms to conduct his works in Moscow. He was disappointed when this offer was declined. The two men parted on excellent terms.

The successful German première three days later, after a total of four rehearsals and 'terrible drunkenness' shortly before the concert, somewhat restored Tchaikovsky's belief in the symphony. The occasion was marred only by the absence of Ave-Lallemant, who was unwell. The composer was flattered by a reception at the Society of Musicians. 'German humour', hé noted in his diary. 'Pleasant people, though.'

If Tchaikovsky failed to shake Ethel Smyth's faith in the sovereignty of Brahms, he nevertheless did succeed in influencing her attitude towards orchestration, as she mentions in *Impressions that Remained*.

On one point we were quite of one mind, the neglect in my school . . . of colour; 'not one of them can instrumentate,' he said, and he earnestly begged me to turn my attention at once to the orchestra and not be prudish about using the medium for all it is worth. 'What happens,' he asked, 'in ordinary conversation? If you have to do with really alive people, listen to the inflections in the voices . . . there's instrumentation for you!' And I followed his advice on the spot, went to concerts with the sole object of studying orchestral effects, filled notebook upon notebook with impressions, and ever since have been at least as much interested in sounds as sense, considering the two things indivisible.

After writing to Ethel Smyth, Tchaikovsky made preparations, that included 'drunkenness', for the evening's concert. The concert went well, the audience calling for an encore of the *Marche miniature*. 'Vasya had a huge success', the composer reported in his diary. Sapellnikov was, in fact, so warmly received that he immediately established himself with the London public. Despite the cavillings of George Bernard Shaw, he became a perennial favourite and in time acquired a world reputation. (He was one of George Gershwin's boyhood heroes; a magazine photo of him appears in the scrapbook kept by the American composer when he was a teenager.) Sapellnikov's most important legacy is perhaps his recording of the First Piano Concerto, which he played with Tchaikovsky not only at their 1889 London concert, but on several other occasions. He was altogether a most winning man, 'an Artist through and through', said Berger, 'and I call him a true "Natur-kind" (nature's child), because of his un-affected, un-assuming, un-worldly character. I have never heard him say an ungenerous word of any brother-Artist.' In his *Reminiscences*, Berger also writes of Sapellnikov's way of bringing his hands down from quite a height and, 'just when you expect a big, coarse crash, he touches the keys with the most delightful delicacy, as though the tips of his fingers were covered with india-rubber thimbles.'

After the concert, Tchaikovsky returned to the Dieudonné, where, according to his last diary entry for the day, he had dinner with 'an old Jewish acquaintance'. Perhaps this was again the Jew posing as a Czech. By the following evening, he was in Marseilles, *en route* for Tiflis.

He did not visit London again till 1893. In 1890, he needed a rest from the strenuous life of travel and concert-giving in which he had recently become involved. At the beginning of that year, he had the rehearsals of *The Sleeping Beauty* to deal with in St Petersburg and then *The Queen of Spades*, a further commission from the Imperial Theatres, to compose. There were also conducting engagements in Russia, including a performance in Moscow of Beethoven's Ninth Symphony, in aid of musicians' widows and orphans. In 1891, he travelled to America, where he had been invited to take part in the ceremonies and concerts marking the inauguration of Carnegie Hall. His next letter to Berger was written in Rouen on 12 April 1891, six days before he embarked for the United States from Le Havre on the SS *Bretagne*, which put in at Southampton en route to New York. In this letter, he recommended the Russian violinist Yuly Konyus, who had graduated with the gold medal from the Moscow Conservatoire three years earlier. Anybody recommended by Tchaikovsky, replied Berger, would be 'esteemed by me as an artist and accepted as a friend.' He then raised another matter: 'You are a very perverse man. For some years you've been promising me your portrait, but I have yet to receive it. You fraud! I can only forgive you if you now rectify this omission by sending me your photo.' The photo was duly dispatched a fortnight after the composer's return to Russia that June; it was inscribed, 'to my dear friend Mr. Francesco Berger'.

The year 1892 was another busy time, with work on *Nutcracker* and *Iolanta* and visits to Vienna, Salzburg and Prague. In October, Tchaikovsky again wrote to Berger, recommending the pianist Alexander Ziloti, a pupil of Rubinstein and Liszt, and later to be recognised as one of the greatest of all Russian virtuosos. In answering, Berger took the opportunity of enclosing his own portrait. Two months later, Tchaikovsky informed his friend that he would once more be coming to London.

No sooner had he reached the Dieudonné, on the morning of 29 May 1893, than he came across the French pianist Louis Diémer, who was also staying at the hotel. Writing, later that day, to his nephew Bob, he admitted that 'to my great astonishment, I found myself delighted to see him.' His normal shyness at meeting people had perhaps been subdued by a need for companionship in this 'quite horrible city'. 'Isn't it strange', he reflected to Bob, 'that, of my own free will, I have elected to undergo this torture?'

> Several times during my journey yesterday I resolved to throw up the whole thing and go home. But what disgrace to turn back for no good reason! Yesterday, I suffered so badly that I could neither sleep nor eat, which is most unusual for me. I suffer not only from an inexpressible sadness that cannot be put into words (in my new symphony, there's one place that seems to depict this well), but also from a hatred of strangers – and from heaven knows what else also. This state affects me physically with a pain in the lower part of my stomach and a gnawing pain and weakness in my legs. However, it's for the last time in my life. Only for a pile of money will I ever go anywhere again, and never for more than three days at a time. And to think that I must kick my heels here for another fortnight!! It seems like eternity.

In a letter to his brother Anatoly, also written on 29 May, he said, 'I never realize how deep is my affection for you until I am away from home and oppressed by loneliness and nostalgia.' Diémer was not a stranger to Tchaikovsky. The pianist, then fifty, was one of his most ardent champions and always gave him a cordial welcome to Paris, inviting him to his home and generally trying to make his stay pleasant. During the 1888 visit, he and his pupils at the Conservatoire put on a private chamber concert of Tchaikovsky's works in the presence of the composer, whose diary records that he was 'touched' by this kindness. Diémer and Tchaikovsky took part in two Paris concerts together: on 4 March 1888, they performed the Concert Fantasy; on 11 March, Diémer played two of the solo piano pieces and Liszt's paraphrase of the polonaise from *Eugene Onegin*. At the home of the conductor Colonne, they performed *Francesca da Rimini* in the arrangement for four hands. Tchaikovsky also attended two of Diémer's recitals.

As a young man, Diémer had been befriended by Rossini, who often invited him to play at his celebrated soirées, where he met Liszt, Auber, Verdi, Rubinstein, Sarasate, Patti and other notable musicians. When his career was threatened by the prospect of seven years' national service, Rossini helped to buy him out. At Rossini's, he formed his lifelong friendship with Saint-Saëns. They were the pianists in the first performance of *The Carnival of the Animals*, and Saint-Saëns dedicated his Fifth Piano Concerto to him. Other works written for Diémer were Massenet's and Lalo's Piano Concertos and César Franck's *Symphonic Variations*. Among his pupils were Alfred Cortot, Marcel Dupré, Robert Casadesus and Lazare Lévy, who said, 'The astonishing precision of his playing, his legendary trills and the sobriety of his style made him the excellent pianist we all admired.'

Diémer had previously mentioned to Tchaikovsky how thrilled he would be if the composer would write a work especially for him; he probably again expressed this desire when they met in London.

On the afternoon of Monday 29 May, the day of the composer's arrival in the capital, he went to Diémer's recital, at St James's Hall, which began at 3.00 pm. The programme consisted of works by Rameau, Couperin, Handel, Mendelssohn, Schumann, Chopin, Brahms, Widor and Goddard, and also included one of Diémer's own compositions. According to *The Musical Times*, he gave 'a very French performance of Schumann's *Études Symphoniques*, and his interpretation of pieces by Chopin lacked distinction and poetic feeling. As regards technique, however, his playing . . . was well-nigh faultless, and this fact goes far to account for the great esteem in which he is held in Paris as a teacher.'

After the recital, Tchaikovsky spent a while with Berger and 'reached an agreement about the rehearsals', he told Bob. No doubt vividly remembering the scarcity of rehearsal time available to him in 1889, he was anxious about the preparations for Thursday's concert, which was clearly going to present even greater problems. Mackenzie, who had succeeded Cowen as the Philharmonic Society's conductor, was to direct Sterndale Bennett's overture *The Naiades* and accompany the soprano Margaret Macintyre in Rossini's 'Bel raggio lusinghier' from *Semiramide* and in the 'Liebestod' from *Tristan und Isolde*; Tchaikovsky was to conduct his Fourth Symphony, the first performance in London of any of his symphonies; Saint-Saëns was to play his Second Piano Concerto, accompanied by Mackenzie, and to conduct *Le Rouet d'Omphale*. In Hamburg Tchaikovsky was given four rehearsals for the Fifth Symphony. Now, for the Fourth, he was faced with the prospect of being allocated only a quarter of that time. Fortunately, the rest of the programme was made up of works with which the orchestra was already familiar. Mackenzie would be accommodating enough, but what of the pernickety Saint-Saëns and his *two* pieces? It is hardly surprising that Tchaikovsky should plead with Berger for as much time as he could get and, perhaps, for a precise rehearsal schedule.

Tchaikovsky wrote a vast quantity of letters, several thousand of which have so far been discovered. Until the age of fifty, he maintained a prolific output. With his habitual orderliness and discipline, he set aside specific hours of specific days of the week in which to write to specific people. Modest would be on a certain day; Madame von Meck, on another; Anatoly, on yet another – and so forth. 'He answered every single letter he received and never kept anybody waiting for a reply', Laroche recalled. 'Ardent and impatient, he walked quickly, wrote quickly and read quickly.' But, with the increasing demands made on his time during the late eighties and early nineties, the volume of his correspondence declined. The letters themselves became not only fewer, but less detailed. In addition, his diary came to a stop in May 1891. We are therefore left with a

comparative dearth of personal information about the composer's
fourth and longest stay in London. With a fortnight at his disposal, he
may well have ventured out of the capital, to visit, say, Oxford,
Brighton or Stratford-on-Avon. Regrettably, we are not yet able to
account for most of his movements.

We know from the diary for 1888 that, on 20 March of that year,
Tchaikovsky perused the '*Dayly-Télégraphe*'. If he did so again on 29
May 1893, he might have come across the sad information that,
owing to poor health, Grieg would not be coming to Cambridge.
This, said the paper, 'will awaken general regret, for the Scandinavian composer is perhaps the most popular of the five musicians who
accepted invitations to take the honorary degree of "Mus. Doc." on
that occasion. Of the remaining four, Messrs. Saint-Saëns and
Tschaikowsky will appear at the Philharmonic Concert on Thursday,
and Messrs. Boito and Max Bruch will arrive early next week.'

Such news must have been disappointing to Tchaikovsky, but
more so to the university. Not one of the world's seven most illu-
strious musicians – Brahms, Verdi, Gounod, Dvořák, Rubinstein,
Grieg and Joachim – would be gracing the jubilee celebrations. Saint-
Saëns would now be the star attraction, with Bruch, Boito and
Tchaikovsky as supporting cast.

On either Monday or Tuesday, Tchaikovsky received the following
letter, written in French, from Stanford.

> 50 Holland Street,
> Kensington, W.
>
> *May 28, 93.*
>
> My dear Mr. Tschaikowsky,
>
> We are hoping to invite some friends for a little soirée on Friday the 9th of
> June at 10.00 p.m. Would you do us the honour of coming? It will be a sort of
> general rehearsal for Cambridge!
>
> With very kind regards,
>
> > Your devoted,
> >
> > Ch. Stanford.

Jurgenson's London agents were Stanley Lucas, Weber, and Co., of
84 New Bond Street. It is a sign of Tchaikovsky's growing stature in
English eyes – he was, after all, to become a doctor – that this

publishing house, should now contact him and put at his disposal during his time in London one of their senior executives. The man they chose was Émile Hatzfeld, who would probably have introduced himself to the composer on the Monday or Tuesday. Hatzfeld was born in Mulhouse, Alsace, on 5 June 1857. His father, a Parisian, was a professor of languages. During the Franco–Prussian War of 1870, the family home was occupied by invading German forces, and, after the annexation of Alsace, the Hatzfelds moved further down into France. While he was still at school, Émile decided that he would like to work in music publishing. He subsequently attempted to find employment with Durand & Cie, of Paris, who published Saint-Saëns, Bizet, César Franck, Fauré and Lalo, but there was nothing for him. Not content with working for a lesser publisher, he came over to London, arriving with fourpence in his pocket. He tried the major English publishers and again failed to secure a position. He therefore took a job in the wine trade. Being a bright young man and coming from Cognac country, he did well enough, but, after a while, left to become a French teacher. Like his father, he had a gift for languages and could also have taught German or Italian. His teaching career lasted for four years. In 1879, he was taken on by Stanley Lucas, Weber, and Co. Charming, good-natured and witty, he quickly made his mark in the firm. In 1881, with his future secure, he married an English girl, Louisa Palmer. Their son Cecil was born a year later; he was named after Hatzfeld's sister Cécile, a governess. In 1888, they had a daughter, Maude, named after her godmother, the composer Maude Valérie White.

Hatzfeld developed into a formidable expert on copyright law, which was still in a dauntingly complicated and muddled state. He made friends with a number of leading musicians, including Grieg, Clara Schumann, Cowen, Mackenzie, Paderewski and, later, Henry Wood and Arnold Bax. He also turned to composing and had some piano pieces published by his own firm. By 1893, he was settled in a spacious house in Goldhawk Road, next to Ravenscourt Park, and was on the verge of being given a partnership.

His daughter, Maude, who became a singer, is the principal source of information about Hatzfeld. She recalls that her father was enchanted by Tchaikovsky and saw a good deal of him during the composer's stay in London.

It is apparent from Tchaikovsky's letters that the forthcoming concert and the trip to Cambridge caused him great anguish. Yet, this was rarely manifest to Hatzfeld. He did, however, consider the composer to be a person of essentially serious mood. Tchaikovsky seems to have enjoyed Hatzfeld's company; he asked his advice on a multitude of everyday matters relating to both London and Cambridge.

Hatzfeld's favourite restaurant was Pagani's, 44–48 Great Portland Street. Renowned for French and Italian dishes, its telegram address was Soufflé, London. Maude Hatzfeld remembers that her father took Tchaikovsky there on more than one occasion. In *Palmy Days*, J. B. Booth compares Pagani's with the Dieudonné in the magnificence of its cuisine. But that was not all they had in common.

. . . each possessed a room the walls of which were decorated with autographs, notes of music, and drawings by *habitués* who were, or were to become, famous, and each restaurant had achieved prosperity after the humblest of beginnings . . .

As long ago as 1871, when the Queen's Hall was still to come, and the St. James's Hall, on the site of which the Piccadilly Hotel now stands, was the musical centre of London, Mario Pagani started his catering career with a little *pâtisserie*, which speedily grew into a small restaurant specialising in Italian cooking, attracting a *clientèle* of painters, singers, and writers, which included Signor Tosti, Carlo Pellegrini, the famous *Vanity Fair* cartoonist, and the inevitable George R. Sims, who wrote regularly in his columns in *The Referee* of the good food to be obtained. In later years, when success had come, Pagani was not ungrateful to 'Dagonet', and his portrait, on a china plaque, occupied the centre of one of the walls in the 'Artists' Room'.

Mario Pagani, the founder, died in 1887, and the restaurant was carried on by his brother and a cousin for a time, until the cousin was left sole proprietor, taking into partnership Meschini, who, in his turn, eventually became sole proprietor, leaving when he died the establishment to his widow and son.

In the course of years Pagani's had undergone many changes, increasing vastly in size and ornamentation, until it developed into a large and important restaurant. But throughout all structural changes it contrived to retain its character. It might pile floor on floor, blossom into a lift and a Masonic banqueting-room, enlarge its kitchen, increase its staff, but the old atmosphere and the type of *clientèle* to a large extent remained. It was always definitely Italian; its waiters were Italian – and generally wore moustaches – and its 'special' dishes were invariably Italian.

The building of the Queen's Hall was to bring fresh custom, for the musicians and singers who performed there soon discovered Pagani's, and its fame spread to the opera stars at Covent Garden.

An amusing memory comes back to me. One evening I was quietly supping in the big restaurant of the ground floor, with its brown walls, and its mirrors with their painted trellis-work, when I became aware of a suppressed excitement amongst the Italian waiters. Through the glazed screen which cut off the dispense bar and the entrance to the kitchens I could see chefs in white caps bobbing their heads excitedly round the kitchen doors, and then, as excitement grew, service of every kind ceased, and amid a hum of excitement and faint cheering, a befurred Caruso, smiling and gesticulating, followed by his little court, burst into the restaurant. He had been singing at Covent Garden, in *La Bohéme*, with Melba, and an atmosphere of excited triumph still enveloped him.

On the second floor of Pagani's was the Artists' Room, one of the most interesting rooms in any London restaurant, for the walls were covered with autographs, caricatures, sketches, and musical notes.

Mascagni himself had written the first bars of one of the famous airs from *Cavalleria Rusticana*; Caruso had caricatured himself; Denza had written the opening bars of *Funiculi, Funicula*; Lamoureux had written a hymn of praise to the cook; Yadya [Ysaye; this is incorrectly cribbed from The Dwarf of Blood. *Dinners and Diners* has 'Mascagni has written the first bars of one of the airs from 'Cavalleria Rusticana', Denza has scribbled the opening bars of 'Funiculi, Funicula', Lamoureux has written a tiny hymn of praise to the cook, Ysaye has lamented that he is always tied to "notes", which, with a waiter and a bill at his elbow, might have a double meaning.'] had lamented that he was tied to notes, and the autographs included those of Paderewski, Puccini, Chaminade, Tosti, Tschaikovsky, Calvé and Melba. Amongst the photographs were a large autographed portrait of Sir Henry Irving as Becket, and Phil May on horse-back, and nearby were caricatures by May, and drawings in sepia and pastel by Mario, Val Prinsep, and others.

The composer Isidore de Lara was one of the first musicians to frequent Pagani's and in *Many Tales of Many Cities*, he considerably extends the list of celebrities who used to go there.

I became an 'habitue' of Pagani's, where I met daily the composer of 'Goodbye' [Tosti]; Denza, whose song 'Funiculi Funicula' was gathering laurels for him all over the world, was a daily customer, and also Carlo Pellegrini, a Neapolitan nobleman, who had become the renowned caricaturist, 'Ape' of *Vanity Fair*; he was the life and soul of Pagani's restaurant.

There is a very remarkable room there, and when young we all wrote our names on the panels of the walls; this has stimulated later visitors to do the same, and there, now, is the most wonderful collection of autographs in the world. The walls are covered with the signatures of nearly all the great artistes of the nineteenth and twentieth centuries. Mario (1870), Caruso, Tamagno, Calvé, Nellie Melba, Sarah Bernhardt, Mancinelli, Toscanini, Richard Strauss, Tchaikowsky, Lamoureux, Mascagni, Leoncavallo, Kreisler, Kubelik [Jan], Paderewski, Pachmann, Damala (the husband of Sarah Bernhardt, who wrote, 'Lasciate ogni speranza o voi che sortite', 'Abandon all hope, Oh ye who go out!'), Victor Maurel, Bottesini, Maeterlinck and Marie Corelli are a few of those who have signed. What magical recollections these names evoke! I assisted at the gradual development and aggrandizement of the little restaurant to its present [1928] important proportions. Its success was in a great measure due to Tosti, Pellegrini, and myself, who brought to Great Portland Street all our many distinguished and fashionable friends. Pagani fully recognized this, and his gratitude caused him to efface from his books a sum of hundreds of pounds owing for luncheons and dinners by Pellegrini, at the moment of his death . . .

Other musicians visited the restaurant in Great Portland Street . . . among them Elgar, then unknown, Percy Pitt, Joseph Hollman, famous for his 'cello playing and his forest of hair; it must have taken him several hours a day to brush it. Alexander Mackenzie, afterwards head of the Royal Academy of Music; Saint-Saëns, whose fine symphony with organ had just been performed at the Philharmonic; Goring Thomas, the composer of 'Esmeralda'.

One evening I saw Pellegrini dining with a man I had never seen before. I asked his name; it was General Gordon, known as 'Chinese Gordon', the tragic hero of Khartoum and a great Christian soldier, and I was introduced to him, and I am proud to think that I had the honour of shaking hands with one of England's most noble sons.

Pagani's was totally destroyed by bombing during the Second World War. Since it seems probable that Tchaikovsky also inscribed his name on the wall of the special room in the Dieudonné, we can presume that we have lost two specimens of his signature.

Wednesday 31 May was the day of the first rehearsal, and Tchaikovsky would have set out, that morning, along the now-familiar route from the Dieudonné to St James's Hall, probably going from Ryder Street into Duke Street and then along Piccadilly.

Few eminent men have lived in the immediate vicinity of the path that he followed. Swift took rooms in Ryder Street for a brief period in 1712 and, ten years later, wrote to Vanessa, 'Remember . . . Rider Street.' The only other person of note to live nearby was the physician John Snow, who made the discovery that cholera is waterborne and whose home, between 1813 and 1858, was at 18 Sackville Street, a few yards north of Piccadilly. From the top of Duke Street, one had a good view of the Hotel Albemarle, perhaps the smartest hotel in the West End, where, at this time, Oscar Wilde held court and Lily Langtry entertained the Prince of Wales.

Piccadilly itself was then perhaps the most fascinating, crowded
and expensive shopping street in the world. Tchaikovsky would
have passed Fortnum and Mason's at around 10.00 am, when, as
W. Macqueen-Pope relates in *Goodbye Piccadilly*, that splendid store
was already well into its day's work.

> By nine a.m. the heads of all departments and the partners themselves
> were busy. The senior assistants were at their posts in their swallow tailed
> coats. The juniors, who were called 'roundsmen', were already off on their
> daily job of calling on customers – at the Best Houses in Mayfair, Belgra-
> via, Bayswater and Kensington, at Marlborough House, Clarence House
> (where the Duke and Duchess of Edinburgh lived) and at Buckingham
> Palace itself. Sometimes the orders from the Palace were very modest –
> 'Two pots of marmalade, 1/8d' or 'Four bottles of oil at 2/6d'. The Prince
> of Wales however wanted apricot pulp, Parmesan and Gruyère cheese.
>   But fashionable people of all nationalities, resident nobility or those on
> a visit from abroad, preferred to call at the shop itself. To them it was the
> centre of Piccadilly, they met their friends, they saw novelties, and the folk
> from overseas regarded the place as being marvellous, a real piece of
> Piccadilly magic. Piccadilly has never been a woman's shopping centre –
> but women could and did shop of course at Fortnum's. Men with great
> names, famous in every walk of life, who would never have entered an
> ordinary provision shop, went into Fortnum and Mason's as readily as
> into their own club. They ordered all sorts of things – for the Victorians
> lived well and were hearty eaters – caviar, pâté de fois gras, Perigord
> Pies, guava jelly, Spanish hams, boars' heads, truffles, mangoes, Chinois
> and Carlsbad plums – everything was available in this Piccadilly
> emporium.

Today, however, was a very special day for Fortnum's: it was Derby
Day, about which Macqueen-Pope also writes.

> Derby Day in the Victorian Age and Edwardian Era was a test not only of
> the speed and stamina of the picked three-year-old thoroughbred race-
> horses but of the speed and stamina of the staff of Fortnum and Mason's.
> Every man jack of them was on duty and standing by ready at 4 a.m. And
> very shortly afterwards a long unbroken line of coaches, and carriages of
> all kinds, queued up and were duly loaded with the hampers ordered –
> containing the luncheon to withstand the fatigues of race-going and the
> champagne wherewith to salute the winnings or drown the memory of the
> losses on the Turf.
>   That is a sight which nobody will ever see again, that almost endless
> line of coaches and carriages, their bodies shining like the skin of their
> horses, the metal work gleaming in the sun; an outward and visible sign of

the richness and prosperity of the British Empire and the sportsmanship of its people, a sight which could be seen nowhere else in the world except Piccadilly.

Charles Dickens, a regular customer of Fortnum's, put the whole thing into words: 'Well, to be sure, there never was such a Derby Day as this present Derby Day! Never, to Þe sure, were there so many carriages, so many fours, so many twos, so many ones, so many horsemen, so many people who have "come down by rail", so many fine ladies in so many broughams, so many Fortnum and Mason hampers, so much ice and champagne. If I were on the Turf and had a horse to enter for the Derby, I would call it Fortnum and Mason, convinced that with that name he would beat the field. Public opinion would bring him in somehow. Look where I will – in some connection with the carriages, made fast upon the top, or occupying the box or peeping out of a window – I see Fortnum and Mason. And now, Heavens! All the hampers fly wide open and the green Downs burst into a blossom of lobster salad . . . And if one recalls that famous picture by Frith – "Derby Day", the figure of the child acrobat in the foreground is delaying rushing into his father's arms to do his trick – because he is gazing at a footman who is laying out the contents of a hamper – doubtless by Fortnum and Mason . . .'

The other world-famous shop on Tchaikovsky's route was Hatchard's, managed, in those days, by the eminent bookseller A. L. Humphreys. Among his customers were Rudyard Kipling, George Moore, Oscar Wilde, and other leading writers. If Hatchard's did not stock the book they wanted, he could frequently remember where he had seen a copy, and, by the next day, he would have it for them. He supplied entire libraries to the nobility, once meeting a request for the 100 worst books ever written. In the spring of 1893, Cecil Rhodes instructed him to acquire, for the library of his house at Table Mountain, a copy of every book that Gibbon had consulted when writing *The Decline and Fall of the Roman Empire*. This commission was speedily and satisfactorily discharged.

St James's Hall consisted of a music-hall, restaurant, two dining-chambers and kitchens on the ground floor, with a concert hall, seating 2,500, on the first floor. The St James's Restaurant, says Macqueen-Pope, was

. . . a good place for a man to dine alone; if he did not want to remain alone, he would soon find a companion of the opposite sex. No gentleman would take his wife to Jimmy's in the evening but he might take somebody else's wife . . . The ladies one met there were very free from inhibitions – there was little of the so-called Victorian severity and starchiness about them. They were dressed in the full flight of fashion and perhaps a little overdressed too, and, where they could, they made full display of their anatomical charms. Most of the ladies who were said to be 'On the Dilly' liked to go to Jimmy's; to be escorted there, or even casually met there by a gentleman, marked them as successes in their own line of business. There was noise, chatter, laughter, and popping of corks and, one presumes, a good time was had by all.

In the music-hall, Moore and Burgess's Christy Minstrels, with blacked-up faces, performed, year in, year out, to packed houses.

The concert hall, according to Fuller-Maitland, had 'beautiful acoustics', and, in *When Soft Voices Die*, Helen Henschel writes, 'I do not suppose that any concert hall has existed with more perfect acoustics.' However, the hall was by no means impervious to either the gaiety of the diners, the twanging of the minstrels, or the effluvia of the kitchens. George Henschel, in *Musings and Memories*, could recall Joachim pouring forth 'sounds that seem to come straight from heaven', accompanied by a 'distant jingle of castanets and tambourines'. In addition, the seats were uncomfortable; they were, says Henschel, 'long, narrow, worn-out, green-upholstered benches, with the numbers of the seats tied over the straight back with red tape.' The entire building was somewhat curiously designed. Outside doors were deceptive, leading to distant, rather than adjacent, rooms. Memory, not commonsense, was the best guide; otherwise, like Grove in Windsor Castle, one could end up in the kitchens.

Arriving at St James's Hall, Tchaikovsky was introduced to Mackenzie, whom he had not met on his previous visits to London. In *A Musicians's Narrative*, the Scottish composer relates that his first reaction was to consider him 'a spent man'. He came to the unhappy conclusion that 'the weak voice, intense nervousness, and exhaustion after rehearsal, plainly indicated failing health.' As to Tchaikovsky's personality, 'His unaffected modesty, kindly manner and real gratitude for any trifling service rendered, all contributed to the favourable impression made by a lovable man.'

On the morning of Thursday 1 June, Tchaikovsky probably received the second of Stanford's letters.

> 50 Holland Street,
> Kensington, W.
> 31 May, 93

Mon cher Monsieur Tschaikowsky,
  Je vous prie de nous faire l'honneur de déjeuner chez nous à une heure Dimanche prochain (le 4 Juin),
  au revoir

> Bien à vous

> Ch. Stanford.

Maude Hatzfeld remembers her father telling her that, for the second rehearsal, he called on Tchaikovsky at the Dieudonné and escorted him to St James's Hall. He now perceived the composer to be in an extremely agitated condition and accordingly stayed near to him throughout the rehearsal, assisting him, as did Mackenzie, in any way he could. Also at this rehearsal was Henry Wood, who, eight months earlier, had conducted the English première of *Eugene Onegin*. In *My Life in Music*, he writes, 'At the final rehearsal I remember how staggered we were when Tchaikovsky, failing to get the reckless Russian spirit he wanted in the *finale*, eventually obtained it by exclaiming "Vodka – more Vodka!!"'

When the rehearsal was over, Hatzfeld, who calculated that Tchaikovsky's nervousness would probably get even worse as the hour of the concert approached, told him that he would call for him in the evening. The composer, though, said that he had already caused enough trouble and would come over on his own and meet Hatzfeld in the artists' room.

Mackenzie, too, may have been worried about Tchaikovsky and, perhaps in the hope of calming him down and occupying the awkward hours ahead, invited him to meet his wife and daughter for tea that afternoon at his home, at 15 Regents Park Road.

At the Mackenzies', Tchaikovsky wrote out and signed for them the opening of the principal theme from the second movement of the Fourth Symphony. This is displayed in Ernest Markham Lee's *Tchaikovski*, published in 1906. It is accompanied by an explanatory note.

The autograph reproduction of the melody of this canzona is, by the kindness of Sir Alexander Mackenzie, printed opposite this page. Sir Alexander says with regard to it: 'The occasion on which Tchaikovski wrote the autograph (at my house in Regent's Park Road, when he was having tea with us) was when he was in London conducting this same *Fourth Symphony* at the Philharmonic, when I was the official conductor.'

In regard to the second movement of the symphony, Tchaikovsky wrote to Madame von Meck, on 1 March 1878, that it 'expresses another aspect of suffering. This is the wistful melancholy that steals over us in the evening, when, sitting alone, tired after work, we let slip from our hands the book we are reading. A host of memories fills the mind. And it is sad to think that so much is already *past and gone*; and it is pleasant to recall our youth. We regret the past, yet have neither the desire nor the will to start life afresh. We are weary of existence . . .'

The concert was scheduled to begin at 8.00 pm. The occasion was completely sold out. The *Daily News* of the following day, 2 June, sets the scene.

The happy accident that MM. Saint Saëns and Tschaikowsky, as representative musicians, respectively of France and Russia, happen to be passing through London on their way to receive the degree of Doctor of Music at Cambridge, enabled the directors of the Philharmonic Society to secure their services at the concert at St. James's Hall last evening, when a splendid audience, which numbered most of the eminent musicians of the metropolis, assembled to give them a warm greeting. Indeed, so great was the crush that Señor Sarasate had to find a place in a back row under the gallery, while little Koczalski [a child-prodigy pianist], with his father, was in the orchestra.

Sterndale Bennett's overture was the opening work, to be followed by the Rossini aria and Tchaikovsky's Fourth Symphony. Saint-Saëns' concerto and symphonic poem, with the 'Liebestod' intervening, made up the second half.

'Vodka – more Vodka!!' might have been the composer's exhortation to himself when touring abroad; drink was his recipe for survival during the lonely, empty hours preceding a concert. Prior to conducting engagements in Russia, too, there are such diary entries as 'slept restlessly. Preparing myself. Vodka.' The result could be 'drunkenness' or even, with the German première of the Fifth Symphony, '*terrible* drunkenness'. No doubt he fortified himself in this way for the Philharmonic concert, numbing a mind racked by anxiety.

In such condition, it does not seem surprising that the complicated geography of St James's Hall should have defeated him. After a 'futile search' for the appropriate entrance, he presented himself at the box office. On occasions like these, his command of foreign languages almost completely disappeared; when introduced to the Leipzig Gewandhaus Orchestra, his usually excellent German abandoned him, and he stuttered, 'Gentlemen, I cannot speak German, but I am proud that I, with such a . . . such a . . . that is . . . I am proud . . . I cannot . . .' Now, at the box office, his scant English deserted him altogether. 'Tchaikovsky', he informed the cashiers. They, however, assumed he was asking if this was the Tchaikovsky concert. Yes, they said; but it was full; there were no seats left. 'Tchaikovsky', Tchaikovsky repeated, pointing at himself. Correct, they said, but every ticket had gone. This exchange, capable of considerable elaboration, was cut short by the arrival of the vigilant Hatzfeld, who, worried by the composer's absence, had decided to go in search of him. No longer barred from his own concert, Tchaikovsky proceeded to the artists' room. By this time, the programme was on the verge of beginning, but, within the twenty minutes prior to his journey to the rostrum, the composer, with Hatzfeld's encouragement, was once again able to 'conquer' himself. He thus finally stepped before the public with much greater peace of mind; his nervousness was no longer evident. But the audience noticed something else. 'M. Tschaikowsky has somewhat altered in appearance since he last visited these shores. His hair is now quite white', wrote the *Daily Chronicle* correspondent, 'but he wields the baton with undiminished spirit.'

'Last evening's concert should be marked with a red letter in the annals of this Society', said Joseph Bennett in the *Daily Telegraph* of 2 June. Both composers, he reported, were loudly cheered. Saint-Saëns was the recipient of tumultuous applause from the audience, who, 'by five times recalling him after a brilliant performance of the concerto, expressed in manner unmistakeable the cordiality of their feeling towards a musician of whom not France alone but all musical countries are proud.' According to the *Illustrated London News*, 'M. Saint-Saëns was greeted as a friend of many years' standing, and, after he had played his concerto with splendid vigour and *aplomb*, he was treated to one of the loudest and longest ovations that has been witnessed lately in a concert room.'

The Fourth Symphony failed to provoke the same high level of excitement, but was nevertheless applauded at the conclusion of each movement. The critics, on the whole, accorded it a warm welcome, with Joseph Bennett being the most cogently enthusiastic.

The Russian composer brought with him a symphony which, though it has been in print for some years [fifteen years], was new to all save those who make a point of following the development of Sclavonic art – the art that has lately taken such enormous strides, and seems destined to exert the highest influence upon music in general. One movement excepted, Tschaikowsky's Symphony in F minor (No. 4) strikes us as possible only to Sclavonic genius. It would be easy for a master of any other race to write themes like those found in it, seeing there are models to work upon, but only one to the manner born could make such free and full use of the national idiom, and give forth the spirit as well as employ the forms of the national art. If it be asked what in the symphony is characteristic, an answer must indicate the evanescent excitement and more prolonged plaintiveness of Sclavonic music; the iteration and reiteration of short phrases with the monotonous regularity of an Eastern chant; and the fantastic passages of ornament, having an air of improvisation, which come from the same source. In these respects the work can scarcely be said to suggest a European origin. Though its form be that of a Western classic, in manner and spirit it is of the East and of the race which last began to take its way along the route trodden by the march of empires. Need we add that the Symphony, being thus so distinguished, was received with the utmost interest? It was something to find the familiar outlines filled in afresh, and to see that the stubborn elements of national music lent themselves, with readiness and even a certain grace, to the imperative requirements of their new use.

In examining the symphony in detail, Bennett notes 'the exuberance of the first movement with its multiplied themes and large development'; the second movement is 'a masterpiece of plaintive expression'; the third is 'the least remarkable' and least Russian; 'but in the Finale the composer is Russian again – perhaps we should say more Russian than ever.' The work, says Bennett, made a great impression and, 'judging by loud and persistent applause, called forth no feeling save admiration. The composer, who conducted, was cheered again and again.' Writing, a few weeks later, in the July issue of *The Musical Times*, Bennett re-expressed his feelings about the symphony.

The work in question (key, F minor) might with entire propriety be known as the Russian Symphony, since three of its four movements are intensely characteristic in that sense, and idiomatic to a remarkable degree. The exception is, however, the movement which will everywhere meet with the greatest measure of popular favour. A delightfully sportive *pizzicato*, with short episodes for the wind, it went straight to the heart of the audience, who, applauding long and loudly, would have heard it again with pleasure. For the rest, the half-melancholy, half-bizarre features of Eastern art made an interesting study, and came with an agreeable freshness to Western ears, although comprehended, it may be, but in part. Bustling, strenuous, at times extravagant, the first and last movements were more an appeal to the judgment than the emotions; but the *Andantino* came as an expression of pure feeling, and with this the Russian master may fairly be allowed to have best vindicated his country's music. The Symphony met with a very cordial reception – more so than any other work from the same pen, and at its close the composer stood higher than before in English estimation.

Bennett's thoughtful and conscientious attempt to grasp the entirely new idiom of Russian music (which had been so much less apparent in Rubinstein's works), as well as his painstaking reports on the first Bayreuth *Ring* cycle, and many other excellent reviews, like that from Milan on *Falstaff*, show him to be one of the finest critics of the nineteenth century. Klein, too, ranks far above the average critic of the day, and, with the Fourth Symphony, seems to have reached a much better understanding of Tchaikovsky.

M. Tschaikowsky, albeit a less familiar figure [than Saint-Saëns] to English amateurs, is well remembered by those who witnessed his first appearance here under the auspices of this [Philharmonic] Society in 1888. The works then heard were scarcely representative of his genius at its best, but the Symphony in F minor which he conducted the other night may without hesitation be set down as a masterpiece, and, considering that it has been written nearly twenty years, ought certainly to have been heard here before. We reserve a definite opinion upon the first movement, which seems unduly long and over-elaborated. The andante 'in form of a song' is simply beautiful; the *pizzicato* scherzo is a gem of ingenuity and skill without a particle of trickery; and the finale, bar an occasional tempest of sound and fury, is replete with characteristic and energetic spirit. The performance was superb, and M. Tschaikowsky received a well-earned ovation.

Almost all the reviewers were agreed that the symphony's first movement was the least satisfactory, and, here, we can turn to the *Daily Chronicle*.

The opening movement (*moderato con anima*, prefaced by a few bars *andante sostenuto*) is the least effective, but the work – of course, we are recording the impressions derived from a first hearing – improves as it goes on, and the final section is sure to be a favourite wherever heard . . . As will be seen, the symphony does not closely adhere to classic lines, but it is wonderfully inspiriting music. The effect upon the ear might not be the same at a second performance; on the other hand, beauties not perceived last night might come to the surface. The work was capitally played with Mr. Carrodus as leader, and each movement was loudly applauded, the composer being warmly greeted at the close by a very large and fashionable assemblage.

The favourite movements appear to have been the second and third. The *Daily News* reports, 'That the work is not in the form or fashion which the westerns are accustomed to expect in a symphony may be admitted, and indeed the principal subject of the opening movement is a species of waltz, while the finale would probably shock Philharmonic subscribers of the old school. The two middle movements are undoubtedly the best and both are strongly marked by the national characteristics.' The *Standard* also detected the Russianness of the third movement. 'In the delightful *scherzo pizzicato estimato*, the national element is perceptible throughout, and the audience would gladly have heard this movement a second time, but the *encore* was wisely declined.'

There seems generally to have been an attempt on the part of the reviewers to accept the symphony for what it was, and this attitude is typified by the *Morning Post*.

The Sclavonic element is very marked, and it may safely be asserted that no one but a Russian could have written it. The wild, restless tonality, the melancholy nature of the themes, and a certain ruggedness in the method of their development bear the unmistakable *cachet* of the author's nationality. Instinctively the mind wanders away to vast plains covered with their mantles of snow and weird pine forests shaken by the winds. The Symphony is so far constructed upon the usual model that it consists of four movements; but there its orthodoxy ceases. It would have been as well if the composer had supplied a key to his poetical intentions . . . the Symphony is a work of high value, and one that we shall look forward to hearing again.

We may note here that the *Morning Post* speaks of 'the melancholy nature of the themes', and this is echoed by the *Observer*, which finds the work to be 'mostly of a pathetic character'.

For some reviewers, the Russian idiom of the symphony, however superficially attractive, debarred it from consideration as a major work of art. This idea is expressed, for instance, in the *Academy*.

One often reads about the new Russian school, but – in this country at any rate – little is known of it. Among the representatives of that School, Tschaikowsky holds a distinguished place; and yet it is by his works of small calibre, pianoforte pieces, and songs, that he has made a name in this country. The Symphony in F minor will do much to increase his reputation here. The national element in it is strong, but is worked up with consummate art . . . A first hearing leaves one with the idea that the composer had a definite programme in his mind, and that he would have done well to reveal it . . . With subject matter of a more earnest, ambitious character, the composer would probably achieve still higher success. The nature of the thematic material, indeed, prevents one from speaking of this Symphony as a great work, in the sense that those of Schumann and Brahms are great; but it is one of exceeding high merit.

Despite the fact that the symphony's themes were not founded in German *volkslieder*, the *Academy* was prepared to give praise where it was due. Other journals were less charitable. *Musical Opinion* was affronted by the work's 'Scythian savagery and overpowering noise . . . Basing our standard upon classical models, from Haydn to Schumann and Brahms, we can hardly call it a symphony.' In like manner, the *Daily Graphic* identified it as 'an interesting example of what may be called Decadent Music. Neglecting the rules and outlines of symphonic form, the composer is curious in research of novel orchestral combinations, strange rhythms and subtle contrasts. Judged as a symphony the work must be found wanting, but it bristles with a hundred brilliant and clever devices to pique the jaded musical palate. It is like a late Gothic Cathedral, encrusted with ornament and at times almost viciously florid.'

One of the reasons why, earlier, Joseph Bennett suggested that 1 June 1893 should be regarded as a red-letter day in the history of the Philharmonic Society was because of the astonishing playing of the orchestra. George Bernard Shaw also noted the quality of their performance.

We had the orchestra under the command of conductors who, as their own works were in hand, were strongly interested in making the most of the occasion; and the result was instructive.

. . . in the scherzo of Tschaikowsky's symphony, a movement of purely orchestral display, the quality of tone in the *pizzicato* for the strings and in the section for the brass was wonderful. Probably Tschaikowsky could not have achieved such a result anywhere else in the world at equally short notice. But why is it that but for the occasional visits of strangers like Grieg, Tschaikowsky, and Saint-Saëns, we should never know what our best London band can do? Solely, I take it, because the visitors are virtually independent of that impossible body of hardened malversators of our English funds of musical skill, the Philharmonic directors. For their displeasure the distinguished foreign composer does not care a brass farthing: he comes and he instals himself at the rehearsals, making their insufficiency suffice for his own work by prolonging and monopolizing them.

On the other hand, the official conductor is the slave of the directors: if he complains to them they take no notice of his complaints: if he complains to the public, as Mr. Cowen did in desperation, they dismiss him . . .

This season, thanks to the scandal of Mr. Cowen's complaint and dismissal, and to such tweaking of the Philharmonic nose, and tripping up of its heels and unexpected hurling of sharp cornered bricks at its third waistcoat button as those critics who have the Society's interests really at heart can find time for, there has been an improvement . . .

Of Tschaikowsky's symphony apart from its performance I need only say that it is highly characteristic of him. In the first movement, the only one with a distinctly poetic basis, he is, as ever, 'le Byron de nos jours'; and in the later ones, where he is confessedly the orchestral voluptuary, he is Byronic in that too. The notablest merit of the symphony is its freedom from the frightful effeminacy of most modern works of the romantic school. It is worth remarking, too, considering the general prevalence in recent music of restless modulation for modulation's sake, that Tschaikowsky often sticks to the same key rather longer than the freshness of his melodic resources warrants. He also insists upon some of his conceits – for example, that Kentish Fire interlude in the slow movement – more than they sound worth to me; but perhaps fresh young listeners with healthy appetites would not agree with me. The symphony, brilliantly performed, was handsomely received; and neither Saint-Saëns nor Tschaikowsky can complain that they were not made as much of as they deserved, especially Saint-Saëns, who was recalled again and again after playing his G minor concerto in the hope that he would throw in a solo. This, however, he evidently did not understand; and the audience had at last to give over the attempt.

In *Le Figaro*, Johnson rhapsodised on Saint-Saëns' triumph, adding, however, that 'un success semblable était réservé à M. Tschaïkowski.' In conclusion, he observed, 'S'il n'y avait à Londres que des concerts de cet ordre-là, les comptes rendus en seraient agréables, malheureusement il en est rarement ainsi et pour beaucoup il est préférable de garder un silence prudent.'

At 3.00 pm on Friday 2 June, the Polish prodigy Raoul Koczalski, aged eight, gave a piano recital in St James's Hall, performing works by Beethoven, Schubert, Mendelssohn and Chopin, his own *Rhapsodie polonaise*, Op 46(!) and 'October' from *The Seasons*. Tchaikovsky may have been among the audience. 'I have to go to concerts every day, because they come to invite me, and it's awkward to refuse', he told Modest in a letter written the following day. In this instance, it would have been 'awkward to refuse' for two reasons: firstly, Koczalski had attended the Philharmonic Concert, and it would have been discourteous not to go, if invited, to the boy's own recital; secondly, he was playing 'October'. In addition, Tchaikovsky liked children and often went out of his way to help young artists.

On the evening of the same day, 2 June, Saint-Saëns and he were guests at a Philharmonic Society dinner given in their honour at St Stephen's Club, Westminster. 'It was unbelievably chic and elegant', he informed Modest the day afterwards; 'we sat down to table at seven and rose at eleven-thirty. (I am not exaggerating.)'

The club was then situated on the corner of Bridge Street, on the Embankment; it had been founded in 1870 to provide a meeting-place for Conservative Members of Parliament. There was a fine view of the Thames from the upper floors, and an underground passage led directly into the Houses of Parliament. Disraeli is thought to have played an important role in the founding of the club. Primrose Day originated in St Stephen's, when the dining-room tables were decked with flowers on the first anniversary of Disraeli's death. In the following year, 1883, this was extended to decorating his statue in Parliament Square. In 1960, the club's premises were taken over by Parliament and absorbed into the Palace of Westminster. Its new premises are in Queen Anne's Gate.

At the dinner, Tchaikovsky and Saint-Saëns were seated on either side of Francesco Berger. Each, says Berger, was keen to know on what work the other was then engaged, 'and it was most interesting to hear how appreciative and complimentary they were to each other.' Berger hardly touched his meal, 'for I was taking in their words, which had for me the weight of oracular pronouncements.' There was a marked contrast between their voices; Tchaikovsky's was soft and melodious, while Saint-Saëns' was 'loud and very shrill', and he spoke so rapidly that it was sometimes difficult to follow him, the words flashing 'like sparks from the anvil'.

Of course they conversed in French, and very choice French it was. Although they had their Art in common, they were outwardly very different men. Tschaikowsky was the taller of the two, more subdued, less voluble, and – may I say it? – more aristocratic (or more bureaucratic) in manner; Saint-Saëns far more animated, more voluble, with much gesture and vehemence, to emphasise his conversation, and – may I say it? – more democratic in manner.

The two composers had known each other for seventeen years. Their first meeting is recorded by Modest.

In November 1875, Camille Saint-Saëns came to conduct and play some of his works in Moscow. The short, lively man, with his Jewish type of features, attracted Tchaikovsky and fascinated him not only by his wit and original ideas, but also by his masterly knowledge of his art. Tchaikovsky used to say that Saint-Saëns knew how to combine the grace and charm of the French school with the depth and earnestness of the great German masters . . .

During Saint-Saëns' short visit to Moscow a very amusing episode took place. One day the friends discovered they had a great many likes and dislikes in common, not merely in the world of music, but in other respects. In their youth, both had been enthusiastic admirers of the ballet and had often tried to imitate the art of the dancers. This suggested the idea of doing a dance together, and they brought out a little ballet, *Pygmalion and Galatea*, on the stage of the Conservatoire. Saint-Saëns, aged 40, played the part of Galatea most conscientiously, while Tchaikovsky, aged 35, appeared as Pygmalion. Nikolay Rubinstein provided the accompaniment. Unfortunately, apart from the three performers, no spectators witnessed this singular entertainment.

Saint-Saëns liked Tchaikovsky's music, particularly the First Piano Concerto and *Romeo and Juliet*. When Adolf Brodsky visited Paris in 1881 and tried, unsuccessfully, to interest conductors in Tchaikovsky's yet-unplayed Violin Concerto, Saint-Saëns accompanied him at the various auditions. Tchaikovsky, as we have just read, greatly respected Saint-Saëns. *Danse macabre* and *Phaëton* gave him especial pleasure, and he found the Second Piano Concerto 'exceptionally beautiful, fresh, elegant and rich in fascinating detail'.

Mackenzie was also at the dinner. He had met neither Tchaikovsky nor Saint-Saëns before the first rehearsal, two days earlier, but had immediately warmed to both of them. He remarks, in his memoirs, that Saint-Saëns' 'snappy manner of speech, by no means observable in his elegant music, may be best described in his own tongue as "sec".' Tchaikovsky, as recounted, he described as 'a lovable man'.

At the evening's end, these two left St Stephen's together, and

he and I started on a long ramble through the streets until past one o'clock in the morning. I then learned he was neither a perfect Wagnerite nor a devout worshipper at the shrine of Brahms, and gathered that his reception at Vienna had not been a pleasant one. Probably friend Hanslick had been at his courteous tricks again: '*Stinkende Musik*' ['*Musikstücke geben könne die man stinken hört*'] was not a pretty expression to use in connexion with the popular Violin Concerto. He stated to me that the fight for recognition had been a hard one everywhere – but in England.

Without showing discontent or bitterness, the amiable Russian appeared melancholy and lonely; devoid of self-assertion and giving no sign of the passion and force revealed in his music.

Tchaikovsky's gracious suggestion that his fight for recognition in England had not been a hard one is ironical when we remember that, until twenty-hours earlier, none of his symphonies had been heard in London. Nevertheless, his own three appearances in the capital had all been warmly received.

In his contribution to the treasury *In the Days of My Youth*, published in 1901, Mackenzie refers to the years he spent in Florence during the early 1880s and to his friendship, there, with Liszt. 'While I was in Florence I saw a great deal of Liszt, and through him became acquainted with the works of Tschaikowsky, Borodin, and Rimsky-Korsakov, thus being familiar with the Russian school of music long before it became popular in London.' Tchaikovsky would have been surprised to know this. He had always imagined that Liszt, whom he met at Bayreuth in 1876 and in Rome in 1881, 'was not particularly interested in my pieces', as he mentioned to Jurgenson in a letter of 13 July 1892. In turn, he felt that Liszt's works possessed 'more poetical intention than actual creative power, more colour than form – in short, despite their external effectiveness, they lack depth. Liszt is exactly the opposite of Schumann, whose vast creative force is not in harmony with his colourless manner of expression.' He had no doubts about Liszt's genius, though; nor about his stature as a man, considering him to be 'one of the very few great artists who have never known envy (Wagner and, to some extent, Anton Rubinstein owe their success to him; he also did much for Berlioz).' He was shy of meeting the venerable Hungarian master, and, during his lengthy stay in Rome in 1881, made no attempt to contact him; the only time they met was at a concert in Liszt's honour, on 6 December of that year.

Liszt, in fact, had a keen regard for Tchaikovsky and was disappointed, says Arthur Friedheim, then Liszt's secretary, that 'the Russian had not come to see him' when in Rome. Tchaikovsky really had little cause for supposing his fellow Slav was not interested in him. Liszt's *Eugene Onegin* paraphrase, written in 1880, should, alone, have changed his mind; so, too, should a letter from the cellist Wilhelm Fitzenhagen, in the summer of 1879, telling of his successful performance of the *Rococo Variations* at the Wiesbaden Festival and how Liszt had declared, 'At last, here is real music!' Perhaps it was Tchaikovsky's lack of faith in himself that led him to discount Liszt's commendation. Had he been able to read Liszt's correspondence he would undoubtedly and delightedly have altered his opinion. The letters contain several references to him. On 15 November 1876, for instance, in a letter to the Leipzig publisher Constantin Sander, Liszt says, 'The compositions of Tschaikowsky interest me. Some of my pupils here [in Budapest] play his concerto and a number of his other pieces quite excellently. I have also recommended Riedel [a conductor in Leipzig] to include Tschaikowsky's symphony in the programme of the next *Tonkünstler-Versammlung*.'

In passing, we should not forget that Liszt was writing a paraphrase on themes from Mackenzie's *The Troubadour* at the time of his death. Another link between Tchaikovsky and Mackenzie was Florence, where the former composed *The Maid of Orleans* and *The Queen of Spades*, and the latter, the first two *Scottish Rhapsodies* and the celebrated *Pibroch* for violin and orchestra.

At 3.00 pm on Saturday 3 June, Pablo Sarasate gave a concert in St James's Hall; the conductor was Cusins. The works performed were Mozart's Symphony No 40, Beethoven's Violin Concerto, Mackenzie's *Pibroch*, Lalo's *Norwegian Fantasy*, for violin and orchestra, and the overture to *Die Meistersinger*. Sarasate, who was at Thursday's concert 'in a back row under the gallery', probably invited Tchaikovsky to his own concert; perhaps Mackenzie also suggested the idea of going, or Saint-Saëns, who would almost certainly have been there and whose First and Third Violin Concertos and *Introduction et rondo capriccioso* are dedicated to Sarasate.

In a letter of the same day, the composer tells Modest that he has been to Sarasate's concert. 'He is most kind and amiable towards me', he says. The great violinist, we will recall, introduced the *Sérénade mélancholique* to England. Like Saint-Saëns, he habitually stayed at the Dieudonné, and it may possibly be that

Tchaikovsky, Saint-Saëns, Sarasate and Diémer all had rooms there.

In another part of his letter to Modest, the composer mentions that the concert was a success and then adds, 'Of course, this is pleasant enough, but what an infliction London life is during the "season"!'

> ... Last time, I was here in the winter and in the bad weather, so that I got no idea of what the town is really like. The devil knows Paris is a mere village compared to London! Walking in Regent's Street and Hyde Park, one sees so many carriages, so much splendid and luxurious equipment that the eye is fairly dazzled. I have been to afternoon tea at the Embassy with the Ambassador's wife. Our Secretary at the Embassy, Sazonov, is a charming man. What a number of people I see, and how tired I become! In the morning, I suffer terribly from depression and, later, I feel in a kind of daze. I have but one thought: to get it all over ...

The Russian Embassy was at Chesham House, Chesham Place. The wife of the ambassador was Baroness de Staal. Sergei Sazonov, was not, in fact, the secretary, but the junior of the two second secretaries, the senior of whom was N. Boulatzel; the secretary was A. Kroupensky.

Sazonov, a gentle and deeply religious man, served in London for six years before promotion took him elsewhere. Married to the sister of Stolypin's wife, he progressed rapidly and, by 1906, was minister-resident at the Vatican. In 1908, he became assistant minister of Foreign Affairs and, two years later, minister, a post he held until 1916, when he was dismissed by the Tsar and appointed ambassador to Great Britain. On the eve of his departure for London, the Tsar was deposed, and the Provisional Government took power. A year later, he was again made minister of Foreign Affairs, by the short-lived Russian Government at Omsk. After it was crushed by the Bolsheviks in 1920, he managed to escape from Russia and settled in Versailles. He died in Nice in 1927.

It was often said, during the eighties and nineties that the ambassador of the Russian Government lived at Chesham Place, but the ambassadress of the Russian Nation was to be found at Claridge's. The extraordinary woman to whom this referred was Olga Novikov. Just a day younger than Tchaikovsky, born into one of Russia's noblest families and inheriting her mother's good looks, which had once inspired Pushkin, she arrived in London in the 1870s, decided she liked the place and took up residence, dedicating herself, through her writings, to explaining Russia to the English and England to the Russians. She contributed to *The Times*, the *Pall Mall Gazette* and other London newspapers and journals, and became London correspondent for the *Moscow Gazette*. She held public meetings, made her suite at Claridge's a haven for Russian émigrés, won the friendship of Gladstone, Carlyle, Tennyson, Matthew Arnold and Mark Twain, and still found time, each year, to return to Russia for a month or two. Disraeli, whom she disliked, called her 'the M.P. for Russia'. Journalists and writers seeking information about Russia tended to consult her rather than the Russian Embassy. Even the easy-going Baron de Staal, himself, would take a cab over to Claridge's when he occasionally felt it necessary to acquaint himself with some recent development in his Government's policies. 'They never tell me anything until they have definitely decided on doing it', he cheerfully admitted.

In her book *Russian Memories*, Madame Novikov speaks of her love for music. She recalls how Anton and Nikolay Rubinstein and the violinists Wieniawski, Laub and Auer used to come to play at her family home. 'Among other well-known musicians whom I have known in my early years, were Litolff (who, like Thalberg, dedicated a composition to my mother), Ferdinand Hiller, Halevy, Stockhausen, Ole Bull, Madame Pauline Viardot, Liszt, Tchaikovsky and others.' She adds, 'I knew Liszt well in Weimar.'

> Once when he called on me at the Hotel de Russie, I happened to be changing my dress after a long walk. As I began to hurry my toilette, I heard enchanting sounds from my piano below. Judge of my delight to be listening to Liszt's improvisations. Instead, therefore, of hurrying, I prolonged my change of dress to what I considered would be the extremity of my visitor's patience. But I found him friendly and smiling, not in the least annoyed, when I at last entered the room. Indeed, he evidently guessed why I had delayed so long, and was even amused at my little stratagem.

In mentioning the notable Russians who visited her when they came to London, Madame Novikov says, 'Tchaikovsky was also here.' From this, we can infer that he went to see her at Claridge's. Because of her status in the capital and because they already knew each other, it seems likely she may have invited him to one of her special Thursday evening gatherings, which, according to a contemporary journalist, were 'the rendezvous of the light, learning, and wit of London society'. That would have been, from a hostess's point of view, the best time to introduce him to her friends. Such a Thursday would have been 8 June, rather than 1 June, the day of the concert.

The composer's letters do not recount whether he accepted the invitation for luncheon with the Stanfords on Sunday 4 June. But, we have no reason to suppose that he did not attend. Saint-Saëns could well have been a fellow guest. Bruch and Boito were to arrive in the capital during the early part of the following week.

George Henschel's autobiography reveals that Tchaikovsky came to his home at 45 Bedford Gardens, Kensington. The two men first became acquainted when Henschel went to Russia in 1875. 'And it was in Moscow that I first met Tschaikovsky, a most amiable, kind, gentle, modest man, with just that touch of melancholy in his composition which to me seems to be a characteristic of the Russian.'

It is perhaps worth remembering that Henschel conducted the first two performances in England of *1812* and, in addition, the London and American premières of *Marche slave*.

Tschaikovsky, whom I had the pleasure of seeing nearly every day during his short stay in London, seemed to me, though then on the uppermost rung of the ladder of fame, even more inclined to intervals of melancholy than when I had last met him; indeed, one afternoon during a talk about the olden days in Petrograd and Moscow, and the many friends there who were no more, he suddenly got very depressed and, wondering what this world with all its life and strife was made for, expressed his own readiness at any moment to quit it. To my gratification I succeeded in dispelling the clouds that had gathered over his mental vision, and during the rest of the afternoon as well as the dinner in the evening he appeared in the best of spirits.

In *When Soft Voices Die*, his daughter Helen Henschel remembers Tchaikovsky being a 'frequent visitor to our house'. She was not aware of his depressed state.

The melancholy was naturally enough not evident to me as a small child, but the gentleness and kindness were. Nobody could have been more charming than he was. One of my life's minor tragedies is that he wrote me a long letter when he left London, that the wind blew it off the table into the waste-paper basket, and that the housemaid lit my fire with it . . . But I do possess a personal remembrance of Tschaikovsky – the photograph he gave to my mother [the American singer Lillian Bailey], inscribed: 'A Madame L. B. Henschel, de la part de son fervent admirateur, P. Tschaikovsky.'

Tchaikovsky also signed Mrs Henschel's fan. This survives and consists of twenty-four sandalwood sticks on which are eighty signatures, including those of Mark Twain, Henry James, Patti, Melba and Sullivan. Tchaikovsky shares a stick with Longfellow.

On one occasion, when visiting the Henschels, the composer accompanied Henschel in 'None But the Lonely Heart'. Helen Henschel recalled to Dr David Brown many years later that his piano-playing seemed wooden and cold. It is possible that nervousness was the cause.

Stanford had asked Henschel to sing the solo part in the prologue to *Mefistofele* at Cambridge, and, soon after his arrival in London, Boito also called at Bedford Gardens, to ask whether he could be of assistance. Henschel recalls his impressions in his autobiography.

The first impression he made on me, a most agreeable one in every respect, furnished a remarkable illustration of the mystery of heredity and, in the case of the two parents being of different nationalities, of the strange way in which the one sometimes predominates over the other. I had never seen Boito before, nor known anything about him save his opera *Mefistofele*, which I greatly admired as a fine, grandly conceived, sincere work of art. The moment Boito entered my room, accompanied by his London host, our mutual friend Albert Visetti, there appeared before my mind's eye the vision of my old home in Breslau in the days of my youth. Every year during the famous Breslau Wool-fair-week Polish noblemen would come to my father's office and occasionally honour our humble home by staying to the mid-day meal. Those Polish land-owners had always impressed me as the most charming people I had ever seen. Their stately carriage, graceful gestures, refined manners and address, their unfailing politeness and bonhomie had made them appear in my youthful eyes the perfect realization of my idea of a gentleman. And now one of these stood before me in the person of Boito, whose very smile, on shaking my hand, I seemed to have seen long years ago. I could not help telling him my impression, when to my surprise he said, 'Well, this is indeed strange, or perhaps it is not – My mother was a Polish Countess.'

Another musician whom Tchaikovsky appears to have visited was Cowen, then living at 73 Hamilton Terrace. At that time, the English composer was hard at work on his opera *Signa*, which received its première in Milan the following November. Tchaikovsky's visit is alluded to in J. F. Barnett's *Musical Reminiscences and Impressions*.

Tschaikowsky I met two or three times whilst he was in London. The first time in the artists' room at the Philharmonic; again at one of those interesting 'at homes' Frederic Cowen so frequently gave in Hamilton Terrace. Tschaikowsky had a striking personality. He was a finely-built man and held himself so well that he looked quite military in appearance.

John Francis Barnett, then fifty-five, was principally a pianist and teacher, but had also achieved some success as a composer. He had been a fellow student of Grieg and Sullivan at the Leipzig Conservatoire, had seen Berlioz conduct the English première of *Roméo et Juliette*, and had heard Bülow play in time to the footsteps of a latecomer. During one of his own recitals he had looked up to discover Liszt among the audience, and Costa had turned down one of his compositions because, after the Sterndale Bennett affair, Costa had vowed never to conduct anything that had never previously been conducted.

On Monday 5 June, Tchaikovsky received a letter from Jurgenson. Enclosed was another letter, which had been sent to the composer, care of Jurgenson. It had reached Moscow without sufficient stamps. 'I was fined', said Jurgenson. The enclosed letter, written in English, was dated 21 May and bore the address The West Lodge, Downing College, Cambridge.

Dear Sir,

I am permitted by the President of the Cambridge Musical Society to ask you whether when you come to Cambridge in next June you will do me the honour of being my guest. My house will be at your service for as long as you please before and after the musical celebration, but in any case I hope that you will sleep here on the night of June 12th.

I have before now had the pleasure of entertaining Professor Paul Vinogradoff of Moscow who is a great friend of mine and may be known to you.

Hoping to hear that you will come

Believe me

Yours very faithfully

F. W. Maitland.

Tchaikovsky at once replied to this, writing in French and dating his letter, in error, 5 May.

> Sir,
>
> Only at this moment have I received your extremely kind letter addressed to Moscow. I do not know how to express my thanks for the hospitality you offer me, which I accept with the greatest pleasure.
>
> I will be arriving next Monday and will then have the honour of shaking your hand. Meanwhile, please take this as the expression of my deepest gratitude.
>
> With respect,
>
> P. Tschaikovsky.
>
> I beg your forgiveness for replying in French, but unhappily I neither write nor speak English, and I am very much afraid, dear Sir, that it may be disagreeable for you to receive somebody who does not speak your language.

On the same day, Tchaikovsky also sent a reply to Jurgenson.

> I've been here a week. The Philharmonic Society concert has taken place, and I had a real success with the Fourth Symphony.
>
> Life here is absolutely frantic, and I don't have a moment's peace. The lunches and dinners are particularly boring. It's all so ceremonial and boring and long-drawn-out that I practically go numb with boredom. I'm so homesick and tired that I feel like running away, but there's nothing to be done. I have to sit out the torture to the end. The letter you sent on to me is an invitation from a professor to stay at his house in Cambridge. I'm going there on 12 June early in the morning. By the 13th, everything will be over, and I'll hurry away from England.

It now seems apparent that London society, having ignored the composer on his previous two visits, was going to the other extreme by mercilessly lionising him. Brahms's suspicions about the English had been right.

There are grounds for supposing that, on the evening of Tuesday 6 June Tchaikovsky was a guest of the famous painter Lawrence Alma-Tadema, who lived at 17 Grove End Road, St John's Wood. In support of this supposition, we should begin by looking at the following extract from *Chords of Remembrance*, the memoirs of the pianist Mathilde Verne.

This was the period of the great *salons*, when hostesses scorned to seek publicity by sending accounts of their parties to the society column of the daily papers, mentioning royalties and all the titled people present, the clothes they wore, etc.

The most notable reunions of those days took place at Sir Lawrence and Lady Alma Tadema's beautiful house in St. John's Wood, where all the arts met in a lovely setting and brought together people distinguished in every walk of life.

Small wonder that all artists were heard at their very best, for not only were the acoustics in Sir Lawrence's wonderful studio, with its vaulted roof, perfect, but the distinguished hosts were an inspiration in themselves.

It was considered an *entrée* into the musical world of London for foreign musicians to have been heard at one of the celebrated Tuesday evenings . . .

As I write, the memory of one special Tuesday evening comes back to me at which we met Monsieur Paderewski for the first time. Tschaikowsky was present at another when Mademoiselle Yrac (who afterwards married the brother of Eugene Ysaye) and I were asked to play.

Tchaikovsky was in London on three Tuesday evenings: 30 May, 6 June and 13 June. By 30 May, the second day of his visit, few Londoners, apart from Stanford, Berger and Hatzfeld, were likely to have been aware of his arrival in the capital. Social interest in the composer probably did not begin until after the concert on 1 June. Writing to Modest, on 3 June, Tchaikovsky gives details of where he has been: to the Embassy, to the Sarasate concert, to the Philharmonic dinner; but there is no mention of Alma-Tadema. Thenceforth, bemused by the onrush of luncheons, dinners, concerts and parties, he abandons factual reporting, replacing it with a long, low, exhausted *cri de coeur*. Since we will later account for his movements on the evening of 13 June, we are therefore inclined to believe that his visit to Alma-Tadema's took place on 6 June.

In June 1893, Alma-Tadema was at the height of his fame. As we have mentioned earlier, painters now ruled the roost in London social life; Tennyson, Browning and Carlyle were all dead, and Swinburne had withdrawn to his crèche in Putney; of native musicians, probably only Sullivan could challenge the sovereignty of men like Leighton, Millais and Alma-Tadema, and, owing to copyright laws and his addiction to horse-racing and the gaming-table, he was certainly not able to match them in wealth, the touchstone of artistic achievement. Alma-Tadema amused his friends by protesting that he usually earned no more than £10,000 a year. But he was industrious and prolific and, by as early as 1874, could command almost £10,000 for a single canvas. With income tax at threepence in the pound, he was thus exceptionally rich. He was reputed to have spent £70,000 on the house that Tchaikovsky visited, and many people believed that parts of it were paved in gold. Tchaikovsky's invitation may have come via Henschel, a close friend of the painter. Henschel's daughter Helen could remember going there when she was little, and she speaks of the Alma-Tadema mansion in *When Soft Voices Die*.

I can still throw myself back into the atmosphere of Arabian nights splendour and fairy-tale glamour with which my young imagination invested this extraordinary house. It was, quite literally, like nothing on earth, because to enter any of its rooms was apparently to walk into a picture. Lady Tadema's studio, for instance, might have been a perfect Dutch interior by Vermeer or de Hoogh. Tadema's, on the other hand, conjured up visions of all the luxury, the ivory, apes, and peacocks of the Roman civilization with which his art was largely preoccupied.

Looking back upon these, after all, not so desperately distant days, when week after week the studio was crammed with highly intelligent and cultured people from all over the world, acclaiming Tadema as one of the greatest artists of his time, it is strange to realize that most of the present generation [*c*. 1940] have never even heard of him.

I am not in any way qualified to speak of him as an artist, but as a host he was undoubtedly a genius, and the Tadema parties played an important and attractive part in the social life of artistic London for nearly thirty years.

. . . come with me to one of the famous Tuesday evening parties . . . the outer gate being opened by the porter, we walk up a long flower-banked, tiled pathway, on either side of which we are dimly aware of lawns and trees stretching away into the darkness. We reach the front door, an arresting and unusual front door composed of one huge piece of golden-coloured wood beautifully grained, and this admits us into a square lobby, where we are faced by a straight flight of solid *brass* stairs. When I was small, I of course thought they were gold. It is a big formal party to-night, so we are at once taken up these fantastic stairs into Tadema's great studio, to be received by both host and hostess with that particularly comforting charm which convinces each of us that we are the one person needed to ensure the success of the party. Lady Tadema is wearing a dress of flame-coloured brocade, showing up the high-lights in her lovely red-gold hair, and her gentle happy voice is a fitting descant to Tadema's deep, 'So glah . . . d!' with which all his guests so soon became familiar.

A vast room is this studio, its domed roof of silver, its walls of sea-green marble. On a shallow platform stands the piano, the case heavily inlaid with various coloured woods and edged all around with ornaments looking like ivory tear-drops. Inside the lid little oblongs of ivory are inset, and upon these apotheoses of visiting-cards are inscribed the signatures of the artists who have made music in the studio.

What a galaxy! Right back to Clara Schumann, Mme. Essipoff, Sophie Menter, Joachim, Anton Rubinstein, Saint-Saëns, Tschaikovsky, Sarasate, Boïto, and a hundred others . . .

I was too young to have gone to many of the Tademas' dinner-parties, dinners which preceded the Tuesday evenings, and reserved for closely intimate friends or guests much older and very much more distinguished than I. On the occasions when I *was* present I found the atmosphere round the table at the end of the evening parties wholly delightful. Both the dining-room itself and the table were long and narrow, making for intimacy and general conversation, as befitted gatherings so often including many brilliant talkers.

Alma-Tadema was passionately interested in music, and scattered throughout the house were his portraits of men like Joachim, Richter, Henschel and Paderewski. The artist's studio, with its aluminium-plated 'domed roof of silver', had a special alcove for the celebrated piano. This was raised above the level of the rest of the studio, and two steps of glistening brass led up to it. One foot of the piano rested on the main floor; the front pedestals were on a dias. The piano-chair was like a throne, and had a painting by Alma-Tadema on the back. The legs of the piano were made of ivory and rosewood. The body was of oak, but invisible beneath encrustations of ebony, tortoise-shell, mother-of-pearl, brass, ivory and mahogany. A frieze running along the lower edge of the case was inspired by a similar decoration in the Church of St Sophia in Istanbul. The magnificence of the piano was enhanced by being bathed in an astonishing translucence of colour emanating from an upper window fashioned from finely cut Mexican onyx.

This instrument, manufactured by Broadwood in 1878 was world-famous and, in 1885, had been displayed at the International Inventions Exhibition. The lid was lined on the inside with six pieces of parchment arranged to form a design consistent with the overall Byzantine character of the decorations. It was on one of these parchments that Tchaikovsky signed his name. Apart from the signatures mentioned by Helen Henschel, the lid also bore those of Bruch, Melba and Paderewski. There is thus the possibility that Tchaikovsky, Saint-Saëns, Boito and Bruch were all at Alma-Tadema's on the same evening.

In 1927, the piano and chair were acquired by Maple's and put on permanent display. They were destroyed by bombing during the Second World War, the third of Tchaikovsky's signatures perishing with them.

We must now return to Mathilde Verne and the evening at Alma-Tadema's.

> Tschaikowsky's appearance was utterly opposed to the mental picture I had formed of the creator of such passionate and stirring music.
>
> I saw at once that he was painfully shy and retiring, but I imagined that if he took part in any actual musical performance he would lose all self-consciousness and disclose some fire and sparkle, so when he accompanied the great singer Augusta Redeker (Lady Semon), in his own lovely song, 'Nur wer die sehnsucht kennt', I was more than ever astonished at his listless attitude. I can only say that his playing struck me as diffident and unsympathetic.

Augusta Redeker was a successful singer, but, from what we can tell, hardly a great one. Born in Hanover and trained at the Leipzig Conservatoire, she married the throat surgeon Felix Semon in 1879. Tchaikovsky was not the only composer to have accompanied her, as Semon relates in his autobiography.

> During our stay in Rome we visited Franz Liszt. Though he had left the concert stage and had become a priest, he was still as much surrounded by ladies as in the days of his phenomenal career. Tadema, who knew him of old, had paid him a visit, during the last days of our stay and had told him of us. The result was an invitation to call on him. We found the old gentleman very imposing. His stately figure in simple black abbé's attire, with a fine sharp-cut face, an artist's high forehead, eyes full of spirit, long white smoothly-combed hair, was most fascinating. A large circle of enthusiastic admirers, mostly ladies, surrounded him. He received us most kindly. The general conversation was carried on in many languages. After a while Liszt addressed my wife, and said he had heard so much about her beautiful singing from our friend Tadema, would she allow him to hear her voice?

Redeker sang a song by Liszt himself. The accompanist, however, was one of the female admirers, who turned out to be a poor pianist, unsettling Redeker and completely spoiling the performance. 'That was beautiful', exclaimed Liszt when it was over, '*so* beautiful that you must give us an encore to my accompaniment.' This time, Redeker sang excellently.

Liszt's poetic accompaniment was above all praise. The whole company held their breath. I still see Tadema before me, leaning against the wall, his hands folded, his head on his breast, and big tears rolling down his cheeks. When the song had ended, and during the stormy applause, Liszt took my wife's hands in his, and kissed her forehead, thanking her again and again.

As a tailpiece to this section, we must refer again to Mathilde Verne, who relates that her sister Adela, who was also a pianist, met Saint-Saëns while he was in London. After she had been introduced, his first words to her were 'Do you play anything of mine?' 'Yes, the G minor concerto', she eagerly replied. '*Mon Dieu!*' he cried. 'Everyone plays that. Why don't you play my *Africa?*'

At 3.00 pm on Wednesday 7 June, the Russian contralto Alexandra Svyatlovskaya gave a recital at The Grafton Salon, 8 Grafton Street. According to the 13 June edition of *Life*, this was 'an exceedingly interesting affair. M. Tschailowsky [*sic*] was present and several of his compositions were included in the programme.'

Tchaikovsky and Svyatlovskaya were well acquainted. She sang the part of Solokha in the first performance of *Cherevichki*, which the composer conducted in Moscow on 31 January 1887. She also created the role of Filipievna in the English première of *Eugene Onegin*, conducted by Henry Wood in London on 17 October 1892. Tchaikovsky had already met her outside Russia, at a supper-party, in Berlin on 24 February 1889, from which he escorted her home. He admired her singing sufficiently to recommend her to Édouard Colonne in Paris and to František Šubert, director of the National Theatre in Prague. He had originally agreed to accompany her in his songs at her recital, but then decided against it, perhaps as a result of his unsatisfactory performance at Alma-Tadema's and almost certainly because of his growing agitation over the trip to Cambridge.

In *My Life in Music*, Henry Wood, who had met the composer for the first time a week earlier, states that Svyatlovskaya sang a number of Tchaikovsky's songs at the recital, and also some arias from *Eugene Onegin*.

As a matter of fact, Tchaikovsky was to have played for her but he told her he was too nervous. I cannot remember accurately what happened or how I came to play instead, but I do remember being asked to do so, and also have a very faint recollection of receiving a telegram in French which said something like 'Too nervous to play this afternoon; please play for me.' Whether it came from Tchaikovsky himself or his agent [Hatzfeld would probably have written it in English] is more than I can be certain of now. However, I do remember him sitting there with an expression of great sadness on his face. He was – and looked – the man who was to compose the *Pathetic Symphony*. He said very little but bowed with great courtesy every time he was addressed.

On the evening of Thursday 8 June, Alberto Visetti gave a reception at his home, at 14 Trebovir Road, Earl's Court, in honour of Boito, who was staying with him while in London. Visetti had been a contemporary of Boito at the Milan Conservatoire and, for his final exam, composed a cantata to verses by Boito. In 1870, he wrote an opera based on *The Three Musketeers,* the libretto of which was provided by Dumas himself. This work was lost in Paris, before it could be produced, during the hostilities. Visetti then moved to London, eventually becoming Professor of Singing at the Royal College of Music.

Luigi Arditi, who conducted the English première of *Mefistofele,* was a guest and, in his autobiography, observes that, for the occasion, Visetti's wife, 'a charming American lady, decorated her house most lavishly with the costliest flowers according to true American fashion.' The 9 June edition of the *Daily News* refers to this 'splendid reception' and lists the principal guests in the following order: Sullivan, Grove, Cusins, Barnby, Bridge, Saint-Saëns, Tchaikovsky, Garcia, Tosti, Beringer, Goldschmidt, Henschel, Randegger, Ganz, Shakespeare, Littleton. Mancinelli, Bevignani, Albani, Nordica, Ravogli, Palliser, Cole, Mrs Henschel, Redeker, Meislinger, Lennox Browne, Semon, the Duchess of Wellington, the Italian Ambassador, Millais and Leighton. Missing here, is Bruch, who was either unwell, engaged elsewhere, or not yet arrived from Berlin.

Visetti had done Boito proud in assembling such an array of celebrities. In terms of the composer's own work, there was an equally impressive representation. Arditi, we may recall, had also conducted the première of *Inno delle nazioni.* Bevignani conducted the English première of *La gioconda* (also of *Aida* and *Pagliacci,* the second performance in England of *Capriccio italien* and the first Bolshoi *Eugene Onegin*). Mancinelli was to conduct the English première, a year later, of *Falstaff* (and, later still, of *Tosca* and Stanford's *Much Ado*

About Nothing, as well as the American première of *Samson et Dalila*). Albani was an acclaimed Desdemona; Nordica, a famous Gioconda. Ravogli was to be the first English Dame Quickly.

Of the less prominent guests, we may note the inventor of the laryngoscope, Manuel Garcia, a singing teacher and the brother of Malibran and Pauline Viardot, whom Wagner unsuccessfully tried to lure to Bayreuth to coach the cast of the first *Ring*. Tosti was teacher of singing to the royal family. Beringer had been soloist in the first English performance of Brahms's Second Piano Concerto. Goldschmidt was the husband of Jenny Lind. Ganz conducted the London première of the *Fantastic Symphony.* Shakespeare was the singing teacher whose wife failed to persuade Brahms to visit England. Littleton was chairman of Novello's, Boito's English publisher. Lennox Browne was senior surgeon to the Central Throat and Ear Hospital and aural surgeon to the Royal Society of Musicians. His *Voice, Song and Speech,* written in 1883, had, by now, reached its fifteenth edition. He did much to explode the popular theory that Italian air had a beneficial effect on the singing voice, maintaining, 'there was nothing to show that peroxide of hydrogen existed in a greater proportion in the towns and cities of Italy than elsewhere and that, on the contrary, the air in most Italian towns was most insanitary.' The Italian ambassador was Giuseppe Tornielli.

In passing on to Felix Semon, the husband of Augusta Redeker, we come to a considerable figure, who was probably the most famous throat surgeon in Europe. His patients included Patti, Melba, Marchesi, Hauk, Nevada, the de Reskes, Henschel and a galaxy of other stars, as well as Queen Victoria and the Prince of Wales, all of whom, whatever their status in other spheres, obediently responded to his well-known introductory command, 'Open your mouse and breeze qvite qvietly'. Born in 1849, at Gdańsk in Prussia, he was educated in Berlin, Heidelberg and Paris before continuing his research in Vienna, where, in 1874, he began practising as a laryngologist. Because his profession brought him into contact with singers, he was soon mixing in musical circles. In this way, he came to know Brahms.

Brahms of 1874 was a rather small, thick-set man, with a clean-shaven, round face. Only the fine high forehead and the smooth hair combed back, gave an artistic smattering to his appearance. His rather small, piercing, greyish-blue eyes, the somewhat sensual mouth, the lips usually pouted as if about to whistle, and a rather round belly, were not at all artistic. Add to this a sharp, high voice, a markedly North-German accent, and – as his main characteristic – a rare sarcasm in speech and thought, and it will be admitted that the ensemble did not tally with an idealistic conception of the personality of the composer.

Alas, that sarcasm! Undoubtedly by nature, Brahms was kind-hearted, but he was a 'rough diamond'. Mordant irony had become his second nature, and when the devil was in him, he spared his friends as little as strangers. Whether he was deficient in observing how cruelly he sometimes hurt people; whether he experienced a grim pleasure in chaffing and torturing others; or whether he only wished to incite opposition – I cannot say. But the fact was undeniable . . .

Brahms, says Semon, did not 'wax enthusiastic' about any of his contemporaries, except Dvořák. Rubinstein, for instance, was simply 'a travelling virtuoso'. Nor, unlike Schumann, Berlioz, Liszt and Tchaikovsky, did he encourage his juniors. Semon was once present when a young Viennese musician brought Brahms one of his compositions that had just been published. 'How beautiful, how very beautiful!' remarked Brahms, to the young man's joy. 'It is the most beautiful title-page I have seen for a long time! How sensible! How tasteful!'

In 1875, Semon moved to London, the ideal city in which to practise laryngology. Singers poured into the English capital from all over the world and often had lengthy engagements. The season was strain enough in itself, but there were, in addition, Costa and the fog. Using his all-powerful position to purposeful effect, the obdurate conductor had stood out against the internationally adopted *Diapason normal* of 1859, with its fixed pitch of 435 vibrations, committing London – and, thereby, the rest of England – to the retention of a more brilliant, but taxing, 458. This took its toll on vocalists until 1895, when England at last reduced to 435. The higher pitch was also inconvenient to instrumentalists; Joachim, for instance, found it necessary to start screwing up his violin two months before coming to London, to avoid damaging it by a sudden change. Joachim took his English appearances very seriously. 'At luncheon in Stanford's rooms in Trinity, Cambridge, about 1876,' Edward Lyttelton recalls in *Memories and Hopes,* the violinist mentioned 'that in avoiding the ugly scraping noise when the wood of the bow presses on the strings of the violin in moments of excitement, he had to be far more careful in England than at home. "In Berlin they do not mind; but your ears in England are more sensitive."'

Semon quickly made his mark in England, producing a number of important papers on laryngology. He gained world interest in 1878, when he challenged Lord Lister's decision to remove an innocent growth from the larynx by external operation, suggesting that it could have been taken out internally with the aid of a laryngoscope. In 1886, he propounded the theory that thyrotomy should not be undertaken for cancer of the larynx. Soon afterwards, he formulated the highly important 'Semon's Law', which states that 'in all progressive organic lesions of the centres and trunks of the motor laryngeal nerves, the abductors of the vocal cords succumb much earlier than the adductors.' His subsequent research led to the thyroid treatment of myxoedema.

'I do not know any profession that shows itself so strangely selfish, particularly towards musical advisers, as that of vocalists', Semon wrote in his autobiography. 'As a rule they only think of themselves; every time they get stage fright, they develop vocal symptoms; they are self-important, and it never occurs to them that a physician may have other duties. They besiege him at all possible and impossible hours, they are indignant when they are not at once admitted, and, usually, they ultimately disappear without paying their fees.' Semon may have married a singer, but he was otherwise not attracted to them. His friends included Browning, George Lewes, du Maurier, Olga Novikov, Leighton, Millais, Alma-Tadema, Herkomer, Bülow, Joachim, Richter and Hallé. But, above all these, he valued Rubinstein: 'his personality towered above all my intimates . . . He was so irresistible in his charm that ladies pardoned his broad jokes . . . He was genuinely indifferent to his triumphs as a *virtuoso*, but in his heart lay the deep sorrow that his talents as a composer were not appreciated.' We find this admiration echoed in the words of Rubinstein's best known pupil, who may perhaps have conversed with Semon at the reception. Rubinstein, he told the German journalist Eugen Zabel in June 1892, was 'a man of rare nobility, frank, loyal, generous, incapable of petty and vulgar sentiments, clear and right-minded, of infinite goodness – in fact, a man who towers far above the common herd . . . Rubinstein's personality shines before me like a clear guiding star.'

Visetti was fortunate to have Sullivan at his reception, the foremost of British musicians. Yet, in a deeper sense, Sullivan was lucky to be there, for, a year earlier, in Monte Carlo, he had come perilously close to death. His recurrent kidney trouble had developed alarmingly, and it was generally believed that he was dying. The Queen telegraphed for news of him; the Prince of Wales dispatched a surgeon to his bedside. The composer himself was convinced that the end was approaching and 'arranged his affairs', wrote Herbert Sullivan in his biography of his uncle, 'with the care and detail of one who knew that he had finished with the world . . . A fresh paroxysm of agony ensued, and those by the bedside believed it must be the last. Then his nephew and the servants carried him from his bed and put him in a hot bath, an action that saved his life.' Sullivan and Boito may have formed a friendship during the Italian composer's visit to London; the following December, Boito sent Sullivan a New Year present, which was a copy of *Mefistofele* inscribed 'A l'illustre Auteur de The Golden Legend.'

At Visetti's, Boito was assuredly a musician among musicians, but he was hardly a poet among poets, or, indeed, among writers of any sort. The painters now held sway, and not just in the persons of Leighton, Millais and Alma-Tadema. They had strength in depth, too, with such imposing figures as Watts, Burne-Jones and Herkomer. Their wealth added to the aura. When, in his autobiography, Trollope meticulously and touchingly calculated his literary earnings over thirty years to have been £68,959 17s 5d, he was simply doing his best to convince his contemporaries that he had worked hard and achieved success in the world. But, at the height of his fame, he could command no more than £3,000 for a novel. Millais could earn £40,000 in a single year.

Celebrating his sixty-fourth birthday on the day of the reception, Sir John Millais had been a baronet since 1885. He was made an officer of the *Légion d'honneur* in 1878 and received an Oxford doctorate in 1880. In 1882, he was elected a foreign associate of the *Académie des Beaux Arts,* in preference to Liszt. In the same year, he was awarded the German order, *Pour le mérite,* four years ahead of Verdi and Brahms. Reproductions of his paintings sold by the million throughout the world. Among those who sat for him were Gladstone (three times), Disraeli, Cardinal Newman, Tennyson, Carlyle, Sullivan and Irving. He appealed to the masses, yet was equally admired by men as shrewd as W. S. Gilbert, Henry James and Mark Twain.

Millais adored music. 'Those who knew him best knew that second to his Art came the sister Art of music', wrote Alice Millais in her brother's biography of their father; 'an inherited taste and a fine musical ear developed in him surprising discrimination and love of

music, and made music at all times a necessity for him . . . He heard
and knew nearly all the great singers, executants, composers of his
generation.' Rubinstein, Sullivan, Joachim, Hallé and Henschel
were often his guests; Wagner called on him during his visit to
London in 1877. Millais knew a great deal about music and frequently went to Manns's concerts at the Crystal Palace. Of modern composers, his favourites were Brahms, Grieg, Bizet, Massenet, Sullivan
and Parry.

Even the remarkable Millais was overshadowed by Sir Frederic
Leighton, the compleat Victorian superman. Heroically built, roman-
tically bearded, majestically handsome, he gave every appearance of
having just descended from Mount Olympus. Painter, sculptor and
architect, he had been everywhere, seen everything, met everybody.
He spoke perfect French, German, Italian and Spanish. This
included the dialects of these languages; when in Carrara, selecting
marble, he would chat with the quarrymen in Tuscan. He also knew
Russian and an assortment of Eastern tongues. Browning once heard
him talking to his Romanian manservant in what he presumed must
be Romanian. He had a vast knowledge of Greek and Roman literature; he was a brilliant orator, a charming conversationalist and a
superb dancer. 'And he paints a little, too, I believe', remarked
Whistler drily to a woman who was brightly listing Leighton's accomplishments.

The first painting he submitted to the Royal Academy was purchased by Queen Victoria for £600 and hung in Buckingham Palace.
His career simply moved on from there. Before reaching thirty, he
was mixing easily and naturally with people like Rossini, Liszt,
Pauline Viardot, Rubinstein, Thackeray and the Brownings. At
thirty-eight, he became president of the Royal Academy, was
knighted and served as president of the international jury of painting
at the Paris Exhibition. During the following year, he received
honorary doctorates from both Oxford and Cambridge. Over the
next decade, he was made honorary member of academies in Rome,
Florence, Turin, Genoa, Berlin, Vienna, Brussels and Antwerp. In
1886, he was created a commander of the Order of King Leopold of
Belgium; in 1887, he was awarded the German order, *Pour le mérite;*
in 1889, he became a commander of the *Légion d'honneur.* As a sculpt-
or, he won the Gold Medal at the Paris Salon of 1885. In 1894, he
received the Gold Medal of the Royal Institute of British Architects.
In 1896, he was raised to the peerage.

Leighton's house, at 12 Holland Park Road, was so magnificent that Alma-Tadema's dwindled into insignificance by comparison. Its centrepiece was a huge Arab hall, over the entrance to which were inscribed, in Arabic, five lines from the Koran. In the middle of the hall was a pool, from which rose a single jet of water. High above, was a gilded dome, with eight little arched windows of exquisite stained glass. The floor was of black and white marble; the columns were of white marble, with green bases, and their richly carved capitals supported the arches of alcoves, in which were placed deep-cushioned divans beneath windows shuttered with meshrabiyehs from Cairo. The walls were decorated with tiles from Rhodes, Damascus and Persia. The hall was filled with the most beautiful pots and vases and other rare ornaments made from bronze, copper, ivory and alabaster. In the other rooms – too many and detailed to describe here – hung paintings by artists of all periods, including canvases by Tintoretto, Gainsborough, Corot and Constable. Each room abounded in flowers and priceless carpets, and each contained some attraction: a massive stuffed peacock, for instance, or casts of the frieze on the Parthenon.

Leighton, too, loved music. As a student in Rome, he wrote to his mother, 'How I yearn for music, which I never hear in the land best adapted to foster it; music, that humanises the soul, that calls forth all that is refined and elevated and glowing and impassioned in one's breast, and without which the very lake of one's heart ("il lago del cuore," Dante) stagnates and is congealed. I express myself extravagantly, but my words flow from my heart.' He had an excellent singing voice. When he first went to Italy, he hoped it would improve, and was disappointed to find it 'instead of strengthening in an Italian climate, getting, if possible, weaker than it was.' His favourite composer was Mozart. He was interested in modern music and visited Bayreuth, but he preferred the Viennese masters.

His musical evenings were more formal than Alma-Tadema's, and his guests were fewer and more carefully selected. They were rewarded with the most sumptuous banquets of the choicest food and wine. On one occasion, the wine was altogether too choice for Chorley, who, says Frederick Lehmann, became 'very wrong and tottery'. After dinner, a full-scale chamber concert would be given, in which Joachim and Hallé might play Beethoven sonatas. Among other musicians who performed at Leighton's were Rubinstein, Piatti, Pauline Viardot and Henschel. These recitals were listened to in complete silence; unlike so many private musical gatherings in

London, they were not intended as a background to conversation. Stanford was one of Leighton's keenest admirers.

As a figure-head, Leighton was unsurpassable. During his Presidency I sat next Burne Jones at an Academy dinner, and B J burst out suddenly, 'Look at him! Look at Jupiter Olympus! Who on earth can ever succeed him?' [Millais did] I sometimes wonder that it never entered into the head even of the unimaginative governments of this country to follow the precedent of Rubens and make him an ambassador. He had all the equipment for such a post at his fingers' ends; spoke German, French and Italian like a native, even so far as to be an adept at foreign slang, and was a born diplomat with an iron hand in his velvet glove. His death was almost as great a loss to the art of music as to his own. His active sympathy with every musician of high aim and sincerity of purpose brought together the two professions in closer relations than they had ever experienced before. He set thereby an example which was followed by many of his brethren to the mutual advantage of both branches of the artistic world.

When Leighton died, in 1896, Swinburne wrote an ode in his honour. As befitted a universal man, the pall-bearers at his funeral included not only the painter Millais, but the physician Lister, the musician Mackenzie and the historian Lecky.

At 4.00 pm on Friday 9 June, the first orchestral rehearsal for the Cambridge concert took place at the Royal College of Music, in Kensington Gore. (This building now houses the Royal College of Organists.)

Tchaikovsky also visited the Royal Academy of Music, in Tenterden Street, off Hanover Square. Mackenzie writes: 'I fear to have unwittingly provided an uncomfortable hour for him when, honouring the R.A.M. by a quite unexpected visit at a time when I happened to be exceptionally busy, I placed the baton in his hand and called upon a student to play his *B Flat Minor Concerto* at an orchestral practice.' Writing thirty-four years after the event, Mackenzie may not have been correct about the unexpectedness of the call. As principal of the Royal Academy, he may well have persuaded Tchaikovsky to come at a prearranged hour and then prepared his students in the concerto, a work that was not yet on their syllabus.

The visit may well have followed (or preceded) a photographic session with Herbert Barraud, in Oxford Street, where the composer sat for his portrait while in London.

On the evening of 9 June, Tchaikovsky went to the Stanfords' soirée. Stanford refers, in his *Pages from an Unwritten Diary*, to this occasion, at which the other three graduands were also present.

I was able to give this European quartet a hearing of some of the best madrigals and part-songs of the English school, which the Magpie Minstrels, conducted by their founder Mr. Lionel Benson, sang admirably in the garden of my house in London. The evening was none too cold for any of the performers, but even so was rather trying to the draught-fearing Bruch, who looked like an Arctic explorer, having armed himself with goloshes, a waterproof wideawake and a thick mackintosh to combat the rigours of an English June.

In fact, the weather had been perfect over the last fortnight, and, as far as one can tell, the temperature on Friday evening would have been around 70°F. However, on 29 May, Joachim had written to Bruch, 'I very much regret to hear that you have been suffering from influenza for such a long time.' Perhaps Bruch was taking no chances.

Stanford's garden was surrounded by tall trees. It rose sharply in the direction of Notting Hill and, at the end, had been levelled into a platform, at almost the same height as the first floor, from which, perhaps, Geraldine and Guy were surveying the scene in their pyjamas. The guests would have sat outside the drawing-room, while the singers would have been on the platform.

Formed in 1886, the Magpie Minstrels originally numbered 80, but, by 1893, they were up to 150. They sang only for charity and tended to draw their members from the upper reaches of society. In June 1893, they included such people as the Marchioness of Lorne (Princess Louise, the fourth daughter of the Queen), Viscountess Folkestone, Alfred Scott-Gatty (York Herald of the College of Arms), Alice Millais, Gerard Cobb, Alfred Lyttelton (the current English tennis champion), Lady Mary Lygon and the Hon H. W. Hepburn-Stuart-Forbes-Trefusis. Every year, they gave a special gala concert in London, and, in 1893, this was held at the Princes' Hall on 22 June, a fortnight after their evening at 50 Holland Street. Among the pieces they performed at the concert were Wilbye's 'Sweet Honey-Sucking Bees,' Linley's 'Let Me, Careless and Undying', Leslie's 'Thine Eyes So Bright', Somervell's 'O, My Sweet Sweeting', Stanford's 'The Knight's Tomb' and 'Sing, Heigh Ho', and works by Sweelinck, Brahms and Henschel. It would not be surprising if some of these songs were included in the programme on 9 June.

Harry Plunket Greene, who was to be a soloist at the gala concert, was also at the soirée. Another guest, he says, commented on the striking contrast between Tchaikovsky and Bruch: the first looked like 'an ambassador and the other like a store-keeper from the Middle West'. Poor Bruch never seemed to excite enthusiasm in anybody. When Edward Dent once asked whether it would be a good idea for him to study with Bruch, Stanford replied, 'I wouldn't wish me worst enemy to go to Max Bruch!'

On Saturday 10 June, Tchaikovsky wrote again to Modest.

This is an infernal life. Not one pleasant moment: perpetual agitation, dread, homesickness, fatigue. However, the hour of liberation is at hand. Besides which I must say I find many excellent folks here, who show me every kind of attention. All the doctors designate have now arrived, except Grieg, who is too ill. Next to Saint-Saëns, Boito appeals to me most. Bruch is a most sickeningly arrogant figure. I go to Cambridge the day after tomorrow and will not be staying at a hotel, but in a flat set aside for me in the house of Dr. Maitland, who has written me a very kind letter of invitation. I'll be there only one night. On the day of our arrival, there will be a concert at 2.30 and a dinner, and, on the following day, the ceremony. By 4.00, it will all be over.

Certain details in this letter make it clear that Tchaikovsky had been asking Stanford about Maitland and the Cambridge arrangements. His anxiety was probably only heightened by the recognition that, in one way or another, the sublime Saint-Saëns, the smug Bruch, and the amused and detached Boito were actually looking forward to the ordeal.

Berger's fifty-ninth birthday fell on Saturday 10 June, and there is the possibility that he invited Tchaikovsky for the occasion. He says, in his *Reminiscences,* that the composer came to dinner during this visit to London, but he gives no date. Tchaikovsky begged him not to make it a dinner-party, just a normal family meal, without evening dress.

Accordingly we were only four: Madame Berger, myself, the Composer, and one young lady (a talented Pupil of mine, Phoebe Hart, who has since distinguished herself by writing some very clever 'Monologues', published in various magazines).
    Like most foreigners, Tschaikowsky was fond of English food, cooked English fashion, so our dinner consisted mainly of such. He told us that before he came as a Composer of Music he had once paid a flying visit to this country in another capacity. His conversation, carried on in French

and German (for I do not speak Russian), was easy without being brilliant, and in all he said there was apparent the modest, gentle spirit which was so characteristic of the man. I noticed on this and other occasions that he never spoke of 'politics', and if in the course of conversation that topic cropped up, he would remark that 'Music and Art generally were fit matters for Musicians to discuss — not politics.'

Before leaving London he made a point of calling in York Street and leaving his card for my wife.

Towards the end of his second week in the capital, Tchaikovsky received the following letter, written in German and dated 7 June.

Deeply Esteemed Mr. Tschaikowsky,

100, 000, 000, 000, 000, 000, 000, 000, 300, 050, 000, 039, 000, 008, 005, 400 thanks for the beautiful photograph of yourself! It's truly kind of you.

You say, as Rubinstein has put it: 'I write a better symphony than a letter'? Well, in that case, please be kind enough to write me a symphony, ha, ha! May I hope that you will dine with me this coming Sunday at 7.00 (at *Monico, upstairs,* as before).

Please write to me only: YES (or NO) on the card (enclosed). Naturally, this will be YES, and so I am expecting you without fail – Sunday at 7.00 in Monico.

With the kind regards of your obedient servant,

Frits Hartvigson.

Hartvigson, by now a professor at the Royal Academy of Music, gave the second performance in England of the First Piano Concerto, in March 1877; a month later, on 25 April 1877, Tchaikovsky wrote to him, 'I am endlessly grateful, dear Hartvigson, for the honour you've shown me in playing my concerto. . . . I have always admired you, and I like the way you play very much, full of courage, energy and verve, and full, too, of poetry.' Earlier, in the 19 December 1873 issue of *Russian News,* reviewing a Hartvigson recital in Moscow, the composer described him as one of the finest pianists in Europe. 'His technique is faultless; he also has remarkable strength of tone and the most elegant phrasing.' Hartvigson may have renewed his acquaintance with Tchaikovsky when the latter visited the RAM; indeed, he may have coached the student who played the concerto. We know from a diary entry of two years earlier that Tchaikovsky was apt to confuse Hartvigson with Dannreuther, who was soloist in the English première. Hartvigson's letter tells us that the two had already dined

at Monico, near Piccadilly, at 46 Regent Street, but we do not know
whether they met there again on Sunday 11 June. For information on
that restaurant, we can do no better than turn to The Dwarf of Blood.

> I went to the Monico and interviewed the manager, Signor Giulio C.
> Nobile, a gentleman of stalwart figure, with a pleasant smile, and a small,
> but carefully-tended moustache . . .
> 'We have five minutes to spare, Signor Nobile,' I said, 'and while they
> are putting the *hors-d'oeuvre* on the table, will you take us round the house
> and show us the different rooms?' . . .
> First we went into a great hall on the first floor, where a smoking-
> concert was in progress, and thunders of applause were greeting a gentle-
> man in evening dress who had just concluded a song. 'It is someone going
> abroad, and they are giving him a send-off,' was Mr. Nobile's explanation.
> Next we went down to the ground-floor through a hall, where people were
> sitting at little round-topped tables drinking various beverages, and down
> some steps into a German beer saloon, with pigmies and other strange
> creatures painted on the walls. Up again to the first floor, through a long
> grill-room with little white-clothed tables in four rows, then a peep into a
> restaurant, and a flight in the lift up to the second floor, where solemn
> gentlemen in black were eating a dinner of ceremony in a very pretty
> saloon with an Egyptian room as a reception-room next door. Our five
> minutes were over, we had seen most of the big rooms of the house, and,
> descending, we took our places at a table by one of the windows in the
> renaissance Saloon on the first floor.

During the two weeks of Tchaikovsky's sojourn in the capital, more
than a hundred concerts took place. The *Daily News* of 2 June commented on this profusion of music.

> We are informed by somebody who has taken the trouble to count, that
> next week upwards of ninety concerts and other musical performances are
> announced in London, the list of course including certain semi-public
> affairs in clubs, private drawing rooms, pianoforte saloons, and other
> places for which tickets are openly sold by the librarians. Singers and
> players of various degrees of merit are still pouring in upon us from the
> provinces and abroad, and, despite the outcry about hard times and the
> general scarcity of money, the present bids fair to be the busiest musical
> June on record. The absurdity of so wholesale an invasion of London at a
> time when music is placed in serious competition with private entertain-
> ments and social functions has frequently been pointed out, but quite
> without avail. Although concert givers ought to know by experience that
> not half of them can possibly make their expenses, nor one fourth obtain
> that newspaper recognition of their merits which they might reasonably

claim at a less pressing period of the year, they come here from mid May to mid July in greater numbers than ever. One reason of course may be found in the fact the London season occurs in the months during which musical performances are suspended in the country, and in the leading capitals of Europe. The winter is the happy hunting time of the provincial and Continental vocalist or virtuoso. A portion of his (or her) vacation might as well be spent in the English metropolis as anywhere else, for there is always an off chance of a London success which may increase the reputation elsewhere.

The *Saturday Review* of 24 June makes similar observations.

During the last six weeks concerts have been given at an average of nearly fifty a week. It is hard to account for the folly of artists who persist in coming forward at a time of year when it is almost impossible for their claims to be properly considered. The operatic performances have alone been almost enough to occupy the limited space usually allowed by newspaper editors for musical notices, and even if a critic were allowed unlimited license as to the length of his 'copy', it would be a physical impossibility for one man to attend all the performances to which he is invited.

Principal among the concerts to which we have not already alluded were one conducted by Henschel, on 30 May; another, conducted by Richter, on 5 June; and Sarasate's second concert, on 10 June, which was attended by Saint-Saëns. These were all held at St James's Hall and were concerts to which Tchaikovsky might well have gone. Henschel, Richter and Sarasate had each given first performances in England of his pieces.

Operas staged during the composer's visit included *Tannhäuser, Lohengrin, Faust, Roméo et Juliette, Les Pêcheurs de perles, Carmen, La Juive, Cavalleria rusticana, Pagliacci, La favorita* and *Orfeo ed Euridice.* Mascagni and Leoncavallo, who went to the Derby, for the premières of *I Rantzau* and *Pagliacci.* Melba, Albani, Calvé and Edouard de Reske were appearing at Covent Garden, and Patti gave a recital at St James's Hall.

Among notable theatrical productions were *A Woman of No Importance,* at the Haymarket, with Beerbohm Tree; *The Second Mrs Tanqueray,* at St James's, with Mrs Patrick Campbell; *Charley's Aunt,* at the Globe; *Becket* and *The Bells,* at the Lyceum, with Irving and Ellen Terry. At the Lyric, could be seen Eleonora Duse in *Antony and Cleopatra, La Dame aux camélias, Cavalleria rusticana* and *La locandièra.* Stanford may have suggested that Tchaikovsky should see *Becket.*

Boito presumably visited the Lyric, for he and the beautiful Duse, were lovers; it was his translation of *Antony and Cleopatra*, made specially for her, that she used in her performances.

Thomas Hardy, who was the same age as Tchaikovsky and still not widely recognised, made one of his infrequent trips to London during the fortnight that the composer was in town; there is no record of their having met but Tchaikovsky and Grieg were among Hardy's favourite composers. When he met Grieg in May 1906, he remarked that Wagner's music suggested to him wind and rain whistling through the trees. 'I would rather have the wind and rain', said Grieg. While in London, the novelist went to the Opera Comique for performances of *Hedda Gabler, Rosmersholm* and *The Master Builder*, and was deeply moved by all three. London was having its first taste of Ibsen and did not particularly relish the experience. The *Observer* found *The Master Builder* almost impossible to digest, owing to wether 'its profundity or its craziness'.

In lighter vein, George Grossmith was at the Shaftesbury; Arthur Roberts at the Gaiety; Eugene Stratton at the London Pavilion; Dan Leno and Vesta Tilley at the Tivoli; Marie Lloyd at the Oxford; Little Tich at the Royal, Holborn.

London was at the height of the season. Thousands of banquets, dinners, luncheons, receptions, soirées and parties were crammed into each week. Men like the Prince of Wales, Gladstone and Leighton were in perpetual motion, their status dictating that they attend function after function after function. For the general public, too, there were myriad entertainments: the Derby, on 31 May; The Oaks, on 2 June; the Trooping of the Colours, on 3 June . . . One could go to the Royal Military Tournament, to the Earl's Court Exhibition of Gardening and Forestry, and, at the Royal Aquarium, to the Great Bull Dog Show – 'Absolutely the Largest Ever Held'. Or one could venture out to the Crystal Palace to ogle

The Famous Amazons, Natives of Dahomey, A Regiment of Women Warriors, captured in Dahomey by the French Army under the command of General Dodds, the greatest and most thrilling novelty to be seen in England during the season of 1893. Fighting women, with their black shining arms and shoulders, their naked feet with anklets of the cowrie shells which form their coinage, their sinewy strength, and their dexterity in the use of the arms they have borne in various engagements against the French in the recent campaign.

CHAPTER 9

CAMBRIDGE

We do not know which train Tchaikovsky took to Cambridge on the morning of Monday 12 June. He had the choice of two stations: King's Cross and Liverpool Street. From King's Cross, the journey lasted about ninety minutes; from Liverpool Street, approximately eight minutes less. King's Cross, however, was much nearer to the Dieudonné, and was the station normally favoured by university people travelling to and from the West End, and Stanford would no doubt have recommended it. The first-class fare was 8s 9d.

The final rehearsal, in the Guildhall, began at 10.30 am. If it followed the order of the concert – Bruch, Saint-Saëns, Boito, Tchaikovsky, Stanford – there was probably no need for Tchaikovsky to appear until around 11.45. The 8.45 from King's Cross, reaching Cambridge at 10.12, might satisfactorily have suited his purpose, giving him time to call on Maitland before going on to the Guildhall.

With so many people travelling to Cambridge that morning, it is hardly surprising that Tchaikovsky should encounter on the train somebody whom he already knew. This proved to be Herman Klein, who had been introduced to the composer at the end of the Philharmonic concert, on which occasion, says Klein in *Musicians and Mummers*, Tchaikovsky confessed that he had been as nervous as a schoolgirl, particularly since he had feared the Fourth Symphony would be too modern for the traditionally conservative Philharmonic audience. Klein left two descriptions of their meeting on the train. The first appeared in the *Sunday Times* of 12 November 1893; the second, in *Thirty Years of Musical Life in London*, published a decade later. The second account appears to have been written without reference to the first, and each contains a certain amount of information not present in the other. For the sake of convenience, these reports are here blended into one, retaining Klein's own words.

> By a happy chance I travelled down to Cambridge in the same carriage with Tschaikowsky. I was quite alone in the compartment until the train

was actually starting, when the door opened and an elderly gentleman was unceremoniously lifted in, his luggage being bundled in after him by the porters. A glance told me who it was. I offered my assistance, and, after he had recovered his breath, the master [a word used only in the second account] told me he recollected that I had been presented to him one night at the Philharmonic. Then followed an hour's delightful conversation. It was one of the pleasantest hours I ever spent in the company of a celebrated musician.

Tschaikowsky chatted freely about music in Russia. He thought the development of the past twenty-five years had been phenomenal. He attributed it, first, to the intense musical feeling of the people which was now coming to the surface; secondly, to the extraordinary wealth and characteristic beauty of the national melodies or folk-songs; and, thirdly, to the splendid work done by the great teaching institutions at St. Petersburg and Moscow. He spoke particularly of his own Conservatory at Moscow, and begged that if I ever went to that city I would not fail to pay him a visit. He then put some questions about England and inquired especially as to the systems of management and teaching pursued at the Royal Academy and the Royal College. I duly explained, and also gave him some information concerning the Guildhall School of Music and its three thousand students. It surprised him to hear that London possessed such a gigantic musical institution. 'I don't know,' he added, 'whether to consider England an "unmusical" nation or not. Sometimes I think one thing, sometimes another. But it is certain that you have audiences for music of every class, and it appears to me probable that before long the larger section of your public will support the best class only.'

The last person he wished to speak of was Tschaikowsky, but when he found that the subject could not be altogether avoided, he ventured to express some curiosity as to the manner in which his opera, 'Eugeny Onégin', had really been performed here and asked me to what I attributed its failure – the music, the libretto, the performance, or what? I replied, without flattery, that it was certainly not the music. It might have been due in some measure to the lack of dramatic fibre in the story, and in a large degree to the inefficiency of the interpretation and the unsuitability of the locale. 'Remember,' I went on, 'that Pushkin's poem is not known in this country, and that in opera we like a definite dénoument, not an ending where the hero goes out at one door and the heroine at another. As to the performance, the only figure in it that lives distinctly and pleasantly in my memory is Eugene Oudin's superb embodiment of *Onégin*.'

'Then I must not wonder,' he replied, 'that it was not a success. The subject naturally could not appeal to English audiences as it does to Russian, and only a very first-rate performance would have given it a chance. I have heard Oudin, and I am sure he at least must have been excellent. But, to tell you the truth, I am not sure to what extent you actually care for my music in England. I only have an idea that you like it better now than you did when I first conducted the Philharmonic in '88. Well, everything takes time, and I find it a great encouragement as well as a great compliment to be included among the musicians whom Cambridge has selected for this honour.' And then he went on to tell me that he was only troubled by one thing, namely a feeling of extreme nervousness as to the formalities and ceremonies he would have to go through on taking his degree. In vain we tried to assure him that the function was a very simple one. He was convinced that without a special rehearsal there would be some muddle.

Tschaikowsky was to be the guest of the Master of Merton[!], and I undertook to see him safely bestowed at the college before proceeding to my hotel. Telling the flyman to take a slightly circuitous route, I pointed out various places of interest as we passed them, and Tschaikowsky seemed thoroughly to enjoy the drive. When we parted at the College, he shook me warmly by the hand and expressed a hope that when he next visited England he might see more of me.

'I don't know whether to consider England an "unmusical" nation or not' is a reference to the widely held belief, emphatically propagated by Rubinstein, that the English were not musical. Saint-Saëns referred to this in his essay on the 1879 Birmingham Festival.

Strange as it may seem, English musical life is still scarcely known on the Continent, and one is amazed at the odd ideas, current in Paris, about the musical outlook of our neighbours. Simply because one of Shakespeare's compatriots has been heard to sing with a cracked voice, the conclusion has been reached that the English are unmusical . . . I should like all those who have been speaking about the unmusicality of the English to hear the Birmingham choir. They have everything: intonation, perfect rhythm, fine shading of dynamics and a lovely sound. If people like this are unmusical, they nevertheless perform as if they were the best musicians in the world.

Yet, despite the good opinions of Saint-Saëns and other leading foreign musicians, including Grieg and Boito, many preferred to believe journalists like Hanslick: 'If Sterndale Bennett, in his time, was a tired, listless conductor, his successor, Sir Arthur Sullivan is a veritable nightcap.' (As recently as 1918, the German journalist Oscar Schmitz produced a book about England, entitled *The Land without Music*.) For his part, Tchaikovsky had been delighted by the Philharmonic orchestra, he had seen the RCM and RAM, and, clearly, he was now beginning to wonder whether to believe any longer what he had so often heard.

Klein's two accounts differ in regard to Oudin. In the first, Tchaikovsky says he has heard Oudin; in the second, he states, 'I have heard a great deal about him.' Our reasons for preferring the earlier version will be made apparent at the end of this chapter.

Klein may have dropped Tchaikovsky in Regent Street, outside Downing College, at the Porter's Lodge, or he may have taken him into the college and put him down at West Lodge. Downing is compact and straightforwardly laid out. Most of the spacious quadrangle is occupied by two large lawns, with a pathway running from east to west between them. At the west end of the pathway is West Lodge, in the centre of the buildings bounding that side of the quadrangle. To the rear of West Lodge is a garden backing on to Tennis Court Road.

We cannot be sure whether Maitland himself was available to greet the composer. It does seem likely, though, that his wife, Florence, one of the loveliest women in England, would have been there, together with their two little girls, Ermengard, five, and Fredegond, four, and their dog, Chloë. Florence Maitland's sister Adeline was also staying with the Maitlands over May Week.

Having been welcomed to West Lodge, Tchaikovsky presumably made his way to the Guildhall, about 600 yards to the north, at the top of Corn Exchange Street. There, he would have joined Bruch, Saint-Saëns, Boito, Stanford, the singers George and Lillian Henschel and Marie Brema. Stanford must have heaved a massive sigh of relief to have them all at last in Cambridge after so many months of planning and replanning, of hope and disappointment. Yet, even at the eleventh hour, he was presented with one final worry: there was no sign of Harry Plunket Greene. 'I have cause to remember the occasion', wrote the Irish baritone in his biography of Stanford. 'My hansom came to grief on the way to King's Cross and, for the only time in my life, I was late for rehearsal. "On this day of all days, my boy!" was all he said.'

A great deal of work had gone into trying to make the concert a success. Preparations began shortly after Austen Leigh had written to all CUMS members, on 15 February, giving them news of the event. Choral rehearsals for the works by Bruch, Boito and Stanford were held in the Alexandra Rooms in Alexandra Street, off Petty Cury. These took place on 27 April, 4 May, 11 May, 18 May, 25 May, 1 June and 8 June. Nobody was allowed to attend the final rehearsal and sing in the concert unless he or she had been to at least five of the seven earlier rehearsals.

The orchestra had been selected at the time when Stanford was concluding his correspondence with Tchaikovsky and had rehearsed under him on several occasions before the composers themselves took charge at the RCM on 9 June. It consisted of ten first violins, ten second violins, eight violas, five cellos, five double-basses, two flutes, piccolo, two oboes, cor anglais, two clarinets, two bassoons, one double-bassoon, four horns, four trumpets, three trombones and tuba, and was completed by two harpists, drummer and two timpanists – the entire personnel amounting to sixty-six.

The printed programme, which ran to twenty-four pages, contained a brief history of the CUMS, written by Charles Wood; the text of the Banquet Scene from *Odysseus*, with an English translation by Natalie Macfarren; the text of the Prologue to *Mefistofele*, with translation by Oscar Browning; the text of Stanford's *East to West*; notes on the six works to be performed, including the nine themes, 'kindly supplied by the composer', on which *Africa* is based; short biographies of all the composers. At the end of the programme was an announcement of the society's next concert, in which Joachim would play his *Hungarian Concerto*. We can add that, since receiving his doctorate sixteen years earlier, the great violinist had declined any fee for performing at Cambridge.

After the rehearsal, which, for *Francesca da Rimini*, probably finished at around 12.45 or 1.00, Tchaikovsky returned to the Maitlands' for lunch. He then retired to his room to change and prepare for the concert. His nervous state must surely have been apparent to Florence Maitland, for Maitland himself was no stranger to nerves. The calming presence of children, whom the composer so loved, probably made things easier, and Florence seems to have recognised this, if we judge correctly from what she wrote that evening in the little diary she kept for Fredegond.

I want them both to remember that on this day Tschaikowsky came to stay with us.

I sent them both up to his room to tell him it was time to start for the concert at which he was to conduct his Francesca da Rimini. They were in their pink cashmeres with white sunbonnets.

He came down with them and was enchanted with them and later on in the day, when he was taking tea, he kissed their hands.

The concert was scheduled to begin at 2.30 pm, but since the Large Room of the Guildhall was full well before then, Stanford launched into the National Anthem sung by the 200-strong choir, at 2.28.

'The appearance of the hall was brilliant', reported the *Cambridge Chronicle*, 'most of the lady visitors being in light summer costumes, while the orchestra and hall were handsomely decorated by Mr. Parish, florist, Chesterton Street, with flowers and ferns.' The flowers filled all the window bays and were also in baskets suspended from the ceiling. Behind the choir, on either side of Alan Gray at the organ, were draped the flags of Germany, Italy, France and Russia. The flag of Norway, wrote the *Cambridge Review*, 'was left pathetically unfurled. May we soon have Edward Grieg among us!'

Shortly after 2.30, Bruch arrived on the platform, accompanied by the four soloists: Henschel, Mrs Henschel, Marie Brema and Harry Plunket Greene. The performance of the Banquet Scene went extremely well; Bruch was heartily applauded and recalled to bow his acknowledgements. In the opinion of the *Cambridge Review*, the choir had never been heard to better advantage. Next came Saint-Saëns and Stanford to perform *Africa*. The *Daily Graphic* takes up the story.

The work, which was now heard for the first time in this country, has none of the darkness of Africa about it. It is, on the contrary, of the gayest, most brilliant, and exhilarating character. M. Saint-Saëns himself took charge of the pianoforte part, and played it with a verve and unfaltering dexterity which fairly brought down the house. Next followed the prologue to 'Mefistofele', the most romantic and original of all the musical works inspired by Goethe, conducted by its composer, Arrigo Boito, undoubtedly one of the most gifted sons of modern Italy. Mr. Henschel, whom an Irishman once described as 'a heaven-born Mephistopheles', gave a fine rendering of the title *rôle*, and both chorus and orchestra exerted themselves with excellent results. On reaching the magnificent final section, in which all the heavenly hosts burst out with their 'Ave Signor degli angeli e dei santi', Signor Boito closed the pages of his score and conducted from memory. His beat grew more animated, and chorus and orchestra responding to his indications, the superb peroration was given with splendid impressiveness. Signor Boito was enthusiastically recalled and applauded to the echo.

It must have been around 3.30 as Tchaikovsky walked out towards the platform to conduct *Francesca da Rimini*. Among the choir, sitting behind the orchestra, was Ernest Markham Lee, an undergraduate at Emmanuel; he recalled this moment, in his biography of Tchaikovsky, published thirteen years later.

How well I remember, from my distant seat far back on the orchestra, my first impression of Tchaikovski, as I saw him then on that sunny June afternoon: a man with sorrow-lines upon his brow, and grey, almost white hair, stepping up to the conductor's desk, amid the plaudits of the throng!

I remember his serious set expression as he faced round to his band, his wildly energetic baton, and the awful fury and madness of his music. I fancy, to most of us present, it was our first introduction to the music of this master, for although his works had gained some following in London, we country cousins had not been so fortunate as to hear them; and the rushing scale-passages, weird, frenzied, wild, were something in music to us that was uncanny and new. Some of us knew Canto V. of the 'Inferno' of Dante, and his description of his entry 'into the second circle of hell, where he witnesses the punishment of carnal sinners, who are tossed about ceaselessly in the dark air by the most furious winds', but a musical interpretation of such an idea was a revelation. Needless to say that the impression of that day, that music, and the man, has never been obliterated.

This first English performance of *Francesca da Rimini* was extremely well received. 'The composition gave most wonderfully the effect of Dante's lines', wrote the *Cambridge Express*. 'The rushing wind was portrayed with terrible effect by the orchestra . . . M. Tschaikowsky was re-called and loudly applauded.' The *Cambridge Chronicle* reported, 'M. Tschaikowsky conducted a capital performance, and, like all the other foreign composers, was cheered to the echo.' The *Cambridge Review*, while acknowledging 'the majesty and directness and insistence' of the symphonic poem, nevertheless found it 'hard to believe at certain moments that the composer's treatment of the orchestration can be legitimately styled music.' Klein, the only London critic of stature to attend the concert, told the readers of the *Sunday Times* on 18 June, 'The rushing and whirling of the cruel winds are depicted with the full force of the orchestra, and amidst a grateful lull Francesca's recital of her sad story is suggested by an impassioned strain for the violins, followed by a delicious duet between the strings and wood-wind. Like his predecessors, Dr. Tschaikowsky was rapturously applauded and recalled.' In the article *Docteur à Cambridge*, included in his *Portraits et Souvenirs*, which was published in 1899, Saint-Saëns wrote, 'Brimming with pungent flavours and coruscating Catherine Wheels of sound, Tchaïkovsky's *Francesca da Rimini* bristles with difficulties and shrinks from no violence of effect; the gentlest and kindest of men has unleashed a terrifying hurricane, with as little pity for his interpreters and listeners as Satan for the damned. But, such are his talent and colossal technique, that one takes pleasure in this damnation and this torture.' Saint-Saëns, as we have noted, was an admirer of Tchaikovsky, preferring music of this sort to that, for instance, of Brahms, which he found full 'of a heaviness that is mistaken for depth of thought.' We do not know Boito's reaction to *Francesca da Rimini*, nor Bruch's, on this occasion; he had heard the piece in September 1878 in Berlin and, when asked for his opinion, replied, 'I am far too stupid to criticize such music'; the *Berliner Fremdenblatt* had called the symphonic poem 'a musical monstrosity', but Joachim, who was also in the audience, enjoyed it, as did Bülow.

After the performance of *Francesca da Rimini*, Stanford conducted Grieg's *Peer Gynt Suite No 1*, which the audience greatly liked, particularly relishing 'Anitra's Dance' and 'In the Hall of the Mountain King'. 'The suite', said Saint-Saëns, 'created an impression of sadness, due to the absence of the composer, who had to stay at home, because of ill health. Everybody knows this work by now. Grieg and Tchaïkovsky belong to posterity.'

In fact, Grieg was not actually at home, but convalescing in a sanatorium at Grefson, near Oslo, where, as chance would have it, Ibsen was on holiday at that moment. Among Norwegians, Ibsen was Grieg's only rival in fame; it is interesting to recall that, while *Peer Gynt* inspired some of Grieg's best music, this music in turn introduced Ibsen to many who had been previously unaware of his existence. There is a certain irony here, for Ibsen was practically tone-deaf. In 1895, when *Brand* was to be staged in Christiania, he asked the producer August Lindberg if he had selected anybody to write the incidental music. 'I'd thought of Grieg, naturally', replied Lindberg. 'Why Grieg?' Ibsen inquired. Because, Lindberg reminded him, Grieg had composed the music for *Peer Gynt*. 'Oh', said Ibsen, 'You think that's good, do you?' The two men came face to face at Grefson, renewing a friendship that had lapsed for several years. Bolette Sontum, the daughter of Grieg's doctor, was present at their meeting, which she recounted in 1913, in Volume 37 of the American magazine the *Bookman*.

Ibsen sat brooding, solemn and relentless. But suddenly his face lighted up radiantly as Grieg, light-hearted and buoyant as a sunbeam, tripped up the steps. The two masters clasped hands. They had not met for years, and there was a shot of questions and answers as between two boys, Ibsen's deep basso vibrating thunders to Grieg's piping Bergen soprano. Half-serious, half-jesting, they discussed the plan of Grieg's setting *The Vikings at Helgeland* to music.

Unfortunately, nothing came of this scheme to turn Ibsen's tragedy, written in 1857, into an opera.

After Stanford had finished conducting the *Peer Gynt Suite*, there was an interval of a few minutes. At around 4.15 or 4.20, he returned to the rostrum to direct his ode *East to West*. 'Perhaps the greatest enthusiasm', said the *Cambridge Chronicle*, 'was reserved for the University professor, whose beautiful setting of Mr. Swinburne's ode for the Chicago Exhibition, "East to West", concluded the concert. The orchestration is on a level with the beauty of the composition itself.' The *Cambridge Express* reiterated this opinion. 'The setting will surely rank among the finest work Professor Stanford has done. The orchestration is magnificent, and besides the work of foreign musicians the concert showed that our own are not left behind.' In *Docteur à Cambridge*, Saint-Saëns declared that the ode was 'brilliant and the work of a master'.

East to West is one of the few English choral works of the latter part of the nineteenth century to have received its première in London; such compositions were usually introduced at the provincial music festivals, in cities like Leeds, Birmingham, Norwich, or Hereford. The programme note gives us more information about the piece.

> The poem of this work was written by Mr. Swinburne at Prof. Stanford's request. This is the second performance of the work, the first having been given at the Albert Hall on the 10th of last month. It will be one of the most important of the English works performed at the Chicago Exhibition this year, and is appropriately dedicated to the President and People of the United States of America.

In normal circumstances, Stanford would probably have sought a text from the poet laureate for a work of this importance. But there was no poet laureate. So stupendous had been Tennyson's standing that when he died, in October 1892, it was considered almost unseemly to appoint a successor, and neither Queen Victoria nor Gladstone, both of whom knew him so well, was eager to find one. Moreover, Tennyson himself had succeeded another colossus, Wordsworth; the job could not be given away lightly. Eventually, in 1896, Lord Salisbury selected the Tory journalist Alfred Austin, then sixty-one, who at once proved to be a disastrous choice, inaugurating his laureateship with an unbelievably bad poem on the Jameson Raid, that prompted the Queen to rebuke her Prime Minister for his choice. None of this would have happened if the nature of Swinburne's life and poetry, instinct with erotic depravity, had not debarred him from consideration as laureate. He stood head and shoulders above the rest, and Stanford, with his fine ear for poetry, knew it. The Queen knew it, too. 'I am told Mr. Swinburne is the best poet in my dominions', she is said to have remarked regretfully to Gladstone soon after Tennyson's death. 'Mr Swinburne is already the Poet Laureate of England', wrote Oscar Wilde in the April 1895 edition of the *Idler*. 'The fact that his appointment to this high post has not been degraded by official confirmation renders his position all the more unassailable.'

Swinburne does not appear to have been at the concert. However, this was very much a Cambridge affair, and the poet was an Oxford man. He made sporadic visits to his old college and used to call on the Master of Balliol, the omniscient classicist Benjamin Jowett, whose legendary infallibility incited Henry Beeching's

> First come I; my name is Jowett.
> There's no knowledge but I know it.
> I am Master of this college:
> What I don't know isn't knowledge.

Swinburne, himself a brilliant classical scholar, would sometimes look through Jowett's work in progress while the don was preoccupied with students in an adjoining room. His occasional cheery cry, 'Another howler, Master!' – to which Jowett would quietly answer, 'Thank you, Algernon, thank you' – caused considerable merriment.

In *Portraits and Sketches*, Edmund Gosse maintained that Swinburne was unmusical, that when a friend played him 'Three Blind Mice' describing it as a Florentine *ritornello*, the poet commented on how it caught to perfection 'the cruel beauty of the Medicis'. In truth, he was not unmusical. He used to go to Clara Schumann's recitals and particularly liked Schumann, Berlioz and Wagner. The eroticism of *Tristan und Isolde* brought him great happiness. This would not have pleased Clara Schumann, who found the opera 'the most repulsive thing I ever saw or heard . . . every feeling of decency was outraged . . . it was the saddest experience of my whole artistic career.'

The concert finished at a little after 4.30. Normally the college boat races would have begun at 5.00, but they were put back until 5.30, so as not to draw people away from the concert at the interval. 'The union of music and gymnastics, as conceived by Plato in his ideal Republic, is beautifully illustrated by this act of homage', remarked the *Daily Graphic*.

Everybody agreed that the concert had been a spectacular success. 'The audience was so diplomatic as could be wished', says Stanford in his memoirs. 'Whatever may have been their sympathies, their reception of each composer was so similar in warmth and in length that it might have been timed by a watch.' The *Cambridge Review* believed that the concert

> . . . will ever stand out as one of the most memorable – it is hardly too much to say the most memorable – in the annals of Cambridge Music. Those who have studied our musical history of the past may well look with satisfaction upon this performance, and the eyes of our successors must always revert to this, as a landmark – to quote Mr. Swinburne's words from the Ode itself which were made use of in a similar connexion later in the day – 'of her days that have been and shall be.'
>
> It is too early to congratulate all concerned in the performance. We are standing too much in the gaze of those who in a few years will come upon much of today that will be forgotten. It is better to turn to our successors through the next fifty years and conclude in Goethe's words – *Wir heissen euch hoffen.*

After the concert, Tchaikovsky was invited over to Trinity College, some 300 yards north of the Guildhall. We do not know who invited him; probably it was either Stanford himself, Sedley Taylor, or Gerard Cobb, all of whom were Trinity men. By now, Stanford had come to know Tchaikovsky quite well, and appears to have liked him.

> He reminded me, in more ways than one, of his countryman Tourgéniew, whom I once met at Madame Viardot's. He had none of the Northern roughness, was as polished as a Frenchman in his manner, and had something of the Italian in his temperament. These international qualities may have been due to a dash of Hebrew blood, for Tschaikowsky means the 'Son of Jacob'. For all the belief which he had in himself, he was to all appearances the acme of modesty. A very curious conversation took place in the train to Cambridge between him and a musical friend of mine. He told my friend of his having written the Pathetic Symphony (which had not yet been performed); that it originally was designed in three movements, but that after he had finished the third, something compelled him to add a tragic slow movement at the end; and he added that perhaps it was prophetic.

This tale of the conversation on the train is a little disturbing; it lacks conviction, which is reflected in the slightly slapdash final lines, that fall some way below the level of Stanford's normally attractive prose style. It should not deflect us from believing in the veracity of Klein's accounts.

Tchaikovsky would probably not have stayed long in Trinity; he was expected back at the Maitlands' for tea. Moreover, by 7.00 pm, he had to be at King's, where the Jubilee Dinner was being held.

Tea is likely to have been at around 5.30. Afterwards, the composer retired to his room, and Florence and Adeline wrote to their sister Cordelia. Tchaikovsky, said Adeline, was

> . . . so tired after his Symphonic Poem that he c^{d}nt speak till Henschel had given him some brandy and water. He pointed pitiably to his shirt collar w^h hung limp and wet around his neck. He had met friends and had been taken to Trinity. He is now lying on his bed before dressing for dinner. He is rather fat and getting bald. He has blue eyes and a short white beard and moustache – this last slightly curled up like a Prussian's. He is a great friend of Grieg. Tschaikowsky and Boito are far the greatest men I think. I hope to see Boito tonight. We will collect relics for you without fail. Now I must dress for our party.

Florence's note said, 'The hand that writes this has just been kissed by the composer! I am too excited to write more.'

It is interesting that Adeline should find Tchaikovsky 'rather fat', since this conflicts with practically all other descriptions of him. A little above average height, he often struck people as being tall, because of his excellent figure and carriage. In recent years, he had certainly put on some weight, but there are no photographs that indicate anything approaching a Brahmsian girth or even a Schubertian *embonpoint*. G. K. Jones's drawing of him, in the *Daily Graphic* of 14 June, depicts a man of undoubtedly solid build, reminiscent of Schumann, who also had a powerful physique. Her assessment is nevertheless supported by Stravinsky, who, as a ten-year-old, saw Tchaikovsky six months earlier, on 9 December 1892, at a performance of *Ruslan and Ludmilla* in St Petersburg. In *Expositions and Developments* he writes, 'Suddenly my mother said to me: "Igor, look, there is Tchaikovsky." I looked and saw a man with white hair, large shoulders, a corpulent back, and this image has remained in the retina of my memory all my life.' However, we must remember that the birdlike Stravinsky viewed others through Lilliputian eyes: Aldous Huxley was a giant, Rakhmaninov was 'a six-and-a-half-foot-tall scowl', T. S. Eliot had a 'big, rather stolid and cumbrous frame'. Gershwin, too, 'was a tall man – taller than I am, anyway.'

The Jubilee Dinner was held in King's because Austen Leigh, the president of the CUMS, was provost of that college. King's is situated directly opposite the Guildhall, on the other side of King's Parade. Tchaikovsky and Maitland, who was also attending the dinner, could have left Downing at 6.45 and still had time to spare.

Places were set for a hundred diners in the hall of the college. There were four separate tables, with twenty-eight at the high table and twenty-four at each of the other three. The three smaller tables ran at right angles to the high table, so that the four together formed a disjointed E. The guests principally comprised past and present members of the CUMS, supplemented by a number of distinguished Cambridge men who had no direct connection with the Society; in addition, there were a few guests from outside the university, seated at the high table. The most important guests at the high table sat facing out over the other three tables. At one end of the high table was the historian Oscar Browning; at the other was Sedley Taylor. In the middle of the row of diners facing into the hall was Austen Leigh. To his right, towards Oscar Browning's end of the table, sat, in order, Saint-Saëns, Leighton, Boito, Stanford, Richard Jebb and Mackenzie.

We have, here, further recognition of Saint-Saëns' pre-eminence in the consort of graduand composers. Moreover, he was also Austen Leigh's guest at King's. In *Docteur à Cambridge*, he relates how this came about.

> Contrary to my usual practice, I had to accept the hospitality of the President of the Music Society, the Provost of King's College, which I at first refused. 'It is so much part of the English custom', he wrote to me, 'to receive under one's roof the most honoured guests, that the Committee would be exposed to many reproaches from the members of our Society if it consented to abandon France's representative to the hospitality of an hotel.' I naturally had to yield to an insistence expressed in such terms. Everything has been said about English hospitality, and, really, one could not praise it too highly. Never obsequious, it surrounds you with attention, without embarrassing you in the least, without ever seeming forced or disguised; and in these enormous establishments, supplied with every conceivable comfort, one never has the feeling of being an embarrassment in the slightest.

According to William Austen Leigh's biography of his brother, Saint-Saëns, in his letter of acceptance, cautioned Austen Leigh, 'Vous savez que je ne parle pas anglais, sauf avec les cabmen at les waiters.'

We should mention that Jebb now fifty-one, had become Professor of Greek in 1889 and MP for the university in 1891. The seating arrangements made no demands on Leighton, who, godlike between Saint-Saëns and Boito, conversed in French and Italian, moving serenely from one language to the other.

To Austen Leigh's left, sat, in order, Bruch, Lord Kelvin, Canon Kynaston, Arthur Coleridge, Walter Damrosch and Tchaikovsky.

Kelvin, whom we first met as William Thomson, was down from Glasgow for the celebrations; for him, the absence of Grieg was perhaps not an undue disappointment. Herbert Kynaston, who stroked the university eight in 1857, and was the author of *Exercises in Greek Iambics*, had become Canon of Durham in 1889. Arthur Coleridge, Stanford's friend from his Liepzig days, was now a distinguished barrister and a pioneer in English Bach scholarship. Damrosch, who was spending the summer months in England, was conductor of the New York Symphony Orchestra.

Among those on the opposite side of the high table, with their backs to the three smaller tables, were Barnby, Bridge, Gerard Cobb, Henschel and Stanford's revered teacher Sir Robert Stewart, now sixty-seven and still completely abreast of every aspect of contemporary music.

Of those whom one might have expected to be present, Sullivan, who had originally accepted an invitation, was 'indisposed' (at Ascot); Parry was yachting in the Mediterranean; Hallé was conducting abroad. Grove presumably had other commitments. And Cowen? Alas, he was probably not invited.

Tchaikovsky, who, according to the seating plan, was at place number 13, sat next to Sedley Taylor, at the end of the high table. On his right, was Damrosch; opposite him, was Henschel, on Sedley Taylor's left. This appears to have been no arbitrary apposition, for, unless we are mistaken, Henschel, Damrosch and Sedley Taylor were more ardent admirers of Tchaikovsky's music than anybody else present at the dinner.

We know already of Henschel's regard for Tchaikovsky, but it is worth noting that Tchaikovsky, in turn, much respected Henschel's talent as a composer. We are so used to encountering Henschel the conductor and singer that it is easy to lose sight of his compositions, which include operas, choral works, songs and piano pieces. In 1892, he wrote incidental music for Beerbohm Tree's production of *Hamlet*. When this was published in September of the same year, *The Musical*

Times welcomed it most enthusiastically, predicting that it would 'assuredly win troops of friends.' Tchaikovsky may have come across the *Hamlet* score in Henschel's home, for, two months later, in August 1893, he replied to an application from a theatre asking to use his own incidental music to *Hamlet* by saying that, better than his, was 'the excellent music for *Hamlet* by George Henschel'.

It was fitting that Austen Leigh and Stanford should have put Walter Damrosch next to Tchaikovsky, for no man outside Russia, except perhaps Bülow, had done more than he to win popularity for the composer's music. And no country, apart from Russia, more deeply loved his works than did America.

Bülow introduced American concert-goers to Tchaikovsky when, on 25 October 1875, he took the solo part in the world première of the First Piano Concerto, in Boston, with Benjamin Lang conducting. A month later, he played the work in New York; it was so well received that it was repeated a week afterwards. The conductor in New York was Leopold Damrosch, the father of Walter Damrosch. The following April, *Romeo and Juliet* was given its first performance in America, at a New York Philharmonic concert; this, too, was warmly greeted. We may recall that these two compositions were also the first to be heard in England. The concerto was played at the Crystal Palace in March 1876, five months after the Boston première; *Romeo and Juliet* was presented, again at the Crystal Palace, in November 1876, a little over six months after the New York performance. In England, as we have seen, these works did little to stimulate curiosity in Tchaikovsky, but in America they created great interest and were followed, in 1878, by *Francesca da Rimini*, which was given in New York, almost fifteen years ahead of the English première in Cambridge. The Third Symphony was introduced in 1879, and, thereafter, during the eighties, practically all of the available orchestral works were performed. Notable premières include those of the Second Piano Concerto, conducted by Theodore Thomas in New York in November 1881; *Marche slave*, conducted by Henschel in Boston in February 1883; *Capriccio italien* and *1812*, conducted by Walter Damrosch in New York in November 1886; the *Manfred Symphony*, conducted by Theodore Thomas in New York in December 1886; the Fifth Symphony, conducted by Theodore Thomas in New York in February 1890. By now, Tchaikovsky was completely established in America. The First Piano Concerto, *Romeo and Juliet*, *Marche slave*, *Capriccio italien*, *1812* and the Third Suite had all become familiar concert items. *Hamlet* was introduced in Chicago in March 1890, conducted by Theodore Thomas, and was soon heard in Boston and New York. Thomas also conducted the *Nutcracker Suite* in Chicago in October 1892, two months before the ballet's first performance in St Petersburg. The most popular of the composer's works was probably the Fifth Symphony, which, by 1893, had been played in Cincinnati, Boston, Philadelphia, Brooklyn and, twice, in both New York and Chicago.

When Carnegie Hall was nearing completion towards the end of 1890, it was decided to invite a European composer to come and take part in the inaugural ceremonies. Walter Damrosch, as conductor of the New York Symphony Orchestra, was allotted the task of making the choice, and he selected Tchaikovsky. The invitation was accepted, and, on 26 April 1891, the composer arrived in New York on board the *La Bretagne*. 'The nearer we came to New York', he wrote to Modest, 'the greater grew my fear and homesickness, and I regretted ever having made this insane trip. When it's all over, I may look back on it with pleasure, but at present it's not without suffering.' A deputation of five met him at the docks and escorted him to the Hotel Normandie. Once they had left him, he burst into tears and, at the end of the day, wept himself to sleep.

Over the next month, he conducted concerts in New York, Baltimore (where he met Victor Herbert) and Philadelphia. He went to Washington, where he was guest of honour at the Metropolitan Club; he visited the Washington Monument and the Capitol and had luncheon with the Russian ambassador, who travelled down from New York to receive him at the Embassy. He also visited the Niagara Falls. 'On the Canadian side, I was forced, so as not to be tortured by thoughts of cowardice, to put on a very ugly overall and go down under the Falls in a lift, walk along the tunnel and finally stand right under the Falls, which is very interesting, but also quite terrifying.'

In New York, where he spent most of his time, he was constantly being fêted, entertained and lavishly dined. One newspaper described him as 'the first of modern composers after Wagner'; another listed him, together with Bismarck, Edison, Herbert Spencer, Ibsen, Sarah Bernhardt, Tolstoy and Dvořák, among the greatest geniuses of the age. At one of his concerts, 'the enthusiasm was such as I never succeeded in arousing even in Russia.' He told his nephew

Bob, 'I'm certain I'm ten times better known in America than in Europe. At first, when they spoke to me about it, I thought it was just excessive kindness on their part. But now I see it's really true. Several of my works, which are unknown even in Moscow, are frequently played here. I seem to be much more important than I am in Russia.' He was besieged by reporters, musicians and other well-wishers and inundated by letters, from all over America, asking for his autograph, 'to which I reply very conscientiously.' He also received a multitude of little gifts, like cigar-cases, boxes of cigarettes, bags of cookies, also a replica of the Statue of Liberty, of which he noted in his diary, 'But will I be allowed to bring it into Russia?' This sardonic reflection was not without justification, as Ronald Hingley underlines in his chapter on censorship in *Russian Writers and Society, 1825 to 1904*.

Absurd examples of censors' interference are often quoted, such as the ban on the phrases 'forces of nature' and 'free currents of air', and the insistence (to deter would-be assassins?) that Roman emperors always 'perished', and were never 'killed'. Musical scores were suspected of cloaking sinister cyphered messages, and one censor even objected to a poet calling a woman's smile 'heavenly' because he thought that no woman deserved such high praise.

The Americans were eager for information about their visitor. Few of the leading composers of the age had made the long journey to their shores. Johann Strauss and Anton Rubinstein had come over in 1872 and 1873, but, since then, apart from Bruch in 1883, they had welcomed nobody of any consequence. (While Tchaikovsky was in America, attempts to lure Dvořák to the National Conservatory in New York were already underway, but he did not arrive until September 1892.) During Tchaikovsky's visit, concert reviewers took pains to acquaint their readers with the composer's appearance and behaviour on the rostrum. In Philadelphia, the *Public Ledger* described him as 'an energetic and authoritative conductor, and under his direction the men evidently felt the spirit of his music as they could not have felt it under another leader.' In Baltimore, the *American* called him 'a czar among musicians and directors'.

His personal appearance alone shows him to be a great man. As he stands to direct, he looks as if the commander of all the armies of Russia had for the moment laid aside the sword of conflict and destruction and taken up the baton of harmony and peace. He has, indeed, a 'front like Mars' and 'an eye to threaten or command.' In fact, he does more directing with his

eye alone than other directors do with all the means at their command.
. . . it is hard for any one to be unmusical in his presence. His magnetic
personality sways all who are about him. Yet he does nothing for effect.
He directs, and all follow; he commands, and all instinctively obey, as
though grateful in their serfdom; art governs him, and all whom he can
govern. If he makes them slaves, they delight in his chains.

Tchaikovsky's sufferings in the last few hours before these concerts
were as bad as ever. 'Never, I'm sure, have I been so afraid', he wrote
in his diary. 'Is it not because they scrutinize my outward appearance
here and therefore will detect my shyness?' When he was on the
rostrum, it was only his intense personal contact with the orchestral
players that carried him through. In one diary entry, he notes that
the performance of his First Piano Concerto had pleased the audience
and that the soloist had been excellent, 'but especially dear to me was
the enthusiasm of the orchestra.' A comment on his appearance, in
the 6 May edition of the *New York Herald*, so upset him that he copied
it into his diary, though somewhat imperfectly. 'Tschaikovsky is a
tall, gray well built interesting man, *well on the the sixty* (?!!) He
seems a trifle embarrassed, and responds to the applause by a succession of brusque and jerky bows. But as soon as he graps the baton
his self confidence returns.' Of course, nobody likes being considered
'well on the the sixty' when he is still only fifty. As for being embarrassed or nervous, the *Musical Courier*'s report would have pleased
him, for it went so far as to suggest that, in the same concert, his
conducting showed greater self-possession than Damrosch's. 'The
Beethoven overture received a very loose reading. Everybody, including Mr. Damrosch, was evidently too excited to play smoothly. When
Mr. Peter Tschaikovsky took the band in hand this was changed. The
great Russian's beat is firm, forcible, a little harsh, but as to its
effectiveness there can be no doubt, for the orchestra followed him
implicitly, and not he the orchestra.' The *World* concurred: 'The musicians followed him involuntarily. There is no mistaking his
meaning.' And the *Sun*, too, commented, 'Tschaikovsky is a genial
looking and very gentlemanly appearing man, with a bright complexion, gray hair and beard and a quick, decided manner, which is
emphasized and accentuated when he is conducting.'

Much as he was moved by the cordiality and openheartedness of
the Americans, the composer's overpowering homesickness never
allowed him to be completely happy, as his diary makes plain.

Amazing people, these Americans! Compared with Paris, where, at every approach, in every stranger's amiability, one feels an attempt at exploitation, the honesty, sincerity and generosity of this city [New York], its hospitality without hidden motives, its eagerness to help you and to be thought well of are all simply astonishing and, at the same time, touching. This, and indeed American customs and American manners, and American habits generally, I find very attractive – yet I enjoy all this in the same spirit as a man who, sitting at a table laid with every marvel of gastronomy, finds himself without hunger. Only the near prospect of returning to Russia will awaken my appetite.

To his nephew Bob, he wrote, 'New York, American customs, American hospitality – all their comforts and arrangements – everything, in fact, is to my taste. If only I were younger, I should very much enjoy my trip to this fascinating and youthful country. But, now, I just accept everything as if it were a punishment mitigated by many delightful things. All my thoughts, all my aspirations are concentrated on Home, Home!!!' He did all he could to hide his homesickness, but without success. When he suddenly chanced on a Russian woman who began to speak to him in Russian, his eyes filled with tears and he had to rush away to hide his sobbing. 'Burn with shame to recall this unexpected incident', he put in his diary. American food and drink did much to cheer him up. He notes in his diary, 'Some kind of *whiskey*, *bitters* and *lemon* were served – extraordinarily delicious', and, of supper at Delmonico's, 'We ate oysters, a sauce of small turtles (!!!) and cheese. Champagne and some kind of peppermint drink revived my sinking spirits.'

He got on very well with Damrosch and his wife, whom he describes as 'a very charming and graceful woman'. Through Damrosch, he was introduced to Carnegie.

The latter, affluent, possessing thirty million dollars, and resembling Ostrovsky, is an elderly man whom I liked very much, mainly because he adores Moscow, which he visited two years ago. No less than Moscow, he loves Scottish songs, and Damrosch played many of them for him on an excellent Steinway. His wife is young and extremely pretty . . . Carnegie – this remarkable person, who has risen over the years from messenger boy to one of America's wealthiest men, but who has remained simple, modest and not in the least turning up his nose at people – inspires me with unusual affection, probably because he is interested in me too. Throughout the whole evening, he displayed his regard for me in an unusual manner. He grasped my hands, declaring that I am the uncrowned but true king of music, embraced me (without kissing – here men never kiss), expressed my greatness by standing on tiptoe and raising his hands on high, and finally threw the whole company into raptures by imitating how I conduct. He did it so seriously, so well, so similarly that even I found it delightful. His wife, an extremely simple and pretty young lady, also showed her interest in me in every way. All of which was extremely pleasant, but, at the same time, rather embarrassing.

Damrosch recorded his impressions of Tchaikovsky in his autobiography, *My Musical Life*, published in 1923.

In all my many years of experience I have never met a great composer so gentle, so modest – almost diffident – as he. We all loved him from the first moment – my wife and I, the chorus and orchestra, the employees of the hotel where he lived, and of course the public. He was not a conductor by profession and in consequence the technic of it, the rehearsals and concerts, fatigued him excessively; but he knew what he wanted and the atmosphere which emanated from him was so sympathetic and love-compelling that all executants strove with double eagerness to divine his intentions and to carry them out. The performance of his Third Suite, for instance, was admirable, although it is in parts very difficult; and he was virtually the first of the great composers to visit America, the public received him with jubilance.

He came often to our house, and, I think, liked to come. He was always gentle in his intercourse with others, but a feeling of sadness seemed never to leave him, although his reception in America was more than enthusiastic and the visit so successful in every way that he made plans to come back the following year. Yet he was often swept by uncontrollable waves of melancholia and despondency.

This despondency only began to lift once the composer, having said farewell to 'my dear American friends', was on board the *Fürst Bismarck* and bound for Europe. His spirits and confidence rose so sharply that he even found the courage to talk to the American passengers in English, the first time he had ever conversed in that language.

Damrosch states in his autobiography that, while on holiday in England in May 1893, he 'received an invitation from Charles Villiers Stanford, then professor of music at Cambridge, to visit the old university during the interesting commencement exercises.' It seems more than likely that Stanford and he agreed that he should sit next to Tchaikovsky.

In the evening a great banquet was given in the refectory of the college, and by good luck I was placed next to Tschaikowsky. He told me during the dinner that he had just finished a new symphony which was different in form from any he had ever written. I asked him in what the difference consisted and he answered: 'The last movement is an adagio and the whole work has a programme.'

'Do tell me the programme,' I demanded eagerly.

'No,' he said, 'that I shall never tell. But I shall send you the first orchestral score and parts as soon as Jurgenson, my publisher, has them ready.'

We parted with the expectation of meeting again in America during the following winter . . .

On Tchaikovsky's left, sitting in a place of honour at the end of the table, was, as we have mentioned, Sedley Taylor. Destined shortly to succeed Austen Leigh as president of the CUMS, he had probably done more than anybody over the last twenty-five years, apart from Stanford, to make the Society 'a power in the country', as Grove's *Dictionary* put it. A distinguished physicist and Fellow of Trinity, he published, in 1873, the important book *Sound and Music*, which for many years was a standard work on acoustical theory. He also carried out experiments at the Cavendish Laboratory demonstrating how the vibrations of a tuning-fork created particular colour patterns on soap film. Another influential book, published in 1890, was on Tonic Sol-fa notation. Equally valuable was his scholarly *The Indebtedness of Handel to Works of Other Composers*, which, for the first time, established the extent of Handel's borrowings, but also revealed the genius of his adaptations. His involvement in the co-operative movement led to the writing of *Profit-Sharing between Capital and Labour*, which became another standard text. He regularly contributed to scientific journals and, in addition, produced pamphlets relating to the 'Eastern Question' and church doctrine. He was a tireless campaigner for equal rights for women and was instrumental in the founding of Girton College. He helped to found, as well, a free dental clinic in Cambridge, the first of its kind in England, and contributed to its upkeep out of his own pocket. He sounds, on the face of it, to have been an alarmingly earnest man, but, as his obituary notice in the *Cambridge Review* of 14 May 1920 makes clear, he was quite the opposite.

He was an accomplished scholar in both French and German, and spoke both languages fluently. He was a genial and entertaining companion, the more attractive for a slight air of diffidence which, however, wore off in the progress of a talk. His keen sense of humour and fund of good stories were always at command. His enjoyment at hearing or telling a joke was itself irresistible, emphasized as it was by the sudden lighting up of the face and vigorous action of the hands. Till his later days, he was always ready to promote the fun of an after-dinner party or a smoking concert with his repertory of comic songs, the absence of all self-consciousness making his appeal to his audience the more charming and irresistible. At the same time there was in him a serious and uncompromising honesty of mind; he was keenly impatient of all intolerance and intrigue, a strong protestant, but singularly free from all personal animosities.

Sedley Taylor was greatly revered by his contemporaries and in 1911 was granted the freedom of the borough of Cambridge. He was unfailingly kind to people. The blind organist Alfred Hollins writes in his autobiography of how Sedley Taylor looked after him when he once went to Cambridge to take part in a CUMS concert. 'The late Professor Sedley Taylor of Trinity College, the great authority on acoustics, showed me all round Trinity, and I remember clearly the kitchen and the old-fashioned spits for roasting. He introduced me to Professor Stanford, who showed me the organ in Trinity Chapel built by Hill & Sons ... Sedley Taylor was a charming man and very musical; extremely learned and possessed of a vivid sense of humour.' Stanford himself, in *Interludes*, wrote of him, 'His great human gift was an all-pervading sense of humour.' James Stuart maintained in his *Reminiscences*, 'Of all raconteurs of humorous stories he is the very best.'

On 8 November 1878, Tolstoy, who loved Tchaikovsky's music, wrote to Turgenev, in Paris, asking him what he thought of the opera *Eugene Onegin*. Turgenev replied, on 14 November.

Tchaikovsky's *Eugene Onegin* has arrived here in piano score. Mme. Viardot has begun to study it during the evenings. It is undoubtedly wonderful music; the lyrical and melodic parts are especially good ...

Tchaikovsky's reputation has grown here since the concerts of Russian music at the Trocadéro; in Germany, he has long enjoyed, if not esteem, at least attention. At Cambridge, an English professor of music told me quite seriously that Tchaikovsky was the most remarkable personality of our times in music. My jaw dropped ...

In his biography of George Eliot, Gordon S. Haight recounts how the novelist and her husband, George Lewes, came to meet Turgenev during his visit to Cambridge, or, more correctly, to Six Mile Bottom, just outside Cambridge.

> In October the Leweses left the Heights for a few days to visit the Bullock-Halls at Six Mile Bottom. A number of Cambridge men were there – Munro and Sedley Taylor and Oscar Browning. But the great attraction this time was Turgenev. Lewes had known him on the Continent in student days, and Turgenev came to the Priory during his London visits. There was no literary man whose society Marian enjoyed so thoroughly and unrestrainedly. His conversation was delightful. She sat next him at the races at Newmarket and heard him discuss the difference between Russian and English sport. At dinner, when Lewes proposed the health of Turgenev as 'the greatest living novelist' he parried the compliment by transferring it sincerely to George Eliot.

We have noted that Turgenev wrote to Tolstoy of 'an English professor of music'. The Professor of Music at Cambridge in October 1878 was Macfarren. The likelihood of this man praising Tchaikovsky is about as remote as his hope that the earth would open and swallow up Bayreuth. Nor did he mix in literary circles. It seems probable that Turgenev used the term 'professor' in a loose sense.

This means that Stanford could, within Turgenev's use of the word, have been the 'professor of music'. However, Stanford wrote of Tchaikovsky, 'He reminded me in more ways than one, of his countryman Tourgéniew, whom I once met at Madame Viardot's.' Stanford would certainly have mentioned any meeting in Cambridge, or at Six Mile Bottom, especially if George Eliot had also been there.

It is suggested, therefore, that Sedley Taylor was perhaps Turgenev's 'professor of music'; his talk was much concerned with music and showed great knowledge of it, and could easily lead somebody to this conclusion. Furthermore, Sedley Taylor, despite his interest in Bach and Handel, had written for the *Cambridge Review*, on 11 June 1891, an article about Dvořák that was so sympathetic and complimentary that, as we remember, the composer was deeply moved by it. This shows that Sedley Taylor was obviously enthusiastic about modern music, and, more particularly, in the case of Dvořák, about Slavonic music. However, it could be asked: what access would anybody at Cambridge have had to Tchaikovsky's music as early as 1878, by which time London was acquainted only with the First Piano Concerto and *Romeo and Juliet*? Speaking of the mathematician

Richard Pendlebury and his music collection at Cambridge, Stanford says, in *Pages from an Unwritten Diary*, 'Pendlebury's researches in the course of forming his library were so thorough and world-wide, that he was probably the first man in this country to discover the modern Russian School, and the shelves of the collection contain all the important early works of Tschaikowsky, which he sent to Russia to acquire as far back as the seventies.'

Finally, we have, at the dinner in King's, Tchaikovsky sitting on Sedley Taylor's right. We feel entitled to assume that Damrosch and Henschel were placed next to and opposite the composer because Stanford knew of their regard for him. Could not the same have been true of Sedley Taylor? Moreover, Sedley Taylor was a sufficiently prominent member of both the university and the CUMS that he would probably have been asked whom he would like to have sitting on his right at the dinner. Tchaikovsky was perhaps his own choice.

With Damrosch on his right, Sedley Taylor on his left, and Henschel opposite him, Tchaikovsky was accessible to only one other diner. This was the university librarian, Francis Jenkinson, who sat opposite Damrosch and next to Henschel. Jenkinson had married Jennie Stanford's sister Marian in 1887, and Stanford had played the organ at their wedding in Croydon, performing the Bridal March from Parry's *The Birds*. He was a classics scholar whose principal interest was music. He had an elegant prose style and beautiful handwriting, and used to draft a number of the CUMS reports and circulars. 'And now let us give it all to Jenkinson to translate into English', Austen Leigh used to say at the end of committee meetings. Jenkinson was often at Stanford's house in Harvey Road, where he met and became friendly with Parry and Joachim. He was also well acquainted with Grove and Alma-Tadema, who painted his portrait and used him as a model in one of his historical paintings. He loved Bach, Beethoven, Schubert, Chopin, Schumann and particularly Mozart, whose birthday he honoured each year. He preferred Sterndale Bennett to Mendelssohn. He was pro-Brahms, anti-Wagner. 'I have no doubt that Brahms is the great man of this generation', he wrote in 1875. In later life, he quite liked some of Debussy, despite the 'dreary lingo', but Ravel was too much. At one Cambridge musical gathering when Ravel was performed, he sought solace by correcting some proofs he happened to have with him, while, on another occasion, no proofs apparently being to hand, he gasped, 'I'm afraid I can't stand it; I must go', and went.

MENU OF THE DINNER

Potages
Consommé Sévigné
Purée d'Asperges

*

Poissons
Saumon, Sauce Capres
Blanchailles Frites au Naturel et Diable

*

Entrées
Corbeilles à la Financière
Timbales de Volaille à l'Essence

*

Relevé
Selle de Mouton
Fonds d'Artichaut à l'Italienne. Haricots Verts

*

Roti
Canetons et Petits Pois

*

Entremêts
Soufflée à la Vanille
Gelée à la Champagne aux Fruits
Bombe Glacée aux Amandes Pralinées

*

Savourie
Croûtes à la Darmstadt

At around 9.00 pm, or perhaps a little beforehand, the speechmaking began, with Austen Leigh proposing a toast to 'the Queen and Royal Family' and making, said the *Cambridge Review*, 'a happy reference to Her Majesty's friendship with Mendelssohn'.

Professor Stanford followed with 'the health of MM. Saint-Saëns, Bruch, Tschaikowsky, Boito and Grieg.' With well-affected apprehension at the outset he trembled lest, in the presence of so many representatives of the Great Powers, he should drop a word which might endanger the peace of

Europe. He had been struck in the afternoon with the boldness of these composers in invading foreign territory. Max Bruch had pounced upon Greece, Boito had scaled Heaven through Germany and Goethe, Tschaikowsky had dived down to Hell by way of Italy and Dante, while Saint-Saëns, boldly plunging into the wilds of Africa, had lit upon some smiling oasis amid its Saharas. M. Saint-Saëns replied in graceful terms.

In *Pages from an Unwritten Diary*, Stanford writes about the problem with which he was faced when making his toast.

Whatever friction there might be between the composers' respective foreign offices, there was in Cambridge an *entente cordiale* which embraced the whole of Europe.

The only debatable question arose as to the order of precedence at a banquet which was given to the new Doctors in King's College Hall. It fell to my lot to propose their healths, and after much heartburning I found the solution of my difficulties in Lumley's 'History of the Opera'. When Lumley was director, he produced the historically famous *pas de quatre*, in which Taglioni, Carlotta Grisi, Fanny Elssler and Cerito danced. They each had a solo and each lady insisted on having hers first. Threatened with a wreck of his great scheme, Lumley hit upon the simple device of giving the solo dances in the order of the dancers' ages: the eldest to come first and the youngest last. He was nearly checkmated again by the claims of each dancer to be the youngest, but, presumably with the help of a biographical dictionary or of some baptismal certificates, he stuck to his ship and weathered the storm. I adopted his principles with the happy result that France, the country which was most likely to feel a slight, came out first, Germany second, Russia third, and Italy fourth. I confessed in my after-dinner speech the method by which I had tried to avoid complications which might cause a European war, and Saint-Saëns in his reply most wittily thanked me for comparing four weather-beaten composers to 'quatre jolies femmes'.

Saint-Saëns, too, refers to the dinner, in *Docteur à Cambridge*.

I had the place of honour, to the right of the President, and I had been warned that I would have the task of replying, on behalf of my fellow composers, to Mr. Stanford's toast, this distinction being due not to my fabled merits, but to the dolorous privilege of age. Partly through lack of practice, partly through natural timidity, I dread speaking in public; nevertheless, it had to be done. Usually, on such occasions, a multitude of ideas spring to mind, which I keep to myself, not daring to express them; this time, encouraged by an extremely cordial reception, and reflecting that, after half a century's existence, timidity is no longer in fashion, I said everything that came into my head, mingling, as they say, the weighty with the light, the solemn with the humorous, and thus following the tradition in England, where, at such functions, one speaks without pretension or pedantry. My fellow doctors declared themselves well satisfied with the words that I expressed on their behalf.

Tchaikovsky must have offered a prayer of thanks that he was not called on to speak. He could still remember the terror of speaking, in French, at a banquet in honour of Berlioz, during the latter's visit to Moscow in December 1867. (However, Berlioz liked the speech.)

Saint-Saëns was followed by Mackenzie, deputising at short notice for Sullivan. The Scottish composer was used to being saddled with this function, since Sullivan was in the habit of suddenly becoming 'indisposed' and appointing him in his place. 'I am always terrified when I have to speak', Mackenzie pleaded in a letter of December 1886, but to no avail. In proposing 'Prosperity to the C.U.M.S.', he trusted that his audience would escape the sort of Inferno that M. Tchaikovsky had so vividly depicted in his symphonic poem. The speech, according to Mackenzie in his memoirs, was 'deplorable'. The concluding speeches are described by the *Cambridge Review*.

> Lord Kelvin and Professor Jebb replied, the former, with peculiar charm and vivacity, tracing the beginnings of the C.U.M.S. to an occasional comic song in Peterhouse rooms in the forties, recalled the time when he was 'second horn to Blow' and President of the Society, spoke with enthusiasm of the Classical works rendered from year to year by the Society, till it reached its climax under the leadership of Professor Stanford, who by a happy stroke in 1872 reinforced the chorus, by the introduction of ladies. Professor Jebb dwelt with his wonted grace upon the refining influence of music, and discerned still further glories for Cambridge in the momentous resolution of the Senate only last week 'by an overwhelming majority' to reorganise the whole procedure in Musical Degrees. A cordial vote of thanks to Mr. Sedley Taylor (proposed by Mr. J. W. Clark) for his untiring labours in behalf of the Jubilee celebration, followed by a similar one (proposed by Mr. Sedley Taylor) to the College for the use of the Hall, brought this portion of the proceedings to a close.

The dinner was followed by a conversazione, in the Fitzwilliam Museum, starting at 9.00 pm, which was given by the women of the university. There were five hostesses, from the Ladies Committee of the CUMS, and twenty-two auxiliary hostesses. This was the 'party', to which Adeline referred in her letter to her sister, and at which she hoped to meet Boito. The main feature of this reception was to be the presentation of a gift to Stanford on his retirement as conductor of the CUMS. The *Cambridge Independent* gives an excellent report of the conversazione, which was attended by between 900 and 1,000 people.

The Fitzwilliam Museum, in which the Conversazione was held, is an ideal building for such an occasion. The portico of the noble entrance afforded of most convenient arrangements being made for the reception of superabundant wraps, etc., and the interior of the building is admirably adapted for a reception. The magnificent marble staircase never looked better than when the hostesses were receiving their guests, and from nine o'clock until considerably after ten o'clock there was a continual flow of visitors . . . The lighting of the noble building is interesting from the fact that had it not been for the advances made in electrical engineering the Museum could not have been thrown open in the evening, the use of gas or oil being on good grounds undesirable. The ease with which a building can now be temporarily lighted by electricity without the least damage to its fabric was shown on this occasion by Messrs. J. Stone and Co., of London, who, under the superintendence of Mr. Arthur B. Gill, their electrical manager, installed the spacious entrance hall and picture galleries with incandescent lights equivalent to about 370 lamps of eight candle power in less than three days. The current was sent stored in accumulators from Messrs. Stone and Co's. works in London. The soft glow of the incandescent lights, which were absolutely steady, produced a most pleasing effect upon the beautiful building, the dresses and the pictures, and gave general satisfaction.

The *Cambridge Chronicle* reports, 'The refreshments, which were dispensed in a room in the basement, were supplied by St. John's College, and the floral decorations were executed by Mr. Parish, florist, Chesterton Road.' (Mr Parish seems to have had a full day, decorating both the Guildhall and the Fitzwilliam Museum.) The *Cambridge Chronicle* also records that 'The Blue Hungarian Band discoursed music of the most ravishing description in the left hand corner of the central gallery, and throughout the evening the bandsmen were surrounded by an admiring crowd.' No wonder the people all gathered round! The Blue Hungarian Band was one of the most popular ensembles in London. Tom Tit, ace reporter on *Life*, heard them at a ball on 8 June and, in the 13 June issue, told his readers about the evening.

The youthful Countess Bianca Deym who has inherited the beauty of her mother, and who is distinguished by the graceful bearing with which birth has stamped her, looked charming in pink . . . Mrs. Crispe brought her two charming daughters, and Miss Carey looked very pretty, as did also Miss Hughes-Hughes . . . Miss Muriel Maitland King looked very pretty and radiantly happy enjoying her first ball in a rich white silk, very simply made, but fresh as herself . . .
As to the Hungarian music, as discoursed by the Blue Hungarian Band,

it is difficult to find adjectives of sufficient strength to express its undoubted beauty and fascination. There can scarcely be, I fancy, anything more enthralling than those passionate minor progressions and startlingly weird harmonies.

The tempestuous headlong rushes of sound, the unexpected pauses, the vehemence and force of the Magyar music is certainly a change to our ears, but it affects one powerfully, as a new kind of intoxicant. At least, that is how it affected me. The curious accompaniment of the 'Czimbal', an instrument which combines the sound of running water with that of ringing glass, is most beautiful and effective. It seems to follow and underlie every glowing phrase. Yes, one has not known what real music is until one has listened to the Hungarian version of it!

From King's College to the Fitzwilliam Museum is a distance of some 600 yards down King's Parade and along Trumpington Street. Maitland, who had been seated at one of the three lower tables, or Sedley Taylor, or Henschel may have escorted Tchaikovsky on this pleasant walk on a warm summer's evening, with the sun setting on the other side of the Cam. The Fitzwilliam Museum must have made an attractive prospect. 'The spacious picture galleries and noble Grecian entrance hall "with store of ladies, whose bright eyes" and dresses lost nothing of their charm by the soft rays of the incandescent light, formed a picture not soon to be forgotten,' said the *Cambridge Review*. By now, at around 10.00 pm, the central gallery would have been densely thronged. As the *Cambridge Independent* recounted, there were many delights beyond those of conversation.

> The galleries presented a very animated appearance during the evening, and though the masterpieces which adorn the walls did not receive a great share of attention from the majority of the visitors, there were a few who were deeply interested in them, notably Sir Frederic Leighton, who was shown some of the best canvases by Dr. Stanford. In the north gallery, near the ivory copy of the Hindoo Mausoleum, were displayed a number of music MS. and autographs. These included a portion of Handel's 'Rinaldo', a study of 'He was despised', Joseph Haydn's symphony in F at the letter W., Domenical parodies, Queen Elizabeth's Virginal Book (so called), and specimens of MS. of Alessandro Stradella (cir. 1670), Dr. Wm. Boyce, Agostino Steffani (1653 to 1730), and Hy. Purcell (1673), and near the refreshment room, in the basement, was a MS. choir book of Naples (1596-1604).

During Leighton's visit to the university, Stanford took him on a tour of the colleges, 'showing him at his request all the nooks and crannies of Cambridge which few visitors trouble about, and even residents are too familiar with to admire.' The painter had no doubt been particularly interested to hear *Francesca da Rimini*; when his own 'Paola and Francesca' was exhibited in 1861, it was criticised for being too earthy. Another point of contact between Leighton and Tchaikovsky was that Leighton's grandfather had been court physician to Tsar Nicholas I.

We know very little of what happened to Tchaikovsky at the Conversazione. He spoke to Wilhelm Ganz, who recalls their meeting in his memoirs.

That evening there was a reception at the Fitzwilliam Museum, and I had a long talk with Max Bruch, whom I had not seen since 1878, and chatted with Boito and Saint-Saëns. Seeing Tchaikowsky standing alone, I went up and spoke to him. He was most affable. On my referring to the frequent performances of his works in London at that time he said, 'Je ne demande pas mieux.'

If Ganz did speak of 'frequent performances', he was exaggerating the composer's popularity in England. It seems more likely that he simply mentioned the success of the Philharmonic concert.

Frederick Bridge also conversed with the composer in the Fitzwilliam Museum

. . . and was charmed with his modest, quiet, little manner ('little' seems just to describe my meaning, and does not convey small in dignity or significance). It was difficult to associate this quiet personality, this lined face and thin hair, with the man who produced such a work as the '1812' . . . he disclosed none of his feelings to those who met him at Cambridge on that lovely day in June, and certainly he revealed to me only an engaging courtesy.

Late in the evening, around 10.45, came the presentation, and Austen Leigh called on Sedley Taylor to say a few words. The authority on acoustics, standing on a chair to make himself heard, delighted the guests, says the *Cambridge Review*, 'with his inimitable force and humour', provoking much laughter and applause. Stanford, he asserted, was entitled to be called the second founder of the Society; he was regarded with great affection, even when descending with the flight of an eagle on a wrong note. He would be sadly missed. Mrs Dunn, who, it will be remembered, was Stanford's strong ally in bringing women into the CUMS, and whose singing of Bach earned the praise of Joachim, also made a short speech, saying that Stanford had helped them to love the music they had performed and had inspired them with his genius. Austen Leigh added that 'the greatest lesson Professor Stanford had taught them was that, if they wanted to make people enthusiastic, they must be enthusiastic themselves.' He now presented Stanford with his gift, which is described in the *Cambridge Chronicle*.

> The testimonial consisted of eight silver octagon footed chased Queen Anne pattern table candlesticks, in a brass bound polished oak case, fitted with divisions, and lined with purple cloth. On each candlestick there was engraved round the foot, in plain block capitals, 'Presented on June 12th, 1893, by members and associates of the C.U.M.S. to Professor C. V. Stanford, its conductor from 1872 to 1893.' A testimonial to Mrs. Stanford consisted of a solid silver ½ fluted Queen Anne pattern 5 o'clock tea service in morocco cases. A suitable inscription was engraved on each of the articles. The goods were supplied by Messrs. T. Reed & Son, silversmiths to the Queen, Market Place, Cambridge.

Warmly applauded, Stanford said he thanked the members of the Society from the bottom of his heart for the beautiful presents. Even dearer to him, though, was the loyalty and support he had received from everybody, going back to that first occasion when he conducted them, at the age of nineteen. They must show the same faith towards their new conductor and towards new music.

It was approaching 11.30 pm when the guests began to make their departures. 'The Hungarian Band now played with redoubled force', reported the *Cambridge Review*, 'as if resolved that no sad regrets should mar the festivity of the gathering. Perhaps it was with the same object that a dance, lasting five minutes, was extemporised, as the numbers thinned, in one of the galleries.'

The Maitlands and Tchaikovsky would now have walked back to Downing, crossing Trumpington Street, going down Fitzwilliam Street, turning right into Tennis Court Road and entering the College by the Kenny Gate – a distance of no more than 350 yards. It had been a long and exhausting day for the composer.

The degree ceremony was scheduled for noon on the following day, and Tchaikovsky therefore at last had a chance to spend some time with the Maitlands and get to know them during Tuesday morning. His letters, which we will come to a little later, reveal that he found Florence Maitland 'very attractive', but he was no less enchanted by her husband. This is hardly surprising, for Frederic Maitland was one of the most brilliant and popular men in the university. He was born in London in May 1850 and educated at Eton and Trinity College, Cambridge. In 1873, the year in which Stanford was appointed Trinity organist, he became president of the Union. He gained a first-class honours degree in Moral Sciences, being placed at the top of the list, and won a blue for cross-country. In 1876, as a student of Lincoln's Inn, he was called to the bar and practised as an equity lawyer. In 1884, he was elected reader in English Law at Cambridge and, in 1888, Downing Professor of Law. He was internationally recognised as one of the most promising legal historians of that time. The subject of English legal history had hardly been developed by then, and his inaugural lecture 'Why the History of Law Is Not Written' can retrospectively be seen as promise of his massive future achievement. He had already published the important and pioneering *Pleas of the Crown for the County of Gloucester*, in 1884, and he followed this, in 1887, with a masterly introduction to Bracton's *Note-Book*. He had an astonishing gift for being able to bring to life and present with the greatest clarity a wealth of complicated information, much of which had never before appeared in print. Because of the nature of his research, he acquired a hard-won but enviable understanding of medieval handwriting, and he was among the first to stress to law students the practical necessity of developing such skills.

He was a compelling lecturer. C. H. S. Fifoot, in his matchless life of Maitland, quotes the following reminiscence, which J. N. Figgis contributed to the 5 January 1907 issue of the *Athenaeum*.

Maitland was not merely a writer; he was also an orator. Although as a lecturer he was extremely nervous and read nearly every word, he had the orator's power of thrilling his listeners both by his voice and his intense preoccupation with his subject . . . His style was like that of no one else, compact of extraordinary Biblical and other archaisms, intensely individual, vivid and striking, packed with allusion, sparkling with humour and suggesting even more than it stated . . . It had an extraordinary quality of reproducing the atmosphere of the time he was discussing.

Maitland was engaged in writing the work that was to become his masterpiece, *The History of English Law Before the Time of Edward I*, when Tchaikovsky visited Cambridge. He had begun the book in 1890; it was completed in 1894 and published in March 1895. It won instant recognition, says Fifoot. 'English and American opinion was unanimous. Vinogradoff in Russia, Brunner and Gierke in Germany, Tardif and Saleilles in France, all acclaimed it. Henceforth, throughout England, young historians were to be "excited by the latest work from the hand of Maitland." Four months after publication it was selling so well that Maitland could anticipate the opportunity of revision.'

The great American lawyer Oliver Wendell Holmes wrote of Maitland that 'he was acknowledged to be supreme', and the English legal historian Sir Frederick Pollock said simply, 'Maitland was a genius.' Nor was his brilliance confined merely to scholarship. Oscar Browning rated him the best after-dinner speaker he had ever heard. G. M. Trevelyan compared his conversation to 'the play of lightning'. Walter Leaf, in his autobiography, was equally panegyrical.

> Maitland was beyond comparison the wittiest man I have known; and his papers and speeches overflowed with the finest humour. I can give an example from another sphere, when the Chit-Chat Club held a dinner of its old members at Cambridge a good many years later. Maitland made a speech. As he sat down, my two neighbours turned to me simultaneously and said, 'That is the best speech I ever heard.' It was always the same with Maitland; his wit bubbled out spontaneously, whether in writing, in speeches, or in private talk, and was always of the same high quality. Hardly any of it has been recorded just because it was so fresh and impromptu; but something can be gathered from the sparkle with which he invested the dryest details of legal history . . . With all this intellectual equipment went all that could attract affection as well as admiration. One of the bonds between us was a love of music combined with a very inadequate technical power of expression.

While still at Eton, Maitland made the acquaintance of men like Sullivan, Grove and Dannreuther. He was old enough to remember Costa conducting Handel and Mendelssohn, but he preferred to go to Manns's concerts at the Crystal Palace, where he once heard a memorable performance of the *Emperor Concerto*, with Hallé as soloist. In 1873, he went to the Schumann Festival at Bonn, where, it will be recalled, Stanford met Brahms for the first time. During the following year, he heard *Tannhäuser* at Mannheim and was immediately converted to Wagnerism. *Die Meistersinger* later became his favourite Wagner opera. Unlike so many of his contemporaries, though, he felt no burning allegiance to Wagner and was equally attracted to Brahms.

Florence shared her husband's love of music and was an admirable violinist and singer. Fifoot paints an attractive portrait of her:

Gwen Raverat, who was two years older than Ermengard, wrote of Florence Maitland as 'strange and beautiful.' That she was beautiful nobody doubted: tall, slender, brown eyes, hair brighter than brown but not so bright as red-gold. That she was strange depends upon definition. She came to Cambridge from a country life where she had not been encumbered with convention – certainly not the convention of a university town, with its mélange of intellectual pressure, or pretension, and the gossip of a closed society. She was amazed to hear the dons' wives talking of servants and 'marrying off their daughters' . . . Florence was hard to tame and she had interests which she pursued to unseemly lengths. Photography might perhaps be condoned, especially in one whose great aunt had been the celebrated Mrs. Cameron . . . Music was an elegant accomplishment, but it had a time and a place whose limits Florence did not or would not understand. She was a good pianist, a very good violinist, and experimented with the guitar even upon Bach. She was not content to play for her husband's delectation or to set the tone of an informal party: she gave violin lessons and invited young men to join her in trios and quartets.

Among the undergraduates who often came to West Lodge to take part in the music-making was Ralph Vaughan Williams. Aged twenty in June 1893, he had sat at one of the lower tables at the dinner in King's, for which, like all but the honoured guests, he had paid one guinea, a sum The Dwarf of Blood might have considered steep, were it not for the attractions of the high table. Ursula Vaughan Williams writes of her husband's visits to West Lodge in her wonderful biography *R.V.W.*

> Ralph admired both Maitland, a vivid and attractive man whose lectures and writings illuminated the dusty archives of legal history with humanity and wit, and his wife, who was a beautiful and original young woman and a fine amateur violinist. Among the most constant visitors to their house were Ralph's friends Nicholas and Ivor Gatty; Nicholas was a violinist, Ivor played the horn, Ralph the viola, and other undergraduate musicians joined the group for 'scratch' chamber music. Sometimes Florence's younger sister, Adeline, stayed at the Lodge and, as she was able to play the cello if no one else was available to do so, though her real talent was for the piano, she was a welcome addition to the party.

Florence's unconformity extended also to pets, which included not only innumerable dogs and cats, but a piebald mouse, a white rat, a Peruvian cavie, a mongoose, and a meerkat that walked like a kangaroo and followed people all over the house. Maitland, says Fifoot, looked on this menagerie 'with affectionate amusement. Others, indeed, thought the atmosphere of West Lodge unbecoming to a scholar. R. L. Poole once entered Maitland's study to find it shared by a monkey which had to be put in a box on a chair with Madox's *Exchequer* as a lid.'

A similar unorthodoxy prevailed both in the choice of their daughters' names and in their education. They were not sent to school; Florence instructed them in French and music, Maitland helped with arithmetic, but, otherwise, teachers were brought in from outside. They were not taught English, but encouraged to read and to write down anything that came into their heads. Both parents read to them a great deal. Maitland read them, Ermengard later recalled, 'most of Scott's novels. I never knew how brilliant was his skipping till, long after, I tried to read Scott to myself.' Stories and plays were made up for the girls, and, not content with turning the house into a zoo, Florence also filled it with imaginary animals that had fantastic names and were, for the children, as real and vivid as anybody else. In addition, Ermengard became Gaga, and Fredegond became Vuff. Maitland was Gougou. Ermengard inherited her parents' love of music and on one occasion, at Florence's suggestion, serenaded some porters on a railway platform with her violin while the family was waiting for a train. 'Really, Gaga,' Maitland once assured her, 'I see no difference between you and Joachim, upon my soul I don't.'

West Lodge was a lovely home for the children to be brought up in, and there is a description of it in Fifoot's book.

> The front of the house was covered with virginia creeper and the back with ivy and with wistaria. A large garden ran behind most of the west side of the court and as far as the lane [Tennis Court Road] beyond Addenbrooke's Hospital. Hiding the lane were large trees with wild parsley beneath them. The lawn was cut up by a fountain and by a flowerbed in which Maitland grew the dark velvet roses and the parrot tulips that he loved. On the ground floor was the study, a plain square room looking on to the court, and the dining room. The drawing room was upstairs – a set piece with Morris paper, black and gold cabinet with matching chairs, and chintz curtains inherited from Maitland's predecessor. The family preferred the lecture room which opened out of the dining room and had steps into the garden. Here Florence Maitland made a sitting space with comfortable chairs and a piano, and here she indulged her music, had small tea parties, and sat after dinner.

Both girls had such happy memories of their childhood that they wrote about it in later life. In *F. W. Maitland, A Child's-Eye View*, Ermengard said of her father, 'He dressed as one who had seen himself, disliking his necessary blacks, choosing rather to wear brown tweeds, low collars when others wore high, and plain, warm-coloured ties when convention said dots and stripes. His love of music was well known. Long, long after his efforts to play his grandfather's organ, or his undergraduate piano, long after press of work kept him from opera or concert, the tunes of Wagner, Beethoven, Mozart and Schubert were whistled through our house as he moved about.' She speaks also of his modesty. He could not deny his proficiency in French and German, but maintained that his Spanish was practically non-existent. 'Yet my mother had his worn copy of Calderón's poems re-bound for his birthday', and, when he once ran out of books on holiday in the Canary Islands, he read Tolstoy's *Resurrection* in Spanish translation.

> In those days a child took its parents' happiness together for granted, but I had a good nose for trouble and I never smelt a whiff of fire save over miracles and the Boer War and he for Dickens and she for Thackeray. I do not believe that her menagerie of animals, her hours of violin playing, her feeding of tramps and gypsies, her photography and pony-driving, her story-telling and play-writing were ever anything but a pleasure to him. Nor do I think she minded his dedication to the laws of England, though it must have called for self-abnegation on her part at times.

In her short autobiographical essay, Fredegond's thoughts turned more to her mother.

> My mother was a Grecian goddess to me . . . She was only twenty-two when she married, so that all our early remembrances of her were destined to be bright ones, she being as beautiful as she was young, vivid and distinct . . . I see my mother's beauty as if it were beauty alone, the only true and perfect sort that I have ever tried or tested – tinted like a shell at sunset upon a lonely shore unharmed by life or time. Her vivid presence and talk I can recall as one recalls things not difficult or distant, but the only image of her that I find in my deepest recollection is the singing one to me. Thinking upon that I can still feel the hands, and the brow is secure above me still, the breath warm . . . I am in my mother's arms and she is singing to me while she walks up and down: up and down all over the nursery floor . . .
> My mother played her violin sometimes alone in a bare white room, and the sound of it was like the speaking of some wounded, wild, woodland animal, half fairy and wholly desolate and alone. My father was surrounded by the dark and soothing presence of books, and the gold dust of tobacco went around him . . . I thought of them like this: my mother – violin; my father – books, tobacco, forests.

Fredegond remembered, too, the grace and beauty of Adeline.

> She had fair hair coloured like spring sunshine in a wintry world, soft and cool as snow, slender and very gentle, she breathed rather than walked into the house and then breathed away again. To us she was a sister – someone dimly connected with apple blossom, snow showers and a cashmere shawl – also with tall fair tapers such as burn in churches in July evenings when Vespers are sung. She was a sister of the order of springtime, of starlight and of the fragrance of lilies . . .

Little Vuff was also much smitten with the Trinity undergraduate Ralph Vaughan Williams; she confided to her mother that he was 'so dark and splendid'. Nor was she the only one to be thus affected. Adeline, too, eventually fell in love with him, and, in October 1897, they were married. Just before the wedding, he wrote the girls a letter telling them that he was going to wear puce spats and blue boots with red heels. He enclosed a drawing of a giraffe and concluded by saying, 'I want to see the new monkey.' When Maitland died in December 1906 in his beloved Canaries, Vaughan Williams went there to look after Florence and the girls and bring them home. He dedicated to Florence *Toward the Unknown Region*, which was given its première, under his baton, at the Leeds Festival in October 1907; the first London performance was conducted by Stanford two months later. In 1925, he set four of Fredegond's poems to music. When Vaughan Williams died in 1958, there were two photographs in his bedroom: one was of Gustav Holst; the other was of Frederic Maitland.

Tchaikovsky found Frederic and Florence 'two of the most charming people I have ever met', but they, too, were delighted by him, and Stanford says that Maitland 'spoke to me with enthusiasm of his culture and grasp of extra-musical subjects.' Such praise from Maitland is not surprising, for Tchaikovsky appears to have been better read than any other leading composer of his time. Not only was he well informed on everyday matters – 'he could read three or four newspapers in a row at amazing speed', says Laroche – but his knowledge and love of literature seems likely to have surpassed even that of Berlioz, Schumann, Liszt and Wagner. In the opinion of Laroche, 'Literature was second only to music among his preoccupations.' From childhood, he was an avid reader and fascinated by literature. At school, he edited the students' magazine; he later wrote poems and many articles about music. When he was in New York, he contributed an essay on Wagner to the *Morning Journal*. His library included books and journals in Latin, French, German, Italian, English and Czech, as well as Russian, and amounted, including bound scores, to over 1,400 items. Many books, like Jahn's four-volume life of Mozart, he read over and over again. He was acquainted with the classics of ancient literature and had a considerable knowledge of history, particularly of the eighteenth century, and of natural science. He was also interested in travel books. He read a good deal of philosophy, especially admiring Spinoza, but not warming very much to the German philosophers. He found Schopenhauer 'dry and egotistical, lacking in love of mankind'.

He had read every classic of Russian literature and even tried a French translation of Pushkin to see what effect his poetry created in a foreign language. He ranked Tolstoy, whom he knew personally, as the greatest of living novelists, though he had reservations about him as philosopher and teacher; *What I Believe* astonished him by 'its combination of wisdom and childish *naïveté*'. He had no doubts about Dostoyevsky's genius. He was moved to tears by *The Brothers Karamazov*, but sometimes found Dostoyevsky unnecessarily harrowing. He adored Chekhov, predicting that he would eventually be regarded as one of the great Russian writers. He made a point of meeting the young author to tell him of his admiration, and Chekhov, in turn, dedicated his next volume of short stories to Tchaikovsky. They even made plans to write an opera together.

Of French literature, he delighted in Molière and Corneille among the older writers. In modern literature, he set Flaubert above everybody else: 'I think there is no more sympathetic personality in the entire world of literature.' Maupassant he put second. He did not like Hugo, being irritated by his 'grimaces and buffoonery'. He had mixed feelings about Zola and doubted his artistic sincerity.

Tchaikovsky tackled many authors, including Dante and Goethe, in their original languages, overcoming any problems this involved by reading for long periods at a time, so as to become completely immersed in the foreign idiom. 'Reading is one of the greatest delights', he told his brother Anatoly, 'if your mind is at peace and if you read continuously and not in snatches.'

He absorbed his Shakespeare in Russian translation, even working through the history plays, and his Byron in French – a happy choice.

His acquaintance with modern English literature seems to have begun in his mid-twenties, with a Russian translation of *The Pickwick Papers*, which completely bowled him over. 'I am laughing at *Pickwick Papers* heartily and unwitnessed', he wrote to the twins Anatoly and Modest (then fifteen) on February 1866, 'and sometimes the thought that nobody can hear me laughing makes me laugh all the more. I recommend you to read this book; when one wants to read fiction, it's best to begin with an author like Dickens. He has much in common with Gogol: the same inimitable and innate humour, and the same masterly power of portraying a character in just a few strokes.' He now became a voracious reader of Dickens and was inspired to investigate Thackeray, whose psychological insight into character he compared to Tolstoy's. Despite his deep affection for Dickens, who always totally gripped him at the time of reading, he did not rank him in any way with Tolstoy. His feelings were well expressed in a letter of 10 November 1889 to his friend the Grand Duke Constantine Constaninovich.

Tolstoy surveys his characters from such a height that they appear to him as poor, insignificant pygmies who, in their blindness, injure one another in an aimless, purposeless way – and he pities them. Tolstoy has no malice; he loves and pities all his characters equally, and all their actions are the result of their own limitations and basic egotism, their helplessness and insignificance. Therefore he never punishes his heroes for their misdeeds, as Dickens does (who is a great favourite of mine), because he never depicts anybody as absolutely bad, but simply blind, as it were. His humanity is far above the sentimental humanity of Dickens; it attains almost to the view of human wickedness that is expressed in Christ's words, 'they know not what they do.'

By the end of the seventies, English literature had come to occupy a place in the composer's esteem second only to the literature of his own country, and he determined to learn English to enjoy it the better. In August 1880, he told Madame von Meck, 'I hope in about six months I'll be able to read in English. This is my only aim. I realize that at my age [forty] I can't hope to speak English freely; but to be able to read Shakespeare, Dickens and Thackeray in the original – that will be the pleasure of my old age.' His studies were interrupted, though, by the press of work, and, two years later, he was still reading in translation. He confined most of his comments on literature to Modest, who had become a playwright, telling him in May 1882, 'I have just finished *Bleak House*. I cried a bit, firstly because I'm sorry for Lady Dedlock, secondly because I'm really sad to part from all these characters with whom I've lived for two months, and thirdly out of gratitude to such a great writer as Dickens. In spite of a slight feeling of artificiality at the end of the novel (as there always is with him), I nevertheless experienced such enjoyment that I felt I had to put my gratitude down on paper.' Of *Little Dorrit*, he wrote to Modest, 'My goodness, what a wonderful book! If you have not read it, buy it at once.' In the autumn of 1883, he again took up his English studies; on 13 November, he told Madame von Meck, 'I am conscious of a burning desire to learn enough of the language so I'll be able to read Dickens with ease, and therefore I give up several hours each day to my lessons, with the result that, except for breakfast and lunch and my walk, I spend all my time as if I were trying to finish something very quickly. It's almost like an illness.' By August 1884, he at last felt confident enough to embark on Dickens in English and started on *David Copperfield*. In mid-September, he informed Madame von Meck, 'Now I am able to read Dickens without difficulty and without looking up words in the dictionary every minute. Reading him in the original has endowed his work with a new charm.' It was nevertheless not all plain sailing, as the many pencilled annotations and queries in his copy of the book testify. At the bottom of the final page is written, 'I finished reading this on 28 April 1885 and began in August 1884, so that makes nine months. Let's see whether this pregnancy has given birth to a knowledge of the English language.' To a degree, it did, for he went on to read *The Pickwick Papers* in English, but his time henceforward was so consumed by composition and travelling abroad on conducting tours that his English lapsed, and thereafter, for ease and speed, he read in Russian translation. He was usually too timorous to attempt a conversation in English. He was even unhappy about writing in English, as witness his reply in French to Maitland's letter, which he would have had no difficulty in understanding.

Towards the end of the 1880s, he discovered George Eliot, beginning with *The Mill on the Floss* and then quickly going on to *Adam Bede*, *Silas Marner* and *Middlemarch*. He was so delighted with these that he read them all over again. George Eliot now became his favourite English novelist, and, among all modern writers of any country, he rated her second only to Tolstoy. Because of its historical context, he cared less for *Romola*, finding it difficult to relate to people from a bygone age. (He experienced the same problem with *Aida*.) He was particularly fond of *Scenes of Clerical Life* and at one time considered making *The Sad Fortunes of the Rev. Amos Barton* into an opera.

One can imagine with what enthusiasm he might have listened to Francesco Berger's remembrances of Dickens or of Sedley Taylor's meeting with George Eliot.

In *R. V. W.*, Ursula Vaughan Williams, who married the composer in 1953, two years after Adeline's death, states that Florence and Adeline played for Tchaikovsky 'and pinned roses in his buttonhole before he joined Boito, Saint-Saëns, and Max Bruch for the ceremonies at which they all received their honorary degrees.' Mrs Vaughan Williams heard this from Adeline herself, whom she had known since 1940. Ermengard Maitland confirmed to Fifoot that her mother and Adeline had played to Tchaikovsky. This would presumably have taken place in the ground-floor lecture room, at the back of the house, where the piano was. It probably happened on the Tuesday morning. Florence would have played the violin, and Adeline would have accompanied her at the piano. If they performed any of Tchaikovsky's works, one might guess that the *Andante cantabile*, over which Tolstoy once wept, could have been among them. It was probably, at the time, the most popular arrangement for violin and piano of any of Tchaikovsky's compositions. The roses pinned in his buttonhole were probably Maitland's 'dark velvet roses'.

At about 11.15 am, it was time to go over to the Senate House for the degree ceremonies. This would have involved a walk of about half a mile, going up Tennis Court Road and then working over towards King's Parade, since Senate House Green is about 150 yards north of King's College. Florence's entry for that day in Ermengard's diary speaks of the great occasion,

> Gaga and Vuff walked down to the Senate House with Tschaikowsky, Fred, Adeline, Annie [the girls' nursemaid] and myself. I managed to get places in the Gard and in the House and they saw both the Procession and the degrees. They saw a magnificent Rajah all with diamonds and precious stones, Lord Roberts & Boïto, Saint-Saëns, Max Bruch and Tschaikowsky in their doctor's robes.

On arriving at Senate House Green, Tchaikovsky and Maitland went into the Old Schools building, on the west side of the square, to prepare for the procession and ceremony. Here, the composer put on his doctor's robes of cream, red, gold and black, and a wide black velvet beret trimmed with gold cord, in the style of Henry VIII. After receiving instruction in the procedure of the ceremony, he took his place in the procession, which was scheduled to come out of Old Schools at noon, proceed round the square in an anticlockwise direction and enter the Senate House by the south door, on the north side of Senate House Green.

Tchaikovsky, Saint-Saëns, Bruch and Boito were by no means the principal attractions of the day, for five other distinguished men were also to receive doctorates. Indeed, the 15 June edition of the magazine *Figaro* went so far as to suggest that these four composers were not even stars in the musical firmament, each being a substitute for a better man.

> Honorary degrees were conferred almost by wholesale at Cambridge on Tuesday, the occasion being the 50th anniversary of the local musical society. The choice, however, fell mostly upon the dii minores . . . Professor Stanford, it is understood, had offered the degree to Brahms and Verdi, as representatives respectively of Germany and Italy, but neither could accept, and consequently the choice fell upon Max Bruch and Boito. Scandinavia would have been represented by Grieg, but that composer is suffering from ill-health, and could not come. Saint-Saëns, in the absence of Gounod, represented France, and Tschaïkowski Russia, Rubinstein, doubtless, being afraid of a ninety minutes of sea voyage.

The phrase 'in the absence of Gounod' is nicely put. The composer of the *Ocean Symphony* was known to be a poor sailor; he passed the voyage to America without moving from his cabin.

The best known of the five other graduands was Lord Roberts of Kandahar, in many ways the most successful of Queen Victoria's generals and certainly the most popular and likeable. Now sixty, he had just given up his command in India, where, by the age of twenty-eight, he had already been awarded the Victoria Cross and mentioned seven times in dispatches. Although his had long been a household name, he had spent practically all his army life abroad, and it was only on his return to England in the winter of 1892 that most people had the chance of seeing him for the first time. He was given a tumultuous reception on taking his seat in the House of Lords, but he refrained from voting on any motions, saying, 'I do not see how a soldier can serve any Government in a satisfactory manner if he takes part in politics.' Many banquets were given in his honour and, by June 1893, he had received the freedoms of Bristol, Newcastle, Cardiff, Edinburgh, Glasgow, Dundee and other major cities. Everywhere he went, crowds gathered to see him and were delighted by his modesty and simplicity and by his short, almost boyish figure. It was during this period that he wrote the popular ballad that begins

> There's a little red-faced man,
>   Which is Bobs,
> Rides the tallest 'orse 'e can –
>   *Our* Bobs.
> If it bucks or kicks or rears,
>   'E can sit for twenty years
> With a smile round both 'is ears –
>   Can't yer, Bobs?

For Bobs, even greater military triumphs lay ahead; under his command came the relief of Ladysmith in February 1900 and the relief of Mafeking three months later.

Another notable graduand was Lord Herschell, the Lord Chancellor, now fifty-five, who had first achieved prominence in 1880, when Gladstone appointed him solicitor-general. His father was Polish, and Herschell was educated in Bonn before going on to London University. He was respected for his great common sense and broad and compassionate handling of social and constitutional problems.

Two of the remaining three non-musical doctors were scholars. Standish Hayes O'Grady, from Dublin, was renowned for his work on medieval Irish literature. Julius Zupitza, from Berlin, was an equally eminent authority on medieval English literature.

Finally, there was the colourful and majestic Sir Takhtsinhji Bhaosinhji, Maharajah of Bhaonagar, who was one of the most estimable of Indian rulers, having devoted much of his vast personal wealth to improving the lot of his subjects, giving them hospitals and schools. Saint-Saëns was captivated by the Maharajah's appearance. The Indian ruler had been excused from wearing his doctor's cap and had been permitted to retain his normal head-dress. This was a magnificent turban studded with gold, diamonds and other precious jewels. Around his neck was a diamond necklace. Beneath his doctor's robes, he wore beautiful crimson and gold robes of his own. In *Docteur à Cambridge*, Saint-Saëns says how enchanted he was by this resplendent contrast 'to the banalities and neutral tones of our usual modern-day clothing'.

As the great bell of St Mary's tolled the hour of noon, all the participants in the forthcoming ceremony formed up in procession and prepared to make their way out into Senate House Green. At the head of the procession were the bedels, followed by the Vice-Chancellor, John Peile, accompanied by the University Registrary. Then came the Maharajah and behind him, in pairs, Lord Roberts and Lord Herschell, O'Grady and Zupitza, Saint-Saëns and Bruch, Tchaikovsky and Boito. Next, in their scarlet robes, were the heads of the colleges, doctors of divinity, doctors of law, doctors of medicine, doctors of the sciences and letters, doctors of music (including Mackenzie), the public orator, the librarian (Jenkinson), the professors (including Stanford and Maitland), members of the Senate Council and, bringing up the rear, the proctors.

At a little after five minutes past midday, the doors of Old Schools were thrown open, and the bedels led the procession out into the square. The sun was directly overhead, blazing down out of a cloudless sky; it was, says Saint-Saëns, 'torride'. The temperature was around 80°F.

The degree ceremony was one of the highlights of May Week and was vivaciously described in the *Daily Graphic*.

Cambridge has been, like all the rest of the world, exulting in the glorious weather. More so, perhaps, than most of the world just now, for the joys and glories of the May week are in full swing, and a May week of fine weather and happy festivities is an experience which gilds the undergraduate's recollections far down the vale of years. Yesterday, was, academically, the great day of the year, for then the Prolusiones Academicae were recited in the Senate House by the winners of the various medals for Greek and Latin and English verse; and – a function of more general interest beyond the college walls and family circles of the prizemen – the ancient University conferred degrees *honoris causâ* upon a number of distinguished men . . . Cambridge is full to overflowing with the usual fair bevies of sisters and cousins, the even more desirable bosom friends of the sisters and cousins, and the seemingly inevitable chaperon. For not only are the boat races an unfailing source of attraction, and the mere hospitalities of undergraduate relations and their even more desirable friends, but there is scarcely a college which has not some form of entertainment wherewith to speed the sunny or starry hours. Garden parties are nowhere as pretty as in the choice spacious gardens of the grey old colleges. Music is keenly cultivated at Cambridge, and numbers of the colleges have given excellent concerts during the week. But, best of all, there is dancing galore, in some cases in the college halls, in others in the Guildhall, or other suitable external spot. With so much going on, no fair visitor can fail to find it somehow an ideal time, and the ceremony in the Senate House yesterday morning will be among the most characteristic and picturesque recollections.

Crowds had been gathering since 11.30 to watch the procession. The galleries of the Senate House were also packed by those who had acquired tickets to see the ceremony itself. The first intimation that the procession was about to emerge from Old Schools came with the sudden appearance of four of the Maharajah's retinue, 'brilliantly attired in scarlet and gold', who made their way over to the Senate House and took up positions around the entrance, ready to salute their ruler's arrival. They were boisterously bidden by the undergraduates to enter the building, but they calmly and dignifiedly ignored such entreaties.

As the assemblage, grave and gay, lively and severe, was gathering, the big bell in St. Mary's Tower opposite tolled according to custom, clanging out with somewhat funereal suggestion at intervals. But the funereal suggestion died upon the ear as soon as it was made. One undergraduate alone, who had charge of three very pretty girls and a by-no-means unpleasing mamma, was enough to banish every thought but that of supreme felicity and the pride which only comes about twice in a lifetime. A man in his first year may languish in the shade of neglect among his fellows for no real failing of his own. But if in the May his 'people' come up and turn out to be pretty and generally conducive, hey presto! the ugly duckling finds himself a swan at once. The schoolboy with the large hamper is not in it with the undergraduate upon whom Heaven has conferred attractive womankind, if he can only manage to get them up for the May festivities. The crowd inside was matched by the crowd outside, which lined the railings on King's Parade, and watched with lively interest the arrival of the ticket holders, and waited for the procession of dons and doctors . . .

Shortly after noon a brilliant procession, consisting of the Vice-Chancellor, University officials, heads of houses, the new honorary doctors, and lastly – the most important person of all, in one sense, on this occasion – the Public Orator, Dr. Sandys, of John's, came into the view of the admiring crowd, and entered the Senate House in state. The Vice-Chancellor, Dr. Peile had on either side of him the men whom the University were delighting to honour. Long and loud cheers greeted the appearance of Lord Roberts, who was in full uniform, his doctor's gown sitting well on his soldierly shoulders . . . The Maharajah of Bhaonagar was the first to be called forth. Dr. Sandys, standing beside his victim, who was clad in rich red and gold robes of his own, as well as in the doctor's gown and hood, began his oration, *ore rotundo*, in such wise that every word of his Latin, pronounced in the rather heart-breaking 'correct' fashion of which Dr. Sandys is so distinguished an exponent, was distinctly audible and intelligible, though what the Indian prince thought it all meant does not sufficiently appear. The Public Orator has a knack of saying very neat things in very sounding phrases, and he seems to enjoy them in the spirit of a true artist. He had the undergraduate ear yesterday. The necessary rather silly little jokes from the gallery never put him out, and his points were taken almost as quickly as the points in a modern farcical comedy. The Vice-Chancellor conferred the degree upon the Maharajah in the accustomed formula, only omitting the words, 'In nomine Patris, et Filii, et Spiritus Sancti.'

The *Cambridge Review* reported, 'The Maharajah of Bhaonagar, resplendent in diamonds and other jewels, was warmly received, and listened with attention, not unmixed with suspicion, to the Public Orator's Speech.' He might certainly have been a little surprised at Dr Sandys' concluding reference to the fact that the Maharajah's country was at the moment represented by one of the best known members of the University Eleven. This was an allusion to K. S. Ranjitsinhji, the Maharajah of Nawanagar, who had come up to Trinity in 1890 and distinguished himself as a cricketer, winning his blue just a few days before the degree ceremony. On the previous Saturday, going in at No 4, he had carried his bat against the Australians, scoring 37 not out, in the second innings of the match at Fenners. A crowd of nearly 5,000 spectators cheered him into the pavilion. Cambridge lost by 117 runs.

Next to step before Dr Sandys was Lord Herschell, who was also enthusiastically applauded. The Lord Chancellor, a 'vir iuris peritissimus', was, at the conclusion of the oration, presented to John Peile, who pronounced him Doctor of Laws, 'in nomine Patris, et Filii, et Spiritus Sancti'; he then resumed his seat.

Now it was the turn of Lord Roberts, and, as he rose to take his place in front of Dr Sandys, 'the house rose too, and there was a prolonged roar of cheers, which for some time checked the proceedings,' said the *Daily Graphic*. According to the *Daily News*, 'General Lord Roberts came in for a tremendous ovation, which lasted some minutes.' The oration that followed was frequently interrupted by bursts of applause from the gallery, and the words 'Unus homo nobis properando restituit rem' excited especially fervent cheering. Once John Peile had admitted him to his degree, the undergraduates broke into 'For He's a Jolly Good Fellow', which, commented the *Cambridge*

Review, 'was sung with more vigour than musical ability.' The *Pall Mall Gazette* noted the musical graduands' reactions to this performance, which caused 'M. Saint-Saëns to twist his fingers, Herr Max Bruch to look pensive, Signor Boïto to smile, and M. Tschaïkowsky to sink into ineffable meditations.' Tchaikovsky's 'ineffable meditations' were more likely to have been a fearful apprehensiveness of the tortures that still lay ahead; Saint-Saëns' twisting fingers may have betrayed the same anxiety.

The virtual anonymity of Julius Zupitza and Standish Hayes O'Grady brought a welcome lull to the proceedings, with the undergraduates confining themselves to aiming sporadic insults at the proctors and calling for speeches from the two literary scholars, once they had been admitted to their doctorates. Now, at last, Saint-Saëns came forward; interest was rekindled, and he was given a lively round of applause. The gallery called not for a speech, but a song. Thereafter, thankfully for Tchaikovsky, the four composers were granted safe passage and polite rather than animated applause. Clearly, the Maharajah, Lord Herschell and Lord Roberts had been the star attractions. Nevertheless, *Punch* maintains that an undergraduate shouted, 'Good old Shakemoffski', which was greeted with 'roars of laughter'.

Dr Sandys began his oration in praise of 'Carolum Camillum Saint-Saëns' by saying, 'Yesterday a certain society, dedicated to the encouragement of music in our midst, held the most auspicious celebrations, to mark fifty years of activity since its foundation. Its leader and champion was himself present. Like Apollo Musagetes in the choir of the muses, he has so long and so successfully held the office of conductor of that society.' This was graceful acknowledgement of the fact that the previous day's concert marked Stanford's retirement from the conductorship of the CUMS. Dr Sandys continued, 'There were also present other illustrious masters of this happy art, including those, representing a number of different nations, whom we decorate today. One stands above the rest, both in age and experience, a man from a neighbouring country, counted among the greatest, who, endowed with an almost incredible memory, has clearly shown by his own example that the Muses were the daughters of Mnemosyne.' The rest of the oration was in praise of Saint-Saëns' various accomplishments.

The oration for Bruch made oblique reference to *Die Loreley*, *Arminius* , the *Frithjof Scenen*, *Das Lied von der Glocke*, *Odysseus* and other works, but did not lay stress on particular characteristics of the composer's art, as had been done with Saint-Saëns. This deficiency was redressed by a quotation from Homer and a translation in Latin of lines by Schiller.

Dr Sandys' enthusiasm returned when he came to Tchaikovsky.

Russorum ex imperio immenso hodie ad nos delatus est viri illustris, Rubinsteinii, discipulus insignis, qui neque Italiam neque Helvetiam inexploratam reliquit, sed patriae carmina popularia ante omnia dilexit. Ingenii Slavonici et ardorem fervidum et languorem subtristem quam feliciter interpretatur! Musicorum modorum in argumentis animo concipiendis quam amplus est! in numeris modulandis quam distinctus! in flexionibus variandis quam subtilis! in orchestrae (ut aiunt) partibus inter se diversis una componendis quam splendidus! Talium virorum animo grato admiramur ingenium illud facile et promptum, quod, velut ipsa rerum natura, nulla, necessitate coactum sed quasi sua sponte pulcherrimum quidque in luminis oras quotannis submittit. Audiamus Propertium:

'aspice quot submittit humus formosa colores;
et veniunt hederae sponte sua melius.'

Etiam nosmet ipsi hodie fronti tam felici hederae nostrae corollam sponte imponimus. Duco ad vos Petrum Tschaikowsky.

This has been well rendered in the translation by Vronwy Hankey.

Today a brilliant pupil of the famous Rubinstein has come into our presence from the vast empire of Russia. He is a man who knows Italy and Switzerland intimately, but whose chief delight is in the popular songs of his native land. How well he interprets the passion and melancholy of the soul of the Slav! How broad is his conception of musical form! How individual is his development of musical themes! How subtle are his modulations! How magnificently he welds together the different departments of the orchestra! We admire and rejoice in such men's genius, which, like Nature herself, spontaneously produces something beautiful every year. As Propertius has said, 'Consider how many flowers the fair earth produces. Even the ivy grows best of its own accord.' Today we, too, of our own accord place the ivy wreath upon the head of this most successful composer.

I present to you Peter Tschaikowsky.

When we put beside this oration the following extract from Dannreuther's article in Grove's *Dictionary*, Dr Sandy's source of information becomes apparent.

His compositions, more or less, bear the impress of the Slavonic temperament – fiery exaltation on a basis of languid melancholy. He is fond of huge and fantastic outlines, of bold modulations and strongly marked rhythms, of subtle melodic turns and exuberant figuration, and he delights in gorgeous effects of orchestration. His music everywhere makes the impression of genuine spontaneous originality.

The quotation from Propertius consists of lines nine and ten from the second poem in Book One of his poetry. The mention of 'the famous Rubinstein' in the very first sentence of the oration neatly acknowledges 'the King over the water' (*ut aiunt*).

How immense must have been Tchaikovsky's relief as John Peile pronounced him doctor and shook him by the hand! How welcome the seat to which he returned as Dr Sandys summoned Boito to rise and stand before him!

Boito, said Dr Sandys, had received a double gift from the Muses, the gift of music and the gift of poetry. Apart from his success as a composer, he had written the librettos of '*Hamleto*' (for Faccio), '*Othello*' and '*Falstaffio*'. But '*Nero*' had remained too long '*in scriniis suis*'. Nobody had more vividly exemplified the precept of the great German poet – who sang of Mephistopheles – that was embodied in the lines '*ipsum pectore prodeat necessest,/quidquid pectora permovere sumet*' ['*Denn es musz von Herzen gehen,/Was auf Hersen wirken soll*']. Dr Sandys concluded, 'Perhaps we shall yet praise others [Grieg] on a future occasion, but, today, we rest content with the number of the Muses and end our eulogy to this assembly of nine distinguished men.'

The *Daily Graphic* says that all four composers were well applauded, 'particularly M. Saint-Saëns, and most of all Signor Boito, who looked strikingly handsome in his gorgeous gown.' Boito was quite taken with his doctor's robes, which he put on for the amusement of his friends when he returned to Milan.

After the orations came the recitation of the prize exercises; this finale to the ceremony was recounted by the *Daily Graphic*.

Mr. Barnett, of King's led off the Prolusiones, by reading excerpts from his Greek prize poem on 'Marie Antoinette'. The Greek is admirable, but Mr. Barnett has not Dr. Sandys' gift of clear utterance. The gallery boys guyed the Greek poet, and the young and fair seemed to enjoy the fun. But Mr. Barnett stuck to his guns like a Roberts and got through all right. His reading of the Greek epigram subsequently was rewarded with loud acclamations – because it was very short. The Latin ode was read by its author, Mr. Ramsey, of King's, in the old-fashioned English style of pronunciation, which presented a marked contrast to the official utterances of the public orator. The Latin epigram is by Mr. Taylor, of Caius. Mr. Taylor was encouraged by friends among the gods, with whom he seemed to find favour. On receiving his medal from the Vice and making a very proper obeissance of obligation, there was a shout of, 'You practised that, Tim,' though it was scarcely equal to a *débutante's* courtsey in elaboration. The English prize poem on 'Delphi' was reserved to the end. This had been won by Mr. J. H. B. Masterman, of John's, and is a very good prize poem indeed. Mr. Masterman has now won the English verse medal three years in succession, and as somebody in the crowd said, 'Oh, then he ought to keep it altogether.' But she was thinking of a challenge cup. Mr. Masterman poured forth his Pindaric strophes with good effect, and there was, apparently, sympathy between the gallery and the poet. When he spoke of a 'seven-tongued lyre', they seemed horrified for a moment at such possibilities of mendacity, but soon got over it, and the interruptions were rather encouraging than embarrassing. The poem is in the manner of Gray's Pindaric odes, and very excellent work it is.

The exercises being over, the stately procession returned by the south door, and the great assembly broke up; but before they all dispersed to lunch in the flower-decorated rooms in sunny courts and cloistered quads there was a great demonstration as Lord Roberts drove away from the Senate House. Then quiet settled over Cambridge, and cooks' boys with covered trays were busy carrying lunches up quaint, twisting staircases to merry parties in college and in lodgings, wherever the hospitable don or equally hospitable undergraduate had his abode.

On quitting the Senate House at just before one o'clock, Tchaikovsky and his fellow doctors made their way to Christ's College, a distance of some 350 yards to the east, at the junction of St Andrew's Street and Petty Cury. Here, they were the luncheon guests of John Peile, who, as well as being Vice-Chancellor, was Master of Christ's. For this meal, three large tables had been brought together to assume the shape of a horseshoe. At the central table sat the principal guests, among whom were Lord and Lady Roberts, Lord and Lady Kelvin, The Maharajah of Bhaonagar, the Italian Ambassador, and Lord and Lady Herschell. The Maharajah sat on John Piele's right, and Lady Roberts, on his left.

Saint-Saëns, Bruch and Boito were all on one of the secondary tables, and Tchaikovsky was at the other. Saint-Saëns sat opposite Austen Leigh and had on his left the University Registrary, J. W. Clark, who four years earlier had run against Jenkinson for the librarianship. He had been registrary since May 1891. Saint-Saëns would have found Clark an intriguing table companion. The registrary's biographer Arthur Shipley relates that he 'was absolutely unmusical, and it was literally true of him that he was only conscious of the National Anthem being played by seeing the people stand up. He would remark when questioned on the subject that he did not mind music more than any other noise. Yet he sat with pleasure through Wagner's *Ring*, and at one time used to go regularly to the Handel Festival. His dramatic instincts on these occasions made up for his lack of musical sense.' Clark was deeply interested in *The Ring*. 'It was always a wish of his to attend some of the performances at Bayreuth as a dramatic experience; but I do not think that this wish of his was ever gratified.' Saint-Saëns usually divided Wagnerites into three categories. The first consisted of those who, though knowing little of music, regarded Wagner's operas as the alpha and omega of all musical creations and had scant regard for any other composers; these people were straightforward maniacs. In the second category came those who, understanding little of Wagner, nevertheless were thrilled by the way his music washed over them; these people were not dissimilar to drug-takers. In the third category were the sane, who, having studied Wagner's works, had no illusions about their defects, yet found in them many beauties. Being perplexed to understand what literary merits anybody could discover in *The Ring*, Saint-Saëns had not thought to invent a fourth category. But this category, for tone-deaf people of a serious and philosophical disposition, would have included many English Wagnerites, Clark being among them. And it often seemed to be precisely those falling within this category who were most blind to the nationalist propaganda disgorged through the master's doggerel. Even the bestiality of *A Capitulation*, written in 'a jovial hour' at the time of the fall of Paris, with its depiction of Victor Hugo, in ram's horns, setting fire to himself, did nothing to disturb their calm belief in Wagner's stature as a literary artist of vision and depth. When Wagner told Saint-Saëns that *A Capitulation* could hardly be held against him, since it was no more than a joke, Saint-Saëns replied, 'It would have been so easy for you not to have made it', to which the master could find no answer.

Further down the same table on which Saint-Saëns was sitting were Bruch and Boito, opposite each other, with Stanford on Boito's left. Interestingly enough, Boito had found the Banquet Scene from *Odysseus* the most absorbing of the works that were performed at the Guildhall. 'I cannot deny that it is somewhat heavy', he later told a friend, 'but the structure and treatment are marvellous, and it is inexhaustible in its changing ideas, which are sometimes harmonic, sometimes rhythmic, sometimes contrapuntal, sometimes instrumental.' It was his intention to make a special study of the score of *Odysseus*.

At the other of the lesser tables, Tchaikovsky sat with John Peile's daughter Hester on his right. She had married the Reverend John Kempthorne three years earlier and moved to Gateshead, where her husband was curate of St Aidan's. He became Bishop of Hull in 1910.

On the composer's left was the celebrated philosopher Henry Sidgwick, the author of *Principles of Political Economy, Scope and Method of Economic Science, Outlines of the History of Ethics* and *Methods of Ethics*. He was one of the founders of the Society for Psychical Research and became its first president. He was also a member of the Metaphysical Society. He took a keen interest in the affairs of the university and played an important role, along with Sedley Taylor, in the founding of Newnham College, of which his wife was created principal in 1892. Her brother was Arthur Balfour.

Sidgwick was a delightful conversationalist. J. N. Keynes wrote of him, 'It was extraordinary how illuminating he would be, whatever turn the conversation might take: on one topic after another he had something interesting to say, and what he said was always to the point and suggestive. He had an excellent memory, and there seemed to be no limit to his range of knowledge . . . And all his talk was touched by a subtle, delicate humour that added to its charm.' He had a slight impediment of speech, but he turned this to his advantage. 'His skill in using his stammer was often noticed', recalled Leslie Stephen. 'His hearers watched and waited for the coming thought, which then exploded the more effectually. Sidgwick not only conceded but eagerly promoted contributions of talk from his companions. He would wait with slightly parted lips to an answer to some inquiry, showing a keen interest which encouraged your expectation that you were about to say a good thing, and sometimes, let us hope, helped to realise the expectation.' His nephew A. C. Benson said, 'The actual manner of his talk was indescribably attractive; his gentle voice, his wise and kindly air, as he balanced arguments and statements, the gestures of his delicate hands, his lazy and contented laugh, the backward poise of his head, his updrawn eyebrows, all made it a pleasure to watch him. Yet his expression as a rule tended to be melancholy, and even wistful.'

Seated opposite Tchaikovsky was John Sandys. He was one of the greatest classical scholars of his time. He came up to St John's in 1863. In 1864 he won the Bell Scholarship; in 1865, the Browne Medal for a Greek Ode; in 1865 and 1866, the Porson Prize for Greek Verse; and also in 1866, the Member's prize for a Latin Essay. In 1867, he became Senior Classic. In 1869, at the remarkably early age of twenty-five, he was appointed Tutor of St John's. He succeeded Jebb as Public Orator in 1876 after one of the most exciting elections in the history of the university. Charles Moule, his senior by ten years, had been expected to take over from Jebb virtually unopposed, but Sandys' decision to stand against him captured the imagination of the academic world. On the day of the election, special trains were run to and from London to cater for all those who determined to cast their vote. By the time the poll had closed, 1,288 members of the Senate, from throughout the British Isles, had voted, breaking all records, and Sandys was elected by a tiny majority. He held the post for the next forty-three years – another record. During that time, he delivered orations in favour of nearly 700 recipients of honorary degrees, including, up to 1893, Dvořák, Stanford, Mackenzie, Joachim, Maitland, Jowett, Watts, Matthew Arnold, Henry Irving and Oliver Wendell Holmes. Sandys took immense pains not only in the composition of his orations, but in researching the achievements of those in whose honour he spoke. 'He was extraordinary, even among scholars of that day, at once for the width and the accuracy of his scholarship', wrote T.R. Glover; 'he knew so much and knew it so well; he remembered everything with such precision, that it was dangerous to try to catch him tripping, and probably few people tried it twice.' He published and edited a large number of books, but his finest work was the *History of Scholarship*, which came out shortly before his death in 1922. This monumental and encyclopaedic study was, says Glover, 'quite out of the range of most scholars'. Sandys also deserves recognition for leading the forces that opposed and eventually defeated the Government's proposal to hand over the British Museum to a department of the War Office.

He was an extremely dignified and serious man, with a superb voice that was capable, as it had to be, of riding majestically over the banter of undergraduates at a degree ceremony. To some, he seemed pompous, cold and even unintelligible. His propriety, Glover maintained, 'often quite obscured the kindliness of his nature.' *The Times* echoed this in its obituary, saying, 'As a matter of fact he was by nature intensely generous, affectionate and warm-hearted.' Nor was he above seeking the advice of others, when preparing his orations, in matters of syntax or biographical detail. He may, indeed, have asked Stanford to look over the orations he produced for the four composers; it is hard to tell, for there is a slight discrepancy in his reference to *Nerone*. But Boito was so cagey about the opera that Sandys could hardly be expected to know much about it, and Stanford may well have been equally in the dark. Sandys enjoyed music and was for some years president of the St John's Musical Society. He had attended the previous day's concert. A year earlier, he and his wife went to Bayreuth and heard *Tannhäuser*, *Die Meistersinger*, *Tristan und Isolde* and *Parsifal*. He might have spoken to Tchaikovsky about Wagner, particularly in light of the fact that the following item of information had been published in the most recent issue of the *Cambridge Review*, which came out on 8 June.

A contemporary London journal gives this account of M. Tschaikowsky's views upon Wagner as recently delivered at Brussels, and it may be interesting to some of our readers during the next week:
'If you were to ask me whether Wagner is the last word on musical art, I should answer, No, – though I have a profound admiration for his immense talent. I should not like all future music to be composed according to the recipe of the Tetralogy. The constant preponderance of the orchestra appears to me to be a false principle. I do not deny the great genius of Wagner. His Tetralogy is a mighty fine thing; but when all is said and done, an opera ought to be sung.'

Tchaikovsky went to the first Bayreuth Festival in 1876 and saw the complete cycle of *The Ring*, which he considered to be, according to Laroche, 'an epoch-making work of art'. Nevertheless, says Laroche, 'the sincere attempt to understand the language and style of the text – which is so clumsy and difficult in its composition that, even to the Germans themselves, it is almost inaccessible – produced in Tchaikovsky a feeling of great depression.' The composer wrote to Modest, 'After the last notes of *Götterdämmerung* sounded, I felt as though I'd been let out of prison.' Tchaikovsky, of course, was never in any doubt about Wagner's musical genius, and *Francesca da Rimini*, the very next work that he composed after visiting Bayreuth, bears unmistakable signs of Wagner's influence. He was always ready to learn from his contemporaries; the Sextet even has a touch of Brahms about it, not least in a near-quotation from the finale of the Double Concerto.

The vice-chancellor's luncheon concluded with a time-honoured ceremony, in which a huge loving-cup was passed round the tables in celebration of the new doctorates. Boito's biographer Piero Nardi says that this made a vivid impression on the composer; it may well have appealed to his sense of romance and nostalgia for the fabled days of medieval chivalry.

After the meal, John Peile showed his guests the beautiful and spacious gardens of Christ's College, drawing their attention in particular to 'Milton's Tree', which, says Saint-Saëns, 'we were charitably informed, has no connection with the author of *Paradise Lost*.' Legend originally had it that the tree was planted by Milton, when he was an undergraduate at Christ's. However, Arthur Shipley, who was Master of the college in the early part of the present century, writes in *Cambridge Cameos*, 'My knowledge of the undergraduate, and it is a long one, leads to the belief that he is rather more apt to pull up trees than to plant them.' Shipley feels that the tree, a mulberry, was planted in 1609, a year after Milton's birth, when 300 mulberry plants were purchased by the college for eighteen shillings. It should be noted that the poet's biographer David Masson states, 'No fact in universal biography is better attested than that great men, wherever they go, plant mulberry trees.'

After their stroll through the gardens, the vice-chancellor's guests were entertained at an *al fresco* tea-party by Mrs Peile and other 'femmes charmantes', according to Saint-Saëns, among whom was presumably Hester Kempthorne. The Frenchman hardly had time to meet these hostesses before he set out for another appointment. He had at last succeeded in upstaging his fellow doctors once and for all by allowing Stanford and Alan Gray to persuade him to give an organ recital in Trinity College Chapel. The organ, one of the finest in Cambridge, had been renovated in 1889, and a pneumatic system had been installed. In particular, a 32 ft Open Wood on the pedal had been added and, rare for that time in England, a Doppel Flute. Saint-Saëns arrived about half an hour late for his recital. After a quarter of an hour's wait, Alan Gray filled in by playing Bach's *St Anne Fugue* and *Wachet Auf* Chorale Prelude. By then, Saint-Saëns had reached the organ-loft and, before a large audience, immediately launched into a brilliant extemporisation, following it with a second, that took the form of a fully developed fugue. He next performed his own Fantaisie in E flat and concluded with Bach's Prelude in E flat. This accumulation of E flat leads one to assume that Saint-Saëns was unaware that Alan Gray had played the *St Anne Fugue*, which is also in the same key. The performances, said the *Cambridge Review*, 'were nothing short of marvellous'. Saint-Saëns found the organ 'excellent et d'un maniement commode'.

Tchaikovsky left Mrs Peile's garden-party at about 3.20 or so and returned to Downing, which was some 600 yards along St Andrew's Street and its continuation Regent's Street.

Florence Maitland took some photographs of him in his doctor's robes, probably in the garden behind West Lodge. It seems likely that this happened immediately following his return. The roses that she and Adeline pinned in his lapel are not apparent in the photographs. At around four o'clock, he took his leave of the Maitlands and set out for the station. Florence and Adeline kept his soap as a memento.

He probably caught the train to King's Cross, for, as Gwen Raverat writes in *Period Piece*, 'Liverpool Street was unknown to the genteel.' Bruch, according to the *Pall Mall Gazette*, was to be seen 'philosophically standing by a lamp-post of the station, leaving frivolous colleagues to travel by another line, and preserving a magnificent solitude.' By 6.15 or 6.30, Tchaikovsky would have been back at the Dieudonné. The reason for the composer's early return from Cambridge was that he had already arranged to give a farewell dinner at the Dieudonné for some of his London friends. These are likely to have included George and Lillian Henschel, Émile Hatzfeld and his wife, and possibly Hatzfeld's brother Louis and his wife. Louis Hatzfeld, thanks to his brother's influence, had been taken on by Lucas, Pitt and Weber as one of their representatives. Modest Tchaikovsky gives us to understand that Eugène and Louise Oudin were also among the dinner guests, which brings us back to Klein's conversation with Tchaikovsky on the train to Cambridge. If Oudin and his wife were present – and the likelihood is that Modest is correct in suggesting that they were – then the composer must have become acquainted with them while he was in London and perhaps went to the first part of the concert in which they participated at 3.00 pm on 1 June in St James's Hall, going on to the Mackenzies's for tea at around 4.30. This was on the same day as the Philharmonic Concert in that building. Tchaikovsky was there for rehearsals until 1.30, and it would not have been unnatural for Oudin, who took the title role in the English première of *Eugene Onegin*, to have been on hand to introduce himself and invite the composer to his own recital an hour and a half later. In his letter of 3 June to Modest, Tchaikovsky said that he was invited to concerts every day and could not refuse to go.

Later that evening, after the dinner-party had finished, Tchaikovsky and Hatzfeld went to the Alhambra and saw the ballet *Chicago*, which was among the most successful entertainments running in London. The first performance had taken place on 27 March, and the ballet had been playing to packed houses since then. The *Observer* gave it an excellent review on 2 April.

> The new ballet, entitled *Chicago*, produced on Monday last at the Alhambra, is one of the most splendid works ever introduced at that popular establishment, and was received with enthusiastic applause by a crowded audience. The scenery, representing the Chicago Exhibition and grounds, with the Michigan Lake in front, is a masterpiece by Mr. T. E. Ryan, of itself worthy of a visit, and surpassing all the previous works of that gifted artist. The music has been arranged and partly composed by Mr. Jacobi; the costumes are the most superb and graceful that Mr. Alias has constructed, and the stage business has been admirably arranged by MM. Gredelue and Burleigh. It would be useless to attempt descriptions of the dazzling scenes which rapidly succeed each other; they must ᴗe seen in order to be appreciated.

The ubiquitous Dwarf of Blood, reporting for the *Sporting Times*, was equally commendatory.

> If ever Yankee Doodle came to town with success, he did so on Monday evening when the new ballet of *Chicago* was danced at the Alhambra, and the applause which brought Mons. Agoust, Mons. Gredelue, and finally Mons. Jacobi before the curtain was well deserved . . . A very bright ballet, with pretty dresses, tuneful music by that past-master of the art, Mons. Jacobi, and not a dull second from the rise of the curtain to the fall. Signora Pollini achieved a very real success in her Spanish dance, and the Agousts and Almontes supplied the necessary comic element.

In an interview that appeared in the December 1895 issue of the *Strand Musical Magazine*, which was then edited by Hatzfeld, Jacobi stated that, during Tchaikovsky's visit to London, in June 1893, he 'called on me at the Alhambra in company with your Editor'. The interviewer, who was probably Hatzfeld, adds, 'I may explain here that on the evening of the day on which the University of Cambridge conferred upon him the degree of Doctor of Music, Tchaikowsky visited the Alhambra, and so charmed was he with M. Jacobi's ballet music that he called on the composer and warmly congratulated him on his artistic work.' It will be recalled, however, that, when the composer saw Jacobi's *Enchantment* at the Alhambra, on 20 March 1888, he was not so enthusiastic.

Jacobi's career was similar to Offenbach's in that, though born in Berlin, he moved early in life to Paris and later became a naturalised Frenchman. In 1861, at the age of twenty-one, he took first prize for violin playing at the Conservatoire. He went on to become first violin at the Opéra, which brought him into contact with all the leading French musicians of the day. He became friendly with Berlioz, Auber, Meyerbeer, Rossini, Gounod, Wagner, Saint-Saëns, Bizet, Massenet, Delibes and other composers. In 1869, Offenbach engaged him as conductor at the Théâtre des Bouffes-Parisiens. Placed in an unhappy position, again like Offenbach, during the Franco-Prussian War, he fled to London, where Costa took him on as first violin at Covent Garden. Shortly afterwards, he was appointed conductor at the Alhambra, for which theatre he wrote dozens of successful ballets and comic operas.

He would have known of Tchaikovsky's interest in ballet through the Belgian choreographer Joseph Hansen, who was ballet master at the Alhambra from 1884 to 1887. Hansen had been director of ballet at the Bolshoi from 1879 until his departure for London. He was attracted to the myth of the Swan-Maiden as a subject for ballet and, in January 1880, revived Tchaikovsky's *Swan Lake*, which had failed disastrously three years earlier on its première in Moscow. The revival proved equally unsuccessful, but Hansen, undeterred, staged a new version in October 1882. This was also a failure, and, by June 1893, no further attempt had been made to produce the ballet. Hansen was still convinced, though, that the Swan-Maiden legend, given the right music, could be turned into a satisfactory ballet. He put the idea to Jacobi on his arrival at the Alhambra, and the French composer supplied him with a score. Hansen thus made his début in England with *The Swans*, which was staged at the Alhambra on 1 December 1884. It achieved a huge success, further adding to Jacobi's reputation, which by now was international, and much increasing the fame of Hansen, who, five years later, was engaged as ballet master of the Paris Opéra, which post he filled for eighteen years, until his death in 1907.

We do not know if Jacobi was acquainted with Tchaikovsky's

ballet music. This seems unlikely, for none of it had yet been heard in England. His second ballet, *Sleeping Beauty*, had been well received in St Petersburg in January 1890, but *Nutcracker* failed to excite much interest when produced in the same city in December 1892. Tchaikovsky's reputation as a ballet composer was practically non-existent outside Russia; it was certainly nothing compared to Jacobi's. Moreover, the French composer had numerous – more than thirty – successful ballets to his credit and was still writing an average of three a year. Since the triumph of his *Sleeping Beauty* in December 1890, he had furnished another seven scores for the Alhambra.

All four of the new doctors returned to London during the afternoon and evening of 13 June. From Bram Stoker's *Personal Reminiscences of Henry Irving*, we learn that Boito went to see *Becket*.

> Boito came to the Lyceum on June 13, 1893, when we were playing *Becket*. I talked with him in his box and in the little drawing-room of the royal box. He afterwards came round on the stage to see Irving. He was wonderfully impressed with *Becket*. He said to me that Irving was 'the greatest artist he had ever seen.' Two nights later, 15th June, he came to supper in the Beefsteak room. Irving had some musicians and others to meet him. The following were of the party: A. C. Mackenzie, Villiers Stanford, Damrosch . . .

Earlier in the evening of 15 June, Boito had been to Bruch's Philharmonic concert, which was well attended and well applauded.

Like Saint-Saëns, Tchaikovsky crossed over to Paris on the morning of 14 June, arriving in the French capital towards the end of the afternoon; he stayed in his usual hotel, in the Rue Richepanse (named after the famous general). On 15 June, he wrote four letters. In the first, addressed to Hatzfeld, he asked him to be kind enough to recover the orchestral parts of *Francesca da Rimini*, 'which I forgot to bring with me when I left Cambridge.' The second letter was to Jurgenson, in which he told him, 'Cambridge, with its peculiar customs that retain much that is medieval, with its colleges that resemble monasteries and its buildings recalling a remote past, made a very agreeable impression on me. Now, I find it pleasant to think about – but, there, it was both hard work and exhausting.' In the third of his letters, to Konradi, the composer wrote at greater length.

At Cambridge, I stayed with Professor Maitland.This would have been dreadfully embarrassing, if he and particularly his wife had not proved to be two of the most charming people I ever met; and Russophiles into the bargain, which is the greatest rarity in England ... Now everything is over, it's pleasant to look back on my success in England and to remember the extraordinary cordiality shown to me everywhere, though, thanks to my peculiar temperament, the whole time I tormented and worried myself terribly. My legs hurt badly all the while I was there as a result of the continual upset and strain on my nerves. It was a special sort of pain, and, towards the end, I started sleeping badly. Only here, where I've at last been on my own again, have I recovered a bit.

His fourth letter was to his brother Anatoly.

I suffered in London and Cambridge. I can't tell you how pleased I am it's all over, and, in fact, it went successfully. The triumph of being elevated to the rank of doctor lasted for two days. I stayed not in a hotel, but in an apartment set aside for me in a professor's house. This could have been very embarrassing, were it not that the professor is the kindest of men and a Russophile as well. I was completely captivated by his wife, who is very attractive ... *Francesca* went very well and got great applause. Then we had a tip-top dinner, with a splendid party afterwards. The next day, there was the ceremony. At 11.30, we gathered in a special place, where the whole body of professors of the university and other officials were present while we were being dressed up in our ceremonial outfits. These consist of a white silk mantle sewn round with ermine and a beret made of black ermine. After this, the official in charge put us in a certain order, and then the procession across the huge courtyard into the Senate began. A big crowd watched the procession. The greatest stir was caused by a rajah ...

In describing the ceremony, Tchaikovsky told his brother, 'The students shriek and scream and make an awful noise, and you have to bear all this without batting an eyelid.' It was only since coming to Paris that he had been able to catch up on his rest after a fortnight of 'unbelievable exhaustion and nervous tension. In comparison with London, Paris seems like a desert, for the traffic in London is so dreadful.'

After leaving Paris, Tchaikovsky spent a week with the delightful pianist Sophie Menter at her castle twenty kilometres west of Kitzbuhel, in the Tyrol. (This magnificent establishment, Schloss Itter, is now a first-class hotel with fifty bedrooms.) Sophie Menter was Liszt's favourite woman pupil; in a letter of 13 September 1884, he tells her, 'My few days' stay at your fairy-like castle Itter will remain a magic memory.' Tchaikovsky, who visited the pianist on more than one occasion, found the castle 'a devilish pretty nest . . . The great thing is the exquisite, picturesque neighbourhood.' He was much attracted to Menter. 'She was very good-looking, wore magnificent diamonds, and dressed beautifully', says Ganz; Berger describes her as 'strikingly handsome'; 'I confess to a weakness, not altogether musical, for Madame Sophie Menter', wrote George Bernard Shaw in April 1890.

Following further visits, to his brothers Modest and Nikolay, the composer eventually arrived back at Klin on 30 July. A letter from his old nurse, who had retired to Switzerland, was waiting for him. 'Did you get very tired?' she asked. 'Did you enjoy your stay in Cambridge? Do you like the English?' Yes, he replied, he did get tired, but he was fully recovered now; he liked the English very much; and he told her all about the ceremony.

Two days later, he began the orchestration of the Sixth Symphony. A few days after that, there came another letter from his nurse. 'I would so much love to see my little Piotr in all the grandeur of his robes', she wrote. 'When you were a child, you wanted to go to England, you also wanted to speak to your Sovereign, and now all this child's dream has come true . . . The English people should be very happy to hold so high a place in your esteem.'

CHAPTER 10

TCHAIKOVSKY

Tchaikovsky was back in his beloved Russia, in the country that revered him above all other living composers. In Catherine Drinker Bowen's book on the composer, the soprano Ella Eichenwald, the first Bolshoi Tatyana, speaks of the affection in which he was held.

> Everyone fell in love with him, women and men and children and grand-mothers. A train of people used to follow him around Moscow . . . He had no mannerisms. Not one affectation . . . I have rehearsed under many directors. Rimsky-Korsakov would roar out upon the stage and frighten us all to death. But Tchaikowsky! He would speak to us like sisters, like children, and then in a little while someone would ask, 'Where is Tchaikowsky? The rehearsal is nearly over and he has told us nothing.' And they would find him in a corner somewhere, just watching. He would say everything had been wonderful . . . He was the simplest man that ever lived.

Tchaikovsky's enormous popularity in Russia can be said to date from October 1884, when *Eugene Onegin* was first staged in St Petersburg in a superb interpretation, under the baton of Eduard Nápravník, that eclipsed the two earlier Moscow productions, conducted by Nikolay Rubinstein and Enrico Bevignani. From the second performance onwards, it drew packed audiences. 'This success not only marked an important event in the history of Russian opera', wrote Modest Tchaikovsky, 'but proved to be the beginning of a new era in the life of Tchaikovsky himself. Henceforward, his name, hitherto known and respected among musicians and a fairly wide circle of musical amateurs, was now recognized by the public at large, and he acquired a popularity which no Russian composer had yet attained in his own land.' In *My Long Life in Music*, Leopold Auer recalls the first night of the St Petersburg production.

> The première, given with a most brilliant *mise en scène*, was applauded from the very beginning – as I well remember, for I was in the audience – and the success of 'Eugene Oniegin' was established beyond question. The

composer was feted in every possible way, but what testified more eloquently than anything else to the favour enjoyed by the work was that it
kept its place in the repertoire from that day to the outbreak of the Revolution, not only in St. Petersburg and Moscow, but all over Russia as well.
From that day forward Tchaikovsky became the best beloved, the most
widely popular of all Russian composers. There has been much argument
pro and con regarding the question of whether Tchaikovsky's music is
truly Slavic, truly representative of Russian musical instincts and national
feeling. But to those who dwell upon his eclecticism and the alleged
absence of a truly national note in his compositions, we may oppose the
verdict which we have just recorded, that of the Russian people itself.

By the time Tchaikovsky was discussing with Klein, on the train to
Cambridge, the bleak reception of *Eugene Onegin* in London eight
months earlier, the work had already become the favourite opera of
the Russians. It remains, to this day, the most frequently performed
opera in Russia, rivalled in popularity only by *The Queen of Spades*. In
Russian Symphony, Boris Yarustovsky places *Eugene Onegin* in the
context of Russian musical history.

It is difficult to overestimate the significance of this opera, which not only
blazed new trails in Tchaikovsky's own work, but played a role of inestimable importance in the rise of Russian national opera as a whole . . .
Although he wrote in all operatic genres – grand, comic and lyrical –
Tchaikovsky invariably concentrated his attention mainly on the inner
world of his heroes. In this sense, his operas might in all justice be called
lyrico-psychological. In this genre, Tchaikovsky was an innovator, and
this is perhaps his most valuable contribution to world opera . . . Through
the medium of his operas, Tchaikovsky revealed the spiritual world, the
psychological make-up of Russian men and women.

Eugene Onegin was the first opera that Shostakovich ever saw. His
mother took him to a performance in Petrograd in 1915, when he was
nine years old. He recalled the impression the work made on him in
an autobiographical article contributed to the September 1956
edition of *Soviet Music*. 'I already knew much of the music by heart. It
was often played and sung in our house. But, when I first heard the
opera performed by an orchestra, I was amazed. A new world of
orchestral music was unfolded before me.' Soon afterwards, he had
committed the entire composition to memory, and Tchaikovsky,
'both the man and the musician', came to occupy 'a special place in
my heart'. On the fiftieth anniversary of Tchaikovsky's death, he
wrote, 'I, like everybody else brought up in the spirit of Russian

culture, find in him a part of myself.'

In a letter to *The Times* of 18 October 1921, Stravinsky said, 'Tchaikovsky's music, which does not appear specifically Russian to everybody, is often more profoundly Russian than music which has long
since been awarded the facile label of Muscovite picturesqueness.
This music is quite as Russian as Pushkin's verse or Glinka's song.
Whilst not specifically cultivating in his art the 'soul of the Russian
peasant', Tchaikovsky drew unconsciously from the true, popular
sources of our race.' Stravinsky's opera *Mavra*, first performed in June
1922, was dedicated to the memory of Pushkin, Glinka and Tchaikovsky. The purpose of this dedication, Stravinsky explained in
Expositions and Developments, was 'to show a different Russia to my
non-Russian, and especially to my French, colleagues, who were, I
considered, saturated with the tourist-office orientalism of the
maguchia kuchka, the "powerful clique", as Stassov used to call the
Five. I was, in fact, protesting against the picturesque in Russian
music, and against those who failed to see that the picturesque is
produced by very small tricks.' He went on to add that 'Tchaikovsky's talent was the greatest of any Russian musician' and that his
principal virtues were elegance and a sense of humour. In his letter to
The Times, Stravinsky pointed out that Tchaikovsky was blessed by
nature with the priceless gifts of simplicity, naïveté and spontaneity.

> That is why he never feared to let himself go, whereas the prudes, whether
> *raffinés* or academic, were shocked by the frank speech, free from artifice,
> of his music.
>   Tchaikovsky possessed the power of *melody*, centre of gravity in every
> symphony, opera or ballet composed by him. It is absolutely indifferent to
> me that the quality of his melody was sometimes unequal. The fact is that
> he was a creator of *melody*, which is an extremely rare and precious gift.
> Among us Glinka, too, possessed it; and not to the same degree, those
> others. And that is something which is not German. The Germans manu-
> factured, and manufactured music with themes and leitmotives, which
> they substituted for melodies.

We can now see more clearly why Tchaikovsky – and Berlioz –
whose works contained 'something which is not German', made such
slow progress in England. Within the space of little more than sixty
years, Germany had produced Beethoven, Spohr, Weber, Mendelssohn, Schumann, Wagner and Brahms. The English became so used
to a nineteenth-century orchestral masterpiece sounding German

that, in a sense, they could not recognise its Germanness; it seemed simply to speak a universal language. Similarly, in the opera-house, they expected a work to sound Italian; Wagner's operas were initially performed in London in Italian, and, for many years, he made greater headway in the concert hall, through orchestral excerpts. In training gifted young composers and instrumentalists, it was only natural to send them to the land of Beethoven and Brahms, where they would hopefully absorb the ethos and methods of the universal language (with its characteristically German idioms and procedures). Likewise, singers would be sent to Italy so their voices could benefit from the Italian air.

Sterndale Bennett, Sullivan, Stanford, Cowen, Berger and Delius all went to Leipzig, and Mackenzie and Parry, too, trained in Germany. Vaughan Williams studied with Bruch in Berlin, though he later rectified this by persuading Ravel, his junior by two years, to take him as a pupil. He admired Tchaikovsky for writing 'his national music as naturally as he spoke his own language', and he eventually came to do the same. But, a generation earlier, young musicians modelled themselves on the Germans. And, to them, how perfect an exemplar Brahms seemed, upholding the great German symphonic tradition, not straying beyond the bounds of absolute music.

The Russians have never been greatly attracted to Brahms's music. In her autobiography *Recital*, the German mezzo-soprano Elena Gerhardt remembers when she visited Moscow in 1909 with Nikisch and was perplexed to find the hall half-empty at one of his concerts, despite all the tickets having been sold. The explanation was that one of Brahms's symphonies occupied the opening half of the programme, and, after the interval, the hall was full. 'They wanted Beethoven, and all the other classics – Russian composers, of course, in particular Tschaikowsky, but not Brahms . . . They fought for tickets when Nikisch conducted, and he stubbornly put Brahms' symphonies on the programme again and again, but I do not think he ever succeeded in conquering their aversion to Brahms, who was one of his most beloved composers.'

Russians like to feel the heartbeat of a composer, to hear him speaking to them through his music, and they warm to men like Beethoven, Berlioz, Schumann, Liszt, Dvořák and Mahler, whom they have come to love as if they were members of their own families. But, however much they respect his music, Brahms is to them little more than a disembodied name. Tchaikovsky's antipathy to Brahms, which is now familiar to us, was typically Russian.

In *Composer and Nation*, Sydney Finkelstein examines the differences between Brahms and Tchaikovsky.

Where Wagner read voluminously, turning everything, however, to his own irrational and subjective uses, Brahms seems to have been, of all the great composers, the most lacking in broad cultural interests, whether concerning the world at large or his own Germany and Austria. The thought central to Beethoven's personality, and taken up in a grotesque perversion by Wagner, that an artist had to know what the past of society made it possible for him to know, that he was a 'teacher of the nation', was foreign to Brahms . . . Since his vocation was that of a musician, to him the monuments of Germany were the great musicians: Johann Sebastian Bach, Handel, Haydn, Mozart, Beethoven, Schubert. Their work at least was solid and real. Brahms worshipped them, studied them, and tried to digest their art and make it his own . . . But he was unable to see these giants as real people, in their historical setting. They were ancestral gods. Where Wagner saw his art as the culmination of the past, Brahms realized there had been an element of greatness in the classic past which was missing in the present. The reason, its social thought, eluded him. It is a sad picture: this mind, so innately sensitive, thoughtful, sceptical of all myths and fantasies thrown up against reality, preferring to keep his feet solidly planted in the 'world of necessity', yet having so little to feed on . . .

Nietzsche described Brahms' character as 'the melancholy of impotence.' This cannot refer to any lack of strength or creative power. It does point up Brahms' inability to find a pathway to satisfy his deepest yearnings . . . He lived a rather lonely, outwardly loveless life, sometimes driving people away from him by his pride and his harsh and brusque manner, as if he had made a resolution never to show a weakness. He is perhaps the most enigmatic figure among the great composers . . .

In all of the four symphonies we find the typical and unclassical complexity of Brahms' style; a complexity which caused him to be looked upon as a cold, 'over-intellectual' and even mathematical composer, but which actually reflected the introspective complications of his own emotional life. Rarely can he make a direct and forthright statement. Every thought brings up a counter-thought, every feeling evokes its opposite, and everything is said with reservations.

A striking example is the Third Symphony. It opens with one of Brahms' most propulsive, declamatory themes, but, only a few bars later, the urgency is dissipated in reflective music. Then comes the second subject, a sweet, lilting melody in a folk waltz or *landler* style, but this, too, soon loses its momentum. A fiery transformation of the first theme follows, and this ushers in the development section, without appreciable break or demarcation. But in the development the storm again quiets down. So the music proceeds, with its propulsive force constantly halted by meditation.

Finkelstein sees Tchaikovsky as a man of equal complexity, but with one particular attribute that Brahms lacked.

> He had a social mind. His favourite writers were those with social minds: Tolstoi and Chekhov in Russia, Dickens and George Eliot in England. His symphonic works are deep personal expressions, in which the conflicts revealed are a parallel to the conflict in the real life of Russia in his time; the yearning for love, for human relations among people, and the protest against the harsh, oppressive, and, as he saw them, mysterious forces stifling such hopes. And just as his operas, with their naturalness in viewing contemporary life, opened up a path different from those of the other Russian composers of his time, so his symphonies marked a stage in the development of the form, with their architectural strength, their absolute clarity, their long-drawn beautiful melodies, and their combination of integrity with the ability to capture the heart of great masses of people.

In an article in the 15 April 1942 edition of the Russian publication *Literature and Art*, Shostakovich wrote, 'The symphonic epoch launched by Beethoven produced such outstanding musicians as Berlioz, Liszt, Wagner and Mahler, but the honour of being the true successor to Beethoven fell to Tchaikovsky. To the profundity of the Beethoven symphony, Tchaikovsky added that passionate lyrical emotion and clear expression of intimate human feelings that rendered the symphony – the most complex genre of musical art – accessible and dear to the masses.' ILN *Russian Symphony*, Boris Assafyev also considers Tchaikovsky to be the successor to Beethoven, as an essentially dramatic symphonist, with Schumann being the connecting link.

> For Schumann, music served not only as a medium of self-expression, but as a means of depicting spiritual conflicts in accordance with the laws of drama; in other words, it was the artistic vehicle by whose means the emotions of the audience could be involved in the portrayal of human passion. The influence of the psychologically realistic principles inherent in Schumann's works proved stronger and more fruitful than the results he himself achieved. He was incapable of applying his own magnificent lyrical qualities to the Beethoven principles of elaborate musical thinking in harmony with the principles of Shakespearean drama. This was left to Tchaikovsky . . .

Assafyev cites, in addition, Tchaikovsky's 'profound insight into the spiritual life of the men and women of an epoch of heightening nervous sensibility', an insight prompted by 'feelings of sympathy and compassion'. These qualities account for 'that particular flavour to his lyricism, which seems to caress the soul. In a word, there is nothing of passionate abandon or emotional anarchy in Tchaikovsky's music. It comes closer to the aesthetic characteristics peculiar to such Russian writers as Pushkin, Tolstoy, Chekhov and Gorky.'

Because of his interest in other people, Tchaikovsky's musical world is a distinctly human world. One thinks of Romeo and Juliet, Francesca and Paolo, Tatyana and Onegin, Lisa and Hermann, Odette and Siegfried, Aurora and Prince Désiré, Manfred, Kuma, Caliban, Carabosse, the Lilac Fairy and many other memorable creations; and one thinks of Tchaikovsky himself. In contrast, the musical world of Brahms is devoid of human beings. The *Tragic Overture* is not concerned with the plight of any particular hero or heroine. *Romeo and Juliet* is also a tragic overture, but it is about two familiar people, as real to us as Coriolanus was to Beethoven; or as Othello to Verdi; or as King Lear to Berlioz. And, for the Russians, this is important.

By the summer of 1893, Tchaikovsky's standing in Russia had reached remarkable heights. Chekhov ranked him second only to Tolstoy in the history of Russian art and told Modest, in a letter of 28 March 1890, 'I'm ready to stand, day and night, as guard of honour at the entrance to Piotr Hmyich's house – such is the extent of my admiration for him.' Seven months later, at the time when he dedicated his collection of stories *Gloomy People* to the composer, Chekhov sent Tchaikovsky a copy of his most recently published book and a photograph of himself, assuring him in an accompanying letter, 'and I would send you even the sun, if it belonged to me.' Tchaikovsky had earlier presented Chekhov with a signed photograph, inscribed 'To A. P. Chekhov, from his ardent admirer P. Tchaikovsky.' In return, Chekhov signed both the book and photograph that he sent the composer, referring to himself, in the inscription in the book, as 'the future librettist, A. Chekhov'. Their intention to collaborate on an opera based on Lermontov's *A Hero of Our Time* was never realised.

Another man of the theatre who venerated Tchaikovsky was Constantin Stanislavsky, who wrote, in *My Life in Art*, of the composer's 'kindness . . . timidity and eternal shyness . . . He was always nervous and afraid of society.' There is an interesting passage in Stanislavsky's book about Chekhov's visit to the Hermitage Theatre in the summer of 1899, when the Moscow Art Theatre company were rehearsing their first production of *Uncle Vanya*.

. . . we talked of the role of Uncle Vanya himself. It is accepted that Uncle
Vanya is a member of the landed gentry who manages the estate of the old
Professor Serebriakov. It would seem that we had not far to look. The
costume and the general appearance of a landed gentleman are well
known: high boots, a cap, sometimes a horsewhip – it is taken for granted
that he rides a great deal. Thus, we pictured him to ourselves. But
Chekhov was most indignant.

'Listen,' he said in great excitement, 'everything is made clear. You
didn't read the play.'

We looked at the text, but could find no hint there, unless we were to
attach significance to several words about a silk tie that Uncle Vanya
wore.

'Here it is, here it is written down,' Chekhov tried to persuade us.

'What is written down?' we asked in amazement: 'A silk tie?'

'Of course. Listen, he has a wonderful tie; he is an elegant cultured man.
It's simply not true that our landed gentry walk about with tar all over
their boots. They are wonderful people. They dress well. They order their
clothes in Paris. It's all written down here.'

These few remarks suddenly helped to explain the play . . . From that
time on, Uncle Vanya became for us a cultured, soft, elegant, poetic, fine
type of man, almost like the unforgettable and enchanting Piotr Ilyich
Tchaikovsky.

The composer, like so many other Russians from his background, did
indeed purchase many of his clothes from Paris. He felt more at ease
in France than in other foreign countries and he had a particular
affection for the music of contemporary French composers. 'What
pleases me', he wrote to Madame von Meck on 17 February 1883, 'is
their effort to be eclectic, their sense of proportion, their readiness to
break with time-honoured routine, while keeping within the limits of
musical grace . . . If we compare modern French music with what is
being composed in Germany, we shall see that German music is in a
state of decay . . . In France, on the contrary, we hear much that is
new and interesting, much that is fresh and forceful.' His love of
things French seems to have exerted a further influence, for says
Leopold Auer, he had 'the personality and the manners of a French
marquis of the eighteenth century; but very modest, with a modesty
which could not be mistaken for a pose. He was too intelligent ever to
attempt playing a part among his artistic comrades, to whom, incidentally, he was always most cordial . . . Tchaikovsky was excessively sensitive; modest and unassertive in his dealings with all, he
was deeply appreciative of any interest shown in him or his works.'
Even the cynical and acidulous Rimsky-Korsakov was completely

won over by Tchaikovsky and said of him in his autobiography, 'He was a pleasing and sympathetic man to talk with, one who knew how to be simple of manner and always to speak with evident sincerity and heartiness.' Laroche wrote, 'By his presence alone, he bought warmth and light'.

Tchaikovsky appears to have made the greatest impression on the young, many of whom worshipped him. Among these was Alexander Grechaninov, who recalled him in his autobiography, *My Life.*

My years at the Moscow Conservatoire [1881–90] coincided with the rise of Tchaikovsky's star on the musical horizon. Every new symphony that he composed was immediately included in the programmes of the Russian Imperial Musical Society. His songs were avidly snatched up by Moscow music lovers as soon as his publisher, Jurgenson, printed them. As a boy, I had the good fortune to be present at the first performances of both *Eugene Onegin* and *The Queen of Spades*. I have never forgotten the overwhelming effect these operas had on me.

The orchestra for the symphony concerts was usually supplemented by violinists, cellists and other players from the ranks of the Conservatoire students. Theory students were sometimes assigned percussion instruments to play, as long as the parts were not too prominent. I once got the chance to play the glockenspiel in Tchaikovsky's *Mozartiana,* when the composer himself was conducting. Naturally, I was nervous, but everything went all right. During the interval at the last rehearsal, I was talking to Kashkin, when I noticed Tchaikovsky coming towards us. Kashkin introduced us, Tchaikovsky shook hands with me and for the sake of saying something nice to me (which was in keeping with his kindly nature), remarked 'Young musicians should always be allotted such parts. Professionals never play them so well.'

I, of course, was in seventh heaven, and my friends, laughingly, said that for a week I did not wash the hand that Tchaikovsky had shaken.

Reinhold Glière also met Tchaikovsky at a concert, when the composer came to Kiev in December 1890 to conduct *The Queen of Spades* and a programme of his works, including *1812* and the Third Suite. In the concert hall, Tchaikovsky passed by Glière, who later recalled, 'I saw his face, so well known from so many portraits, and I involuntarily bowed, and Tchaikovsky smilingly returned my bow. The concert was fantastically successful. It was the first time in my life that I'd witnessed such ovations.' The young man had never before realised the degree to which music could thrill a whole mass of listeners. At the time, he was studying at the Kiev Conservatoire, but he now determined to complete his education in Moscow and become a composer. His aspirations were shortly afterwards fulfilled, and he went on to win the gold medal for composition at the Moscow Conservatoire.

Alexandre Benois was another upon whom Tchaikovsky's music had a profound effect. 'It was Tchaikovsky's *The Sleeping Beauty* that transformed my complete ignorance, and even contempt, for Russian music into enthusiastic admiration', he wrote in his *Memoirs*. He was nineteen at the time of the first production of the ballet in January 1890. A year later, he was equally moved by *The Queen of Spades*. 'Now, suddenly, the past of St Petersburg came closer to me. Until this was revealed to me by the opera, I had not been aware of my spiritual affinity with my native town. Because of *The Queen of Spades*, my environment took on a further dimension. Everywhere I went, I found something enchanting and poetic, at whose existence I had hitherto merely guessed.' In *Reminiscences of the Russian Ballet*, Benois spoke more fully of his reactions to Tchaikovsky's music.

I went to the second performance of *The Sleeping Beauty* and left the theatre in a rather hazy state, only feeling that I had just heard and seen something that I was *going* to love. When I try to analyse the feeling that came over me then, it seems to me that I simply could not believe in my own joy; that, subconsciously, I was already completely in the power of something entirely new, but for which, nevertheless, my soul had been waiting, for a long, long while. As soon as possible, I saw *The Sleeping Beauty* a second time, and then a third and a fourth. The more I listened to the music, the more I seemed to discover in it greater and greater beauty – a beauty that was not universally understood, but that was absolutely in harmony with me, that aroused the tenderest moods and an almost celestial joy . . .

Gradually my visits to the ballet became practically a sort of obsession. Not only did I know the entire score by heart, but I *had* to hear it played by the orchestra, again and again . . . It seemed to have penetrated my entire being.

Let me repeat, Tchaikovsky's music was what I seemed to have been waiting for since my earliest childhood. It generally happens that each generation is influenced and most deeply stirred by the art and music created *within its time*. Their understanding and perception is aided by certain cultural conditions that both the creator and those who enjoy his creations have in common. Bach, Handel, Gluck, Mozart, Beethoven seem sublime to us, but I do not doubt that those who heard their work when it had just been created experienced a joy and rapture that is beyond comparison with ours. It is true that Tchaikovsky did not belong strictly to my generation, for he was 50 when he composed *The Sleeping Beauty*, whereas I was only 20, but there was not a great difference in the cultural conditions that had helped to form his personality and mine. One word would have been enough to make our understanding of each other complete. This kind of understanding between human beings is the greatest happiness that can be attained by mankind; the joy that is born of spiritual union and relationship is so intense that any other fades into insignificance in comparison with it . . .

Those who love Tchaikovsky as I do, who love his way of thinking and feeling in music, the wonderful mastery with which he conveys the most varied sensations – whether they be of a purely psychological nature, or merely descriptive – will already have understood me. On the other hand, there is no use in arguing with those who profess to have 'ideas that are more advanced', who consider Tchaikovsky's music as old-fashioned as some Victorian table or sofa, or that it is not sufficiently 'national' – we Russians know that, although Tchaikovsky did not draw much from folk-lore, he is nevertheless the most national of our composers. Let those people hold their own opinion; they are sufficiently punished for it by being debarred from a region so vast and so enchanting . . .

The production of *The Sleeping Beauty* was a most significant turning-point . . . Interest in ballet, which had been somehow declining, was suddenly regenerated with fresh vigour and has never lessened since. It can be said with confidence that, had this production not proved to be such an outstanding success, the whole history of ballet in general – not only that of Russian ballet – would have been totally different. The *Ballets Russes* themselves would never have seen the light of day had not *The Sleeping Beauty* awakened in a group of Russian youths a fiery enthusiasm that developed into a kind of frenzy. It is a curious fact that Diaghilev had not at that time arrived in St Petersburg. When he came, he did not at first share our enthusiasm, possibly because he was not as fully prepared as we were for artistic appreciation; but, later on, he also became infected.

Diaghilev, two years younger than Benois, became a passionate admirer of Tchaikovsky's music. The Tchaikovsky and Diaghilev families were distantly related, and Diaghilev found, in this, sufficient justification for referring to the composer as 'Uncle Piotr'. The small group of young men that formed round Benois and Diaghilev idolised Tchaikovsky, who, Walter Nouvel later wrote, 'alone knew how to render the soul of the Russian nineteenth century and find a spontaneous and sincere echo in the people, while the music of the "Five" was a somewhat artificial reconstruction of popular melodies, strongly Germanized by the influence of Liszt and Wagner.' Stravinsky, incidentally, agrees with Nouvel. 'The "nationalists" Europeanized their music', he says in his autobiography, and names Wagner, Liszt and Berlioz as their models. He feels that Tchaikovsky owed more to Schumann. 'But, though he was under the influence of Schumann, that did not prevent him from remaining Russian any more than Gounod, for example, was prevented from remaining French. Both profited by the purely musical discoveries of the great German ... They borrowed his phraseology and his distinctive idioms without adopting his ideology.'

Tchaikovsky was revered by the younger Russians not only because of his music, but because of the kindness he showed towards his junior colleagues. He gave money to needy young composers and persuaded impresarios to bring out their works. He used his influence to help secure posts at the Moscow Conservatoire for Ippolitov-Ivanov, Arensky, Ziloti, Safonov and Taneyev. 'A composer who has won success and recognition stands in the way of younger men who want to be heard', he wrote to the Grand Duke Constantin, and on occasion he would request that one of his works be removed from a programme and replaced with a particular composition by a younger colleague. Both Ippolitov-Ivanov and Arensky profited from this. He also sometimes secretly bought as many as twenty tickets to concerts given by young Russian composers and distributed them to friends. He was always happy to devote time to young artists. When the eighteen-year-old Sergei Koussevitzky, then a double-bass player, called on him in Moscow, the composer took the trouble to accompany him at the piano in Koussevitzky's arrangement of the *Andante cantabile*. He gave similar encouragement to the twenty-year-old ballerina Mathilda Kschesinskaya. 'Tchaikovsky was a delightful man', she wrote in her memoirs. 'Before the first performance of *The Sleeping Beauty* he often came to rehearsals and accompanied us himself at the piano; we were very fond of him ... The greatest thing that happened to me was my appearance, on January 17th 1893, as Aurora in *The Sleeping Beauty*. Of all the praise I received, that which meant most to me was from Tchaikovsky, who came and congratulated me in my dressing-room.' Felix Weingartner and the cellist Carl Fuchs also had pleasant memories of meeting Tchaikovsky at the very beginning of their careers. Weingartner remembered him as a 'delightful man', while Fuchs recalled, 'The impression he made on me was that of a gentlemanly, simple, amiable man.'

The musician who probably reaped the greatest benefit from Tchaikovsky's friendship and encouragement was Rakhmaninov. They met for the first time in 1886, when Rakhmaninov was only twelve years old, but already showing remarkable ability as a pianist. He made clear how much Tchaikovsky meant to him in an article contributed to the June 1930 edition of *The Musical Times*.

To'him I owe the first and possibly the deciding success in my life. It was my teacher Zverev who took me to him. Tchaikovsky at that time was already world-famous, and honoured by everybody, but he remained unspoiled. He was one of the most charming artists and men I ever met. He had an unequalled delicacy of mind. He was modest, as all really great people are, and simple, as very few are. (I met only one other man who at all resembled him, and that was Chekhov.)

Tchaikovsky became a real friend to Rakhmaninov and showed such genuine admiration for him that the boy could not fail to develop rapidly in his studies. At thirteen, he was admitted to the Moscow Conservatoire. By the age of fifteen, he had been accepted into the classes of Ziloti and Arensky. In the 1888 examinations, he gained the maximum mark, five plus, in composition. Tchaikovsky attended the examinations, which 'gave the event a special character that year', as Rakhmaninov told Oskar von Riesemann in 1930.

After I had finished playing my pieces, I saw Tchaikovsky go over to the examination journal and write something in it. Not until a fortnight later did Arensky let me know what had been written; he was probably worried that I might become vain, and so had kept it a secret from me. The board had given me a '5 plus', the highest mark; but Tchaikovsky had added three more plus signs, over, below and behind the original plus.

In 1892, Rakhmaninov graduated from the Conservatoire, again with the highest possible marks. He was also awarded the Great Gold Medal, which had been bestowed on only two other students in the entire history of the college. Shortly afterwards, his opera *Aleko* was accepted for production at the Bolshoi, where it was to be presented during the spring of 1893. Meanwhile, in December 1892, Tchaikovsky gave an interview to a St Petersburg newspaper and mentioned Glazunov, Arensky and Rakhmaninov as the most promising of Russia's younger composers. 'This was a true joy for me', Rakhmaninov wrote to his friend Mikhail Slonov. 'Thanks to the old man for not forgetting me.' Tchaikovsky went to the rehearsals of *Aleko* and was an invaluable aid to the young composer, who later told Riesemann of the help he received.

We sat together in a corner of the darkened theatre. The way that Altani, the conductor, handled some sections of the opera did not please me. I remember the following dialogue between Tchaikovsky and myself:
'Do you like this tempo?' he asked.
'No.'

'Then why not say so?'

'I'm afraid to.'

During a break in the rehearsal, Tchaikovsky said to Altani, 'Sergey Vasilyevich and I feel that the tempo here could be taken a little faster.'

He was always scrupulously polite in making such suggestions.

Rakhmaninov also recalled that, during one of the rehearsals, Tchaikovsky said, 'I've just finished an opera, called *Iolanta*, that is not long enough to fill an entire evening. Would you object to its being performed together with yours?' Rakhmaninov could hardly believe his ears, but 'Would you object?' was distinctly what he remembered Tchaikovsky saying.

Aleko received its première on 9 May 1893 and was greeted with marked enthusiasm by the Moscow audience. Much of its success, Rakhmaninov believed, was due to Tchaikovsky's generally known liking for the opera, which he publicly displayed at the conclusion of the work by leaning out of his box and applauding 'for all he was worth'. Tchaikovsky had further espoused Rakhmaninov's cause by persuading Vsevolozhsky, the director of the Imperial Theatres in St Petersburg, to attend the performance.

Glazunov was another who had reason to be thankful for Tchaikovsky's support, and in gratitude he dedicated his Third Symphony to him. He was among the first to recognise that Tchaikovsky's later symphonies were essentially dramas. Interestingly, he was far less attracted to their thematic material than to 'the inspired development of ideas and the cast and perfection of their overall musical form, the coherence of which always leaves me with a feeling of satisfaction.' This was echoed many years later, when Shostakovich wrote, 'In development of musical idea and in orchestration, he has no equal.'

Glazunov felt that Tchaikovsky 'combined simplicity with dignity and refinement' in his character; 'everybody loved him everywhere', he wrote, and this applied not only to musicians but to people from all walks of life. It included his many nephews and nieces, with whom he never tired of playing and on whom he continually showered presents. It included friends whom he nursed when they were ill. It included the lazy but gifted music critic Laroche, whom the composer would sometimes help out by completing an article that had fallen behind deadline, and from whom he even took dictation in an effort to get Laroche started again. Nor should one forget his public acts of generosity, like the founding of a village school near his country home.

His attitude towards his famous contemporaries was no different. He arranged for Dvořák and Massenet to give concerts in Russia and invited Saint-Saëns and Brahms to do the same. He conducted Borodin's first two symphonies. After hearing the rehearsal of Rimsky-Korsakov's *Capriccio espagnol*, he was so full of admiration for the work that he immediately went out and had a silver medallion engraved, which he presented to the composer at the première. 'Rimsky could not conceive of Tchaikovsky otherwise than as a "rival",' Stravinsky informed Robert Craft in *Memories and Commentaries*; moreover, Rimsky often proclaimed that 'Tchaikovsky's music is in abominable taste.' Nonetheless, Stravinsky observed, he chose to exhibit the medallion in his workroom.

'The Five' – Balakirev, Cui, Borodin, Mussorgsky and Rimsky-Korsakov – were never openly very enthusiastic about Tchaikovsky, and the Russian press did much to suggest that The Five, in St Petersburg, and Tchaikovsky, in Moscow, were violently opposed to each other's work. In the end, many people – including, typically, the press itself – believed there really was a bitter feud, even though Tchaikovsky always denied it. In an interview in *Petersburg Life* on 12 November 1892, he told a reporter that this division into parties was 'a sort of colossal muddle, and it is time the confusion came to an end.' How could he be opposed, he asked, to Rimsky-Korsakov, 'whom I esteem more than any other living composer? . . . This is a strange misunderstanding, that has brought, and continues to bring, sad results. It prevents the public from properly grasping what is happening in Russian music, and gives rise to a totally pointless enmity . . . The future historian of Russian music will laugh at us as we now laugh at the nagging critics who disturbed the peace of Sumarokov and Trediakovski [two eighteenth-century Russian writers].' To which the reporter replied, 'I must confess, I never thought I would hear that from you.' 'Well, there you are!' said Tchaikovsky.

This interview is important, also, because of the composer's answer to the question 'What do you think about the present state of music in the West and about its future?'

I feel that music in Western Europe is undergoing some sort of transitional phase. For a long time, Wagner was the only great figure in the German school. This man of genius was in a state of splendid isolation, and there is no European composer of the second half of this century who has not been influenced by him. He had no equal during his lifetime, and there is now nobody who can replace him. It is true that, in Germany, there is Brahms, a highly respected and esteemed composer, but the cult of Brahms can be interpreted more as a protest against the overindulgences and excesses of Wagner. In spite of his undoubted mastery and the purity and seriousness of his aims, Brahms has hardly brought anything eternal or valuable into the great stream of German music. One can, of course, name two or three other outstanding German composers: Goldmark, Bruckner and young Richard Strauss . . . On the whole, though, there is a certain decline of talent . . . a kind of deadness and stagnation. There is plenty of life only in Bayreuth, the centre of the Wagner cult – and, whatever we think of Wagner's music, it is impossible to deny its force, and its extraordinary significance and influence on contemporary musical art.

On 24 August 1893, Tchaikovsky wrote to Jurgenson to say that he had finished the orchestration of the Sixth Symphony. 'I'm very proud of the symphony', he told him, 'and I think it's the best of my compositions.' By now, the torments of London and Cambridge were long since forgotten. 'Tchaikovsky was as serene and cheerful as at any period in his life', Modest states in his biography of his brother. After the creatively unproductive June and July and the comparatively quick completion of the symphony, the composer was now eager to embark on another opera and asked Modest for suggestions about subject matter. Already, too, the urge to travel was returning, and he accepted an invitation from Berger to conduct the Sixth Symphony at a Philharmonic concert the following spring. He also accepted an invitation from Eduard Strauss to conduct the Royal Viennese Orchestra in the early spring. The idea of this second engagement was a particularly pleasing one, since the first public performance of any of his orchestral works had taken place on 12 September 1865 in Pavlovsk, when Johann Strauss conducted the *Characteristic Dances*, which later became *Dances of the Hay Maidens* in the opera *The Voyevoda*. Edouard Strauss was an admirer of Tchaikovsky's music and of Russian music generally. His performance of Borodin's *In the Steppes of Central Asia*, in Vienna in 1883, was among the very first to be given outside Russia. Johann Strauss's influence on Tchaikovsky should not be underestimated. In as late a work as the *18 Morceaux*, written between his sketching the Sixth Symphony and leaving for London, one encounters *L'Espiègle*, with its echoes of *Die Fledermaus*; and perhaps we should recall that Strauss's Op 226 is also entitled *L'Espiègle*, a by-product of his Pavlovsk affair with Olga

Smirnitzki. It is worth remembering, too, that the *Pizzicato Polka*, written in Pavlovsk in June 1869 and first performed there, may well have had as great an impact on the Fourth Symphony as had Delibes' *Sylvia*.

Tchaikovsky received a letter, as well, from Damrosch, who, still holidaying in England, wrote from Uxbridge, on 30 July, to inquire about the Sixth Symphony.

> It gave me such great pleasure to see you again at Cambridge, and I have much regretted that we had so little time together there.
>
> I eagerly await your new symphony and I'd love to hear from you whether it will be published in time to be given in New York this coming season. To be truthful, what I really ask is the honour of being the first to perform it in America, that is, if it's published before you yourself come over to conduct it.
>
> It would be impossible for you to find more wholehearted admirers than those in America, who, because of this, look forward with impatience to each new product of your genius.

In the August edition of the *British Musician*, there appeared a short biography of Tchaikovsky, which seems to have been prompted by nothing more than the magazine's desire to supply information about a modern composer whose name was becoming tolerably well known. The article immediately follows a biography of Mascagni, which is three-and-a-half times as long. Mascagni was still only twenty-nine, but *Cavalleria rusticana* had already taken the world by storm. The biography of Tchaikovsky refers to him as 'the greatest living Russian composer', without feeling it necessary to justify placing him above Rubinstein, and then proceeds to lift familiar sentences out of Grove's *Dictionary* ('His compositions, more or less, bear the impress of the Slavonic temperament – fiery exaltation on a basis of languid melancholy. He is fond of huge and fantastic outlines, of bold modulations and strongly marked rhythms, of subtle melodic turns and exuberant figuration, and he delights in gorgeous effects of orchestration. His music everywhere makes the impression of genuine spontaneous originality . . .'). What, however, is so significant about this article is its second and concluding paragraph.

> Mr. Walter Damrosch says of Tschaikowsky: 'His natural melodic genius is stronger than that of any living composer, and his music is the more interesting because it has a national colouring. Furthermore, owing to the vast extent of the Russian Empire, comprising so many races of different

characteristics and tastes, Tschaikowsky's music has the additional merit of wonderful variety in style, colouring and effects. I consider Brahms, St.-Saens, and Tschaikowsky the three greatest living composers, and in most respects Tschaikowsky is the greatest of this trio of illustrious means.'

This must undoubtedly have astonished many readers of the *British Musician*. Beside it we can usefully set the review, in the following month's *The Musical Times*, of twenty-four of Tchaikovsky's songs, which had just been published by Novello, Ewer & Co.

Among modern Russian composers Tchaïkowsky occupies a distinguished place, and his works include sonatas, concertos, symphonies, and operas. Some of these have been heard in England, but it is by his short pianoforte pieces and songs for one or more voices that his name has become so familiar to us. One must not, of course, infer from this that the works of smaller calibre are of greater merit; but they appeal to a wide circle and are constantly being played or sung, while the opportunities of hearing the orchestral or stage compositions are few and far between. The songs, however, fully deserve their reputation . . .

We may note here that Tchaikovsky 'occupies a distinguished place' not among modern composers, but among 'modern Russian composers'. His output includes 'sonatas, concertos, symphonies, and operas', the sonatas apparently ,taking precedence over the symphonic poems and ballets.

On 4 September, the composer travelled to Hamburg to attend a performance of *Iolanta*, at the invitation of Bernhard Pollini, the director of the Hamburg Opera. Pollini was an ardent admirer of Tchaikovsky's music and had staged the first German production of *Eugene Onegin*, in Hamburg on 19 January 1892, and of *Iolanta*, in the same city on 3 January 1893. Both operas were directed by the resident conductor, Gustav Mahler. It was originally intended that Tchaikovsky should conduct the première of *Eugene Onegin*. He arrived in Hamburg for the final rehearsal, but found the German translation of the libretto so confusing that he wisely asked Mahler, who had meticulously prepared the work, to take his place on the first night. The two men had met previously on 28 January 1888 at a supper-party in Leipzig at the home of the violinist Henri Petri. The evening before, Tchaikovsky had been present at a performance of *Don Giovanni* that Mahler had conducted, and on 30 January he saw him direct what appears to have been the second performance of *Die drei Pintos*. On 10 February 1888 he attended a presentation of *Die Meistersinger*, also conducted by Mahler.

Tchaikovsky was perfectly happy to let Mahler take the baton for the German première of *Eugene Onegin*, for he regarded him, he told his nephew Bob, as 'a man of genius'. This opinion was confirmed by a 'wonderful rendering' of *Tannhäuser* on 18 January 1892 and by the performance of *Eugene Onegin*, which was 'positively superb'. According to Henry-Louis de la Grange, in his remakable biography of Mahler, the two composers had a long talk at the dinner given by Pollini after the première. Mahler later described Tchaikovsky, in a letter to his sister Justine, as 'an elderly gentleman, very likeable, with elegant manners . . .'

They were again dinner companions, at Pollini's home, on the evening of 8 September 1893, following the performance of *Iolanta*. The Russian composer stayed a further day in Hamburg and then returned to St Petersburg. Shortly afterwards, Mahler became desperately unwell, writes Henry-Louis de la Grange.

> The son of Mahler's landlady died suddenly and mysteriously. Almost simultaneously, the boy's grandmother became seriously ill, and the same night Mahler suffered pain and violent diarrhoea. The next morning, a doctor diagnosed cholera and told him that there were still a few isolated cases in the town. The previous autumn, 17,000 people had contracted cholera in Hamburg, half of whom died. He warned him that, if there was no improvement, the case must be reported to the health authorities and he would be sent to a hospital . . . After hovering between life and death for several days, Gustav Mahler's strong constitution finally overcame the disease, which only left him with unpleasant memories and an added tendency toward intestinal troubles.

On his return to Russia, Tchaikovsky spent a couple of days with Modest in St Petersburg and then went to stay with Anatoly in Mikhailovskoye. He eventually arrived back at Klin on 6 October. Nine days later, he completed the Third Piano Concerto, on which he had been working intermittently since June 1892; he dedicated it to Diémer. On 19 October, he journeyed to Moscow to attend a memorial service for his friend Nikolay Zverev and to listen to a private rehearsal of the Sixth Symphony. This was performed by students and members of the staff of the Moscow Conservatoire and was conducted by Vasily Safonov, who had succeeded Taneyev as director of the Conservatoire in 1889. At Taneyev's home a few weeks earlier, the composer had heard the symphony played in an arrangement for four hands, prepared by Lev Konyus. The pianists were Taneyev and Konyus himself; among the other listeners were Ippolitov-Ivanov and Rakhmaninov. In his recollections,kpublished in 1934, Ippolitov-Ivanov says that the four-hand performance of the symphony made little impression and that Tchaikovsky was agitated and downcast. However, when Rakhmaninov played his recently completed symphonic poem *The Rock*, he brightened up. 'The symphonic poem pleased us all very much', wrote Ippolitov-Ivanov, 'especially Piotr Ilyich, who was delighted by its colourfulness. The performance of *The Rock* and our discussion of it must have diverted Piotr Ilyich, for his usual goodjspirits returned.' He asked Rakhmaninov if he could conduct the work that winter in St Petersburg. According to Riesemann, Tchaikovsky also said he would like to perform the symphonic poem during the conducting tour he was planning to make in western Europe in the early part of 1894. By now, Rakhmaninov was beginning to gain recognition as a composer and had just been invited to Kiev to conduct *Aleko*. In wishing him good luck, Tchaikovsky said, 'So now we're both famous composers! One of us goes to Kiev to conduct his opera, and the other goes to Petersburg to conduct his symphony!'

The première of the Sixth Symphony had been arranged to take place in St Petersburg on 28 October. Tchaikovsky left Moscow by the overnight train on the evening of 21 October, after having dinner at the Moscow Restaurant with his good friend Nikolay Kashkin and other acquaintances, including Safonov and Pollini; the latter was visiting Russia to try to promote a concert tour. Kashkin refers to this dinner in his recollections.

We talked over Pollini's ideas of arranging an extensive concert tour through Russia with a German orchestra under a Russian conductor . . . Tchaikovsky was to conduct his own works, and Safonov, the rest of each programme . . . After the others had gone, and Piotr Ilyich and I were left to ourselves, he told me about his trip to Cambridge and spoke with great warmth of the professor of that university in whose home he had stayed; he spoke, too, of one of his fellow doctors, Arrigo Boito, whose mind and culture had been a delight to him . . . the conversation turned to our recent losses: to the deaths of Albrecht and Zverev. We thought of the gaps that time had made in our circle of old friends and of how few now remained.

Involuntarily, the question arose: who would be next to take the road along which no traveller returned? With absolute confidence, I predicted that Tchaikovsky would outlive us all. He disputed this, but concluded by saying that he had never felt better or happier in his life. He had to catch the night mail to St Petersburg, where he was going to conduct his Sixth Symphony, which was still unknown to me. He said he had no doubts about the first three movements, but the finale worried him; after the premiere he might replace it with something else. The Russian Musical Society's next concert in Moscow was to be on 5 November. We arranged that, if we did not see each other there, we would meet at the Moscow Restaurant, since Tchaikovsky was anxious to introduce the singer Eugene Oudin to musical circles in Moscow. Here our conversation ended, and Tchaikovsky went to the station.

It seems probable that, before leaving for St Petersburg on the evening of 21 October, Tchaikovsky learned of the death of Gounod, who had died four days earlier, on 17 October. The French composer was universally mourned as a great master. Queen Victoria was among the many prominent figures who sent condolences to his widow. 'Poor old man – how I did love him', Georgina Weldon wrote in her diary; shortly afterwards, she sent letters to the press, enjoining that he be interred in the *Panthéon*. The November issue of *The Musical Times* carried, as its opening article, a two-page obituary within a black border. Its concluding sentences confirm the high regard in which Gounod was held.

Alike in his gayest and his gravest moods he was an ideal representative of the charm, the elegance, and the stately grace of the best type of Frenchman. He was a very great melodist, with an unerring sense of beauty and symmetry, and his instinct for colour was so keen that with the minimum of means he never failed to produce the richest and most impressive effects. Lastly, to his rare accomplishments as a musician he added the fascinations of a most winning personality and the attractions of a highly cultivated intellect. He sang exquisitely, he was a brilliant conversationalist, a fine scholar, a most suggestive and witty writer, and a master of the art of irony and badinage. Gounod was not a genius of the inaccessible order. He found it hard to close his doors to any one, so great was his *bonhomie*. His optimism remained with him to the end. And although he had achieved his task on earth, and earned the rest into which he has entered, his loss has evoked the most genuine regret all over the civilized world in the hearts of scores of thousands whom he has cheered, delighted, and soothed by the magic of his music.

Tchaikovsky would have been moved by Gounod's death. He first met him in Paris on 1 March 1888, and his diary comments, 'He is very nice.' He also liked Gounod's music and, on 2 May 1892, conducted a performance of *Faust* in Moscow. Apart from his own stage works and Rubinstein's *The Demon*, it was the only other opera he ever directed. The baritone and opera manager Ippolit Pryanishnikov told Modest Tchaikovsky that Tchaikovsky's interpretation of *Faust* added much that was 'fresh and original' to many passages in the opera.

———————————

The composer arrived in St Petersburg on the morning of Sunday, 22 October and went to Modest's flat in Morskoy Street, where he normally stayed when visiting the capital. The première of the Sixth Symphony was on the following Saturday, and much of the week was devoted to rehearsals. The members of the orchestra were not particularly enthusiastic about the new work. 'The adverse opinions of others often caused Tchaikovsky to lose faith in his compositions', wrote Modest. 'But, on this occasion, his judgement remained unshaken, and even the indifference of the orchestra did not alter his belief that this symphony was "the best thing I've ever composed or will ever compose."'

There was more to rehearse than the symphony, for this occupied only the first half of the programme. The second half was made up of Laroche's *Karomzina* Overture, the First Piano Concerto, dances from Mozart's *Idomeneo* and Liszt's *Spanish Rhapsody*, which was performed by Adele Aus der Ohe, who was also the soloist in the concerto. Among those who attended the final rehearsal were Diaghilev and Walter Nouvel. Nouvel's memories of the occasion are preserved in Arnold Haskell's biography of Diaghilev.

> 'As with all the works of this great composer,' says Nouvel, 'we awaited with impatience the first performance of his latest symphony, *The Pathetic*, which he was to conduct himself at the symphonic concert of the Imperial Music Society.
>
> The day before, at nine in the morning, Diaghileff and I went to the *répétition générale*. With what eager attention did we listen to his rehearsal of the symphony, and to his piano concerto. We drank in each note. I remember, also, that in the same programme were Mozart's *Danses d'Idoménée*. I shall never forget the expression of beatitude on Tchaikovsky's face while he played the work of the composer for whom he had an admiration amounting almost to worship.

The following night the performance took place before a packed and enthusiastic house. We were all especially impressed by the fact that the symphony was concluded by a melancholy *adagio*, whose last bars diminished like a dying breath.'

Leopold Auer was another who later recalled the première. 'All of us in the concert hall that night were not only impressed by the beauty of the work, but also profoundly moved by the dramatic poignancy of the final chords. When I went up to congratulate Tchaikovsky, he appeared entirely happy and content with the success he had achieved, joked and laughed; and, at the same time – there was this strange finale, unique of its kind as the closing movement of a symphony!' Grechaninov, who was also among the audience, felt that the symphony achieved 'only a mediocre success', because Tchaikovsky had conducted disappointingly, but Rimsky-Korsakov wrote in his autobiography that 'it had gone very well in the composer's hands.' In his opinion, the audience 'had simply not fathomed it at the first hearing, had not given it enough attention.' The press tended to be of the same opinion as Grechaninov, preferring to believe that the work would have made a greater impact under Nápravník or Auer. Tchaikovsky seems to have been undismayed by this qualified success. Two days later, writing to Jurgenson on Monday, 30 October, he said, 'It was not exactly a failure, but was received with some hesitation. As for me, I'm prouder of it than any of my previous works. However, we'll soon be able to talk about it, since I'll be back in Moscow on Saturday.' Modest confirms that his brother's mood after the première was 'contented and jovial'. He was already looking to the future, planning a revision of *The Maid of Orleans* and adding Odessa to the itinerary of his winter concert tour. On Tuesday evening he went to a performance of Rubinstein's *The Maccabees*. On Wednesday, 1 November, Modest and he saw Ostrovsky's *The Burning Heart* at the Alexander Theatre. They visited the actor Varlamov in his dressing-room and discussed spiritualism, which Varlamov said he detested because it reminded him of the existence of death. Tchaikovsky told him, 'It will be a good while before we need reckon with that snub-nosed monster; it won't come to snatch us off just yet!' and added, 'I feel I shall have a long life.'

On the following morning, the composer woke feeling unwell. His condition worsened as the day proceeded, and during the late afternoon Modest sent for Tolstoy's doctor, Lev Bertenson, who had attended Mussorgsky in his final illness. Bertenson was at once alarmed and summoned his brother Vasily, an equally distinguished physician, for a second opinion. After a brief consultation, they diagnosed cholera.

Glazunov visited Tchaikovsky that same afternoon and saw how sick he was. By evening, many others had also been informed. Then came the announcement of the Bertensons' diagnosis; 'the fame of the composer was so great', wrote Stravinsky in *Expositions and Developments*, 'that after he was known to have caught cholera the government issued bulletins about the progress of his illness.' According to Rimsky-Korsakov, 'the news of his grave illness was in everybody's mouth. The whole world filed to his apartment several times a day to inquire about his condition.' Grechaninov recalled, 'I met a friend on the street, and he told me that Tchaikovsky had the dreaded disease. I was thunderstruck by this news. Refusing to believe it, I immediately went to Modest Tchaikovsky's house, where the composer was staying. The news was true . . . The doctors struggled desperately to save his precious life. Intensely worried, I went several times a day to Modest Tchaikovsky's house in Morskoy Street. There were always large crowds of people standing around looking at the bulletins posted on the wall.' Walter Nouvel remembered, 'There had been a serious epidemic the previous year, but now it was abating, only mild cases remained, and deaths were few and far between. We had great hopes for his recovery. Diaghileff was living near the composer, and went several times a day to find out the latest news, which he communicated to me.'

Throughout Thursday, 2 November, Tchaikovsky struggled for survival. 'His courage was wonderful', wrote Modest, 'and in the intervals between the paroxysms of pain he made little jokes with those around him.' He begged his nurses, who included his nephews Litke, Buxhövden and Bob Davidov and his brother Nikolay, to think of themselves and get more rest. He constantly thanked them for their attention and apologised for the trouble he was causing and for the unattractive nature of his illness.

On Friday, he rallied and believed himself to be recovering, but, by Saturday, his condition had again deteriorated. When his servant Alexey Sofronov arrived from Klin, Tchaikovsky was no longer able to recognise him. As a last resort, he was immersed in a hot bath, but to no effect. He now passed into unconsciousness and, at 3 o'clock on the morning of Monday 6 November, he died.

The news of the composer's death travelled quickly across St Petersburg. 'Neither before nor since, have I ever witnessed such deep universal grief', wrote Alexander Grechaninov. Diaghilev and Nouvel were among the first to go and pay their respects; 'there were few people there save relations and close friends. All were weeping.'

By mid-afternoon, the news had reached Moscow. In *Souvenirs d'un temps disparu*, Marie Scheikevitch relates how, as a little girl, she was walking with her father along the Prechistenka, when a man distinguished by 'high boots, wide trousers, a great beard and, in the middle of his face, two holes, two enormous nostrils, surmounted by bushy eyebrows' came towards them. It was Tolstoy.

'I have just received very distressing news,' he said. I gave all my attention to this grave voice. 'Tchaikovsky died last night in St Petersburg.' I looked up at my father. His head was bowed, and tears glistened on his cheeks. I had never seen him cry. His hand clenched mine so that it nearly hurt. His tears formed a stream that dripped from his white beard that was swaying above my head . . . Then Tolstoy's huge fist, clutching the telegram that he was showing my father, obscured my view, like a small yellow screen shutting out the darkening sky.

Leopold Auer also writes of the 'deep universal grief' to which Grechaninov refers.

The death of Pierre Tchaikovsky in 1893 struck musical circles in Russia like a bolt from the sky . . . In the full flower of his strength and at the apogee of his glory, he was carried off after a few days' illness, a victim of the cholera which was ravaging the city at the time and against whose onslaughts the medical science of the day was helpless . . .

His death plunged the whole of artistic and intellectual Russia into the deepest mourning. Since the deaths of Tourgueneff and Dostoievsky no funeral like that of Tchaikovsky had been seen, nor one which called forth so many tears. Deputations from the theatres of St. Petersburg and Moscow, from all the universities and the other superior institutions of learning, the entire teaching personnel of the St. Petersburg Conservatoire, together with hundreds of students from these academies marched in the ranks of the funeral procession, which followed the Nevsky Prospect to the Alexander Nevsky monastery . . .

The funeral was paid for by the state, on the orders of Tsar Alexander. The service was held in Kazan Cathedral. 'Deputations came from every corner of Russia, bearing a sea of flowers and wreaths', says Grechaninov.

I walked in the funeral procession and carried a silver wreath bought with money contributed by my friends. To give you some idea of the length of the procession, when its head was at Nikolaevsky Station, its end was at Kazan Cathedral, half a mile away. Tchaikovsky was buried in the cemetery of the Alexander Nevsky Monastery. Only about half the mourners could find room within the cemetery gates . . .

Tchaikovsky was only 53 when he died. Everybody loved him while he was alive as perhaps no other living composer has ever been loved. Many more works of genius had been expected from him. That is why all Russia mourned him so deeply and inconsolably.

Grechaninov wrote an orchestral elegy in memory of Tchaikovsky; similarly, Rakhmaninov composed a piano trio.

The first memorial concert took place in Moscow on 11 November, the day after the funeral. There were two more shortly afterwards in Moscow and two in Kiev, as well as many throughout the provinces. Nápravník conducted the second performance of the Sixth Symphony at a memorial concert in St Petersburg on 18 November, winning a tremendous ovation; Auer played the Violin Concerto on the same programme. On 12 December, in St Petersburg, Rimsky-Korsakov directed a concert that included the Fourth Symphony, *Francesca da Rimini* and *Marche slave*. A month later, he conducted a memorial concert in Odessa that featured the Third Symphony, First Piano Concerto and *Romeo and Juliet*.

Eugène Oudin, who, through Tchaikovsky's influence, had secured engagements in Russia in November 1893, made his début in Moscow on 4 November. Tchaikovsky had promised to be there, but by then was mortally ill. When Oudin and his wife arrived in St Petersburg three days later, he was dead. The baritone had the sad honour of singing Onegin's *arioso* from *Eugene Onegin* and two songs in the concert, on 18 November, at which Nápravník conducted the Sixth Symphony.

Another artist who owed his Russian début to Tchaikovsky was the Scottish pianist Frederic Lamond, who, with Manns, performed the First Piano Concerto in Glasgow in 1890, when he was twenty-two. He met the composer in Frankfurt and soon afterwards wrote him an admiring letter, telling him how much he loved his piano concertos. In reply, addressing him as 'Fellow Artist', Tchaikovsky spoke of the joy that Lamond's letter had given him, adding 'Perhaps an opportunity may be found for you to play in Moscow. I have spoken warmly about it to Monsieur Safonov.' After the composer's death, Lamond understandably gave up any immediate hopes of appearing in Russia, but in 1896 he suddenly received an invitation to play the First Piano Concerto in Moscow and, on 31 October of that year, scored a great success with it at an Imperial Russian Musical Society concert conducted by Safonov. He then learned that Tchaikovsky had pleaded just before his death that Lamond be given an engagement. This had been the society's first opportunity of fulfilling that wish, since their concerts were always arranged well in advance. On the day after the concert, Lamond attended a Requiem Mass for Tchaikovsky at a cathedral in Moscow 'and found all the professors of the Conservatoire gathered in a small side-chapel', he relates in his autobiography. 'I stood between Scriabin and Taneiev. When the officiating priest began to read the Mass for the dead I was aware of an unnatural paleness on the part of Scriabin. Taneiev wept and sobbed; knelt down and kissed the icy flags of the chapel . . .'

During his visit to Moscow, Lamond heard that Tchaikovsky would often supplement the 300 roubles paid to young artists making their débuts with the Imperial Russian Musical Society, by adding 100 roubles (then about £12) from his own pocket – 'for travelling expenses', he would tell the treasurer.

Recalling his meeting with the composer, Lamond wrote, 'Tchaikowsky had the exquisite manners of the arisotcrat of former times. But he was more than an aristocrat. He was, to wit, a nobleman of the spirit: one of God's chosen, and his memory will for me remain unforgettable.'

The British daily press greeted Tchaikovsky's death with dignity and economy, making appropriate use of Dannreuther's article in Grove's *Dictionary*. The *Manchester Guardian* deemed him 'one of the most remarkable of Russian composers'. *The Times* said that his death 'has been received with great regret throughout the country.' Very few opinions of his worth were advanced that had not been previously stated in concert reviews.

In William Barclay Squire's article in the *Saturday Review* of 11 November, however, there are glimmerings of a more generous assessment.

The sudden death, from cholera, last Monday, of the Russian composer, Petr Iljitsch Tschaikowsky, removes one more from the small list of living composers of European reputation. The bald record of Reuter's despatch describes him as having 'arranged several works for orchestra' – a

curiously inadequate tribute to one who was classed among the most
brilliant orchestral writers of the day, and who was selected last May by
the University of Cambridge as the representative of Russian music in an
international distribution of the academic honour of Mus. Doc. That the
choice of the University fell upon the most characteristic Russian
composer is open to question. His music is imbued with a less degree of
national spirit than that of either Cui or Rimsky-Korsakoff, and his
adherence to the latest Russian school was strongly tempered by the eclecticism which proceeded from his wide culture and intimate knowledge of
the compositions of the great French and German masters . . . Personally
he was distinguished by a singular charm; and he will be deeply regretted
by all with whom he came in contact.

Musical News's obituary, also published on 11 November, shows a
similar enthusiasm, though it still leans heavily on Dannreuther and
is marred by inaccuracies.

In Tschaïkowski the world has lost a famous musician, one who appealed
to a wide circle. He was esteemed and appreciated throughout Europe,
and few living musicians were so generally known and admired as he . . .
    Tschaïkowski is remarkable for the width of his sympathy and for his
varied power. He has composed music of almost every kind; in opera,
symphony, chamber music and in instrumental and vocal solos he has
been successful . . . Tschaïkowski has written four symphonies; the one in
F minor was performed at a Philharmonic concert last season . . . His first
visit to England was in June last when he received the honorary degree of
Mus. Doc. of Cambridge University as a representative of Russia. On this
visit he conducted his symphonic poem, 'Francesca', at the Jubilee concert
of the Cambridge University Musical Society. The London Philharmonic
Society was negotiating with him to come and conduct one of his works at
the forthcoming concerts. Tschaïkowski's music is characterised by fire
on the one hand and melancholy on the other. It is truly Slavonic; the
ideas are bold and the rhythm forcible. He was a great master of harmony,
he knew how to invent melody and to elaborate details. His skill in instrumentation was also remarkable. By the death of Peter Tschaïkowski, not
only Russia but Europe has lost one of the greatest of modern musicians.

Writing in the *Sunday Times* a day later, on 12 November, Herman
Klein produced what was hitherto the most thoughtful and independent judgement.

Following so soon after the death of Gounod, the extinction of a lesser light
in the person of Peter Tschaikowsky has hardly received the measure of
comment that it deserves. Yet the 'lesser light' was, in his own orbit, a star
of the first magnitude, and, indeed, for some time had been shining with a
brilliancy that was visible throughout the entire musical firmament. Ten

years ago we might not have noted the loss. To-day we know that Russia has been deprived of her greatest composer and Slavonic music of one of its most capable and distinguished exponents. There is something infinitely pathetic in the sudden manner in which this gifted man, the pet of his compatriots, the most favoured of his brother-musicians in a land where favour can do so much, has been carried off by cholera at the comparatively early age of fifty-three. That terrible scourge, which attacks its victims without respect to 'class', might well have seized upon some other Russian among the high places who could have been so much more easily spared than Tschaikowsky. For he was a man not only of great attainments, but of kind heart, gentle disposition, and liberal mind.

But with all his diffidence Tschaikowsky had plenty of dignity, and, though by no means a model conductor, he knew how to keep an orchestra under perfect control. In his compositions he was boldness itself. There he would dare anything and everything – sometimes too much. He might, in fact, have been called the Tartar of Russian music. He laid his colour on with an unsparing hand; his effects, gorgeous, grandiose, sonorous to the point of excess, were often coarse and blatant, if not right down vulgar. Nevertheless he had a poet's imagination in addition to a magician's art of weaving the folk-tunes of his country into the warp and woof of his symphonic designs. Despite a certain tendency to eccentricity, his music was undeniably original – far more so, to our thinking, than Rubinstein's, whose works, side by side with his, have carried musical art in Russia to a stage of development that it had never before attained. As yet we know comparatively little of Tschaikowsky's music, and even that, it is said, does not comprise his finest efforts. Perhaps, now that he is dead, our concert-*entrepreneurs* will look his scores up more industriously.

Monthly Musical Record followed Klein in recommending that more of Tchaikovsky's works be brought forward.

The Russian musician lately deceased was one of the foremost men of his day, and by his death our art has suffered a distinct loss; for he had only just arrived at the age of maturity, and there is every reason to believe that he would have still added to his reputation. So far, however, as England is concerned, the question is not so much what might have been, but what Tschaïkowsky actually accomplished. His name is tolerably familiar among us, but, somehow or other, we know very little of his music . . .

In an article on Tschaïkowsky in our columns [November 1892], the few instrumental works by which he was known here were mentioned; to these must now be added the 4th Symphony in F minor, produced under the composer's direction at a Philharmonic Concert only last June. But Tschaïkowsky wrote six symphonies, and has left, we believe, one in manuscript. Then, besides, there are symphonic poems, suites, quartets for strings, and other chamber music – works which have never been given here. From the one opera, and the few instrumental compositions known

to us, it is quite impossible to form a serious, solid opinion of Tschaïkowsky as a musician – impossible to assign the place which he is likely to
occupy in the pages of musical history. His sudden death may draw attention to his music; Mr. A. Manns or Mr. A. Chappell would find it an easy
matter to draw up an interesting programme selected entirely from his
works, and such a scheme appears to us by no means unreasonable. If not
earlier, the first anniversary of his death might prove a suitable occasion;
that of his birth is out of the question, for he was born – at least, so say the
dictionaries – on Christmas Day. But his death may serve a wider
purpose, and through Tschaïkowsky the claims of modern Russian music
to consideration may become more fully recognised. Not to mention the
works of Glinka and Rubinstein, why should not some enterprising
manager let us hear some of the symphonic works of Dargomijsky, or the
symphonies of Borodine, or the King Lear music of Balakireff?

The Musical Times devoted just over a page to Tchaikovsky's obituary, which, unlike Gounod's, was neither bordered in black nor
placed at the front of the magazine. As with the other obituaries of the
composer, there is no suggestion that Tchaikovsky should be ranked
among the masters or compared with Brahms, Gounod or Saint-
Saëns; he is seen as an important, but minor composer. The list of his
works is far from accurate: he has written five symphonies, two violin
concertos and 'two or three ballets'. But in this obituary there
breathes something new, something that his visits to England had
unintentionally fostered: a real affection for the man himself.

A very serious loss has befallen the musical world by the sudden death,
while still in the prime of life and activity, of P. I. Tschaikowsky, who only
four months ago, as the honoured representative of Russian music, visited
Cambridge to receive the complimentary Degree conferred upon him by
that University. He was, however, no stranger to our shores, having previously visited England in 1888 and 1889, appearing in both years as the
conductor of his own compositions at the Philharmonic Society's Concerts. And it is, perhaps, not too much to say that of all foreign contemporary composers who have been our guests, none inspired a more cordial
liking than the genial and unaffected Russian whose premature removal
we so deeply deplore. He was absolutely free from any affectation, and, in
the fullest and best sense of the word, a thorough gentleman . . .
 The predominant characteristics of Tschaikowsky's music have been
described by Mr. Dannreuther as essentially Slavonic – fiery exaltation
alternating with languid melancholy, a fondness for huge outlines and
barbaric gorgeousness of colour. This is no doubt true to a very considerable extent, but although Tschaikowsky undoubtedly made considerable
use of national themes and rhythms in his works, and in the choice of
subjects almost invariably drew upon the treasures of Northern literature,

his wide culture and extensive acquaintance with German music inclined him to an eclecticism which in his earlier days aroused the hostility of Chauvinistic critics in Russia. 'Eugen Onegin' might have been written by a cultivated musician of any nationality, so free is it from local or national colour. It is, perhaps, the most popular Russian opera ever written, and the moderate impression it created when given in London a couple of years ago may be accounted for, in part at least, by the inadequateness of the performance . . .

Latterly Tschaikowsky had resided in St. Petersburg, where he enjoyed a personal popularity second to no artist throughout the length and breadth of Russia. He was an especial favourite with the Imperial family, but remained unspoiled by his social success. Thanks to the munificence of the Czar and the profits of his copyrights, he was the possessor of a handsome income, but it is stated that he has left next to nothing. Having no wife or family dependent upon him he never saved his money, but spent it freely in charity. As an instance of the chivalrous and gentlemanly feeling which was so marked a feature in his character, we may conclude this notice with the following anecdote. When M. Lamoureux, the famous French conductor, visited Russia early this year, he was entertained at a dinner in Moscow, at which some of his hosts went out of their way to institute invidious comparisons between him and Von Bülow, whose name was greeted with derision and abuse. Tschaikowsky had no sympathy with this mixing up of art and politics, which was at the bottom of this demonstration, and though it involved no little courage to run counter to the popular current of Gallomania, he issued a most spirited protest in the Russian and French papers against the indecency of the attack on Von Bülow, who was then lying dangerously ill, and who, whatever his faults and extravagancies, had done more than any other foreign musician to popularise Russian music outside Russia.

A month later, in the January 1894 edition of *Musical Opinion & Music Trade Review*, appeared the best informed and most complimentary obituary of all. This was written by Robin Legge, who eventually became music critic of the *Daily Telegraph*.

Hardly had the tomb closed upon all that was mortal of Charles Gounod, hardly had the echo of M. Saint-Saëns's panegyric passed away, ere the news of the death of the famous Russian master came upon the musical world with a shock that was all the greater for being quite unexpected . . . That the news of his death evoked expressions of universal regret from the whole musical world goes without saying; and many were the enquiries made during his brief illness, not only by musicians, but also by the Czar himself, who has invariably showed a deep interest in the music and musicians of Russia.

On November 9th, the remains of the composer were accorded a state funeral at the Kazan Cathedral by order of the Czar, at which many of the

highest officials were present. It is significant to note, too, that when the
funeral procession passed the Opera House, it was joined by the principal
singers of the Czar's private opera company. An immense crowd attended
the obsequies, no less than ninety-one deputations from all parts of Russia
taking part; and, as if to show how deeply Russia felt her loss, nearly one
hundred and eighty wreaths (some seventeen of which were of silver) were
placed upon the grave.

Legge goes on to give a very full account of Tchaikovsky's life,
covering his visits to London and Cambridge, and referring to the
'fine performance' of *Francesca da Rimini*. 'Tschaïkowsky was an
extraordinarily versatile composer', he says, reciting the list of his
successes in all forms of music. 'Among the songs – many of which are
quite superb – I cannot refrain from pointing out at least his setting of
"Nur wer die Sehnsucht kennt", which, in spite of what Beethoven
and Schubert have done with the beautiful poem, I am bound to
confess I prefer above all.' The operas and ballets 'one and all are
characteristic of his master mind.' Legge concludes, 'In the *technique*
of composition and in orchestration, Tschaïkowsky had no living
superior; and by his lamented death not only Russia but the whole
musical world loses a veritable master at a time when it can ill afford
the loss. Amiable, kindly, and genial to all with whom he came in
contact, his death creates a void in present day musical life which it
will be immensely difficult to fill.'

When one considers the composer's limited popularity in England
at the time and the prevailing lack of acquaintance with most of his
orchestral compositions and virtually all his works for the stage, this
article is all the more extraordinary.

On 28 February 1894, the Sixth Symphony was given its English
première at a Philharmonic Society concert conducted by Alexander
Mackenzie, almost exactly four months after the first performance in
St Petersburg. It thus received a hearing in England sooner after its
completion than any other of Tchaikovsky's pieces. Moreover, the
Philharmonic performance appears to have been the first outside
Russia, ahead even of Damrosch's, in New York on 16 March. But
Mackenzie's rendering was not strictly the first in England, for, as he
readily admits in his autobiography, the symphony 'had been pre-
viously run through by Manns at a rehearsal at the Crystal Palace.'

Unlike any previous English premières of the composer's works, that of the Sixth Symphony caused a sensation, moving the Queen's Hall audience to a frenzy of enthusiasm. From this moment, Tchaikovsky was suddenly looked on in a new light, and *The Musical Times* henceforward speaks of him as a master, commenting favourably, in its April issue, on the symphony's 'bold innovations upon established form . . . Here then we have an enlargement of the scope of a first movement, and a model which composers are not at all unlikely to work from.'

The work was greeted with wide critical praise; Klein at once called it a masterpiece. George Bernard Shaw, however, was not to be deceived.

Tschaikowsky had a thoroughly Byronic power of being tragic, momentous, romantic about nothing at all. Like Childe Harold, who was more tragic when there was nothing whatever the matter with him than an ordinary Englishman is when he is going to be executed, Tschaikowsky could set the fateful drum rolling and make the trombones utter the sepulchral voice of destiny without any conceivable provocation.

This last symphony of his is a veritable Castle of Otranto, with no real depth of mood anywhere in it, but full of tragic and supernatural episodes which, though unmotivated, and produced by a glaringly obvious machinery, are nevertheless impressive and entertaining. There are, besides, abundant passages of romance and revelry, with the usual Tschaikowskian [possibly the first appearance of this word in English] allowance of orchestral effects which are so purely that and nothing else that they have absolutely no sense if played on a pianoforte. Take, for instance the basso ostinato at the end of the first movement, and the rushing scale passages for strings and wind in the march. These are, from the symphonic point of view, simple humbug.

Mackenzie's inspired interpretation of the Sixth Symphony, on which all were agreed, played no small part in Tchaikovsky's rapid change of fortune in England, but the greatest credit must go to Francesco Berger. He had programmed the symphony for the first Philharmonic concert of the 1894 season; if the composer had lived, he himself would have been there to conduct it. 'It had been arranged that at his next visit to England, in the following year,' wrote Berger, in *Reminiscences, Impressions and Anecdotes*, 'he should accept the invitation of a friend of mine to stay with him at his charming house; but on the very morning when I received a letter from this friend enquiring on what day he might expect his guest, I took up the *Daily Telegraph* to read he had passed away.' (Olga Novikov states that the composer 'had indeed accepted the invitation of an English friend to be his

guest during the forthcoming visit.') Berger's affection for Tchaikovsky never diminished. In 1931, at the age of ninety-seven, he
produced a second volume of autobiography. He certainly had cause
for reminiscing: he had seen Berlioz conduct *La Fuite en Égypte* in
Leipzig in December 1853; he had met Verdi in Trieste, Wagner at
the Royal Albert Hall, Spohr and Meyerbeer at Covent Garden; he
had known Dickens, Thackeray, Wilkie Collins, Liszt, Gounod,
Saint-Saëns, Dvořák, Grieg, Sullivan, Clara Schumann, Joachim
and many more. But his favourite was Tchaikovsky.

> . . . as one who knew and loved him personally, I may venture to say here,
> that in the course of a very wide acquaintance with men and women of
> mark, I have never met with such a remarkable combination, as in this
> man, of eminent talent with complete modesty. When he died, the loss to
> the world of such a musician was not greater than was the loss to his
> friends of such a man. His death has left a void in their hearts which time
> nor the genius of others can never fill.

After Mackenzie's triumph with the Sixth Symphony on 28
February, Berger took the unprecedented step of programming the
work as the opening item in the following Philharmonic concert, on
14 March. Again it excited thunderous applause. Stanford was the
next to conduct the symphony, on 22 June, when the third movement
created 'a veritable *furore*'. By the end of the year, it had also been
played, predictably, by Manns and Hallé. On 24 May 1894, Mackenzie introduced another of Tchaikovsky's works, the *Concert
Fantasy*, to England. The soloist in this Philharmonic performance
was the beautiful Sophie Menter, with whom the composer had
stayed on his way home from Cambridge. It is now noticeable that
Tchaikovsky's music was being ardently championed by those who
had known him personally.

On 27 May 1895, the final seal of approval was set on the Sixth
Symphony when it was conducted in London by Richter, who was
generally regarded as the greatest conductor of the day. *The Musical
Times* spoke of the 'barbaric splendour and passion' of this 'noble,
picturesque and moving work'. A month later, on 29 June, Nikisch
directed the first London performance of the Fifth Symphony, which,
wrote *The Musical Times*, 'immediately won the hearts of all present.'
On 21 October, Richter repeated the Sixth Symphony and then took
it on tour to Edinburgh, Glasgow, Birmingham and Bradford; this
composition, *The Musical Times* maintained, 'has brought the Russian

composer more fame after his death than he enjoyed during his life.'
The Fifth Symphony received its second London performance, on 16
November, when Manns conducted it at the Crystal Palace. The
'impressive Fifth Symphony', in the opinion of *The Musical Times*,
possessed 'great breadth of treatment, rhythmic strength, sustained
thematic interest, and splendour of orchestral colouring . . . The
thanks of all admirers of Tschaïkowsky's genius – a steadily increasing class – are due to Mr. Manns for his inclusion in the programme
of that master's fine Symphony.' Richter's performance of the Fifth
Symphony, on 18 May 1896, established that work, too, in the
English orchestral repertoire. Meanwhile, the Fourth Symphony had
been performed in Manchester, by Mackenzie on 5 December 1895,
and in Bradford, by Stanford on 7 February 1896.

Therefore, within the space of three years, the Fourth, Fifth and
Sixth Symphonies had all been introduced and had won complete
acceptance. The First Piano Concerto had also achieved permanent
popularity; but, for practical purposes, Tchaikovsky was the very
latest discovery in English musical life, twenty years after Brahms,
ten years after Dvořák, three years after Mascagni and Leoncavallo
– and, let it be added, no more than a dozen years after the full
greatness of Wagner had been recognised. Tchaikovsky's slow and
erratic climb to fame before coming to Cambridge was but vaguely
remembered, and, when Richter conducted *Romeo and Juliet* in
London on 8 June 1896, *The Musical Times* stated that this composition 'had not been heard in England since its first performance here
at the Crystal Palace in November, 1876, five years after its publication in Berlin.' This was incorrect, but it does show the infrequency
with which the piece had been presented and the comparatively small
impact it had made. In addition, since the last three symphonies take
their place among Tchaikovsky's very finest concert works, any
further composition that was introduced was likely to be viewed as
falling short of his highest capabilities. England was thus getting to
know his works generally in the opposite order in which they were
written. *The Musical Times*, comparing *Romeo and Juliet* with the 'three
magnificent Symphonies', found in it little of 'the Tschaïkowsky
whom we have learnt to admire' other than 'certain outward characteristics which are probably less individual than national.'

In the autumn of 1895, the impresario Robert Newman introduced
his new Queen's Hall Promenade Concerts and made Henry Wood,
then twenty-six, permanent conductor. This must rank as one of the

most inspired appointments in English musical life. Wood was four years younger than Manns had been when Grove gave him the Crystal Palace conductorship in 1855, and four years younger than Hallé when he began his reign in Manchester in 1849. He proved as daring an innovator as either of them, and the chief beneficiary at once became Tchaikovsky. The Fifth and Sixth Symphonies became regular items at the Promenade Concerts. As we may recall, Wood had directed the English première of *Eugene Onegin* in October 1892; on 17 October 1896, he added to this the first English performance of the *Nutcracker Suite*. Three of the numbers had to be encored. *The Musical Times*, though finding the suite 'grotesque in character and scored in a most *bizarre* manner', nevertheless was delighted by 'that keen sense of tonal colour which is so striking a characteristic of this composer's production'. On 20 February 1897, Wood introduced *The Storm* in a programme that also included the Sixth Symphony and *Nutcracker Suite*.

A month later, on 19 March 1897, Stanford, who had given his third performance of the Sixth Symphony on 5 November 1896, conducted the RCM orchestra in the London première of *Francesca da Rimini* at St James's Hall. *The Musical Times* reported that 'the orchestra has never played better – in fact, the performance of Tschaïkowsky's very difficult Fantasia, 'Francesca da Rimini', was extremely fine, even if judged by the highest standard. This work was new to London, and, to judge from its reception, it scored a great success.' Stanford repeated it on 22 July. A month earlier, on 23 June 1897, he conducted the first performance in England of the Third Piano Concerto, with Maud Gay as soloist.

Tchaikovsky was now becoming very popular, and his compositions were arousing great interest. Wood again conducted the Sixth Symphony, on 6 March 1897, and, two weeks later, the Fifth. *The Musical Times* came to the conclusion that the latter was 'a worthy companion of the magnificent "Pathetic" Symphony.'

The work grows more fascinating on further acquaintance, and particularly by the discovery of Mr. E. F. Jacques, the writer of the historical and analytical programme, that the most important theme of the work, which is heard in each movement and is especially prominent in the *Finale*, bears a 'striking resemblance to the opening phrase of the *Trio* of Chopin's Polonaise in E flat minor (Op. 26, No. 2) – itself said to be founded on a Polish Death Song.' Mr. Jacques has also noted that 'the first two bars of the chief subject of the *Allegro* are found in a Polish folk-song, "Mialem ja kochanke jux nie mam nic", classed under the head of "Love songs of serious character." ' These facts, combined with the tragic nature of the music, seem to indicate that the symphony has a poetic basis connected in some way with Poland.

Equally alive to the growing interest in Tchaikovsky, the *Musical Standard* of 27 March published a lengthy article signed by R. Peggio.

Surely of all composers Tchaïkovsky is the most tantalising to the critic. He was capable of writing the veriest trash, the most obviously melodramatic stuff, such as the 'Orage' overture [Op 76, but a student work published posthumously]; he could be as dainty and as piquant as the Frenchiest of the French, as in the 'Nutcracker' ballet music; he could be as bright as an Auber, as in 'Eugen Onegin'; he could even descend to the commonplace in sentiment; and yet he could be sincere and touching and poetic as in his fifth and sixth symphonies. When the 'Pathétique' was introduced to London, the most of us were astonished, crying, 'surely this is not the Tchaïkovsky we know' – and rightly, too, because we had not then heard the fifth symphony which Arthur Nikisch conducted for the first time in London, unless my memory is all astray. Until quite lately I must confess Tchaïkovsky *was* a puzzle to me, but I am now beginning to understand the man.

We must look upon him as a composer who had never finished developing, for, as you all know, he did not die from any constitutional disease, but from cholera. He was only fifty-three years of age, and he had a good ten years of work before him. Considering that the 'Pathétique', by far the best of his works, was his latest composition I do not think we can go wrong if we suppose that he might have done something still better . . .

The Russian national temperament is supposed to be alternately gloomy and vivacious . . . I am inclined, indeed, to look upon the composer as two men: the bright, vivacious man of the world and the curiously gloomy sentimentalist with a cast of fatalism. To disarm criticism it would be as well to state that 'sentimentalist' is not used as a term of reproach, but as the nearest word that will distinguish such a composer as Tchaïkovsky, so full of human feeling, from such a one as Brahms or Beethoven, each of whom aims at being more sublime and impersonal: with Tchaïkovsky the feeling is intimate and subjective; with Beethoven much more objective and remote, and with Brahms still more so – even to the length of being quite unhuman at times.

On 3 April 1897 – the day of Brahms's death – Wood performed the Fifth and Sixth Symphonies at the Queen's Hall, while, at St James's Hall, the Bohemian String Quartet gave what seems to have been the English première of the Second Quartet. Three weeks later, on 24 April, the *Musical Standard* devoted its entire front page to an article on Tchaikovsky.

No work of recent times has achieved such a measure of popularity as the Pathetic Symphony of TCHAIKOVSKY . . . In 1893 the symphony was first produced in America under the bâton of Mr. WALTER DAMROSCH, the well-known conductor. It was received here with enthusiasm by the press and public. To the Philharmonic Society and to Sir ALEXANDER MACKENZIE [knighted in 1895] all credit is due for having first performed it in London, on February 22nd [28th], 1894. It was repeated at the next Philharmonic Concert of the same season. Then Dr. RICHTER took it in hand and gave a performance which still remains in the mind as a thing of absolute perfection. Since then the Symphony has often been performed at the Queen's Hall, by Mr. HENSCHEL; and by Mr. F. H. COWEN at the Hallé concerts [Hallé had died in 1895] in Liverpool and Manchester . . .

It is such genuine, vital works as the 'Pathetic' symphony that convince one the symphony is not dead. In the Russian composer's composition there is a vast amount of musical cleverness which cannot but enchain the attention of the practical and analytical musician, and yet, with it all, there is a pathos and emotion which carry away the least learned of listeners. This is what art should do. To sacrifice beauty of workmanship to emotional expression is the characteristic of the half-baked composer; to make beauty of workmanship subserve beauty of expression is the work of a genius. The 'Pathetic' and Fifth symphonies with all their transparent melodic charm and emotional effect are full of touches of the subtlest musicianship, in harmony, melody, rhythm, treatment of themes, and orchestration. In the latter alone the 'Pathetic' symphony is a model to young composers, second only to the works of WAGNER. The Russian composer thoroughly understands the tone-colour of different instruments, not only from the standpoint of mere musical beauty but from that of poetic meaning. His instruments are voices . . . it might very well be argued that a good deal of the charm of TCHAIKOVSKY's music is due to this fact: that his feeling is so sincere, so wavering between the sublime and the human. Sometimes he suggests the comparative triviliality of outside life, the brightness of the ball-room, the gaiety of clinking spurs, the fascinating smiles of beautiful women, the lighthearted songs of soldiery on the march, their fierce exultance in victory, the heart-arresting boom of the cannon; and then, at a turn, as it were, he becomes introspective and shows the soul of a man at work: the brightness was only assumed, the exultance was but a momentary forgetfulness of the spiritual tragedy of life; in one step he leaves the ball-room, the opera-house, the camp, all the glitter and fascination of outside life, and is face to face with the infinite sadness of existence, with the ceaseless struggle of the burdened spirit upwards towards the light. That he does not conquer is his weakness and yet is something of his fascination. BEETHOVEN rises above the melancholy that paralyzes smaller men; his head is among the stars if his feet be on earth; he speaks to us, sometimes, as a god to men; TCHAIKOVSKY always speaks as man to man, and his voice is full of sympathy and tenderness.

This is committed, vulnerable writing; it is also remarkably perceptive – and penned, less than four years after the composer's death, in a
country that had hitherto imperfectly grasped the nature of his
musical idiom.

On 15 May 1897 at the Queen's Hall, Henry Wood conducted what
appears to have been England's first all-Tchaikovsky concert, including the *Capriccio italien* and Fourth Symphony, and introducing the
overture to *The Voyevoda* and the entire Third Suite. The *Rococo Variations* received its English première, with Leo Stern as soloist, on 17
June 1897 at a Philharmonic concert directed by Alexander Mackenzie. *Mozartiana* was introduced by Wood on 24 September 1897.
On 3 November 1897, Charles Lamoureux, conducting the Queen's
Hall orchestra, gave the first performance in England of *Hamlet*,
which, said *The Musical Times*, 'arouses and sustains the attention by
reason of its tragic character and intensity, and leaves an impression
not easily effaced.' Lamoureux was one of the composer's leading
French admirers and a good friend; he had recently introduced the
Sixth Symphony in Paris. The French were not particularly taken
with Tchaikovsky's music; it was not Russian enough for them.
Fauré greatly liked it, but the younger men – Debussy, Ravel, Dukas
– held it in scant regard. The next English première was of *The Tempest*, which George Halford conducted in Birmingham on 18 January
1898.

By now, the *Nutcracker Suite* had taken its place as a popular favourite, and, when Wood conducted it on 12 February 1898, the *Musical
Times* declared that Tchaikovsky 'challenges the best French composers of ballet music and easily beats them on their own ground . . .
Nothing could well be more charming than these delicious little
pieces or of Mr. Wood's manner of playing them.'

The Sixth Symphony, however, was by now beginning to take on a
popularity of astonishing proportions, holding its own against the
simultaneous Wagner boom, and overshadowing the 'New World'
Symphony, which had also reached England in 1894. In the spring of
1898, Lamoureux conducted the work three times, and Felix Mottl
became another addition to its interpreters in London. Separate
ballots at the Crystal Palace, Queen's Hall and in Glasgow voted it
the work that subscribers wanted to hear most. When Richter conducted the symphony on 13 June 1898, *The Musical Times* commented:

... poor Tschaïkowsky was yet once again made to perform his gruesome task of giving an enormous audience shivers of emotional excitement. 'Pathetic' Symphony indeed! The barbarous doing to death of this splendid *opus summum* of the great Russian, and the consequent utter neglect of so many other masterpieces, form perhaps the gravest indictment which musical history can bring against the London concert managers of the end of this century. Not that we suppose those gentry feel any qualms at such a dreadful prospect! They will exploit Tschaïkowsky's very heart's blood and agony, so long as the public pay their silver pieces. Meanwhile, we begin to almost dislike the work and would as lief listen to the dullest symphony on record if it were only new! Dr. Richter's reading was not much more to our taste than M. Lamoureux's. He seems bent on introducing order and calm into that terrific first movement which so evidently suggests the chaotic state of a brain on fire. We greatly prefer Mr. Wood's reading, though nobody, in our opinion, has reproduced the spirit of the work better than Professor Stanford at the Royal College of Music, where the third and fourth performances in England took place. His fine reading (though he was necessarily somewhat handicapped by the inexperience of his juvenile players) should not be allowed to be forgotten.

Two days later, on 15 June, Wood conducted an all-Tchaikovsky concert that included the first English performance of the *Festival Overture on the Danish National Anthem*. *The Musical Times* duly presented its report.

The programme was devoted to the composer of the end of the century, Tschaïkowsky, and, it is scarcely necessary to say, included his 'Pathetic' Symphony. Of the recent readings given of this work, that of Mr. Henry J. Wood is the finest, as most completely in sympathy with the spirit of the work. Nor is this astonishing. Mr. Wood has for years past identified himself with Slavonic music, with which his temperament would seem to be in entire accord, and no conductor has succeeded in so forcibly expressing the fierce and wild passion which surges like a mighty under-current in its strains, or in so brilliantly producing the barbaric glitter of its orchestration. With regard to the much debated subject of the *Andante* in the first movement, Mr. Wood adopts a happy middle course between the over-hurried passion of M. Lamoureux and the most tranquil expression of Dr. Richter. Under Mr. Wood's baton the beautiful melody seems to come into the turbulence of the struggle with fate like a treasured memory of a past ecstasy, and, in the second portion of the theme, to cry out with poignant grief bordering on despair in the conviction that that past will never return. This interpretation is chiefly secured by subtleties of tempo varying but in slight degree from those of other conductors, but providing a reading that furnishes the required contrast to the storm and stress of the rest of the number, and gives consistency to the subsequent appearances of the subject. The exuberant, half-savage triumph of the martial third movement was also given with pulse-stirring intensity, and the whirl of the wonderful *crescendo*, which leads to the return of the principal theme, was worked up with startling force.

In the autumn of 1898, Wood conducted the first English performance of the *Manfred Symphony* at the Queen's Hall on 28 September and first London performance of *The Tempest* on 5 October. When he again played the Sixth Symphony, on 29 October, *The Musical Times* recorded that this 'hobby-horse was once more ridden to the admiration of a crowded house. Moral for all orchestral conductors everywhere: Play the "Pathetic" for the remainder of your days and you will please the dear public evermore.' On 30 October, there took place at South Place, near Finsbury Circus, the first all-Tchaikovsky chamber concert. The principal pieces were the Piano Trio and the First Quartet. During the following autumn, Wood gave the English première of the Second Suite on 2 September, the overture to *Cherevichki* on 22 September, and *Fatum* on 28 October. On 29 October, the Sextet received its first London hearing at another all-Tchaikovsky chamber concert at South Place.

Meanwhile, on 4 March 1899 at the Crystal Palace, Manns, showing that, at seventy-three, he had lost nothing of his pioneering spirit, directed the first performance in England of the Third Symphony. (Contrary to accepted belief, he did not christen the symphony 'The Polish'; it was already known as that on the Continent.) In 1899 on Good Friday, the Sixth Symphony was played in the Brompton Oratory, Knightsbridge.

As normally happens, the provinces lagged a little behind London in assimilating the new music. Nevertheless, the new-found interest in Tchaikovsky spread throughout the country. Manchester, in the fine tradition nurtured by Hallé, responded ahead of the rest, and, on 20 January 1898, Cowen conducted the first all-Tchaikovsky programme in that city, only eight months after Wood's initial London concert devoted exclusively to the composer.

The visits of celebrated conductors did much to gain acceptance for Tchaikovsky in the provinces. Richter conducted the Sixth Symphony at the Birmingham Festival in 1897; Sullivan conducted the Fifth Symphony at the Leeds Festival in 1898, telling Henry Wood, in a letter of 4 September, 'And what a lovely work it is!' But, in one town in England, no imported advocacy was needed: at Bournemouth, young Dan Godfrey was already in full spate.

Godfrey's career was similar to Manns's. Born in 1868, the son of a bandmaster, he entered the Royal Academy of Music in 1885; he played the clarinet in the student orchestra conducted by Stanford and made the memorable trip to Windsor when Grove led everybody into the kitchens. In 1889, he became bandmaster of the Corps of Commissionaires and, shortly afterwards, helped by a recommendation from Sullivan, bandmaster, also, of the London Military Band. To supplement his income, he took on a wide variety of engagements, conducting at society balls and, in 1889 and 1890, at Cambridge during May Week. 'The work was hard', he wrote, in his autobiography, of the university gigs; 'dancing was quite as strenuous in those days as now. We commenced about 9 p.m. and, with one short interval, the dance went on till 5 a.m. the next morning. Even then the undergraduates were not tired and wanted to borrow the musicians' instruments, which request was, of course, politely but firmly refused.' On one occasion, he was invited to join an early-morning boating party – 'and made the acquaintance of cold water in an unexpected manner.' His most unusual assignment was to write and conduct incidental music for a boxing match at Her Majesty's Theatre, in the Haymarket. Since he was naturally unable to predict what course the contest would take, this presented some difficulty. However, with the bass drummer alerted to punctuate the landing of a heavy punch, he managed successfully to follow the fight, mostly using changes of tempo and volume. His efforts were crowned with success when, by a happy stroke of fate, one of the protagonists put an end to the bout by dispatching the other through the ropes and into the crowd. Godfrey and his band at once responded with a thrilling coda that drew an enthusiastic ovation from the audience.

In 1893 he went to Bournemouth as a bandmaster and, the following summer, was appointed musical director to the Corporation. With his twenty-four players, he gave concerts on the pier, he and the band being dressed in pillbox hats and artillery cadet uniforms that he purchased secondhand. By 1895, the band had increased to thirty-three and was giving symphony concerts in the Winter Gardens Pavilion. These were exceptionally well supported. Beginning with programmes that included marches, waltzes, entr'actes and selections from light opera, Godfrey rapidly moved on to Mendelssohn, Spohr and Beethoven, using a number of the bandsmen as string-players. In

1896, he was appointed general manager of the Winter Gardens. This was the green light he had been waiting for; he immediately turned the band into an orchestra of forty players, and proceeded to cut loose, raining on the docile burghers of Bournemouth, on its many invalids and retired couples, on its peaceful holidaymakers, the glories of the modern repertoire: Berlioz, Liszt, Brahms, Dvořák, Grieg, Rubinstein and Saint-Saëns. Less musically sophisticated than London concert-goers, they reacted in a surprising way – by warming to what they heard and applauding Godfrey's enterprise. In January 1897, Manns happened to visit Bournemouth, attended one of the concerts and called on the young conductor to congratulate him. Godfrey promptly invited the distinguished veteran to direct the next concert, three days later. Manns accepted, performing Schubert's Ninth Symphony and Schumann's Fourth. He followed this with a glowing letter to Godfrey. 'The artistic achievement is something of which Bournemouth may well be proud', he wrote, 'and which cannot fail to produce most beneficial results for musical art in England . . . What was especially gratifying to me was the great attention and enthusiastic display of appreciation of the audience. Such programmes as you had on the two days last week would have been an impossibility when I began my conductor's work at the Crystal Palace, now more than 41 years ago.' He added that the orchestra would benefit from the addition of certain further instruments. Godfrey wasted no time in savouring Manns's letter, but, after sending copies to the local newspapers, placed it before the town council. Manns's final words, 'let me assure you that it will always delight me to hear of the work which you are doing at Bournemouth', were duly noted, and civic pride sanctioned the hiring of the extra personnel, as Manns had suggested.

Inspired both by local support for his endeavours and by the ardent encouragement from the legendary champion of new music, Godfrey now set forth with a vengeance, introducing, during March 1897, Tchaikovsky's Fifth and Sixth Symphonies and the *1812* Overture. Two months later, came the Violin Concerto, and, in December, the Third Suite. In January of 1898, he conducted the First Piano Concerto and, in February, the Fourth Symphony. In December of the same year, he presented the *Manfred Symphony*; this was only the second English performance of the work, less than three months after the première in London. Godfrey was, by this time, almost matching Wood stride for stride, and, on 9 October 1899, he overtook him, giving the first performance in England of the Second Symphony. On 8 October 1900, he again pipped Wood, by conducting the English première of the First Symphony. Since he had also performed the Third Symphony at the Winter Gardens in May 1900, Bournemouth thus became the first town in England to hear all of Tchaikovsky's symphonies. Godfrey appears also to have given the première of the suite, Op 66a, arranged by Ziloti from *The Sleeping Beauty*, on 7 January 1901. It seems likely that the Winter Gardens witnessed, too, the first performance in England of the Andante and Finale, Op 79, on 19 November 1900.

We are now in a position to see that Tchaikovsky's symphonies were performed in England in the following order: No 5 (Hallé), No 4 (Tchaikovsky), No 6 (Mackenzie), *Manfred* (Wood), No 3 (Manns), No 2 (Godfrey), No 1 (Godfrey). In London, the order was: No 4 (Tchaikovsky), No 6 (Mackenzie), No 5 (Nikisch), *Manfred* (Wood), No 3 (Manns), No 1 (Wood), No 2 (Wood). In length of time between the Russian and English premières, they follow precisely the reverse order of composition: No 6 (four months), No 5 (four years), *Manfred* (12 years), No 4 (15 years), No 3 (23 years), No 2 (26 years), No 1 (32 years).

Wood introduced the First Symphony to London audiences on 27 August 1902 and the Second Symphony on 3 September 1902. His was not even the second English performance of the First Symphony, but the third. Alfred Rodewald conducted the work in Liverpool on 13 October 1900, only five days after the première in Bournemouth. A year later, he led the Liverpool Orchestral Society in the world première of Elgar's *Pomp and Circumstance* Marches Nos 1 and 2, the first of which is dedicated to him. 'He was the dearest, kindest, *best* friend I ever had', Elgar told August Jaeger after Rodewald's death in November 1903. His grief for Rodewald is expressed in the *larghetto* of his Second Symphony.

So great was the impression made by Tchaikovsky's music during the second half of the 1890s that people became eager to hear the works of other Russian composers. This interest unfortunately did not extend to Rubinstein, who died in November 1894 and whose popularity simultaneously declined.

On 17 February 1896, Mackenzie conducted the first performance in England of Borodin's Second Symphony, at a Philharmonic concert. According to *The Musical Times*, 'the audience listened in some wonder, and considerable doubt what to make of it. But we are glad to have heard the Symphony. It indicates that which, according to present appearances, will be, in some more or less modified form, the "music of the future." Not the Philistines, but the Slavs are upon us.' On 24 September 1896, Wood conducted the English première of *Capriccio espagnol*, following it with *Sheherazada*, on 5 December of the same year. On 10 October 1896, Manns presented the orchestral suite from *Mlada*. All three of these works by Rimsky-Korsakov met with a promising response, and Wood repeated the *Capriccio espagnol* on 20 March 1897. Two weeks later, London heard the *Polovtsian Dances* for the first time; these, wrote *The Musical Times* 'are scored in too noisy a manner for entire enjoyment in the concert-room, but the wild force of the themes and the virility and glowing colour with which they are treated make the music memorable.'

In February 1897, Wood directed Glazunov's Fifth Symphony. Five months later, the composer himself came to London and conducted the Fourth Symphony. By now, *The Musical Times* had been subjected to rather more Russian music than it was prepared to stomach.

Mr. Glazounow's symphony is his Op 48 and stands in the key of E flat. It is not so characteristically Russian as his No. 5, which Mr. Henry Wood produced some months ago, and we almost like it better for that reason, for we confess that we do not care one jot for the much vaunted 'nationalism' in music unless the nationalism produces beautiful as well as 'characteristic' music; and a great deal of the Russian music lately introduced to Londoners, though very characteristic, appears to us almost devoid of beauty. We refuse to believe that Englishmen will ever become greatly attached to the effusions of the Russian school unless the latter assimilates Western ideas – *i.e.*, comes more strongly under the influence of the great classic masters of music. In this connection we may point out that what in England is considered the greatest achievement of the Russian school so far – viz., the stupendous first movement of Tschaikowsky's 'Pathetic' Symphony, is also the least essentially Russian of that master's pieces. It is great *not* because it is Russian, nor merely because it displays phenomenal strength, superb workmanship, gorgeous colour, etc., though these qualities go for much, but because it is heart-music in which a master speaks to us in accents of suffering and despair, hope and resignation, which go straight to the heart and move us to tears in spite of ourselves. This *is* beautiful, great music, and of such the Russians have given us all too little. They have, in fact, revealed to us next to nothing of the *heart* of their great people. When they begin to do so, they will produce beautiful music which will appeal with equal force to all music-lovers irrespective of nationality,

for the human heart is the same all the world over. At present we are too
frequently reminded of Bismarck's 'Scratch a Russian and find a Tartar'
when listening to the wild effusions which some Russian composers inflict
upon us. There is little depth of feeling in Mr. Glazounow's symphony,
and it almost seems as if we must not expect much from him in this
respect, seeing that he has refrained (wisely, perhaps) from attempting a
slow movement in this work, while that in his subsequent symphony (No.
5), though agreeably melodious, displays but a sentimental kind of
passion.

On 29 January 1898, Borodin's Second Symphony was given its
second London hearing, under Henry Wood's baton. *The Musical
Times* gleefully recorded that the audience 'seemed terribly bored by
one of the most Russian of Russian compositions. In fact, we have
never, in all our long experience, heard any symphonic work received
so coldly . . . We have no desire to hear Borodine's masterpiece
again.' *The Musical Times*, in attributing Joseph de Maistre's dictum
to Bismarck, had betrayed its 'blood and iron' intentions towards the
gathering Tartar invasion. The snickering reference to Borodin's
symphony as a 'masterpiece' was probably occasioned by the knowledge that it was extremely popular in Russia; in *Expositions and Developments*, Stravinsky recalls that, in pre-war St Petersburg, 'Rimsky's
Antar and Borodin's Second were played a dozen times for every
performance of a symphony by Brahms or Bruckner.' The next
arrival, which was very much grist to *The Musical Times*'s satanic mill,
happened to be *A Night on Bald Mountain*, 'as hideous a thing as we
have ever heard. The "story" is of that gruesome, childish description
so fascinating to Slavonic composers.' The piece was performed by
Wood on 19 February 1898. It was 'an abomination. May we never
hear it again.' Three months later, reversing its previously indulgent
attitude towards Rimsky-Korsakov, the journal made Richter's first
English performance of *Sheherazada* the pretext for further obloquy.

Verily, the average Russian composer, he of the band of *real* Russians, who
look askance at Tschaïkowsky as 'under foreign influence', is a past
master of the gentle art of making bricks without straw! Strip this precious
Suite of its glittering orchestral garb and search for what we Westerners
consider the kernel and substance, the very heart and soul of music,
Melody, and there seems not enough to furnish material for a Strauss
waltz. There are some pretty tunes in the two middle movements . . . But
the rest is notes, notes *et praeterea nihil*! Even the wonders of the brilliant
orchestration soon pall, even as to look into the sun becomes unendurable

after a short while, and we rebel against the utter lack of emotional qualities in a very lengthy work. Do Slavonic music-lovers admire this kind of music, we wonder, and must we Anglo-Saxons, Celts, and Teutons first become Slavs before we can appreciate these strange effusions at their full and proper value? We suppose our Russian friends do derive some satisfaction from them, something more, we mean, than a mere tickling of the senses. To us, we confess it with sorrow and all due humility, they seem like 'linked boredom long drawn out,' to vary a famous quotation. Brahms's C minor Symphony supplied the longed-for contrast to Rimsky-Korsakoff's piece, and never has the great master's magnificent epic seemed greater or moved us more deeply than on this occasion. Its glories seemed to 'bring all Heav'n before our eyes', as its ravishing beauties and touching accents brought tears into them.

One might imagine that the work had not generally pleased, but, in October 1898, Richter repeated *Sheherazada*. It remained an 'empty, irritatingly prolix effusion'. The suite from *Mlada*, performed by Wood in November, was 'very Russian music, of little account as regards subject-matter or its development . . . It leaves us utterly unmoved, and all too soon we grow weary of the gorgeous apparel in which its pretty, harmless little ideas are dressed.'

By the end of 1898, Newman and Wood had introduced, in less than four years, a large body of previously unknown Russian music, including works by Dargomyzhsky, Arensky, Cui, Serov, Sokolov, Volkov and Ilinsky. To these were added, in 1899, pieces by Liadov, Balakirev's First Symphony and *Overture on Themes of Three Russian Songs*, both on 26 September, and, on 7 September, Ippolitov-Ivanov's *Caucasian Sketches*. But by 1899 *The Musical Times* had had enough. It made this plain in its February issue. 'The programmes of Mr. Robert Newman's forthcoming season of Symphony concerts at the Queen's Hall have been published, and we cannot feign any surprise at observing that they do not contain a single note of British music, old or new.' The present fashion for Russian music was to blame.

The craze, such as it is, is of Mr. Newman's and Mr. Wood's creating. Tschaïkowsky's last great symphony proving a phenomenal success, they let loose a flood of Russian music – good, bad and indifferent, without discrimination and without mercy. We admire the brilliant band of young Russians, with Glazounoff at their head, and believe that before long they will produce music of lasting value; but why their every note should be deemed worthy of production at the Queen's Hall, while our own composer's best works are ignored, is a mystery.

Several of the other music journals echoed this opinion, and, in the *Strand Musical Magazine*, even the pro-Russian Arthur Hervey drily suggested that England's five leading composers might fare better if they were named 'Sullivanski, Cowenkoi, Mackensikoff, Stanfordtscheff and Parrykine'.

In April 1899, *The Musical Times* reproved Wood for his neglect of Brahms, following his performance of the Third Symphony on 25 February, by observing that 'the orchestra was none too well acquainted' with the work. Moreover, 'Mr. Wood's *tempi* are not those of Dr. Richter; *ergo*, they cannot be Brahms's.' The magazine must have been somewhat nonplussed when, on 29 May, Glazunov's Sixth Symphony was introduced in a performance conducted, not by Wood, but by Richter. It nevertheless stuck to its guns.

> Time was when we built great hopes on Alexandre Glazounow. We believe in him less and less as he goes on producing symphony after symphony with the facility and rapidity of a Mozart or Schubert. To be sure, he is a great architect, and can raise a splendid monument of learning and ingenuity with anybody. But, alas! the life-giving breath of melodic inspiration is sadly wanting, and the whole astounding fabric seems doomed to a short life.

The performance was 'magnificent'; the work was 'coolly received'.

On 25 November, Wood conducted the English première of the suite from *Raymonda*, prompting *The Musical Times* into thinly veiled repetition.

> Upon Alexander Glazounoff used to rest the fond hopes of those who rightly or wrongly expect Slavonic composers to shape the course and make the history of music in the near future. To us the gifted young Russian [now forty-four] has proved a disappointment, for every fresh work from his pen seems to take him farther away from the path that leads towards greatness. He gains in facility of execution as he pours forth work after work with the ease of a Schubert, but he seems to exercise less and less self-criticism . . . We doubt whether we shall ever hear the Suite again . . .

The performance was given 'with the most wonderful finish'; the work's reception was 'chilling'.

The Musical Times, in its December issue, rounded off the century with a rapturous salute to Brahms and Richter.

A Brahms symphony under Hans Richter! O great and all too rare delight, that makest us forgive those of our friends who love not the great Johannes, and even them who will persistently inflict upon our long-suffering good nature the barbarous noises and the unspeakable dulnesses of much unripe, bill-poster art *à la Tartare*. Seriously, Brahms's strong, sane, noble, beautiful music seems a perfect godsend when one has been compelled to listen long to the orgies of blatant Muscovite futilities with which the Queen's Hall resounds on untold afternoons and evenings. It was the Viennese master's great No. 1 in C minor that Dr. Richter played to the delight of a crowded audience . . . and never has he conducted it with happier results. There was a dignity about his reading that caused the music to stand more than ever aloof from all things mundane and common. No nervous excitement was there, no frantic hurrying up to sensational climaxes, no explosion of musical powder magazines, so to speak; but order and strength, beauty and nobility reigned supreme and braced us up after the day's labour instead of merely exciting and irritating us as so much modern music does. It was a great performance of a great work.

Immediately following this, came a review of a Henry Wood concert that had been given two days earlier.

At the Tsar's – beg pardon, the Queen's Hall in Langham Place, the sentimental and unhappy hero of the 'Pathetic' Symphony has once more been killed with stroke of tam tam and decently buried with much growling of double-basses . . . But weep not, gentle reader, he is not really dead; alas! he will come to life again to be scotched and killed many more times ere we have quite done with him. Not that we would really object to the gentleman, for we have taken the liveliest interest in his 'life and death' ever since he made his appearance (and disappearance) at the Queen's Hall in 1894, under the aegis of kind and sympathetic Sir Alexander Mackenzie. But even you, gentle reader, cannot deny that the *toujours perdrix* of tam tam suicides (for it *is* a suicide, of that we are convinced) and weeping double-bass funeral mutes does become monotonous. Mr. Wood and his merry men played the work quite magnificently. This much is due to them.

At the same concert, *Fatum* was played for the first time in England. It should, remarked *The Musical Times*, have been consigned to oblivion.

If Mr. Wood spent half as much time in the preparation of some representative British work as he must have devoted to this wretched 'Fatum', how happy some native composer might be made! British art is just good enough for the Promenade concerts, in the estimation of the Queen's Hall

authorities; but 'taboo' is their motto for the higher class Symphony concerts. In no other country in the world is such an unjust and unpatriotic
insult to native art possible or even conceivable, and nowhere in England
except at the Queen's (save the mark!) Hall.

By 1900, Tchaikovsky was securely established in the orchestral
repertoire and had become immune to such criticism as we have just
read. By 1902, there was a weekly Tchaikovsky night at the Queen's
Hall. Beethoven, Schubert, Wagner, Brahms, Gounod, Grieg and
Sullivan nights were also tried out, but only the Beethoven and
Wagner nights proved to be sufficiently popular to justify their
continuance.

Wood extended his list of Tchaikovsky premières, on 14 Septem-
ber 1901, with the *Swan Lake* suite published by Jurgenson in
November 1900 and, again, possibly arranged by Ziloti. 'The suite is
not a brilliant example of Tschaikowsky's genius', wrote *The Musical
Times*, 'but it is pleasing music and very picturesquely scored.'
During 1904 and 1905, Wood performed excerpts from *The Oprichnik*,
Mazeppa, *The Queen of Spades* and *Iolanta*, concluding his pioneering
work on behalf of Tchaikovsky by conducting the symphonic ballad
The Voyevoda at the Queen's Hall on 28 September 1905.

He continued to champion the other Russian composers, conducting, notably, the English premières of Rimsky-Korsakov's *Antar*
Symphony, on 19 September 1900, and Rakhmaninov's First Piano
Concerto, on 4 October 1900, but, here, partly due to opposition from
the critics, progress was slower. Nevertheless, by the end of the first
decade of the twentieth century, Rimsky-Korsakov, Borodin and
Rakhamaninov had each gained a permanent place in English
musical life. Moreover, the way had been prepared for Stravinsky
and Prokofiev, and, later, Shostakovich. Wood conducted the first
English performance of *The Firebird* suite in September 1913, following it, during 1914, with *Feu d'artifice* and the *Scherzo fantastique*. The
degree to which Russian music had by then become established in
England is apparent in the programmes for the 1915 season of the
Philharmonic (now Royal Philharmonic) Society. The opening
concert, conducted by Thomas Beecham, consisted of Balakirev's
Tamara, the 'Letter Scene' from *Eugene Onegin*, Borodin's *Polovtsian
Dances* and Stravinsky's *Petrushka*. *Antar* was played at the second
concert; *The Firebird*, at the third; Rakhmaninov's Second Suite, at

the fourth; *Sheherazada*, at the seventh; and *Petrushka* again, at the eighth and last.

It would be a mistake to regard Henry Wood as a specialist simply in Tchaikovsky or in Russian music generally. As James Agate wrote in *Ego* in 1933, 'All conductors find it advisable to let their names be associated with some particular composers; Beecham specializes in Mozart and Delius, Harty in Berlioz, Weingartner in Beethoven, Coates in Wagner and Russian music, and Wood in everything.' The breadth of his interests is apparent in the works that he introduced to England. Russian music, as we have mentioned, had truly come into its own by the time of Beecham's opening Royal Philharmonic concert of 1 November 1915. But, by then, Wood had also given the English premières of Strauss's *Sinfonia domestica*; Debussy's *Prélude à l'après-midi d'un faune, L'Enfant prodigue, La Damoiselle élue* and *Images*; Ravel's *Rhapsodie espagnole, Mother Goose Suite* and *Valses nobles et senti-mentales*; Sibelius's *En Saga, Karelia Overture* and *Karelia Suite, King Kristian II Suite, Pelléas et Mélisande Suite*, First Symphony and Violin Concerto; Bartók's *Two Portraits* and First Suite, His Mahler advocacy is even more remarkable: he conducted the first perform-ance in England of the First Symphony, in October 1903; the Fourth Symphony, in October 1905; the *adagietto* from the Fifth Symphony, in August 1909; the Seventh Symphony, in January 1913; 'Das Lied von der Erde', in January 1914. By then, no other major work of Mahler had been played in England. Wood championed him almost singlehanded, apart from Beecham, who directed the Fourth Symphony in December 1907. Wood had intended performing more of Mahler's compositions, but was impeded by lack of rehearsal time. He introduced the Eighth Symphony in April 1930, having been granted adequate time in which to prepare it by the BBC. He conduc-ted it again at the opening concert of the 1938 Sheffield Festival. Unique among his achievements was the world première of Schön-berg's Five Orchestral Pieces, at the Queen's Hall on 3 September 1912. 'Stick to it, gentlemen!' Wood had exhorted his orchestra during rehearsals. 'This is nothing to what you'll have to play in 25 years' time.' The performance was greeted with hisses and laughter; one woman quietly wept for the death of music; Fuller-Maitland, still critic for *The Times*, meditated on retirement from the musical life. Wood's reaction was to invite Schönberg to come and conduct the Five Orchestral Pieces himself, and this second performance took place in January 1914. Afterwards, the composer wrote a letter of thanks to the orchestra, praising their 'precision, beauty of sound and noble taste, and careful thoroughness of every detail, which are to the credit of each one of you and the success of all of you together. I must tell you that on the Continent, as far as my knowledge goes, there are, at the most, only two orchestras that could be compared with yours – the Amsterdam Concertgebouw and the Vienna Philharmonic.'

Two months later, Wood welcomed the equally controversial Scriabin, who had only a year to live before his sudden, premature death. On 1 February 1913, Wood had conducted the English première of *Prometheus*, and now, with Scriabin, he again performed it, together with the Piano Concerto, on 14 March 1914 at the Queen's Hall, provoking a furore. 'I've got a mountain of letters asking for my autograph', Scriabin wrote from the Welbeck Palace Hotel to his wife Tatyana. 'Tillett tells me I have to comply with Londoners' requests for these, and it will take me all of three hours to become their victim. Where will I find the time?' On 25 March, he visited Cambridge to discuss his theories about colour and music with two of the professors.

It is little wonder that Russian musicians have always held Henry Wood in the highest regard. Rakhmaninov came to London in October 1938 especially to take part in the concert celebrating his fifty years as a conductor. On Wood's seventy-fifth birthday, Shostakovich sent him a telegram, and a special party in his honour was held in Moscow, at which speeches were made and his records were played. This was attended by Prokofiev; both he and Shostakovich – and Miaskovsky – owed much to him, for Wood conducted English premières of their works, too. But, as we have said, Wood was no mere Russian specialist. Other composers whose compositions received their first performances in England under his baton include Janáček, Kodály, Dohnányi, Berg, Webern, Krenek, Hindemith, Roussel, Honegger, Ibert, Casella, Malipiero, Villa-Lobos and Loeffler.

Nor, as was often so strenuously alleged, did he neglect English music. Elgar, Holst, Delius, Vaughan Williams, Ireland, Bax, Rubbra, Ethel Smyth, Moeran, Howells, Berkeley, Bliss and Walton all benefited from the frequency with which he played their works. Malcolm Sargent wrote after Wood's death in August 1944, 'Sir Henry has done more for English music than any other man.'

Within ten years of his death, Tchaikovsky had become more popular in England than in any other country in the world, apart from Russia and America. Indeed, although it is difficult to gauge, his English popularity may have equalled his American.

We have just seen that, by 1902, Wood was devoting one programme a week to Tchaikovsky at the Queen's Hall Promenade Concerts and that Beethoven and Wagner were the only other composers also to have their own evenings. We estimate that, by then, Tchaikovsky was on the verge of becoming the third most popular composer in England, having already overtaken Gounod, Grieg, Saint-Saëns and Rubinstein, and being about to overtake Verdi, Brahms and Dvořák, as well as Bach, Handel, Haydn, Mozart, Schubert, Mendelssohn, Schumann and all English composers. In America, the situation was almost identical, with Tchaikovsky moving past Dvořák into third place, again behind Beethoven and Wagner, in about 1902. In addition, according to John H. Mueller's invaluable *The American Symphony Orchestra*, by around 1898, Russian music was second only to Austro-German music in popularity, due largely to the fact that Rimsky-Korsakov and Borodin had made headway more quickly than in England and that Rubinstein had suffered a less sharp decline. The arrival of Debussy and Ravel during the next decade made the French level, though this was counterbalanced for a while by Glazunov. However, the emergence of Rakhmaninov, Stravinsky and Prokofiev then lifted the Russians decisively into second place.

In New York, Damrosch continued his ardent championship of Tchaikovsky, conducting the New York Symphony Orchestra in all-Tchaikovsky programmes, though not as frequently as Wood was doing with the Queen's Hall Orchestra. In 1906, Safonov was appointed conductor of the New York Philharmonic for three years. During that period, says Mueller, Russian composers occupied over 30 per cent of the orchestra's repertoire, of which around 20 per cent was allotted to Tchaikovsky. With Damrosch still conducting the New York Symphony Orchestra, Tchaikovsky became the most performed composer in New York, with Beethoven a close second.

On the Continent, he did not gain anything like the popularity that he was accorded in England or America. In Italy, he made little impact, though *The Queen of Spades* was well received at La Scala in January 1906. In France, despite the efforts of Lamoureux, his music failed to convince the French that it was as Russian as Russian music should sound. For the Germans and Austrians, it was not sufficiently German. In this respect we should recall that, when Webern gave a series of sixteen historical lectures on the development of music, delivered in Vienna in 1932 and 1933, he found it necessary to mention only two composers, Palestrina and Debussy, who were not either German or Austrian (Mahler being considered Austrian). The German attitude towards Tchaikovsky is made clear in Richard Specht's biography of Brahms, published in 1928. Alluding to the meeting between Tchaikovsky and Brahms at Brodsky's home in Leipzig, Specht says that Brahms 'could establish no contact with Tchaikovsky.' It is understandable, suggests Specht, that Brahms, with 'his thoroughly sound nature', should be 'instinctively repelled' by Tchaikovsky – by 'the perfumed Cossack's savagery and gilt-edged melancholy of the composer of the "Pathetic" Symphony, who was so elegant and yet so inwardly torn by the tragedy of his unhappy disposition, which finally drove him to voluntary death. Brahms was unable to like him, and silently dismissed him.' The German antipathy to Tchaikovsky manifested itself most notably when the Nazis defaced and pillaged the Tchaikovsky Museum in Klin during the Second World War.

On the whole, the Austrians have had a better liking for Tchaikovsky, though he made a very slow start in that country. This is clear from Hanslick's review of the Austrian première of the Sixth Symphony, which Richter conducted in Vienna on 3 March 1895.

> We know very little of his work, and our initial acquaintance was not a happy one. The only larger orchestral works of Tchaikovsky hitherto presented in Vienna – *Romeo and Juliet* and the Violin Concerto – both fell flat . . .
>
> The 'Pathetic' Symphony has a special place among the compositions of Tchaikovsky, for it contains no trace of national colour. What woefully trivial Cossack cheer we had to stomach in the finale of his Serenade for Strings, in his Violin Concerto, in his D major Quartet, or in the third [fourth?] movement of his Suite, opus 54 [55?]! There is nothing like this in the symphony, the character of which is fundamentally Western, revealing a nobler mind . . .

Hanslick added that the five-four time of the third movement was 'disturbing to listeners and players alike . . . Moreover, it is superfluous, since the piece could be perfectly well adapted to six-eight time.'

From having at first described *Eugene Onegin* to his sister Justine as 'a very commonplace pot-boiler', Gustav Mahler developed into a warm admirer of Tchaikovsky's music and gave several first performances in Vienna, conducting *Eugene Onegin* in 1897, *Iolanta* in 1900, and *The Queen of Spades* in 1902. In January 1899, he directed the première of *1812* and, in January 1901, that of the *Manfred Symphony*. In *Die Wiener Oper*, Max Graf recalls that Mahler was so enthusiastic about the *Manfred Symphony* that he covered it in markings to ensure he kept to the correct tempi. Mahler also conducted the American première of *The Queen of Spades*, in New York on 5 March 1910.

Tchaikovsky's influence on Mahler, which is as extensive as Rimsky-Korsakov's on Ravel, makes such an attractive subject that musicologists have generally devoted much less time to uncovering his influence on other composers of Mahler's generation, like Puccini, Delius and Janáček. Sibelius, for instance, observed in a letter written to his wife at the time of his First Symphony, 'There is much in that man which I recognize in myself', thus repeating almost word for word what we have already heard from Grieg and Shostakovich. Nor should Tchaikovsky's influence on Richard Strauss and Elgar be discounted. It clearly extends beyond the literal quotation from the Twelves Pieces, Op 40, in the *Sinfonia domestica*, and from *Romeo and Juliet* in the lovers' music in *Cockaigne*. The imprint of Tchaikovsky and Wagner can be seen across the entire face of twentieth-century music, even in as characteristic a work as Sibelius's Seventh Symphony, which presents us with a chunk of the *Tristan und Isolde* prelude.

Tchaikovsky would have been delighted and probably surprised to know of his great popularity in England by the turn of the century. He would also have been pleased to learn that Queen Victoria was one of his fans. In her declining years, the Queen, true to her times, had become a devotee of Wagner, and when she commanded Henry Wood and the Queen's Hall Orchestra to give a concert at Windsor Castle on 24 November 1898, she chose to hear the *Good Friday Music*, the overture and prelude to Act III of *Die Meistersinger*, the *Siegfried Idyll* and the prelude to *Parsifal*. As an encore, she requested *The Ride of the Valkyries*. But she selected, as well, the overture to *Hansel and Gretel*, Saint-Saëns' *Le Rouet d'Omphale* and the last two movements from Tchaikovsky's Sixth Symphony. She wrote in her diary, 'the Adagio out of Tschaikowsky's *Symphonie Pathétique* was most touching and wonderfully beautiful. Mr. Wood conducted quite admirably, and the orchestra was quite perfect in every little detail. It was a real treat to hear it.' Edward VII was another who greatly enjoyed Tchaikovsky and once especially asked for *1812* to be played at a concert he attended in the Queen's Hall in 1904. The Sixth Symphony was performed at his memorial concert in May 1910.

The composer would have been disappointed, though, at the slow progress of his operas, which were as dear to him as any of his other compositions. When *Eugene Onegin* was revived in London in 1906, it ran for three performances. *The Queen of Spades*, which received its English première, conducted by Gurovich, at the London Opera House on 29 May 1915, fared no better. It failed again, at Covent Garden, in 1950, 1952, 1953 and 1956. Like *Eugene Onegin*, it has only recently attracted real enthusiasm. None of the other operas has made any headway. Perhaps *The Sorceress* will be the next to find acceptance in England.

With the ballets, of course, it has been a different story. The first to be produced was *Swan Lake* (at the Hippodrome Theatre in London on 16 May 1910) which was danced by a Russian company led by Olga Preobrajenska. However, this was a condensed version of the ballet and lasted no more than an hour. The following year, Diaghilev brought his Ballets Russes to London for the first time and, on 30 November at Covent Garden, presented another heavily abbreviated edition of *Swan Lake*, with Kschesinskaya and Nijinsky. The orchestra was conducted by Pierre Monteux, and Mischa Elman played the solo violin. Two weeks earlier, on 14 November, Kschesinskaya and Nijinsky danced the *pas de deux* for Princess Aurora and Prince Désiré from the last act of *The Sleeping Beauty*. The Ballets Russes repeated *Swan Lake* during their visits to London in 1912, 1913 and 1914. In 1918, at the Coliseum Theatre, Diaghilev introduced the 'Blue-Bird' *pas de deux*, from the last act of *The Sleeping Beauty*, which was danced by Lopokova (who, in 1925, married John Maynard Keynes) and Idzikowsky, on 16 September. The *pas de deux* for Princess Aurora and Prince Désiré was again performed, on 30 July 1921.

By this time, London had been familiar with *The Firebird* (1912), *Petrushka* (1913) and *The Rite of Spring* (1913) for eight years. It had also witnessed the introduction of *Jeux* in 1913, *Daphnis and Chloé* in 1914 and *Parade* in 1919. More recently, it had become acquainted with *Pulcinella* (1920) and *Chout* (1921). It had already had the chance to see *The Rite of Spring* in both Nijinsky's and Massine's choreographies. Yet, of Tchaikovsky, it had been treated to no more than a few fragments and scenes from *Swan Lake* and two *pas de deux* from *The Sleeping Beauty*.

Hitherto, Diaghilev had not attempted to give any of his ballets much of a run, but, during each season in London, had shuffled them about from night to night or week to week in an effort to provide greater variety. Now, in 1921, impressed by the staying power of *Chu Chin Chow*, which had arrived five years earlier, in August 1916, at His Majesty's Theatre and was still going strong, he decided to experiment by putting on a ballet that would occupy a whole evening and be allowed to run continuously. He settled on *The Sleeping Beauty*, whose title he wisely changed to *The Sleeping Princess*, lest it be mistaken for a pantomime. This was lavishly and painstakingly presented on 2 November 1921 at the Alhambra Theatre, which had just become available, following the failure of its latest production. By coincidence, therefore, the first of Tchaikovsky's ballets to be given practically complete in London was produced at the theatre that he had visited on his final evening in England. In order to cover the vast financial outlay, *The Sleeping Princess* was played right through the winter, but, in face of falling receipts and mounting debts, it was at last withdrawn on 4 February 1922, after 115 performances. The deficit amounted to around £10,000. Despite a cast that included Spessivtseva, Vladimirov, Lopokova, Idzikowsky and Nijinska, with Carlotta Brianza (the original Aurora in St Petersburg in 1890) as Carabosse; despite the appearance of the legendary Enrico Cecchetti (the original Blue-Bird) as Carabosse in the 100th performance; despite the visit, on 12 December, by King George V and Queen Mary; and despite the excellent conducting of Eugene Goossens, the ballet never really caught the public's imagination. Audiences were not yet ready for the revival of classical ballet, nor for the weightiness of Tchaikovsky's music. However, the importance of the production, in the history of English ballet, can hardly be exaggerated. As Arnold Haskell has written in his biography of Diaghilev, 'to-day in England its influence in retrospect is tremendous. No one who saw those performances could ever think the same about dancing again.'

The Sleeping Princess had nevertheless pleased a great many people, and, on 31 March 1924, Lopokova and Idzikowsky, with a small company, appeared at the Coliseum in a selection of *divertissements* from the ballet, including their now-famous 'Blue-Bird' *pas de deux*. Diaghilev also prepared a ballet, *Aurora's Wedding*, that featured a number of the character dances from the third act, and this was presented at the Coliseum on 15 December 1924. It proved immediately popular and was thereafter given in every year until 1929. In 1926, 1927, 1928 and 1929, he also revived his condensed *Swan Lake*.

Diaghilev's death, on 19 August 1929, stunned the world of ballet, robbing it of the greatest figure in the history of that art. The world of music also owed him an incalculable debt. A number of the scores that he commissioned – *Petrushka, The Rite of Spring, Daphnis and Chloé* – rank among the supreme masterpieces of the twentieth century, and, besides these, there are *The Firebird, Les Noces, Jeux, Parade, The Prodigal Son, Les Biches, The Three-Cornered Hat* and many others. Moreover, the Ballets Russes were the making of conductors such as Monteux, Ansermet and Desormière. Nor should we forget that Beecham, Boult and Sargent all conducted for Diaghilev (and that Boult's *The Rite of Spring* was once an ornament of the orchestral repertoire).

The death of Diaghilev created a vacuum in the life of English ballet. This was filled in 1931 by the formation of the Sadler's Wells Ballet, which, under the brilliant guidance of Ninette de Valois, who had danced with the Diaghilev company, made such rapid progress that, on 30 January 1934, it was able to present *Nutcracker*. Amazing as it may seem, this was the first production of the ballet in Western Europe. At long last, on 29 November 1934, Sadler's Wells also produced the complete *Swan Lake*, almost sixty years after its première in Moscow, and more than forty years after Tchaikovsky's death. By then, Elgar, Delius and Holst were all dead. The first Sadler's Wells production of *The Sleeping Beauty* took place on 2 February 1939; it has since been staged more than 500 times by that company.

When we consider how much was achieved by men like Hallé, Manns, Berger, Stanford, Wood, Godfrey, Mackenzie, Cowen and Diaghilev to acquaint the English with Tchaikovsky's music, it comes as a shock to discover how little our critics have done to increase our understanding and enjoyment of it. Indeed, it is no exaggeration to say that, on the whole, they have not, until recently, even attempted to deepen our understanding, and many have done all they can to lessen our enjoyment.

The tone for much of their criticism was set by Parry in his address to students at the Royal College of Music in May 1897, following the death of Brahms. He had been appointed director of the college in 1894 on the retirement of Grove. By the middle of 1897, as we will recall, London was in the grip of Tchaikovsky fever, with Wood still pushing through première after première at the Queen's Hall. Students at the RCM were wildly excited about Tchaikovsky. Among them was John Ireland, who, in 1956, told Alfred J. Swan, the author of *Russian Music and Its Sources in Chant and Folk-Song*, 'When we were at the College, we all thought he was the last word in music. I heard the first performance in England of his Sixth Symphony. It simply swept us off our feet. We had never heard such music before . . .' It is obvious from Parry's address that he felt the great European tradition and the universal language were being threatened; through an exotic dialect and an unscrupulous appeal to their emotions, the young were being seduced by a nine days' wonder. Moreover, many of their elders had proved equally susceptible to the spicy blandishments of the barbarian Pied Piper, for several London newspapers greeted Brahms's death with an insouciance that would have been inconceivable four years earlier, at the time when Parry was plying the waters of the Mediterranean, in the very cradle of European civilisation. Thus he stood before his pupils and spoke.

An overwhelming loss seems to make a void in the musical world which we cannot hope to see filled in our time. The great heroes of the world are so rare that it is fortunately but seldom in the brief spell of our lives that we have to try and realise what parting with them means. When the career of a great hero ends we stand amazed, and wonder how the immense powers it represented can have really ceased.

When we think of the vital force which the work of a man like Johannes Brahms represents, we can scarcely bring ourselves to face the fact that there will be no more symphonies, quartets, 'Schichsalslied', requiems, songs, sonatas, part-songs, nor any other treasures of art marked by the strong and noble individuality of that particularly heroic tone-poet. Not heaven itself, nor all the combined ingenuity of all the cleverest scientists and artists in the world can ever produce one single work which would represent truly and adequately the noble type of thought and the essentially characteristic qualities in the now familiar works of that single-hearted man.

The life-work is ended and nothing of quite the same order can again be done in the world. The mortal part of him lies fitly in close proximity to the resting-places of Beethoven and Schubert in the cemetery at Vienna. And what comfort have we? Truly, the comfort of heroic work heroically done – a noble life lived out in untainted devotion to generous ideals . . .

The man Johannes Brahms has gone from us, but his work and his example are our possession still, and will be, not for us only, but for the generations that come after us . . . the example of Johannes Brahms is full of encouragement for us. His was no nature always laid open to receive any chance external impression. He was no expansive, neurotic, ecstatic, hysterico-sensitive bundle of sensibilities, but even as full of dignified artistic reserve and deliberate artistic judgement as the most serious of our own people. But he joined with it the great nature, the cultivated, comprehensive taste, the imagination fostered and fed by dwelling on noble subjects and keeping far from triviality and conventions . . .

The first books on Tchaikovsky to be published in England were written, as one might expect, by enthusiasts, and these initial volumes stand out like beacons against the long black night of critical carnage that was to follow them. The earliest, by Rosa Newmarch, appeared in 1900 and was an excellent introduction to the composer's life and work, being both informative and explanatory; it was dedicated to Henry Wood. In 1904, Ernest Markham Lee produced an equally helpful study, devoted almost exclusively to the music. Two years later, came his second book, which concentrated more on Tchaikovsky's life, but, at the same time, made a number of general and valuable observations.

> . . . . it is not merely that he appeals by means of known media of expression; rather is it that his matter and his methods both find ready response in our hearts. His matter does not often run him into extravagant riot, yet you would hardly call him restrained, although there *is* control; and then there is, to counteract any diffuseness of idea or over-emotional tendency, all that gorgeously beautiful power of melody, that consummate mastery of colour and of orchestral resource, and that general lovableness which commands and draws us to the man, we know not why. Such warm-hearted fellow-feeling we do not offer to Bach or Brahms: we respect them too much, and the heights on which they reign appear sometimes a little cold and distant; we cannot always soar to them in our every mood. But there are others, of whom, to my mind, Tchaikovski is one, who have just that amount of human weakness that makes us love them all the more. . . . There is something more akin to the fierce impetuosity and unresting strain of Schumann's music in him, with that undercurrent of kept-down grief which we can trace through all the work of the Zwickau master . . . It is indeed somewhat wonderful that a man so easily discouraged, and withal so timid, should have accomplished all that he did. When we consider his late start in musical life, the many difficulties he had to overcome, and the very slow appreciation which was felt for his music, we may indeed look with reverence and love upon one who bequeathed to the world so much of enduring excellence and beauty.

Published also in 1906 was Mrs Newmarch's abridged translation of Modest Tchaikovsky's biography of his brother, which was completed in 1902. This has remained, for over seventy years, the fullest account in English of the composer's life. Yet another volume to come out in 1906 was a complete study by Edwin Evans junior, both of the man and his music. Two years later, Mrs Newmarch's original 1900 biography was reprinted in a greatly expanded edition, with additional material, by Edwin Evans senior, consisting of essays on different aspects of Tchaikovsky's music, with detailed analyses of the Piano Trio, First Piano Concerto, and Fifth and Sixth Symphonies. Evans father and son both write with enthusiasm and perception, and the son often reveals, as in the following passage, a real understanding of his subject.

> Much has been made of Tchaikovsky's pessimism, but it is at least open to doubt whether this was personal or racial. In every Slav there lies hidden a fatalist, and, combined with a certain fluidity of emotion, running rapidly over the whole gamut of human joy and sorrow, this fatalism engenders in every true Russian moments of gloom and depression such as we Westerners can little appreciate. That modern sensation for which Germans coined the word *Weltschmerz* has little in common with it.
>
> On the whole, Tchaikovsky's works, with their strong emotions and occasionally violent contrasts, form the most reliable basis for a clear estimate of his character, and even where conclusions formed from them may not strictly correspond with what we know of his life, the wise man will nevertheless give them the preference, for as time goes on, a man's biography pales into insignificance beside the monument he has set himself.

Edwin Evans junior's *Tchaikovsky* proved such a fine book that it went unchallenged by any other publications on the composer until the 1940s. In the preface to the 1935 edition, the author stated that, in revising his original text, he had come across passages in which 'the enthusiasm of my younger self seemed exaggerated, until I recalled that in those days the need of proselytism still existed.' He nevertheless made hardly any changes, for, by now, the wheel had come full circle: Tchaikovsky had been so reviled by English critics during the previous two decades that proselytising was as much, if not more, necessary than at the beginning of the century.

During that period, a new breed of critic had risen in the land. These men were masters of critical analysis, and their gods were Bach, Mozart, Beethoven, Wagner and Brahms. They set the greatest store by structure and the manipulation of form, particularly sonata form. They were distinguished by Olympian poise, omniscience and an elitist attitude towards music. Their views were proclaimed with immense self-confidence, violence of expression, and contempt for any composer who, in their eyes, fell short of the highest intellectual standards. They wore their erudition on their sleeves, delighted in paradox, sudden references to the most obscure compositions, and vague and sweeping generalisations. They tended to accept Hanslick's view that 'a musical idea requires only beauty without any concern for meaning' and that it was not the purpose of music to represent feelings: 'the beauty of a work is specifically musical; it inheres in its combination of musical sounds and is independent of all alien, extramusical notions.' They put their formidable powers of analysis at the service of those composers whom they esteemed and at the disservice of those whom they despised. Thus, a curious or perplexing passage in Beethoven could be brilliantly and convincingly analysed to reveal further dimensions of his greatness, while a comparable passage in Liszt served only as additional proof of his ineptitude. Finally, they looked on most performing musicians with disdain for their lack of real musicality.

For forty years or so, these men held sway with such sovereign authority that many music-lovers were made to feel guilty about their likes and dislikes. A penchant for Grieg could be regarded as an amusing foible in somebody who made the yearly pilgrimage to Bayreuth or knew Brahms's quartets by heart, but to suggest that Grieg was one's favourite composer was to surrender all hope of being considered musical.

We can laugh at these critics now, but we should remember that, over a lengthy period of time, they severely impeded the growth of appreciation of many important composers. They also insidiously limited people's understanding of composers who were near to being fully appreciated: by asserting, for instance, that Dvořák's Seventh Symphony, the most Germanic of his major works, was his masterpiece, they succeeded in distorting the nature of his overall achievement, thereby lessening enjoyment of the wealth of music that does entitle him to greatness. Ultimately and paradoxically (a paradox that, with their icy detachment, they might have relished) they managed, through the weight they gave to structure and technique, to diminish the stature of even Bach, Mozart, Beethoven, Wagner and Brahms by virtually ignoring most of the attributes that made them great composers.

Their inspiration was Donald Francis Tovey. Born in 1875 at Eton, where his father was a master, he quickly showed musical promise, coming to the attention of Parry, with whom he began to study when he was fourteen. With Parry's help, he secured a scholarship to Balliol College, Oxford, in 1894. By now, he was already omniscient. The college was used to this sort of thing, having endured Benjamin Jowett for several decades, but in a nineteen-year-old it was less palatable. Although he was meant to be studying Greek and Latin, he devoted most of his time to music. He derived the greatest pleasure from Bach, Mozart, Beethoven and Brahms. Brahms stood head and shoulders above all other modern composers; Dvořák came next, and then Joachim, whom Tovey had known personally for several years. But even Dvořák could be a little trying, and a hearing of the Czech master's *Requiem* failed to move him because of 'the false touches in Dvořák's views of death, and the errors in his structure and vocal writing, and the amazing badness of the performance.' He meditated on music constantly and would return from a walk 'with a new theory about consecutive 5ths (and a very good one too)'. In the summer of 1897, he visited Beethoven's birthplace, in Bonn, travelling on to Bayreuth, where he saw *Das Rheingold*. This opera shed new light on Beethoven. 'I found myself quite fit to read the Beethoven D Major Mass through for the third time this week. These two impressions can exist side by side with no more difficulty than they make by the side of Cologne Cathedral.' The following year, he took his finals. Only two of the exam questions really interested him, and he used practically all the time available in answering them, with the result that he just managed to scrape a third-class pass.

On leaving Oxford, he embarked on a career as a pianist. He made a second trip to Bayreuth, where he became friendly with Edward Marsh. Shortly afterwards, Marsh wrote to a friend, 'I don't think you'd like him at all, unless you took some trouble to understand him, but I saw a great deal of him at Bayreuth and got accustomed to him. He is the incarnation of Brahmsness, and lives almost entirely by the intellect. When he talks to one he gives the idea that he looks on one exclusively as a listener and not in the least as a human being.' On a train journey with Marsh, Tovey sat 'moping in the corner' for a while, then astounded the rest of the carriage by starting to sing 'in an unearthly kind of murmur occasionally swelling into a roar; and then without a moment's notice he burst into a lecture on Bach, with floods of the most recondite information.' A few months later Tovey descended on Marsh in London. This proved embarrassing; Marsh felt he would rather not introduce him to his family, since Tovey was 'apt to be the most fearful bore on any subject but music; and when I take him to my clubs I live in terror of his bursting into a Bach fugue when the waiter is giving him potatoes.' In 1899, Tovey went to Meiningen for the unveiling of the Brahms memorial. Edward Dent, who met him there, found him 'rather overpowering'. Dent later maintained that Tovey was not actually conceited; he simply displayed his musical erudition 'because he wanted his friends to share the joy of it.'

In 1900, Tovey produced his first analytical notes and brought forward his Trio, Op 1, dedicated to Parry. In the *Sunday Times*, Herman Klein described the trio as 'little beyond an unconscionably dull imitation of Brahms'. Tovey's accompanying programme note was 'not exactly calculated to aid the comprehension of his own somewhat complex and obscure productions'. Fuller-Maitland, in *The Times*, suggested that the note 'went far to create an impression that the trio was a feat of erudition and nothing else.' Undaunted, Tovey pressed on with more compositions, more notes and more piano recitals. 'Mr. Tovey threatens three concerts in May', warned one journal. He continued to provoke the same response. Klein referred to some new notes as 'turgid stuff which he glorifies by the name of "Analytical Essays", and worries the hearers withal.' When Tovey supplied notes for a series of Brahms concerts in 1902, *Musical Opinion* also showed its irritation.

> In this country Brahms' music has attracted a curious clique of worshippers who are not happy unless they are dull. Secretly ashamed of the emotional appeal of music, they have hailed Brahms as the representation of pure musical thought which can only be grasped by those who have not too much blood in their veins . . . The scores of the master make a Brahms specialism easy. They delight a mind such as that of Mr. D. F. Tovey, who wrote the analytical programmes for these concerts. He is the kind of musical analyst who finds an unholy pleasure in noting the diminution or augmentation of a theme on its repetition, and an addition of a new counterpoint sends him into chaste ecstasies of delight . . . Brahms, in short, has become the refuge of the half-educated in music, who find it easy to analyse his complexities on paper.

Tovey's notes were nevertheless a new departure, for nobody had previously analysed music in such minute and painstaking detail. Moderately detailed programme notes already existed, among the earliest of which were Grove's for Manns' concerts at the Crystal Palace. Grove's notes are extraordinarily good, full of interesting biographical information, enthusiasm and unobtrusive scholarship; they whet one's appetite and increase one's enjoyment; they can be assimilated before a performance and need not be consulted during it. Tovey's notes, however, relate almost entirely to the score itself and really have to be followed throughout the performance; they are rightly called 'analytical essays'. After reading one of Grove's notes, one feels how much one would like to hear the piece of music about which he has been writing; after one of Tovey's notes, one reflects, 'What a brilliant man this Tovey is', and hopes one will be able to follow him adequately while the music is playing. With Tovey, the music becomes the background to the note.

By 1905, his notes had excited such enthusiasm in certain quarters that he was invited to contribute the principal articles on music to the eleventh edition of the *Encyclopaedia Britannica*. From this year, his real influence began. In 1914, he became Professor of Music at Edinburgh University, where he remained until his death in 1940. His *Essays in Musical Analysis* were published in six volumes, between 1934 and 1939. They were greeted as Holy Writ. By then, he was regarded as the Einstein of music, and neither the abuse of Constant Lambert nor the adulation of Neville Cardus could diminish his stature. In 1935, he was knighted.

In truth, Tovey was not an Einstein, for he lacked the great scientist's vision, imagination, curiosity, wonderment and humility. Far from being a scientist, he was simply a mechanic, dexterous at stripping down a 6-litre Beethoven or a Brahms Family Saloon, but often utterly and belligerently useless when confronted with a Berlioz Supercharged Drophead Coupé or, indeed, anything other than a German or pseudo-German model. He worked from a Leipzig manual and stuck to it with myopic assiduity. So accomplished and perceptive were his analyses of German masterpieces that both he and many others were never in doubt that he had originated a critical method by which the worth of any composer could be definitively assessed. After all, his method proved that Bach, Mozart, Beethoven and Brahms were the supreme composers, and this tallied with generally accepted critical opinion. His method also revealed that many of the Romantics were considerably lesser figures, and the demolition work he carried out on them won the approval of the 1920s and 1930s avant-garde, whose music was incomprehensible to him, but who were in reaction against the Romantics. Tovey's views were therefore acceptable to both conservatives and moderns alike. He exerted a vast influence on younger musicologists. The beauty of his method was that, deftly manipulated, it could quickly win a critic a reputation for intellectual brilliance; no scholarship was necessary, since all one had to study was often a single score; and, perhaps most importantly, one need not actually be musical. Also, it was fun: with Mozart, one could be brilliantly *con*structive; with Tchaikovsky, brilliantly *de*structive. Moreover, since Tchaikovsky was the most popular of the Romantics and beloved of the 'man in the street', who simply relied on his ears and his heart, he was more frequently abused than any other composer. And critics were confident that the 'man in the street' could never find the arguments with which adequately to fight back. In addition, the flaws in the method were extremely difficult to prove; a disbeliever had only to be drawn on to intellectual ground to be annihilated. In *Dialogues and a Diary*, Stravinsky says, 'analysis as little explains a masterpiece or calls it into being as an ontological proof explains or causes the existence of God.' But how seriously should we take the remarks of a man who never earned his living as a music critic?

Tovey's articles for the *Encyclopaedia Britannica*, which were revised in 1910, 1922 and 1926 and substantially rewritten in 1929, give us a clear perception of the bizarre critical ethos that he was responsible for creating. The entry for 'Aria' is principally concerned with Bach, Handel, Gluck, Mozart and Wagner; there is no mention of Rossini, Bellini, Donizetti, Verdi, Puccini, Gounod, Massenet, Bizet, Debussy, Weber, Meyerbeer, Richard Strauss, Glinka, Tchaikovsky or Mussorgsky. In 'Concerto' he refers only to the Bach family, Mozart, Beethoven, Hummel, Spohr, Mendelssohn, Schumann, Brahms, Joachim, Saint-Saëns and Elgar; 'the case where the concerto as a whole is a fantasia (as with Liszt) needs no discussion.' 'Instrumentation' is almost wholly devoted to Bach, Handel, Mozart, Beethoven and Wagner; nothing is said of Weber, Mendelssohn, Mahler, Liszt, Dvořák, Tchaikovsky, Stravinsky, Debussy, Ravel or Sibelius. The solitary Russian to be cited is Rimsky-Korsakov, whose orchestration 'comes within the aesthetic range of Russian ballet-music.' And Berlioz?

It seems paradoxical to leave Berlioz out of account in a history of instrumentation. Yet, short of a detailed appreciation of his individual strokes of
genius, all that can be said of him is that he drew attention to the subject
in an epoch-making but capricious treatise, and that he achieved all that
was possible to a highly imaginative musician who happened to hate
polyphony. And that is more than some critics might expect. But it cannot
have much direct influence on more ordinary musicians.

In the article on 'Music', alluding to modern music, Tovey states,
'There is at present no Brahms; the twentieth century must enlarge
its musical experience before another renascence of classical form can
either be expected or recognized when it comes.' In 'Programme
Music', he observes that explicit programme music 'has never been a
thing of cardinal importance'; Berlioz 'is utterly incapable of focuss-
ing his attention on either his music or his programme'; Liszt's 'conscientious plan of deriving the whole piece from transformations of a
single figure was quite irrelevant even when it was effective.' There is
no mention of any Russian composer. Beethoven's bird imitations in
the *Pastoral Symphony* should not be looked on as explicit programme
music.

> The real cuckoo, nightingale, and quail happen to be musical birds whose
> themes are exactly what Beethoven wants for a break in the rhythm at a
> point of repose in the coda of his slow movement. Similar final digressions
> can be seen in slow movements with no programme at all, e.g. in the
> Violin Sonata, op. 24, the Pianoforte Sonata in D minor, op. 31, No. 2,
> and the String Quintet in C major, op. 29. Not a bar of the 'Pastoral'
> Symphony would be otherwise if its 'programme' had never been thought
> of.

The representation of a flock of sheep in Richard Strauss's *Don
Quixote* is, however, 'childish'; Strauss 'has as much right as Humpty
Dumpty' to call the work a set of variations. The article on 'Sonata
Form' is longer than the combined entries for 'Aria', 'Melody',
'Opera' and 'Symphonic Poem'. In 'Symphonic Poem', the inventor
of the genre is given short shrift: 'Liszt's efforts on a larger time-scale
. . . achieve no sense of movement at all, and the device of deriving all
their themes from a single figure is totally irrelevant.' Tchaikovsky is
not mentioned in this article; the only other names to appear are
Beethoven, Schubert, Wagner, César Franck, Saint-Saëns and
Richard Strauss.

As early as 1903, the pre-Cardus *Manchester Guardian* deplored

Tovey's 'startling narrow-mindedness . . . His total misapprehension of what is called the modern spirit in music is simply astonishing.' By 1929, these characteristics had become even more grotesquely exaggerated. The *Encyclopaedia Britannica* articles are a sad blemish in the history of that fine publication.

In the *Essays in Musical Analysis*, published between 1934 and 1939, Tovey reaches the point where one is inclined to believe that he was occasionally indulging in self-parody.

Schumann cannot develop an idea, he can only make sequences on it. He cannot even state an idea that is capable of development . . . he does not know the difference between a symphonic theme and a lyric arabesque. The sequences are such as every competent teacher promptly weeds out of his pupils' first exercises . . .

Berlioz's technique is as unquestionably defective as beri-beri is a disease of defect in the vitamins. The defects are neither punctilios for pedantry, nor signs of immaturity or struggle; they are not wrestlings like the harshness of Beethoven's counterpoint, nor youthful exuberances like the redundancies of Schubert, nor primitive squalors like the counterpoint of Gluck and of Handel's cook. They are ordinary students' blunders . . .

Bruckner conceived magnificent openings and Götterdämmerung climaxes, but dragged along with him throughout his life an apparatus of classical forms as understood by a village organist. His was the fallacy of the popular natural-history writer who tells us that a flea magnified to the size of a dog could jump over Mount Everest, whereas the poor creature could not support its own weight with a vertebrate anatomy. Your pocket working model has — I forget what inverse-geometrically greater power than the full-sized machine . . . his defects are obvious on a first hearing, not as obscurities that may become clear with further knowledge, but as things that must be lived down as soon as possible. No other defects will appear; this art has no tricks. Listen to it humbly; not with the humility with which you would hope to learn music from Bach, Beethoven and Brahms, but with the humility you would feel if you overheard a simple old soul talking to a child about sacred things . . . an out-and-out Brucknerite was, in his day as now, a person of slow intellectual processes to whom subtleties were as unintelligible as they were to Bruckner himself, and for whom Brahms's mind was eight times too alert . . .

Rimsky-Korsakov's brilliant mastery was the perfect expression of a perky and conceited little mind, which was no more capable of telling a blunder from a stroke of genius or feature of style, than Herbert Spencer was capable of producing an authoritative edition of Plato . . .

How closely these extracts approach the manner of Chorley and George Bernard Shaw.

Volume Four in the *Essays*, entitled *Illustrative Music*, is among the oddest of all Tovey's productions, the largest sections being devoted to Mozart, Beethoven, Weber, Schubert, Mendelssohn and Wagner. It includes no Liszt and no Tchaikovsky, but does contain Joachim's *Overture to a Comedy by Gozzi*, Parry's *Overture to an Unwritten Tragedy*, Röntgen's *Old Netherlands Suite*, Voormolen's *Baron Hop Overture* and other delights. There are also four tone poems by Reger, whom Tovey's method inexorably raised to dazzling eminence. It is significant that a place can be found for Bantock's symphonic poem *Dante and Beatrice*, but not for Liszt's *Dante Symphony* or Tchaikovsky's *Francesca da Rimini*.

Tovey, predictably, could see little to admire in Tchaikovsky, and his dislike of him was exacerbated by the fact that the Russian's 'huge and splashy compositions' had overtaken those of Brahms in popularity. Although he drew some comfort from his belief that the Sixth Symphony was 'beginning to show signs of wear', he nevertheless deployed his method zealously to combat the pernicious hold that Tchaikovsky exerted over the general public. He did this to good effect: the 'man in the street' came to believe that Tchaikovsky was indeed a third-rate composer, and felt slightly guilty for liking him. Moreover, Tovey prepared the way for a new generation of critics, who, as we shall shortly discover, treated Tchaikovsky far less scrupulously than their master had done. Let us now take our leave of him with a few lines from his essay on the Fifth Symphony.

It cannot be too often pointed out that the duty of a writer of programme notes is that of counsel for the defence. Whatever the discerning critic may find to say against a composition, the programme writer has no business to say anything that interferes with the listener's enjoyment of the music . . . If in 1907 a programme writer had dared to insinuate that Tchaikovsky was primarily a writer of light music and that his tragedy was melodrama, the only effect would have been to excite the exultant fury of the 'Brahminen' against the numerically overwhelming opposition of all more persuasive and popular critics . . . To-day the situation is different . . . A clear distinction between good music and bad ought to be absolute for responsible persons. The distinction between bad good music and good bad music is an excellent conversational topic for talkers who can keep their tempers, but I have never ventured to prescribe it as a subject for students' essays . . . I am afraid that my *locus classicus* for impotence . . . is the finale of Tchaikovsky's Fifth Symphony. If the composer had intended to produce the nightmare sensation, or the Alice-and-Red-Queen sensation, of running faster and faster while remaining rooted to the spot, he might have been said to have achieved his aim here; but the melancholy fact remains that this finale resembles all other compositions in which the vitally necessary problem of movement has simply not occurred to the composer at all. I have been generously praised for my defence of Bruckner, whose popularity, now at best-seller height in Germany and Austria, has not yet begun in England; and, that being so, nobody has objected to my saying frankly that you must not expect Bruckner to make a finale 'go'. But the popular Tchaikovsky is in worse case than Bruckner, for he evidently expects his finales to 'go', and neither the naïve listener, nor the still more naïve *Heibrau*, can at this time of day be helped by an analysis that leaves it to him to discover the fact that Tchaikovsky's finale wants to go and cannot.

Among the most brilliant young men reaching maturity in the shadow of Tovey was Gerald Abraham, who was born in 1904. He decided to make a special study of Russian music and in 1927 produced his first book, on Borodin. This was followed, in 1935, with *Studies in Russian Music* and, in 1936, with extensive contributions to *Masters of Russian Music*. In 1939, came *On Russian Music* and, four years later, *Eight Soviet Composers*. His biography of Tchaikovsky was published in 1944; *Tchaikovsky: a Symposium* appeared in 1945. These last two works installed Abraham as the leading Western authority on the composer. For many years, those who loved Tchaikovsky's music and wanted to find out more about it and about the man himself would turn to Abraham's books, just as we now turn to the incomparable H. C. Robbins Landon when we want to learn about Haydn.

Abraham's interests are not confined purely to Russian music. He has also written books on Beethoven and Chopin and edited works on Handel, Schubert, Schumann and Grieg. His very successful *A Hundred Years of Music*, covering the period from Beethoven's death to the Second World War, published in 1938 and revised and expanded in 1949 and 1963, is perhaps our best introduction to his general views.

Tchaïkovsky, so fertile in attractive tunes, was completely incapable of writing a true 'theme' and apparently never tried to write one till he reached the *Pathétique*, for the first movement of which he hatched the not very striking four-note motive which by no means dominates it . . .

The great difference between the symphonic lyricism of Brahms and that of his more naïve contemporaries – Tchaïkovsky and the Dvořák of the Eighth and Ninth Symphonies – is that Brahms was so much more skilful in covering up his tracks. Tchaïkovsky presents his tunes, usually very attractive tunes, comparatively naked, or at any rate, dressed only in brilliant orchestration, counter melodies and savoury accompanying harmonies, trimmed with rushing scales and the like. Bruckner gravely entangles his Schubert-and-Wagner-and-water melodies in webs of obvious and very organist-like counterpoint and blobs of rather Wagnerian harmony, decked out with baroque, rather crude orchestration . . . But with Brahms the statement of a subject in its simplest form is, in his instrumental music, quite exceptional; even the simplest of the forms in which it actually appears is generally reducible to still lower terms, in other words, is itself a variation. The purely melodic, perhaps even strophic, origin of much of his texture is completely concealed. It is this constant avoidance of the obvious that makes so much of his music profoundly and enduringly satisfying; it never seems to have revealed the last of its secrets.

It is no doubt true also that Brahms's personality was stronger than that of any of his contemporaries except Wagner, that his fine, bracing pessimism is stronger and healthier than Tchaïkovsky's neurotic melancholy . . .

Tchaïkovsky frequently introduces folk-song themes but his own melodic style has so little affinity with the folk-idiom, especially in his later works such as the finale of the Fourth Symphony (1877) and the finale of the String Serenade (1880), that they seldom or never coalesce . . . *Russia* and *Islamey* [both by Balakirev] are almost the only instances in Russian music of genuinely inspired treatment of folk-material . . . The preference of Balakirev and other composers for borrowed folk-material rather than invented material as the bases of works absolutely original and individual in essence, for instance, has literary parallels in the borrowing by Pushkin and Gogol of folk-tales as the bases of so many of their most characteristic stories. That which gives the music or the story enduring value as a work of art is in each case the treatment, the elaboration; and that is completely individual. But the *given* basis seems to be almost indispensable; without some form of it, Russian art is usually painfully insipid . . .

Another peculiarity of the Russian creative mind in general is its inability to conceive organic wholes. The Russian thinks most naturally in episodes and produces his general effects by the accumulation of episodes . . . It is obvious in the plays and novels of Tolstoy, in Dostoevsky's novels, in Chekhov's plays; Pushkin's *Boris* is actually more episodic than the opera Mussorgsky based on it. Naturally the same disjointedness (and the same lack of dynamic 'drama' in the ordinary sense of the word) is very apparent in Russian opera. From Glinka's *Ruslan* to Borodin's *Prince Igor* and Korsakov's *Sadko* (completed 1896; perf. 1898), it is difficult to think of one really characteristic Russian opera that is not essentially episodic in structure and lacking in conventional 'dramatic interest.'

The same peculiarity can be detected in Russian music in general. With the exception of Borodin's symphonies and one or two other works, Russian symphonic music in general is patchy and sectional – with the sections badly joined. That is particularly true of Tchaïkovsky's instrumental works; as he himself confessed, 'my *seams* always showed and there was no organic union between the separate episodes.' Even in the first movement of the *Pathétique* Symphony (1893), where the intensely felt episodes are more or less fused together by the emotional heat, the impression left by the parts obliterates in retrospect that made by the whole. Mussorgsky was almost completely lacking in a sense of independent musical form and Rimsky-Korsakov's so-called 'symphonic' music has only an artificial form produced by sedulous aping of Liszt's 'wallpaper pattern' methods of construction . . .

No composers in the world have written more avowedly fantastic music than the Russians. But this fantastic music of theirs always turns out on examination to be essentially mathematical: a logical working out of a certain rigid symmetrical pattern or device, seducing and tickling the ear by its strangeness and harmonic ruthlessness. Harmonic tricks (particularly use of the piquant 'ambiguous' chords, the augmented and diminished triads with all their possibilities of enharmonic change) and artificial scales (the whole-tone scale, and the scale of alternate tones and semitones invented by Rimsky-Korsakov) are also an important part of the stock-in-trade of these dealers in mathematical sound-fantasy . . .

The interaction of melody and harmony so often apparent in the music of the great German masters is comparatively rare in Russian music . . . the bulk of Russian music seems to have been conceived primarily in terms of line and timbre; the harmony is support, spice, sound-padding – but not living tissue.

That is true of the contrapuntal element in Russian music. Genuine, spontaneous contrapuntal thought seems to be quite foreign to the Russian nature.

In Abraham's book on Borodin, whom he describes as 'the supreme justification of the amateur in music', there are further references to Tchaikovsky. The Sixth Symphony is 'notorious'. Borodin's orchestration is preferred to 'the vulgar laying on of instrumental colours with which such men as Tchaïkovsky have bedecked their works.' Tchaikovsky's compositions are 'intoxicating but obviously programmatic and unbalanced'. In this regard, they exhibit characteristics also to be found in the works of Stravinsky.

. . . Stravinsky is very frequently unable to control his self-expression. Hence his large-scale works, hampered by the requirements of choreographic scenarios, which, whatever he may say to the contrary, cannot permit of thought in purely musical terms, are structurally almost boneless, so to speak. Yet this faculty of orderliness, control, selection, call it what you will, is often all that distinguishes the ravings of a lunatic from the outpourings of a genius. Nobody would be foolish enough now seriously to consider Stravinsky a lunatic, but there is no doubt that this failure to control an over-heated imagination and to prune and train its products is a serious defect in an artistic mentality.

Borodin never had this, and, whereas by far the greater proportion of Russian art and literature is as mentally unbalanced as Stravinsky's music in this respect, one's prevailing feeling as to the older man is a strong conviction of his unfailing fundamental sanity. He is, for all that, more accurate in his expression of the Russian mind and soul than any of the excitable neurotics, and while their paroxysms are merely repellent to the sober Western mind, we are able to enjoy Borodin even when he is depicting the most frightful traits of national character.

Before moving on, we must at least do Abraham justice by hearing him on one of Borodin's compositions.

There is no doubt that the 'Steppenskizze' [*Eine Steppenskizze aus Mittelasien*] is a very attractive little work and one well-calculated to catch the ear of the man-in-the-street; the latter gentleman always likes something with a tune in it, and, if possible, something with a story in it, and he gets *both* in this case. The workmanship is clever enough to interest the musician. . . .

In *Studies in Russian Music*, Abraham suggests that Tchaikovsky's Fifth and Sixth Symphonies should be viewed principally as 'psychological (or pathological) studies'; the Sixth, unlike his earlier symphonies, does not achieve 'artificial shapeliness through padding and vain repetitions, but it remains a collection of episodes.'

The impression of something-less-than-greatness that we get from Tchaikovsky's biggest and most tragic works may be largely due to the fact that he had not at his command a musical speech adequate to express what he wanted to say. But it is also caused by his morbid egotism, his inability to be universal.

Abraham's interest in Tchaikovsky's personality is expressed in the introduction to his 140-page biography of the composer, published in the Duckworth series, *Great Lives*.

Far from being a great man, he was not even a great personality, like Wagner, or a striking one, like Berlioz; some of his fellow-Russians – for instance, Balakirev and Skryabin – led far more fantastic lives. But Tchaikovsky was more puzzling than any of them; his character offers more interesting material to the amateur psychologist than any musician from Jubal to the present day. The contrast between the outward man seen by his acquaintances (the pleasant companion, somewhat shy, but still a polished man of the world) and the real man (the neurotic, the secret drinker) is striking enough to begin with. 'His manner was simple and natural and he always appeared to speak with warmth and sincerity', says Rimsky-Korsakov. And intellectually he was simple; he seems to have been completely lacking in petty affectations; he did try desperately all his life to be sincere. Yet many instances in his correspondence betray that it was his habit to say one thing to one person and something very different to someone else, and in everyday life, often in quite trivial matters, he seems never to have shrunk from a convenient lie (often naïvely confessing to it later), and it is hardly too much to say that his whole outward life was a façade carefully built up and desperately preserved, to give the world a certain impression and conceal his true nature.

At the end of the book, Abraham summarises Tchaikovsky's achievements as a composer.

The true nature of Tchaïkovsky's musical gifts is most easily studied from his earlier works. From these we see that he had a genuine lyrical talent, spontaneous, but easily lapsing into the commonplace and often forced into it by the pressure he put upon himself to keep on producing. His orchestration was always colourful in a crude, garish way, and it became rather more refined later. As a symphonic architect he was, from first to last, as inferior to Borodin as he was superior to Rimsky-Korsakov; in other words, he was able to develop organic sections but not organic wholes. Taneev summed up the nature of Tchaïkovsky's music in general with deadly accuracy when he spoke of the Fourth Symphony as 'ballet music'.

All Tchaïkovsky's earlier works are as objective as those of most Russian composers; that is, they are either 'abstract' music, or frankly pictorial or programmatic. And it was some time before his growing subjectivity – the inevitable consequence of unrelieved introspection – really began to show itself in his music ... The essential material of Tchaïkovsky's musical mind remained the same, of course, but it was now brutally forced into a sort of expressiveness which it did not really possess. The quasi-ballet-tune no longer remained a pleasant, innocuous symbol of, say, 'desire'; the composer now really used it as the – sadly imperfect – instrument of his self-expression; and so we get things like the slow movement of the Fifth Symphony and the second subject of the Pathétique ...

It is probable that much of this music written during the eighties served Tchaïkovsky as a cathartic. It is certainly this later, intensely emotional music of his, with its effective colours and pretty, obvious tunes, which has done almost as much as the comparatively early B flat minor Concerto to endear him to the musical man-in-the-street – who seldom detects the essential falseness of the curious, self-deceiving, self-torturing personality behind it.

In 1945, Abraham produced another biography, of Rimsky-Korsakov, for Duckworth's *Great Lives* series and also edited and contributed to *Tchaikovsky: a Symposium*, the most comprehensive survey of the composer's works to be published outside Russia. In choosing the other contributors for this volume, to which so many Tchaikovsky-lovers have turned during the last thirty-five years, Abraham was clearly successful in recruiting just the men he wanted, and, as he mentions in the preface, they 'show a surprising unanimity on many general points.' The symposium commences with Edward Lockspeiser's 'Tchaïkovsky the Man', the qualities of which are apparent in the following extract.

Tchaïkovsky's mind, seen for a moment from a scientific viewpoint, constitutes a text-book illustration of the borderland between genius and insanity. If by genius we mean that abnormally acute vision of human values brought into reality by a highly organised mind, then insanity, too, reveals the same abnormal vision, no less true in its fundamental elements, but incapable of any creative expression and condemned to chaos and destruction.

It is only by constant effort and suffering that an artist of Tchaïkovsky's mental constitution can manage to orientate his mind towards sanity and productiveness. The explanation of his prolific output must surely be that he felt compelled to produce ceaselessly so as to create some sort of equation between his work and his unsatisfied and insatiable passions , , , These perpetual fears made social life impossible for him, his despondency and self-pity are all signs of his failure to divert his energies into music completely . . .

It is not always necessary, in the study of an artist's character, to delve into the malformation of his mind. In some cases it may have no more effect on his creative powers than a physical ailment that incapacitates without in any way obscuring the artist's vision. It is admittedly difficult to indicate where the inroads of a neurosis commence and still more difficult to isolate it . . . In Tchaïkovsky's case, however, the neurotic elements are inseparable from his development as a composer. The man and his music are one – unsatisfied and inflamed . . . Beginning with the Fourth Symphony and *Eugene Onegin*, Tchaïkovsky's music now reflects all the indulgent yearning and the garish exteriorisation of a composer who can never refrain from wearing his heart on his sleeve – if, indeed, it is not music which suggests a less modest image than that . . .

Behind the exterior of a successful composer, decorated by the Tsar, journeying to Cambridge to receive an honorary doctorate or to America for a concert tour, there is the whining tone of so many of Tchaïkovsky's declarations, and that parading of his inmost thoughts with the persistence of an exhibitionist . . .

The man and his music combine to show that his grief and sorrow remain imprisoned within himself, so that it is never pity that he expresses, but self-pity and with it self-love and self-hatred. The dignity of suffering was unknown to him, but not its pleasures. He is the musician of indulgence. Power is evident in his character, but one suspects at the same time a strain of impotence which far from reducing his creative force, excites and enhances it with an unnaturally vivid imagination. It may be unorthodox to point, in a symphony, to a sense of guilt or of sin; but they are there, in his letters as in his music, expressed with the same horrifying terror as in the poetry of Baudelaire. If there is no humour in his character there is also no irony, no embittered sarcasm. Nor is there cleverness in Tchaïkovsky. His is not the 'art of concealing art'; it is music to gorge on, shameless in its sensuousness and splendour. And it was no accident that such music was conceived by a warped neurotic, shy and tortured.

This fascinating article raises many tantalising questions which, probably from lack of space, Lockspeiser had to leave unanswered. One would love to know which bars of which symphony exhibit a sense of guilt and sin, and one wishes he could have found room to quote those pieces of music that are shameless, unsatisfied and inflamed. And what particular malformation of the mind made Tchaikovsky a warped neurotic? And what is it that might have looked more appropriate worn on Tchaikovsky's sleeve?

The section in the symposium on 'miscellaneous orchestral works' is written by Ralph Wood, the composer of *Overture to a Tragedy*. According to the 1954 edition of Grove's *Dictionary*, Wood's article 'made his name more widely known', which, as we shall see, is understandable, in the light of the prevailing critical ethos. Here is Wood discussing *Francesca da Rimini*, 'a very low-grade piece of music':

The necessary elaborate transitions are effected with Tchaïkovsky's customary skill, that art which never conceals art. When it is said that the oft-repeated main theme of the slow movement is one of Tchaïkovsky's loveliest the reservation has, of course [of course], to be made that Tchaïkovsky's loveliest is still, emphatically, Tchaïkovsky's; never, surely, was there a composer who so constantly – above all in his best passages – makes the listener reflect, if reflection comes at all, that silk purse just cannot be made out of sow's ear . . . The material of the allegro vivo must be the very worst that ever came from Tchaïkovsky's pen; beside it, *1812* ['one of the most dreary and repulsive works in the whole of music'] seems attractively made of good, solid, honest, academic bread-and-butter. It is just empty blood-and-thunder, and its only appropriate context would be a storm [or even, by a stretch of imagination, '*crudelissimi venti*'], or cowboys chasing Red Indians, on the old silent screen. It is over-full, just

– and 'just' means everything – goes beyond the limit, of diminished sevenths and of Tchaïkovsky's relentless, immaculate, ineluctable sequences and repetitions.

The opening motive has something to be said for it . . .

Wood is equally perceptive in his comments on the non-programmatic works. The finale of the Serenade for Strings

> . . . is founded on one of those tiresome moto perpetuo Russian themes – and Tchaïkovsky had the audacity to make the movement into what at any rate was *his* usual idea of sonata form, complete with slow introduction . . . Instead of bringing back that introduction as a coda (which, in any case, its character would have precluded) he breaks a little before the end into a re-statement of the opening material of the *Pezzo in forma di sonatina,* and then works out of it again in very trite, perfunctory, schoolboy manner into a boisterous close concerned with the 'merry-go-round' tune.

In dealing with the orchestral suites, Wood eloquently observes that the first movement of the First Suite is 'quite a pleasant affair'; the second movement is 'quite a nice little piece, if rather undistinguished'; the fourth is 'trivial, undistinguished'; the fifth possesses 'no spark of inspiration'; the sixth is 'nor any more inspired'. The first movement of the Second Suite is 'quite pleasant music'; the second is 'quite unattractive'; the fourth, 'A Child's Dream', is 'a pleasant, conventional berceuse, not very original and not very distinguished'; the fifth is 'a very typical example of the more obvious Russian style with which Westerners have become so very, very familiar, full for them of the atmosphere of knee-boots, beards and frog-dancing'. Of particular interest, returning to 'A Child's Dream', is Wood's suggestion, in regard to the middle of the movement, that 'the part one may assign such a section in a child's dream is too obvious to need naming' – just as, of course, one need not name what would have been more appropriate on Tchaïkovsky's sleeve. The contributors to the symposium do, indeed, 'show a surprising unanimity on many general points.'

Tackling the Third Suite, Wood lists in full the composer's markings (*allegro vivace, moderato mosso,* etc.) and then asks,

> A meaningless string of words, you say? No more meaningless, as a whole, than the string of bits and pieces that the composition itself is. If, on the other hand the string of words is not quite meaningless, if it conveys

anything (say to an experienced reader of programme-notes), it will convey – that résumé – a pretty good idea of what the thing is like. For those who enjoy such things this is a fair-to-average specimen, making up in verve and brightness what it lacks in profundity or subtlety. It is a good deal less than Tchaïkovsky at his best, whichever view one happens to take of what *is* Tchaïkovsky's best.

Among the random observations in Wood's essay are that 'Tchaïkovsky's conception of himself as above all a symphonist was hopelessly wrong', that his orchestration is not 'intrinsically, essentially, exclusively, spontaneously orchestral', that the programme of the Fourth Symphony is 'notorious', that the Fifth and Sixth Symphonies contain 'slobbering vulgarities'.

We need not go much further into *Tchaikovsky: a Symposium*, though we should note that Arnold Alshvang, a Russian, is enthusiastic about the songs and that Edwin Evans junior, who was then seventy and deals with the ballets, mars the general unanimity by telling the reader that the Russian approach to music is not inherently inferior to the German.

> In their [the Russian] conception, musical form is shapeliness rather than constructive elaboration, and they could, if they chose, quote in support the meaning of the Latin adjective *formosus* . . . The English musical world was so long exclusively swayed by Teutonic ideas that until comparatively recent times it accepted these as final and beyond challenge. Even now there are some who cling to those views and regard as heretics those who admit the possibility of there being other conceptions of the art of music. But much of the best music of non-German countries such as France and Russia testifies to another, more liberal creed.

However, we must not conclude our examination of *Tchaikovsky: a Symposium* on a discordant note and will therefore finish with an extract from the section on the piano music – 'a document in weeds rather than flowers', according to its author, A. E. F. Dickinson, who like Tovey, went to Balliol.

> Even his Piano Concerto in B flat minor [Wood refers to it as 'notorious'] owes its force to certain haunting themes and to an adroit treatment of the orchestra in conjunction with the soloist rather than to the cheerful Lisztian swagger (but not Lisztian accomplishment) of the piano rhetoric. After all, when the piano *enters* with nothing more than loud reiterations of the tonic chord (and a false tonic at that), one experiences emptiness

rather than *élan;* and there is a good deal more pianistic vanity to live down. A verdict on the Piano Concerto as a whole is not my concern here, but if its original contribution to pianistic development is in question, the burden of proof lies undoubtedly with the Concerto's admirers.

In other words, if there is anything good to be said for Tchaikovsky's music, 'the burden of proof' lies with its admirers (readers of the *Symposium?*), rather than with the contributors to that unusual publication.

The 1940s were dark days for Tchaikovsky in England. The *Symposium* attempted to destroy him as a composer. German bombs erased his connections with London by obliterating Alma-Tadema's piano and his signature at Pagani's and by razing Queen's Hall, which witnessed more premières of his works than any other auditorium in the land. And Otto Deutsch, in his article 'Haydn in Cambridge', published in the *Cambridge Review* of 7 March 1941, annulled his trip to Cambridge.

> Cambridge is hardly aware that Haydn came here as a visitor soon after his Oxford degree, yet he was, apart from Dvořák (1891), the only one of the great Masters of Continental Music who stayed at Cambridge at all, if only for a short time . . .
> A few months hence it will have been 150 years since Haydn came twice to Cambridge. It were the more fitting, therefore, that his memory be preserved here, since Cambridge has now twice missed the opportunity of making a Continental Master of Music honorary doctor. (Brahms twice declined to undertake the journey from Vienna to Cambridge.) Perhaps it may be possible to put up a plate in the Guildhall to commemorate the concert of Nov. 30, 1791.

What a host of composers – Rossini, Verdi, Saint-Saëns, Tchaikovsky, Grieg, Paganini (who gave a recital at the Theatre Royal on 30 October 1833), Rimsky-Korsakov (who declined a doctorate in 1907), Scriabin – fail to qualify as either 'Masters of Continental Music' or 'Continental Masters of Music'!

Even by the end of the forties, critical opinion had little changed. Martin Cooper, who had written about Tchaikovsky's symphonies in the symposium, was invited to reiterate his opinions in Penguin's *The Symphony*, published in 1949, 'Tchaikovsky was not a symphonist by nature' was how he began his article. The Sixth Symphony was 'a grim ballet danced between Death and the Neurotic.' (In *French Music*, published in 1951, Cooper opens, 'French music is not generally popular in England, for it lacks the quality which most endears any work to the public. It lacks, that is to say, a strongly flavoured emotional content, either moral and uplifting as in Beethoven or introvert and lowering as in Tchaikovsky.')

Despite the prevailing unwillingness of critics to make any effort to understand the true nature of Tchaikovsky's music, the forties nevertheless produced a few stray seeds of hope. As early as May 1940, Constant Lambert wrote in the *Listener*, 'In my opinion, Tchaikovsky had a gift for thinking naturally in musical terms which has been granted a few composers in the course of history.' In 1946, in his excellent book on Fauré (who so greatly esteemed Tchaikovsky), Norman Suckling also pursued a new line of thought.

> Fauré's limpidity is sometimes deceptive as to his real intellectual depth . . . I make the remark in order to clear up . . . a . . . misunderstanding; the word 'intellectual' being commonly used by German and German-inspired critics in as misleading a manner as the word 'profound'. They use it to denote sheer ingenuity, rather than mental grasp of an artistic design and of its parts in relation to the whole. That is the only sense I can discover, for example, in a verdict of Adolf Weissmann (*The Problems of Modern Music*) upon Tchaikovsky: 'He scarcely knows the meaning of intellectual construction.' That is to say, he does not exhaust the permutations and combinations of his material for the sake of exhausting them; but it has always seemed to me that to keep one's ingenuity thus in subordination to one's judgment is evidence rather of intellectual strength than otherwise.

He adds the suggestion that, although they may be 'very solidly built', a great many late nineteenth-century German compositions are 'devoid of aesthetic direction'.

During the fifties and early sixties, the shadow of Tovey began to recede, and, simultaneously, composers at whom he and his followers had scoffed began to enjoy a new respect and a new popularity. Among these were Berlioz, Liszt, Mendelssohn, Schumann, Bruckner, Mahler – and Satie, who, wrote Abraham, in *A Hundred Years of Music*, 'is merely what Sir Donald Tovey loved to describe as an Interesting Historical Figure.' But the Toveyites had so thoroughly reduced Tchaikovsky, their principal target, that he took longer to regain his position; their propaganda had been so successful that a new generation of music lovers almost unquestioningly accepted that Tchaikovsky was not entitled to a place among the masters, for his compositions, however appealing, amounted, as Ralph Wood implies, to little more than glorified film music. (In his article 'Is There Any Music at the Movies?' published in the September 1969 edition of *Stereo Review*, Paul Kresh speaks of the composers 'who unabashedly thank Tchaikovsky and Rimsky-Korsakov when they walk off with an Academy Award'; while one of the finest of film composers, Shostakovich, has said, 'whenever I encounter difficulty in the course of my work, I invariably find the solution to my problem by studying Tchaikovsky's technique.')

Tchaikovsky suffered a similar, though much slighter reversal in America during the 1930s and 1940s, but in that country, steeped in the tradition of building rather than destroying, he found ready champions to pioneer his revival and set an example to English critics. Prominent among these pathfinders was Richard Leonard, who put forward his views in *A History of Russian Music*, published in 1956.

> For many years it has been the fashion to dwell upon the lack of formal excellence in Tchaikovsky's music, its inability to develop properly, and the fact that his symphonies turned out to be, in the academic sense, mere suites; his melodies are dismissed as overly sentimental and too facile, his harmonies as all gilt and plush, his orchestration as blatant. His music is summed up as sensational and obvious when not actually hysterical, and thus fit only for the masses but not for the urbane and intelligent listener . . . The easiest way to damn any creative artist is to subject him to comparisons, especially in fields where he had no intention of going; the more honest way to appraise him is to seek the special merits of his finest, not his worst, works . . . Tchaikovsky . . . is an exemplar of an art which is remarkable for its directness, its ability to reach swiftly and move deeply a wide audience . . . its great strength, and its great mystery, is the clarity of its thought and at the same time the abundance of the creative ideas which crowd into every line or every measure. Thus it is expressive and communicative in the highest degree. That it is also comparatively easy to absorb and appreciate should be accounted among its virtues instead of its faults.

The statement that 'the more honest way to appraise him is to seek the special merits of his finest, not his worst, works' shows a vast divide between Leonard and English critics of a generation earlier. But 'the more honest way' must necessarily be the more painstaking way and perhaps the more imaginative.

The advantage of Richard Leonard's attitude is that it encourages other critics to think afresh, as did James Bakst in his *A History of Russian-Soviet Music,* published in New York in 1962.

Tchaikovsky's melodies and themes are very individual and bear the imprint of his personality. They are expressive and reproduce and transmit moods, thoughts, psychological states, dramatic elements, developments of the heroes' feelings as well as those of Tchaikovsky himself. The melodies are seldom regular musical periods or sentences. They are usually constructed of small links, motives, or fragments which Tchaikovsky builds into an overflow of feeling by means of sequences, intonational changes, chromatic additions, suspensions, simultaneous contrasting movement of upper and lower voices and resolution of the tension by dividing the melodic structure into individual links, motives, and figures . . .

Tchaikovsky is a musical orator who influences audiences, not by pathos and rhetoric but by emotional suggestions concentrated in the particular turns and lilts of his melodies, that is, in his musical intonations. The significance of these intonations transcends national boundaries and becomes universal. In the words of the Soviet critic Asafiev, 'The appeal of Tchaikovsky's intonations is different from those of Schubert, Beethoven, Chopin, Schumann, and Brahms. It echoes voices of people one loves, of friends, of a mother, a father, whose kindness and endearments mean so much to everyone.'

Tchaikovsky's lyricism contains emotional characteristics which, in the relationships among people, represent a distinctive dictionary of the intonations of sympathy, interest, compassion, romance, and friendliness. Tchaikovsky is a sensitive psychologist, equal to the greatest Russian writers and poets including Tolstoy, Dostoyevsky, Chekhov, and Pushkin. This is remarkably revealed in Tatyana's letter scene in *Eugene Onegin,* in which Tchaikovsky sympathetically and caressingly discloses emotional conflicts and experiences. These qualities are present in the Sixth Symphony, in the *Romeo and Juliet Overture* and in *Francesca da Rimini.* Impetuous melodic flashes are followed by lyrical themes full of heartfelt sympathy, love, and humanity. These qualities relate Tchaikovsky to Dante and Shakespeare.

As an operatic composer, Tchaikovsky is unique in Russian music. In *Eugene Onegin,* in *Queen of Spades,* and in his ballets, Tchaikovsky is a master of dramatic collisions growing out of psychological situations. In this sense, Tchaikovsky's operas are related to the plays of Chekhov and the psychorealistic productions of Stanislavsky in the Moscow Art Theater.

Tchaikovsky's musical psychorealism can be traced to Robert Schumann, whose music exerted a profound influence on nineteenth-century Russian composers. Schumann's emotional impressions of reality and introspections are musically expressed in nervous, improvisational imagery calling forth the listener's participation in the emotional experience . . .

Uncompromising struggles between good and evil, darkness and light, and love and death are reflected in Tchaikovsky's music. Love and kindness triumph in *Swan Lake* and *Sleeping Beauty* . . . Love of life and happiness restore the vision of the blind princess, Iolanthe. Although Liza and Herman perish, the idea of eternal human love underlies *Queen of Spades*.

The programmatic basis of Tchaikovsky's last three symphonies is the conflict between the hope and aspiration of man and the obstacles he encounters in life . . . The word 'fate', used by Tchaikovsky, does not mean that he believed in the existence of a fatal or mystical power which prevented the attainment of happiness. The concept of 'fate' in Tchaikovsky's thinking was a complex of objective factors or causes which prevented a free individuality from attaining happiness . . .

The romantic symphony, after Beethoven, lost the social and ideological significance of Beethoven's heroic conceptions. Post-Beethovenian passive romanticism stressed the struggles and contrasts of psychological sensations and sentiments or the descriptive genres in Mendelssohn's *Italian* and *Scotch Symphonies*. Brahms was interested in containing romantic esthetic forms within classical designs . . . After Beethoven, Tchaikovsky was the first composer whose music exercised a tremendous social influence, although the heroic ideology of Beethoven's music was alien to Tchaikovsky. Tchaikovsky's interest was concentrated on eternal human problems, such as man and fate, struggle for happiness, and life and death . . .

There are similarities in Tchaikovsky's and Beethoven's thematic developments. Both preferred dynamic treatment of symphonic forms, especially of the sonata form, development of expressive elements in a theme and dynamic intensification preceding cadential climaxes . . . Tchaikovsky's symphonic developments chiefly represent the contrasts and comparisons of cumulative emotional states rather than the manipulation of thematic motives . . . In Tchaikovsky's symphonies, contrasts of extensive and unified emotional states dominate the tonal flow. The effect of such emotional states is intensified or weakened by means of dynamics, harmonic elements, and orchestral timbres . . . Tchaikovsky's symphonic forms represent successions and contrasts of emotional cycles . . .

Beginning with the Fourth Symphony, Tchaikovsky's thematic developments disclose realistic intonational elements in which thoughts and imagery become sounds which displace the schematic features of classical developments. His developments are often intensifications of the intonations of main themes, rendered in accumulations of rising dynamic tonal waves. The climactic wave is reached before the return to the recapitulation. The final coda, as a second development, is the culminating point of the movement . . . While intensifying the excitement of thematic intonations, Tchaikovsky often contracts the theme by gradually narrowing its tonal range until the emotional possibilities of the theme seem to be exhausted. This is found in the first movement of the Fourth Symphony in which the theme is enriched by chromatic elements and is gradually contracted. The contractions eventually reduce the theme to repetitions of two thematic tones . . .

Tchaikovsky's music is neither heroic nor epic. It is humane music which expresses love, compassion, truth, and justice. Hence the wholesome effect of his music and its growing popularity among listeners all over the world. It is an art which speaks of the beautiful and the good in life . . . Tchaikovsky speaks of the emotions of ordinary people, the joys, sorrows, tribulations, and struggles one encounters in daily existence. The road to happiness is not strewn with roses. Thus, Tchaikovsky's music speaks from heart to heart. It is a call to something better, more beautiful in life. These elements were not new in Tchaikovsky's music. Tchaikovsky, through his art, was able to find simple, convincing musical means and intonations which have the articulation of speech. The hero in Tchaikovsky's music is the common man. Tchaikovsky was not a disciple of Schopenhauer's philosophy. He expressed the eternal problem in his music: the clash between dream and reality, the transitory quality of human experience, and the vanity of existence.

If Beethoven is the greatest dramatic symphonist, Tchaikovsky should be called the greatest lyrical symphonist. The lyricism of nineteenth century romanticism in music found its greatest exponent in Tchaikovsky the symphonist.

Tchaikovsky is a realist as well as a lyricist. One cannot listen to his music without experiencing an imaginative transformation. The imagery in his music becomes real and personal. One seems to recall something forgotten or slumbering in the unconscious. The recollection has become real, almost palpable to the imagination. The result is that a listener thinks: I have also experienced it; it is true.

Bakst has clearly approached Tchaikovsky in the belief that he is a major, not a flawed minor, composer. He has thus provided us with a new way of looking at Tchaikovsky and the possibility of increasing our understanding and enjoyment of his music.

Because of critics like Bakst, Tchaikovsky's stock continued to rise in America during the 1960s, and, in 1970, in *Russian Music*, Alfred J. Swan could write, 'Tchaikovsky's greatest strength lies in his uncanny faculty for symphonic construction and development . . . His orchestral eloquence is phenomenal', which comes very close to Shostakovich's 'In development of musical idea and in orchestration, he has no equal.'

At long last, in 1966, an English (Austrian by birth) critic, Hans Keller, produced an article, for a new edition of Penguin's *The Symphony*, that followed in Bakst's footsteps, by being completely positive, and simultaneously hoisting the Toveyites by their own petard.

> Our age has produced the notion of the neurotic artist. Is he to blame or it? The critic of Tchaikovsky cannot help being interested in this question, because for many, Tchaikovsky is the neurotic artist *par excellence*. The so-called 'Pathetic' symphony (Tchaikovsky withdrew the title) fills the Albert Hall. Do eight thousand people assemble at a time in order to hear Tchaikovsky pitying himself? No doubt there are emotional complexes in the 'Pathetic' which, in life, can give rise to neurosis. (There are no neurotic complexes as such: it all depends on what you do with them.) No doubt some of the emotions which Tchaikovsky expresses with ruthless frankness can stimulate a self-pitying operation in many listeners, who may promptly project their feelings onto him. If they do so, *they* are behaving neurotically, not because they have been subjected to neurotic art but, on the contrary, because they are incapable of facing this particular piece of artistic reality – incapable, perhaps, of coping with strongly expressed emotion altogether. It may indeed be primarily because of the unambiguous clarity of his emotional expression that many sophisticated music lovers still underestimate Tchaikovsky as a symphonist . . .

Of the Fourth Symphony, Keller says that 'sundry anti-romantic, emotion-fearing neurotics' have devoted most of their criticism of the work to sniping at its literary programme (which Tchaikovsky made up after completing the symphony and never published) instead of concerning themselves 'with one of the most towering symphonic structures in our whole literature'. Speaking of the first movement, he points out that the 'gradual emergence of a rhythmic character, which at first remains latent if not indeed contradicted, is entirely a discovery of Tchaikovsky's. The procedure was to have a far-reaching if unobtrusive effect on the history of composition; even in so advanced a structure as the third movement of Schoenberg's violin concerto we can detect the ultimate influence of Tchaikovsky . . .' The Fifth Symphony is so popular 'that one feels slightly embarrassed to write about it; it is as if one were invited to write an essay recommending the "Blue Danube" waltz.' 'The integration of folkloristic material' reveals Tchaikovsky 'at the height of his powers . . . the orchestration offers original sounds at every change of texture.'

> The *Pathétique?* No other work has survived so many intellectual burials. Gerald Abraham has shown that . . . [etc.]

> The symphonic world never was the same again after this Sixth symphony had been performed. We speak of Tchaikovsky's overstatements, but had full-scale sonata form ever been so drastically, and so consistently understated, compressed, as in the first movement, with its violent shortening of the second subject and its grippingly compact coda? Is there a more original transformation of scherzo function, a more breathtaking contrast, than the ultimate metamorphosis of the Tchaikovsky waltz that is the second movement in 5/4 time? . . . Where would Mahler's and indeed Schoenberg's symphonic structures be without Tchaikovsky's 'many formal innovations' – above all, without that *Adagio* finale itself, which was to cast an illuminating shadow [a delightful image; the inverse of Milton's 'Dark with excessive bright'] over the whole future history of the form?

'The symphonic world never was the same again', remarks Keller. Nor, as we have seen, was the critical world, and Alfred J. Swan surely did not exaggerate in declaring, 'When Tchaikovsky's music penetrated into the western capitals, it caused complete consternation.' Parry, Tovey, 'the children of Tovey' and the rest of the English musical Establishment put up strenuous opposition. 'A powerful idea', said Proust, 'communicates some of its strength to him who challenges it.'

If one of the marks of a great composer is that many of his works, written in a wide variety of forms, are still frequently performed a long time after his death, then Bach, Mozart and Beethoven are pre-eminently among the great composers. And so, too, is Tchaikovsky. Yet, in England, he continues to await full recognition. Abraham, now president of the Royal Musical Association and chairman of the editorial board of the sixth edition of Grove's *Dictionary*, is still active and, as recently as 1974, repeated his views in *The Tradition of Western Music*.

> One need only study Mussorgsky's struggles with his operas or read Rimsky-Korsakov's own account of his fumblings with his First Symphony and his first opera, to see the difficulties that beset even the most gifted dilettante. But facility easily becomes fatal. Technical facility not only enabled Chaykovsky and the later Rimsky-Korsakov to turn out great quantities of music in which inspiration runs rather thin; it encouraged a great outpouring of beautifully made, euphonious music which sounds no greater depths and scales nor many greater heights than the dilettante music of the earlier part of the century. Only it is much more skilfully made and much greater in quantity.

In his biography of Tchaikovsky, dating from the earlier part of our own century, Abraham referred to the composer's 'terrifying industry, his insistence on talking whether or not he had anything to say'. But this 'terrifying industry', which took Tchaikovsky, by the end of his life, to Op 74, somehow seems less terrifying when measured against the 122 opus numbers of Brahms (who, Berger once wrote, 'spoke admirably, but . . . had so little to tell'). Perhaps it depends on one's point of view.

It could be argued, of course, that the 'man in the street' is unlikely to read as scholarly a work as *The Tradition of Western Music,* which comprises lectures originally delivered by the author when he was Ernest Bloch Professor of Music at the University of California. However, the thoughts of an influential critic can be transmitted to the market-place in a variety of ways. For instance, in Robin Golding's note that accompanies the currently available recording of Lorin Maazel's distinguished interpretation of the Sixth Symphony, we find the following statement. 'Though melancholy and extravagant self-pity are characteristics of Tchaikovsky's music, particularly of his three great symphonies (and are factors which undoubtedly account for their immediate and widespread appeal), it is tempting to think that he knew his sixth was to be his last.' This sentence not only reflects Abraham's own views (if not his syntax) and attitude towards the 'man in the street' (who is apparently a sucker for 'melancholy and extravagant self-pity' and likes to be told so), but, in the use of the word 'undoubtedly', echoes his style. And, again, no music is quoted to show examples of 'extravagant self-pity', let alone common-or-garden self-pity.

Perhaps all this will be rectified now that the splendid first volume of David Brown's biography of the composer has been published.

Men like Bakst and Keller have pointed the way towards a greater understanding of why Tchaikovsky's music exerts such a powerful appeal, but the fact remains that we are still in the Stone Age of music analysis.

When we attend a performance of *Hamlet,* are we purged by pity and terror, or do we marvel at Shakespeare's superb manipulation of iambic pentameter? When we see the 'Mona Lisa', might we reflect, 'She is older than the rocks among which she sits; like the vampire, she has been dead many times, and learned the secrets of the grave', or do we admire Leonardo's exquisite *sfumato*? In music analysis, we still concentrate like mechanics on how a piece is put together. But we know next to nothing about why it creates the impression it does. Modern technology has surely granted us the means by which we can begin to find out much about our reactions to music, and it should be possible to plot these reactions, note by note, against a score. This could lead to a different kind of analysis and to a more convincing explanation of why certain composers affect us so strongly.

In regard to traditional analysis, there are many ways in which the computer can help us. With a composer's entire works stored in such a machine, we should be able to discover more about his methods and intentions. Integral analysis of this sort is already being undertaken by Soviet musicologists. In the most modest of investigations, they have determined that 36 per cent of Tchaikovsky's melodies are slow, 34 per cent are of moderate tempo and 30 per cent are fast. For Rimsky-Korsakov, the figures are 60: 10: 30; for Scriabin, 30: 10: 60. These findings perhaps tell us little, but they are probably not without some value. A subject that might better repay examination is the remarkable variety of Tchaikovsky's melodies.

When music analysis has left its infancy, it may reveal why we regard Beethoven so highly and why the 'Blue Danube' is so popular. It may even show that the reactions and tastes of the 'man in the street' are not so dissimilar, dear reader, to our own.

CHAPTER 11

STANFORD

On 10 May 1894, ten weeks after Mackenzie conducted the English première of Tchaikovsky's Sixth Symphony, Grieg received his doctorate in the Senate House at Cambridge. It was an occasion saddened for him by the knowledge that 'my honoured friend Tschaikowsky' had stood on the same spot eleven months earlier. When, in January 1906, he read Modest's biography of Tchaikovsky, Grieg wrote to Frants Beyer, 'It goes to my heart. Often it's as though I were looking into my own soul. There's so much of him that I see in myself.' Of the Sixth Symphony, he declared in a letter to August Winding, 'And God help you if you have not rejoiced in it! Is it not remarkable!' He probably also regretted not having been there, the previous year, to meet Saint-Saëns and Boito, whom he much respected. Missing Bruch would have been less of a disappointment; having taken part in a concert with him in Breslau in November 1883, Grieg decided that he was 'a frightful bore'.

Like Saint-Saëns, the Norwegian composer and his wife stayed at King's College as the guests of Austen Leigh, who was now not only provost of that college but vice-chancellor of the university, having succeeded John Peile. Sedley Taylor took Austen Leigh's place as president of the CUMS.

The ceremony, graced by one of John Sandy's elegant eulogies, provoked more than the usual amount of mirth from the undergraduates, the cause being Grieg himself. By some oversight, a Mus Doc gown had not been provided for him, and, at the last moment, it was discovered that the only one available belonged to Alan Gray, the new CUMS conductor. Since Gray was of above average height and Grieg was under five foot tall, this caused a further complication, and, according to William Austen Leigh, in his biography of his brother, lightning repairs were effected, in order to eschew the impression that Grieg was taking part in a coronation, not in a degree ceremony.

537

The gown was hastily flounced and pinned up in the background till it assumed a shape calculated to move the muscles even of the uninstructed male portion of the audience. The Vice-Chancellor preserved his gravity as long as he was in the Senate House, but he was much amused when his guest insisted on going straight to the post office to despatch a telegram. He knew well a (medical) Doctor Grieg at Bergen, and he had now become a (musical) Doctor himself. The message was, 'Doctor Grieg, Bergen, Norway. Kollega, jeg hilser Dem' ('Colleague, I greet thee') – 'Doctor Grieg'.

A fortnight later, Grieg appeared at a Philharmonic concert, conducting the English première of his suite from *Sigurd Jorsalfar*. George Bernard Shaw, who, two years earlier, had described Grieg as 'only a musical grasshopper in comparison with the musical giant of Bayreuth', called the suite 'trumpery stuff'. This serves to remind us that Grieg, like Tchaikovsky, was considered fair game by the Toveyites during the first half of this century. In *A Hundred Years of Music*, published in 1938, Abraham described the Piano Concerto as 'essentially salon music put under a microscope'. Few of the piano pieces are 'particularly pianistic; those that are are trivial and schoolgirlish.'

> The most serious of all Grieg's weaknesses is his inability to conceive more than two bars of music at a time .*. Broadly speaking, his chromatic harmony is an individual twig of the Wagnerian tree, a demonstration that Wagner's harmony could be employed in the charming salon-piece as well as in heroic and passionate drama.

In 1948, Abraham edited a symposium on Grieg, to which he contributed an essay on the Piano Concerto. In the preface, he poses the question, 'Was Grieg, with his narrow range, his limited fertility, his defective technique, a "master" in any sense of the word?' The nineteenth century seems to have been rich in composers with 'defective technique'.

Grieg's arrival in Cambridge made few demands on Stanford. As Professor of Music, he had to attend the degree ceremony, but, beyond that, nothing was really required of him. No longer Trinity organist, no longer conductor of the CUMS, he now had much more time for composition.

Over the coming thirty years, he used that time to such effect that he became one of the most prolific of all British composers. By the end of his life, he had produced nine operas, more than a dozen large choral works, incidental music to seven plays, a great deal of church music, 7 symphonies, 6 concertos, 8 quartets, 20 organ pieces and over 160 songs.

Before embarking on a brief survey of Stanford's later music, we can do no better than preface it with some extracts from Vaughan Williams's essay on his teacher, which first appeared in 1952.

Stanford was a great composer, a great teacher, a skilled conductor, and as befits a true Irishman, a lovable, quarrelsome, and generous man.

He has written some of the most beautiful music that has come from these islands. He realized that all art which is worth while must spring from its own soil . . .

Of course in Stanford's enormous output there is bound to be a certain amount of dull music; but, after all, so there is in Beethoven and Bach. At times his very facility led him astray. He could, at will, use the technique of any composer and often use it better than the original, as in 'The Middle Watch' [from *Songs of the Fleet*], where he beats Delius at his own game . . . The bright young things of the younger generation do not seem to know much about Stanford, and not having had the advantage of his teaching are inclined to ignore what he did and what he taught. But I believe that he will return again. With the next generation the inevitable reaction will set in and Stanford will come into his own. His smaller works are still known and loved by our choral societies, and I cannot but believe that such splendid music as the *Stabat Mater*, *Requiem*, and *Songs of the Fleet* will not strike home as soon as opportunity is given to hear them. It is up to our concert societies, in this centenary year, to give us these works as well as the 'Irish' Symphony and Rhapsodies and the many fine songs. In any continental country the centenary of a composer of Stanford's calibre would have been celebrated in every opera house in the country. Covent Garden and Sadlers Wells cannot even give us an opportunity of hearing such splendid works with all the certainty of popularity as *Much Ado* and *Shamus O'Brien* . . .

The belittling of Stanford's work was encouraged by one who ought to have known better. The late Bernard Shaw, in the first number of *Music and Letters*, used Elgar as a stick to beat what he called 'the Academic clique' . . . Shaw was rather proud of having called Stanford a 'gentleman amateur' since he repeated the expression more than once. Apparently the word 'gentleman' was to Shaw a term of abuse, and as to 'amateur', who could have been more professional in his methods than Stanford? . . .

Stanford had none of the clumsiness of his contemporaries. Though a great admirer of Brahms, he did not imitate his awkward execution. Stanford's orchestration, though perhaps unadventurous, is a model of clarity: every stroke tells . . .

Stanford's career, after his childhood and youth in Dublin, may be divided into two periods. The first dates from his appointment as organist at Trinity College, Cambridge, and afterwards as Professor in the University . . .

Stanford's second period begins when he left Cambridge, about 1893, and lived in London. He was already conductor of the London Bach Choir, and later became conductor of the Leeds Festival: still continuing his immense output of music, often inspired, sometimes less inspired, but keeping always within the bounds of classical beauty.

An artist cannot always control his inspiration, but Stanford saw to it that his tools were bright and sharp and fashioned of tempered steel. His music is educated music, founded on the great traditions by one who was determined to uphold the nobility of his art.

In speaking of Stanford's second period, we can possibly even put an exact date to its beginning: 12 June 1893, the day of the jubilee concert, on which he resigned the conductorship of the CUMS. What distinguishes this period from the first is his full blossoming as an Irish composer; after forty years, the child at last proved to be father of the man.

Such a development was presaged eleven years earlier, in 1882, by his folk-tune arrangements *Fifty Songs of Old Ireland* and, of course, by the *Irish Symphony*, of 1887. Then, in 1893, came *Thirty Irish Songs and Ballads*; in 1894, *Six Irish Fantasies* for violin and piano; in 1895, *Moore's Irish Dances Restored, Edited and Arranged*; in 1896, the choral ballad *Phaudrig Crohoore* and the opera *Shamus O'Brien*. This sudden upsurge of Irishness was followed, over the next decade, by the *First Irish Rhapsody*, *Songs of Erin*, *Four Irish Dances*, the song-cycle *An Irish Idyll*, and the *Second Irish Rhapsody*, subtitled *Lament for the Sons of Ossian*. During 1902–5, he edited and arranged more than 1,500 numbers from the Petrie Collection of Irish folk-songs. Among his later Irish works are *A Sheaf of Songs from Leinster*, *Six Songs from 'The Glen of Antrim'*, the song-cycles *Cushendall* and *A Fire of Turf*, *Six Irish Sketches* for violin and piano, the *Irish Concertino* for violin, cello and orchestra, and the *Irish Rhapsodies Nos 3, 4, 5 and 6*.

Although the Irishness of Stanford's music has pleased his countrymen, it has not always been to the taste of English critics, who, in the same way that the French found Tchaikovsky wanting in Russianness, have deemed Stanford insufficiently Irish. In *Music in Ireland*, Arnold Bax asserts that Stanford 'never penetrated to within a thousand miles of the Hidden Ireland', and he says the same of Charles Wood and Hamilton Harty: 'these three undoubtedly proficient musicians were assiduous and dutiful disciples of the nineteenth century German tradition, even whilst clothing their native melodies in all too conventional dress.' Similarly, in *A Hundred Years of Music*, Abraham, who is usually not amused by the Russianisation of German symphonic processes, depreciates the achievements of Mackenzie and Stanford, who, 'in their Scottish and Irish Rhapsodies had employed native folk-themes – though only as the material for thoroughly Teutonic methods of working-out.' Again, Frank Howes, in *The English Musical Renaissance*, pronounces the 'total effect' of the *Irish Symphony* to be 'like leaving and returning to Ireland for a holiday in Germany'. And, for good measure, just as the Toveyites dismissed Berlioz, Schumann and Liszt because of their 'defective' techniques, Howes reproves Stanford for the faultlessness of his: 'It meant that he found the solutions to all problems too easily.'

In essence, it seems, Stanford's works fail to evince Irish symphonic thinking. But what is Irish symphonic thinking? Or Danish? Or Finnish? In *Marching Along*, John Philip Sousa touches on this matter.

If nationalism were a factor in music, would it be Wagner or Brahms in Germany who would represent the German in music, Debussy or Gounod in France, Sullivan or Elgar in England, Puccini or Respighi in Italy? We speak of music which is typically Irish; I have in my library nearly five hundred compositions by Irishmen and not one of these works shows the slightest trace of what we have been pleased to call the Irish note in music.

In practice, therefore, Irish symphonic thinking may be a way of thinking that comes naturally to whichever Irishman happens to be doing the thinking. For Stanford, it was natural to think generally in a Teutonic manner, and this caused him no difficulty when manipulating his native music. He thus resembles the originator of German symphonic thinking, who so immaculately wove his native Croatian folk-tunes into his compositions. Moreover, there is nothing about Irish folk-tunes that makes them inherently unadaptable to traditional symphonic procedures; indeed, a melody like 'Shandon Bells' could almost have come from the pen of Haydn himself. Conversely, an Irish flavour informs parts of the finales of Beethoven's Seventh Symphony and Brahms's Piano Quintet, while the first two bars of. the opening theme from the second movement of Brahms's Fourth Symphony are identical to the beginning of 'Lament of the Sons of Usnach'.

Stanford has also been charged with being a sort of musical stage-

Irishman, exploiting his country's music to tickle the palate and add spurious sparkle to an otherwise bald and unconvincing style. It does not seem to have occurred to many critics that the 'academic' Stanford may have had roots less deep than the Irish Stanford – and not the other way round. In *A Musician's Narrative*, Mackenzie appears to be in no doubt. 'That he could cast off his Irish brogues at will and adapt himself to any particular subject in hand added to my appreciation of an outstanding ability;' a parallel can be found in the poetry of Burns. Those who doubt Stanford's sincerity and oneness with his native music need only turn to Harry Plunket Greene, a pure Irishman born in County Wicklow, who writes of their first meeting in 1888.

We were smoking after supper when he asked me if I knew the tunes in the *Songs of Old Ireland* volume which he and Alfred Graves had brought out between them some time before. I was more or less German minded still and had never heard of them. He sat down at the piano and played them to me one after another. He began with 'My Love's an Arbatus' and went on with 'Owen Roe O'Neill' and 'The Flight of the Earls' and 'Emer's Farewell' (the Londonderry Air) and 'When She Answered Me'. When I think back on it now I can understand the secret of his semi-miraculous teaching powers. I remember that he never said a word as to how the tunes should be handled; yet with his playing he seemed to reveal not only how they should be played but how all music should be felt. True phrasing is not a mechanical act made by order of the intelligence; it is a trained response to an emotional call. Only a man so completely unself-conscious as he could work such magic with the 'beauty will out' which came warm from his singing touch and showed in the lines of his architecture. It was a lifelong lesson, over in an hour or so, and given without a word.

In *Pages from an Unwritten Diary*, we discover more about the composer's attitude to Ireland's folk-music. It is, he says, 'a mine of riches which no other country could surpass, if indeed it could equal, either in quality or quantity.' Its originality and distinctness of style are as marked 'as in the Keltic type of ornament, of which the finest examples are in the Book of Kells and the Missals at St Gall.' He regrets the influence of Thomas Moore, who would often 'ruthlessly twist' a melody to fit his verses.

If he found a tune in the scale of G with an F natural, he would sharpen the unfamiliar note, regardless of the character of the modal scale which gave the whole distinction to the melody. In a way the charm and wide appeal of his polished and musical verse were a drawback to the very plan which he set out to accomplish, for many of the distorted tunes, which he, Procrustes-like, lengthened and lopped, became so familiar to the world in their 'transmogrified' shape and contents that their fine old flavour became obliterated and forgotten. Unfortunately his collaborator, Stevenson, who was a man of a certain genius, was such a devotee of the great Haydn, that he read all the native music through Austrian spectacles and acquiesced in, if he did not suggest, the destruction of modal scales . . . It is almost a tragedy, that Ireland to this day [1914] is so loyal to the memory of her best-known poet, that she resents the alteration of a note of his work, looks on it as a blasphemy to restore his tunes to their natural and proved form, and is still, under official sanction, teaching her young children to sing the wrong and wholly un-Irish scales which Moore and Stevenson stereotyped.

The most eloquent and persuasive justification of Stanford's style is his music. Alluding to the andante from the *Irish Symphony*, Henry Krehbiel wrote in the *New York Tribune* in February 1917 that it was 'the finest monument to the spirit of Celtic folk-song which artistic music has produced.' Another work that has always been deeply admired is the *Irish Rhapsody No 4* subtitled *The Fisherman of Lough Neagh and What He Saw*, which was first played by Mengelberg and the Royal Philharmonic Orchestra on 19 February 1914. Of this, Thomas Dunhill said the following in 1935, in his contribution to Harry Plunket Greene's biography of the composer.

If I wanted to impress a foreign unbeliever with the real beauty of British music at its best I should take him to hear a performance of the 'Ulster' Rhapsody, that he might have a glimpse of what the 'Fisherman saw at Lough Neagh', and of what the great Irish composer was able to reflect of this vision in his music. 'Dark and true and tender is the North' is the quotation attached to the closing page of the score – a mere expression of an Orangeman's sympathies, probably – but the three adjectives describe the loveliness of the music itself in a way that no other words could do. It is a work of imperishable quality.

The treatment of Irish material usually brought out the best in Stanford, and taking their place among his finest pieces are works like *Shamus O'Brien, Phaudrig Crohoore, An Irish Idyll, Cushendall, A Fire of Turf*, the *Irish Symphony* and the first and fourth of the *Irish Rhapsodies*. But these compositions have a further significance, for, together with the restoration of the folk-songs, they were an inspiration and example to his students Holst and Vaughan Williams, thereby also contributing to the development of English music. And these roots, these Irish rhythms and cadences sprang up not only in the pieces to which an Irish label is attached, but fertilised much else that he composed. We find them, for instance, in the scherzo of the Piano Quintet of 1887; in the third movement of the Second Piano Concerto of 1915 (first performed at the Norfolk Festival in Virginia); in the third and sixth movements from *Night Thoughts*, completed in 1917; in the finale of the 1918 Third Piano Trio. We find them even in the *Judex crederis* section of the Diamond Jubilee *Te Deum*, presented at the 1898 Leeds Festival.

Stanford was undoubtedly an Irish composer. That his music should show the influence of composers of other nationalities is not a defect, but a virtue. In *A History of Music in England*, Ernest Walker casts aside the shallow accusations that have been made against him.

His Irish blood had shown itself not only in his frequent researches into the rich store of his native folk-music, but also in his versatile susceptibility to many and various influences; individual as his utterance is, it is, so to speak, a very composite blend. Quite apart from the Irish folk-songs that he has edited, and many movements coloured more or less by such influences, he has produced in the opera *Shamus O'Brien*, or the choral ballad *Phaudrig Crohoore*, something that is virtually Irish folk-music itself; *Shamus O'Brien* in particular – one of the most deliciously 'open-air' works in all British music – is crammed full of tunes which, without any suspicion of plagiarism, seem to suggest that their composer has lived in the wilds of Ireland all his life. We see French influence, especially that of Bizet, in considerable tracts of *The Three Holy Children* and *The Veiled Prophet*, signs of the later Verdi in the *Requiem* and the *Te Deum*, of Sebastian Wesley in the Anglican anthems and services, of Brahms in the chamber-music; and yet all this roving results in something really characteristic, something that is unmistakably Stanford himself.

In recalling that Holst and Vaughan Williams were students of Stanford, we come to another of his great achievements. Those who also trained under him include Herbert Howells, John Ireland, Arthur Bliss, Ivor Gurney, Ernest Moeran, Arthur Benjamin, Charles Wood, Frank Bridge, Samuel Coleridge-Taylor, Dan Godfrey and Leopold Stokowski. That one or two of his students should go on to be highly successful musicians could be ascribed to coincidence or luck; equally, there have been teachers like Reinecke through whose hands several notable composers have passed; yet, if we read what Stanford or Svendsen had to say about Reinecke, we can see that they – and Grieg and Sullivan – prospered not because of him, but despite him; indeed, as far as one can judge, Reinecke was conspicuously inferior to the comparatively obscure Hamburg pedagogue Edward Marxsen, who taught Brahms. Stanford's students, with a very few exceptions like Arthur Bliss, make it clear that he exerted an enormously beneficial effect on their development.

Remarkably, he seems to have had no set procedure. His approach was practical and flexible. He did not attempt to teach any particular style. He had an uncanny gift for divining what a student was trying to do and, as long as it appeared worth doing, he would help him to make the best of it. As often as possible, he gave his students the priceless opportunity of hearing their works. He was harsh, sometimes even brutal, but a student soon began to realise that becoming a second Beethoven was not necessarily accomplished with one's first compositions.

In Harry Plunket Greene's biography of Stanford, a number of his students recall their teacher and his methods. Among these is Edgar Bainton.

> It is a curious paradox that in spite of his dominating personality (at times aggressively dominating) hardly one of his many pupils' works shows any influence of Stanford . . . And this fact in itself is surely the finest tribute to his teaching that he kept his own personality in the background and helped them whether they were conscious of it or not to express themselves, to say clearly what they wanted to say.

In George Dyson's opinion,

> . . . his technical advice was impeccable . . . There has certainly been no other teacher of composition in England who has approached Stanford in the number and distinction of his pupils. If to be a great teacher is to produce neat samples after one's own model then Stanford failed. If the proper criterion is an inculcated virility of speech, a sustained harvest of decided and coherent personalities, then Stanford was phenomenal in his success.

It is amusing to note how many of his students remember with affection the rough ride that he gave them. Samuel Liddle's experiences are fairly typical.

> I had the privilege of three years' lessons from Stanford at the Royal College, having been lucky enough to gain a scholarship. He seemed to

know at once what treatment was good for me and I certainly got it. I was 'for it' from the beginning, and my first year with him was not a bed of roses. There was no softness in his methods with me, and he was right. A few effective sentences of criticism, startling in their candour and absolutely unanswerable; a few enlightened sarcasms followed by a few hints on methods of study and he handed me back my work with his usual smile and an invitation to 'Tear it up, my boy, it's no use.'

Such terse suggestions abound in the recollections of his students. 'I'd burn it, me boy', Stanford told Vaughan Williams. To another, he remarked more expansively, 'Your music comes from hell. From hell, my boy. H E double L.' Eugene Goossens received the comparatively mild 'Damned ugly, me bhoy'.

This abrasiveness might have proved unbearable, had it not been tempered by something else. 'As a teacher he was a severe critic, often very satirical in his remarks', writes Dan Godfrey in his autobiography. But the derision would eventually be followed by a look 'in that delightfully whimsical manner which used to make us forget his harsh though just criticisms and made us all love him.' In *Up To Now*, Martin Shaw has memories of a less dramatic relationship.

> Stanford inspired me with the utmost admiration for his qualities as a teacher and also with affection for his personality. Some found him difficult, but all I can say is that I always got on very well with him; though I was a bad pupil, being undisciplined by nature . . . Stanford was not fond of talking, nor was his attitude to music ethical. He was essentially practical and sane, with a thorough grasp of form, balance, and construction. With an Irish grunt he would suddenly cause your mind to jump over the obstacle that had been in the way for a week . . . I don't suppose there has ever been a time when such a galaxy of young composers studied at the same period under one master.

Just as he adopted a practical approach to his students' compositions, so he invariably struck the right relationship with each of the students. With the brilliant, modest and diligent Charles Wood, he gave particular attention to orchestration, otherwise not attempting, writes Sidney Waddington 'to interfere with a taste marvellously just and impeccable, but content to let him expand in his own way'. Towards the timid, gentle and self-doubting Samuel Coleridge-Taylor, he was kind and enthusiastic. After reading through Coleridge-Taylor's Clarinet Quintet, he exclaimed to the apprehensive student, 'You've done it, me bhoy'; shortly afterwards, he took the work with him to Berlin and persuaded Joachim and his quartet to play it. He was of further service to Coleridge-Taylor by conducting the first performance, on 11 November 1898, of *Hiawatha's Wedding Feast*, which was attended by Sullivan. Stanford had supervised the composition of this cantata. Coleridge-Taylor worshipped his teacher and once declared, 'If Stanford's activities had not been displayed over so many and various fields, he would have been as great as Beethoven.' Throughout his life, he always composed with Stanford's photograph, framed in a velvet horseshoe, on the piano in front of him. His opinions on music were often Stanford's. When asked whether Tchaikovsky's Sixth Symphony should be regarded as the product of a diseased mind, he answered, 'I don't think there was much the matter with the mind to which we owe the *Pathétique*' – the sort of reply that one might expect from Stanford.

The temperamental Ivor Gurney both enchanted and exasperated Stanford, who told Harry Plunket Greene that, 'of all the pupils who came under him at the College, the one who most fulfilled the accepted idea of genius was Ivor Gurney' – but he was 'the least teachable'. As Michael Hurd points out in his notable book on Gurney, Stanford also recognised his pupil's poetic talent and, in an effort to forward his career, sent his 'Severn and Somme' to Robert Bridges, who had succeeded Alfred Austin as poet laureate. Gurney was almost obsessively untidy; his student scores were textbook models of cacography. Understandably he described Stanford as 'difficult to please', though adding 'and most glad to be pleased'. Stanford had an affectionate regard for his pupil and was unusually tolerant towards him. At times, however, his patience could become exhausted. Herbert Howells speaks of the day when Gurney and he were having a tutorial in Room 51 (now the Stanford Room) at the RCM. Gurney had submitted a song that delighted Stanford sufficiently for him to deliberate for some time on how the final bars could be improved. At length, having made a number of adjustments, he smilingly passed the score back to Gurney, remarking, 'That'll be half a crown' and holding out his hand. Gurney, with knitted brow, peered intently at the alterations for a full three minutes and then muttered, 'You've jiggered it!' In a flash, Stanford rose to his feet, grabbed Gurney by his collar, opened the door and, with the words 'Out you go, sir!' – more a running commentary than a command – pitched him into the corridor. After watching him scuttle away, he stood for a moment in the doorway and, turning to Howells, said, 'I love him more each time.'

John Ireland decided by the age of sixteen that he wanted to study with Stanford; he therefore called on him, begging to be accepted. 'We'll see, m' bhoy, we'll see' was all he was promised. Two years later, his wish came true, as he related to Murray Schafer in *British Composers in Interview*.

> I had studied a great deal of Brahms before I went to him and this may have displeased him a little. He said to me 'Your music is all Brahms and water, me boy. I shall have to do something with you which I have never done with anybody else.' He put me to work on sixteenth-century style and methods and I wrote music in the style of Palestrina for a year. After that he made me study Dvořák.
>
> I think the best quality Stanford possessed as a teacher was that he made you feel nothing but the best would do. He wouldn't let you write in pencil. He held that you would have more respect for what you did if you wrote in ink.

In Ireland's memories of Stanford that were recorded by Norah Kirby and appear in the biography by John Longmire, the composer acknowledges the benefit he derived from the special course of study he had to undertake. 'I have since had every reason to bless him for it.'

> I remember him so well as he was then . . . He was about forty-five, and at the height of his powers. To look at he was tall and loosely built. He had a commanding presence and an alert, challenging face which generally wore an expression of humour tinged with irony, quickly warming to kindly quizzical interest.
>
> Week by week he would let a score progress with practically no comments. When it was finished he would say, 'Now, me b'hoy, go home and copy out the parts and we'll try it over.' In due course one's piece *was* tried over by the orchestra. I stood beside Stanford whilst he conducted it. When the more or less appalling sounds had subsided, the Master would close the score, and handing it back with a grin would say, 'Well, you see, it won't do – you'll have to find some other way.'

'And one did, you know', Ireland told Murray Schafer.

Holst began studying with Stanford in May 1893, a month before the Cambridge jubilee. Imogen Holst describes his relationship with Stanford in her biography of her father.

He went to Stanford for composition, and week after week he was to hear that distingushed teacher say: 'It won't do, me boy. It won't do.'

This verdict acted like a tonic. He appreciated the way that Stanford insisted on sincerity, and he readily accepted the creed that a composer, however gifted, must learn his technique so completely that he can afford to forget it. He envied Stanford's genius for quoting exactly the right musical example to illustrate any point he was criticizing, and he delighted in his refusal to rely on cast-iron rules. Although he often disagreed with Stanford's opinions, he was always grateful to him, especially for having taught him to become his own critic.

Harry Plunket Greene recalls that when Stanford encountered insincerity, he 'saw red'. But if a student's composition, however alarmingly modern, appeared entirely sincere, he would respond with the almost playful 'That's damned ugly, me boy.' This would seem, says Plunket Greene, 'to be a negative criticism barren of instruction, but it made the pupil ask "Why?" and never failed to rouse his imagination or his opposition and keep his mind alert for other inventions.' Stanford once observed, 'Originality, like murder, will out' and he made it his job, if necessary, to goad it out. 'One is tempted to wonder', concludes George Dyson, 'whether there is really anything better a teacher can do for his pupils than drive them into various forms of revolution.'

In *A Musical Autobiography*, Vaughan Williams's description of his time with Stanford, beginning in 1895, reads frequently like a report of guerrilla warfare: 'I was hopelessly obstinate.' In one of their skirmishes, Stanford, feeling that Vaughan Williams was too preoccupied with modes and needed a lighter touch, instructed him to write a waltz. Vaughan Williams riposted with a modal waltz. Many of his pieces were declared to be '"damnably ugly" and that was the end of it.' However,

> When all is said and done, what one really gets out of lessons with a great man cannot be computed in terms of what he said to you or what you did for him, but in terms of the intangible contact with his mind and character. With Stanford I always felt I was in the presence of a lovable, powerful, and enthralling mind.
>
> This helped me more than any amount of technical instruction.

The student with whom Stanford was closest over the years was Herbert Howells. More than fifty years after Stanford's death, Howells was still wearing the signet ring that he bequeathed to him.

His most cherished memory was Stanford's smile, 'which seemed to forgive all the wrong one had ever done.' In December 1952, he spoke to the Royal Musical Association about his teacher.

> For his students, learning at his feet was a blending of Paradise and Purgatory, Heaven and Hell. For the weak and timorous, it was early death; for the fellow who had lost his way, Ariadne's thread. It had no high-sounding method, no sacrosanct principles. It was guidance, penance and defiance coming from a man who solved few of his own problems but was passionately concerned to solve those of his pupils. On the day of his death his pupil, Holst, said to me: 'The one man who could get any one of us out of a technical mess is now gone from us.' One agreed: recalling the hovering pencil, the caustic commentary, the surgeon-like dexterity with which the keen mind cut through to the seat of trouble, and the seraphic smile and childlike pride when the operation was over.

Stanford was not only Professor of Composition at the RCM, but also conductor of the college orchestra for more than thirty years. Harry Plunket Greene doubts whether any other student orchestra in the world received such a complete grounding in essentials during that period.

> The result was that they could read anything at sight, were ready for any emergency and had a practical knowledge of the world's masterpieces. One student after another passed almost automatically into the great orchestras of the country and never failed to make good. Sixty years ago British orchestras were mainly foreign; today they are British to a man – and the training grounds have been the R. A. M. and R. C. M. and Stanford their greatest trainer.

As we have already discovered, he was a born conductor, being entirely unselfconscious. Vaughan Williams mentions in his essay on Stanford that Eugene Goossens regarded him as 'the finest interpreter of Brahms that he had ever heard'. At the same time we may recall that his performance of Tchaikovsky's Sixth Symphony was preferred to those of Mackenzie, Manns, Wood and Richter, which says a great deal. In matters of technique, he was aided by a clear beat, the ability to convey precisely what he wanted and an extraordinary ear for orchestral texture. When a student conductor somehow felt that what he was hearing did not tally with the score, but was unable to identify the cause, Stanford would whisper something like 'See what the second clarinet is doing, m' boy', and there would be the answer. He was a disciplinarian, as one might expect, and a quiet 'Out you go, sir' would quickly banish anybody rash enough to misbehave. He once remarked, 'A conductor need never be nervous; he can't make any wrong notes', and he was wont to train students in the spirit of this belief. In *Farewell, My Youth*, Arnold Bax recalls how, having been sent over from the RAM, he was greeted with 'So here ye are, you're Bax, aren't you? Well now, ye can go up there and work your wicked will on the orchestra.' When the young man protested that he had never before conducted, Stanford responded, 'Never mind that. You've got to begin some time, my bhoy. Go on with ye.' Stanford's concerts with his student players were not lacking in incident, as Martin Shaw testifies.

> On one occasion [4 November 1896] the whole orchestra went down to Cambridge to give a concert. Among other things we played Tchai-kovsky's overture *Francesca da Rimini* [the second performance in England], Holst clashing the cymbals, Dunhill tinkling the triangle, and I thumping the big drum. Unfortunately I miscounted my bars and delivered a *fortissimo* bang, solo about three seconds after the overture had finished, causing Stanford to shake his fist at me from the conductor's desk.

Stanford and the students also gave performances of operas, despite the opposition of Parry, for whom opera was 'the shallowest fraud man ever achieved in the name of art ... the appanage of the wastrels, the home of the humbug'. Earlier, Grove had been keen about presenting opera, and fortunately a tradition was established that Parry could not break. For Stanford, opera was in his blood; of all his achievements at the Royal College, he was proudest of having brought the production of operas to a high standard. He conducted a large number of popular masterpieces, including *Orfeo ed Euridice*, *Così fan tutte*, *The Magic Flute*, *Fidelio*, *Der Freischütz* and *Falstaff*, and did not shirk *Euryanthe*, with all its staging problems. The presence in the cast of *Orfeo ed Euridice* of the nineteen-year-old Clara Butt – all willowy six feet two inches of her – came to the attention of the Prince of Wales, resulting in yet another command performance for Stanford. Miss Butt played Orfeo in deliciously boyish attire, and when presented to the Prince further bewitched him by asking whether he would like her to bow or curtsy. He suggested a curtsy, which she executed so delightfully that he complimented her on it. 'Then I'd like to do it again', she said, and did.

Stanford was responsible for several notable productions. On 9 December 1891, at the Savoy Theatre, he conducted the English première of Cornelius's *The Barber of Baghdad*. On 6 December 1893, at the Drury Lane Theatre, he conducted the English première of Schumann's *Genoveva*. He did the same for Delibes's *Le Roi l'a dit* on 13 December 1894, at the Prince of Wales Theatre, followed by a command performance at Windsor Castle. On 20 November 1895, at the Lyceum Theatre, he staged one of the few productions of *Dido and Aeneas* since 1704. At the Lyceum again on 11 December 1896, he conducted the first English-language performance of *Falstaff*.

Harry Plunket Greene says that 'there was a joyousness in the air' when Stanford was producing an opera. His thoughts were mostly with his singers, whom he seems to have hoped would all become stars overnight. When one of them, Harold Samuel, gave a recital at the Aeolian Hall, he went along, though ill at the time. Samuel recollects that after each group of songs, Stanford came backstage and, 'for all the world like a fellow-student', greeted him with 'That was all right, wasn't it?' or 'Go back and bow! Don't waste the applause!'

The second half of Stanford's life realised a greater number of important compositions, but was less rich in external excitement. There were fewer memorable encounters with other artists, for the heroes of his youth were passing away.

In 1895, he brought forward his Fifth Symphony, *L' Allegro ed il Penseroso* which he conducted at a Philharmonic concert on 20 March. On 27 May, the First Piano Concerto was also introduced in London, with Leonard Borwick as soloist and Richter conducting. During the same year, *The Bard*, after Thomas Gray, was enthusiastically received at the Cardiff Musical Festival. In the early part of the following year, he gave a number of concerts on the Continent. During the second week in January, he was in Berlin, where, seven years earlier, on 14 January 1889, he had conducted the world première of his Fourth Symphony in an all-Stanford programme. Now, on 10 January 1896, he attended an all-Brahms concert, conducted by the composer and consisting of the *Academic Festival Overture* and the two piano concertos. At a dinner in Brahms's honour, Stanford spoke to him for the last time. Joachim began proposing a toast to 'the greatest composer', but Brahms cut him short with 'Quite right! Here's to Mozart's health!' and then, says Stanford in *Studies and Memories*, 'walked round clinking glasses with us all.'

On 2 March 1896, *Shamus O'Brien*, Stanford's operatic masterpiece, was presented at the Opera Comique in London, conducted by Henry Wood. Five days later, on the Saturday of the same week, Gilbert and Sullivan's *The Grand Duke* came on at the Savoy. *Shamus O'Brien* was rapturously acclaimed, and *The Grand Duke* suffered by comparison, not only at the box-office, but in critical reception. Almost every music magazine devoted greater space to *Shamus*. *The Musical Times* considered the work to be such a success that the première was likely to become 'historically memorable'. The opera ran for more than one hundred performances. This was followed by a lengthy tour of the provinces and Ireland, with Granville Bantock as conductor. The presentations in Ireland, at Belfast, Waterford, Limerick, Cork and Dublin, excited fervent applause. Its reception in Waterford was reminiscent of the first night of *I Lombardi*, with the audience so absorbed in the unfolding of the drama that, at the point where Mike Murphy betrays Shamus to the police, a voice cried out, 'O, ye dirthy blagyard' with such fury that the production was brought to a halt. The opera was also performed in America, in Germany, at La Scala and in many countries throughout the world. Thomas Beecham produced it at His Majesty's Theatre in June 1910. In *A Mingled Chime*, he describes it as 'a colourful, racy piece'.

Shamus O'Brien has never lacked admirers. In *Songs and Song Writers*, published in 1901, Henry Finck wrote that this work, 'imbued with the genuine spirit of Irish folk-music, is the most delightful opera ever written on the British isles.' The finale, 'with its ever-persistent drum taps for over 60 bars, produced an effect alike on the audience and musicians never to be forgotten', recalled Henry Wood; Holst, who played the trombone in the first production told Harry Plunket Greene that it was 'the most wonderful finale he had ever seen upon the stage.'

J. A. Fuller-Maitland, in *English Music in the XIXth Century*, says of Stanford, 'it was not until *Shamus O'Brien* was brought out at the Opera Comique that he was recognised as a master of the art of high comedy in music.' We, being already acquainted with his sense of humour, are apt to forget that so far this had rarely penetrated his compositions. Now, with the full flowering of his Irishness, it, too, emerged with engaging frequency. Indeed, his next work, also based on Le Fanu, was the rollicking *Phaudrig Crohoore*, introduced at the Norwich Musical Festival a few months after the première of *Shamus*. Like the opera, this piece, for all its merriment, concludes in affecting pathos. It would probably be even more popular today than it was in the 1890s, for, as Sydney Grew writes in *Our Favourite Musicians*, the average nineteenth-century member of a choral society was 'a trifle self-conscious when asked to throw himself interpretatively into any subject other than one of grave character.' In addition, few would now regard the text as indecent; yet a number of choral groups rejected the work on the grounds of its impropriety. Phaudrig was 'the broth of a boy' and behaved like one; this was apparently beyond the English pale.

The *Requiem* of 1897, introduced at the Birmingham Musical Festival, was written in memory of Frederic Leighton, who had died the previous year. Its Italianate, almost cosmopolitan style is a fitting tribute to a man whose second home was Italy and who had surveyed mankind, at firsthand, from China to Peru. The *Te Deum*, another large-scale work, in celebration of Queen Victoria's jubilee, followed a year later, being presented at the Leeds Festival. On 4 May 1899, the brilliant Concert Variations on 'Down among the Dead Men', for piano and orchestra, were played by Leonard Borwick at a Philharmonic Society concert, with Stanford conducting. In the summer of 1900, one of his finest shorter choral works, *The Last Post*, was performed at the Hereford Musical Festival.

On St Cecilia's Day, 22 November 1900, at Stanford's recommendation, Edward Elgar received an honorary degree from Cambridge University. The occasion could hardly have been more symbolic, for, on that same day, Sullivan died, and, thirteen years later, to the day, Benjamin Britten was born. Elgar was already forty-three, only five years younger than Stanford, but, after many years of obscurity, had suddenly and rapidly achieved recognition, principally through the *Enigma Variations*, first performed in June 1899. He was conscious of the significance of the doctorate and suggested, in a letter of 26 October 1900 to August Jaeger, that *The Musical Times* should print a list of those composers on whom it had previously been conferred. This reaction was amusingly reminiscent of Bruch and Saint-Saëns.

In his Elgar oration, John Sandys mentioned *From the Bavarian Highlands* (1895), *The Light of Life* (1896), *Scenes from the Saga of King Olaf* (1896), *Imperial March* (1897), *The Banner of St George* (1897), *Caractacus* (1898), *Enigma Variations* (1899), *Sea Pictures* (1899) and even 'Praise to the Holiest in the Height' from *The Dream of Gerontius*, which had received its first, and unsatisfactory, performance seven weeks earlier. This final reference must surely have been suggested to Sandys by Stanford.

Now comes something to warm the cockles of our hearts. For Elgar was not the only man to be honoured on 22 November. Immediately prior to the conferring of his degree, the Senate House resounded to the final words of Sandys's earlier oration: 'Duco ad vos Fredericum Hymen Cowen'.

> This hon. degree was conferred upon Elgar at the same time as upon myself, and I shall never forget what we both looked like on the occasion . . . Elgar's [gown] did not reach much below his knees, and mine trailed upon the ground, and we presented the funniest picture imaginable . . .
>
> I recollect, also, that on our way back to London we concocted between us a musical postcard to a mutual friend – the only time that he and I have ever collaborated in a composition. This consisted of a ground bass founded on my three initials, F. H. C. (H in German notation is B natural), to which Elgar put a counterpoint, beginning with *his* initials E. E. The words were something like this: 'We are two Mus. Docs. newly made, returning to our homes'; and we signed ourselves, 'Yours by *degrees*', which ending, the one who suggested it (I forget which of us it was) considered a real stroke of genius.

Elgar had originally intended to turn down the doctorate, because of his irritation at the success enjoyed by composers who had been educated at university, but he was persuaded to accept it by his friend Rosa Burley. In *Edward Elgar: the Record of a Friendship*, she relates that the prospect of the ceremony made him nervous. Like Tchaikovsky, though, he managed to 'conquer' himself.

> When he returned to Malvern I found that he enjoyed his visit. The honour had been shared by Cowen [a non-university man], for whom at that time Edward had a certain affection and regard, and it was evident that he had been treated, as might have been expected, with great tact and courtesy. In particular he had been delighted with an especially happy quotation from the *Aeneid* [The *Odyssey*, XXII 347: 'I am self-taught, but God has planted in my mind all manner of songs'] in the address of the Public Orator (Dr Sandys).

On 30 May 1901, at Covent Garden, Luigi Mancinelli conducted the première of Stanford's *Much Ado About Nothing*. It ran for two performances, as did Lalo's *Le Roi d' Ys*, which was introduced six weeks later. It therefore failed in good company. The world of opera does not lend itself easily to logical discussion, and it is impossible to explain why as fine a work as *Much Ado About Nothing* foundered and has since been neglected. In Klein's opinion, 'the music in the main proved delightful.' John F. Porte considered it to be 'very tuneful'. Herbert Howells has called it 'enchanting'. Vaughan Williams, we may recall, described *Much Ado* and *Shamus O'Brien* as 'splendid works with all the certainty of popularity'.

In 1901, Stanford succeeded Sullivan as conductor of the Leeds Festival and at once began a nine-year battle with the committee, trying to drag them into the twentieth century. 'Get out of this eternal rut of *Messiah* and *Elijah*', he implored them in a letter of 28 November 1900. 'Set the example of what ought to be done at a Festival like yours.' On 18 January 1901, he exhorted them to let him perform 'a big Berlioz', and was rewarded with the overture to *Benvenuto Cellini*. On the whole, though, the committee gradually accepted his more progressive ideas.

In 1901, he persuaded Joachim to appear at the festival; in 1904, Kreisler came and played Stanford's First Violin Concerto. Also performed that year, for the first time, at Leeds, were the *Songs of the Sea*.

In 1902, Stanford was knighted. By then, Mackenzie and Parry had also gained that distinction. In 1904, he became the first British composer to be elected a member of the Royal Academy of Arts in Berlin. In 1906, he received the same honour from the Maatschaapij tot Bevoorderung der Toonkunst in Amsterdam. In addition, he was made an honorary member of the Beethoven Haus in Berlin and a *membre correspondent* of the Société des Compositeurs de Musique in Paris.

Because of his commitments in Leeds, where he had also taken over the conductorship of the Philharmonic Society, he relinquished the conductorship of the Bach Choir in 1902. He still continued, though, to accept a number of conducting engagements in London, often giving young artists a place on his programmes. He did much to forward the career of Percy Grainger, with whom he performed the variations on 'Down among the Dead Men' during the winter of 1904. In January 1906, he conducted Beethoven's Ninth Symphony with the London Symphony Orchestra at a concert in Paris that Boito came specially from Milan to hear. During the same month, and with the same orchestra, he introduced his Sixth Symphony, in memory of G. F. Watts; according to Harry Plunket Greene, this was his own favourite among his symphonies.

At the Leeds Festival of 1907, owing to Stanford's advocacy, Vaughan Williams conducted the première of *Toward the Unknown Region*, dedicated to Florence Maitland and, in effect, a memorial to Frederic Maitland, who had died the previous year. Other works, by students of Stanford, to be given a first hearing at the festival included Arthur Somervell's 'Intimation of Immortality' Ode and Rutland Boughton's *Two Folk Songs with Variations*. With Percy Grainger, Stanford performed Grieg's Piano Concerto. Grieg himself was to have conducted, but had died on 4 September, five weeks before the festival. Stanford had met him for the last time on 9 April in Berlin, where Grieg had come to conduct two concerts.

On the same day, 10 October, on which *Toward the Unknown Region* was given, he conducted his *Stabat Mater*, another impressive italianate work. Agnes Nicholls, who, as his pupil, had sung in *Le Roi l'a dit*, and was now the wife of Hamilton Harty, fell ill on the evening before the performance and so could not take the leading soprano part. In desperation, another pupil, Gladys Honey, was summoned from London. She recalls this episode in Harry Plunket Greene's book on the composer.

> I thought at the time that he would be the gloomy one, but not a bit of it. I was met with 'Come along, my child, I'll take you through it'; which he proceeded to do and just was sweet to me all the time. I was awfully anxious to do my best for him because I felt he must have been so terribly disappointed at his new work being spoilt, but he never once gave a hint that he was upset, and I might have been the best soprano in the place by the way he talked to me. The rest you know. How the great moment came and how I got through, entirely owing to him . . . and then at the end when he flung his arms around me and hugged me I was quite upset as I had only known him as a very BIG MAN with capital letters! at College, and everything seemed topsy-turvy. Why he ever chose me, I can't imagine [Plunket Greene describes her as 'very pretty, with great charm'] . . .

There is a reminder here that Stanford was indeed a BIG MAN. 'The impression he made on me was, primarily, one of brilliance', wrote Sidney Waddington in the RCM magazine in 1933. 'His personality had a sort of splendour, as if the hero of a fairy-tale, incredibly gifted, miraculously omniscient, had strolled unconcernedly into a world of ordinary mortals. Until I got used to it his very appearance awed me . . . His speech added to the wonder he created in me: his Irish brogue grafted on to a Cambridge idiom . . . he was a force such as this generation can hardly realize.' It is interesting that his female students do not seem to have been frightened of him in the same way that the men were. Some were, in fact, not beyond flirtation. When he was once examining a young Irish instrumentalist and asked, after consulting the list in front of him, whether she was Annie De Vine or De Vine Annie, she replied in a soft brogue, 'You'll be able to tell me after you've heard me play.'

Stanford's inharmonius relationship with the committee brought about his resignation as conductor of the Leeds Festival. His fourth and last appearance was in 1910. Once again, at this festival, he attempted to introduce more modern works. In a letter of 21 October 1909, he suggests that two pieces by Brahms are sufficient.

> The *Song of Destiny* is piling on a *third* Brahms. I strongly recommend in preference a great contrast and a lovely thing (which curiously enough much delighted Brahms himself), the *Blessed Damozel* [published in 1893 and first performed in England, under Henry Wood, in 1908] of Debussy, 20 minutes, mostly pianissimo. Fascinating stuff. That will represent most modern France, Germany (Strauss), England (Vaughan Williams) and Russia (Rachmaninoff).

The Strauss was *Don Juan*. Rakmaninov conducted his Second Symphony and, with Stanford, played the Second Piano Concerto. Vaughan Williams conducted the première of *A Sea Symphony*. Stanford much admired this exceptionally modern work, which was well received. So, too, did Jennie Stanford, who, alluding to Vaughan Williams's success, told Adeline, 'You must be very proud of him.' When Parry eventually heard the symphony, he noted in his diary that it was 'Big stuff, but full of impertinences as well as noble moments'. Stanford took the 'impertinences' in his stride. Edward Bairstow, who played the organ in the first performance of *A Sea Symphony*, recalls one of the rehearsals.

> The composer was conducting. The work was new to everyone and was written in what was a strange idiom in those days. Stanford sat down in the hall with only a vocal score to follow and picked out mistakes in the manuscript parts and the playing of them. I remember particularly one or two missing accidentals which he spotted in a rapidly moving viola passage in the middle of the ensemble. His keenness of ear absolutely took my breath away.

Also introduced at the 1910 festival was *Songs of the Fleet*, which occupies a place alongside *The Revenge* and *Songs of the Sea* as the most popular of all Stanford's shorter works for chorus and orchestra. Although, in practice, the sea made him queasy, it nevertheless exerted an almost magical effect on him as a composer. These three works are saturated with the many moods of the sea and of life at sea. Their impact is immediate and considerable; there seems little doubt that *A Sea Symphony* was partially inspired by *Songs of the Sea*. High spirits abound in *Songs of the Sea* and *Songs of the Fleet*, but in *Homeward Bound* we find great beauty and in *Farewell* a grief that can move one to tears.

Both cycles are set to poems by Henry Newbolt, who, together with Tennyson, inspired some of Stanford's finest compositions. The two men became acquainted in October 1886, when Newbolt, then twenty-four, visited Cambridge as the guest of Augustus Austen Leigh. The occasion is described in Newbolt's *My World as in My Time*.

This was my first stay in Cambridge, and it gave me a friend – Charles Stanford – to whom I afterwards owed some of the most stirring moments of my life. He was then organist of Trinity College and had gone up to the Leeds Festival to conduct his new Cantata, founded on Tennyson's *Ballad of the Revenge* [performed on 14 October]. I. had dined with the Vice-Provost [Austen Leigh] and was smoking with him and several others in his rooms after Hall, when the door was noisily opened and a gust of Irish humour blew in among us. That something fortunate had happened was evident, and in the hurly-burly of questions and replies I gathered that Stanford's success had been overwhelming . . . [The *Daily News* reported that the work's reception 'produced the greatest scene of enthusiasm we have yet had. Cheer after cheer greeted the composer from audience and chorus, and three times had he to appear . . .']

My own partnership with Stanford did not begin till some years after this and it was a happy one throughout. He was the most subtly appreciative critic and interpreter of poetry that I ever met with. Again and again he would receive my verses by the morning post, and set them before noon to irresistible music. I always felt that to hear those songs, given as Harry Greene could give them, was to be told secrets about myself, to see my own thoughts reflected with perfect accuracy but irradiated with the magic lights of a dream. He could set a ballad to a hornpipe so perfectly as to make my ears hear the wind in the rigging and my nerves dance, as it were, to my own tune. Better still, he could tell me in my own language what it means to some of us to sight the White Cliffs after a long voyage, and what it may mean to any of us to be Outward Bound at last.

In May 1928, a few years after Stanford's death, Newbolt was at the Wiltshire Musical Festival, where he heard a performance of *Songs of the Fleet*. The baritone was Harry Plunket Greene, 'like a noble ghost from some older period', Newbolt wrote to his wife; 'there was Charles Stanford's ghost too and his music made me weep – the restrained wailing of "Farewell" (writ so long before the War) and the marvellous beat of "The Little Admiral", like 10,000 pulses in one and a thunderstorm over it all, and the sad courage of "Sailing at Dawn".' A year later, in October 1929, he was visiting his daughter and granddaughter when they played him a record of 'Drake's Drum' and 'The Old Superb' from *Songs of the Sea*. 'Too loud, of course', he told his wife, 'and the singer not a patch on Harry Greene; but I was quite overcome with admiration of old Charles Stanford's genius . . . I wrote that Old Superb all in one piece and next day he set it in one morning. Could one enjoy life more gloriously?'

The idea of 'old' Charles Stanford seems to come abruptly upon us, but in 1912, he celebrated his sixtieth birthday. Yet, in these last few years before the First World War, he remained in the thick of musical life. Some of his finest works date from this period. Among them are the three song-cycles *Cushendall* (1910), *A Fire of Turf* (1913) and *A Sheaf of Songs from Leinster* (1914); the wonderful part-songs, opus 119, which include 'The Bluebird' and were written in a fortnight in August 1911 on a fishing holiday at Achanalt, in Scotland; the sunny Seventh Symphony, presented at a Philharmonic Concert on 22 February 1912; the Irish Rhapsody No 4, introduced by Mengelburg. Also composed at this time was the Second Piano Concerto, played by Harold Bauer at the Norfolk Musical Festival, in Virginia, on 3 June 1915.

His music was still widely performed. Choral works like *Songs of the Fleet* were frequently programmed. *Shamus O'Brien* was conducted by Beecham in June 1910. After a quarter of a century, the *Irish Symphony* maintained its popularity; Godfrey scheduled it on eight occasions during his time at Bournemouth, and, in the winter of 1910, Mahler twice conducted it with the New York Philharmonic.

Stanford himself was busy as a conductor, again directing performances of *Genoveva*, in November 1910, and *Falstaff*, in 1913, as well as taking part in presentations of his own compositions. The works other than his own that he chose to conduct reveal an endearing characteristic. The last sentence of *Pages from an Unwritten Diary*, written at this time and published in 1914, states, 'My only hope is that there may be a few crumbs of incident or record to comfort the reader and redeem the book from uselessness, and that they may recall to some of my contemporaries a few happy memories of old times, old haunts, and (best of all) old and valued friends.' It seems that, by conducting certain pieces, he may have been reviving his own happy memories. It was, for instance, at the première of *Falstaff* in Milan that Boito introduced him to Verdi. We have noticed, also, that he conducted *Francesca da Rimini* on several occasions, and this must certainly have brought back memories of the Cambridge jubilee. In November 1911, we find him conducting, at a Philharmonic concert, Brahms's Violin Concerto, a work that, *sans pareil*, links Brahms with Joachim. To conclude the same concert was Dvořák's Eighth Symphony, which the composer conducted when he came to Cambridge for his degree and stayed with the Stanfords. Possibly there were associations, too, in his conducting the première of the revised version of Mackenzie's *Colomba*, which was produced at His Majesty's Theatre on 9 December 1912. Mackenzie and he first met at the original presentation of the opera at Drury Lane in 1883 and became firm friends; Stanford's *Interludes*, published in 1922, is dedicated to the Scottish composer.

It is perhaps difficult for many of us, so far removed from those terrible events, to comprehend how deeply the onset of the First World War shocked and stunned men and women of Stanford's generation. For him, in particular, with his acute sensitivity and oneness with Europe, the unfolding of the conflict occasioned the most appalling anguish. This distress was soon magnified when Guy was ordered to the front and Geraldine went to France as a nurse. He clung pathetically, for some time, to the belief that hostilities were almost at an end, sending messages to friends, saying he had just heard from such-and-such a general that the latest reports were optimistic. Sometimes he imagined that these reports were meant to be secret, and so he relayed them in Greek. There was a genuine fear that spies were everywhere and that anything smacking of the Teutonic could be suspect. Hermann Klein changed his name to Herman; Gustav von Holst became Gustav Holst. Stanford wondered for a time whether he should resign his membership of the Royal Academy of Arts of Berlin, but, after consulting with Widor, who held the same distinction, he decided against it.

Stanford, says Harry Plunket Greene, 'bore the early stages of the war without any apparent damage', but, with the coming of the air raids, his constitution began to decline. His doctor was sufficiently alarmed by this deterioration to direct him to sleep outside the London area, in Windsor. From there, he would journey up to London every day, returning at nightfall.

> Looking back on it now, it becomes plain that from this time he headed slowly downward. It was imperceptible at first. He carried on with his work and taught and conducted and examined apparently as well as before, but as time went on the boundaries of his interest seemed gradually to shrink, giving one the feeling that he was concerned only with the things in front of him and that those on either side passed him by unnoticed . . .
>
> Politics, fishing and cards did not play their old part. There was no more picquet or poker-patience and even bridge seemed to have lost its interest. All honour to those good men of the Savile who played with him and followed his pace and never said a word. Recreations meant nothing to him any more; the only thing that absorbed him was the routine of his daily work. His creative brain continued to function in a semi-miraculous manner.

Stanford produced a few more works of major importance. His opera *The Critic* was completed in September 1915, before his health began to suffer, and was performed at the Shaftesbury Theatre on 14 January 1916, with Eugene Goossens conducting. 'Press and public enthusiastically praised the work and its performance', wrote Goossens in *Overtures and Beginners*, 'and dear old Stanford literally shook with excitement at the end of the evening when, hand in hand with his erstwhile pupil [Goossens was then twenty-two], he took many curtain calls . . . That this witty and beautiful opera should have passed so completely out of the current repertory shows how unsafe it is to prophesy about matters operatic in England.'

His last opera, *The Travelling Companion*, adapted by Henry Newbolt from Hans Christian Andersen's fairy-tale, was also written during the war. It was first produced in Liverpool on 30 April 1925 and, in October of the following year, was presented in Bristol. The London première took place at Sadler's Wells in 1935; many who saw the opera on that occasion found it extremely moving.

The last choral work to bear comparison with his most successful essays in this genre is *Merlin and the Gleam*, based on Tennyson's poem and completed in August 1919. It was John F. Porte's opinion that this piece exhibited 'a loftiness of thought and consummate musical beauty not surpassed by any other modern composer'.

We have reached a point from which it is possible to survey the extent of Stanford's achievement. In the realm of orchestral and instrumental music, he produced a number of works of indisputable importance, these being the *Irish Symphony*, the first and fourth of the *Irish Rhapsodies*, the Second Piano Concerto, the First Piano Trio, the Fourth Organ Sonata (*Celtica*) and the incidental music to *Becket*; time will probably show that other pieces should be added to this list, such as the variations on 'Down among the Dead Men'. Of his choral works, one would similarly cite *The Revenge, Songs of the Sea, Songs of the Fleet*, and possibly *Phaudrig Crohoore, The Voyage of Maeldune* and the *Stabat Mater*.

Apart from *Shamus O'Brien*, none of the other operas has won any lasting success. But they were produced at a time when the idea of an English opera was considered strange, and the possibility of singing in English was, for many years, not even countenanced. Neither was the opera-going public keen to see English singers; they primarily wanted Italians, and the Italian stars that they created had no intention of singing in anything other than Italian. The first English productions of *Der fliegende Holländer, Tannhäuser* and *Lohengrin* were all sung in Italian; in July 1895, during a vogue for opera in French, *Tannhäuser* was sung in French at Covent Garden. *The Veiled Prophet of Khorassan* was introduced in Hanover, in German translation, on 6 February 1881 and was sufficiently successful to be presented in several other German cities. Yet the English première did not take place until 26 July 1893, when the opera was given a single performance, in Italian, on the antepenultimate night of the season. The conclusion to be drawn is that English operas stood little chance of success. *Savanarola* also did well in Germany before arriving at Covent Garden, where it, too, received only one performance, in German. In his essay *Music and the War*, published in 1916, Stanford recalls that 'Wagner, when he visited London in 1877, openly expressed his preference for use of the English language in the English presentation of his operas. He knew, as we should know, if we were not such inveterate depreciators of our own possessions, that the language which was good enough for the Bible, Shakespeare and Milton, is good enough for the operatic stage, provided that it is written in a style worthy of the literature of the country.' Yet thirty years after Wagner's visit, the situation had hardly changed, as Stanford recognised in his essay *The Case for National Opera*, written in 1908.

One of the idosyncrasies of England is to identify the term Art with only one of its branches. All other countries, with the exception of our own, include music under this head. So has it been also with official England's attitude towards music. While every possible assistance, state and munici-pal, is given to painting and to literature, none is forthcoming to her. What wonder if this gives occasion to the foreigner to write us down unmusical? He sees our national galleries and our museums endowed and enriched with the best of ancient and contemporary works, and the building to which he gives equal prominence in all his centres of popula-tion, the National Theatre, non-existent. Small wonder that he presumes that we possess no works to produce in it and no talent to perform in it. If this reproach were removed, what an awakening he would have! The English School of Painting he has learnt to appraise at its true value because he can see it. The English School of Dramatic Music he knows nothing of, because he cannot hear it. He therefore makes haste to supply the deficiency himself; and as we cannot get on without some form of it, least perchance we forget that there is such a thing as opera and dramatic singing at all, he makes us pay so prodigiously for the pleasure of hearing him, that the music-loving masses of the people are precluded from hearing operas even in a language which fails to convey to them the sense of what is being performed. In other words we, who are perfectly capable of growing fine fruit in open-air orchards of our own, are compelled to eat foreign produce at hot-house prices or go without it. There follows the natural result that this foreign opera becomes a rendezvous for society, that fashion and not musical taste dictates its policy, and that its votaries go, not to hear an opera, however great, but to hear the singer or singers who are to appear in it. Perform the *Meistersinger* with an excellent all-round cast, of which the singers' names are unknown, and empty benches are the reward, as long as the empty benches are at prices beyond the reach of the music-loving rather than the diamond-loving public. Announce an ancient and worn-out work (which even its composer grew to despise), to show off the roulades of one *prima donna*, and to give them the chance of comparing them with the roulades of another, and society will see the prospect of some such excitement as wrestling contests and football matches provide for the poorer brethren, and will rush in all its finery to 'assist'.

He points out that, while the annual grants to the National Portrait Gallery and the Wallace Collection, in 1908, are around £6,000 (and to the British Museum, £170,000), the toal sum expended by the state on music is £1,000: £500 each to the RCM and RAM. 'Is this a fair proportion? Is this calculated to raise the position of England in the eyes of the world?' In contrast, he mentions that Frankfurt and Breslau both make annual grants of £10,000 to their municipal theatres; Brussels provides the same sum; with Geneva, it is £7,500.

A special point must be made of encouraging (as the Paris Opera House is compelled to do by law) the native production of dramatic music, by performing a certain fixed minimum of new English work. The recent competition for a prize opera by Englishmen, which was lately instituted by Messrs. Ricordi, made it abundantly clear that there is no lack of supply in this respect. The sequel of the competition is a curious comment upon our present doleful state. The prize opera was promised a production during the present season [May to July 1908]. It has not been given, because after the promise was made, a condition was imposed that it, an English Opera written to an English book by an English composer, would have to be translated into Italian in order to be presented to an English public in an English theatre during the opera season. Imagine the authorities of the Scala, having promised Puccini a production of his first opera, insisting upon its translation into Russian for presentation to an Italian audience! Our country is producing in curiously large quantities anti-English Englishmen, but no more glaring example could be found than this of the unpatriotic spirit which prevails in operatic ventures run for profit at fancy prices.

Thanks to the pioneering efforts of a German, Carl Rosa, Stanford's opera, *The Canterbury Pilgrims*, was performed in English and produced at Drury Lane in April 1884. It was extremely well received, so much so that the price of seats was nearly doubled; but Rosa seems to have been unprepared to trust his luck, and, after no more than a handful of performances, it was withdrawn. It was Fuller-Maitland's view that, had the opera been allowed to establish itself, 'it would certainly have taken in England something like the place that the *Meistersinger* had enjoyed all over the world.'

In face of such dispiriting results, it is not surprising that several years passed before he embarked on his next opera, *Shamus O'Brien*. Its success is significant: its appeal was not primarily to the 'diamond-loving' public; it fitted recognizably into the *métier* that Sullivan had so triumphantly instituted; it benefited from the opportunity of an unlimited run. *Much Ado*, though also sung in (Shakespeare's) English, availed itself of none of these advantages and managed only two performances before being withdrawn. 'Judged on its merits this was a rank injustice', states Harry Plunket Greene. 'Full of the loveliest tunes, sparkling with humour, beautifully scored, and sung and acted by a splendid cast it made a great hit. I was there and can testify to this.' In *A Quaker Singer's Recollections*, David Bispham, who took the part of Benedick, writes, 'This really fine work was rehearsed and played with great enthusiasm by those of us who sang, and had been written with equal gusto; as Stanford told me in his delightful Irish way, "It ran right out of the end of my pen."' The cast, says Bispham, could not have been bettered, and Marie Brema was 'enchanting' as Beatrice. 'The work is beautiful and will well repay study by those interested in opera in English.' This is no mean opinion; Bispham was an outstanding artist, who sang under Richter, Mahler and Richard Strauss.

Although *The Critic* has many admirers and was described by its first conductor, Goossens, as 'witty and beautiful', its failure is perhaps understandable. Despite the delightfulness of the music, the plot, adapted by Lewis Cairns James, is somewhat artificial and lacking in continuous interest. As a result, Stanford's subtle references to *Ein' feste Burg*, Beethoven's Ninth Symphony, *Tristan, Blest Pair of Sirens* and other compositions fail to make their full impact. However, perhaps this can be overcome through imaginative staging.

Newbolt had doubts about the libretto he prepared for *The Travelling Companion*, being unhappy over the alterations for which Stanford asked. Nevertheless, Andersen's story remains intact both in spirit and letter, and the opera proved dramatically effective at Sadler's Wells in 1935.

Shamus O'Brien and *Much Ado About Nothing* undoubtedly merit revival and could easily gain permanent places in English musical life. If that were to happen, it would be sufficient cause for the remaining operas to be heard again.

Despite his comparative lack of success, Stanford is an important figure in the history of English opera. He did much to further the cause of national opera through his works and writings. He played as vital a role in re-establishing Purcell as he did, in a different sphere, in reviving Bach. He conducted, on 16 July 1890, what appears to have been the first performance of *Così fan tutte* to be heard in London for more than sixty years. He introduced *Genoveva* to England. By example, he showed his students that British composers could and should write operas.

Because of the age in which we live, we tend either to forget or to deem forgettable the fact that Stanford composed much of our finest church music. 'When we have grown up, passed through the mange of revulsion from our grandfathers' artistic expression', writes Arthur

Hutchings in *Church Music in the Nineteenth Century*, 'we shall see Stanford's operas, part-songs, solo songs and church music as better than
those of any British composer between the seventeenth century and
ours.' In *The Singing Church*, C. Henry Phillips makes much the same
assessment.

> . . . with his lyrical gift, his well of melody, his refreshing harmony and
> rhythm, Stanford released many needed draughts of fresh air into the
> stuffy or quasi-dramatic work of his contemporaries. By the time he had
> passed his sixtieth year Stanford indeed found himself the doyen and
> teacher of all serious-minded church composers; church music could not
> have wished for a better master. He is never dull and always emotionally
> clean; if his work is sometimes more lyrical than ecclesiastical, that was all
> to the good: church music is all the better for an occasional breeze from
> such work as the spiritual part-song *Glorious and Powerful God*. As an in-
> spiration to his pupils his work has a historic importance.

Dr Phillips attributes Stanford's success in church music to his symphonic approach, which was influenced by Brahms. Professor Hutchings, however, regards the composer's method as typically
Wagnerian; he did not write vocal parts 'from verbal phrase to verbal
phrase and then dull them with an accompaniment', as was almost
traditional; instead, he produced 'a total score, as Wagner did for
each act of a drama', and gave the voices a part in it. This latter
concept of Stanford as the Wagner of church music is certainly appealing, but Professor Hutchings also detects the influence of Purcell.
Nevertheless, the voice that speaks to us through his church music is
unmistakably Stanfordian, and, in its almost conversational intimacy, possibly comes as near in spirit to Schumann as to some of the
other composers that have been mentioned.

Five of Stanford's church services are still regularly sung, as are
several hymns, anthems, settings of the psalms and the two groups of
motets. It is a pity that the prevailing attitude towards church music
prevents these works being more widely known. Perhaps the time will
come when they will regain the currency they once deservedly
possessed.

As a song-writer, Stanford is at his most individual and masterly.
He is virtually unrivalled in his feel for the English language. He
commands an exceptionally wide range of moods and emotions. He is
consistently economical, yet usually manages to encompass every
facet of the atmosphere of a poem. For Harry Plunket Greene, who
sang them better than anybody else, Stanford's songs offered

all that I want in song – lilt, rhythm, sense of words, sense of atmosphere, musical imagery and illustration, directness of purpose and – guiding them all – imagination, humour and economy.

But in one thing Stanford stands in a place by himself. I say unreservedly, in the light of a pretty wide acquaintance with the anthology of song, that in his knowledge of the handling of the voice he stands higher than any writer since Schubert. In all the years I have sung his songs I can never remember having had to ask him to alter a passage or note on account of technical difficulty . . .

In the wide range of Stanford's songs, from grave to gay, there is not one that is not ridiculously easy to sing, and that is the highest tribute you can pay to workmanship. Why are the 'Sea Songs' and the 'Fleet Songs' sung every day throughout the country? Because the composer knew how to bring them within the scope of every singer who knew his business – not by writing down to him, but by his intimate knowledge of his instrument. He knew too, that that instrument is melodic and horizontal and that the true song *never stops*.

Harry Plunket Greene speaks as highly of the accompaniments; he suggests that 'there is not a passage or chord in any of them which has not a definite meaning and which is not friends with its neighbour; and that technically it is as easy to play as the voice part is to sing.' He believes Stanford's sense of humour 'to be the driving power of everything he has written. He is the only British composer that I have ever come across whose humour is non-sporadic. Most of our song writers have written on odd song or two either frankly humorous or leaning towards humour, just to say they could do it. But it is part of Stanford's permanent mental outfit, and comes out in everything he writes.'

Stanford produced more than 150 songs, very many of which show him at the height of his powers. 'Some of the songs are among the most perfect written by any composer', said Arthur Benjamin in *British Composers in Interview*, 'and some of the short choral works such as *The Bluebird* are unsurpassed.' The cycles *An Irish Idyll, Cushendall, A Fire of Turf* and *A Sheaf of Songs from Leinster* have hardly a weak number among them and scattered through their pages are such masterpieces as 'The Fairy Lough', 'Johneen', 'Did You Ever?', 'A Soft Day', 'The Bold Unbiddable Child' and others. There are also, separately, songs like 'La Belle Dame sans merci', 'A Corsican Dirge', 'The Radiant Dark' and 'The Monkey's Carol', as well as the part-songs 'Heraclitus', 'The Blue Bird' and 'My Heart is Thine'. Compositions as fine as these, says Herbert Howells, 'are remarkable

even against an international background . . . By their subtlety and
fine-spun texture, their general reticence, their high sensitivity to the
colours, tensions and characteristics of even our most hackneyed
words, and by their astonishing flair for the placing and changes of
emphasis in any single phrase or succession of phrases – by any of
these criteria – the songs are rare and lovely things.'

At present, Stanford's music is neglected. 'But I believe that he will
return again', wrote Vaughan Williams in 1952. 'With the next
generation the inevitable reaction will set in and Stanford will come
into his own.' A quarter of a century has passed since this prediction;
the reaction has not yet occurred. But, reaction to what?

The answer, at its simplest, is reaction to Stanford's being a Victorian gentleman who composed church music and happened to be a
professor at the Royal College of Music when Holst, Vaughan
Williams and others were there as pupils. Yet was not Tchaikovsky
also a Victorian gentleman who composed church music and was a
professor? Yes; but he was Russian, and Stanford was British.

Our lack of belief in the possibility of our native composers being
men of importance seems to be at the heart of the matter. Often it
appears to go deeper than that; the lack of belief approaches contempt. And, if we have contempt for our own composers, can we
expect other countries to be at all interested in them? Until recently,
we did such an effective demolition job on Elgar, the Edwardian
Imperialist, that he was practically unknown outside the British
Isles. As eminent a musician as Georg Solti admitted that, up to a few
months before recording Elgar's First Symphony for Decca in 1972,
when he was sixty, he knew nothing of either of the symphonies. Such
was the success of the anti-Elgar propaganda. Though, as Michael
Kennedy points out in his biography of the composer, there is no
reference to the Boer War in any of Elgar's correspondence. With
Purcell, there was no such propaganda; we simply ignored him for a
couple of centuries.

This national sickness is not confined to music. In the nineteenth
century, Shakespeare was rather better admired in France, Germany
and Russia than in England. The letters of Berlioz, Brahms and
Tchaikovsky reveal a far more intimate acquaintance with Shakespeare's plays than do those of most British artists of the time.

It has been said that, if an artist was once extremely popular, then
the likelihood is that his works will contain something of interest for
succeeding generations. The recent Meyerbeer revival adds credence

to this assertion. There can be no doubt whatever about the level of popularity that Stanford's works once obtained. The *Irish Symphony*, for instance, was conducted at its première in 1887 by Richter; twenty-three years later, it was conducted by Mahler; in the intervening period, it received performances under the batons of such men as Bülow, Damrosch, Nikisch and Mengelberg.

The Elgar revival has brought forth a torrent of recordings; EMI and Decca, two of the world's largest record companies, have been especially prominent in making available a wide range of his music, including such pieces as the ballet *The Sanguine Fan*, the incidental music to *King Arthur, The Starlight Express* and the symphonic prelude *Polonia*. Of Stanford's orchestral music, they had released, up to the end of 1978, nothing. The implication must be that he is barely worth anybody's consideration. For Cowen and Mackenzie, it is the same.

If we consider, not unreasonably, perhaps, that Stanford was the equal of contemporaries like Stenhammar, Suk and Svendsen, then we must conclude that, had he been Swedish, Czechoslovakian or Norwegian, he would now be more widely known. For, in regard to recordings of their works, each of these composers has been well served by his respective country. Svendsen's symphonies, symphonic poems, and concertos, for instance, are all available in excellent interpretations.

Had Stanford been a Czech, not only would there be many records of his music, but his portrait would have travelled the world on postage stamps, as has Suk's. Italy celebrated the 50th anniversary of Boito's death with a 50 lire stamp, but Purcell, Sullivan and Elgar have yet to be acknowledged in a similar way. In 1957, the Elgar centenary year, the Czech government issued stamps commemorating Jan Stamitz, Laub, Foerster, Novák, Ostrčil and Ondřéček; the German Democratic Republic honoured Ramin and Abendroth, while Yugoslavia produced a Mokranjać stamp. Tchaikovsky's likeness has appeared on eight stamps; his home at Klin, on three; his statue in Moscow, on two.

Before we proceed to Stanford's final years, we should perhaps briefly mention a few of his compositions that fall outside the main body of his work. These felicitously endorse Harry Plunket Greene's contention that humour was one of the mainsprings of his creative urge.

Among the earliest of these pieces, dating from 1894, is a pseudo-Beethoven quartet, 'the last of the so-called *Poniatowski Quartets*' (dedicated to 'Prince Poniatowski'), which, apart from occasionally drifting into snatches of Schubert, includes analytical notes.

> Beginning with the third tributary of the finale, its first subject is never heard at all, and the second theme, in strong contrast to the first, is played frequently in the provinces but seldom in London. The introduction, which appears first towards the close of the composition, prepares the mind most suitably for the silence which follows. As a rule, in performance, this silence is broken by expressions of opinion, not always favourable, on the part of the audience, but such interruptions were not originally part of the composer's scheme . . . Of this fragment Schumann said, 'One glance at this trio, and all the woes of life disperse.' Mendelssohn, overhearing the remark, said with his usual urbanity and strict accuracy, 'But it's a quartet, not a trio.' 'What does that matter?' was the former composer's caustic reply . . .

Another piece in similar vein, written a dozen years later, is the *verismo* aria 'Elegia Maccheronica', consisting of a jumble of Italian phrases and names of Italian singers and operas. Equally alluring are the limericks 'There was an Old Man in a Pew' sung to an adaptation of Sullivan's *The Lost Chord*, and 'There was a Young Lady of Joppa', based on the opening bars of *Tristan und Isolde* and the 'Venusberg Music' from *Tannhäuser*, and concluding with the final chords of *Erlkönig*. Against this second work should be set, incidentally, the superbly judged reference to the *Magic Fire Music* when Daddy-Long-Legs singes his wings in *Cushendall*. The most substantial of these entertainments, probably stimulated by the appearance of Richard Strauss's *Elektra*, was *Ode to Discord*, 'a chimerical bombination in four bursts', scored for soloists, chorus and a huge orchestra, including organ, hydrophone and dreadnought drum. Dedicated to the Amalgamated Society of Boiler Makers and featuring the aria 'Hence, Loathed Melody', it employs the whole-tone scale and other contemporary *derniers cris*. The first performance, given at the Queen's Hall on 9 June 1909 by the New Symphony Orchestra, was conducted by Landon Ronald. The work, described by Ronald, in *Myself and Others*, as 'amazingly clever', was well received by a large audience.

It is worth remembering that Stanford's humour was usually as spontaneous as it was polished. One day, after lunch at the Royal College, Sir Fredrick Bridge propounded to his colleagues a theory that the elements of music could be taught by gestures, and then proceeded to demonstrate how he would signal a crochet, a minim and so on. 'There's one ye've forgotten, Bridge', said Stanford quietly, cocking a magnificent double-handed snook in the direction of his earnest fellow-professor: 'Consecutive fifths, me boy'.

By the time the Armistice was signed in November 1918, Stanford was sixty-six. In the summer of 1916, the lease of 50 Holland Street having expired, he was forced to move, and went to 9 Lower Berkeley Street, off Baker Street. (In 1935, Lower Berkeley Street became Fitzhardinge Street. A branch of Lloyd's Bank now stands on the site once occupied by his house; it is just around the corner from the head office of EMI, in Manchester Square. The chain of events is almost allegorical.)

Stanford was distressed to leave Holland Street. The house contained a multitude of happy memories. These were shared by many of his students; more than a dozen years later, Herbert Howells was walking along Holland Street 'and put my hand on the door of No. 50 as I went by.' Now, in 1918, though Guy and Geraldine had returned safely from the war, Stanford's health continued to decline. Depressed, racked by nerves, exhausted from a life of immense activity, he had become a frail ghost from a far-off age, disorientated in a new, alien world. Of the other survivors from those two radiant June days in Cambridge, Boito had died on 10 June 1918, with *Nerone* still uncompleted; elected a senator in 1912, he had made a trip to the front that too greatly taxed his strength and hastened his end. Bruch died on 2 October 1920. He had lost a son, who had been a painter. Perplexed and despondent over Germany's defeat and the waning popularity of his works, he found little reason for holding on to life. 'Into the dust with all the enemies of Germany!' he wrote in a letter of August 1914. 'England's declaration of war upset me so much that my hands shook. I thought the blow might finish me off. I hate nothing so much as England.' He told his daughter Margarethe that he was thinking of 'flinging my doctor's certificate at the feet of the English university of Cambridge with a few choice words.' On 6 August 1921, at the age of eighty-five, Saint-Saëns gave a concert, in Dieppe, at the end of which of which he announced to the audience, 'J'ai joué aujourd'hui pour la dernière fois.' This time, by some chance irony, he was telling the truth. Four months later, on 16 December, he died in his beloved Algiers.

Stanford continued to compose and teach. He was still Professor of Music at Cambridge, but his relationship with the university authorities had gradually deteriorated over the years. 'Towards the end of his life', says Harry Plunket Greene, 'it very nearly came to open warfare.' He was even asked to resign, but he refused, and the matter was taken no further. In normal circumstances, he would have been granted a fellowship of Trinity College, but this was denied him. His repugnance for the university took a physical form and he eventually gave his lectures in the Station Hotel, at some distance from the colleges; it also meant that, quite literally, he hardly set foot in Cambridge. Nevertheless Edward Dent, who became professor in 1926, recalled in 1934 how much the lectures had meant to him.

> I believe I can honestly say that I think of Stanford every day at Cambridge; I am always trying to pass on to my composition pupils what he taught me, and I know that the immense respect in which Music (as a University Department) is now held by the Council of the Senate and similar authorities (even when they are individually unmusical) is all due to Stanford's struggles in the face of opposition long ago.

As a student, with hopes of becoming 'the world's next great composer', Dent had been advised by Stanford, 'I tell ye what ye ought to do; why don't ye translate operas? Ye write very good English, and y're *quite musical*.' At length, Dent took up this suggestion and became probably the most celebrated of all Mozart translators. 'Stanford was always right; but it sometimes took one a very long time to convince oneself of that.'

In the introduction to his masterly treatise *Musical Composition*, published in 1911, Stanford wrote, 'The author has not (as is usually the case) to express his obligation to any authorities for help or assistance . . . But he has to put on record a very deep sense of gratitude to a numerous and many-sided body of pupils who, in learning from him, have taught him how to teach, and by their unvarying loyalty and keen endeavour have minimised the anxiety and magnified the interest of his labours on their behalf.' His own loyalty to his pupils was equally unvarying. He once refused for six months to speak to a critic and fellow-member of the Savile Club who had given one of his pupils a bad review.

After the war, his links with the Royal College remained, but his health was such that Adrian Boult and Malcolm Sargent had to assist him with the orchestra. He conducted his last concert at the college on 3 June 1921. He was much altered in other ways. Thomas Wood studied with him at this time and has left a sombre portrait in his autobiography *True Thomas.*

I got the beginnings of my own technique from Stanford: Sir Charles Villiers Stanford, Professor of Music at Cambridge, Professor of Composition at the Royal College of Music. He was an Irishman, a scholar, a talker clever enough for six, a composer of brilliance, a gifted teacher and a fighter first and last, who trailed the tail of his coat for his enemies and his friends alike to tread on and exultantly assailed them when they trod. In short, a great man. When I knew him he was already an old one, still tall, but stooping a little in the shoulder and bent at the knee; and his fires were burning low. Yet there was heat in them. I never had dealings with anyone of whom I was more thoroughly scared. I used to go for my composition lesson at four o'clock on Wednesdays in room 51 at the R.C.M. It was a biggish room, carpeted red. The door was glazed in the upper half and through the pane I could see him, sitting huddled by the hearth. The windows were tight shut. I plucked my heart up, knocked, tiptoed in.

'Good afternoon, Sir Charles.'

He would stare at me sideways without moving his head – very typical – and look away again.

'And what have ye brought for me this time?'

The familiar challenge He waited, dour and austere, while I produced my week's work – a sketch for string quartet or another movement of a suite – which he took, spread out on the table and peered down at short-sightedly, in silence. A most unnerving silence. The explosion was bound to come. But he would delay it: pick up the manuscript to get a closer view: droop his heavy lower lip petulantly and then purse his mouth and twist it sideways: suck his cheeks in and puff them out till the pouches under his eyes grew dark: then fumble in his waist-coat pocket. His pencil lived there. A silver one. It would emerge half-way, and be fiddled with, absently, until some passage in my music damnable beyond endurance brought him upright with a jerk that sent his glasses flying. They would swing and dangle elusively at the end of a cord immensely long, and that kind of secret and painful and ill-timed laughter which all of us have known assaulted me, as he tried to pick up the manuscript and capture his glasses and find his pencil in one tumultuous sweeping movement. He was curiously unhandy, contemptuous of help; and there always seemed to be very fair odds that he would fit the pencil on his nose and prepare to write with the glasses. But he sorted them out: settled himself: scored through the passage with a vicious black cross. Then the mine exploded.

'It won't *wash*, me boy. Have a look at it!'

Every pupil of Stanford heard that phase. It roused in a second the very emotion he must have wanted to be met with – resentment. Resent, and you expostulate: expostulate to a first-class mind and you must argue for your life. And argue we did about the washability or unwashability of that miserable clot of notes, ineffectively, on my side, for I was new at the game: ruthlessly on his, in words picked to sting. If the point was merely technical peace would come. He knew every road there could be: through, round, or over. His emendments were ingeniously neat. I was forced to acknowledge that. He would smile. But if we differed about *music* there was trouble. For him, the works of the experimenters held neither truth nor beauty. 'That's dam' ugly, me boy,' was the mildest reproof that met any attempt to toy with these riches, and rejoicing in them brought open war. Once I took him an overture. I was proud of it. Full-blooded stuff, I thought, the real thing – seas bursting over the fo'c'sle and the wash-ports clanging, just as I knew they did. And in order that this delectable scrunching should not be missed by an inattentive ear I led off in two keys, which was a device that had a faint air of novelty at the time. Stanford studied the score. He took a noisy gulp of tea when the maid brought in the tray, and ate a piece of cake. He took another piece of cake. Still not a word. And then came an outburst that was genuinely terrifying: measured and restrained, but savage. '. . . and if they ever *did* play this, ye'd sweat till y'r shirt was a rag.'

I have kept that overture. It is packed away in a suitcase labelled 'Earlies and Bads'. My shirt on that count will perpetually be dry. But it served its turn. I might go away in a fume, muttering 'There's no pleasing the old devil. If I write what I think he wants it's called milk-and-water and if I write what I want to write he goes off like a bomb'; but doubts came unbidden, later, and with them misgivings. Did I really believe that those yowps were the sea turned into music? No; they were a vainglorious sham. I wanted to show how clever I was. And wasn't it about time I stopped being clever and got down to business?

. . . that hot and airless room at the R.C.M. comes back with Stanford in it: his eyeglasses askew, a crumb clinging to his ragged grey moustache; and he is talking in that Leinster brogue that defies phonetic reproduction, of economy of means, and art that conceals art, and simplicity.

If I could have gone to him ten years earlier I should have less uncomfortable memories and this would make more pleasant reading. It is honest in showing the Stanford that I knew, but he was not the Stanford of the legends. The old truculence was there, but not the warmth or the tenderness or the wit. These had died in the War. He had changed. So had we all. I found him bitter . . . He made me angry, he made me unhappy, he made me rebel, but he taught me my job; and I still do not know whether he whole-heartedly wished to do so or whether he could not help himself. He was Irish; and the Irish have ever been the puzzlers.

It should be said again that Stanford was never averse to modern music, as long as it satisfied his belief in simplicity and economy of means. He once said that anybody was capable of producing an acceptably avant-garde score. 'It is largely a matter of having enough spare time to put in the extra notes.'

His last few years, like those of the equally disillusioned and disconsolate Elgar, were a gradual withdrawal from the outside world. We glimpse him only now and then in society. In March 1920, he went to Drury Lane for a production of *Parsifal*, conducted by Eugene Goossens. In *Overture and Beginners*, Goossens recalls that

> Stanford sat behind me during the whole evening, and afterwards came back to tell me how much he'd enjoyed the performance. So affected was he by the music that he burst into tears – something I'd never seen him do before! (I was much moved by the sight and had difficulty restraining my own.) 'Damned beautiful, me bhoy, but ye took the Grail march a mite too fast. Maybe though 'tis myself's been playing it too slow these last years. The Old Man's spirit surely hovered over ye this night.' And he wiped his glasses, took up his hat, and left. That was the last time I saw him.

His final appearance as a conductor was on 5 March 1921 at the Royal Albert Hall. 'For the first time in his life he lost his nerve', writes Harry Plunket Greene. 'When I arrived in the Artists' Room he said to me that he knew he could not conduct without breaking down and that he was going to ask someone else to take his place.' In the end, after a strong dose of sal volatile, he found the necessary courage and 'never conducted better'. During the same month, he received an honorary degree from Trinity College, Dublin; knowledge of a celebrated man's slackening grasp on life is sometimes a spur to recognition by the city of his birth.

One evening in November of the following year, he walked out of the Savile Club in a dense fog. An hour later, a stranger brought him back, having discovered him wretchedly wandering about in Down Street, less than a hundred yards away. It seems he had had a stroke. He managed to hold on for more than another year, giving a final dinner party in July 1923 and even going to Leeds four months later for a concert of his works and a dinner in his honour. On the evening of St Patrick's Day, 17 March 1924, he suffered a further stroke. He died twelve days afterwards, on the morning of 29 March. On 3 April, his ashes were interred in the North Choir Aisle of Westminster Abbey. They lie, appropriately, between the graves of Sterndale Bennett and Vaughan Williams and are marked by a stone on which is simply and factually inscribed, 'A GREAT MUSICIAN'.

SELECTIVE BIBLIOGRAPHY

Stanford

Fuller-Maitland, J.A., *A Door-Keeper of Music* (John Murray, London, 1929)
—— *The Music of Parry and Stanford* (W. Heffer & Sons, Cambridge, 1934)
Greene, Harry Plunket, *Charles Villiers Stanford* (Arnold, London, 1935)
Howells, Herbert, 'Charles Villiers Stanford' from *Proceedings of the Royal Musical Association* (Session LXXIX, London, 1952)
Porte, John F., *Sir Charles V. Stanford* (Kegan Paul, London, 1921)
Stanford, C.V., *Interludes* (John Murray, London, 1922)
—— *Musical Composition* (Macmillan, London, 1922)
—— *Pages from an Unwritten Diary* (Arnold, London, 1914)
—— *Studies and Memories* (Constable, London, 1908)
Stanford, C.V. and Forsyth, C., *A History of Music* (Macmillan, London, 1916)
Willeby, Charles, *Masters of English Music* (Osgood, McIlraine, London, 1893)

Tchaikovsky

In Russian
Laroche, H., *Sobraniye Stati (Collected Articles)*, Vol 2: *P.I. Chaykovsky* (Leningrad, 1975)
Tchaikovsky, M.I., *Zhizn P.I. Chaykovskovo (The Life of P.I. Tchaikovsky)* (Moscow, 1902)
Tchaikovsky, P.I., *Polnoye Sobraniye Sochineny: Literaturniye Proizvedeniya i Perepiska (Literary Works and Correspondence)* (Moscow, 1953, Vols 1–16, and still in progress)
—— *Pisma k Blizkim (Letters to His Family)* (Moscow, 1955)
—— *Dnevniki (Diaries)* (Moscow, 1923)
—— *Muzikalno – Kriticheskiye Stati (Critical Articles on Music)*, (Moscow, 1953)
Yakovlev, V., *Dni i Godi P.I. Chaykovskovo (The Days and Years of P.I. Tchaikovsky)* (Moscow, 1940)

In English
Brown, David, *Tchaikovsky* (Gollancz, London, 1978, Vol 1; Vols 2 and 3 still in progress)
Garden, Edward, *Tchaikovsky* (Dent, London, 1973)
Shostakovich, D. *et al*, *Russian Symphony: Thoughts about Tchaikovsky* (Philosophical Library, New York, 1947)
Tchaikovsky, P.I., ed Lakond, Vladimir, *Diaries*, (Greenwood Press, Westport, Connecticut, 1973; reprinted with index from Norton edition, 1945)
Volkoff, Vladimir, *Tchaikovsky: A Self-Portrait* (Robert Hale, London; Crescendo Publishing, Boston, 1975)
Warrack, John, *Tchaikovsky* (Hamish Hamilton, London, 1973)
—— *Tchaikovsky Ballet Music* (BBC Publications, London, 1979)
—— *Tchaikovsky Symphonies and Concertos* (BBC Publications, London, 1969)
Weinstock, Herbert, *Tchaikovsky* (Cassell, London, 1946)

Miscellaneous

Auer, Leopold, *My Long Life in Music* (Duckworth, London, 1924)
Austen Leigh, W., *Augustus Austen Leigh* (Smith, Elder & Co, London, 1906)
Bantock, Myrrha, *Granville Bantock* (Dent, London, 1972)
Beaumont, Cyril W., *The Diaghilev Ballet in London* (Putnam, London, 1940)
Bennett, J.R. Sterndale, *The Life of William Sterndale Bennett* (CUP, Cambridge, 1907)
Benois, Alexandre, *Reminiscences of the Russian Ballet* (Putnam, London, 1941)
Berger, Francesco, *97* (Elkin Mathews and Marrot, London, 1930)
—— *Reminiscences, Impressions and Anecdotes* (Sampson Low, London, 1913)

Blanche, J.E., *Portraits of a Lifetime* (Dent, London, 1937)
Boito, Arrigo, *Critiche e cronache musicali* (Fratelli Treves, Milan, 1931)
Bonnerot, Jean, *C. Saint-Saëns* (Durand, Paris, 1923)
Booth, J.B., *The Days We Knew* (Werner Laurie, London, 1943)
—— *Palmy Days* (Richards Press, London, 1957)
Bülow, Hans von, *Briefe und Schriften* (Breitkopf und Härtel, Leipzig, 1896)
—— *Neue Briefe* (Drei Masken, Munich, 1927)
Damrosch, Walter, *My Musical Life* (Scribner's, New York, 1923)
Davison, J.W., *From Mendelssohn to Wagner* (William Reeves, London, 1912)
Elkin, Robert, *Royal Philharmonic* (Rider, London, 1946)
Fellerer, K.G., *Max Bruch* (Arno, Cologne, 1974)
Fifoot, C.H.S., *Frederic William Maitland* (Harvard University Press, Cambridge, Massachusetts, 1971)
Foster, M.B., *The Philharmonic Society of London, 1813–1912* (Bodley Head, London, 1912)
Fowler, J.T., *Life and Letters of John Bacchus Dykes* (John Murray, London, 1897)
Gardner King, Agnes, *Kelvin the Man* (Hodder & Stoughton, London, 1925)
Geiringer, Karl, *Brahms: His Life and Works* (Allen & Unwin, London, 1936)
Graves, C.L., *The Life of Sir George Grove* (Macmillan, London, 1903)
—— *Hubert Parry* (Macmillan, London, 1926)
Godfrey, Dan, *Memories and Music* (Hutchinson, London, 1924)
Grechaninov, Alexandre, *My Life* (Coleman-Ross, New York, 1952)
Grierson, Edward, *Storm Bird: The Strange Life of Georgina Weldon* (Chatto & Windus, London, 1959)
Hallé, Charles, *Life and Letters* (Smith, Elder & Co, London, 1896)
Harding, James, *Gounod* (Allen & Unwin, London, 1973)
—— *Saint-Saëns and His Circle* (Chapman & Hall, London, 1965)
Haskell, Arnold, *Diaghileff* (Gollancz, London, 1935)
Henschel, George, *Musings and Memories of a Musician* (Macmillan, London, 1918)
Henschel, Helen, *When Soft Voices Die* (John Westhouse, London, 1944)
Hewlett, Henry G., *Henry Fothergill Chorley* (Richard Bentley, London, 1873)
Jebb, Caroline, *The Life and Letters of Sir R.C. Jebb* (CUP, Cambridge, 1907)
Kennedy, Michael, *The Hallé Tradition* (MUP, Manchester, 1960)
—— *Portrait of Elgar* (OUP, London, 1968)
Klein, Herman, *Musicians and Mummers* (Cassell, London, 1925)
—— *Thirty Years of Musical Life in London, 1870–1900* (Heinemann, London, 1903)
Lehmann, John, *Ancestors and Friends* (Eyre & Spottiswoode, London, 1962)
Lehmann, R.C., *Memories of Half a Century* (Smith, Elder & Co, London, 1908)
Mapleson, J.H., ed Rosenthal, Harold, *The Mapleson Memoirs*, (Putnam, London, 1966)
May, Florence, *The Life of Brahms* (William Reeves, London, 1905)
Mueller, John H., *The American Symphony Orchestra* (John Calder, London, 1958)
Nardi, Piero, *Vita di Arrigo Boito* (Mondadori, Verona, 1942)
Osborne, Charles, *Letters of Giuseppe Verdi* (Gollancz, London, 1971)
Pope, Macqueen W., *Goodbye Piccadilly* (David & Charles, Newton Abbot, 1960)
—— *The Melodies Linger On* (W.H. Allen, London, 1950)
Prod' homme, J.-G. and Dandelot, A., *Gounod* (Delagrave, Paris, 1911)
Riesemann, Oskar von, *Rachmaninoff's Recollections* (Books for Libraries Press, Freeport, NY, 1934)
Saint-Saëns, C., *Portraits et Souvenirs* (Calmann-Lévy, Paris, 1909)
Saxe Wyndham, H., *August Manns and the Saturday Concerts* (Walter Scott Publishing Co, London, 1909)
Scholes, Percy A., *The Mirror of Music, 1844–1944* (Novello and OUP, London, 1947)
Smyth, Ethel, *Impressions That Remained* (Longmans, London, 1919)
Thomas, Rose Fay, *Memoirs of Theodore Thomas* (Moffat, Yard & Co, New York, 1911)
Vaughan Williams, Ursula, *R.V.W: A Biography of Ralph Vaughan Williams* (OUP, London, 1964)
Walker, Frank, *The Man Verdi* (Dent, London, 1962)
Wood, Henry J., *My Life of Music* (Gollancz, London, 1938)

SELECTIVE INDEX